European Yearbook of International Economic Law

EYIEL Monographs - Studies in European and International Economic Law

Volume 34

EYIEL Monographs is a subseries of the European Yearbook of International Economic Law (EYIEL). It contains scholarly works in the fields of European and international economic law, in particular WTO law, international investment law, international monetary law, law of regional economic integration, external trade law of the EU and EU internal market law. The series does not include edited volumes. EYIEL Monographs are peer-reviewed by the series editors and external reviewers.

Andrés Eduardo Alvarado-Garzón

Environmental Counterclaims in Investment Arbitration

Deconstructing the Requirements of Jurisdiction, Connection and Cause of Action

Springer

Andrés Eduardo Alvarado-Garzón
Frankfurt am Main, Germany

ISSN 2364-8392 ISSN 2364-8406 (electronic)
European Yearbook of International Economic Law
ISSN 2524-6658 ISSN 2524-6666 (electronic)
EYIEL Monographs - Studies in European and International Economic Law
ISBN 978-3-031-46390-7 ISBN 978-3-031-46391-4 (eBook)
https://doi.org/10.1007/978-3-031-46391-4

This Springer imprint is published by the registered company Springer Nature Switzerland AG
The registered company address is: Gewerbestrasse 11, 6330 Cham, Switzerland

Paper in this product is recyclable.

Preface

This book is the result of a doctoral dissertation accepted by the Faculty of Law of Saarland University in winter 2022/2023. It was written during my time as a research associate at the Chair for Public Law, Public International Law, European Law and International Economic Law of Professor Dr. Marc Bungenberg at Saarland University. The manuscript reflects legal literature and case-law until January 2023.

Many people accompanied and supported me during this academic endeavour. Thus, fully expressing my gratitude to all and every single one of them in these few lines is well-nigh impossible. Yet, I cannot miss the chance to single out certain people by name, without whom this work would not have been completed. First of all, I am extremely grateful to my doctoral supervisor, Professor Dr. Marc Bungenberg, whose insightful comments and unwavering support for this and many other projects have paved the following years of my career. I would like to thank Professor Dr. Torsten Stein, who kindly undertook the second evaluation of my doctoral dissertation. I would also like to thank the members of the defence committee, Professor Dr. Thomas Giegerich, Professor Dr. Marc Bungenberg, Professor Dr. Torsten Stein and Professor Dr. Annemarie Matusche-Beckmann, for the pleasant and thought-provoking discussions.

Furthermore, I would like to thank the editors of this series, Professor Dr. Marc Bungenberg, Professor Dr. Christoph Herrmann, Professor Dr. Markus Krajewski, Professor Dr. Jörg Philipp Terhechte and Professor Dr. Andreas R. Ziegler for including this dissertation in the *EYIL Monographs—Studies in European and International Economic Law*.

This work has enormously benefitted from the experience gained at the International Centre for Settlement of Investment Disputes (ICSID) and the United Nations Commission on International Trade Law (UNCITRAL), particularly, from my work with Paul-Jean Le Cannu, Marisa Planells-Valero and Ana Conover at ICSID and with Judith Knieper and Corentin Baslé at UNCITRAL. Furthermore, I am grateful to Professor Hélène Ruiz-Fabri for hosting me at the Max Planck Institute Luxembourg for Procedural Law and for providing me with a scholarship to complete my research.

From the bottom of my heart, I am thankful to my dear friends and colleagues Dr. Pieter Van Vaerenbergh, Bianca Böhme and Vishakha Choudhary, who reviewed and proof-read the book and provided invaluable feedback for improvement.

During the writing process, I was fortunate to enjoy an excellent research environment at the Europa-Institut of Saarland University. In particular, thanks to my friends and former colleagues Anna, Pieter, Angshuman, Fabian, Bianca, Björn, Afolabi and Romy, who each contributed in their own way to a pleasant and inspiring atmosphere. My sincere thank you to Dr. Patricia Nacimiento for motivating me during the last stages of this process and to my colleagues Adilbek, Alessandro, Bajar, Elmar, Jacky and Gani, who have warmly welcomed me in the disputes team.

My deepest and most heartfelt thanks, however, go to my family: To the love of my life, Claudia, whose patience and unconditional love have become the bedrock of everything I do; to my dad, Luis Eduardo, the reason and inspiration for everything I have achieved; to my mom, Graciela and my brother, Sergio, whose constant support and affection I have felt despite the distance.

Frankfurt am Main, Germany
August 2023

Andrés Eduardo Alvarado-Garzón

Contents

Abbreviations

Algiers Accords	Declaration of the Government of the Democratic and Popular Republic of Algeria (General Declaration) of 19 January 1981
ARSIWA	Articles on the Responsibility of States for Internationally Wrongful Acts
ATCA	US Alien Tort Claims Act
BIT	Bilateral Investment Treaty
Brundtland Report	Report of the World Commission on Environment and Development of 1987
CAO	Compliance Advisor/Ombudsman of the IFC
Claims Settlement Declaration	The Declaration of the Government of the Democratic and Popular Republic of Algeria concerning the Settlement of Claims by the Government of the United States of America and the Government of the Islamic Republic of Iran of 19 January 1981
CSR	Corporate and Social Responsibility
DIS	*Deutsche Institution für Schiedsgerichtbarkeit—DIS* [German Arbitration Institute]
DSU	Understanding on the Rules and Procedures governing the Settlement of Disputes at the WTO
EU	European Union
First Hague Convention	Convention for the Pacific Settlement of International Disputes of 1899
FTA	Free Trade Agreement
GATT	General Agreement on Tariffs and Trade
HKIAC	Hong Kong International Arbitration Centre
IBA	International Bar Association
ICC	International Chamber of Commerce

ICJ	International Court of Justice
ICSID Convention	Convention on the Settlement of Investment Disputes between States and Nationals of other States
ICSID	International Centre for Settlement of Investment Disputes
IFC	International Finance Corporation
IIA(s)	International Investment Agreement(s)
IISD	International Institute for Sustainable Development
ILC	International Law Commission
ILO	International Labour Organization
ISDS	Investor-State Dispute Settlement
ITLOS	International Tribunal for the Law of the Sea
IUSCT	Iran-US Claims Tribunal
LCIA	London Court of International Arbitration
MFN	Most-Favoured Nation Treatment
New York Convention	Convention on the Recognition and Enforcement of Foreign Arbitral Awards
OECD	Organization for Economic Co-operation and Development
OSPAR Convention	Convention for the Protection of the Marine Environment of the North-East Atlantic
PCA	Permanent Court of Arbitration
PCIJ	Permanent Court of International Justice
Rio Declaration	Rio Declaration on Environment and Development of 1992
SCC	Stockholm Chamber of Commerce
Second Hague Convention	Convention for the Pacific Settlement of International Disputes of 1907
SIAC	Singapore International Arbitration Centre
Stockholm Declaration	Declaration on the Human Environment of 1972
TFEU	Treaty on the Functioning of the European Union
UN	United Nations
UNCITRAL Arbitration Rules	Arbitration Rules of UNCITRAL
UNCITRAL Model Arbitration Law	UNCITRAL Model Law on International Arbitration
UNCITRAL Working Group III	Working Group on Investor-State Dispute Settlement Reform at UNCITRAL
UNCITRAL	United Nations Commission on International Trade Law
UNCLOS	UN Convention on the Law of the Sea
UNCTAD	UN Conference on Trade and Development

UNFCCC	UN Framework Convention on Climate Change
UNIDROIT Principles	UNIDROIT Principles of International Commercial Contracts
US	United States of America
USD	US Dollar
VCLT	Vienna Convention on the Law of Treaties
VIAC	Vienna International Arbitral Centre
WIPO	World Intellectual Property Organization
WTO	World Trade Organization

Chapter 1
Introduction

The notion of sustainable development condenses the close relation between the goal of economic development and environmental protection. Sustainable development is '*development that meets the needs of the present without compromising the ability of future generations to meet their own needs*'.[1] Pursuant to Principle 4 of the Rio Declaration on Environment and Development of 1992 (Rio Declaration),[2] environmental protection constitutes an integral part of sustainable development. Accordingly, sustainable development connects the goals of economic and social development with the goal of environmental protection,[3] based on the principles of intergenerational and intragenerational equity.[4] Therefore, the notion of sustainable development evolves according to the circumstances such as time, the area or the subjects concerned.[5]

One may argue that sustainable development seems to entail a political ideal, which undermines its normative value.[6] Thus, it cannot have the status of a norm of

[1]Report of the World Commission on Environment and Development (04 August 1987) UN Doc A/43/427 and Annex 'Our Common Future' (Brundtland Report) 54.

[2]UN Conference on Environment and Development, 'Rio Declaration on Environment and Development' (12 August 1992) UN Doc A/CONF.151/26 (Vol I), Principle 4: ('In order to achieve sustainable development, environmental protection shall constitute an integral part of the development process and cannot be considered in isolation from it').

[3]Beyerlin (2013), mn. 11; Bjorklund (2019), p. 40.

[4]According to Virginie Barral, intergenerational equity '*posits that in their development choices states must preserve the environmental capital they hold in trust for future generations and ensure that it is transmitted in conditions equivalent to those in which it was received*', whereas intragenerational equity '*requires equity in the distribution of the outcomes of development within one generation as much internally (within one national society) as internationally (between developed and developing states)*', see Barral (2012), p. 380.

[5]Barral (2012), p. 382.

[6]Beyerlin (2013), mn. 17–18.

A. E. Alvarado-Garzón, *Environmental Counterclaims in Investment Arbitration*, EYIEL Monographs - Studies in European and International Economic Law 34,
https://doi.org/10.1007/978-3-031-46391-4_1

international law given its incapability of being couched in normative terms.[7] Even though there is no obligation to achieve sustainable development, this does not deprive this concept of reflection in custom.[8] At least, sustainable development, as an objective to aspire to, represents a principle of customary international law.[9] This might be '*by reason not only of its inescapable logical necessity, but also by reason of its wide and general acceptance by the global community*'.[10] The International Court of Justice (ICJ) in the *Gabčíkovo-Nagymaros* case mentioned for the first time the concept of sustainable development and underscored the pivotal role of environmental protection in international law and the need to reconcile it with economic development.[11]

Yet, international environmental law is deemed as a relatively emerging field in the broader spectrum of public international law and subject to a state of steady and dynamic evolution.[12] This might explain the gradual development of environmental considerations in investment arbitration. Investment arbitral tribunals traditionally exhibited certain reluctance to consider environmental concerns as a decisive element in their reasonings.[13] In fact, until 2005 there was a tendency for arbitral tribunals to decide conflicts between environmental protection policies and investment protection in favour of the latter.[14] This clash between environmental policies and investment protection has functioned as a 'catalyst' for the reformulation of international investment agreements (IIAs) more amenable to non-investment considerations.[15] Various IIAs have indeed incorporated into their preambles the

---

[7]Lowe (1999), pp. 23–25.

[8]In this regard, Virginie Barral refers to the decision in *US-Shrimp*, *Gabčíkovo-Nagymaros*, *Iron Rhine Railway* and *Pulp Mills*, as well as the multitude of international law documents recognising the need to pursue sustainable development and the national strategies implementing environmental considerations, see Barral (2012), pp. 386–388. For a different opinion *see*, Chi (2018), p. 13.

[9]Barral (2012), p. 388. Similarly, Sands et al. (2018), p. 219: ('There can be little doubt that the concept of 'sustainable development' has entered the corpus of international customary law, requiring different streams of international law to be treated in an integrated manner').

[10]*Case concerning the Gabčíkovo-Nagymaros Project (Hungary v Slovakia)* (Judgment) [1997] ICJ Rep 7, Separate Opinion of Vice-President Weeramantry, 95.

[11]*Case concerning the Gabčíkovo-Nagymaros Project (Hungary v Slovakia)* (Judgment) [1997] ICJ Rep 7, para 140: ('Throughout the ages, mankind has, for economic and other reasons, constantly interfered with nature. *In the past, this was often done without consideration of the effects upon the environment.* Owing to new scientific insights and to a growing awareness of the risks for mankind - for present and future generations - of pursuit of such interventions at an unconsidered and unabated pace, new norms and standards have been developed, set forth in a great number of instruments during the last two decades. Such new norms have to be taken into consideration, and such new standards given proper weight, not only when States contemplate new activities but also when continuing with activities begun in the past. *This need to reconcile economic development with protection of the environment is aptly expressed in the concept of sustainable development*') (emphasis added).

[12]Boyle (1999), p. 62.

[13]Kulick (2012), pp. 258–259.

[14]Behn and Langford (2017), p. 44.

[15]Asteriti (2016), p. 146. Similarly, Chi (2018), p. 90.

protection of the environment and/or the promotion of sustainable development as objectives worth pursuing through foreign investment or at least consistent with investment protection.[16] In some cases, the objective of protecting the environment might have been further reflected in exception clauses or carve-out provisions,[17] or even indirectly, through the inclusion of corporate social responsibility provisions.[18]

As such, treaty provisions reflecting environmental objectives, carve-outs or even obligations upon the contracting states seem to alleviate to a certain degree the conflicts an environmental measure may generate in the investment protection regime.[19] Such treaty practice of introducing environmental considerations in investment treaties suggests that those IIAs should be construed under the light of sustainable development, or at least that investment and environmental protection cannot be treated separately.[20] In this sense, such new language in IIAs indicates that the activity of foreign investors cannot impinge on environmental protection.[21]

Investment tribunals seemed to have heeded these developments. In various cases, tribunals have considered that environmental concerns merit an analysis in investment arbitration either by informing the scope of application of other treaty provisions or by assessing the reasonableness of a state's conduct.[22] This intricate

[16] *See* for instance: NAFTA (1994), Preamble; US-Uruguay BIT (2005), Preamble; Colombia-US TPA (2006), Preamble; Korea-US FTA (2007), Preamble; US-Rwanda BIT (2008), Preamble; Japan-Switzerland FTA (2009), Preamble; Japan-Colombia BIT (2011), Preamble; Canada-China BIT (2012), Preamble; Canada-Benin BIT (2013), Preamble; Canada-Burkina Faso BIT (2015), Preamble; Austria-Kyrgyzstan BIT (2016), Preamble; Slovak Republic-Iran BIT (2016), Preamble; Morocco-Nigeria BIT (2016), Preamble; Rwanda-UAE BIT (2017), Preamble; Ethiopia-Qatar BIT (2017), Preamble; Argentina-UAE BIT (2018), Preamble; Belarus-India BIT (2018), Preamble; USMCA (2019), Preamble; Hungary-Kyrgyzstan BIT (2020), Preamble.

[17] *See* for instance: Turkey-Gambia BIT (2013), Art 5; Guatemala-Trinidad and Tobago BIT (2013), Art 2(2); Switzerland-Georgia BIT (2014), Art 9; Mexico-Panama FTA (2014), Art 10.9(2); Colombia-France BIT (2014), Art 10; Colombia-Turkey BIT (2014), Arts 6 and 11; Japan-Uruguay BIT (2015), Art 22; Australia-China FTA (2015), Art 9.8; Canada-Burkina Faso BIT (2015), Art 18; Canada-Guinea BIT (2015), Art 18; Argentina-Qatar BIT (2016), Art 10; Colombia-UAE BIT (2017), Arts 10 and 11; Rwanda-UAE BIT (2017), Art 9; Israel-Japan BIT (2017), Art 15; Turkey-Cambodia BIT (2018), Art 4.

[18] *See* for instance: Canada-Benin BIT (2013), Art 16; Canada-Cameroon BIT (2014), Art 15; Colombia-France BIT (2014), Art 11; Canada-Burkina Faso BIT (2015), Art 16; Canada-Guinea BIT (2015), Art 16; Nigeria-Singapore BIT (2016), Art 11; Canada-Mongolia BIT (2016), Art 14.

[19] Asteriti (2016), p. 149. Similarly, Boisson de Chazournes (2017), p. 380: ('These can be classified in three categories. First, preambular provisions often refer to environmental protection in general terms as an objective. Second, by way of exception or derogatory language, environmental concerns may be part and parcel of the State's regulatory power. Third, environmental obligations may be incorporated with provisions on corporate social responsibility and the obligation to conduct an environmental impact assessment').

[20] Martini (2017), pp. 582–583.

[21] Choudhury (2020), p. 5.

[22] *See* for instance: *Chemtura Corporation v Government of Canada*, UNCITRAL Case, Award (02 August 2010) paras. 134 et seqq.; *Yuri Bogdanov and Yulia Bogdanova v Republic of Moldova*, SCC Case No V091/2012, Award (13 April 2013) paras. 192 et seqq.; *Adel A Hamadi Al Tamimi v Sultanate of Oman*, ICSID Case No ARB/11/33, Award (03 November 2015) paras. 387–390;

relation between environmental protection and investment protection delineated by treaty drafting and arbitral jurisprudence suggests that international investment law should contribute to sustainable development, and consequently, foreign investors should not affect a state's goals in this regard.[23]

Nowadays, the facilitation of foreign investment (including its protection) is even deemed critical for achieving sustainable development.[24] Particularly, the possibility to harness the financial and technological resources of foreign investors may pave the way towards sustainable development.[25] Illustratively, with respect to climate change, the Paris Agreement's objectives would require approximately USD 90 trillion investment, which renders the channelling of foreign investment towards those objectives indispensable.[26]

These developments reveal, perhaps ironically, a two-sided relation between investment law and environmental protection: synergetic and supportive, on the one hand, and conflicting, on the other hand.[27] The synergetic and supportive relation epitomises the idea of harnessing the financial and technological resources of foreign investors for fostering environmental protection.[28] The conflicting relation appears from the origins of investment protection, which was characterised by the commodification of natural resources in complete disregard of potential environmental effects.[29]

While environmental awareness has increased over the years, globalisation has turned investment activities more complex and in some cases more detrimental to environmental protection.[30] For instance, investments in industries such as mining, oil, or hazardous waste disposal always pose a latent threat to the environment of the host state,[31] irrespective of being heavily regulated.[32] In certain cases, environmental damage may ensue from investors' misconduct, such as in the case of the oil spills caused by Shell Oil Company in Nigeria or by Chevron in Ecuador.[33] This conflicting relation between investment law and environmental protection,

---

David R Aven and Others v Republic of Costa Rica, ICSID Case No UNCT/15/3, Award (18 September 2018) para. 412; *Cortec Mining Kenya Limited, Cortec (Pty) Limited and Stirling Capital Limited v Republic of Kenya*, ICSID Case No ARB/15/29, Award (22 October 2018) paras. 346–347.

[23] Choudhury (2020), p. 14.

[24] UNCTAD (2017), p. 125. Similarly, UNGA, 'Transforming our World: The 2030 Agenda for Sustainable Development' (21 October 2015) UN Doc A/RES/70/1, Sustainable Development Goals 2, 7, 10.

[25] Viñuales (2019), p. 34.

[26] Miles and Lawry-White (2019), p. 2.

[27] Dupuy and Viñuales (2018), pp. 453–454.

[28] Viñuales (2019), p. 34.

[29] Miles (2013), p. 140.

[30] Chi (2018), p. 157.

[31] Dünnwald (2015), p. 17; Sullivan and Kirsey (2017), p. 107.

[32] Mistura (2019), para. 23.10.

[33] Miles (2013), pp. 134–135.

particularly with respect to the environmental damage caused by foreign investors, constitutes the premise or starting point of this monograph.

Certainly, domestic courts may rule upon environmental damages caused by non-state actors, including investors, within the territory of the country. However, relying on domestic courts might often not be efficient for two reasons: *first*, host states may suffer from limited financial, technological and human resources for the implementation and enforcement of environmental law.[34] For instance, after the disastrous gas leak in a pesticide factory at Bhopal, India, the victims resorted to the domestic courts to obtain compensation against the foreign investor operating the factory. However, those court proceedings were strategically stalled at different instances,[35] and finally, the Supreme Court ruled that the parties should agree on a settlement for an amount insufficient to pay for the treatments of the Bhopal victims.[36]

Second, domestic proceedings might be nevertheless thwarted by the impending threat of foreign investors commencing investment arbitration against the state.[37] Adjudication by domestic courts on environmental damage caused by foreign investors is therefore far from ideal, and as the *Chevron* saga has proven,[38] it may turn one dispute into a mushrooming series of claims all across the world.

At this juncture, environmental counterclaims come to play, which are the focus of this book. For this, the first point to necessarily address is the state of play of environmental counterclaims in investment arbitration from a structural and practical point of view [Sect. 1.1]. This would lay down the foundations for the subsequent delimitation on the scope of this manuscript and research questions [Sect. 1.2].

1.1 State of Play

The structure of investment arbitration, and in particular treaty-based investment arbitration, may portray an asymmetrical system, whereby host states are deemed the '*perpetual respondents*'.[39] Even if the respondent state is successful in defeating an investor's claim, the former can only expect a beneficial cost-allocation at best,

34 Morgera (2020), pp. 26–28. Similarly, Thomé (2021), pp. 669 et seqq.

35 Cassels (2001), p. 328.

36 Mathur and Morehouse (2002), p. 73.

37 Douglas (2013), p. 417; Shao (2021), p. 158.

38 Multiple claims in multiple fora have been filed against or by Chevron/Texaco related to Chevron's oil spillage in Ecuador, including the Aguinda Litigation in New York, the Lago Agrio litigation in Ecuador, some commercial arbitration cases at the Hague, the state-to-state arbitration between Ecuador and the US, an AAA arbitration in New York, and the Chevron v Ecuador treaty-based investment arbitration *see*, *Chevron Corporation and Texaco Petroleum Corporation v Ecuador (II)*, PCA Case No 2009-23, Second Partial Award on Track II (30 August 2018) paras. 4.75 et seqq.

39 Popova and Poon (2015), pp. 223–224.

which normally does not cover all the expenses of the proceedings.[40] As a result, one may argue that in investment arbitration, '*investors have much to gain, and states everything to lose*'.[41] In this context, the instrument of counterclaims breaks with this traditional appraisal of investment arbitration.

Counterclaims are different to defences: while defences seek to fend off a claimant's claims or to reduce compensation, counterclaims seek independent relief for the claimant's illegal actions, including in the form of monetary compensation. Accordingly, an environmental counterclaim in investment arbitration would seek redress for the environmental damages caused by the claimant investor. One may argue that this instrument thus offers the opportunity to develop investment arbitration '*into an enforcement tool for environmental law*'.[42] Indeed, environmental counterclaims in investment arbitration would serve as a viable tool to alleviate the tensions between investment law and environmental protection. This would not only exalt the role of environmental protection at the international level, but it would also serve procedural economy by centralising an investment dispute and its related environmental counterclaim before one single tribunal. Yet, these benefits have been often overlooked in practice.

From all publicly available decisions in investment arbitration, this monograph has found 47 cases where the respondent host state has raised a counterclaim against the claimant investor, of which only eight have been successful or at least partially successful on merits.[43] While the success rate might seem strikingly low, the reasons for rejecting counterclaims have ranged between jurisdiction, admissibility and ultimately merits-related issues. Out of all the surveyed counterclaims, only six of these cases have involved an environmental-related issue, where the respondent has requested relief for some sort of environmental damage.[44] Among those six environmental counterclaims, only two have been successful: in the *Perenco v Ecuador* case and in the *Burlington v Ecuador* case. Interestingly, both cases are related.

Both investors, Burlington and Perenco, acquired interests in two oil concession sites in the Ecuadorian Amazon region and were operating as a consortium. Essentially, both disputes arose from the same legislative measures increasing the tax rate on extraordinary profits or 'windfall taxes' for oil companies, and the subsequent expropriation of the investments. Burlington and Perenco initiated investment arbitration independently, and Ecuador raised counterclaims (including for environmental damage) against them. Although the possibility of consolidation of both proceedings was discussed, the parties could not reach an agreement in that regard.

---

[40] Choudhury (2020), p. 35. However, statistics show that tribunals usually shift the allocation of costs for winning investors, whereas for winning host states, tribunals tend to adopt a '*pay-your-own-way*' approach, meaning that each party pays its own costs *see*, Franck (2019), p. 218.

[41] Vohryzek-Griest (2009), p. 87.

[42] Asteriti (2015), p. 270.

[43] *See* this book "Annex 3: *Counterclaims in Numbers*".

[44] These are: *Paushok v Mongolia; Perenco v Ecuador*; *Burlington v Ecuador; Chevron v Ecuador*; *David Aven v Costa Rica* and *Metro de Lima v Peru*, *see* this book "Annex 1: *Counterclaims with an Environmental Related-Issue*".

While these two cases are the only examples of successful environmental counterclaims in investment arbitration, increasing environmental awareness might be conducive to host states filing this type of counterclaims more often. For instance, the *Perenco v Ecuador* tribunal opined that:

> Proper environmental stewardship has assumed great importance in today's world. The Tribunal agrees that if a legal relationship between an investor and the State permits the filing of a claim by the State for environmental damage caused by the investor's activities and such a claim is substantiated, the State is entitled to full reparation in accordance with the requirements of the applicable law.[45]

However, the decisions in *Perenco v Ecuador* and in *Burlington v Ecuador* have begotten mixed reactions. Some authors consider the *Perenco v Ecuador* and *Burlington v Ecuador* decisions on environmental counterclaims as a turning point, opening investment arbitration as a forum for adjudicating environmental damages caused by the investors.[46] These cases thus evince that environmental counterclaims in investment arbitration are not a '*totally hopeless venture*'.[47] Other authors are more cautious on the importance attributed to those decisions. They do so either by highlighting that in both cases, Ecuador obtained '*pyrrhic victories*' as the damages Ecuador had to pay for the claimants' claims were significantly higher,[48] or by underscoring that the prospect of investors' liability in investment arbitration is rather extremely exceptional.[49]

At this stage, the discourse on environmental counterclaims in investment arbitration has left more questions than answers: what is the societal and practical relevance of seeking redress for environmental damages in investment arbitration? How do environmental counterclaims function in investment arbitration? Are arbitral tribunals entitled and suited for ruling upon environmental counterclaims? Would do they effectively redress all kind of environmental damages?

1.2 Scope of the Research

This book focuses on the functioning of environmental counterclaims in investment arbitration, particularly on the requirements of jurisdiction, connection between the claim and the counterclaim, and cause of action (or legal basis). While these requirements have been addressed, directly or indirectly, by some legal scholars, and perhaps more restrictively by arbitral tribunals, the deconstruction of those

---

[45] *Perenco Ecuador Ltd v Republic of Ecuador and Empresa Estatal Petróleos del Ecuador (Petroecuador)*, ICSID Case No ARB/08/6, Interim Decision on the Environmental Counterclaim (11 August 2015) para. 34.

[46] Sullivan and Kirsey (2017), p. 115. Similarly, Schill and Djanic (2018), p. 52.

[47] Bilanová (2020), p. 405.

[48] Scherer et al. (2021), p. 434.

[49] Sharma (2020), p. 422.

requirements is indispensable: not only because of the lack of systematisation of the instrument of counterclaims in investment arbitration, but also due to the lack of coherence in its study.

Against this backdrop, Chap. 2 sets the theoretical underpinnings of the research. This Chapter undertakes a comparative analysis of the instrument of counterclaims in the broader spectrum of international dispute resolution. Subsequently, it considers investment arbitration and its particularities, and the possible implications for counterclaims. Finally, given the intricate relation between international investment law and environmental protection, the Chapter specifically explores the utility of environmental counterclaims in investment arbitration.

Chapter 3 analyses the jurisdiction of arbitral tribunals to decide on environmental counterclaims. Accordingly, this Chapter lays out the tribunals' jurisdiction and power to decide counterclaims in investment arbitration in the broader sense. Subsequently, it delves into the jurisdiction of arbitral tribunals over environmental counterclaims both in contract-based and treaty-based investment arbitration. With respect to the latter, this Chapter examines the traditional obstacles for the submission of environmental counterclaims divided in two fronts: the interpretation of the underlying IIA and the possible exclusion of contractual counterclaims in treaty-based investment arbitration. Finally, it critically revises the interpretation of dispute settlement provisions *vis-à-vis* environmental counterclaims and proposes some prospective solutions to overcome the challenges of interpretation.

Chapter 4 scrutinises the requirement of connection between the counterclaim and the main claim, as well as the implications of this requirement for environmental counterclaims. As such, this Chapter firstly explores the justifications for the requisite connection. Subsequently, it reflects on the proper characterisation of this requirement. Finally, this Chapter addresses the dilution of the connection requirement into various balancing factors and the implications thereof for environmental counterclaims.

Chapter 5 provides an assessment on the cause of action (or legal basis) for an environmental counterclaim in investment arbitration and the appropriateness of bestowing an arbitral tribunal with the power to entertain such counterclaims. Accordingly, this Chapter analyses what environmental obligations could give rise to counterclaims in contract-based investment arbitration and in treaty-based investment arbitration. Finally, it delves into the appropriateness of tribunals in investment arbitration deciding environmental counterclaims both from a technical/procedural viewpoint as well as from a policy perspective.

Chapter 6 presents the main take-aways from this monograph and the overall prospects for an environmental counterclaim in investment arbitration. In arriving to its conclusions, this book focuses on an in-depth analysis of the surveyed investment arbitration cases where counterclaims were submitted, legal interpretation of treaties and other instruments, the formulation of provisions rendering investment arbitration more amenable to environmental counterclaims, and in general, the discussion of the theoretical framework supporting the availability of environmental counterclaims.

References

Asteriti A (2015) Environmental law in investment arbitration: procedural means of incorporation. J World Invest Trade 16(2):248–273

Asteriti A (2016) Climate change policies and foreign investment: some salient legal issues. In: Levashova Y, Lambooy T, Dekker I (eds) Bridging the gap between international investment law and the environment. Eleven, The Hague, pp 145–186

Barral V (2012) Sustainable development in international law: nature and operation of an evolutive legal norm. Eur J Int Law 23(2):377–400

Behn D, Langford M (2017) Trumping the environment? An empirical perspective on the legitimacy of investment treaty arbitration. J World Invest Trade 18(1):14–61

Beyerlin U (2013) Sustainable development. In: Wolfrum R (ed) Max Planck encyclopedia of public international law. Oxford University Press, Oxford

Bilanová A (2020) Environmental counterclaims in investment arbitration. Eur Invest Law Arbitr Rev 5:400–411

Bjorklund AK (2019) Sustainable development and international investment law. In: Miles K (ed) Research handbook on environment and investment law. Edward Elgar Publishing, Cheltenham, pp 38–68

Boisson de Chazournes L (2017) Environmental Protection and Investment Arbitration: Yin and Yang? Anuario Colombiano de Derecho Internacional 10:371–400

Boyle A (1999) Codification of international environmental law and the international law commission: injurious consequences revisited. In: Boyle A, Freestone D (eds) International law and sustainable development: past achievements and future challenges. Oxford University Press, Oxford, pp 61–85

Cassels J (2001) Outlaws: multinational corporations and catastrophic law. Cumberland Law Rev 31:311–336

Chi M (2018) Integrating sustainable development in international investment law: normative incompatibility, system integration and governance implications. Routledge, New York

Choudhury B (2020) International investment law and non-economic issues. Vanderbilt J Transnatl Law 53(1):1–78

Douglas Z (2013) The enforcement of environmental norms in investment treaty arbitration. In: Dupuy PM, Viñuales JE (eds) Harnessing foreign investment to promote environmental protection: incentives and safeguards. Cambridge University Press, Cambridge, pp 415–444

Dünnwald S (2015) Bilateral and multilateral investment treaties and their relationship with environmental norms and measures. Duncker & Humblot, Berlin

Dupuy PM, Viñuales JE (2018) International environmental law, 2nd edn. Cambridge University Press, Cambridge

Franck SD (2019) Arbitration costs: myths and realities in investment arbitration. Oxford University Press, Oxford

Kulick A (2012) Global public interest in international investment law. Cambridge University Press, Cambridge

Lowe V (1999) Sustainable development and unsustainable arguments. In: Boyle A, Freestone D (eds) International law and sustainable development: past achievements and future challenges. Oxford University Press, Oxford, pp 19–37

Martini (2017) Balancing investors' rights with environmental protection in international investment arbitration: an assessment of recent trends in investment treaty drafting. Int Lawyer 50(3): 529–584

Mathur C, Morehouse W (2002) Twice poisoned Bhopal: notes on the continuing aftermath of the world's worst industrial disaster. Int Labor Work Class-Hist 62:69–75

Miles K (2013) The origins of international investment law: empire, environment and the safeguarding of capital. Cambridge University Press, Cambridge

Miles W, Lawry-White M (2019) Arbitral institutions and the enforcement of climate change obligations for the benefit of all stakeholders: the role of ICSID. ICSID Rev 34(1):1–31

Mistura A (2019) Integrating civil liability principles into international investment law: a solution to environmental damage caused by foreign investors? In: Sachs LE, Johnson LJ, Coleman J (eds) Yearbook on international investment law & policy 2017. Oxford University Press, Oxford, pp 446–491

Morgera E (2020) Corporate environmental accountability in international law, 2nd edn. Oxford University Press, Oxford

Popova IC, Poon F (2015) From perpetual respondent to aspiring counterclaimant? State counterclaims in the new wave of investment treaties. BCDR Int Arbitr Rev 2(2):223–260

Sands P, Peel J, Fabra A, Mackenzie R (2018) Principles of international environmental law, 4th edn. Cambridge University Press, Cambridge

Scherer M, Bruce S, Reschke J (2021) Environmental counterclaims in investment treaty arbitration. ICSID Rev 36(2):413–440

Schill SW, Djanic V (2018) Wherefore art thou? Towards a public interest-based justification of international investment law. ICSID Rev 33(1):29–55

Shao X (2021) Environmental and human rights counterclaims in international investment arbitration: at the crossroads of domestic and international law. J Int Econ Law 24(1):157–179

Sharma G (2020) Environmental claims by states in investment treaty arbitration. Eur Invest Law Arbitr Rev 5:412–425

Sullivan J, Kirsey V (2017) Environmental policies: a shield or a sword in investment arbitration? J World Invest Trade 18(1):100–130

Thomé H (2021) Holding transnational corporations accountable for environmental harm through counterclaims in investor-state dispute settlement: myth or reality? J World Invest Trade 22: 651–686

Viñuales JE (2019) Foreign investment and the environment in international law: current trends. In: Miles K (ed) Research handbook on environment and investment law. Edward Elgar Publishing, Cheltenham, pp 12–37

Vohryzek-Griest A (2009) State counterclaims in investor-state disputes: a history of 30 years of failure. Revista Colombiana de Derecho Internacional 15:83–123

Other Documents

Report of the World Commission on Environment and Development (04 August 1987) UN Doc A/43/427 and Annex ‘Our Common Future’ (Brundtland Report)

UN Conference on Environment and Development (12 August 1992) Rio Declaration on Environment and Development. UN Doc A/CONF.151/26 (Vol I)

UNCTAD (2017) World Investment Report 2017: Investment and the Digital Economy. UN Publication

UNGA (21 October 2015) Transforming our World: The 2030 Agenda for Sustainable Development. UN Doc A/RES/70/1

Chapter 2
The Contextualisation of Environmental Counterclaims: A Comparative Perspective

Before embarking upon a critical analysis of environmental counterclaims in investment arbitration, their availability, functioning and (in some cases) facilitation, this Chapter sets the theoretical underpinnings of the book. By this means, the first section analyses the instrument of counterclaims from a comparative perspective in the broader spectrum of international dispute resolution [Sect. 2.1]. However, a comparative analysis demands the contextualisation of the specific characteristics and nuances of the system brought into question. The second section thus assesses the instrument of environmental counterclaims through the prism of investment arbitration and its particularities [Sect. 2.2]. Finally, the third section draws some preliminary conclusions on the functioning of counterclaims in investment arbitration, the instrument's rationale and its potential for redressing environmental damage [Sect. 2.3].

2.1 Counterclaims from a Comparative Perspective in International Dispute Resolution

By means of a counterclaim, the respondent seeks something more than the mere rejection of the main claim in the same proceedings.[1] While there is no uniform definition of the instrument of counterclaims across the different forms of international dispute settlement,[2] the practice of various adjudicative bodies suggests that counterclaims are generally accepted in international dispute settlement as a procedural instrument.[3] Accordingly, this section dives into the instruments and

[1] Anzilotti (1930), p. 867; Murphy (2012), para. 1.

[2] Antonopoulos (2011), p. 50.

[3] de Nanteuil (2018), p. 375.

A. E. Alvarado-Garzón, *Environmental Counterclaims in Investment Arbitration*, EYIEL Monographs - Studies in European and International Economic Law 34,
https://doi.org/10.1007/978-3-031-46391-4_2

jurisprudential developments on counterclaims in various forms of international dispute settlement including the International Court of Justice (ICJ) [Sect. 2.1.1], the Iran-US Claims Tribunal (IUSCT) [Sect. 2.1.2], and International Commercial Arbitration [Sect. 2.1.3]. Subsequently, and for the sake of completeness, this section presents some short considerations on the interaction of counterclaims in other institutional frameworks such as the Permanent Court of Arbitration (PCA), the International Tribunal for the Law of the Sea (ITLOS), and the World Trade Organization (WTO) [Sect. 2.1.4]. Finally, this section displays the common features of counterclaims across the board [Sect. 2.1.5].

2.1.1 The International Court of Justice and Counterclaims

Neither the ICJ nor its Statute or Rules of Court defined the term 'counterclaim'. The same was the case for its predecessor, the Permanent Court of International Justice (PCIJ). Perhaps, this lack of definition has provided a considerable room of manoeuvre to the Court for regulating the instrument of counterclaims as it sees fit.[4] The instrument of counterclaims has therefore experienced various reforms to the rules of court and case law-based developments [Sect. 2.1.1.1]. From this, some observations on the requirements for counterclaims may be drawn [Sect. 2.1.1.2].

2.1.1.1 History and Evolution of Counterclaims

The concept of counterclaims used at the PCIJ and ICJ seems to emanate from civil procedural law, with the objective of addressing complex disputes in a comprehensive and effective manner.[5] One cannot overstate that by borrowing a concept from private law such as 'counterclaims', international law is not importing such institution as used in private law, but rather reflecting the policy behind it.[6] Thus, the development of counterclaims at the PCIJ and ICJ must be assessed in its own context. In this sense, the discussion on counterclaims certainly started at the PCIJ with the elaboration of a set of rules that firstly sketched the requirements for submitting counterclaims [Sect. 2.1.1.1.1]. Afterwards, the ICJ took the sample of the PCIJ Rules of Court and, from its own jurisprudential developments, the ICJ modified in several occasions the specific rule on counterclaims [Sect. 2.1.1.1.2].

[4] Kolb (2013), p. 676. Similarly, Thirlway (1999), p. 198; Arcari (2018), para. 38.

[5] Antonopoulos (2011), pp. 7–10.

[6] *International Status of South-West Africa* (Advisory Opinion) [1950] ICJ Rep 128, Separate Opinion by Sir Arnold McNair, 148.

2.1.1.1.1 During the Permanent Court of International Justice

The Statute of the PCIJ did not address the instrument of counterclaims. Rather, when devising its procedural rules, the PCIJ introduced the possibility to submit counterclaims via its Rules of Court.[7] Pursuant to Article 40 of the PCIJ Rules of Court of 1922, counterclaims were merely mentioned:

> (. . .) Counter-cases shall contain:
>
> 1. The affirmation or contestation of the facts state in the case
> 2. A statement of additional facts, if any;
> 3. A statement of law
> 4. Conclusion based on the facts stated; *these conclusions may include counter-claims*, in so far as the latter come within the jurisdiction of the Court;
> 5. A list of document in support; these documents shall be attached to the counter-cases.[8]

The PCIJ discussed this provision for the first time in the famous *Chorzów Factory* case in 1928.[9] In this case, Germany, as the applicant, did not oppose to the admissibility of the counterclaim raised by Poland, the respondent. Thus, the PCIJ concluded that it was competent to hear the counterclaim, given that the Court's jurisdiction was based on the will of the parties.[10] Moreover, the PCIJ considered that, since both claim and counterclaim were based on the Versailles Treaty, they were connected, hence, the counterclaim was admissible.[11] Although in substance, the Polish counterclaim seemed more like a set-off than a counterclaim,[12] the Court dismissed it on the merits.

This case sparked the debate about counterclaims at the PCIJ. Despite the lack of reference in the Statute of the PCIJ to counterclaims, it was considered that a limit to the admissibility of counterclaims should exist, for instance, by requiring the counterclaim to be connected to the main claim.[13] This was not mentioned in the Rules of Court of 1922, but it found its way in the subsequent Rules of Court of 1936.

---

[7] Murphy (2012), para. 5.

[8] PCIJ, Series D—Acts and Documents concerning the organization of the Court, 'Rules of Court adopted by the Court on 24 March 1922', Art 40 (emphasis added).

[9] Larschan and Mirfendereski (1986), p. 15.

[10] *Case concerning the Factory at Chorzów (Germany v Poland)* (Merits) (13 September 1928) PCIJ Rep Series A No 17, 37.

[11] *Case concerning the Factory at Chorzów (Germany v Poland)* (Merits) (13 September 1928) PCIJ Rep Series A No 17, 38.

[12] *Case concerning the Factory at Chorzów (Germany v Poland)* (Merits) (13 September 1928) PCIJ Rep Series A No 17, 38: ('in reality... [the counterclaim] constitutes an objection to the German claim designed to obtain from Poland an indemnity... it is in fact a question of eliminating from the amount of this indemnity a sum corresponding to the value of the rights and interests which [Germany] possessed in the enterprise').

[13] Anzilotti (1930), p. 866.

The *travaux préparatoires* of the PCIJ Rules of Court of 1936 show a lengthy discussion over counterclaims and their requirements.[14] Judge Anzilotti emphasised that the main purpose of counterclaims was to enable '*the respondent to demand, in the course of the same proceedings, what was due to him from the applicant for a reason related to the dispute already pending.*'[15] He considered that, for reasons of justice, it is recommendable to decide the claim and the directly connected counterclaim in the same proceedings, following uniform standards.[16]

A new draft of the Rules of Court was presented, introducing the 'connection' between the main claim and the counterclaim, and the question emerged whether it is a connection in fact, in law, or both.[17] Judge Fromageot opined that the connection could only be on fact, while Judge Schücking observed that the connection is flexible but it would normally be in fact and in law.[18] Judge Anzilotti took a moderated approach, arguing that the direct connection would be for the Court to decide in each case.[19] By introducing an express 'direct connection' requirement, the PCIJ closed the possibility for submitting unconnected cross-claims, which otherwise would impinge on the consensual nature of international courts.[20] Consequently, in 1936 the PCIJ adopted a new set of rules, whose Article 63 provided:

> When proceedings have been instituted by means of an application, counter-claims may be presented in the submissions of the Counter-Memorial, provided that such counter-claims are directly connected with the subject of the application and that they come within the jurisdiction of the Court. Any claim which is not directly connected with the subject of the original application must be presented in the form of a separate application and may form the subject of distinct proceedings or be joined by the Court to the original proceedings.

Respondents in two cases made use of the newly adopted Article 63 of the Rules of Court of 1936 namely in the *Diversion of Water from the Meuse*,[21] and in the

[14] PCIJ, Series D—Acts and Documents concerning the Organization of the Court, Third Addendum to No 2, 'Elaboration of the Rules of Court of March 11th, 1936' (Thirteenth Meeting (28 May 1934a)) 105.

[15] PCIJ, Series D—Acts and Documents concerning the Organization of the Court, Third Addendum to No 2, 'Elaboration of the Rules of Court of March 11th, 1936' (Thirteenth Meeting (28 May 1934a)) 106.

[16] Anzilotti (1930), p. 870.

[17] PCIJ, Series D—Acts and Documents concerning the Organization of the Court, Third Addendum to No 2, 'Elaboration of the Rules of Court of March 11th, 1936' (Fourteenth Meeting (29 May 1934b)) 111.

[18] PCIJ, Series D—Acts and Documents concerning the Organization of the Court, Third Addendum to No 2, 'Elaboration of the Rules of Court of March 11th, 1936' (Fourteenth Meeting (29 May 1934b)) 112.

[19] PCIJ, Series D—Acts and Documents concerning the Organization of the Court, Third Addendum to No 2, 'Elaboration of the Rules of Court of March 11th, 1936' (Fourteenth Meeting (29 May 1934b)) 112.

[20] Antonopoulos (2011), p. 64.

[21] *The Diversion of Water from the Meuse (The Netherlands v Belgium)* (Judgment) (28 June 1937) PCIJ Rep Series A/B No 70.

Panevezys-Saldutiskis Railway[22] cases. However, the Court did not analyse the counterclaims in depth, leaving the new provision untested. Article 63 of the Rules of Court of 1936 did not fade into oblivion since it served as the inspiration for the ICJ and the drafting of its own Rules of Court, containing an almost identical provision on counterclaims.

2.1.1.1.2 From the Establishment of the International Court of Justice Onwards

The evolution of the instrument of counterclaims at the ICJ oscillates between the development on the jurisprudence and the redrafting of the Rules of Court. Yet, the most important legal points therein can be identified. Like its predecessor, the ICJ Statute did not foresee the possibility to submit counterclaims. This has been included in the Rules of Court. Initially, Article 63 of the ICJ Rules of Court of 1946 contemplated counterclaims as follows:

> When proceedings have been instituted by means of an application, a counterclaim may be presented in the submissions of the Counter-Memorial, provided that such counter-claim is directly connected with the subject-matter of the application and that it comes within the jurisdiction of the Court. In the event of doubt as to the connection between the question presented by way of counter-claim and the subject-matter of the application the Court shall, after due examination, direct whether or not the question thus presented shall be joined to the original proceedings.

One may deduce from this provision that the Court had some interpretative room of manoeuvre on the connection between the claim and counterclaim, as long as it would not exceed the limits of its jurisdiction.[23] Under this set of rules, the ICJ decided a counterclaim in the *Asylum* case.[24] Peru, the respondent, filed a counter-claim against Colombia, the applicant, arguing that the prolonged asylum to Victor Raúl Haya de la Torre granted by Colombia was in violation of the Havana Convention on Asylum.[25] Colombia disputed whether the counterclaim was directly connected to the main claim but the Court concluded that one of the applicant's claims rested on the legality of the asylum, thus, there was a direct connection.[26] The counterclaim finally succeeded on the merits. This was certainly the first time the ICJ ruled upon the 'direct connection', however, the Court did not elaborate on this criterion.

In 1972, the ICJ modified its Rules of Court, keeping the provision on counter-claims identical but under a different numbering namely Article 68 thereof. A few

[22] *The Panevezys-Saldutiskis Railway Case (Estonia v Lithuania)* (Judgment) (28 February 1939) PCIJ Rep Series A/B No 76.

[23] Larschan and Mirfendereski (1986), p. 15.

[24] *Colombian-Peruvian Asylum Case (Colombia v Peru)* (Judgment) [1950] ICJ Rep 266.

[25] *Colombian-Peruvian Asylum Case (Colombia v Peru)* (Judgment) [1950] ICJ Rep 266, 280.

[26] *Colombian-Peruvian Asylum Case (Colombia v Peru)* (Judgment) [1950] ICJ Rep 266, 280.

years after, in 1978, a new reform on the Rules of Court was undertaken and counterclaims were included in Article 80 of the new rules as follows:

> 1. A counter-claim may be presented provided that it is directly connected with the subject-matter of the claim of the other party and that it comes within the jurisdiction of the Court.
>
> 2. A counter-claim shall be made in the Counter-Memorial of the party presenting it, and shall appear as part of the submissions of that party.
>
> 3. In the event of doubt as to the connection between the question presented by way of counter-claim and the subject-matter of the claim of the other party the Court shall, after hearing the parties, decide whether or not the question thus presented shall be joined to the original proceedings.

Under this new formulation, the ICJ decided the most emblematic case on counter-claims: the *Application of the Convention on Genocide*.[27] The former Yugoslavia, the respondent, counterclaimed against Bosnia and Herzegovina, the applicant, for violations of the Genocide Convention, particularly acts of genocide against Serbs in the territory of the applicant. The applicant nevertheless disputed the admissibility of the counterclaim.[28] Here, the most important development referred to the 'direct connection' between claim and counterclaim.

Given the lack of definition of 'direct connection', the Court considered that this requirement is to be assessed at its sole discretion, but it usually implies a connection in fact and in law.[29] The Court found no qualms with the connection in fact. Furthermore, the Court noted that both the applicant and the respondent were seeking the establishment of responsibility for the violation of the same Genocide Convention, thus, despite the lack of reciprocity in the obligations therein, the main claim and counterclaim were considered directly connected.[30]

Interestingly, Judge Weeramantry disagreed with the majority of the judges and he explained his position in the following terms: first, a counterclaim must counter the main claim, thus, by its intrinsic nature, it is not applicable for criminal acts—'*A*

[27] *Application of the Convention on the Prevention and Punishment of the Crime of Genocide (Bosnia and Herzegovina v Yugoslavia)* (Order on Counterclaims) [1997] ICJ Rep 243.

[28] *Application of the Convention on the Prevention and Punishment of the Crime of Genocide (Bosnia and Herzegovina v Yugoslavia)* (Order on Counterclaims) [1997] ICJ Rep 243, paras. 4–10.

[29] *Application of the Convention on the Prevention and Punishment of the Crime of Genocide (Bosnia and Herzegovina v Yugoslavia)* (Order on Counterclaims) [1997] ICJ Rep 243, para. 33.

[30] *Application of the Convention on the Prevention and Punishment of the Crime of Genocide (Bosnia and Herzegovina v Yugoslavia)* (Order on Counterclaims) [1997] ICJ Rep 243, para. 35: ('. . .the Parties rightly recognized that in no case could one breach of the Convention serve as an excuse for another; and whereas, however, the argument drawn from the absence of reciprocity in the scheme of the Convention is not determinative as regards the assessment of whether there is a legal connection between the principal claim and the counter-claim, in so far the two Parties pursue, with their respective claims, the same legal aim, namely the establishment of legal responsibility for violations of the Genocide Convention').

murder cannot be set off against another murder, nor a rape against a rape'.[31] Second, the counterclaim was based on different facts, victims, motivations, venues, etc., thus, it did not promote procedural economy in the particular dispute.[32] In any case, the Court never decided the merits of the counterclaim as by a letter dated 20 April 2000, the respondent requested the withdrawal of its counterclaim and the applicant did not object. Whilst the premise that a counterclaim must attack the main claim is questionable, the argument on procedural economy bears significant weight. Hence, the Court could have elaborated further on the complexity the counterclaim might have added to the case.

Some years later, in a similar dispute between Croatia and Serbia, the latter as respondent filed a counterclaim against Croatia, the applicant, for the violations of the Genocide Convention committed against the Serb population in the Krajina region.[33] Without much analysis, the Court concluded that the counterclaim was admissible,[34] but dismissed it on the merits.[35]

In a different dispute, the *Oil Platforms* case,[36] Iran as the applicant instituted proceedings against the US, the respondent, for the destruction caused by several US warships of three Iranian offshore oil production complexes. The US counterclaimed that Iran was engaged in military actions affecting maritime commerce, thus, breaching the Treaty of Amity of 1955.[37] The Court concluded that the counterclaim was both within the jurisdiction of the Court and directly connected to the main claim, thus, it was admissible in the interest of proper administration of justice.[38] Perhaps the most important legal development from this case stems from the Separate Opinion of Judge Higgins with regards to when a counterclaim may be considered 'within jurisdiction' of the Court: '*it is not essential that the basis of jurisdiction in the claim and in the counter-claim be identical. It is sufficient that there is jurisdiction. (Indeed, were it otherwise, counter-claims in, for example, tort*

[31] *Application of the Convention on the Prevention and Punishment of the Crime of Genocide (Bosnia and Herzegovina v Yugoslavia)* (Order on Counterclaims) [1997] ICJ Rep 243, Dissenting Opinion Judge Weeramantry, 289–292.

[32] *Application of the Convention on the Prevention and Punishment of the Crime of Genocide (Bosnia and Herzegovina v Yugoslavia)* (Order on Counterclaims) [1997] ICJ Rep 243, Dissenting Opinion Judge Weeramantry.

[33] *Application of the Convention on the Prevention and Punishment of the Crime of Genocide (Croatia v Serbia)* (Merits) [2015] ICJ Rep 3, para. 121.

[34] *Application of the Convention on the Prevention and Punishment of the Crime of Genocide (Croatia v Serbia)* (Merits) [2015] ICJ Rep 3, para. 123.

[35] *Application of the Convention on the Prevention and Punishment of the Crime of Genocide (Croatia v Serbia)* (Merits) [2015] ICJ Rep 3, paras. 446 et seqq.

[36] *Oil Platforms (Iran v United States of America)* (Order on Counterclaim) [1998] ICJ Rep 190.

[37] *Oil Platforms (Iran v United States of America)* (Order on Counterclaim) [1998] ICJ Rep 190, para. 4.

[38] *Oil Platforms (Iran v United States of America)* (Order on Counterclaim) [1998] ICJ Rep 190, para. 43.

could never be brought, as they routinely are, to actions initiated in contract).'[39] The counterclaim was nevertheless dismissed on the merits.[40]

Another example of the instrument of counterclaims at the ICJ is the *Land and Maritime Boundary between Cameroon and Nigeria* case.[41] Nigeria, the respondent, submitted a counterclaim against Cameroon, the applicant, for the illegal incursions into Nigeria's territory and the ensuing damages caused.[42] The Court concluded that the counterclaim was admissible, emphasising that both the claim and the counterclaim pursued the same legal remedy—the establishment of international responsibility.[43] Although this standard seemingly broadens the scope of when counterclaims may be considered 'directly connected' with the main claim, the Court did not further elaborate on it. The counterclaim was in any case rejected on the merits.[44]

In the *Armed Activities on the Territory of the Congo* case,[45] Uganda counterclaimed against Congo for breaches of international law, such as the prohibition to the use of force and to assist armed groups, and the non-intervention in internal affairs.[46] The Court considered that they were indeed counterclaims because they sought the establishment of international responsibility and reparation on that account.[47] Here, the Declaration of Judge Verhoeven set an important standard. He admitted that the connection requirement should not be applied in a 'mechanical' manner, but rather, taking heed of a counterclaim's purpose namely providing a thorough understanding of the dispute and avoiding contradictory decisions.[48] He belaboured nevertheless for a strict interpretation of the terms 'directly connected' in

[39] *Oil Platforms (Iran v United States of America)* (Order on Counterclaim) [1998] ICJ Rep 190, Separate Opinion Judge Higgins, 218.

[40] *Oil Platforms (Iran v United States of America)* (Merits) [2003] ICJ Rep 161.

[41] *Land and Maritime Boundary between Cameroon and Nigeria (Cameroon v Nigeria)* (Order) [1999] ICJ Rep 983.

[42] *Land and Maritime Boundary between Cameroon and Nigeria (Cameroon v Nigeria)* (Order) [1999] ICJ Rep 983, 984–985.

[43] *Land and Maritime Boundary between Cameroon and Nigeria (Cameroon v Nigeria)* (Order) [1999] ICJ Rep 983, 985.

[44] *Land and Maritime Boundary between Cameroon and Nigeria (Cameroon v Nigeria, Equatorial Guinea intervening)* (Counterclaims) [2002] ICJ Rep 303.

[45] *Armed Activities on the Territory of the Congo (Democratic Republic of the Congo v Uganda)* (Order on Counterclaims) [2001] ICJ Rep 660.

[46] *Armed Activities on the Territory of the Congo (Democratic Republic of the Congo v Uganda)* (Order on Counterclaims) [2001] ICJ Rep 660, para. 4.

[47] *Armed Activities on the Territory of the Congo (Democratic Republic of the Congo v Uganda)* (Order on Counterclaims) [2001] ICJ Rep 660, para. 29.

[48] *Armed Activities on the Territory of the Congo (Democratic Republic of the Congo v Uganda)* (Order on Counterclaims) [2001] ICJ Rep 660, Declaration of Judge Verhoeven, 684.

the rules governing counterclaims, given the consensual nature of the Court's jurisdiction.[49] The counterclaim finally failed on the merits.[50]

In 2001, the ICJ undertook its latest amendment to its Rules of Court with respect to counterclaims. The provision underwent a few changes on the wording, but the list of requirements remained the same. Thus, until date, Article 80 of the Rules of Court reads:

> 1. The Court may entertain a counter-claim only if it comes within the jurisdiction of the Court and is directly connected with the subject-matter of the claim of the other party.
>
> 2. A counter-claim shall be made in the Counter-Memorial and shall appear as part of the submissions contained therein. The right of the other party to present its views in writing on the counter-claim, in an additional pleading, shall be preserved, irrespective of any decision of the Court, in accordance with Article 45, paragraph 2, of these Rules, concerning the filing of further written pleadings.
>
> 3. Where an objection is raised concerning the application of paragraph 1 or whenever the Court deems necessary, the Court shall take its decision thereon after hearing the parties.

Following this latest modification of the Rules of Court, counterclaims came to play in the *Jurisdictional Immunities of the State* case.[51] Italy, the respondent, filed a counterclaim against Germany, the applicant, for the violation of humanitarian law against Italian victims during World War II.[52] The Court recognised that the admissibility of counterclaims pursuant to Article 80 of the Rules of Court depends on whether the counterclaim is within the Court's jurisdiction and whether it is directly connected with the main claim.[53] However, after its analysis, the Court concluded that the counterclaim was beyond the temporal scope of the Court's jurisdiction.[54] Judge Trindade disagreed with the Court's decision, but some of the aspects in its extensive analysis on counterclaims, albeit *obiter dictum*, deserve consideration. First, he recognised counterclaims as a juridical instrument of procedural law.[55] Second, he emphasised that the parties to the claim and the counterclaim must be the same.[56] Third, he suggested that the connection between main claim and

[49] *Armed Activities on the Territory of the Congo (Democratic Republic of the Congo v Uganda)* (Order on Counterclaims) [2001] ICJ Rep 660, Declaration of Judge Verhoeven, 685.

[50] *Armed Activities on the Territory of the Congo (Democratic Republic of the Congo v Uganda)* (Merits) [2005] ICJ Rep 168.

[51] *Jurisdictional Immunities of the State (Germany v Italy)* (Order on Counterclaim) [2010] ICJ Rep 310.

[52] *Jurisdictional Immunities of the State (Germany v Italy)* (Order on Counterclaim) [2010] ICJ Rep 310, para. 3.

[53] *Jurisdictional Immunities of the State (Germany v Italy)* (Order on Counterclaim) [2010] ICJ Rep 310, para. 14.

[54] *Jurisdictional Immunities of the State (Germany v Italy)* (Order on Counterclaim) [2010] ICJ Rep 310, para. 30.

[55] *Jurisdictional Immunities of the State (Germany v Italy)* (Order on Counterclaim) [2010] ICJ Rep 310, Dissenting opinion of Judge Cançado Trindade, para. 4.

[56] *Jurisdictional Immunities of the State (Germany v Italy)* (Order on Counterclaim) [2010] ICJ Rep 310, Dissenting opinion of Judge Cançado Trindade, para. 11.

counterclaim should be in fact and law, but it must be assessed with certain flexibility, mindful of the purposes of counterclaims.[57]

In the *Certain Activities carried out by Nicaragua in the Border Area* dispute, Nicaragua, the respondent, filed a counterclaim against Costa Rica, the applicant, for the violation of the borders by constructing a road, the failure to protect the environment, and for the non-implementation of provisional measures.[58] There are two important legal developments in this case. First, the Court considered that it is not bound by the sequence of requirements set forth in Article 80 of the Rules of Court.[59] Hence, it started its analysis with the direct connection requirement instead of jurisdiction. Second, the Court delineated some criteria to determine the direct connection of the counterclaim with the main claim, for instance, whether the facts relate to the same geographical area, during the same period or to similar types of conduct; or if the parties rely on the same legal principles or instruments.[60] The Court ultimately rejected the counterclaims, but Judge Guillaume disagreed and questioned the Court's restrictive understanding of a connection between a claim and a counterclaim in the particular case.[61]

In the *Alleged Violations of Sovereign Rights and Maritime Space in the Caribbean Sea* case, Colombia, the respondent, filed a counterclaim against Nicaragua, the applicant, for the infringement of Colombia's rights in the Caribbean Sea.[62] The most important legal development on this case was the analysis of whether the counterclaim was within the Court's jurisdiction, which necessitates some context. Colombia denounced the Pact of Bogotá on 27 November 2012, which contains a sunset clause of one year.[63] Within this one-year period, Nicaragua filed its application on 26 November 2013, invoking Article XXXI of the Pact of Bogotá as the basis for the Court's jurisdiction. Colombia filed its counterclaims on 17 November 2016 arguing the same jurisdictional basis, although the Pact of Bogotá ceased to be in force between the parties in the meantime.

---

[57] *Jurisdictional Immunities of the State (Germany v Italy)* (Order on Counterclaim) [2010] ICJ Rep 310, Dissenting opinion of Judge Cançado Trindade, paras. 14–15.

[58] *Certain Activities Carried Out by Nicaragua in the Border Area (Costa Rica v Nicaragua), Construction of a Road in Costa Rica along the San Juan River (Nicaragua v Costa Rica)* (Order on Counterclaims) [2013] ICJ Rep 200, para. 15.

[59] *Certain Activities Carried Out by Nicaragua in the Border Area (Costa Rica v Nicaragua), Construction of a Road in Costa Rica along the San Juan River (Nicaragua v Costa Rica)* (Order on Counterclaims) [2013] ICJ Rep 200, para. 27.

[60] *Certain Activities Carried Out by Nicaragua in the Border Area (Costa Rica v Nicaragua), Construction of a Road in Costa Rica along the San Juan River (Nicaragua v Costa Rica)* (Order on Counterclaims) [2013] ICJ Rep 200, para. 32.

[61] *Certain Activities Carried Out by Nicaragua in the Border Area (Costa Rica v Nicaragua), Construction of a Road in Costa Rica along the San Juan River (Nicaragua v Costa Rica)* (Order on Counterclaims) [2013] ICJ Rep 200, Declaration of Judge ad hoc Guillaume, para. 17.

[62] *Alleged Violations of Sovereign Rights and Maritime Spaces in the Caribbean Sea (Nicaragua v Colombia)* (Order on Counterclaims) [2017] ICJ Rep 289, para. 14.

[63] Article LVI American Treaty on Pacific Settlement 'Pact of Bogotá', signed on 30 April 1948.

By citing the *Nottebohm* case, the ICJ in the *Alleged Violations of Sovereign Rights and Maritime Space in the Caribbean Sea* case considered that '*once the Court has established jurisdiction to entertain a case, it has jurisdiction to deal with all its phases; the subsequent lapse of the title cannot deprive the Court of its jurisdiction.*'[64] Furthermore, the Court highlighted that counterclaims are, albeit autonomous, incidental to the main proceedings. The Court thus concluded that the lapse of the jurisdictional title does not affect the Court's jurisdiction to rule upon counterclaims.[65]

This was a certainly controversial decision. Judge Yusuf opined that the Court needs to establish jurisdiction *de novo* only when the counterclaim is not based on the same jurisdictional title as the main claim, in which case, the Court solely checks whether the counterclaim falls within the scope of consent.[66] Judges Tomka, Gaja, Sebutinde, Gevorgian and Daudet considered that the majority of the Court inappropriately relied on the *Nottebohm* case out of context, and that a claim, in a form of a counterclaim, could not be based on a non-existent jurisdictional basis.[67] Furthermore, they argued that Colombia's counterclaims did not contribute to the administration of justice since they have already delayed the proceedings.[68] Finally, after disagreeing with the factual analysis on the counterclaims, Judge Caron suggested some justifications for counterclaims: they promote procedural economy and the sound administration of justice; they avoid inconsistent results; they should not

---

[64] *Alleged Violations of Sovereign Rights and Maritime Spaces in the Caribbean Sea (Nicaragua v Colombia)* (Order on Counterclaims) [2017] ICJ Rep 289, para. 67.

[65] *Alleged Violations of Sovereign Rights and Maritime Spaces in the Caribbean Sea (Nicaragua v Colombia)* (Order on Counterclaims) [2017] ICJ Rep 289, para. 67: ('The Court notes that the opposite approach would have the disadvantage of allowing the applicant, in some instances, to remove the basis of jurisdiction after an application has been filed and thus insulate itself from any counter-claims submitted in the same proceedings and having a direct connection with the principal claim').

[66] *Alleged Violations of Sovereign Rights and Maritime Spaces in the Caribbean Sea (Nicaragua v Colombia)* (Order on Counterclaims) [2017] ICJ Rep 289, Declaration of Vice-President Yusuf, para. 8.

[67] *Alleged Violations of Sovereign Rights and Maritime Spaces in the Caribbean Sea (Nicaragua v Colombia)* (Order on Counterclaims) [2017] ICJ Rep 289, Joint Opinion of Judges Tomka, Gaja, Sebutinde, Gevorgian and judge ad hoc Daudet, para. 21. Although Judge Greenwood acknowledged that the *Nottebohm* case did not deal with counterclaims, he shared the opinion that a counterclaim is incidental to the main proceedings, *see Alleged Violations of Sovereign Rights and Maritime Spaces in the Caribbean Sea (Nicaragua v Colombia)* (Order on Counterclaims) [2017] ICJ Rep 289, Separate Opinion of Judge Greenwood, paras. 5–6.

[68] *Alleged Violations of Sovereign Rights and Maritime Spaces in the Caribbean Sea (Nicaragua v Colombia)* (Order on Counterclaims) [2017] ICJ Rep 289, Joint Opinion of Judges Tomka, Gaja, Sebutinde, Gevorgian and judge ad hoc Daudet, para. 23.

affect the applicant's rights; and adjudicating counterclaims reflects the Court's role for peaceful settlement of international disputes.[69] The foregoing history at the ICJ boils down to the definition of certain requirements for the submission of counterclaims.

2.1.1.2 Observations on the Requirements for Counterclaims at the ICJ

The ICJ certainly considers that a counterclaim seeks relief beyond the mere dismissal of the main claim,[70] but it has not provided a comprehensive definition beyond the listing of the requirements for a counterclaim. Counterclaims are categorised as part of incidental proceedings in Section D of the Rules of Court, yet this does not mean that they are completely dependent on the main claim.[71] The goal of a counterclaim is to achieve procedural economy and to provide an overview of the whole dispute, which enables the Court to decide more consistently.[72] A counterclaim must nevertheless adhere to the pre-established requirements to prevent its abuse, and it cannot infringe the applicant's rights or compromise the proper administration of justice.[73]

The latest version of Article 80 of the Rules of Court provides that the requirements therein are mandatory given the expression 'only if'.[74] However, even if the requirements are complied with, the Court retains the discretion to reject the

[69] *Alleged Violations of Sovereign Rights and Maritime Spaces in the Caribbean Sea (Nicaragua v Colombia)* (Order on Counterclaims) [2017] ICJ Rep 289, Dissenting Opinion of Judge ad hoc Caron, paras. 22–28.

[70] *Application of the Convention on the Prevention and Punishment of the Crime of Genocide (Bosnia and Herzegovina v Yugoslavia)* (Order on Counterclaims) [1997] ICJ Rep 243, para. 28. Similarly, *Armed Activities on the Territory of the Congo (Democratic Republic of the Congo v Uganda)* (Order on Counterclaims) [2001] ICJ Rep 660, para. 29; Kolb (2013), p. 659.

[71] Considering that counterclaims are essentially, albeit not wholly, incidental, one may argue that the discontinuance of the main claim extinguishes the counterclaim. However, Robert Kolb opines that counterclaims remained as independent claims, even though they are connected to the main claim. Thus, once a counterclaim is admitted under the parameters of Article 80 Rules of Court, the fate of the main claim should not affect the counterclaim, *see* Kolb (2013), p. 659.

[72] *Application of the Convention on the Prevention and Punishment of the Crime of Genocide (Bosnia and Herzegovina v Yugoslavia)* (Order on Counterclaims) [1997] ICJ Rep 243, para. 30.

[73] *Application of the Convention on the Prevention and Punishment of the Crime of Genocide (Bosnia and Herzegovina v Yugoslavia)* (Order on Counterclaims) [1997] ICJ Rep 243, paras. 30–31. Similarly, *Oil Platforms (Iran v United States of America)* (Order on Counterclaim) [1998] ICJ Rep 190, para. 43; *Armed Activities on the Territory of the Congo (Democratic Republic of the Congo v Uganda)* (Order on Counterclaims) [2001] ICJ Rep 660, para. 48.

[74] Kolb (2013), p. 662. Sean D Murphy suggests that even if the applicant does not raise any objections against the counterclaim, the Court should analyse the requirements of Article 80 Rules of Court. *See* Murphy (2012), para. 17; Arcari (2018), para. 15.

counterclaim given the expression 'may entertain'.[75] This would be the case, for instance, where joining the counterclaim to the main proceedings would not serve the proper administration of justice.[76] Until date, there has been no case where the Court had used its discretion to decline a counterclaim despite having found that the requirements of Article 80 Rules of Court were met.[77] Be that as it may, the three requirements a counterclaim must fulfil are: *first*, a counterclaim must fall within the jurisdiction of the Court [Sect. 2.1.1.2.1]; *second*, a counterclaim must be directly connected with the main claim [Sect. 2.1.1.2.2]; and *third*, a counterclaim must be submitted with the counter-memorial [Sect. 2.1.1.2.3].

2.1.1.2.1 Within the Court's Jurisdiction

Since the PCIJ Rules of Procedure of 1926, the first and most important requirement for counterclaims is that they must fall within the jurisdiction of the Court.[78] There is no need for the counterclaim to be grounded on the same jurisdictional title as the main claim, but rather on a valid title whereby the parties submit to the jurisdiction of the Court.[79] The Court has highlighted that when the counterclaim is based on the same jurisdictional title as the main claim there is no need to establish jurisdiction *de novo*.[80] However, some judges have disagreed with this approach.[81] The purpose of this requirement is to prevent that the jurisdictional limits set by the parties are

[75] *Application of the Convention on the Prevention and Punishment of the Crime of Genocide (Bosnia and Herzegovina v Yugoslavia)* (Order on Counterclaims) [1997] ICJ Rep 243, Dissenting Opinion Judge Weeramantry, 288; *Application of the Convention on the Prevention and Punishment of the Crime of Genocide (Bosnia and Herzegovina v Yugoslavia)* (Order on Counterclaims) [1997] ICJ Rep 243, Separate Opinion Judge Lauterpacht, para. 18. For a different opinion *see* Thirlway (1999), p. 223: ('The question is not one of the reasonable application of the rule: if the text lays down certain conditions for the vailidity [sic] of a procedural step, states are entitled to act on the basis that those conditions are exhaustive, and that the Court does not preserve a residual discretion to adjust the application of the Rules unless the rules themselves say so'). Similarly, Antonopoulos (2011), pp. 73–74: ('once both requirements are present the Court is bound to rule that a counterclaim is admissible and does not have the discretion to decide the opposite').

[76] *Alleged Violations of Sovereign Rights and Maritime Spaces in the Caribbean Sea (Nicaragua v Colombia)* (Order on Counterclaims) [2017] ICJ Rep 289, Joint Opinion of Judges Tomka, Gaja, Sebutinde, Gevorgian and judge ad hoc Daudet, para. 4.

[77] Murphy (2012), para. 16; Arcari (2018) para. 14.

[78] Anzilotti (1930), p. 868.

[79] Anzilotti (1930), p. 869. Similarly, *Alleged Violations of Sovereign Rights and Maritime Spaces in the Caribbean Sea (Nicaragua v Colombia)* (Order on Counterclaims) [2017] ICJ Rep 289, Declaration of Vice-President Yusuf, para. 11; Murphy (2012), para. 24. For a different opinion, Antonopoulos (2011), pp. 76 et seqq.

[80] *Alleged Violations of Sovereign Rights and Maritime Spaces in the Caribbean Sea (Nicaragua v Colombia)* (Order on Counterclaims) [2017] ICJ Rep 289, para. 67.

[81] *Alleged Violations of Sovereign Rights and Maritime Spaces in the Caribbean Sea (Nicaragua v Colombia)* (Order on Counterclaims) [2017] ICJ Rep 289, Joint Opinion of Judges Tomka, Gaja, Sebutinde, Gevorgian and judge ad hoc Daudet, para. 23.

exceeded with the counterclaim,[82] since the Court has jurisdiction over a dispute only to the extent of the parties' consent.[83]

2.1.1.2.2 Direct Connection Between Claim and Counterclaim

A counterclaim is a separate claim that 'reacts' to the main claim, thus, both claim and counterclaim are linked.[84] The Rules of Court do not provide a definition of the requirement of 'directly connected' to the main claim. Although the Court on its sole discretion will assess this requirement, it usually refers to a connection in fact and in law.[85] A counterclaim may be connected in fact with the main claim if the facts occurred during the same time, in the same geographical area, or when they refer to the same type of conduct.[86] Certainly, the period of time or location must not be identical between the claim and counterclaim.[87] Moreover, this requirement does not prevent the counterclaim from bringing also new facts, since the connection refers to a same factual matrix instead of identical facts.[88]

A counterclaim may be connected in law with the main claim if the applicant and respondent seek the same legal remedy, or if they rely on the same legal principles or instruments.[89] If the respondent argues a breach of a different instrument, this may

---

[82] *Application of the Convention on the Prevention and Punishment of the Crime of Genocide (Bosnia and Herzegovina v Yugoslavia)* (Order on Counterclaims) [1997] ICJ Rep 243, para. 31.

[83] Renteln (1987), p. 385; Thirlway (1999), p. 202.

[84] *Application of the Convention on the Prevention and Punishment of the Crime of Genocide (Bosnia and Herzegovina v Yugoslavia)* (Order on Counterclaims) [1997] ICJ Rep 243, para. 27.

[85] *Application of the Convention on the Prevention and Punishment of the Crime of Genocide (Bosnia and Herzegovina v Yugoslavia)* (Order on Counterclaims) [1997] ICJ Rep 243, para. 33; *Oil Platforms (Iran v United States of America)* (Order on Counterclaim) [1998] ICJ Rep 190, para. 37; *Armed Activities on the Territory of the Congo (Democratic Republic of the Congo v Uganda)* (Order on Counterclaims) [2001] ICJ Rep 660, para. 36; *Certain Activities Carried Out by Nicaragua in the Border Area (Costa Rica v Nicaragua), Construction of a Road in Costa Rica along the San Juan River (Nicaragua v Costa Rica)* (Order on Counterclaims) [2013] ICJ Rep 200, para. 32.

[86] *Certain Activities Carried Out by Nicaragua in the Border Area (Costa Rica v Nicaragua), Construction of a Road in Costa Rica along the San Juan River (Nicaragua v Costa Rica)* (Order on Counterclaims) [2013] ICJ Rep 200, para. 32; *Alleged Violations of Sovereign Rights and Maritime Spaces in the Caribbean Sea (Nicaragua v Colombia)* (Order on Counterclaims) [2017] ICJ Rep 289, para. 25. Similarly, *Oil Platforms (Iran v United States of America)* (Order on Counterclaim) [1998] ICJ Rep 190, paras. 38–39.

[87] Murphy (2012), para. 37.

[88] Kolb (2013), p. 672.

[89] *Certain Activities Carried Out by Nicaragua in the Border Area (Costa Rica v Nicaragua), Construction of a Road in Costa Rica along the San Juan River (Nicaragua v Costa Rica)* (Order on Counterclaims) [2013] ICJ Rep 200, para. 32; *Alleged Violations of Sovereign Rights and Maritime Spaces in the Caribbean Sea (Nicaragua v Colombia)* (Order on Counterclaims) [2017] ICJ Rep 289, para. 25. Similarly, *Oil Platforms (Iran v United States of America)* (Order on Counterclaim) [1998] ICJ Rep 190, paras. 38–39.

be considered as a lack of connection.[90] Similarly, should the respondent use a different jurisdictional title for its counterclaim, it might be an indication against the connection requirement.[91] One may argue that precisely due to this connection, the withdrawal of the main claim should carry the consequence of the discontinuance of the counterclaim.[92] However, should the counterclaim be already admitted, there is no reason to dismiss it in case of the withdrawal of the main claim since by its nature, a counterclaim is a substantive and independent claim of the respondent.

Some judges posit that connection in law should take precedence over connection in fact.[93] Others, like Judge Caron considered that Article 80 of the Rules of Court does not demand a connection both in fact and in law, but rather, the connection can be either in fact or in law.[94] Should the Court find that the counterclaim is not directly connected with the main claim, the respondent would need to present a separate case.[95] Considering that counterclaims widen the scope of the dispute and allow the Court to decide more consistently, the connection requirement should be interpreted with certain flexibility.[96] In any case, the requirement of direct connection becomes the ultimate standard that differentiates what should or should not be joined to the existing proceedings for reasons of judicial economy.[97]

A final issue is the order of the analysis. The Court has considered that it is not bound to follow the sequence set out in Article 80 of the Rules of Court[98] but a counterclaim must comply with all requirements cumulatively.[99] In this vein, and given the Court's discretion when entertaining a counterclaim, the analysis may start

---

[90] Murphy (2012), para. 37.

[91] Kolb (2013), p. 672.

[92] Antonopoulos (2011), p. 154: ('As a counterclaim is so closely bound with the principal claim both as a matter of procedure and merits it would be a distortion of the entire rationale underlying it to allow it to survive the withdrawal of the principal claim').

[93] *Application of the Convention on the Prevention and Punishment of the Crime of Genocide (Bosnia and Herzegovina v Yugoslavia)* (Order on Counterclaims) [1997] ICJ Rep 243, Declaration of Judge ad hoc Kreca.

[94] *Alleged Violations of Sovereign Rights and Maritime Spaces in the Caribbean Sea (Nicaragua v Colombia)* (Order on Counterclaims) [2017] ICJ Rep 289, Dissenting Opinion of Judge ad hoc Caron, para. 18.

[95] Kolb (2013), p. 659.

[96] *Jurisdictional Immunities of the State (Germany v Italy)* (Order on Counterclaim) [2010] ICJ Rep 310, Dissenting opinion of Judge Cançado Trindade, paras. 14–15.

[97] Kolb (2013), p. 660: ('In short, the direct connection criterion is the essential pivot enabling the Court to reconcile the various applicable principles, enabling it to make the necessary separation between what can be included in existing proceedings and what cannot and must be left to a fresh set of proceedings').

[98] *Certain Activities Carried Out by Nicaragua in the Border Area (Costa Rica v Nicaragua), Construction of a Road in Costa Rica along the San Juan River (Nicaragua v Costa Rica)* (Order on Counterclaims) [2013] ICJ Rep 200, para. 27; *Alleged Violations of Sovereign Rights and Maritime Spaces in the Caribbean Sea (Nicaragua v Colombia)* (Order on Counterclaims) [2017] ICJ Rep 289, para. 20.

[99] Thirlway (1999), p. 203.

with the connection between the claim and the counterclaim and follow to the Court's jurisdiction over the counterclaim.[100] Although such interpretation is not at odds with the wording of the article, it seems more reasonable to start from jurisdiction, which entails a broader analysis, and only if jurisdiction is found, to proceed with the connection, which is a narrower, subject-specific assessment.[101] As such, the Court would have no authority to inquire into the facts of the counterclaim to determine connection if it has no jurisdiction to entertain the counterclaim in the first place.

2.1.1.2.3 In the Counter-Memorial

Article 80 of the Rules of Court provides that a counterclaim must be submitted in the counter-memorial. There is however no legal interpretation on this requirement, since the Court merely acknowledges whether the counterclaim was presented timely.[102] It is argued that this requirement does not prevent the respondent from submitting its counterclaim earlier than the counter-memorial.[103] Furthermore, it is feasible that the respondent submits a broad counterclaim in time, but with the option of developing the analytical exposition afterwards.[104] Conversely, Article 80 of the Rules of Court does not foresee the admission of a belated counterclaim. One may argue that a belated counterclaim should in principle be excluded.[105] However, under exceptional circumstances and only if it serves the proper administration of justice, the Court could admit such a counterclaim, as long as the equality of parties is respected.[106]

2.1.2 *Iran-US Claims Tribunal and Counterclaims*

The IUSCT was established by the Algiers Accords of 19 January 1981.[107] Unlike at the ICJ, the status and use of counterclaims at the IUSCT seem more consistent. The Declaration of the Government of the Democratic and Popular Republic of Algeria

[100] Arcari (2018), para. 17.

[101] Suggesting that the analysis on jurisdiction comes first, and only afterwards the connection requirement is evaluated, *see* Murphy (2012), para. 18.

[102] For instance, *Certain Activities Carried Out by Nicaragua in the Border Area (Costa Rica v Nicaragua), Construction of a Road in Costa Rica along the San Juan River (Nicaragua v Costa Rica)* (Order on Counterclaims) [2013] ICJ Rep 200, para. 19.

[103] Kolb (2013), p. 674.

[104] Antonopoulos (2011), p. 139.

[105] Anzilotti (1930), p. 875; Antonopoulos (2011), pp. 136–137.

[106] Kolb (2013), p. 674.

[107] Declaration of the Government of the Democratic and Popular Republic of Algeria (General Declaration), 19 January 1981.

concerning the Settlement of Claims by the Government of the United States of America and the Government of the Islamic Republic of Iran of 19 January 1981 (hereinafter 'Claims Settlement Declaration') contemplates the IUSCT's jurisdiction over counterclaims. Particularly, Article II(1) thereof sets forth:

> An international arbitral tribunal (the Iran-United States Claims Tribunal) is hereby established for the purpose of deciding claims of nationals of the United States against Iran and claims of nationals of Iran against the United States, and any counterclaim which arises out of the same contract, transaction or occurrence that constitutes the subject matter of that national's claim, if such claims and counterclaims are outstanding on the date of this Agreement (...)

From this wording, there are three clear characteristics of the IUSCT's jurisdiction: *first*, only nationals of the US may bring a claim against Iran and only nationals of Iran may bring a claim against the US. *Second*, the respondent state can nevertheless raise a counterclaim against the claimant as long as there is a connection with the subject-matter of the main claim. *Third*, claims and counterclaims must be outstanding on 19 January 1981. Under Article II of the Claims Settlement Declaration, a myriad of counterclaims have been submitted,[108] for payment of social security premiums, breach of contract, failure to return items, among others.[109] The IUSCT jurisprudence has led to the development of an increasingly nuanced approach to the adjudication of counterclaims.[110]

There are four issues in connection with counterclaims at the IUSCT, which are unique to this form of international dispute settlement. These concern whether the US or Iran may submit a claim against an investor of the other state [Sect. 2.1.2.1]; the availability of counterclaims in inter-state disputes [Sect. 2.1.2.2]; the exceptional admission of belated counterclaims [Sect. 2.1.2.3]; and the limitation of the connection requirement [Sect. 2.1.2.4].

2.1.2.1 Counterclaims Instead of State Claims Against a National of the Other State?

Iran submitted a request for interpretation in 1981 asking whether, under the Claims Settlement Declaration, the Tribunal had jurisdiction over claims by Iran against nationals of the US. The Tribunal considered that the state parties had limited the scope of jurisdiction to specific cases.[111] This certainly included counterclaims by the respondent state against the claimant, but not claims by the state against the

[108] Brower and Brueschke (1998), p. 99. Similarly, Antonopoulos (2011), p. 23.

[109] Marossi (2006), p. 503.

[110] Brower and Brueschke (1998), pp. 100–101.

[111] *Request for Interpretation: Jurisdiction of the Tribunal with respect to claims by the Islamic Republic of Iran against nationals of the United States of America*, Case A/2, Decision No DEC 1-A2-FT (13 January 1982) 1 Iran-US CTR 101, 2.

nationals of the other state.[112] However, three members of the IUSCT disagreed with this decision.

They considered that claims by the state against a foreigner should be allowed for three reasons: *first*, the object and purpose of the Claims Settlement Declaration was to terminate all litigations between a party and the nationals of the other party; *second*, the Algiers Accords pursue reciprocity; *third*, counterclaims are merely defensive tools, thus, insufficient.[113] While the arguments regarding the interpretation of the Claims Settlement Declaration and the Algiers Accords could have been considered in detail by the rest of the Tribunal, reducing the counterclaims' role to a 'defensive tool' is as a misconception of this instrument.

2.1.2.2 Official Counterclaims

Article II(2) of the Claims Settlement Declaration regulates inter-state disputes. Given that such provision does not contain any mention to the possibility to file counterclaims, unlike Article II(1) of the Claims Settlement Declaration, the IUSCT analysed the admissibility of counterclaims under Article II(2) thereof (official counterclaims). The Tribunal concluded that official counterclaims are allowed for two reasons: on the one hand, according to the ordinary meaning of the terms, counterclaims are inherent to the respondent, thus, explicit language is not needed.[114] Article II(2) differs from Article II(1) because under the former, both contracting parties could file a claim, whereas under the latter a contracting party cannot claim against the nationals of the other party, thus, if counterclaims were not included, such claims would be left without a forum.[115] On the other hand, the Tribunal considered the contracting parties have consistently filed counterclaims to official claims under Article II(2) of the Claims Settlement Declaration, thus, this subsequent practice reflects an agreement on the interpretation of such provision, allowing official counterclaims.[116]

---

[112] *Request for Interpretation: Jurisdiction of the Tribunal with respect to claims by the Islamic Republic of Iran against nationals of the United States of America*, Case A/2, Decision No DEC 1-A2-FT (13 January 1982) 1 Iran-US CTR 101, 3.

[113] *Request for Interpretation: Jurisdiction of the Tribunal with respect to claims by the Islamic Republic of Iran against nationals of the United States of America*, Case A/2, Decision No DEC 1-A2-FT (13 January 1982) 1 Iran-US CTR 101, Dissenting opinion of Mahmoud Kashani, Shafie Shafiel and Seyyed Hossen Enayat, 3.

[114] *The Islamic Republic of Iran v The United States of America*, Case B1, Interlocutory Award ITL 83-B1-FT (counterclaim) (9 September 2004) 38 Iran-US CTR 77, para. 87.

[115] *The Islamic Republic of Iran v The United States of America*, Case B1, Interlocutory Award ITL 83-B1-FT (counterclaim) (9 September 2004) 38 Iran-US CTR 77, para. 89.

[116] *The Islamic Republic of Iran v The United States of America*, Case B1, Interlocutory Award ITL 83-B1-FT (counterclaim) (9 September 2004) 38 Iran-US CTR 77, para. 116.

2.1.2.3 Belated Counterclaims

According to Article 19(3) of the Tribunal Rules of Procedure, the respondent must file its counterclaim in the statement of defence or '*at a later stage in the arbitral proceedings if the arbitral tribunal decides that the delay was justified under the circumstances*'. There is thus certain flexibility for the Tribunal with regard to the timing of the counterclaim's submission. In the *American Bell International v Iran* case, the Tribunal admitted a counterclaim for the repayment of tax costs, albeit having been presented in a later stage.[117] The reasons behind its decision were that such belated counterclaim did not prejudice the claimant, and the delay was justified given the voluminous documentary material.[118]

2.1.2.4 Connection Between Claim and Counterclaim

In principle, Article II(1) of the Claims Settlement Declaration allows that claim and counterclaim are based on different contracts, insofar such contracts are closely connected as to represent a 'single transaction'.[119] The situation may be different when the counterclaim does not arise from a contractual relationship at all. In this regard, the Tribunal in the *TCSB Inc v Iran* case held that a distinction should be made between legal relationship arising out of the application of the law, and a contractual relation arising out of the contract, but only the latter could be subject of a counterclaim.[120] In this case, the counterclaim was on tax and social security contributions, including a contractual obligation on 5.5% tax withholding. While the Tribunal considered that the 5.5% tax withholding arose from the contract and it was

[117] *American Bell International Inc v The Islamic Republic of Iran, The Ministry of Defense, The Ministry of Post, Telegraph and Telephone, and the Telecommunications Company of Iran*, Case 48, Chamber 3, Award No 255-48-3 (19 September 1986) 12 Iran-US CTR 170, paras. 181–184.

[118] *American Bell International Inc v The Islamic Republic of Iran, The Ministry of Defense, The Ministry of Post, Telegraph and Telephone, and the Telecommunications Company of Iran*, Case 48, Chamber 3, Award No 255-48-3 (19 September 1986) 12 Iran-US CTR 170, para. 183.

[119] *American Bell International Inc v The Islamic Republic of Iran, The Ministry of Defense, The Ministry of Post, Telegraph and Telephone, and the Telecommunications Company of Iran*, Case 48, Chamber 3, Interlocutory Award No ITL 41-48-3 (11 June 1984) 6 Iran-US CTR 74: ('In light of these particular circumstances, the Tribunal finds that the linkage between all three contracts must be considered sufficiently strong so as to make them form one single "transaction" within the meaning of the Claims Settlement Declaration. Accordingly the Tribunal concludes that it has jurisdiction over the counterclaims'). Similarly, *Westinghouse Electric Corporation v The Islamic Republic of Iran, The Islamic Republic of Iran Air Force, Iran Air, The National Iranian Oil Company*, Case 389, Chamber 2, Interlocutory Award No ITL 67-389-2 (12 February 1987) 14 Iran-US CTR 104, paras. 7 et seqq.

[120] *TCSB Inc v The Islamic Republic of Iran*, Case 140, Chamber 2, Award No 114-140-2 (16 March 1984) 5 Iran-US CTR 160.

within its jurisdiction, the opposite was concluded for the remaining taxes and social insurance contributions.[121]

By considering the obligation to pay taxes and social insurance contributions to arise from the operation of the law rather than from a contract, subsequent tribunals have consistently rejected counterclaims on those issues.[122] Although the Tribunal in the *Houston Contracting Company v Iran* case followed the above-mentioned reasoning, it made two clarifications: *first*, it considered immaterial that tax revenues result from the performance of a contract, since the obligation remains statutory in nature.[123] *Second*, the Tribunal, in line with the *TCSB Inc v Iran* decision on the tax withholding, contemplated that contractual provisions creating tax-related obligations not existing in law, could be considered as counterclaims.[124]

In a dissenting of opinion to the *Sylvania Technical Systems v Iran* award, the arbitrator Seyyed Mohsen Mostafavi considered that the contract had a provision subjecting it to the laws and regulations of Iran in all aspects, thus, social security regulations had become '*an inseparable and integral part*' of the contract.[125] Consequently, the dissenting arbitrator concluded that rejecting the counterclaim on social security premiums was not only a faulty interpretation of Article II(1) of the Claims Settlement Declaration, but it was causing an unjust enrichment as well.[126]

Perhaps the most influential reasoning on counterclaims at the IUSCT is the concurring opinion of Richard Mosk in *William L Pereira Associates v Iran*. Beyond the annotation that counterclaims on tax and social security premiums do not arise out of a contract but rather by the operation of the law, the arbitrator considered the unique features of tax laws, where issues of domestic policy are involved, and where

---

[121] *TCSB Inc v The Islamic Republic of Iran*, Case 140, Chamber 2, Award No 114-140-2 (16 March 1984) 5 Iran-US CTR 160.

[122] *Sylvania Technical Systems Inc v The Islamic Republic of Iran*, Case 64, Award No 180-64-1 (27 June 1985) 8 Iran-US CTR 298; *Questech Inc v The Ministry of National Defence of the Islamic Republic of Iran*, Case 59, Award No 191-59-1 (20 September 1985) 9 Iran-US CTR 170; *International Technical Products Corporation and ITP Export Corporation v The Islamic Republic of Iran and others*, Case 302, Chamber 3, Award No 196-302-3 (24 October 1985) 9 Iran-US CTR 206.

[123] *Houston Contracting Company v National Iranian Oil Company, National Iranian Gas Company, and the Islamic Republic of Iran*, Case 173, Chamber 3, Award No 378-173-3 (22 July 1988) 20 Iran-US CTR 3, para. 117.

[124] *Houston Contracting Company v National Iranian Oil Company, National Iranian Gas Company, and the Islamic Republic of Iran*, Case 173, Chamber 3, Award No 378-173-3 (22 July 1988) 20 Iran-US CTR 3, para. 120: ('the situation is quite different if the contract includes provisions which create specific obligations, which do not exist in the law, of one party towards the other, in relation to the burden of the taxes to be paid, or provisions which set forth conditions for payment of amounts earned under the contract in relation to the payment of taxes').

[125] *Sylvania Technical Systems Inc v The Islamic Republic of Iran*, Case 64, Award No 180-64-1 (27 June 1985) 8 Iran-US CTR 298, Dissenting Opinion of Seyyed Mohsen Mostafavi, para. 7.

[126] *Sylvania Technical Systems Inc v The Islamic Republic of Iran*, Case 64, Award No 180-64-1 (27 June 1985) 8 Iran-US CTR 298, Dissenting Opinion of Seyyed Mohsen Mostafavi, para. 7.

the taxpayer deals in first instance with an administrative agency.[127] Thus, Richard Mosk concluded: '[j]*ust as courts recognize that they are not equipped to apply and enforce the revenue laws of a foreign jurisdiction neither is this Tribunal so equipped.*'[128]

2.1.3 International Commercial Arbitration and Counterclaims

Party autonomy has been praised as the cornerstone of international commercial arbitration,[129] whereby the contracting parties enjoy considerable leeway to tailor their arbitral process. Most importantly, each party has the same rights under the arbitration agreement, and they must be treated equally.[130] Correspondingly, the respondent is normally entitled to raise claims of its own in the same arbitral proceedings *ie* counterclaims.[131] This is the result of the traditional reciprocal relation between private parties, where one-side privileges are to be prevented.[132]

A counterclaim is deemed a *procedural instrument* for the introduction of a substantive claim of the respondent.[133] Its permissibility depends on the particular national arbitration law.[134] Those laws based on the UNCITRAL Model Arbitration Law (2006) normally contemplate the possibility of counterclaims.[135] It thus requires two decisions: one for the claimant and its claim, and another for the respondent and its counterclaim.[136] In this context, this section provides an overview of counterclaims in international commercial arbitration. First, it distinguishes

---

[127] *William L Pereira Associates, Iran v the Islamic Republic of Iran*, Case 1, Chamber 3, Award No 116-1-3 (19 March 1984) 5 Iran-US CTR 198, Concurring Opinion of Richard M Mosk.

[128] *William L Pereira Associates, Iran v the Islamic Republic of Iran*, Case 1, Chamber 3, Award No 116-1-3 (19 March 1984) 5 Iran-US CTR 198, Concurring Opinion of Richard M Mosk.

[129] *See* Böckstiegel (1997), p. 25; Williams and Kirk (2018), p. 87; Born (2021), pp. 81–83.

[130] *Baron v Sunderland Corporation* (10 December 1966) [1966] 2 QB 56 (CA) 64; *Tote Bookmakers Ltd v Development Property Holding Co Ltd* (21 December 1984) [1985] 49 P & CR 232 (Ch) 239. If the arbitration agreement confers and unfair advantage to only one of the parties, it may be declared void afterwards, *see* Bundesgerichthof (BGH) [Federal Court of Justice] (Germany) Az: X ZR 23/87, Judgment (26 January 1989); *RTK v Sony Ericsson*, Case No 1831/12, Supreme Arbitrazh Court (Russia) Decision (19 June 2012); Supreme Court of Cassation (Bulgaria) Case No 1193/2010, Judgment (02 September 2011).

[131] Paulsson (1995), p. 232.

[132] Wälde (2010b), p. 6.

[133] Berger (1999), p. 60; Kee (2005), p. 146.

[134] Binder (2013), para. 21-012.

[135] UNCITRAL Model Law on International Commercial Arbitration (2006), Art 2: ('For the purposes of this Law: ...(f) Where a provision of this Law, other than in articles 25(a) and 32(2)(a), refers to a claim, it also applies to a counter-claim, and where it refers to a defence, it also applies to a defence to such counter-claim').

[136] Berger (1999), p. 60; Kee (2005), p. 146.

counterclaims from a similar instrument *ie* a set-off [Sect. 2.1.3.1]. Second, it deduces the basic features of counterclaims having due regard of the interplay of the arbitration agreement with the arbitration rules [Sect. 2.1.3.2].

2.1.3.1 The Delimitation of the Concept of Counterclaims in Commercial Arbitration

When a counterclaim consists of a claim for money, it may be confused with a set-off.[137] However, they operate differently. The basic notion of set-off illustrates the mutual extinction of claims owned by each party to the other.[138] Both civil law and common law traditions contemplate the possibility to set-off claims,[139] as well as the UNIDROIT Principles, in Article 8.1 thereof.[140] The instrument of set-offs and its characteristics may vary from jurisdiction to jurisdiction. For instance, while in some countries it may be recognised *ipso iure* and be applied independently from the parties' will, in some others the application of a set-off may require a declaration of the other party.[141] This refers to the *lex causae* or applicable law to the merits of the set-off, which plays a significant role on the final admissibility of this instrument.[142] However, the analysis of the applicable law to the merits of the set-off exceeds the purpose of this section.[143] Instead, it is apposite to mention the procedural admissibility of set-offs in international commercial arbitration, and the differences with a counterclaim.

The parties may agree to the possibility of raising set-offs during arbitral proceedings.[144] In the absence of any mention to the admission of set-offs in the arbitration agreement, the tribunal may opt for one of the following theories. *First*, an arbitral tribunal has jurisdiction to rule upon set-offs, given their defensive

---

[137] As eloquently described by Klaus Peter Berger, counterclaims and set-offs are 'only a hair's-breadth away', *see* Berger (1999), p. 58.

[138] Fountoulakis (2011), p. 9; Pryles and Waincymer (2009), p. 457.

[139] The concept of set-off in civil law may harkens back to Roman law, whereas in common law the concept evolved from considerations of equity, through the concepts of abatement or recoupment, *see* Berger (1999), pp. 56–57.

[140] UNIDROIT Principles of International Commercial Contracts (2016), Art 8.1 Set-Off: ('(1) Where two parties owe each other money or other performances of the same kind, either of them ("the first party") may set off its obligation against that of its obligee ("the other party") if at the time of set-off, (a) the first party is entitled to perform its obligation; (b) the other party's obligation is ascertained as to its existence and amount and performance is due. (2) If the obligations of both parties arise from the same contract, the first party may also set off its obligation against an obligation of the other party which is not ascertained as to its existence or to its amount').

[141] Fountoulakis (2011), pp. 8 et seqq.; Koller (2008), p. 61; Mourre (2008), p. 389.

[142] Koller (2008), pp. 67–69.

[143] For a comprehensive analysis on the applicable law to the set-off *see* Fountoulakis (2011).

[144] Koller (2008), p. 70.

nature,[145] unless they are explicitly subjected to a different arbitration agreement or forum selection clause.[146] *Second*, the subject-matter of the set-offs must fall within the scope of application of the arbitration agreement to be admissible.[147] The second theory seems more fitting to arbitration. The consensual nature of international arbitration requires that to be admissible, a set-off must in principle fall within the scope of the arbitration agreement.[148] Parties admittedly may extend the tribunal's jurisdiction afterwards expressly or impliedly to cover a set-off.[149] For instance, if the arbitration agreement is silent on set-offs and the claimant does not object the tribunal's jurisdiction over the set-off, it may be considered to impliedly consent to arbitrating the set-off.[150]

The respondent should consider two possible drawbacks of set-offs: *first*, if the set-off exceeds the main claim, the respondent would need to pursue the exceeding part in a different forum or in a different proceeding, thus, the set-off would not foster procedural economy.[151] *Second*, in cases where there is a different arbitration agreement or forum selection clause covering the subject-matter of the set-off, unless the parties otherwise agree, the tribunal cannot extend the arbitral proceedings to such a set-off because it would imply the violation of the parties' original intention.[152] Thus, the tribunal might be inclined to decline the admissibility of a set-off covered by a different dispute resolution clause.[153]

There are clear differences between counterclaims and set-offs. The instrument of set-off is deemed as an exclusively defensive instrument, '*as shield, not as a sword.*'[154] This marks the first difference with a counterclaim, which embodies a claim in itself.[155] Another difference between a set-off and a counterclaim refers to their independency/dependency to the main claim. A set-off is accessory or

---

[145] Poudret and Besson (2007), p. 277, para. 323. Some consider that the mere defensive character of set-offs does not completely resolve the issue of admissibility of set-offs, since only *inherent* defences—eg mitigation of damages—will fall within the arbitration agreement, *see* Pryles and Waincymer (2009), pp. 483 et seqq.

[146] Poudret and Besson (2007), p. 277, para. 323.

[147] Poudret and Besson (2007), p. 278, para. 323

[148] Berger (1999), p. 62; Poudret and Besson (2007), p. 275, para. 319. Similarly, Mourre (2008), p. 388.

[149] Berger (1999), p. 62.

[150] Koller (2008), p.73.

[151] Pavic (2006), p. 107.

[152] In the words of Klaus Peter Berger, it could imply the introduction of '*consolidation of arbitral procedures through the back-door of the set-off defence*', see Berger (1999), p. 75.

[153] Pavic (2006), p. 107.

[154] *Stooke v Taylor*, Decision (7 August 1880) [1880] 5 QBD 569, 575.

[155] Werner (2002), pp. 5–6: ('Der Widerkläger macht einen eigenen Anspruch geltend und leitet an sich einen eigenen Prozess ein. In diesem Sinne geht die Widerklage auf Verurteilung des Klägers. Damit unterscheidet sich die Widerklage auch von bloßen Angriffs- und Verteidigungsmitteln, welche lediglich der Abwehr eigener Verurteilung dienen').

dependent to the main claim,[156] in contrast to a counterclaim. If the main claim is withdrawn or rejected, the tribunal will still be competent to decide the counterclaim.[157] Whereas in the case of a set-off, this latter will follow the same fate as the main claim.[158] A final difference appertains to the excess of the counterclaim or set-off over the main claim. A set-off is capped by the amount of the main claim,[159] since the main purpose is to free the debtor from the claim.[160] Should the set-off exceed the main claim, such exceeding portion would not be addressed by the tribunal.[161] Whereas if a counterclaim exceeds the main claim, it would lead to 'enforceable entitlements' in favour of the counterclaimant.[162]

2.1.3.2 The Interplay of the Arbitration Agreement, Arbitration Rules and Counterclaims

A counterclaim in international commercial arbitration must adhere to the requirements and time limits stipulated by the parties either in the arbitration agreement or in the arbitration rules.[163] Given the consensual nature of arbitration, a tribunal would rule on a counterclaim only if it falls within the scope of the arbitration agreement.[164] The wording of arbitration clauses such as 'relating to' or 'in connection with' the underlying contract have been construed to allow non-contractual claims, *eg* tort or statutory claims, to be referred to arbitration.[165] By analogy, this implies that in commercial arbitration based on broad arbitration clauses, the respondent could as well bring a counterclaim for tort. In other words, '[t]*he more broadly the terms* [of the arbitration agreement] *are drafted, the easier it is to allow a counterclaim*'.[166] One may argue that as long as the counterclaim arises from the same legal relation as the main claim, it is feasible that the arbitration agreement will cover the counterclaim.[167] Moreover, like with a set-off, implied consent to the submission of a counterclaim is feasible, when, for instance, the claimant does not raise any objections to the submission of the counterclaim.[168] The risk of deciding

156 Poudret and Besson (2007), p. 275, para. 318.

157 Berger (1999), p. 60; Poudret and Besson (2007), p. 275, para. 318; Koller (2008), p. 64.

158 Berger (1999), p. 60; Poudret and Besson (2007), p. 275, para. 318; Koller (2008), p. 64.

159 Pavic (2006), p. 104.

160 Koller (2008), p. 64.

161 Pavic (2006), p. 104.

162 Fountoulakis (2011), p. 21.

163 Fouchard et al. (1999), para. 1222.

164 Pavic (2006), p. 104; Steingruber (2012), para. 7.25; Born (2021), p. 2388.

165 Blackaby and Wilbraham (2016), para. 2.29; Lew et al. (2003), pp. 151–52. Similarly, Douglas (2009), para. 528; Sourgens (2017), p. 197.

166 Pryles and Waincymer (2009), p. 453.

167 Pavic (2006), p. 105; Lew et al. (2003), p. 153, para. 7–68.

168 Pryles and Waincymer (2009), p. 482.

on a counterclaim falling outside the scope of the arbitration agreement must be noted, since this might lead to the refusal of the recognition and enforcement pursuant to Article V(1)(c) of the Convention on the Recognition and Enforcement of Foreign Arbitral Awards (New York Convention).[169]

A different case appertains to the situation when the subject-matter of the counterclaim and of the main claim are covered by separate arbitration agreements. While the arbitration agreement governing the counterclaim need not be the same as the one governing the main claim,[170] claim and counterclaim should be part of the same economic venture, and their respective arbitration agreements should contemplate compatible modalities of arbitration.[171] However, an incompatible arbitration agreement (or a forum selection clause for that matter) may be interpreted as the will of the parties to have separate proceedings for the subject-matter of the claim and counterclaim, which must be analysed by the tribunal on a case-by-case basis.[172] Consequently, either when the counterclaim is subject to an incompatible arbitration agreement or forum selection clause, tribunals might tend to decline the admissibility of the counterclaim.[173]

Arbitration rules[174] vary in the wording of their articles referring to counterclaims. There are nonetheless certain commonalities and differences that are worth

[169] Convention on the Recognition and Enforcement of Foreign Arbitral Awards (adopted 10 June 1958, entered into force 7 June 1959) 330 UNTS 3 (New York Convention). The enforcement court might consider the counterclaim as a matter beyond the arbitration agreement (*ultra petita*), constituting a ground for the refusal of enforcement under the New York Convention, *see* Kurkela and Turunen (2010), pp. 28–32.

[170] Steingruber (2012), para. 7.25.

[171] Koller (2008), p. 83: ('This requires the arbitration agreements to coincide regarding the following issues: procedure for appointing the arbitrators, applicable procedural rules, language and place of the arbitration').

[172] Pryles and Waincymer (2009), p. 498.

[173] Lew et al. (2003), p. 154, para. 7–69.

[174] *See* for instance: Arbitration Rules of the International Chamber of Commerce (*ICC Arbitration Rules (2021)*); Arbitration Rules of the Stockholm Chamber of Commerce (*SCC Arbitration Rules (2017)*); Arbitration Rules of the United Nations Commission on International Trade Law (*UNCITRAL Arbitration Rules (2013)*); Arbitration Rules of the London Court of International Arbitration (*LCIA Arbitration Rules (2020)*); Arbitration Rules of the *Deutsche Institution für Schiedsgerichtbarkeit – DIS* [German Arbitration Institute] (*DIS Arbitration Rules (2018)*); Administered Arbitration Rules of the Hong Kong International Arbitration Centre (*HKIAC Arbitration Rules (2018)*); Arbitration Rules of the Singapore International Arbitration Centre (*SIAC Arbitration Rules (2016)*). Arbitration Rules of the World Intellectual Property Organization (*WIPO Arbitration Rules (2021)*).

mentioning. Under the HKIAC Arbitration Rules,[175] LCIA Arbitration Rules,[176] SCC Arbitration Rules,[177] SIAC Arbitration Rules,[178] UNCITRAL Arbitration Rules,[179] and WIPO Arbitration Rules,[180] the respondent wishing to submit a counterclaim must indicate it from an early stage of the proceedings with the response to the notice of arbitration. Most of these rules contemplate formal requirements for the submission of a counterclaim, such as a brief statement of facts, legal arguments, and relief sought.[181] Conversely, the DIS Arbitration Rules[182] and the

[175] HKIAC Arbitration Rules (2018), Art 5.3: ('Any counterclaim, set-off defence or cross-claim shall, to the extent possible, be raised with the Respondent's Answer to the Notice of Arbitration, which should include in relation to any such counterclaim, set-off defence or cross-claim: (a) a copy of the contract(s) or other legal instrument(s) out of or in relation to which it arises, or reference thereto; (b) a description of the general nature of the counterclaim, set-off defence and/or cross-claim, and an indication of the amount involved, if any; and (c) the relief or remedy sought').

[176] LCIA Arbitration Rules (2020), Art 2.1: ('Within 28 days of the Commencement Date, or such lesser or greater period to be determined by the LCIA Court upon application by any party or upon its own initiative (pursuant to Article 22.5), the Respondent shall deliver to the Registrar a written response to the Request (the "Response"), containing or accompanied by: ... (iii) if not full confirmation, a statement briefly summarising the nature and circumstances of the dispute, its estimated monetary amount or value, the transaction(s) at issue and the defence advanced by the Respondent, and also indicating whether any counterclaim will be advanced by the Respondent against any Claimant and any cross-claim against any other Respondent').

[177] SCC Arbitration Rules (2017), Art 9: (1): ('The Secretariat shall send a copy of the Request for Arbitration and any attached documents to the Respondent. The Secretariat shall set a time period within which the Respondent shall submit an Answer to the SCC. The Answer shall include: ... (iii) a preliminary statement of any counterclaims or setoffs, including an estimate of the monetary value thereof; (iv) where counterclaims or set-offs are made under more than one arbitration agreement, an indication of the arbitration agreement under which each counterclaim or set-off is made').

[178] SIAC Arbitration Rules (2016), Art 4.1: ('The Respondent shall file a Response with the Registrar within 14 days of receipt of the Notice of Arbitration. The Response shall include: ... (b) a brief statement describing the nature and circumstances of any counterclaim, specifying the relief claimed and, where possible, an initial quantification of the counterclaim amount').

[179] UNCITRAL Arbitration Rules (2013), Art 4(2): ('The response to the notice of arbitration may also include: ... (e) A brief description of counterclaims or claims for the purpose of a set-off, if any, including where relevant, an indication of the amounts involved, and the relief or remedy sought').

[180] WIPO Arbitration Rules (2021), Art 11(a): ('Within 30 days from the date on which the Respondent receives the Request for Arbitration from the Claimant, the Respondent shall address to the Center and to the Claimant an Answer to the Request which shall contain comments on any of the elements in the Request for Arbitration and may include indications of any counter-claim or set-off').

[181] For instance, ICC Arbitration Rules (2021), Art 5(5); UNCITRAL Arbitration Rules (2013), Art 4(2); LCIA Arbitration Rules (2020), Art 15.3; HKIAC Arbitration Rules (2018), Art 17.3; SIAC Arbitration Rules (2016), Art 4.1.

[182] DIS Arbitration Rules (2018), Art 7.5: ('Any counterclaim shall, when possible, be filed together with the Answer. Article 5.2 shall apply, mutatis mutandis. The counterclaim shall be filed with the DIS').

WIPO Arbitration Rules[183] merely foresee that counterclaims must comply with the same requirements as the main claim.

The UNCITRAL Arbitration rules are the only set of rules that prescribes as a requirement for counterclaims to be within the jurisdiction of the tribunal.[184] Although not directly addressing the jurisdiction of the tribunal but closely related, the ICC Arbitration Rules[185] and the SCC Arbitration Rules[186] demand to mention the relevant arbitration agreement upon which the counterclaim is made.

A final point to highlight from the analysed arbitration rules refers to the deadline for submission of counterclaims. Most rules contemplate that counterclaims must be submitted with the statement of defence. However, only the UNCITRAL Arbitration Rules[187] and the WIPO Arbitration Rules[188] mention the admissibility of belated counterclaims under exceptional circumstances. One may argue that in any case, even if not mentioned by the arbitration rules, the arbitral tribunal should be

[183] WIPO Arbitration Rules (2021), Art 42(c): ('Any counter-claim or set-off by the Respondent shall be made or asserted in the Statement of Defense or, in exceptional circumstances, at a later stage in the arbitral proceedings if so determined by the Tribunal. Any such counter-claim or set-off shall contain the same particulars as those specified in Article 41(b) and (c)').

[184] UNCITRAL Arbitration Rules (2013), Art 21(3): ('In its statement of defence, or at a later stage in the arbitral proceedings if the arbitral tribunal decides that the delay was justified under the circumstances, the respondent may make a counterclaim or rely on a claim for the purpose of a set-off provided that the arbitral tribunal has jurisdiction over it').

[185] ICC Arbitration Rules (2021), Art 5(5): ('. . . Any counterclaims made by the respondent shall be submitted with the Answer and shall provide: a) a description of the nature and circumstances of the dispute giving rise to the counterclaims and of the basis upon which the counterclaims are made; b) a statement of the relief sought together with the amounts of any quantified counterclaims and, to the extent possible, an estimate of the monetary value of any other counterclaims; c) any relevant agreements and, in particular, the arbitration agreement(s); and d) where counterclaims are made under more than one arbitration agreement, an indication of the arbitration agreement under which each counterclaim is made. The respondent may submit such other documents or information with the counterclaims as it considers appropriate or as may contribute to the efficient resolution of the dispute').

[186] SCC Arbitration Rules (2017), Art 9(1): ('The Secretariat shall send a copy of the Request for Arbitration and any attached documents to the Respondent. The Secretariat shall set a time period within which the Respondent shall submit an Answer to the SCC. The Answer shall include: . . . (iii) a preliminary statement of any counterclaims or setoffs, including an estimate of the monetary value thereof; (iv) where counterclaims or set-offs are made under more than one arbitration agreement, an indication of the arbitration agreement under which each counterclaim or set-off is made').

[187] UNCITRAL Arbitration Rules (2013), Art 21(3): ('In its statement of defence, or at a later stage in the arbitral proceedings if the arbitral tribunal decides that the delay was justified under the circumstances, the respondent may make a counterclaim or rely on a claim for the purpose of a set-off provided that the arbitral tribunal has jurisdiction over it').

[188] WIPO Arbitration Rules (2021), Art 42(c): ('Any counter-claim or set-off by the Respondent shall be made or asserted in the Statement of Defense or, in exceptional circumstances, at a later stage in the arbitral proceedings if so determined by the Tribunal. Any such counter-claim or set-off shall contain the same particulars as those specified in Article 41(b) and (c)').

empowered to admit belated counterclaims as long as it serves the purpose of procedural economy.[189] In this sense, the admission of belated counterclaims should be balanced against the reasons for the delay as well as the procedural stage at which the respondent finally filed its counterclaim. For instance, in the *Peters Fabrics Inc v Jantzen* case, the respondent submitted its counterclaim only seven days before the hearing, without putting the arbitrator on notice of its intention to submit a counterclaim at any previous stage.[190] The US District Court for the Southern District of New York considered that the arbitrator was not guilty of misconduct for refusing to hear the counterclaim, since the counterclaim was clearly untimely.[191]

The abovementioned arbitration rules, albeit mentioning counterclaims, would not overcome the limitations for the admission of counterclaims in the arbitration agreement. Most of those rules contemplate formal requirements and time limits for submissions, but they do not cover what kind of counterclaims may be submitted to the tribunal.[192] Besides explicit provisions in the arbitration rules or the *lex arbitri*, there are no further requirements for the admission of a counterclaim.[193] In principle, a counterclaim need not be connected with the main claim as long as they are based on the same arbitration agreement.[194] The tribunal may nonetheless demand a connection of the counterclaim with the main claim, in order to counterbalance the necessary delay on the proceedings that the admission of a counterclaim would entail.[195] Moreover, in order to preserve the equality of parties, the claimant should be entitled to respond to the counterclaim.[196] Despite the connection with the main claim, a counterclaim remains as independent in respect to the requirements and effects of the main claim.[197]

Some authors posit that the requirements of a counterclaim, including its connection with the main claim, '*should be interpreted liberally, to minimize the risk of inconsistent arbitral awards and to reduce unnecessary costs of constituting an arbitral tribunal and completing initial procedural arrangements*'.[198] Justifications for the admission of counterclaims revolve around procedural efficiency, reducing transaction costs of parallel proceedings, avoidance of contrasting decisions by different arbitral tribunals.[199] Yet, one must be mindful of the risk that counterclaims may be used as a delaying or retaliatory tactic.[200]

---

[189] Berger (1999), p. 69.

[190] *Peters Fabrics Inc v Jantzen Inc* [1984] 582 F.Supp 1287 (SDNY) 1292.

[191] *Peters Fabrics Inc v Jantzen Inc* [1984] 582 F.Supp 1287 (SDNY) 1292.

[192] Pryles and Waincymer (2009), p. 482.

[193] Koller (2008), p. 83.

[194] Fouchard et al. (1999), para. 1222.

[195] Koller (2008), p. 83.

[196] Born (2021), p. 2388.

[197] Werner (2002), p. 5: ('Als grundsätzlich selbständige Klage ist die Widerklage sowohl in Bezug auf die Voraussetzungen als auch die Wirkungen von der Hauptklage unabhängig').

[198] Born (2021), p. 2388.

[199] Pryles and Waincymer (2009), p. 485.

[200] Berger (1999), p. 59.

2.1.4 *Other Frameworks for International Dispute Settlement*

Counterclaims might come into play in other frameworks for international dispute settlement. However, their development is usually more limited. For the sake of completeness, this section briefly addresses the interaction of counterclaims before three of the most representative institutions for international dispute settlement namely the Permanent Court of Arbitration [Sect. 2.1.4.1], the International Tribunal for the Law of the Sea [Sect. 2.1.4.2], and the WTO Dispute Settlement Body [Sect. 2.1.4.3].

2.1.4.1 Permanent Court of Arbitration

The PCA was established by the Convention for the Pacific Settlement of International Disputes of 1899 (First Hague Convention). Some years later, the contracting parties to the Convention undertook a revision, resulting in the Convention for the Pacific Settlement of International Disputes of 1907 (Second Hague Convention). According to Article 20 First Hague Convention, the idea was to facilitate recourse to arbitration to the contracting states '*for international differences, which it has not been possible to settle by diplomacy*'. The first case entertained at the PCA was the *Pious Fund Arbitration*, between the US and Mexico in 1902.[201] Originally, the PCA administered inter-state arbitration exclusively, until 1934 with the *Radio Corporation of America v China* dispute,[202] which was the first arbitration involving a non-state party against a state at the PCA.[203] Until date, the administration of arbitration proceedings involving a non-state party has considerably increased,[204] however, the PCA continues to administer inter-state arbitrations.[205]

The Hague Conventions of 1899 and 1907 do not mention the possibility to raise counterclaims in the arbitration proceedings. Yet, the latest version of the PCA Arbitration Rules (2012) contains several references to counterclaims.[206] These rules seem to be inspired by the UNCITRAL Arbitration Rules,[207] thus, there is no requirement for presenting counterclaims save for the submission in the statement of defence.

---

[201] *The Pious Fund (United States of America v United Mexican States)*, Award (14 October 1902) IX RIAA 1.

[202] *Radio Corporation of America v the National Government of the Republic of China*, Award (13 April 1935) III RIAA 1621–1636.

[203] Daly (2012), p. 40; Ando (2006), para. 28.

[204] Ando (2006), para. 31.

[205] Daly (2012), p. 40.

[206] PCA Arbitration Rules (2012), Arts 2(d), 21(3), 22, 23, 30.

[207] Antonopoulos (2011), p. 16.

2.1.4.2 International Tribunal for the Law of the Sea

The ITLOS was established by the UN Convention on the Law of the Sea (UNCLOS).[208] The ITLOS is a permanent judicial body, competent to adjudicate disputes arising from the interpretation or application of UNCLOS.[209] While there are no provisions in UNCLOS referring to the possibility to submit counterclaims, Article 98 ITLOS Rules of Procedure contains the following provision:

> 1. A party may present a counter-claim provided that it is directly connected with the subject-matter of the claim of the other party and that it comes within the jurisdiction of the Tribunal.
>
> 2. A counter-claim shall be made in the counter-memorial of the party presenting it and shall appear as part of the submissions of that party.
>
> 3. In the event of doubt as to the connection between the question presented by way of counter-claim and the subject-matter of the claim of the other party the Tribunal shall, after hearing the parties, decide whether or not the question thus presented shall be joined to the original proceedings.

This provision is similar to Article 80 ICJ Rules of Procedure, and it is also framed within the section of 'incidental proceedings'. Given this characterisation, one may argue that if the Tribunal finds no jurisdiction to decide the main claim, the incidental proceedings will be consequently terminated.[210] However, a counterclaim at ITLOS has a double nature, while the decision on the admission of counterclaims is part of the Tribunal's incidental jurisdiction, the decision on the merits of the counterclaims belongs to the main jurisdiction of the Tribunal.[211] This characterisation of counterclaims is certainly creative but far from settling the debate. Even the decision on the admissibility of counterclaims differs considerably from other orders issued by the Tribunal since there is a substantive discussion on it, which resembles a judgment.[212]

The *M/V Virginia G* case[213] is an example of counterclaims at ITLOS. The authorities of Guinea Bissau detained a ship with a Panamanian flag and Panama claimed for the damages suffered during the detention period. However, Guinea Bissau counterclaimed that Panama violated UNCLOS by granting nationality to the ship without having a genuine link to Panama.[214] After analysing the facts of the case, the Tribunal considered that the counterclaim had complied with all conditions

[208] United Nations Convention on the Law of the Sea (adopted 10 December 1982, entry into force 16 November 1994) 1833 UNTS 3.

[209] ITLOS Statute, Art 284.

[210] Eiriksson (2000), p. 133.

[211] García García-Revillo (2015), p. 254.

[212] Lekkas and Staker (2017), mn. 5.

[213] *M/V 'Virginia G' (Panama v Guinea-Bissau)*, Order (02 November 2012) ITLOS Reports 39.

[214] *M/V 'Virginia G' (Panama v Guinea-Bissau)*, Order (02 November 2012) ITLOS Reports 39, para. 16

of Article 98 ITLOS Rules of Procedure, thus, it was admissible.[215] However, Judge Treves disagreed and argued that the main claim and counterclaim, albeit based on the UNCLOS Convention, were disconnected.[216]

Neither the Tribunal nor the dissenting judge found any qualms with the jurisdiction over the counterclaim. This has been criticised because the jurisdictional title, in spite of being concluded after the dispute arose, did not contemplate the possibility to submit counterclaims.[217] Such criticism does not seem tenable. Nothing in UNCLOS or in the ITLOS Rules of Procedure demand an express consent to counterclaims in the jurisdictional title even if the parties agreed to arbitrate after the dispute arose. Besides, it is conceivable that the Tribunal's jurisdiction over a counterclaim may be found on the basis of *forum prorogatum*.[218] Thus, an explicit mention to counterclaims in the jurisdictional title should not be required.

2.1.4.3 WTO Dispute Settlement Body

The WTO was established in 1994 by the treaty of Marrakesh.[219] It contemplates a dispute settlement body which decides by *ad hoc* panels, in the first instance, and by a standing Appellate Body, in the second instance. Under the Understanding on Rules and Procedures Governing the Settlement of Disputes (DSU) every WTO Member may request consultations to other WTO Member for any dispute arising from a covered agreement.[220] If the consultations fail, the adjudicative process may start by a request for the establishment of a panel.[221] The provision referring to the instrument of counterclaims, or in this case a counter-complaint, is Article 3(10) DSU, which states that '*complaints and counter-complaints in regard to distinct matters should not be linked*'. Based on this provision, one may argue that the WTO dispute settlement system does not permit to adjudicate counterclaims.[222] Moreover, during the adjudicative proceedings in front of the panel there is no room for counter-complaints since a panel's review only follows failed consultations requested by a complaining party.[223] Additionally, the panel's terms of reference are set based on a panel request, which only contains the complainant's claims.

---

[215] *M/V 'Virginia G' (Panama v Guinea-Bissau)*, Order (02 November 2012) ITLOS Reports 39, paras. 34 et seqq.

[216] *M/V 'Virginia G' (Panama v Guinea-Bissau)*, Order (02 November 2012) ITLOS Reports 39, Dissenting Opinion of Judge ad hoc Treves.

[217] García García-Revillo (2015), pp. 198–99.

[218] Eiriksson (2000), p. 239. In a nutshell, *forum prorogatum* reflects the scenario where an international court assumes jurisdiction based on the respondent's consent expressed through its conduct.

[219] Marrakesh Agreement establishing the World Trade Organization (with final act, annexes and protocol) (adopted 15 April 1994, entered into force 01 January 1995) 1867 UNTS 3.

[220] DSU, Art 4(3).

[221] DSU, Art 4(7).

[222] Carmody (2011), p. 175.

[223] Pauwelyn (1998), p. 241.

Pertaining to the admissibility of counter-complaints at the WTO dispute settlement mechanism, the panel report in *Mexico – Soft Drinks* may be illustrative. Mexico, the respondent, filed a counter-compliant against the US for the violation of a market access commitment under NAFTA (1994), although the main complaint of the US against Mexico was for the violation of the GATT 1994. By referring to Article 3(10) DSU, the panel rejected the counter-complaint based on two reasons: *first*, it was based on a different agreement (NAFTA (1994)); *second*, it was not mentioned in the terms of reference.[224] Furthermore, in an *obiter dictum*, the panel highlighted that '*even if, arguendo, the dispute between Mexico and the United States regarding access of Mexican sugar in the United States market were a matter under the WTO covered agreements, a Panel could not link the complaints and counter-complaints related to distinct matters in one single case.*'[225] Consequently, the respondent party wishing to file a complaint against the complaining party must in turn initiate new proceedings, starting with the request for consultations.[226]

2.1.5 Common Characteristics of Counterclaims in International Dispute Settlement

The foregoing comparative analysis has proven that the instrument of counterclaims shares some features across different forms of international dispute settlement. Primarily, the court or tribunal ought to have jurisdiction to decide the counterclaim in accordance with the underlying instrument of consent. Similarly, the counterclaim should be connected to the main claim for the tribunal or court to entertain it. While there might be some varying time-frames for the submission of counterclaims in each international dispute settlement framework, belated counterclaims could exceptionally be admitted. Of particular relevance for this monograph are the requirement of jurisdiction over the counterclaim and the connection between the main claim and the counterclaim. Accordingly, the interplay and development of such characteristics in their respective frameworks of international dispute settlement might shed some light on the functioning of counterclaims in investment arbitration (where appropriate).

---

[224] *Mexico: Tax Measures on Soft Drinks—Report of the Panel* (07 October 2005) WT/DS308/R, para. 8.232.

[225] *Mexico: Tax Measures on Soft Drinks—Report of the Panel* (07 October 2005) WT/DS308/R, para. 8.232.

[226] Pauwelyn (2001), p. 553. Similarly, Antonopoulos (2011), p. 29.

2.2 Environmental Counterclaims Through the Prism of Investment Arbitration: Distilling the Basic Features

The common features of counterclaims in international dispute settlement must be tested through the prism of investment arbitration, its nature and particular functioning. Although investment arbitration may be considered the *'poster-child of international legalization'*,[227] its conceptualisation is unfortunately far from being settled. Accordingly, a preliminary issue consists of the analysis of the unique and multifaceted nature of investment arbitration [Sect. 2.2.1], and based upon this analysis, the subsequent section elaborates on the underpinnings of environmental counterclaims in the specific framework of investment arbitration [Sect. 2.2.2]. Finally, the third section specifically ascertains the utility of environmental counterclaims in investment arbitration [Sect. 2.2.3].

2.2.1 The Multifaceted Nature of Investment Arbitration

The state may express its consent to international arbitration for solving investment disputes with foreign investors by means of domestic legislation or by an international treaty, as well as by a contract provision concluded directly with the concerned investor.[228] Encompassing all investment disputes arising from these different types of the state's consent within the category of 'investment arbitration' may be seen as an oversimplification, particularly if the instrument by which the state gives its consent would move the dispute settlement procedure from the private to the public sphere.[229] Therefore, this section firstly provides an overview of the functioning of contract-based investment arbitration and some preliminary remarks on the viability of counterclaims [Sect. 2.2.1.1]. Secondly, this section addresses the design of law- and treaty-based investment arbitration and the implications thereof for counterclaims [Sect. 2.2.1.2].

---

[227] Puig (2014), p. 238.

[228] Van Harten (2007), p. 24; Kriebaum (2014), p. 69; Schreuer (2014), pp. 302–303. Even at a substantial level, the obligations arising out of an international investment may be linked to three legal frameworks namely national, contractual and international law, *see* Salacuse (2014), pp. 35–48.

[229] Van Harten (2007), p. 24: ('The form of a state's consent is significant because it correlates strongly with the positioning of investment arbitration in the private or public sphere, and in the domestic or international sphere').

2.2.1.1 Contract-Based Investment Arbitration: Closer to International Commercial Arbitration?

Investment contracts between a state and a foreign investor have been concluded for centuries, for instance, in form of concession agreements.[230] Here, there is a reciprocal (synallagmatic) and defined investor-state relation restricted to the specific transaction.[231] Moreover, investment contracts are ordinarily governed by a domestic law, which can be found in a particular choice of law clause within the contract.[232] Thus, the breach of an investor-state contract does not entail in itself responsibility on the international law level.[233] Nowadays, investment contracts usually contemplate international arbitration as method for dispute resolution.[234] The agreement to arbitrate is concluded directly by the host state and the foreign investor with the aim of submitting future or existing disputes related to that contract.[235] Consequently, one may consider that the state is acting in its private capacity (*jure gestionis*) and the method for solving disputes will basically be a type of international commercial arbitration.[236]

Admittedly, in most of the cases of law- or treaty-based investment arbitrations, there are equally some contractual relations between the investor and the state. This is explained by the fact that in practice, the specificities of the investment are normally condensed in a contractual instrument (joint venture, concession, public private partnership).[237] However, the decisive element to distinguish between a contract-based investment claim and a law- or treaty-based claim is the jurisdictional basis for the arbitration (contract v law/treaty) and the alleged breach.

Should the state seek to raise a counterclaim in contract-based investment arbitration, the counterclaim would most likely reflect the breaches of the contractual obligations owed to the state,[238] or breaches of domestic law in some cases.[239] Given the reciprocal (or synallagmatic) nature of investment contracts, as well as their reliance on international arbitration, one should pay heed to the intricacies of counterclaims in international commercial arbitration as elaborated above.

---

[230] Walter (2015), p. 82.

[231] Van Harten (2007), p. 63. Similarly, De Brabandere (2014), p. 26.

[232] Salacuse (2014), pp. 160 et seqq. Similarly, Bjorklund (2014), p. 272.

[233] Alvik (2019), p. 274. Similarly, *SGS Société Générale de Surveillance SA v Islamic Republic of Pakistan*, ICSID Case No ARB/01/13, Decision on Jurisdiction (06 August 2003) para. 167.

[234] Besch (2015), p. 140.

[235] Schreuer (2014), p. 303.

[236] Van Harten and Loughlin (2006), p. 142; Magnarelli (2020), pp. 46–47. For a different opinion considering that investor-state contracts always concern the exercise of public authority, *see* Alvik (2019), p. 271.

[237] De Brabandere (2014), p. 29. Similarly, Dumberry (2012), p. 241.

[238] Paulsson (1995), p. 247.

[239] *See* Sect. 5.1.

2.2.1.2 Law- and Treaty-Based Investment Arbitration

Law- and treaty-based investment arbitration can be grouped into one category given that in both cases, there is a prospective consent of the state to submit to arbitration with an undefined number of foreign investors to control the exercise of public authority.[240] The first time that arbitral tribunals assumed jurisdiction under such model was in the *SPP v Egypt* case in 1988 for law-based investment arbitration,[241] and in the *AAP v Sri Lanka* case in 1990 for treaty-based investment arbitration.[242] Considering that the majority of cases are based on treaties rather than on domestic laws,[243] this book focuses only on the framework for treaty-based investment disputes. This section consequently starts with the conceptualisations of treaty-based investment arbitration [Sect. 2.2.1.2.1]. It follows with a discussion on the relevant features of this dispute settlement system for the purpose of counterclaims [Sect. 2.2.1.2.2]. Finally, it briefly addresses the backlash against treaty-based investment arbitration as an opportunity for environmental counterclaims [Sect. 2.2.1.2.3].

2.2.1.2.1 Conceptualisations of Treaty-Based Investment Arbitration: A Never-Ending Story

The nature of treaty-based investment arbitration has engendered heated debates among practitioners and academics, who seek to explain the functioning of this relatively new model of international arbitration. In 1995, Jan Paulsson coined the term of '*arbitration without privity*', which sought to describe a new type of international arbitration between a foreign investor and a host state.[244] The novelty lied in a unique consent to arbitration achieved by two distinct steps: the state indicates its consent, as a result of an inter-state bargaining, in a treaty provision, whereas the investor consents by submitting its notice of arbitration against the state, based on the pre-existing treaty provision.

Accordingly, the dispute settlement provisions in IIAs providing for arbitration with the investors of the other contracting state(s) are considered as a 'unilateral offer' to arbitrate, upon which an *arbitration agreement* is concluded when an

---

[240] Van Harten and Loughlin (2006), p. 143.

[241] *Southern Pacific Properties (Middle East) Ltd v Arab Republic of Egypt*, ICSID Case No ARB/84/3, Decision on Jurisdiction (14 April 1988).

[242] *Asian Agricultural Products Ltd v Republic of Sri Lanka*, ICSID Case No ARB/87/3, Award (27 June 1990).

[243] The figures of the ICSID database show this tendency. From the 888 cases registered at ICSID by 30 June 2022, only 8% has been based on a domestic investment law of the host state, *see* <https://icsid.worldbank.org/sites/default/files/publications/The_ICSID_Caseload_Statistics_2022-2_ENG.pdf> accessed 10 January 2023.

[244] Paulsson (1995), pp. 232 et seqq. See also, Alvarez (2011), pp. 46–47.

investor 'accepts the offer', usually by submitting a claim.[245] Consequently, one thing is the dispute resolution provision in the treaty which reflects the consent of the state to submit to arbitration, whereas the arbitration agreement is a separate agreement entered by the host state and the specific foreign investor based on the respective treaty provision.[246] In this vein, in the *Occidental Exploration v Ecuador* case, the Supreme Court of the United Kingdom held '*the agreement to arbitrate which results by following the Treaty route is not itself a treaty. It is an agreement between a private investor on the one side and the relevant State on the other*'.[247]

Given the use of contractual-related terms such as 'offer' and 'acceptance', a first conceptualisation emerged, conceiving treaty-based investment arbitration as akin to international commercial arbitration.[248] Initially, most of the arbitrators dealing with this kind of disputes had a commercial arbitration background, which perhaps supported the characterisation of treaty-based investment arbitration as subset of commercial arbitration.[249] However, commercial arbitration differs from treaty-based investment arbitration on the instrument conferring authority to the tribunal and on the source of the obligations of the parties. The disputing parties certainly select the arbitrators sitting on each case, but the authority of the tribunal to judge the conduct of the state stems from the underlying IIA.[250] Moreover, the tribunal, unlike in commercial arbitration, is asked to assess the possible breaches of public international law obligations embedded in the respective IIA.[251]

This prevents a blind importation of an unmodified principle of party autonomy,[252] which is the cornerstone of commercial arbitration.[253] Certainly, the investor seeks the protection of its private rights,[254] and the procedure in treaty-based investment arbitration contains several similarities with commercial arbitration in regards to party-appointed arbitrators, the rules governing the conduct of proceedings or even the enforcement instruments.[255] However, the principle of party autonomy in treaty-based investment arbitration should play a less controlling role

[245] Bjorklund (2001), p. 183; Magnarelli (2020), p. 40; Marisi (2020), p. 240.

[246] Douglas (2009), para. 674.

[247] *Occidental Exploration & Production Company v The Republic of Ecuador* [2005] EWCA Civ 1116, para. 33. Similarly, *ICS Inspection and Control Services Limited v The Republic of Argentina*, PCA Case No 2010-9, Award on Jurisdiction (10 February 2012) para. 270: ('The formation of the agreement to arbitrate occurs through the acceptance by the investor of the standing offer to arbitrate found in the relevant investment treaty').

[248] Further on investment treaty arbitration as international commercial arbitration, *see* Price (2000), p. 112; Alvarez (2000), pp. 393–394.

[249] Kulick (2012), p. 77.

[250] Roberts (2013), p. 61.

[251] De Brabandere (2014), p. 8.

[252] Roberts (2013), p. 61.

[253] *See* Sect. 2.1.3.

[254] De Brabandere (2014), p. 27.

[255] Van Harten and Loughlin (2006), pp. 139–140; De Brabandere (2014), pp. 49–50.

than in commercial arbitration[256] because the system stems from public international law instruments. Despite the similarity between investment and commercial arbitration, they should not be deemed as interchangeable.[257] Otherwise, this might lead to overlooking the broader context of each one, their principles and more importantly, their differences.[258] Consequently, in spite of the ground-breaking contribution of considering treaty-based investment arbitration as 'arbitration without privity' or containing a unilateral offer to arbitrate, it has been argued that both descriptions may mislead the interpreter exclusively to a private law sphere.[259]

The second conceptualisation consists of framing treaty-based investment arbitration as part of public international law.[260] It is argued that the public international law regime in the broad sense governs the investment regime, given the intersections of investment law with public international law.[261] It has thus been suggested that within the four corners of public international law, one may find similar rules to apply by analogy in treaty-based investment arbitration, for instance, from rules of state responsibility, diplomatic protection, or the law of treaties.[262] A clear example from customary international law that has been applied in investment arbitration constitutes the minimum standard of treatment as developed in the seminal *Neer* case.[263] Still, public international law governs inter-state rather than investor-state relations, which puts into question its suitability for treaty-based investment arbitration.[264]

These discussions reveal that the traditional fields such as public international law or commercial arbitration may not be adequate characterisations of treaty-based investment arbitration.[265] In the latter, foreign investors are entitled to sue the host state in matters related to public administration, which does not correspond to the underlying principle of equality of parties in commercial disputes, nor to the concept of sovereign immunity in inter-state disputes.[266] Moreover, the tribunal might decide on the exercise of regulatory powers, there is a hierarchical relation between the

---

256 Brown (2010), p. 671.

257 Cordero-Moss (2009), pp. 782 et seqq.

258 Cordero-Moss (2009), p. 784.

259 Van Harten (2007), p. 64.

260 For instance, *Loewen Group Inc and Raymond L Loewen v United States of America*, ICSID Case No ARB(AF)/98/3, Award (26 June 2003) para. 233.

261 José E Alvarez identifies ten points of intersection: (1) treatification and other positivist sources; (2) fragmentation; (3) impact of non-state parties; (4) globalization and its discontents; (5) the profession of international law; (6) the move to judicialization; (7) hegemonic international law; (8) global administrative law (9) constitutionalization (10) humanity's law; *see* Alvarez (2011), p. 406.

262 Paparinskis (2014), pp. 74 et seqq.

263 *LFH Neer and Pauline Neer (United States of America v United Mexican States)*, Award (15 October 1926) IV RIAA 60–66.

264 Van Harten (2007), p. 135; Schill (2011), pp. 73–74. Similarly, Kriebaum (2014), pp. 49 et seqq.

265 Schill (2010), p. 12; Kalderimis (2011), p. 149.

266 Wälde (2010b), p. 6.

investor and the state as the former is subject to the exercise of sovereignty of the latter, the obligations arise from a treaty, and there is a generalised and prospective consent.[267]

Although recognising that treaty-based investment arbitration does not fit into one traditional field of law, the similarities on some issues cannot be ignored. Thus, one may be tempted to draw conclusions in treaty-based investment arbitration from analogies in similar fields of law. For instance, from public international law with respect to sources of law, from administrative or constitutional law with respect to the analysis of government conduct *vis-à-vis* private investors, or from commercial arbitration with respect to procedure.[268] This 'clash of paradigms' strives to shed some light on the functioning of treaty-based investment arbitration by focusing only on certain aspects of the system.[269] Certainly, under those paradigms the argument is that given the textual or functional similarities between the fields, it is illustrative to draw comparisons for solving some issues in treaty-based investment arbitration.[270]

However, the emphasis on commonalities or differences with other fields of law is more telling of the perspective and personal background of the person conducting the analysis than it is about treaty-based investment arbitration as such.[271] Thus, the transplant of principles from one field of law to another may not always respond to an oversimplification, but rather sometimes may be the result of a conscious choice to steer the system towards certain direction.[272] Consequently, using analogies with others fields to explain the investment treaty system may fail to capture the whole picture.[273]

In this context, a third conceptualisation of treaty-based investment arbitration comes into play. For the first time in 2003, Zachary Douglas posited that treaty-based investment arbitration presents 'hybrid foundations'.[274] The idea is to look beyond traditional fields of law in order to understand treaty-based investment arbitration as a *sui generis* system.[275] This requires to analyse the different foundational structures of treaty-based investment arbitration to understand its functioning. In any case, this must be undertaken carefully. Sometimes the different hybrid foundations may not provide the same answer to a legal question in treaty-based investment arbitration, or they may even lead to the same answer but for very

[267] Schill (2011), pp. 75–77. Similarly, Van Harten (2007), p. 126.

[268] Schill (2010), p. 17.

[269] Roberts (2013), p. 47.

[270] Roberts (2013), p. 52.

[271] Mills (2011), p. 101.

[272] Cordero-Moss (2009), pp. 796–797.

[273] Roberts (2013), p. 49.

[274] Douglas (2003), p. 159.

[275] Roberts (2013), p. 93.

different reasons.[276] The practical relevance of considering investment arbitration as hybrid has nevertheless been called into question.[277]

A final conceptualisation consists of portraying treaty-based investment arbitration as a 'species of global administrative law'.[278] This conceptualisation, also known as the public law paradigm, describes treaty-based investment arbitration as akin to the administrative or constitutional procedures in domestic law, where the individual seeks compensation for damages against the state.[279] From a substantive point of view, this paradigm conceives treaty-based investment arbitration as providing an adjudicatory framework for the control of the exercise of public authority, dissolving the domestic/international law dichotomy, and handing trump cards derived from public international law to the investor against the state's exercise of public authority.[280] In this sense, treaty-based investment arbitration constitutes an instrument of global governance by means of a strong and persuasive, albeit non-binding, system of precedent, providing how investment treaties should be construed.[281] Thus, it is argued that the public law paradigm of treaty-based investment arbitration provides legitimacy and accountability for the exercise of public authority.[282]

Under the public law paradigm, it may be contended that commercial arbitration rules and instruments are unsuitable for regulatory disputes between a state and a foreign investor.[283] Such assertion might however ignore the fact that since its origins, arbitration has been used for all kind of disputes, including inter-state

---

[276] Paparinskis (2014), p.106.

[277] Pauwelyn (2014b), p. 13: ('[L]imited pay-off can be gain from thinking IIL as a hybrid in search of an appropriate analogy ... what defines IIL is its myriad sources and actors ... and how they interact and have interacted over the time. The appropriate unit of analysis is not the system but its interacting components... the decentralized composition of IIL and its self-organizing qualities'). De Brabandere (2014), p. 4: ('[C]ategorizing investment law and arbitration as "hybrid" fails to take account of the fact that contemporary investment arbitration forms an integral part of public international law, and that (the recognition of) this feature is of paramount importance to the dispute settlement procedure').

[278] Van Harten and Loughlin (2006), p. 122: ('[I]t is precisely because of the potential of these internationally generated adjudicative norms and mechanisms to exert a strong disciplinary influence over domestic administrative programmes that investment arbitration should be seen to constitute a powerful species of global administrative law'). Similarly, Kalderimis (2011), pp. 155 et seqq.

[279] Van Harten (2007), pp. 68–71. This system could be even theorised as judicial review of government conduct in international law akin to the procedures at the ECtHR or the CJEU, *see* Schill (2011), p. 78.

[280] Kulick (2012), pp. 96–97.

[281] Schill (2010), pp. 18–19.

[282] Schill (2010), pp. 17–18.

[283] Van Harten (2007), p. 58.

disputes.[284] In fact, on several occasions, states have relied on international arbitration or arbitration-like proceedings for inter-state disputes as well for claims from citizens of one state against the other state.[285] Critics to the public law paradigm posit that such paradigm obscures or overlooks the crucial features of treaty-based investment arbitration, such as the underlying state-state relation[286] or the choice of commercial-like arbitration.[287]

One may certainly theorise some justifications for treaty-based investment arbitration ranging from procedural justice,[288] corrective justice,[289] and deterrence.[290] However, the fragmented system of IIAs and the unconnected decisions of *ad hoc* arbitral tribunals might not contribute to a single understanding of ISDS.[291] As such, it seems that the abovementioned conceptualisations attempted to square the circle by searching an overarching theme to explain all the features of treaty-based investment arbitration. Thus, for the purpose of this monograph, it seems appropriate to instead focus on the relevant features of treaty-based investment arbitration, which are relevant for the environmental counterclaims.

2.2.1.2.2 Relevant Features of Treaty-Based Investment Arbitration for Environmental Counterclaims

There is not a single point of time where the creation of treaty-based investment arbitration can be traced back, but rather a myriad of factors and historical events, including the development of treaties of friendship, commerce and navigation, the use of diplomatic protection, the decolonisation process, debt crises, the gunboat policy, among others, which gradually mould treaty-based investment arbitration as it currently stands.[292] Thus, instead of a rational design, treaty-based investment

---

[284] Emerson (1970), pp. 155–157; Ager (1996); Lafont (2000), pp. 557–590; Born (2021), pp. 8 et seqq. For a different opinion considering the origins of arbitration as for resolving exclusively private disputes, *see* Mustill (1989), pp. 43 et seqq.

[285] In this regard *see*, Dolzer (2011), paras. 6–7; Brilmayer et al. (2017), pp. 13–14; Happ and Wuschka (2017), pp. 116 et seqq.; Ando (2006), para. 36.

[286] De Brabandere (2014), pp. 5–8.

[287] Roberts (2013), p. 68.

[288] Procedural justice refers to granting access to a neutral and readily available tribunal for the invocation of state responsibility by non-state actors, overcoming the obstacles and formalities of public international law, *see* Puig (2014), p. 243.

[289] Corrective justice or compartmentalisation of investment disputes seeks to create a setting where investment disputes do not affect inter-state relations, *see* Puig (2014), pp. 244–245.

[290] Deterrence refers to the idea that international commitments towards foreign nationals can be upheld, thus, avoiding opportunistic behaviour of host states, *see* Puig (2014), p. 247.

[291] Roberts (2013), p. 75: ('As long as the investment treaty system remains based on thousands of BITs and FTAs interpreted by hundreds of ad hoc tribunals, we will continue to see conflicting analogies and diverse paradigms for understanding the system's nature').

[292] For an analysis on the origins of investment treaty arbitration *see* Newcombe and Paradell (2009), pp. 1–74; Miles (2013); John (2018).

arbitration seems to be the result of 'historical accidents' evolving over decades.[293] Yet, there are some overarching features of the investment treaty regime, which might not only be accepted by each and all of the different conceptualisations discussed above, but also might be relevant for environmental counterclaims.

First, the process for achieving consent to arbitration starts with the state expressing its consent to arbitration in an IIA provision without direct involvement of possible investors.[294] The state consent is thus a sovereign act rooted in a public international law instrument[295] and delineates the tribunal's jurisdiction by limiting the kind of disputes that can be submitted to arbitration.[296] Whilst previous mixed claims tribunals or the IUSCT foresaw a similar system of dispute settlement giving standing to private actors against a state, consent in claims tribunals was always retrospective and circumscribed to specific events, in the aftermath of an international upheaval or internal disturbances.[297] The state consent to treaty-based investment arbitration is markedly different, in the sense that it is *prospective* (for events that may happen in the future) and *generalised* (direct action granted to an indeterminate group of claimants).[298] Naturally, the claimant investor must comply with the requirements set out in the respective treaty provision,[299] but the fact remains that the state could not foresee the particular covered investors at the moment of consent.

As mentioned above, the consent to arbitration is perfected in a second stage with the investor's acceptance, usually when submitting its claim against the state.[300]

---

[293] Pauwelyn (2014b), p. 19: ('[Investment treaty arbitration] is at least partly the result of historical accident; a series of discrete, small steps by both contract and treaty negotiators, international institutions, and arbitrators which, taken together, vegetated into the complex regime with which we are all familiar'). Similarly, John (2018), p. 5: ('Rather than one moment of institutional design, the institution of investor-state arbitration developed incrementally—a transformative political change that occurred in small steps').

[294] Van Harten (2007), pp. 68–70; Bjorklund (2001), p. 183; Douglas (2003), p. 220; Schill (2010), pp. 12–14.

[295] De Brabandere (2014), p. 8.

[296] Consent in treaty-based investment arbitration may be open for all kind of disputes related to the investment, it may be limited to disputes arising out of an investment authorisation, investment agreement or treaty obligation, or it may be even restricted to the quantum payable in cases of expropriation *see*, Douglas (2009), paras. 443 et seqq.; Fontanelli (2018), p. 34.

[297] Brilmayer et al. (2017), pp. 7–9; Dolzer (2011); Pauwelyn (2014b), p. 36; De Brabandere (2014), pp. 50–51.

[298] Van Harten and Loughlin (2006), p. 128; Schill (2011), pp. 75–77; De Brabandere (2014), pp. 50–51.

[299] Bjorklund (2001), p. 190. In any case, it must be highlighted that direct legal standing of the investors was only included in a second generation of IIAs, *see* Pauwelyn (2014b), p. 38.

[300] See for example the investor's acceptance to submit to arbitration in the *Philip Morris v Uruguay* case through the notice of arbitration, whereby the investor expressly stated: '*The Claimants in the present Request for Arbitration accept the Respondent's offer to arbitrate and consent to the jurisdiction of ICSID over their claims*' see, *Philip Morris Brands Sàrl, Philip Morris Products SA and Abal Hermanos SA v Oriental Republic of Uruguay*, ICSID Case No ARB/10/7 (formerly FTR Holding SA, Philip Morris Products SA and Abal Hermanos SA v Oriental Republic of Uruguay), Request for Arbitration (19 February 2010) para. 56.

Accordingly, some authors have pondered the question whether an acceptance limited to the investor's claims could narrow the scope of the arbitration agreement, thereby excluding the possibility of counterclaims. There are three different views in this regard: the first view considers that if the investor's consent is limited to its claims, this excludes the possibility of counterclaims irrespective of the wording of the underlying treaty provision.[301] The second view borrows the terminology of contractual law and posits that if by means of its acceptance the investor aims at modifying the scope of the dispute resolution provision in the treaty (*eg* excluding counterclaims), this constitutes a rejection of the 'offer' to arbitrate accompanied by a 'counteroffer' on the terms of the arbitration agreement directed to the host state.[302] It would be then for the host state to accept (or reject) that 'counteroffer' in order to reach the mutual consent to arbitration.[303] The third view holds that an investor cannot 'pick and choose' from the dispute resolution provision in IIAs, for instance by excluding counterclaims.[304] Thus, the investor can neither limit nor expand the scope of the dispute resolution provision in the IIA, but rather only accept it as it stands.[305]

Consequently, the last two views concord: if the dispute resolution provision can be construed as permitting counterclaims,[306] the investor cannot unilaterally exclude such possibility with its acceptance. This conclusion should be supported given that the state's consent is embedded in an instrument of public international law. On this point, the *Urbaser v Argentina* tribunal considered, in *obiter dictum*, that the restriction of the dispute resolution provision in the treaty via the notice of arbitration could not be upheld.[307] The 18th Commission of the *Institut de Droit International*

---

[301] Alvarez (2000), p. 411: ('since the investor's consent will usually be given only after the dispute has arisen, the scope of its consent can be expected to be quite narrow, thus limiting the possibility of counterclaims by the disputing State Party'); Shihata and Parra (1999), p. 320: ('There would normally be no reason for the consent of the investor to be broader than is necessary to enable the investor's grievance against the State to be submitted to arbitration under the [ICSID] Convention. Other grievances, such as that of the State against the investor, would then fall outside the scope of the consent of the two parties and could not be placed before the arbitral tribunal'). Similarly, Kjos (2007), p. 610.

[302] Ben Hamida (2003), para. 280; Dudas and Tsolakidis (2013), p. 10; Steingruber (2013), p. 297; Huber (2020), p. 330.

[303] Steingruber (2012), para. 14.21; Douglas (2009), para. 129;

[304] Lalive and Halonen (2011), p. 150; Kryvoi (2012), p. 227.

[305] Kjos (2013), p. 135; Ishikawa (2017), p. 723; de Nanteuil (2018), p. 381.

[306] In this respect, *see* Sect. 3.3.

[307] *Urbaser SA and Consorcio de Aguas Bilbao Bizkaia, Bilbao Biskaia Ur Partzuergoa v The Argentine Republic*, ICSID Case No ARB/07/26, Award (08 December 2016) para. 1147: ('Article X of the BIT, which has been invoked by them as basis of this proceeding, covers all disputes in connection with investments within the meaning of the BIT, exactly as the scope of the Argentine Republic's offer to arbitrate has been defined in the very same provision. *Even if it is argued that Claimants' acceptance was more restricted in its scope than the Argentine Republic's offer to arbitrate contained in Article X of the BIT, the appropriate conclusion would have been that no agreement had been concluded between the Parties*') (emphasis added).

holds a similar position. Pursuant to Article 6(3) of the Resolution of 31 August 2019 on Equality of Parties before International Investment Tribunals, the tribunal's jurisdiction is not limited '*by the scope of the dispute as framed by the claimant in its Request for Arbitration*'.[308]

Second, treaty-based investment arbitration involves the adjudication of regulatory disputes. This means, on the one hand, there is a vertical or hierarchical relation between the respondent host state and the investor because the latter is subject to the jurisdiction of the former, and on the other hand, the disputes in treaty-based investment arbitration are centred on the state's exercise of sovereign authority (or acts *jus imperii*).[309] Thereby, treaty-based investment arbitration is more likely to involve concerns of public interest.[310] This is of the utmost importance as environmental protection constitutes the quintessential example of a public interest. As will be elaborated below, this influences the analysis of the connection requirement,[311] and addresses some legitimacy concerns on arbitrators adjudicating public law-related issues such as environmental counterclaims based on domestic law.[312]

Third, treaty-based investment arbitration presents an interaction of multilevel norms. Accordingly, tribunals encounter, on the one hand, a three-layer disposition of norms regulating the substantive obligations allegedly breached, the consent to arbitration and thereby the tribunal's jurisdiction, and the procedural rules for dispute resolution.[313] On the other hand, even within those layers, there is a rich variety of norms, for instance, at the substantive level, tribunals' determinations might involve treaty provisions, customary international law, domestic law, concession contracts, insurance schemes, or at the procedural level, arbitral procedures may be subject to the ICSID Arbitration Rules, SCC Arbitration Rules, UNCITRAL Arbitration Rules, PCA Arbitration Rules among others.[314] Particularly, the multilevel interaction of norms at the substantive level should be taken into account when analysing the appropriate cause of action for an environmental counterclaim.[315]

[308] *See* this book "Annex 4: *Article 6 of the Resolution on the 'Equality of Parties before International Investment Tribunals of the 18th Commission of the Institut de Droit International*".

[309] Van Harten (2007), pp. 45 et seqq.; Kulick (2012), pp. 85 and 146; Schill (2010), pp. 12–14.

[310] Van Harten (2007), pp. 65–67.

[311] *See* Sect. 4.3.3.1.2.

[312] *See* Sect. 5.3.2.

[313] Kriebaum (2014), p. 47. Similarly, McLachlan et al. (2017), para. 398; Thomas and Dhillon (2014), p. 975

[314] Pauwelyn (2014b), pp. 14–15.

[315] *See* Sect. 3.3.1.2 as well as Chap. 5.

2.2.1.2.3 Backlash Against ISDS: An Opportunity for Environmental Counterclaims?

The 'legitimacy crisis'[316] of, or 'backlash'[317] against treaty-based investment arbitration has portrayed an increasing array of concerns surrounding the functioning of this dispute settlement mechanism and the discontent of several groups of the society. Criticisms range from inconsistency of decisions, partiality of arbitrators or the threat to the state's right to regulate, but substantially the rise of environmental protection is one of the factors calling for ISDS reform.[318] On this point, it is perceived that the exercise of public authority, *eg* by enacting environmental regulations, might by threatened by the looming use of treaty-based investment arbitration.[319]

Should the state pursue the protection of the environment under its domestic law, this could potentially conflict with the broad substantive standards of protection in an IIA triggering investment arbitration, where the investor's interests would likely override the state measure.[320] Moreover, the discontent with treaty-based investment arbitration has been further fuelled by 'high-profile' cases of corporate misconduct that considerably affects the environment of the host state.[321] For instance, the never-ending story of *Chevron v Ecuador*,[322] where there is evidence of disastrous oil spillage in the Amazon rainforest.

The criticisms to treaty-based investment arbitration have moved different states to discuss possible reforms at UNCITRAL already in 2017.[323] Particularly, UNCITRAL Working Group III has considered the inclusion of counterclaims as a

[316] For a full analysis *see* Franck (2005), pp. 1521 et seqq.

[317] For a full analysis see Waibel et al. (2010).

[318] See for instance, Miles (2013), p. 106: ('Although a complex interplay of factors is at work in the current pressure to reshape international investment law, environmentalism stands out as a significant challenge to the status quo ... In many ways, therefore, the continued reluctance of the investment sector to engage with host state public interest issues is in conflict with the current globalising culture of environmental consciousness').

[319] Alvarez (2011), pp. 54–56.

[320] Kulick (2012), p. 51.

[321] Miles (2013), p. 133.

[322] Multiple claims in multiple fora have been filed against or by Chevron/Texaco related to Chevron's oil spillage in Ecuador, including the Aguinda Litigation in New York, the Lago Agrio litigation in Ecuador, some commercial arbitration cases at the Hague, the state-to-state arbitration between Ecuador and the US, an AAA arbitration in New York, and the Chevron v Ecuador treaty-based investment arbitration, see *Chevron Corporation and Texaco Petroleum Corporation v Ecuador (II)*, PCA Case No 2009-23, Second Partial Award on Track II (30 August 2018) paras. 4.75 et seqq.

[323] UNCITRAL, Possible future Work in the Field of Dispute Settlement: Reforms of Investor-State Dispute Settlement (ISDS) (20 April 2017a) UN Doc A/CN.9/917, para. 2.

reform option for ISDS[324] but without embarking upon a detailed analysis on the subject. Perhaps this is so because a counterclaim, in the context of ISDS, touches upon the substantive obligations of investors, an issue that has been consistently considered to fall outside of the scope of the Working Group's mandate.[325] Yet, some delegations such as the Government of Morocco[326] and the Government of South Africa[327] have suggested in their submissions to the Working Group III that a comprehensive ISDS reform should, among other things, enable host states to bring counterclaims against the claimant-investors.

The deliberations held at UNCITRAL are still ongoing, and no further prospects for counterclaims have been discussed. Some argue that counterclaims could turn treaty-based investment arbitration more appealing for the states,[328] as well they could rebalance the often-criticised asymmetry of the system.[329] Yet, the implementation of counterclaims via the current UNCITRAL Working Group III might need to focus on the procedural aspects of the instrument exclusively[330] because any discussion on the substance of counterclaims risks either forestalling the ISDS reform process or receiving objections from some participating delegations.[331]

2.2.2 *Finding the Underpinnings of Counterclaims in Investment Arbitration*

Almost dogmatically, different frameworks for international dispute settlement display similar justifications for the availability of counterclaims. This includes the emphasis on counterclaims serving procedural economy,[332] the proper

[324] UNCITRAL, Report of Working Group III (Investor-State Dispute Settlement Reform) on the work of its thirty-fourth session, Part I (26 February 2018) UN Doc A/CN.9/930/Add.1/Rev.1, paras. 3–7. See also UNCITRAL, Possible reform of investor-State dispute settlement (ISDS) Multiple Proceedings and Counterclaim (22 January 2020) UN Doc A/CN.9/WG.III/WP.193, paras. 32–45.

[325] UNCITRAL, Report of Working Group III (Investor-State Dispute Settlement Reform) on the work of its thirty-seventh session (09 April 2019c) UN Doc A/CN.9/970, para. 27; UNCITRAL, Report of Working Group III (Investor-State Dispute Settlement Reform) on the work of its thirty-fourth session, Part II (19 December 2017b) UN Doc A/CN.9/930/Rev.1, para. 20.

[326] UNCITRAL, Possible reform of investor-State dispute settlement (ISDS) Submission from the Government of Morocco (04 March 2019a) UN Doc A/CN.9/WG.III/WP.161, para. 9.

[327] UNCITRAL, Possible reform of investor-State dispute settlement (ISDS) Submission from the Government of South Africa (17 July 2019b) UN Doc A/CN.9/WG.III/WP.176, para. 64.

[328] Pathak (2019), p. 101.

[329] Gleason (2021), p. 428.

[330] In this regard, *see* Sect. 3.3.3.3.2.

[331] EI—IILCC Study Group on ISDS Reform (2022), pp. 51 et seqq.

[332] Werner (2002), p. 14; Koller (2008), p. 64; Antonopoulos (2011), p. 10; Steingruber (2012), para. 7.24; Murphy (2012), para. 3; Kolb (2013), p. 660; Atanasova et al. (2014), p. 359; Bubrowski (2013), p. 214.

administration of justice,[333] the equality of parties[334] among others. Yet, the instrument of counterclaims in investment arbitration has always been controversial, particularly in treaty-based investment arbitration. This is arguably explained by the differentiated functioning of treaty-based investment arbitration:

> This new world of arbitration is one where the claimant need not have a contractual relationship with the defendant and where the tables could not be turned: the defendant could not have initiated the arbitration, **nor is it certain of being able even to bring a counterclaim**.[335]

Against this backdrop, this section assesses the rationale/objectives behind the instrument of counterclaims and to what extent those proclaimed objectives are (or not) fostered by permitting counterclaims in investment arbitration, with especial emphasis on treaty-based investment arbitration. These objectives are the promotion of procedural/judicial economy [Sect. 2.2.2.1], due process [Sect. 2.2.2.2], and the rule of law [Sect. 2.2.2.3].

2.2.2.1 The Principle of Procedural or Judicial Economy

Procedural or judicial economy in international adjudication '*requires the judge to obtain the best result in the management of a controversy with the most rational and efficient use possible of his or her powers*'.[336] Thus, one may wonder about the nature of such mandate either as a principle or as a rule. A principle expresses a fundamental legal idea or a standard of optimisation, which detailed rules are based on.[337] As such, while rules are either complied with or not, and they set out the legal consequences for their breach, principles can be fulfilled in different degrees.[338] Procedural or judicial economy does not reflect a dichotomy of compliance/non-compliance but rather it evinces a standard of optimisation or legal value to be pursued. In other words, procedural or judicial economy epitomises a principle.

As a principle, procedural or judicial economy may justify either the application of a procedural rule or the departure therefrom, but the adjudicator must always

[333] *Jurisdictional Immunities of the State (Germany v Italy)* (Order on Counterclaim) [2010] ICJ Rep 310, Dissenting opinion of Judge Cançado Trindade, para. 15; Murphy (2012), para 84; Kolb (2013), p. 660; Ng (2018), p. 4; Sharpe and Jacob (2018), p. 357.

[334] Larschan and Mirfendereski (1986), p. 34; *Application of the Convention on the Prevention and Punishment of the Crime of Genocide (Bosnia and Herzegovina v Yugoslavia)* (Order on Counter-claims) [1997] ICJ Rep 243, Declaration of Judge ad hoc Kreca; Kjos (2013), p. 131; Kolb (2013), p. 660; Marisi (2020), p. 252.

[335] Paulsson (1995), p. 232 (emphasis added).

[336] Palombino (2010), p. 909.

[337] Alexy (1994), pp. 75–76; Kolb (1999), p. 428.

[338] Dworkin (1977), pp. 24–25; Alexy (1994), pp. 75–76. In a slightly different note, Joseph Raz considers whilst rules prescribe relatively specific acts, principles prescribe highly unspecific actions, thus concluding that the distinction between both is one of degree on the specificity of the prescribed act, *see* Raz (1972), p. 838.

weigh the interests at stake and the particular circumstances of the case.[339] This does not mean that procedural efficiency is a subjective notion, whose meaning depends on the party wielding it.[340] Rather, the objective circumstances of each case will dictate what course of action would better serve procedural efficiency.

In this vein, the principle of procedural or judicial economy appears as the first (and perhaps most important) underpinning of the instrument of counterclaims for two reasons: *first*, counterclaims prevent the commencement of two separate and parallel proceedings for claim and counterclaim because only one tribunal or court would decide upon them in a single proceeding.[341] In fact, parallel proceedings constitute the antithesis of procedural or judicial economy because they burden disputing parties, whose costs would duplicate for appearing in different but related proceedings.[342] This also burdens adjudicators, who are unnecessarily engaged in duplicative tasks, uncapable of relying on the work of the other adjudicators tasked with the parallel proceeding.[343] Thereby, there is a higher risk of contradictory decisions given that the different adjudicators need not consider the decisions taken on the other proceedings.[344]

This is even more pronounced in treaty-based investment arbitration with respect to counterclaims, where the parallel proceedings would run at different levels, usually international arbitration for the investor's claim and domestic court proceedings for the host state's claim. This kind of parallel proceedings could not be prevented by invoking *lis alibi pendens* because while the claimant would most likely seek international arbitration, the respondent might rely on its domestic judicial system, and the legal issues and probably the disputing parties might differ as well.[345] Consequently, the 'triple identity test' would not be fulfilled. Understandably, the dissenting arbitrator Mauro Rubino-Sammartano in the *Gavazzi v Romania* case questioned whether by concluding the underlying treaty, the contracting states '*intended to give rise to parallel proceedings before different*

339 Palombino (2010), p. 926.

340 For a different opinion *see* Pathak (2019), p. 113: ('In fact, procedural efficiency represents a rather eclectic notion, the interpretation of which varies from one disputing party to another. What may be efficient for a respondent State may not be efficient at all for a claimant investor').

341 Renteln (1987), p. 380; Murphy (2012), para. 3; Werner (2002), p. 14.

342 Renteln (1987), p. 391; Pryles and Waincymer (2009), p. 485. Similarly, Magnarelli (2020), p. 94.

343 Shany (2003), pp. 156–157: ('co-existence of two or more simultaneous proceedings before different for a places an unusual heavy burden on the parties to litigation, which are required to maintain two legal teams or shuttle between two or more tribunals. It also entails the investment of unnecessarily duplicative judicial time and resources by courts and tribunals that are faced with similar (if not identical) tasks and yet are unable to rely on the work of each other... Thus the possibility of parallel proceedings may radically increase the costs of the legal process and offer apt room for manipulating it . . . and it might result in inconsistent judgments').

344 Schreuer et al. (2009), Art 46, mn. 1; Dudas and Tsolakidis (2013), pp. 4–5; Bravin and Kaplan (2013), p. 195.

345 Reinisch (2004), p. 51; Shany (2003), p. 26; Magnarelli (2020), pp. 108 et seqq.; Magnayea and Reinisch (2016), p. 271.

courts and tribunals, by preventing the Host State from asserting its rights against the investor in a counterclaim'.[346]

Second, counterclaims in investment arbitration have the potential to prevent a circuity of action, particularly latent in treaty-based investment arbitration.[347] This refers to the scenario where the investor initiates investment arbitration against the host state, but the latter is prohibited to bring a closely connected counterclaim in the same proceedings. The host state would have to resort to its domestic courts to have its failed counterclaim heard. However, if the outcome of the domestic court proceedings is adverse to the investor, the investor could be tempted to return to treaty-based investment arbitration, challenging the negative consequences of the domestic court judgment, for instance, claiming denial of justice or generally the breach of the fair and equitable treatment standard.

Consequently, one may thus conclude that the principle of procedural or judicial economy underpins the instrument of counterclaims in investment arbitration. Yet, counterclaims could be abused of, for instance, by introducing ill-founded claims that complicate the judicial debate and delay the process.[348] As such, counterclaims could be used to slow down the disposition of the main claim[349] or to obscure the central dispute.[350] Paradoxically, this would impinge on the procedural economy counterclaims seek to promote. Therefore, arbitrators ought to be mindful of such risks, particularly when assessing the connection requirement between the claim and counterclaim,[351] and to balance the benefits of admitting a counterclaim against the negative consequences on the overall procedure of such admission.

2.2.2.2 Due Process and Counterclaims: Comparing Apples and Oranges?

Due process may be portrayed as a safeguard '*to reduce the power of the state to a comprehensible, rational, and principled order, and to ensure that citizens are not deprived of life, liberty, or property except for good reason.*'[352] Thus, it represents those norms that control the exercise of adjudicative and sovereign powers.[353] There

[346] *Marco Gavazzi and Stefano Gavazzi v Romania*, ICSID Case No ARB/12/25, Dissenting Opinion (14 April 2015) para. 42(i).

[347] Kryvoi (2012), p. 221; Marisi (2020), p. 239.

[348] Kolb (2013), p. 660.

[349] Bjorklund (2013), p. 477.

[350] Murphy (2012), para. 3.

[351] *See* Sect. 4.3.3.1.

[352] Sandefur (2012), p. 285.

[353] Kotuby and Sobota (2017), p. 1.

are some precepts or basic standards of due process common to all legal systems *ie* the right to be heard or equal treatment.[354]

On the one hand, the right to be heard (*audiatur et altera pars* or *audi alteram partem*) entails that each party, during the course of adjudicative proceedings, must have the opportunity to be heard by the adjudicator.[355] In practice, this implies that each party enjoys the opportunity to present its position, submit evidence and rebut the counterparty's evidence.[356] In investment arbitration, the right to be heard is certainly a core aspect, which, if ignored, may lead to the annulment or setting aside of the award.[357] As recognised by the *Wena Hotels v Egypt* tribunal:

> It is fundamental, as a matter of procedure, that each party is given the right to be heard before an independent and impartial tribunal. This includes the right to state its claim or its defense and to produce all arguments and evidence in support of it. This fundamental right has to be ensured on an equal level, in a way that allows each party to respond adequately to the arguments and evidence presented by the other.[358]

On the other hand, the equality of arms (equal treatment or equality of parties) implies that whilst the opposing parties must not enjoy equal resources or skills, they must have the same procedural rights to present their position in the case.[359] Consequently, neither of the disputing parties should be put at a disadvantage towards the counterparty to present their case.[360] As such, the equality of arms is a central component of adjudicatory systems in domestic and international law, including investment arbitration, without which no effective legal protection is conceivable.[361] It is thus '*a key component of the principle of "procedural fairness", "integrity of process" or "good administration of justice" which tribunals have to apply.*'[362] The difference between the right to be heard and equality of parties is that the former operates vertically (between each party and the adjudicator), whereas the latter operates horizontally (between the parties) and is thereby relative in nature.[363]

The crux of the matter here is whether the availability of counterclaims in investment arbitration might be supported by the right to be heard, the equality of parties or more generally due process. In this vein, the dissenting opinion of the

---

[354] della Cananea (2010), p. 49. One may further suggest those basic standards of due process might have become international through its uniform application across the globe, *see* Friedmann (1963), p. 290; Kotuby and Sobota (2017), p. 55.

[355] Cheng (1953), p. 296.

[356] Bain (2018), para. 8.09.

[357] Sourgens (2017), p. 199. Similarly, della Cananea (2010), pp. 60–61.

[358] *Wena Hotels Limited v Arab Republic of Egypt*, ICSID Case No ARB/98/4, Decision on Annulment (05 February 2002) para. 57.

[359] Silver (1990), p. 1009.

[360] *Dombo Beheer v The Netherlands*, ECtHR Judgment (27 October 1993) Series A No 274, para. 33; *The Prosecutor v Dusko Tadic*, ICTY Case No IT-94-1-A, Appellate Judgment (15 July 1999) para. 48.

[361] Huber (2020), pp. 310–311. Similarly, Wälde (2010a), p. 161; Reinisch (2016), p. 299.

[362] Wälde (2010b), p. 11.

[363] Bain (2018), para. 8.08.

arbitrator Mauro Rubino-Sammartano in the *Gavazzi v Romania* case becomes apposite:

> Since the counterclaim is an extension of the Respondent's defence against the claim, one has to consider whether counterclaims are included within the consent of the Parties to arbitrate before the Tribunal their dispute arising from the investment ... due process includes the right to defend a claim and in my opinion natural justice requires that such defence may include making a counterclaim related to such issues.[364]

Yet, such position might have misconceived due process. As opined by James Crawford, the equality of parties (or more generally due process) '*does not require that the respondent state be able to bring counterclaims*'.[365] Even in the particular case of treaty-based investment arbitration, the *Institut de Droit International* considered that the limitation on counterclaims by itself does not evince a lack of equality between the disputing parties because it might either reflect the contracting parties' choice when framing their IIAs, but most importantly, the state will always have recourse to its domestic courts for seeking relief for the investor's misconduct.[366] Indeed, the availability of counterclaims, by itself, does not protect nor impinge on the right to be heard, the equality of parties, or more generally due process. As long as the respondent is granted the possibility to comment on the claimant's submissions and to present evidence on an equal footing as the claimant, due process in the broader sense would be preserved. Thus, whether a respondent may submit a counterclaim is immaterial to due process.

However, if the respondent files a counterclaim, the tribunal should grant additional rounds of submissions, and adapt the procedure accordingly, in order to safeguard due process. Moreover, a submitted (and eventually, an admitted) counterclaim '*must not infringe due process rights or compromise the proper administration of justice*',[367] including the claimant's rights.[368] This includes the claimant's expectation of having its claims decided within a reasonable time.[369] Here, once

---

[364] *Marco Gavazzi and Stefano Gavazzi v Romania*, ICSID Case No ARB/12/25, Dissenting Opinion (14 April 2015) para. 42(i).

[365] Report of the Eighteenth Commission of the *Institut de Droit International* (Rapporteur Professor Campbell McLachlan) on the 'Equality of Parties before International Investment Tribunals', p. 544 (James Crawford) <https://www.idi-iil.org/app/uploads/2019/06/Commission-18-Equality-of-parties-before-international-investment-tribunals-McLachlan-Travaux-La-Haye-2019.pdf> accessed 10 January 2023.

[366] Report of the Eighteenth Commission of the *Institut de Droit International* (Rapporteur Professor Campbell McLachlan) on the 'Equality of Parties before International Investment Tribunals' para. 187 <https://www.idi-iil.org/app/uploads/2019/06/Commission-18-Equality-of-parties-before-international-investment-tribunals-McLachlan-Travaux-La-Haye-2019.pdf> accessed 10 January 2023.

[367] Sharpe and Jacob (2018), p. 357.

[368] *Application of the Convention on the Prevention and Punishment of the Crime of Genocide (Bosnia and Herzegovina v Yugoslavia)* (Order on Counterclaims) [1997] ICJ Rep 243, Separate Opinion Judge Koroma.

[369] *Application of the Convention on the Prevention and Punishment of the Crime of Genocide (Bosnia and Herzegovina v Yugoslavia)* (Order on Counterclaims) [1997] ICJ Rep 243, para. 40.

again, the tribunal must engage in a balancing exercise, particularly when assessing the connection requirement.

2.2.2.3 The Rule of Law and the Asymmetrical Structure of Treaty-Based Investment Arbitration

Without pretending to provide a definition of the rule of law, there are some elements or principles all conceptions of the rule of law share, namely government by the law, supremacy of the law, equality before the law, and access to an independent legal body for the settlement of disputes.[370] These elements of the rule of law may also be applied to international law, particularly in the adjudication of disputes.[371] Here, adherence to the rule of law by international law becomes a matter of degree: instead of compliance or non-compliance, the appropriate standard consists of '*the extent to which international rule of law principles are operative and can be operative within the international system*'.[372]

Even recognising the application of the rule of law principles in international law, one may question whether they serve for the benefit of the state, or whether applying the rule of law on a state's interest indirectly benefits the people committed to its charge.[373] Such enquiries nevertheless exceed the scope of this book. Suffice it to say that investment arbitration, as an international adjudicative system should adhere to the rule of law basic precepts. This also seems to be the states' goal as indicated by recent ISDS reform processes, which are rule of law oriented. Particularly, the UN has encouraged the rule of law among its member states at the national,[374] and at the international level.[375] Here, common elements such as core notions of due process, access to justice, judicial independence and impartiality, transparency, and consistency and predictability of the dispute settlement decisions can be identified.[376] These elements provide the yardstick for the functioning of investment arbitration and the extent to which such adjudicative system is concordant with the rule of

[370] Chesterman (2008), p. 342; McCorquodale (2016), p. 284.

[371] Crawford (2003), p. 10.

[372] McCorquodale (2016), p. 296.

[373] Waldron (2011), p. 326; Van Harten (2010), p. 629.

[374] See *eg*, UNSC, Report of the Secretary General on 'The Rule of Law and Transitional Justice in Conflict and Post-Conflict Societies' (23 August 2004) UN Doc S/2004/616.

[375] UNGA Resolution 67/1, '*Declaration of the High-level Meeting of the General Assembly on the Rules of Law at the National and International Levels*' (30 November 2012) UN Doc A/RES/67/1, para. 2: ('We recognize that the *rule of law applies to all States equally, and to international organizations*, including the United Nations and its principal organs, and that respect for and promotion of the rule of law and justice should guide all of their activities and accord predictability and legitimacy to their actions. We also recognize that all persons, institutions and entities, public and private, *including the State itself, are accountable to just, fair and equitable laws and are entitled without any discrimination to equal protection of the law*') (emphasis added).

[376] Reinisch (2019), p. 344.

law.[377] The interrelation between investment arbitration and the rule of law has been extensively studied.[378] Of particular interest is whether the asymmetrical structure of treaty-based investment arbitration (in other words, a structure whereby access to arbitration exists exclusively at the investor's behest since states cannot lodge a claim against investors) adheres to the rule of law.[379]

Some authors consider the asymmetrical structure of treaty-based investment arbitration as problematic for the rule of law.[380] One of the options for rebalancing the asymmetrical structure of the system is to allow the respondent to submit counterclaims.[381] It is argued that by conferring the authority to a single arbitral tribunal to decide all related claims from both the claimant and the respondent in a single proceeding, some of the concerns on the legitimacy of the system regarding the disparity between states and investors with respect to rights and remedies could be tackled.[382] Accordingly, the *Institut de Droit International* opined that the '*ability of the State to assert a counterclaim rebalances the asymmetry that otherwise applies where the claimant is always an investor*'.[383] This might explain the inclusion of Article 6 of the Resolution of 31 August 2019 on Equality of Parties before International Investment Tribunals, which sets out an entire provision on counterclaims.[384]

Be that as it may, the argument that the asymmetrical structure of treaty-based investment arbitration undermines the rule of law is difficult to follow. One may argue that treaty-based investment arbitration resembles an administrative review, therefore, it does not demand correction especially given that the states remain the masters of the treaties.[385] Moreover, treaty-based investment arbitration might be

---

[377] Reinisch (2019), p. 345.

[378] On an analysis of investment arbitration and certain components of the rule of law such as impartiality of arbitrators, procedural fairness, access to arbitration, consistency and transparency, *see* Reinisch (2016), pp. 291–307. On a discussion on how the investment treaty regime promotes the rule of law, *see* Schill (2015), pp. 81–102.

[379] Arcuri (2019), pp. 394–413.

[380] Arcuri (2019), para. 22.37. Similarly, noting on the salient problems of the asymmetrical structure *see*, Garcia et al. (2015), p. 870; Amado et al. (2018), pp. 14–15.

[381] Ben Hamida (2003), para. 280; Kryvoi (2012), p. 218; Kjos (2013), p. 131; Bjorklund (2013), pp. 463–464; Rivas (2015), p. 781; Ishikawa (2017), p. 728; Tietje and Krow (2017), pp. 27–28.

[382] Sharpe and Jacob (2018), p. 366. Similarly, Marisi (2020), p. 250; Zin (2020), p. 228; Nacimiento et al. (2021), p. 168.

[383] Report of the Eighteenth Commission of the *Institut de Droit International* (Rapporteur Professor Campbell McLachlan) on the 'Equality of Parties before International Investment Tribunals', para. 186 <https://www.idi-iil.org/app/uploads/2019/06/Commission-18-Equality-of-parties-before-international-investment-tribunals-McLachlan-Travaux-La-Haye-2019.pdf> accessed 10 January 2023. For a different opinion, stating that including the possibility of a counterclaim does not change the inherently unilateral structure of investment-treaty arbitration, *see* Steingruber (2020), p. 598.

[384] *See* this book "Annex 4: *Article 6 of the Resolution on the 'Equality of Parties before International Investment Tribunals of the 18th Commission of the Institut de Droit International*".

[385] Wälde (2010b), pp. 7–16.

more symmetrical than assumed since it shifted investment protection from state power and the use of force to a rule-based dispute settlement system.[386] Furthermore, the host state has the sovereign power to enforce its laws and adjudicate claims against the investor through its domestic courts.[387]

One concern treaty-based investment arbitration could cause to the rule of law is if the system is used to prevent the respondent to submit its claim elsewhere. This was recognised by the *SGS v Pakistan* tribunal. The claimant investor in treaty-based investment arbitration requested a stay of domestic arbitral proceedings, through which the respondent was pursuing damages against the investor, until the treaty-based tribunal rendered a decision on jurisdiction. Accordingly, the *SGS v Pakistan* tribunal stated:

> It would be inequitable if, by reason of the invocation of ICSID jurisdiction, the Claimant could on the one hand elevate its side of the dispute to international adjudication and, on the other, preclude the Respondent from pursuing its own claim for damages by obtaining a stay of those proceedings for the pendency of the international proceedings, if such international proceedings could not encompass the Respondent's claim.[388]

In this context and despite the concerns on the asymmetrical structure of treaty-based investment arbitration, this by itself does not undermine the rule of law. Accordingly, counterclaims appear immaterial to the rule of law and their availability—or lack thereof—simply reflects the contracting parties' limited consent to treaty-based investment arbitration.

2.2.3 The Utility of Environmental Counterclaims in Investment Arbitration

After embarking on the analysis of counterclaims through the prism of investment arbitration, one may argue that, as a procedural instrument, a counterclaim is neutral to the particular interests, for which a host state might seek relief. Given the relation between investment law and environmental protection outlined in the **Introduction**,

[386] Pauwelyn (2014a), p. 403.

[387] For instance, Stephen M Schwebel considered the arguments on the asymmetrical structure of treaty-based investment arbitration as 'misconceived', since the host state has many means for bringing pressure upon the investor, *see* Schwebel (2008), pp. 5–6. Similarly, underscoring the availability of domestic courts for the host state, *see* Report of the Eighteenth Commission of the *Institut de Droit International* (Rapporteur Professor Campbell McLachlan) on the 'Equality of Parties before International Investment Tribunals', para. 83 <https://www.idi-iil.org/app/uploads/2019/06/Commission-18-Equality-of-parties-before-international-investment-tribunals-McLachlan-Travaux-La-Haye-2019.pdf> accessed 10 January 2023.

[388] *SGS Société Générale de Surveillance SA v Islamic Republic of Pakistan*, ICSID Case No ARB/01/13, Procedural Order No 2 (16 October 2002) 302 [reproduced in (2003) 18(1) ICSID Review 293–306].

this section underscores the utility of environmental counterclaims in investment arbitration.

Overall, counterclaims would direct the adjudicator's attention over a series of facts and legal arguments that otherwise would not appear in the case,[389] thereby contextualising the dispute and the different interests involved.[390] In particular, the instrument of counterclaims has the potential to incorporate environmental obligations into investment arbitration permitting an appropriate balance between an investor's conduct and the state's right to protect its environment.[391]

Within this balance, environmental counterclaims may serve a variety of related purposes. *First*, environmental counterclaims may furnish environmental norms with effective enforcement mechanisms. Whilst the state may force compliance with its environmental laws domestically *eg* through administrative law to sanction environmental damage, the enforcement of domestic decisions in third states might be more problematic.[392] Accordingly, respondent host states might want to benefit from the enforcement regime of arbitral awards provided that their counterclaims outweigh the investor's claims.[393] As successful environmental counterclaims in investment arbitration would be reflected in an arbitral award, the respondent host state could enforce such award via the Convention on the Settlement of Investment Disputes Between States and Nationals of Other States (ICSID Convention),[394] or the New York Convention.[395]

Second, the availability of environmental counterclaims might incentivise investors to improve their corporate governance practices and social responsibility. Certainly, environmental counterclaims remain reactionary and their use is subordinated to the investor's commencement of arbitral proceedings,[396] and to the preferences of the host state for the adjudication of environmental issues. However, investors may wish to enhance their corporate governance and social responsibility as to prevent that any proceedings in investment arbitration could be turned into a forum for discussing damages they may have caused in the host state.[397]

[389] Murphy (2012), para. 3; Marotti (2017), p. 84.

[390] Bjorklund (2013), p. 475; Schill and Djanic (2018), p. 52.

[391] Boisson de Chazournes (2017), pp. 392–394.

[392] Huber (2020), p. 312.

[393] Ng (2018), p. 5.

[394] Convention on the Settlement of Investment Disputes Between States and Nationals of Other States (adopted 18 March 1965, entered into force 14 October 1966) 575 UNTS 159 (ICSID Convention).

[395] Convention on the Recognition and Enforcement of Foreign Arbitral Awards (adopted 10 June 1958, entered into force 7 June 1959) 330 UNTS 3 (New York Convention).

[396] Tan and Chong (2020), p. 191. Thus, some authors highlight the limited efficacy of counterclaims as they are only available after the investor brings a claim *see*, Amado et al. (2018), p. 118.

[397] Ishikawa (2019), p. 36; Marisi (2020), p. 250.

Accordingly, investors may not only be inclined to strong adherence to environmental laws but also they may be deterred from engaging in particularly polluting practices.[398]

Third, environmental counterclaims might strengthen and promote environmental policies. In this sense, states might seek, on the one hand, to advance their environmental interests and policies through environmental counterclaims.[399] On the other hand, states may gain political and reputational benefits by upholding their commitments to environmental protection through investment arbitration.[400] Thereby, the environment gains an international forum for its protection (at least indirectly), which may exalt the role of environmental protection within the broader context of sustainable development in the long term.

Fourth, the adjudication of environmental counterclaims in investment arbitration centralises the settlement of related disputes at a neutral forum. Instead of relying on its domestic courts, a host state could submit a counterclaim against the investor for environmental damages in investment arbitration. This would prevent the duplication of related proceedings (and the ensuing risks of inconsistency) by resolving both claim and counterclaim in a neutral forum *ie* investment arbitration.[401] Thereby, the principle of procedural or judicial economy as one of the underpinnings of counterclaims finds its application to full extent.

Furthermore, when the host state's legal system is plagued by corruption or is susceptible to political interference, this may breed investors' distrust of the effectiveness of the judicial system.[402] This in fact could be the investor's reason to resort to arbitration in the first place. All in all, environmental counterclaims would serve as a catalyst to the benefit of the host state (avoiding the unnecessary duplication of proceedings) and of the investor (eluding unreliable domestic judicial systems). These considerations may explain the parties' decision in the *Burlington v Ecuador* case: the claimant committed to not raise jurisdictional objections to the environmental counterclaim, and the respondent waived its right to file the same counterclaim against the claimant or its related entities before any other jurisdiction (whether arbitral or judicial, national or international).[403]

Consequently, the utility of environmental counterclaims in investment arbitration reflects on various aspects such as the availability of an effective enforcement mechanism for environmental norms, the improvement of investors' corporate governance and social responsibility, the strengthening and promotion of environmental policies and the centralisation of related disputes at a neutral forum.

---

[398] Marisi (2020), p. 253; Tan and Chong (2020), fn. 113.

[399] Scherer et al. (2021), p. 440.

[400] Scherer et al. (2021), p. 434.

[401] Kjos (2007), p. 628; Hussin (2019), p. 3.

[402] Ishikawa (2019), p. 35.

[403] *Burlington Resources Inc v Republic of Ecuador*, ICSID Case No ARB/08/5, Decision on Ecuador's Counterclaims (07 February 2017) para. 61.

Nevertheless, an important caveat must be underscored: environmental counterclaims in investment arbitration should be circumscribed to 'pure' environmental damage.

The definition of environmental damage is problematic as it may vary from treaty to treaty.[404] However, one must distinguish between 'pure' environmental damage and the possible damage to persons or property ensuing therefrom: while the former deals with the impairment suffered by the environment (which includes air, water, land, flora and fauna, natural ecosystems), the latter refers to the economic losses due to personal injury or affected property that are consequential to the 'pure' environmental damage.[405]

An environmental counterclaim for damage other than 'pure' environmental damage could be dismissed by an investment tribunal as in the *Chevron v Ecuador* case. The case revolves around a domestic judgment against Chevron where the plaintiffs (the Lago Agrio plaintiffs) won compensation for the damages suffered as consequence of Chevron's environmental contamination. Chevron submitted to treaty-based investment arbitration arguing that it suffered denial of justice since the domestic judgment was procured through corruption. Ecuador thus filed a counterclaim seeking to secure that even if the claimant wins on denial of justice, the Lago Agrio plaintiffs could receive appropriate compensation for the losses arising out of Chevron's contamination.[406]

However, the tribunal concluded that Ecuador based its counterclaim on '*a right belonging only to these individual plaintiffs alleging personal harm. It is not a right belonging to the Respondent*',[407] thereby dismissing the counterclaim. Interestingly, the tribunal opined in an *obiter dictum* that the respondent could have been legitimised for bringing a counterclaim on 'pure' environmental damage (using the terminology of Ecuadorian law, based on a 'diffuse or collective right'), however, since the respondent waived such possibility in the late nineties, this was not possible in the case at hand.[408]

All in all, the main problem with consequential damage as the basis for a counterclaim is the legitimisation both of the state for claiming on behalf of its citizens and of the citizens themselves as gaining indirect access to investment arbitration. Therefore, following the *Chevron v Ecuador* tribunal, it is more likely that, either in accordance with its domestic law or with public international law, a

---

[404] Douhan (2019), mn. 3.

[405] ILC YB [2006] vol II, part II, A/CN.4/SER.A/2006/Add.l (Part 2) 'Draft Principles on the Allocation of Loss in the Case of Transboundary Harm arising out of Hazardous Activities, with Commentaries' (58–90) Art 2, mn. 8ff; Sands et al. (2018), p. 741; de Sadeleer (2020), p. 65.

[406] *Chevron Corporation and Texaco Petroleum Corporation v Ecuador (II)*, PCA Case No 2009-23, Second Partial Award on Track II (30 August 2018) paras. 7.29–7.31.

[407] *Chevron Corporation and Texaco Petroleum Corporation v Ecuador (II)*, PCA Case No 2009-23, Second Partial Award on Track II (30 August 2018) para. 7.40.

[408] *Chevron Corporation and Texaco Petroleum Corporation v Ecuador (II)*, PCA Case No 2009-23, Second Partial Award on Track II (30 August 2018) paras. 7.41 et seqq.

respondent host state is legitimised for asserting a cause of action aimed at the remediation of 'pure' environmental damage.

2.3 Interim Conclusions

This Chapter has set the theoretical underpinnings of this monograph. Preliminary, a comparative analysis of counterclaims in various frameworks for international dispute settlement reveals some common features of counterclaims across the board. For instance, the court or tribunal must have jurisdiction over the counterclaim in accordance with the underlying instrument of consent. Moreover, the tribunal ought to assess whether the counterclaim is connected to the main claim. Time-frames for the submission of counterclaims may vary in each framework, but it appears that belated counterclaims could exceptionally be admitted. While the features (or requirements) of jurisdiction and connection in other frameworks for international dispute settlement might be enlightening for this book, they must nevertheless be tested through the prism of investment arbitration, its nature and particular functioning.

In this vein, one must differentiate between contract-based and treaty-based investment arbitration: given the synallagmatic structure of investment contracts, international commercial arbitration and the operation of counterclaims therein might be of guidance when assessing counterclaims in contract-based investment arbitration. In the case of treaty-based investment arbitration, irrespective of its multiple conceptualisations, there are three overarching characteristics, which will delineate the analysis of counterclaims: the unique process for achieving consent; the adjudication of regulatory disputes; and the interaction of multilevel norms.

Furthermore, all different frameworks for international dispute settlement display similar objectives justifying the availability of counterclaims including procedural economy, the proper administration of justice, the equality of parties, or due process. An analysis in investment arbitration reveals that procedural or judicial economy is the cornerstone of counterclaims, whereas due process and the rule of law are immaterial for the availability of such procedural instrument. Finally, while counterclaims appear neutral to the particular interests they may protect, the evolving relation between investment law and environmental protection supports the particular case of environmental counterclaims in investment arbitration as a means to address instances of 'pure' environmental damage. All in all, these underpinnings support the deconstruction of the requirements of jurisdiction, connection and cause of action for environmental counterclaims.

References

Ager SL (1996) Interstate arbitrations in the Greek world: 337-90 BC. University of California Press
Alexy R (1994) Theorie der Grundrechte. Suhrkamp, Berlin
Alvarez HC (2000) Arbitration under the north American free trade agreement. Arbitr Int 16(4): 393–430
Alvarez JE (2011) The public international law regime governing international investment. Hague Academy of International Law
Alvik I (2019) Investor-state contracts. In: Krajewski M, Hoffmann RT (eds) Research handbook on foreign direct investment. Edward Elgar, Cheltenham, pp 271–298
Amado JD, Kern JS, Rodriguez MD (2018) Arbitrating the conduct of international investors. Cambridge University Press, Cambridge
Ando N (2006) Permanent court of arbitration (PCA). In: Wolfrum R (ed) Max Planck encyclopedia of public international law. Oxford University Press, Oxford
Antonopoulos C (2011) Counterclaims before the international court of justice. TMC Asser Press/ Springer, The Hague
Anzilotti D (1930) La demande Reconventionnelle en Procedure Internationale. Journal du Droit International 57(4):857–877
Arcari M (2018) Counterclaim: international court of justice (ICJ). In: Ruiz Fabri H (ed) Max Planck encyclopedia of international procedural law. Oxford University Press, Oxford
Arcuri A (2019) The great asymmetry and the rule of law in international investment arbitration. In: Sachs LE, Johnson LJ, Coleman J (eds) Yearbook on International Investment law & Policy 2018. Oxford University Press, Oxford, pp 394–413
Atanasova D, Martínez Benoit A, Ostřanský J (2014) The legal framework for counterclaims in investment treaty arbitration. J Int Arbitr 31(3):357–391
Bain E (2018) When some are more equal than others: the need for a more substantive conception of "equality of the parties" in investment arbitration. In: Sachs LE, Johnson LJ (eds) Yearbook on international investment law & policy 2015–2016. Oxford University Press, Oxford, pp 292–326
Ben Hamida W (2003) L'arbitrage Transnational Unilatéral: Réflexions sur une Procédure résérvée à l'initiative d'une Personne Privée contre une Personne Publique. Dissertation, Université Pantheon-Assas Paris II
Berger KP (1999) Set-off in international economic arbitration. Arbitr Int 15(1):53–84
Besch M (2015) Typical questions arising within negotiations. In: Bungenberg M, Griebel J, Hobe S, Reinisch A (eds) International investment law: a handbook. CH Beck/Hart/Nomos, Baden-Baden, pp 93–152
Binder P (2013) Analytical commentary to the UNCITRAL arbitration rules. Sweet & Maxwell, London
Bjorklund AK (2001) Contract without Privity: sovereign offer and investor acceptance. Chic J Int Law 2(1):183–192
Bjorklund AK (2013) The role of counterclaims in rebalancing investment law. Lewis Clark Law Rev 17(2):461–480
Bjorklund AK (2014) Applicable law in international investment disputes. In: Giorgetti C (ed) Litigating international investment disputes: a Practitioner's guide. Brill Nijhoff, Leiden, pp 261–286
Blackaby N, Wilbraham A (2016) Practical issues relating to the use of expert evidence in investment treaty arbitration. ICSID Rev 31(3):655–669
Böckstiegel KH (1997) The role of party autonomy in international arbitration. Disp Resol J 52(3): 24–30
Boisson de Chazournes L (2017) Environmental protection and investment arbitration: yin and Yang? Anuario Colombiano de Derecho Internacional 10:371–400
Born G (2021) International commercial arbitration, 3rd edn. Kluwer Law International, The Hague

Bravin MN, Kaplan AB (2013) Arbitrating closely related counterclaims at ICSID in the wake of Spyridon Roussalis v. Romania. Yearb Int Arbitr 3:185–198

Brilmayer L, Giorgetti C, Charlton L (2017) International claims commissions: righting wrongs after conflict. Elgar International Law, Cheltenham

Brower CN, Brueschke JD (1998) The Iran-united stated states claims tribunal. Martinus Nijhoff Publishers, The Hague

Brown C (2010) Procedure in investment treaty arbitration and the relevance of comparative public law. In: Schill SW (ed) International investment law and comparative public law. Oxford University Press, Oxford, pp 659–688

Bubrowski H (2013) Balancing IIA arbitration through the use of counterclaims. In: de Mestral A, Lévesque C (eds) Improving international investment agreements. Routledge, New York, pp 212–229

Carmody C (2011) The duty to settle in WTO dispute settlement. Asian J WTO Int Health Law Policy 6(1):169–200

Cheng B (1953) General principles of law: as applied by international courts and tribunals. Stevens and Sons Limited, London

Chesterman S (2008) An international rule of law? Am J Comp Law 56(2):331–362

Cordero-Moss G (2009) Commercial arbitration and investment arbitration: fertile soil for false friends? In: Binder C, Kriebaum U, Reinisch A, Wittich S (eds) International investment law for the 21st century: essays in honour of Christoph Schreuer. Oxford University Press, Oxford, pp 782–798

Crawford J (2003) International law and the rule of law. Adelaide Law Rev 24:3–12

Daly BW (2012) Chapter 2: permanent court of arbitration. In: Giorgetti C (ed) The rules, practice, and jurisprudence of international courts and tribunals. Martinus Nijhoff Publishers, Leiden, pp 37–76

De Brabandere E (2014) Investment treaty arbitration as public international law: procedural aspects and implications. Cambridge University Press, Cambridge

de Nanteuil A (2018) Counterclaims in investment arbitration: old questions, new answers? Law Pract Int Courts Trib 17(2):374–392

de Sadeleer N (2020) Environmental principles: from political slogans to legal rules, 2nd edn. Oxford University Press, Oxford

della Cananea G (2010) Minimum standards of procedural justice in administrative adjudication. In: Schill SW (ed) International investment law and comparative public law. Oxford University Press, Oxford, pp 39–74

Dolzer R (2011) Mixed claims commissions. In: Wolfrum R (ed) Max Planck encyclopedia of public international law. Oxford University Press, Oxford

Douglas Z (2003) The hybrid foundations of investment treaty arbitration. Br Yearb Int Law 74(1): 151–289

Douglas Z (2009) The international law of investment claims. Cambridge University Press, Cambridge

Douhan A (2019) Liability for environmental damage. In: Peters A (ed) Max Planck encyclopedia of public international law. Oxford University Press, Oxford

Dudas S, Tsolakidis N (2013) Host-state counterclaims: a remedy for fraud or corruption in investment-treaty arbitration? Transnational Dispute Management 10(3) <https://www.transnational-dispute-management.com/article.asp?key=1962> Accessed 10 Jan 2023

Dumberry P (2012) International investment contracts. In: Gazzini T, De Brabandere E (eds) International investment law: sources of rights and obligations. Brill/Nijhoff, Leiden, pp 215–244

Dworkin R (1977) Taking rights seriously. Harvard University Press, Massachusetts

EI—IILCC Study Group on ISDS Reform (2022) Reform of investor-state dispute settlement: current state of play at UNCITRAL. Zeitschrift für Europarechtliche Studien 25(1):15–74

Eiriksson G (2000) The international tribunal for the law of the sea. Martinus Nijhoff Publishers, The Hague

Emerson FD (1970) History of arbitration practice and law. Clev State Law Rev 19:155–164
Fontanelli F (2018) Jurisdiction and admissibility in investment arbitration: the practice and the theory. Brill, Leiden
Fouchard P, Gaillard E, Goldman B (1999) Fouchard, Gaillard, Goldman on international commercial arbitration. Kluwer Law International, The Hague
Fountoulakis C (2011) Set-off Defences in international commercial arbitration: a comparative analysis. Hart Publishing, Oxford
Franck SD (2005) The legitimacy crisis in investment treaty arbitration: privatizing public international law through inconsistent decisions. Fordham Law Rev 73:1521–1626
Friedmann W (1963) The uses of "general principles" in the development of international law. Am J Int Law 57(2):279–299
Garcia FJ, Ciko L, Gaurav A, Hough K (2015) Reforming the international investment regime: lessons from international trade law. J Int Econ Law 18:861–892
García García-Revillo M (2015) The contentious and advisory jurisdiction of the international tribunal for the law of the sea. Brill Nijhoff, Leiden
Gleason T (2021) Examining host-state counterclaims for environmental damage in investor-state dispute settlement from human rights and transnational public policy perspectives. Int Environ Agreements Polit Law Econ 21:427–444
Happ R, Wuschka S (2017) From the Jay treaty commission towards a multilateral investment court: addressing the enforcement Dilemma. Indian J Arbitr Law VI(1):113–132
Huber S (2020) Die Stellung von Unternehmen in der Investitionsschiedsgerichtsbarkeit (unter besonderer Berücksichtigung von Korruptionsproblemen): Unternehmen als gleichberechtigte Verfahrensparteien? In: Reinisch A, Hobe S, Kieninger EM, Peters A (eds) Unternehmensverantwortung und Internationales Recht. CF Müller, Heidelberg, pp 303–338
Hussin A (2019) Environmental counterclaims under the CPTPP: lessons for Asia from recent investor-state jurisprudence. Transnational Dispute Management 5 <https://www.transnational-dispute-management.com/articleasp?key=2673> Accessed 10 Jan 2023
Ishikawa T (2017) Marco Gavazzi and Stefano Gavazzi v Romania: a new approach to determining jurisdiction over counterclaims in ICSID arbitration? ICSID Rev 32(3):721–728
Ishikawa T (2019) Counterclaims and the rule of law in investment arbitration. AJIL Unbound 113: 33–37
John TST (2018) The rise of investor-state arbitration: politics, law and unintended consequences. Oxford University Press, Oxford
Kalderimis D (2011) Investment treaty arbitration as global administrative law: what this might mean in practice. In: Brown C, Miles K (eds) Evolution in investment treaty law and arbitration. Cambridge University Press, Cambridge, pp 145–160
Kee C (2005) Set-off in international arbitration – what can the Asian region learn? Asian Int Arbitr J 1(2):141–160
Kjos HE (2007) Counterclaims by host state in investment dispute arbitration "without privity". In: Kahn P, Wälde T (eds) Les aspects nouveaux du droit des investissements internationaux/new aspects of international investments law. Brill Nijhoff, Leiden, pp 597–628
Kjos HE (2013) Applicable law in investor-state arbitration: the interplay between national and international law. Oxford University Press, Oxford
Kolb R (1999) Les Maximes Juridiques en Droit International Public: Questions Historiques et Théoriques. Revue Belge de Droit Internationational/Belgian Rev Int Law 32(2):407–434
Kolb R (2013) The international court of justice. Hart Publishing, Oxford
Koller C (2008) The Arbitration Agreement and Arbitrability – Contemplations on Set-Off and Counterclaim in International Commercial Arbitration. In: Klausegger C, Klein P, Kremslehner F, Petsche A, Pitkowitz N, Power J, Welser I, Zeiler G (eds) Austrian Yearbook on International Arbitration 2008. Man'zsche Verlags und Universitätsbuchhandlung, Alphen aan den Rijn, pp 59–85
Kotuby CT, Sobota LA (2017) General principles of law and international due process: principles and norms applicable in transnational disputes. Oxford University Press, Oxford

Kriebaum U (2014) The nature of investment disciplines. In: Douglas Z, Pauwelyn J, Viñuales JE (eds) The foundations of international investment law: bringing theory into practice. Oxford University Press, Oxford, pp 44–72

Kryvoi Y (2012) Counterclaims in investor-state arbitration. Minn J Int Law 21(2):216–252

Kulick A (2012) Global public interest in international investment law. Cambridge University Press, Cambridge

Kurkela M, Turunen S (2010) Due process in international commercial arbitration, 2nd edn. Oxford University Press, Oxford

Lafont S (2000) L'arbitrage en Mésoptamie. Revue de l'Arbitrage:257–590

Lalive P, Halonen L (2011) On the availability of counterclaims in investment treaty arbitration. Czech Yearb Int Law 2:141–156

Larschan B, Mirfendereski G (1986) The status of counterclaims in international law, with particular reference to international arbitration involving a private party and a foreign state. Denver J Int Law Policy 15:11–48

Lekkas SI, Staker C (2017) Annex VI, Article 27. In: Proelss A (ed) United Nations convention on the law of the sea: a commentary. CH Beck/Hart/Nomos, München, pp 2406–2411

Lew J, Mistelis LA, Kröll S (2003) Comparative international commercial arbitration. Kluwer Law International, The Hague

Magnarelli M (2020) Privity of contract in international investment arbitration: original sin or useful tool? Kluwer Law International, The Hague

Magnayea J, Reinisch A (2016) Revisiting res judicata and Lis Pendens in investor-state arbitration. Law Pract Int Courts Trib 15(2):264–286

Marisi F (2020) Environmental interests in investment arbitration: challenges and directions. Kluwer Law International, Alphen aan den Rijn

Marossi AZ (2006) Iran—United States claims tribunal: claims, counterclaims, dual nationality, and enforcement. J Int Arbitr 23(6):493–519

Marotti L (2017) Establishing the existence of a dispute before the international court of justice: glimpses of flexibility within formalism? Quest Int Law 45:77–88

McCorquodale R (2016) Defining the international rule of law: defying gravity? Int Comp Law Q 65(2):277–304

McLachlan C, Shore L, Weiniger M (2017) International investment arbitration: substantive principles, 2nd edn. Oxford University Press, Oxford

Miles K (2013) The origins of international investment law: empire, environment and the safeguarding of capital. Cambridge University Press, Cambridge

Mills A (2011) The public-private dualities of international investment law and arbitration. In: Brown C, Miles K (eds) Evolution in investment treaty law and arbitration. Cambridge University Press, Cambridge, pp 97–116

Mourre A (2008) The set-off paradox in international arbitration. Arbitr Int 24(3):387–404

Murphy SD (2012) Counter-claims: Article 80 of the rules. In: Zimmermann A, Tams CJ, Oellers-Frahm K, Tomuschat C (eds) The statute of the international court of justice: a commentary, 2nd edn. Oxford University Press, Oxford

Mustill M (1989) Arbitration: history and background. J Int Arbitr 6(2):43–56

Nacimiento P, Scharaw B, Covi A, Tussupov A (2021) Counterclaims in investment arbitration. In: Bungenberg M, Giegerich T (eds) 'Europa lässt nicht mit einem Schlag herstellen' 70 Jahre Europa-Institut der Universität des Saarlandes. ZEuS Special Issue, Nomos, Baden-Baden, pp 165–186

Newcombe A, Paradell L (2009) Law and practice of investment treaties: standards of treatment. Kluwer Law International, Alphen aan den Rijn

Ng M (2018) Can human rights counterclaims succeed in investment treaty arbitration?' Transnational dispute management 5 <https://www.transnational-dispute-management.com/article.asp?key=2600> Accessed 10 Jan 2023

Palombino FM (2010) Judicial economy and limitation of the scope of the decision in international adjudication. Leiden J Int Law 23(4):909–932

Paparinskis M (2014) Analogies and other regimes of international law. In: Douglas Z, Pauwelyn J, Viñuales JE (eds) The foundations of international investment law: bringing theory into practice. Oxford University Press, Oxford, pp 73–107
Pathak H (2019) Consenting to counterclaims under the ICSID convention. Pepperdine Disp Resol Law J 19(1):101–126
Paulsson J (1995) Arbitration without privity. ICSID Rev 10(2):232–257
Pauwelyn J (1998) Evidence, proof and persuasion in WTO dispute settlement: who bears the burden? J Int Econ Law 1:227–258
Pauwelyn J (2001) The role of public international law in the WTO: how far can we go? Am J Int Law 95(3):535–578
Pauwelyn J (2014a) At the edge of chaos? Foreign investment law as a complex adaptive system, how it emerged and how it can be reformed. ICSID Rev 29(2):372–418
Pauwelyn J (2014b) Rational design or accidental evolution? The emergence of international investment law. In: Douglas Z, Pauwelyn J, Viñuales JE (eds) The foundations of international investment law: bringing theory into practice. Oxford University Press, Oxford, pp 10–43
Pavic V (2006) Counterclaim and set-off in international commercial arbitration. Annals Facul Law Belgrade – Int Edn 2006:101–116
Poudret JF, Besson S (2007) Comparative law of international arbitration, 2nd edn (trans: Berti S, Ponti A). Sweet & Maxwell, London
Price DM (2000) Chapter 11 – private party vs government, investor-state dispute settlement: Frankenstein or safety valve? Canada-United States Law J 26:107–114
Pryles M, Waincymer JM (2009) Multiple claims in arbitration between the same parties. In: Van den Berg AJ (ed) 50 years of the New York convention: ICCA international arbitration conference. Kluwer Law International, The Hague, pp 437–499
Puig S (2014) No right without a remedy: foundations of investor-state arbitration. In: Douglas Z, Pauwelyn J, Viñuales JE (eds) The foundations of international investment law: bringing theory into practice. Oxford University Press, Oxford, pp 234–256
Raz J (1972) Legal principles and the limits of law. Yale Law J 81(5):823–854
Reinisch A (2004) The use and limits of res judicata and Lis Pendens as procedural tools to avoid conflicting dispute settlement outcomes. Law Pract Int Courts Trib 3(1):37–78
Reinisch A (2016) The rule of law in international investment arbitration. In: Pazartzis P, Gavouneli M (eds) Reconceptualising the rule of law: in global governance, resources, Investment and Trade. Bloomsbury, Portland, pp 291–308
Reinisch A (2019) The UN concept of the rule of law. Zeitschrift für Europarechtliche Studien 22(3):337–348
Renteln AD (1987) Encountering counterclaims. Denver J Int Law Policy 15:379–394
Rivas JA (2015) ICSID treaty counterclaims: case law and treaty evolution. In: Kalicki JE, Joubin-Bret A (eds) Reshaping the investor-state dispute settlement system: journeys for the 21st century. Leiden, Brill Nijhoff, pp 779–827
Roberts A (2013) Clash of paradigms: actors and analogies shaping the investment treaty system. Am J Int Law 107(1):45–94
Salacuse JW (2014) The three Laws of international investment: national, contractual, and international frameworks for foreign control. Oxford University Press, Oxford
Sandefur T (2012) In defense of substantive due process, or the promise of lawful rule. Harv J Law Public Policy 35(1):283–350
Sands P, Peel J, Fabra A, Mackenzie R (2018) Principles of international environmental law, 4th edn. Cambridge University Press, Cambridge
Scherer M, Bruce S, Reschke J (2021) Environmental counterclaims in investment treaty arbitration. ICSID Rev 36(2):413–440
Schill SW (2010) International investment law and comparative public law – an introduction. In: Schill SW (ed) International investment law and comparative public law. Oxford University Press, Oxford, pp 3–38

Schill SW (2011) Enhancing international investment Law's legitimacy: conceptual and methodological foundations of new public law approach. Vr J Int Law 52:57–102

Schill SW (2015) International investment law and the rule of law. In: Lowell J, Thomas JC, van Zyl SJ (eds) Rule of law symposium 2014: the importance of the rule of law in promoting development. Singapore Academy Publishing, Singapore, pp 81–102

Schill SW, Djanic V (2018) Wherefore art thou? Towards a public interest-based justification of international investment law. ICSID Rev 33(1):29–55

Schreuer C (2014) Investment arbitration. In: Romano CPR, Alter KJ, Shany Y (eds) The Oxford handbook of international adjudication. Oxford University Press, Oxford, pp 295–315

Schreuer C, Malintoppi L, Reinisch A, Sinclair A (2009) The ICSID convention: a commentary, 2nd edn. Cambridge University Press, Cambridge

Schwebel SM (2008) A BIT about ICSID. ICSID Rev 23(1):1–9

Shany Y (2003) The competing jurisdictions of international courts and tribunals. Oxford University Press, Oxford

Sharpe JK, Jacob M (2018) Counterclaims and state claims. In: Beharry CL (ed) Contemporary and emerging issues on the law of damages and valuation in international investment arbitration. Brill/Nijhoff, Leiden, pp 347–369

Shihata IFI, Parra AR (1999) The experience of the international centre for settlement of investment disputes. ICSID Rev 14(2):299–361

Silver JS (1990) Equality of arms and the adversarial process: a new constitutional right. Wis Law Rev 4:1007–1042

Sourgens FG (2017) Supernational law. Vanderbilt J Transnatl Law 55:155–216

Steingruber AM (2012) Consent in international arbitration. Oxford University Press, Oxford

Steingruber AM (2013) Antoine Goetz and others v Republic of Burundi: consent and arbitral tribunal competence to hear counterclaims in treaty-based ICSID arbitrations. ICSID Rev 28(2): 291–300

Steingruber AM (2020) Counterclaims: a critical analysis of Article 6 of the 2019 The Hague resolution of the Institut de Droit International on the "Equality of Parties before International Investment Tribunals". ICSID Rev 35(3):595–645

Tan G, Chong A (2020) The future of environmental counterclaims in ICSID Arbitration: challenges, treaties and interpretations. Cambridge Int Law J 9(2):176

Thirlway H (1999) Counterclaims before the International Court of Justice: The *Genocide Convention* and *Oil Platforms* Decisions. Leiden J Int Law 12:197–202

Thomas C, Dhillon HK (2014) Applicable law under international investment treaties. Singapore Acad Law J 26:975–998

Tietje C, Krow K (2017) The Reform of Investment Protection Rules in CETA, TTIP and other recent EU-FTAs: convincing? (19 August 2017). <https://papers.ssrn.com/sol3/papers.cfm?abstract_id=2885279> Accessed 10 Jan 2023

Van Harten G (2007) Investment treaty arbitration and public law. Oxford University Press, Oxford

Van Harten G (2010) Investment treaty arbitration, procedural fairness, and the rule of law. In: Schill SW (ed) International investment law and comparative public law. Oxford University Press, Oxford, pp 627–658

Van Harten G, Loughlin M (2006) Investment treaty arbitration as a species of global administrative law. Eur J Int Law 17(1):121–150

Waibel M, Kaushal A, Chung LKH, Balchin C (2010) The backlash against investment arbitration. Kluwer Law International, Alphen aan den Rijn

Wälde TW (2010a) Equality of arms in investment arbitration: procedural challenges. In: Yannaca-Small K (ed) Arbitration under international investment agreements: a guide to the key issues, 1st edn. Oxford University Press, Oxford, pp 161–188

Wälde TW (2010b) Procedural challenges in investment arbitration under the shadow of the dual role of the state: asymmetries and tribunal's duty to ensure, pro-actively, the equality of arms. Arbitr Int 26(1):3–42

Waldron J (2011) Are sovereigns entitled to the benefit of the international rule of law? Eur J Int Law 22(2):315–343

Walter A (2015) Investor-state contracts in the context of international investment law. In: Bungenberg M, Griebel J, Hobe S, Reinisch A (eds) International investment law: a handbook. CH Beck/Hart/Nomos, Baden-Baden, pp 80–92

Werner M (2002) Widerklage auf Nationaler und Internationaler Ebene. Verlag Paul Haupt, Bern

Williams DAR, Kirk A (2018) Chapter 6: balancing party autonomy, jurisdiction and the integrity of arbitration: where to draw the line? In: Kaplan N, Moser MJ (eds) Jurisdiction, admissibility and choice of law in international arbitration: Liber Amicorum Michael Pryles. Kluwer Law International, Alphen aan den Rijn, pp 87–106

Zin SM (2020) Reappraising access to justice in ISDS: a critical review on state recourse to counterclaim. In: Anderson AM, Beaumont B (eds) The investor-state dispute settlement system: reform, replace or status quo? Kluwer Law International, Alphen aan den Rijn, pp 225–246

Other Documents

ILC YB [2006] vol II, part II, A/CN.4/SER.A/2006/Add.l (Part 2) 'Draft Principles on the Allocation of Loss in the Case of Transboundary Harm arising out of Hazardous Activities, with Commentaries' (58-90)

PCIJ (28 May 1934) Series D—Acts and Documents concerning the Organization of the Court, Third Addendum to No 2, 'Elaboration of the Rules of Court of March 11th, 1936' (Thirteenth Meeting)

PCIJ (29 May 1934) Series D—Acts and Documents concerning the Organization of the Court, Third Addendum to No 2, 'Elaboration of the Rules of Court of March 11th, 1936' (Fourteenth Meeting)

Report of the Eighteenth Commission of the Institut de Droit International (Rapporteur Professor Campbell McLachlan) on the 'Equality of Parties before International Investment Tribunals'. <https://www.idi-iil.org/app/uploads/2019/06/Commission-18-Equality-of-parties-before-international-investment-tribunals-McLachlan-Travaux-La-Haye-2019.pdf> Accessed 10 January 2023

UNCITRAL (20 April 2017) Possible future Work in the Field of Dispute Settlement: Reforms of Investor-State Dispute Settlement (ISDS). UN Doc A/CN.9/917

UNCITRAL (19 December 2017) Report of Working Group III (Investor-State Dispute Settlement Reform) on the work of its thirty-fourth session, Part II. UN Doc A/CN.9/930/Rev.1

UNCITRAL (26 February 2018) Report of Working Group III (Investor-State Dispute Settlement Reform) on the work of its thirty-fourth session, Part I. UN Doc A/CN.9/930/Add.1/Rev.1

UNCITRAL (04 March 2019) Possible reform of investor-State dispute settlement (ISDS) Submission from the Government of Morocco. UN Doc A/CN.9/WG.III/WP.161

UNCITRAL (17 July 2019), Possible reform of investor-State dispute settlement (ISDS) Submission from the Government of South Africa. UN Doc A/CN.9/WG.III/WP.176

UNCITRAL (09 April 2019) Report of Working Group III (Investor-State Dispute Settlement Reform) on the work of its thirty-seventh session. UN Doc A/CN.9/970

UNCITRAL (22 January 2020) Possible reform of investor-State dispute settlement (ISDS) Multiple Proceedings and Counterclaim. UN Doc A/CN.9/WG.III/WP.193

UNGA Resolution 67/1 (30 November 2012) Declaration of the High-level Meeting of the General Assembly on the Rules of Law at the National and International Levels. UN Doc A/RES/67/1

UNSC (23 August 2004) Report of the Secretary General on 'The Rule of Law and Transitional Justice in Conflict and Post-Conflict Societies. UN Doc S/2004/616

Chapter 3
Jurisdiction Over Environmental Counterclaims: The Puzzle of Consent

An arbitral tribunal's jurisdiction to adjudge counterclaims is the most significant obstacle for environmental counterclaims. In approximately 38% of the cases with counterclaims analysed in this monograph, tribunals have declined jurisdiction to rule upon the respective counterclaims.[1] These statistics might work as a deterrent for a respondent state, who despite being entitled to submit counterclaims might be reluctant to expend its time and resources on a counterclaim that most probably would be rejected on jurisdiction. Against this backdrop, it cannot be overstated that the parties' consent plays a central role in the limitation of a tribunal's jurisdiction and the ensuing power to decide on counterclaims.

Accordingly, this Chapter analyses the requisite jurisdiction for an environmental counterclaim in investment arbitration centred around consent. With this purpose, the first section lays out the foundations for a tribunals' jurisdiction to decide counterclaims in investment arbitration [Sect. 3.1]. The second and third sections delve into the jurisdiction of arbitral tribunals over environmental counterclaims both in contract-based [Sect. 3.2] and treaty-based investment arbitration [Sect. 3.3]. Finally, the last section presents some conclusions on parties' consent for contract-based and treaty-based investment arbitration, its implications for environmental counterclaims and possible tools to overcome the jurisdictional obstacles [Sect. 3.4].

[1] *See* this book "Annex 3: *Counterclaims in Numbers*".

A. E. Alvarado-Garzón, *Environmental Counterclaims in Investment Arbitration*, EYIEL Monographs - Studies in European and International Economic Law 34,
https://doi.org/10.1007/978-3-031-46391-4_3

3.1 Tribunals' Jurisdiction to Decide Counterclaims: Covering the Basics

As portrayed in Chap. 2, the requisite jurisdiction is the foremost important requirement for environmental counterclaims or any other kind of counterclaims for that matter. In this sense, some authors find that the failure of counterclaims in investment arbitration is mostly caused by jurisdictional barriers, particularly in treaty-based cases.[2] Yet, the factual background, underlying instruments and tribunals' reasoning for declining or upholding jurisdiction has considerably varied. It is thus necessary to analyse the source of arbitral tribunals' jurisdiction to decide counterclaims. Accordingly, this section starts with parties' consent as the backbone of tribunals' jurisdiction in investment arbitration [Sect. 3.1.1]. Afterwards, it addresses consent over counterclaims [Sect. 3.1.2]. Finally, this section explores other possible bases for an arbitral tribunal's power to decide counterclaims [Sect. 3.1.3].

3.1.1 The Parties' Consent as the Backbone of Tribunals' Jurisdiction in Investment Arbitration

Consent is a foundational idea in international law, which legitimises the submission of a state to an international adjudicative body.[3] Consequently, the jurisdiction of any court or tribunal hinges on the disputing parties' consent.[4] The PCIJ and the ICJ have reaffirmed this in cases such as *Status of Eastern Carelia,*[5] *Mavrommatis*,[6]

---

[2]Popova and Poon (2015), p. 226.

[3]Brilmayer et al. (2017), p. 31; Fontanelli (2018), pp. 100–101. For a slightly different opinion, analysing a shift from a predominantly consensual paradigm towards a compulsory one in international adjudication *see*, Romano (2007), pp. 791–872.

[4]Fitzmaurice (1986), p. 436; Waibel (2015), p. 1213.

[5]*Status of Eastern Carelia* (Advisory Opinion) (23 July 1923) PCIJ Rep Series B No 05, 27: ('It is well established in international law that no State can, without its consent, be compelled to submit its disputes with other States either to mediation or to arbitration, or to any other kind of pacific settlement').

[6]*The Mavrommatis Palestine Concessions (Greece v United Kingdom)* (Judgment) (30 August 1924) PCIJ Rep Series A No 02, 16: ('For this reason the Court, bearing in mind the fact that its jurisdiction is limited, that it is invariably based on the consent of the respondent and only exists in so far as this consent has been given').

Interpretation of Peace Treaties,[7] or *Certain Phosphate Lands in Nauru*,[8] highlighting that without consent a state cannot be compelled to adjudication.

In this sense, consent to the jurisdiction of a court or tribunal in public international law cannot be presumed, but rather it requires strict proof.[9] This however does not mean that only a particular form of consent is accepted. As set out in the *Corfu Channel* case, it is not required that '*consent should be expressed in any particular form*'.[10] Accordingly, consent may be general (every kind of disputes) or partial (certain disputes), it may be given before or after the dispute arose, and consent may as well be explicit or implicit.[11]

The same principle applies for consent to international arbitration.[12] Arbitral tribunals are bound in their jurisdiction to the confines of the respective parties' consent.[13] This is equally true for contract-based and treaty-based investment arbitration. As highlighted by the arbitrator Brigitte Stern in *Impregilo v Argentina*:

> [I]n the framework of BITs, investors are not capable of intervening on the international level against States for the recognition of their rights, unless States grant them such a right under conditions that they determine. An arbitral tribunal – just as the ICJ or any international court – does not have a general jurisdiction, it only has a "*compétence d'attribution*", which has to respect the limits provided for by the States.[14]

'Unlimited' consent by a state to the jurisdiction of an adjudicative body is rather rare, thus, consent must be carefully interpreted.[15] The interpretation of states' consent to the jurisdiction of an adjudicative body (including its scope of application) must be construed neither broadly nor restrictively, but rather following the canons of treaty interpretation.[16] The importance of the delimitation of consent cannot be overstated because if a tribunal decides a claim outside the parties' consent

---

[7] *Interpretation of Peace Treaties with Bulgaria, Hungary and Romania* (Advisory Opinion) [1950] ICJ Rep 65, 71: ('The consent of States, parties to a dispute, is the basis of the Court's jurisdiction in contentious cases').

[8] *Case concerning Certain Phosphate Lands in Nauru (Nauru v Australia)* (Judgment) [1992] ICJ Rep 240, para. 53: ('[the Court's] jurisdiction depends on the consent of States and, consequently, the Court may not compel a State to appear before it, even by way of intervention').

[9] Fitzmaurice (1986), pp. 514 and 738.

[10] *Corfu Channel Case (United Kingdom v Albania)* (Judgment on Preliminary Objection) [1948] ICJ Rep 15, 27.

[11] Tomuschat (2012), mn. 35. Similarly, Fitzmaurice (1986), p. 515.

[12] Carlston (1972), p. 62: ('Arbitration between States, as well as between persons, is contractual in source and arises solely out of consent'); *Ambatielos Case (Greece v United Kingdom)* (Merits: Obligation to Arbitrate) [1953] ICJ Rep 10, 19: ('... the principle, which is well established in international law and accepted by its own jurisprudence as well as that of the Permanent Court of International Justice, to the effect that a State may not be compelled to submit its disputes to arbitration without its consent').

[13] Sharpe and Jacob (2018), p. 352.

[14] *Impregilo SpA v Argentine Republic*, ICSID Case No ARB/07/17, Concurring and Dissenting Opinion of Professor Brigitte Stern (21 June 2011) para. 53.

[15] Fitzmaurice (1986), p. 513.

[16] Fitzmaurice (1986), p. 513; Tomuschat (2012), mn. 35.

this may lead to the unenforceability or annulment/setting aside of the resulting award.[17] In this line, one may use the analogy drawn by Alan Scott Rau, who described that the presence of consent to arbitration reflects a series of concentric circles: the inner circle pertains to whether there is consent at all, followed by wider circles representing questions such as who are the parties, what kind of disputes, what are the procedural rules, etc.[18] The closer to the centre the question is, the stricter the requirement of proof should be.

3.1.2 Consent over Counterclaims: An Unavoidable Requirement?

The consensual nature of investment arbitration, which limits the arbitral tribunal's jurisdiction, engenders the question of whether there must be consent over counterclaims. In principle, all procedural rules conceive that the arbitral tribunal must have jurisdiction over counterclaims as *sine qua non* requirement.[19] Thus, a variety of authors consider that there must be consent to the settlement of a counterclaim, otherwise it would fall outside the scope of the tribunal's jurisdiction.[20] Certainly, a counterclaim cannot be used as a back door for a claim that is out of the tribunal's jurisdiction.[21] However, what does 'consent to counterclaims' entail? Must the dispute settlement clause set out explicitly the tribunal's jurisdiction over counterclaims?

Illustratively, the Claims Settlement Declaration explicitly contemplates the IUSCT's jurisdiction over counterclaims.[22] However, there is no reason to require such express language. Jurisdiction over counterclaims should be analysed similarly as jurisdiction over the main claim without imposing stricter requirements. Moreover, a state's consent to the investor's claims need not appear in the same instrument as the investor's consent to counterclaims.[23] Accordingly, there are four scenarios of parties' consent to counterclaims:

In the first scenario, explicit consent prior to the dispute, there is an express provision on counterclaims either in the investment contract in contract-based

[17] Scherer et al. (2021), fn. 16, referring to Article V(c) New York Convention, Article 34(2)(a)(iii) and Article 36(1)(a)(iii) UNCITRAL Model Law on Arbitration, and Article 52(1)(b) ICSID Convention.

[18] Rau (2008), pp. 203 et seqq.

[19] Renteln (1987), p. 390.

[20] Kjos (2007), p. 602; Bjorklund (2013), p. 466; Rivas (2015), pp. 790–791.

[21] Sharpe and Jacob (2018), p. 352.

[22] *See* Sect. 2.1.2.

[23] Kalicki and Silberman (2012), p. 14. This finds reflection in public international law, where judge Higgins held that claim and counterclaim need not have identical basis of jurisdiction *see*, *Oil Platforms (Iran v United States of America)* (Order on Counterclaim) [1998] ICJ Rep 190, Separate Opinion Judge Higgins, 218.

investment arbitration or in the underlying treaty in treaty-based investment arbitration. Such provision may either explicitly foresee counterclaims to be decided by the arbitral tribunal, in which case there is no obstacle for it,[24] or it may explicitly exclude the possibility of raising counterclaims, in which case the tribunal is prevented from deciding on counterclaims. While this might be the safest route to find consent to counterclaims, arbitration agreements do not normally contain procedural details but rather an outline of the procedure, for instance through the incorporation of institutional rules.[25] Thus, the existence of an IIA (or even investment contracts) explicitly excluding the possibility of raising any counterclaim would rather be an exception.[26]

In the second scenario, explicit consent after the dispute arose, the disputing parties explicitly agree to submit the respondent's counterclaim in the same proceedings as the claimant's claim, or they explicitly agree not to do so. Should the parties agree on having both counterclaim and claim in the same arbitral proceedings, nothing prevents the tribunal from adjudging the counterclaim.[27] This is precisely what occurred in *Burlington v Ecuador*.[28] However, the disputing parties may agree not to submit the counterclaim in the same proceedings as the claim,[29] for instance, with the purpose of submitting such counterclaim to a different forum. This second scenario is based on the premise that the jurisdictional title did not foresee counterclaims, nor did it exclude them from its scope. Thus, by explicitly agreeing to submit counterclaims to arbitration, the disputing parties are 'expanding' the original arbitration agreement to include a previously non-contemplated issue, namely a respondent's counterclaim.[30] This idea relies on the consensual nature of arbitration, whereby any jurisdictional gap may be fulfilled by the parties' agreement including counterclaims not originally foreseen in the arbitration agreement.[31]

In the third scenario, tacit consent after the dispute arose, there is no prior indication of consent over counterclaims but the claimant has expressed its consent to the submission of counterclaims through its conduct. This assimilates to *forum prorogatum* at the ICJ, whereby there is a lack of the respondent's consent to the jurisdiction of the Court, or the applicant's submissions go beyond the jurisdictional title, yet the Court assumes jurisdiction given that the respondent consented to it

[24] Kjos (2007), p. 615.

[25] Hanefeld and de Jong (2019), p. 250.

[26] Bravin and Kaplan (2013), fn. 30.

[27] Kjos (2007), p. 615.

[28] *Burlington Resources Inc v Republic of Ecuador*, ICSID Case No ARB/08/5, Decision on Ecuador's Counterclaims (07 February 2017) paras. 6 and 60.

[29] Steingruber (2013), p. 293.

[30] With regards to the expansion of the arbitration agreement in the framework of counterclaims, *see* Kjos (2007), p. 615; Kryvoi (2012), p. 251. Similarly, Popova and Poon (2015), pp. 226–227; Ben Hamida (2005), p. 266.

[31] Blackaby et al. (2022), para. 5.101.

through its conduct.[32] The respondent's acts or conduct must conclusively establish consent to the Court's jurisdiction[33] and be regarded as '*an unequivocal indication*' of the state to willingly submit to the Court.[34] Similarly, in international arbitration, the parties may express their consent by conduct, even expanding the original arbitration agreement.[35]

Accordingly, it has been considered that if the investor does not raise any objections to the tribunal's jurisdiction to decide a respondent's counterclaim, this should be construed as tacit consent.[36] Examples of tacit consent over counterclaims can be found in the context of contract-based investment arbitration, such as in *Benvenuti v Congo,*[37] *RSM v Grenada,*[38] *Balkan Energy v Ghana,*[39] *Metro de Lima v Peru,*[40] or in the context of treaty-based investment arbitration, such as in *Alex*

[32] Fitzmaurice (1986), p. 753: ('Consent by subsequent conduct constitutes a consent virtually as express as if it were conveyed in a written statement . . . indeed, the conduct will normally take the form of, or be accompanied or manifested by, something in writing, such as a letter of appointment, the deposit of a memorial, thus leaving little room for inferences or implications'). Similarly, Tomuschat (2012), mn. 40.

[33] *Rights of Minorities in Upper Silesia (Minority Schools) (Germany v Poland)* (Judgment) (26 April 1928) PCIJ Rep Series A No 15, 24: ('And there seems to be no doubt that the consent of a State to the submission of a dispute to the Court may not only result from an express declaration, but may also be inferred from acts conclusively establishing it. It seems hard to deny that the submission of arguments on the merits, without making reservations in regard to the question of jurisdiction, must be regarded as an unequivocal indication of the desire of a State to obtain a decision on the merits').

[34] *Case Concerning Armed Activities on the Territory of the Congo (New Application: 2002) (Democratic Republic of Congo v Rwanda)* (Jurisdiction) [2006] ICJ Rep 6, para. 21; *Corfu Channel Case (United Kingdom v Albania)* (Judgment on Preliminary Objection) [1948] ICJ Rep 15, 27.

[35] Carlston (1972), p. 172: ('by their conduct the parties can by tacit consent enlarge the powers of the tribunal. Accordingly, objection should be promptly be made to departures from the course of procedure stipulated for the tribunal if a State desires to avoid the otherwise reasonable inference that its inaction is to be viewed as acquiescence'). With respect to tacit consent for counterclaims, *see* Steingruber (2020), p. 602.

[36] Kjos (2007), p. 616; Kendra (2013), p. 593. Similarly, Ben Hamida (2005), p. 266; Popova and Poon (2015), pp. 226–227.

[37] The tribunal acknowledged that its competence over the counterclaims was not disputed, see *SARL Benvenuti & Bonfant v People's Republic of the Congo*, ICSID Case No ARB/77/2, Award (08 August 1980) para. 4.104.

[38] The claimant simply addressed the merits without challenging tribunal's jurisdiction over the counterclaims, see *RSM Production Corporation v Grenada*, ICSID Case No ARB/05/14, Award (13 March 2009).

[39] The claimant contested the lack of evidence for the merits of the counterclaim without challenging tribunal's jurisdiction over it, see *Balkan Energy (Ghana) Limited v Republic of Ghana*, PCA Case No 2010-7, Award (01 April 2014) para. 570.

[40] Neither did the claimant challenge the tribunal's jurisdiction over counterclaims, nor did the tribunal address the issue of jurisdiction over counterclaims, see *Metro de Lima Línea 2 SA v Republic of Peru (I)*, ICSID Case No ARB/17/3, Decision on Jurisdiction and Liability (06 July 2021).

Genin v Estonia,[41] *Desert Line v Yemen*,[42] *Occidental v Ecuador*,[43] and *Perenco v Ecuador*.[44] In those cases, no jurisdictional objections to the counterclaims were raised and consequently, the respective tribunals assumed jurisdiction over them.

In the fourth scenario, there is no prior expression of consent *vis-à-vis* counterclaims, and the parties have not expressly or tacitly agreed on the submission of a counterclaim after the dispute arose. This is the most recurrent scenario, in which the tribunal ought to interpret the jurisdictional title and decide whether the counterclaim falls within the arbitration agreement or not. In other words, the tribunal would seek to determine whether there is implied consent to counterclaims within the underlying contract or treaty. Determining implied consent consists of interpreting the terms of the arbitration agreement in order to infer if a specific case is covered by the parties' consent or not.[45]

On a related note, one may consider that consent over counterclaims is a jurisdictional question, which must be proven by the respondent.[46] This implies that the respondent must furnish the tribunal with proof of consent together with the substance of its counterclaim. However, as mentioned above, consent over counterclaims may be completed in a later stage, for instance, when the claimant does not object to the tribunal's jurisdiction over counterclaims. In this case, the claimant's actions should suffice for the finding of consent over counterclaims.

---

[41] The claimants did not address the tribunal's jurisdiction over the counterclaim, see *Alex Genin, Eastern Credit Limited, Inc and AS Baltoil v The Republic of Estonia*, ICSID Case No ARB/99/2, Award (25 June 2001).

[42] The claimant did not comment on the respondent's counterclaims, see *Desert Line Projects LLC v The Republic of Yemen*, ICSID Case No ARB/05/17, Award (06 February 2008) para. 221.

[43] This case was based both on a treaty's and on a contract's dispute resolution clause. However, the claimants counter the counterclaims' substance without addressing the tribunal's jurisdiction to decide them, see *Occidental Petroleum Corporation and Occidental Exploration and Production Company v The Republic of Ecuador*, ICSID Case No ARB/06/11, Award (05 October 2012) paras. 288–290.

[44] *Perenco Ecuador Ltd v Republic of Ecuador and Empresa Estatal Petróleos del Ecuador (Petroecuador)*, ICSID Case No ARB/08/6, Decision on Perenco's Application for Dismissal of Ecuador's Counterclaims (18 August 2017) para. 35: ('The Tribunal further observes that Perenco never in the past challenged its jurisdiction to hear Ecuador's counterclaims nor their admissibility').

[45] Fitzmaurice (1986), pp. 753–754.

[46] Sullivan and Kirsey (2017), p. 109.

3.1.3 Beyond the Arbitration Agreement: Other Possible Sources for a Tribunal's Power to Decide Counterclaims?

The arbitral tribunal may be tempted to search its power of determining counterclaims beyond the wording of the arbitration agreement. In this regard, there are two possible sources of a tribunal's powers that might be relevant in the framework of counterclaims, namely, the theory of inherent powers of arbitrators [Sect. 3.1.3.1], and the rules of procedure or arbitration rules [Sect. 3.1.3.2].

3.1.3.1 Inherent Powers

From the outset, inherent powers are intertwined with the judicial function of international courts and tribunals.[47] They are powers necessary to fulfil their mandate as adjudicatory bodies.[48] Inherent powers can be categorised as expressed, discretionary or implied.[49] Expressed inherent powers are set out in the underlying instruments and rules, discretionary inherent powers stem from rules granting discretion to the tribunal to decide procedural or substantive issues, and implied inherent powers rest on the principle of interpretation *effet utile* of the underlying instruments as a whole.[50] In any case, the powers falling within the scope of inherent powers is subject to evolution,[51] and they should '*reflect contemporary views of judicial functions*'.[52]

Under the umbrella of inherent powers of international courts and tribunals, one could consider an arbitral tribunal's decision to adjudge counterclaims.[53] Against this backdrop, the question to solve is whether a tribunal's power to adjudge counterclaims indeed falls within its inherent powers. However, the concept of inherent powers alone cannot justify such a jurisdictional decision.

Considering that international courts and tribunals are based on state consent or party autonomy, the exercise of inherent powers cannot supersede parties' consent.[54] Some inherent powers can indeed be modified or even restricted by agreement of the parties, as long as such modification or restriction does not deprive the court or

---

[47] Holzer (2022), pp. 77 et seqq.

[48] Brown (2010), p. 666. Similarly, Hanefeld and de Jong (2019), p. 253.

[49] Bjorklund and Brosseau (2019), pp. 34–52.

[50] Bjorklund and Brosseau (2019), pp. 34–52.

[51] Wälde (2010), p. 182.

[52] Bjorklund and Brosseau (2019), p. 52.

[53] Brown (2010), pp. 666–669. Similarly, in commercial arbitration, *see* Steingruber (2012), para. 7.26.

[54] Thirlway (2013), p. 693. Nevertheless, Andrea Bjorklund and Jonathan Brosseau argue that when inherent powers are used properly, they actually promote state consent and party autonomy, *see* Bjorklund and Brosseau (2019), p. 34.

tribunal of their judicial nature.[55] In the context of the ICJ, on the one hand, counterclaims are referred to as 'Incidental Proceedings',[56] which fall within the Court's incidental or ancillary jurisdiction as part of the inherent powers of the Court.[57]

Accordingly, given that a tribunal's jurisdiction in a subject-matter encompasses the power to decide all relevant incidental questions,[58] one may argue that counterclaims fall within the category of 'incidental' questions to which the tribunal's jurisdiction extends. However, a decision on counterclaims does not involve a preliminary or incidental matter per se, thus, jurisdiction over counterclaims is '*not independent of, but consequential upon, a determination (even if a negative one), of the question of substantive jurisdiction*'.[59] This means that the Court must analyse whether it is empowered to decide the particular dispute giving rise to the counterclaim.[60]

In international arbitration, on the other hand, inherent powers have been invoked by arbitral tribunals, in the interest of efficiency, to streamline the proceedings, for consolidation and joinder, when bifurcating proceedings, or issuing an early dismissal of a claim.[61] This also includes the inherent power to ensure the equality of parties.[62] However, there are limitations on the exercise of inherent powers. For instance, an international court or tribunal cannot assert an inherent power if by doing so it would be inconsistent with its constitutive instruments.[63] In fact, the International Law Association (ILA) highlighted that inherent powers remain subordinate to the parties' consent.[64]

Thus, consent in investment arbitration has priority and cannot be trumped by efficiency purposes.[65] In other words, inherent powers must not be used as a tool to

---

[55] Bjorklund and Brosseau (2019).

[56] *See* ICJ Rules of Court of 2001, Section D. Incidental Proceedings, whereby Subsection 3, Article 80 thereof, deals with counterclaims.

[57] Fitzmaurice (1986), fn. 5: ('The main types of incidental jurisdiction, besides that relating to interim measures, are in respect of counterclaims, third-party interventions, the control of the proceedings and the interpretation and revision of judgments').

[58] Cheng (1953), p. 266.

[59] Fitzmaurice (1986), p. 535.

[60] On 'substantive jurisdiction' of the ICJ, *see* Fitzmaurice (1986), p. 483.

[61] Certainly, in the absence specific provisions empowering the tribunal, methods such as early dismissal might be controversial, *see* Hanefeld and de Jong (2019), pp. 255 et seqq.

[62] Bain (2018), para. 8.42.

[63] Brown (2010), p. 669; Bain (2018), para. 8.42.

[64] ILA Committee on International Commercial Arbitration, 'Inherent and Implied Powers of International Arbitral Tribunals: Recommendations' (Resolution No 4/2016) <https://www.ila-hq.org/images/ILA/docs/No.4_Resolution_2016_InternationalCommercialArbitration.pdf> accessed 10 January 2023.

[65] Pathak (2019), p. 113. A seemingly opposite view was expressed by Berger (1999), p. 76: ('Aspects of procedural economy in the ongoing arbitration may therefore take priority over the parties' will as expressed in the arbitration agreement covering the cross-claim only in those exceptional cases where the claimant clearly indicates a corresponding will'). Interestingly, Klaus

enlarge the already-defined scope of the arbitration agreement. The same applies for a tribunal's power to adjudge counterclaims. If the jurisdictional title evinces an inconsistency with the exercise of a tribunal's power to decide a counterclaim, then the tribunal must refrain from doing so.

3.1.3.2 Rules of Procedure or Arbitration Rules

Most of the arbitration rules used for the settlement of investment disputes foresee a procedure (and sometimes requirements) for the submission of counterclaims.[66] Interestingly, most of those sets of rules were not drafted for treaty-based investment arbitration, thus, whether the incorporation of arbitration rules suffices to include counterclaims within the scope of the tribunal's jurisdiction in investment arbitration is at least debatable.[67] Understandably, arbitration provisions (either in IIAs or in investment contracts) are hardly ever detailed enough on issues of procedure, which normally is left to the chosen arbitration rules.[68] Consequently, some authors may consider that unless explicitly prohibited by the underlying treaty or contract, counterclaims should be allowed, provided they are contemplated in the arbitration rules.[69]

However, the arbitration rules cannot be used to extend the tribunal's jurisdiction, when the latter has a restrictive scope.[70] In other words, if the arbitration agreement is narrowly drafted, the tribunal cannot entertain counterclaims arguing that the arbitration rules contemplate the submission of counterclaims.[71] The crux of the matter thus lies in the tribunal's jurisdiction, which is solely based on consent.

Peter Berger's argument hinges on the claimant's consent; thus, procedural economy does not take priority over the parties' agreement, but rather procedural economy arguments for the admission of counterclaims presuppose the existence of parties' agreement.

[66] These are: ICSID Rules of Procedure for Arbitration Proceedings (*ICSID Arbitration Rules (2006)* and the newly adopted *ICSID Arbitration Rules (2022)*); UNCITRAL Arbitration Rules (2013); SCC Arbitration Rules (2017); ICC Arbitration Rules (2021); Vienna International Arbitral Centre Rules of Investment Arbitration and Mediation (*VIAC Investment Arbitration Rules (2021)*).

[67] Harrison (2016), p. 479.

[68] Bjorklund (2013), p. 471.

[69] Alvarez (2000), p. 410. Similarly, Larschan and Mirfendereski (1986), pp. 32–33. With respect to the UNCITRAL Arbitration Rules (1976) *see*, Clodfelter and Tsutieva (2018), paras. 17.75 et seqq.

[70] Kjos (2007), fn. 95: ('One may wish to note that a restriction of the tribunal's jurisdiction in this regard cannot be overcome by a reference to explicit provisions for counter-claims in the relevant arbitration rules'). For a different opinion *see* Sourgens (2017), p. 198: ('the question arises whether the scope of the arbitration consent is broadened by reference to the arbitration instruments pursuant to which it is given. . .many arbitration rules in fact expressly contemplate that the parties consent to a tribunal hearing counterclaims that arise out of the same transaction and occurrence as the main claim. This incorporation may well operate to expand even narrowly drafted arbitration consent. . .there is no bar to stating counterclaims if they are appropriately articulated as matter of applicable law') (footnotes omitted).

[71] Popova and Poon (2015), p. 227; Hussin (2019), p. 3.

Moreover, the arbitration rules do not normally address whether parties have consented to counterclaims, but rather they start from that assumption and further regulate the procedure to present a counterclaim.[72]

On the one hand, the ICC Arbitration Rules[73] and the SCC Arbitration Rules[74] contemplate certain requirements that must be included in a counterclaim such as statement of facts, statement of relief and an indication of any relevant arbitration agreement grounding the counterclaim. These requirements seem to evoke the formal requisites for the proper submission of a counterclaim rather than jurisdictional preconditions. Although until date, no investment tribunal has discussed the requirements for submitting a counterclaim under the ICC Arbitration Rules or the SCC Arbitration Rules, it is likely that tribunals following these set of rules would consider the scope of the relevant arbitration agreement as the jurisdictional requirement for the adjudication of counterclaims.

On the other hand, the UNCITRAL Arbitration Rules and the ICSID Arbitration Rules (as some of the most often-used arbitration rules in investment arbitration) establish that a purported counterclaim must fall within the scope of parties' consent. Particularly, Rule 40 ICSID Arbitration Rules (2006) (and cwith similar language Rule 48 ICSID Arbitration Rules (2022)) sets forth:

> 1. Except as the parties otherwise agree, a party may present an incidental or additional claim or counter-claim arising directly out of the subject-matter of the dispute, provided that such ancillary claim is within the scope of the consent of the parties and is otherwise within the jurisdiction of the Centre.

---

[72] Bjorklund (2013), fn. 20. Interestingly, Andrea Bjorklund disagrees with Zachary Douglas when he stated that '*if a general principle can be discerned . . . it is that the jurisdiction* ratione materiae *of an international tribunal extends to counterclaims unless expressly excluded by the constitutive instrument*'. However, in reality Andrea Bjorklund and Zachary Douglas are on the same page because before making such statement, he started from the assumption that the parties' consent is couched in broad terms. Otherwise, as he further explains, an arbitration clause allowing only claims from the investor as to the breach of treaty—such as NAFTA—might not be wide enough to encompass counterclaims, *see* Douglas (2009), paras. 488 et seqq.

[73] ICC Arbitration Rules (2021), Art 5(5): ('. . . Any counterclaims made by the respondent shall be submitted with the Answer and shall provide: (a) a description of the nature and circumstances of the dispute giving rise to the counterclaims and of the basis upon which the counterclaims are made; (b) a statement of the relief sought together with the amounts of any quantified counterclaims and, to the extent possible, an estimate of the monetary value of any other counterclaims; (c) any relevant agreements and, in particular, the arbitration agreement(s); and (d) where counterclaims are made under more than one arbitration agreement, an indication of the arbitration agreement under which each counterclaim is made. The respondent may submit such other documents or information with the counterclaims as it considers appropriate or as may contribute to the efficient resolution of the dispute').

[74] SCC Arbitration Rules (2017), Art 9(1): ('The Secretariat shall send a copy of the Request for Arbitration and any attached documents to the Respondent. The Secretariat shall set a time period within which the Respondent shall submit an Answer to the SCC. The Answer shall include: . . . (iii) a preliminary statement of any counterclaims or setoffs, including an estimate of the monetary value thereof; (iv) where counterclaims or set-offs are made under more than one arbitration agreement, an indication of the arbitration agreement under which each counterclaim or set-off is made').

2. An incidental or additional claim shall be presented not later than in the reply and a counter-claim no later than in the counter-memorial, unless the Tribunal, upon justification by the party presenting the ancillary claim and upon considering any objection of the other party, authorizes the presentation of the claim at a later stage in the proceeding.

3. The Tribunal shall fix a time limit within which the party against which an ancillary claim is presented may file its observations thereon.

This provision replicates the requirements of Article 46 ICSID Convention, whereby the requisite consent is emphasised.[75] Rule 40 ICSID Arbitration Rules (Rule 48 ICSID Arbitration Rules (2022)) envisages further details, such as a deadline for submission and the possibility of the counterparty to file observations to the counterclaim. In the case of the UNCITRAL Arbitration Rules, Article 21(3) thereof provides for the appropriate moment for the submission of counterclaims, but it also states that '*the respondent may make a counterclaim . . . provided that the arbitral tribunal has jurisdiction over it*'. One may assume that such reference to the tribunal's jurisdiction refers to the scope of parties' consent as the underpinning of arbitration. Accordingly, the drafting history of the rules elucidates the intention behind such requirement.

The previous version of the rules namely the UNCITRAL Arbitration Rules (1976) contemplated counterclaims under Article 19 thereof in a similar wording. Nevertheless, instead of '*provided that the arbitral tribunal has jurisdiction over it*', Article 19(3) UNCITRAL Arbitration Rules (1976) contained a different requirement *ie* '*arising out of the same contract*'. From its inception, such wording had caused some concerns, especially in related contracts.[76] Despite the absence of any reference for counterclaims to be within the scope of consent, arbitral tribunals constituted in accordance with the UNCITRAL Arbitration Rules (1976) have consistently analysed whether the instrument of consent is broad enough to cover counterclaims.[77]

In an opposite view, some authors argue that given the absence of any reference to the parties' consent, by selecting the UNCITRAL Arbitration Rules (1976) there is either an *ipso facto* importation of consent or at least an implied consent to counterclaims.[78] This latter view is untenable. The requirement for a counterclaim to fall within the scope of jurisdiction of the tribunal arises from the consensual nature of arbitration, which ought to be assessed by the each tribunal irrespective of the existence of a treaty provision or an arbitration rule in that regard. Thus, the selection of the UNCITRAL Arbitration Rules (1976) cannot obviate this requirement.

---

[75] For a full analysis on Article 46 ICSID Convention *see* Sect. 3.3.1.3.

[76] Binder (2013), para. 21-014.

[77] *See* for instance: *Saluka Investments BV v The Czech Republic*, UNCITRAL Case, Decision on Counterclaims (07 May 2004) paras. 37 et seqq; *Sergei Paushok, CJSC Golden East Company and CJSC Vostokneftegaz Company v The Government of Mongolia*, UNCITRAL Case, Jurisdiction and Liability (28 April 2011) paras. 688 et seqq.

[78] Clodfelter and Tsutieva (2018), paras. 17.75–17.81.

During the deliberations of UNCITRAL Working Group II undertaking the revision of the arbitration rules of 1976, it became clear that the rules should permit counterclaims in wider circumstances than the 'same contract'.[79] Various wordings were proposed striving to strike a balance between investment and commercial disputes, whereby the admission of counterclaims might have different nuances.[80] Considering that references to the 'same arbitration agreement' or 'sufficient link' with the main claim might be construed differently under various legal systems, it was ultimately decided to include the broad wording of '*provided that the arbitral tribunal has jurisdiction over it*'.[81]

Therefore, the rationale behind the introduction of '*provided that the arbitral tribunal has jurisdiction over it*' in Article 21(3) UNCITRAL Arbitration Rules (2013) was to broaden the article's scope of application.[82] Certainly, the tribunal's jurisdiction may stem from the terms of an arbitration agreement, the applicable law or the underlying investment treaty depending on the situation,[83] which is deemed to encapsulate a variety of disputes, promoting procedural efficiency.[84] Some commentators underline that although treaty-based tribunals had interpreted the '*arising out of the same contract*' requirement under the UNCITRAL Arbitration Rules (1976) quite broadly, the change under the UNCITRAL Arbitration Rules (2013) provided greater certainty and clarity on this regard.[85]

Illustratively, the tribunals in *Saluka v Czech Republic* and *Paushok v Mongolia* had construed the '*arising out of the same contract*' requirement under UNCITRAL Arbitration Rules (1976) in a broader sense. Both tribunals assimilated such phrase with the requirement of connection with the main claim,[86] which constitutes a

[79] UNCITRAL, Report of Working Group II (Arbitration and Conciliation) on the work of its fiftieth session (09 March 2009) UN Doc A/CN.9/669, para. 27.

[80] See for instance: UNCITRAL, Report of the Working Group on Arbitration and Conciliation on the work of its forty-fifth session (05 October 2006) UN Doc A/CN.9/614, para. 96: ('the view was expressed that permitting the arbitral tribunal to deal with any such issue arising out of a legal relationship between the parties might raise important issues, especially in the context of investment disputes, where it might be necessary to adopt a particularly broad understanding of the range of counter-claims and set-off that could be dealt with in the same proceedings'); UNCITRAL, Report of the Working Group on Arbitration and Conciliation on the work of its forty-sixth session (20 March 2007) UN Doc A/CN.9/619, para. 158: ('In that context, the view was expressed that removal of any connection between the claim and the counter-claim or set-off might accommodate the needs of specific situations such as investment disputes involving States but might not sufficiently meet the needs of more general commercial disputes').

[81] UNCITRAL, Report of Working Group II (Arbitration and Conciliation) on the work of its fiftieth session (09 March 2009) UN Doc A/CN.9/669, paras. 29–31.

[82] Binder (2013), para. 21-015; Croft et al. (2013), para. 21.15; Paulsson and Petrochilos (2017), p. 170; Webster (2019), para. 21.29.

[83] Caron and Caplan (2013), p. 426.

[84] Paulsson and Petrochilos (2017), p. 171.

[85] Caron and Caplan (2013), p. 428; Paulsson and Petrochilos (2017), p. 172.

[86] *Saluka Investments BV v The Czech Republic*, UNCITRAL Case, Decision on Counterclaims (07 May 2004) para. 76; *Sergei Paushok, CJSC Golden East Company and CJSC Vostokneftegaz*

second step of analysis right after finding whether the scope of jurisdiction covers the counterclaims or not.[87] Certainly, those tribunals addressed the issue of consent over counterclaims regardless of the absence of such explicit requirement—as it should be. It nevertheless seems that the modification of the UNCITRAL Arbitration Rules (2013) pertaining explicitly to the tribunal's jurisdiction over counterclaims might have been warranted in order to avoid confusions.

The modification of the UNCITRAL Arbitration Rules (2013) refers back to the analysis of the consent and its extent as expressed by the parties.[88] In this vein and for the purpose of this section, the foregoing analysis demonstrates that the requirement of '*provided that the arbitral tribunal has jurisdiction over it*' in Article 21(3) UNCITRAL Arbitration Rules (2013) reaffirms this Chapter's premise that a counterclaim must be covered by the parties' consent, upon which the tribunal exercises jurisdiction.

The *Oxus v Uzbekistan* tribunal[89] discussed this issue. The respondent state pointed out that the dispute settlement provision in the underlying treaty, *ie* Article 8 UK-Uzbekistan BIT (1993), did not explicitly exclude counterclaims, but rather such provision referred to the UNCITRAL Arbitration Rules, whereby counterclaims were contemplated.[90] The tribunal rejected the counterclaims and stated that it did '*not consider that this provision creates a jurisdiction where there is none. All it does is stating that counter-claims are admissible and can be submitted to the extent that they already fall under the scope of jurisdiction of the Arbitral Tribunal*'.[91]

Similarly, the *Iberdrola v Guatemala* tribunal[92] considered this point. Here, it was to determine whether a reference in the treaty to a set of arbitration rules foreseeing counterclaims would incorporate consent to counterclaims.[93] Although the tribunal agreed that such arbitration rules are incorporated by reference, it held that '*this is only to the extent that they are not contradicting the treaty... if there is a contradiction between the arbitration rules and the treaty language (as is the case here), the treaty prevails*'.[94] The counterclaims were thereby rejected.

Consequently, one may conclude that a counterclaim must fall within the parties' consent to be permitted. Whether the specific provision explicitly requires the

---

Company v The Government of Mongolia, UNCITRAL Case, Jurisdiction and Liability (28 April 2011) paras. 688–693.

[87] On this issue *see* Chap. 4.

[88] Bjorklund (2013), p. 473.

[89] *Oxus Gold v Republic of Uzbekistan*, UNCITRAL Case, Award (17 December 2015).

[90] *Oxus Gold v Republic of Uzbekistan*, UNCITRAL Case, Award (17 December 2015) para. 908.

[91] *Oxus Gold v Republic of Uzbekistan*, UNCITRAL Case, Award (17 December 2015) para. 944.

[92] *Iberdrola Energía SA v The Republic of Guatemala (II)*, PCA Case No 2017–41, Award (24 August 2020).

[93] *Iberdrola Energía SA v The Republic of Guatemala (II)*, PCA Case No 2017–41, Award (24 August 2020) para. 388.

[94] *Iberdrola Energía SA v The Republic of Guatemala (II)*, PCA Case No 2017–41, Award (24 August 2020) para. 389.

counterclaim to be within the parties' consent (such as ICSID Arbitration Rules) or not (such as ICC Arbitration Rules) is immaterial. Accordingly, a set of arbitration rules by its own does not suffice as a source of counterclaims in investment arbitration because the tribunal must analyse in every case whether its jurisdiction encompasses the said counterclaim.

3.2 Jurisdiction Over Environmental Counterclaims in Contract-Based Investment Arbitration

Investors may choose either contract-based or treaty-based investment arbitration depending on the breach they relied upon. Following the annulment committee in *Vivendi v Argentina*, a treaty breach is determined by the underlying treaty and public international law, whereas a contract breach is determined by the proper law of the contract.[95] Indeed, a breach of contract may at the same time be a breach of the treaty, but only if it is the result of the exercise of sovereign authority ('*puissance publique*').[96] Whether the tribunal's jurisdiction arises from a treaty or a contract may be determinative to the availability of counterclaims, including environmental counterclaims.

As elaborated above, an investment contract embodies a specific transaction between the investor and the host state.[97] Accordingly, the arbitration provisions therein tend to be restricted to the specific contractual relation, but it also entails that the state is entitled to commence arbitral proceedings against the foreign investor.[98] This arises from the synallagmatic character of the contractual obligations which are subject to redress at either party's behest.[99] In principle, the possibility of filing a counterclaim in contract-based investment arbitration is generally accepted,[100] as long as the arbitration clause is broadly worded granting jurisdiction to the tribunal to adjudge any matters arising from the contractual relationship between the

[95] *Compañiá de Aguas del Aconquija SA and Vivendi Universal SA v Argentine Republic*, ICSID Case No ARB/97/3, Decision on Annulment (03 July 2002) para. 96.

[96] *Impregilo SpA v Islamic Republic of Pakistan*, ICSID Case No ARB/03/3, Decision on Jurisdiction (22 April 2005) para. 260.

[97] *See* Sect. 2.2.1.1.

[98] Kjos (2013), pp. 129–130; Sourgens (2017), p. 196.

[99] Report of the Eighteenth Commission of the *Institut de Droit International* (Rapporteur Professor Campbell McLachlan) on the 'Equality of Parties before International Investment Tribunals' para. 80 <https://www.idi-iil.org/app/uploads/2019/06/Commission-18-Equality-of-parties-before-international-investment-tribunals-McLachlan-Travaux-La-Haye-2019.pdf> accessed 10 January 2023.

[100] Lalive and Halonen (2011), p. 146; Kjos (2007), p. 599; Asteriti (2015), p. 258; Clodfelter and Tsutieva (2018), para. 17.46; de Nanteuil (2018), p. 384.

parties.[101] By analogy to international commercial arbitration,[102] such broad wording could include tort counterclaims based on environmental law of the host state.

The foregoing explains that arbitral tribunals did not have many qualms recognising their jurisdiction over counterclaims in the framework of investment contracts.[103] For instance, the *Adriano Gardella v Côte d'Ivoire,*[104] *Benvenuti v Congo,*[105] *MINE v Guinea,*[106] *Zeevi v Bulgaria,*[107] *Balkan Energy v Ghana*[108] and *RSM v Grenada*[109] tribunals did not elaborate on their jurisdiction over the counterclaims raised by the respective respondents.[110] A different situation occurred in the *Klöckner v Cameroon* case. The claimant investor disputed the jurisdiction over a counterclaim, which was based on another arbitration clause in a related contract.[111] By resorting to the intricacies of the contractual relation between the parties and the definitions of investor and investment under the ICSID Convention, the tribunal decided to entertain the counterclaim.[112] Conversely, the dissenting arbitrator reached a different conclusion by delving into the purpose of the various contracts.[113]

The tribunals in *Atlantic Triton v Guinea* and *Elsamex v Honduras* upheld jurisdiction over certain counterclaims while rejecting others for specific reasons.

---

[101] Sourgens (2017), p. 204. As such, the contractual arbitration clause (and the interpretation thereof) would define the tribunal's power to rule upon counterclaims against the claimant investor, *see* Nacimiento et al. (2021), p. 170.

[102] *See* Sect. 2.1.3.2.

[103] Vohryzek-Griest (2009), pp. 83–124.

[104] *Adriano Gardella SpA v Côte d'Ivoire*, ICSID Case No ARB/74/1, Award (29 August 1977).

[105] *SARL Benvenuti & Bonfant v People's Republic of the Congo*, ICSID Case No ARB/77/2, Award (08 August 1980) para. 4.104.

[106] *Maritime International Nominees Establishment (MINE) v Republic of Guinea*, ICSID Case No ARB/84/4, Award (06 January 1988).

[107] *Zeevi Holdings v The Republic of Bulgaria and the Privatization Agency of Bulgaria*, UNCITRAL Case No UNC 39/DK, Award (25 October 2006).

[108] *Balkan Energy (Ghana) Limited v Republic of Ghana*, PCA Case No 2010-7, Award (01 April 2014).

[109] *RSM Production Corporation v Grenada*, ICSID Case No ARB/05/14, Award (13 March 2009) para. 266.

[110] It must be highlighted that the *Benvenuti v Congo* tribunal recognised that the parties did not dispute the jurisdiction over counterclaims, and the *RSM v Grenada* tribunal without much details acknowledged its jurisdiction to decide counterclaims.

[111] For a detailed explanation of this case and the grounds for challenging the tribunal's jurisdiction *see* Sect. 3.3.2.3.

[112] *Klöckner Industrie-Anlagen GmbH and others v United Republic of Cameroon and Société Camerounaise des Engrais*, ICSID Case No ARB/81/2, Award (21 October 1983) 13–16 [reproduced in R Rayfuse (ed), *ICSID Reports vol 2* (CUP 1994) 3-163].

[113] *Klöckner Industrie-Anlagen GmbH and others v United Republic of Cameroon and Société Camerounaise des Engrais*, ICSID Case No ARB/81/2, Award (21 October 1983), Dissenting Opinion Prof D Schmidt, 93 [reproduced in R Rayfuse (ed), *ICSID Reports vol 2* (CUP 1994) 3-163].

For instance, in the *Atlantic Triton v Guinea* case, the arbitration clause was explicitly limited to the scope of the underlying contract (a vessels' management agreement) between the investor and the state. Yet, one of the respondent's counterclaims pursued damages for the alleged failure on the choice of vessels, which was an obligation preceding the contract. The tribunal rejected such counterclaim for being outside of the scope of the contract and the arbitration agreement,[114] whereas the jurisdiction over the rest of the counterclaims was not discussed. In the *Elsamex v Honduras* case, the tribunal upheld its jurisdiction over most of the respondent's counterclaims, except for those based on tort or otherwise outside the contractual relationship.[115] Considering the restrictive wording of the underlying arbitration clause,[116] it is understandable that the *Elsamex v Honduras* tribunal rejected the counterclaims based on tort.

Therefore, in the particular case of environmental counterclaims, nothing prevents the tribunal from deciding on counterclaims seeking redress for the environmental damage caused by the investor, as long as the underlying arbitration clause is broadly drafted. Yet, whether the environmental counterclaim is to be based on contract obligations or on domestic law of the host state appertains to the source of the environmental obligation rather than to the tribunal's jurisdiction, which will be elaborated in Chap. 5.

3.3 Jurisdiction Over Environmental Counterclaims in Treaty-Based Investment Arbitration

In treaty-based investment arbitration, the tribunal's jurisdiction is the result of a two-step process: the state provides a general consent to submit to international arbitration through a treaty, and the foreign investor meets such consent by initiating arbitral proceedings in accordance with the treaty.[117] This particularity of investment arbitration has an impact on the functioning of the procedural mechanism of counterclaims. Therefore, this section analyses the traditional appraisal of an arbitral tribunal's jurisdiction over counterclaims in treaty-based investment arbitration [Sect. 3.3.1]. Then, it examines the obstacles to the contractual counterclaims in treaty-based investment arbitration [Sect. 3.3.2]. Finally, this section proposes a reinterpretation of consent to environmental counterclaims [Sect. 3.3.3].

---

[114] *Atlantic Triton Company Limited v People's Revolutionary Republic of Guinea*, ICSID Case No ARB/84/1, Award (21 April 1986) 39 [reproduced in R Rayfuse (ed), *ICSID Reports vol 3* (CUP 1995) 13–44].

[115] *Elsamex SA v Republic of Honduras*, ICSID Case No ARB/09/4, Award (16 November 2012) paras. 302–305.

[116] For the reproduction of the underlying arbitration clause(s), the sort of disputes subject to arbitration and the tribunal's analysis in this regard *see*, *Elsamex SA v Republic of Honduras*, ICSID Case No ARB/09/4, Decision on Jurisdiction (04 June 2010) paras. 33 and 158 et seqq.

[117] *See* Sect. 2.2.1.2.2.

3.3.1 The Traditional Appraisal of Counterclaims in Treaty-Based Investment Arbitration

Counterclaims in treaty-based investment arbitration have faced an initial reluctance by arbitral tribunals, who remained cautious to decide on them, given the restrictive wording of the underlying treaty provisions.[118] Accordingly, different approaches have been proposed to interpret whether the underlying treaty confers jurisdiction on the tribunal to adjudge counterclaims raised by the respondent host state. Mark Clodfelter and Diana Tsutieva consider three features of investment treaties that might indicate the possibility to adjudge counterclaims[119]: *first*, direct or indirect reference to counterclaims, for instance allowing them or excluding certain type thereof. *Second*, the scope of jurisdiction *ratione materiae*, either by a broad arbitration provision or by a broad applicable law provision including domestic law of the host state. *Third*, the standing granted to the state to bring claims to arbitration.

Ina Popova and Fiona Poon contemplate three kinds of obstacles in investment treaties that might prevent the tribunal from deciding on counterclaims[120]: *first*, treaty clauses limiting the tribunal's jurisdiction to claims raised by investors. *Second*, applicable law provisions excluding the host state's domestic law. *Third*, the effect of the investor's violation of domestic law. Similarly, Arnaud de Nanteuil considers that the tribunal's jurisdiction over counterclaims hinges on the wording of the arbitration clause, and on the possibility to identify an investor's obligations.[121]

All these approaches boil down to two categories: the scope of the arbitration provision foreseen in the treaty [Sect. 3.3.1.1], and the scope of the applicable law *vis-à-vis* an investor's obligations [Sect. 3.3.1.2]. This section thus examines whether these two categories provide the correct approximation to the tribunal's jurisdiction over counterclaims. Additionally, this section addresses the particular case of counterclaims under the ICSID Convention [Sect. 3.3.1.3].

3.3.1.1 The Scope of the Dispute Settlement Provision in the Treaty

The first obstacle that counterclaims face in treaty-based investment arbitration constitutes the wording of the provision referring to arbitration. Considering the consensual nature of investment arbitration, the possibility to raise counterclaims

[118] On that account, Ana Vohryzek-Griest described the instrument of counterclaims in investment arbitration, perhaps provokingly, as a '*history of 30 years of failure*', a label that subsequently has been taken up by several authors *see*, Vohryzek-Griest (2009), p. 83.

[119] Clodfelter and Tsutieva (2018), para. 17.46.

[120] Popova and Poon (2015), p. 228.

[121] de Nanteuil (2018), pp. 377 et seqq.

demands the interpretation of the respective arbitration agreement.[122] There are two kinds of formulations of such provisions that may be construed as restricting the tribunal's jurisdiction over counterclaims: *first*, the state's possibility to bring claims or legal standing [Sect. 3.3.1.1.1]. *Second*, the limited scope *ratione materiae* over treaty breaches [Sect. 3.3.1.1.2]. Although both features may overlap, for the purpose of clarity, they will be explained separately.

3.3.1.1.1 A State's Legal Standing for Submitting Claims: Obstacle or Logical Starting Point?

Treaties use different wordings in providing for investment arbitration. Some IIAs leave the initiation of proceedings open to either the investor or the host state.[123] In case of state claims against the investor, such IIAs presuppose that the investor has consented to international arbitration. Other IIAs grant the investor the exclusive right to initiate arbitration proceedings.[124]

One may argue that state counterclaims can only be admitted as long as the respective dispute resolution provision grants legal standing to the state to submit a claim.[125] Conversely, treaty provisions conferring upon the investor the exclusive right to initiate arbitration proceedings may suggest that the state has not legal

[122] Kryvoi (2012), p. 226; Bjorklund (2013), p. 466; Hoffmann (2013), p. 446; Dudas (2016), p. 395.

[123] *See* for instance: Italy-Chad BIT (1969), Art 7; UK-Singapore BIT (1975), Art 8; Korea-UK BIT (1976), Art 8(1); UK-Sri Lanka BIT (1980), Art 8(3); OIC Investment Agreement (1981), Art 17(1)(2)(a); Romania-Sri Lanka BIT (1981), Art 7(2); US-Panama BIT (1982), Art VII(2); France-Pakistan BIT (1983), Art 8; Senegal-Tunisia BIT (1984), Art 8; St Lucia-Germany BIT (1985), Art 10(2); Sri Lanka-China BIT (1986), Art 13(2); UK-Jamaica BIT (1987), Art 9(1); Malta-BLEU BIT (1987), Art 8(2); Hungary-Denmark BIT (1988), Art 9(2); France-Nigeria BIT (1990), Art 8(2); Netherlands-Czech Republic BIT (1991), Art 8; Germany-Argentina BIT (1991), Art 10(3); US-Estonia BIT (1994), Art VI(3)(b); Russia-Mongolia BIT (1995) Art 6; Peru-Germany BIT (1995), Art 10(3); Germany-Ghana BIT (1995), Art 12(2); China-Saudi Arabia BIT (1996), Art 8(2); UK-El Salvador BIT (1999), Art 8(3); Netherlands-Algeria BIT (2007), Art 9.

[124] *See* for instance: Netherlands-Kenya BIT (1970), Art 11; Japan-Egypt BIT (1977), Art 11; Singapore-BLEU BIT (1978), Art 9; Netherlands-Senegal BIT (1979), Art 10; Korea-Italy BIT (1989), Art 10(2); Poland-Kuwait BIT (1990), Art 10(2)(b); France-Argentina BIT (1991), Art 8(2); Norway-Lithuania BIT (1992), Art IX(2); Germany-Belarus BIT (1993), Art 11; ECT (1994), Art 26(2); Croatia-Canada BIT (1997), Art XII; Indonesia-Bangladesh BIT (1998), Art VIII(2); Israel-Armenia BIT (2000), Art 8(3); Turkey-Greece BIT (2000), Art VII(2); Austria-Iran BIT (2001), Art 11(2); Finland-Uruguay BIT (2002), Art 9(2); Spain-Albania BIT (2003), Art 11(2); Thailand-Jordan BIT (2005), Art 11(2); Mexico-Trinidad and Tobago BIT (2006), Art 13; Panama-Sweden BIT (2008), Art 8(2); China-Malta BIT (2009), Art 9(2); Canada-Czech Republic BIT (2009), Art X(2); Moldova-Estonia BIT (2010), Art 11(2); Japan-Colombia BIT (2011), Art 27; Switzerland-Tunisia BIT (2012), Art 11(2); Canada-Benin BIT (2013), Art 23; Colombia-France BIT (2014), Art 15(4); Russia-Cambodia BIT (2015), Art 8(2); Austria-Kyrgyzstan BIT (2016), Art 14; Israel-Japan BIT (2017), Art 24(2); Turkey-Cambodia BIT (2018), Art 9(2); Hungary-Kyrgyzstan BIT (2020), Art 9(3).

[125] Kjos (2007), pp. 611 et seqq.; Dudas (2016), pp. 401–402; Bilanová (2020), p. 402.

standing to raise a claim, and accordingly, it is prevented from the possibility to raise a counterclaim.[126] This aspect of counterclaims has been referred to, perhaps inappropriately, as 'jurisdiction *ratione personae*'.[127] However, state legal standing and jurisdiction *ratione personae* pertain to different notions.

The tribunal's jurisdiction *ratione personae* alludes to the parties to the dispute in investment arbitration namely the host state and the protected foreign investor.[128] For instance, under the ICSID Convention, the tribunal's jurisdiction *ratione personae* is limited to disputes '*between a Contracting State (or any constituent subdivision or agency of a Contracting State designated to the Centre by that State) and a national of another Contracting State*'.[129] Similarly, each IIA determines the conditions *ratione personae* for submitting a claim to investment arbitration,[130] defining who are protected investors and possible respondent states. If the disputing parties fulfil the requirements or conditions of the underlying treaty with regards to the definition of investor and of host state, the tribunal ought to enjoy jurisdiction *ratione personae* irrespective of the possibility for the state to submit claims (or counterclaims for that matter). Thus, the state's legal standing to submit claims should not be confused with the tribunal's jurisdiction *ratione personae*, as the latter encompasses the disputing parties over which the tribunal has jurisdiction, whereas the former goes one step further and addresses whether one of those disputing parties, *ie* the state, may bring a claim.

It follows from this that the issue is not whether the tribunal's jurisdiction *ratione personae* plays a role for counterclaims (because the disputing parties are the same as to the main claim) but rather whether the state's lack of legal standing to submit claims affects the possibility of counterclaims. The reason behind such conflation may lie in the conceptualisation of a counterclaim as an independent claim of the respondent. If the state lacks legal standing to raise a claim against the foreign investor, it would equally lack legal standing to raise a counterclaim.

By such logic, some tribunals have considered the dispute settlement provisions that do not provide for the state's legal standing to submit a claim as an obstacle for counterclaims. For instance, in the *Roussalis v Romania* case, one of the arguments to decline jurisdiction over the counterclaims was that the treaty did not contemplate claims to be introduced by the host state.[131] Similarly, the *Gavazzi v Romania* tribunal considered that the underlying treaty only conferred upon the investor the

[126] Clodfelter and Tsutieva (2018), para. 17.60. Similarly, de Nanteuil (2018), p. 378; Sharpe and Jacob (2018), pp. 353 et seqq.

[127] Dudas (2016), pp. 401 et seqq.; Kjos (2007), p. 611.

[128] Dolzer et al. (2022), p. 354; Waibel (2015), p. 1241.

[129] ICSID Convention, Art 25(1).

[130] Reed and Davis (2015), p. 616.

[131] *Spyridon Roussalis v Romania*, ICSID Case No ARB/06/1, Award (07 December 2011) para. 869.

right to claim in arbitration against the host state.[132] However, the dissenting arbitrator Mauro Rubino-Sammartano criticised such decision and stated:

> The omission of any express mention of the Host State's right to file a counterclaim may be due to the fact that the drafters of the BIT focused on the protection of the investor. One has then to consider whether this omission excludes any counterclaim by the Host State against the investor before the arbitration forum provided for by the BIT.
>
> ...
>
> Since the counterclaim is an extension of the Respondent's defence against the claim, one has to consider whether counterclaims are included within the consent of the Parties to arbitrate before the Tribunal their dispute arising from the investment.[133]

The tribunal in the *Rusoro Mining v Venezuela* case held as one of the reasons for denying jurisdiction over the counterclaim that, by its literal wording, '*the Treaty affords investors, and only investors, standing to file arbitrations against host States*'.[134] In the *Karkey v Pakistan* case, siding with the tribunal's decision in *Roussalis v Romania*, the tribunal declined jurisdiction over the counterclaims, among other reasons, given that the underlying treaty only enabled arbitration at the investor's initiative.[135]

The tribunal in the *Iberdrola v Guatemala* case noted first that by the wording of the dispute settlement provision in the underlying BIT, the Spain-Guatemala BIT (2002), the right to initiate arbitration was only bestowed on the investor.[136] Consequently, relying on the *Karkey v Pakistan* decision, the tribunal declined jurisdiction over the counterclaim.[137] A last tribunal that deemed the lack of the state's legal standing as an obstacle for counterclaims was in the *Naturgy v Colombia* case. The tribunal analysed in detail the dispute settlement provision of the underlying treaty, *ie* Article 10 Spain-Spain BIT (2005), and concluded '[i]*t is doubtful, in this Tribunal's view, that in the context of such a precisely defined dispute resolution procedure, the Contracting parties would have omitted addressing state counterclaims if it was truly their intention that an arbitral tribunal's jurisdiction should extend to such counterclaims*'. [138]

---

[132] *Marco Gavazzi and Stefano Gavazzi v Romania*, ICSID Case No ARB/12/25, Decision on Jurisdiction, Admissibility and Liability (21 April 2015) para. 151.

[133] *Marco Gavazzi and Stefano Gavazzi v Romania*, ICSID Case No ARB/12/25, Dissenting Opinion (14 April 2015) para. 42(i).

[134] *Rusoro Mining Ltd v Bolivarian Republic of Venezuela*, ICSID Case No ARB(AF)/12/5, Award (22 August 2016) para. 627.

[135] *Karkey Karadeniz Elektrik Uretim AS* v Islamic Republic of Pakistan, ICSID Case No ARB/13/1, Award (22 August 2017) para. 1013.

[136] *Iberdrola Energía SA v The Republic of Guatemala (II)*, PCA Case No 2017-41, Award (24 August 2020) para. 386.

[137] *Iberdrola Energía SA v The Republic of Guatemala (II)*, PCA Case No 2017-41, Award (24 August 2020) paras. 390–391.

[138] *Naturgy Energy Group SA and Naturgy Electricidad Colombia SL (formerly Gas Natural SDG SA and Gas Natural Fenosa Electricidad Colombia SL) v Republic of Colombia*, ICSID Case No UNCT/18/1, Award (12 March 2021) para. 616.

In the same vein, some tribunals have considered that treaty dispute settlement provisions open to both investor and host state support the finding of jurisdiction over counterclaims. In the *Al-Warraq v Indonesia* case, despite the wording of Article 17 OIC Investment Agreement (1981), whereby '*each* [disputing] *party has the right to resort to the Arbitration Tribunal for a final decision on the dispute*', the claimant argued that the treaty did not provide for '*a state's right to a cause of action against an investor*'.[139] The tribunal nevertheless interpreted the state's right to resort to arbitration under the OIC Investment Agreement (1981) as entitling the state to either initiate arbitration or to file counterclaims.[140]

The *Urbaser v Argentina* tribunal found that the dispute resolution provision in the underlying treaty was '*completely neutral as to the identity of the claimant or respondent*'.[141] Consequently, '*it cannot happen that in acting first one party could prevent the other from raising its claim. This can be avoided only by admitting the possibility of a counterclaim*'.[142] Similarly, in the *Tethyan v Pakistan* case, the underlying treaty allowed both the investor and the host state to initiate proceedings, thus, the tribunal considered this as an indication that the state could raise counterclaims.[143]

Conversely, some tribunals have not deemed the lack of the state's legal standing to submit a claim as an impediment for counterclaims either explicitly or implicitly. In the *Amto v Ukraine* case, the claimant argued that the respondent had no standing to file a claim or counterclaim.[144] The tribunal did not analyse the legal standing argument and rather dismissed the counterclaim stating that the respondent failed to present the legal basis for non-material injury to reputation in the treaty or international law.[145] In the *Inmaris v Ukraine* case, despite the fact that pursuant to Article 11 Germany-Ukraine BIT (1993),[146] the submission to arbitration was conferred exclusively on the investor, the tribunal focused on the definition of dispute and

---

[139] *Hesham Talaat M Al-Warraq v The Republic of Indonesia*, UNCITRAL Case, Award (15 December 2014) para. 476.

[140] *Hesham Talaat M Al-Warraq v The Republic of Indonesia*, UNCITRAL Case, Award (15 December 2014) paras. 660–661.

[141] *Urbaser SA and Consorcio de Aguas Bilbao Bizkaia, Bilbao Biskaia Ur Partzuergoa v The Argentine Republic*, ICSID Case No ARB/07/26, Award (08 December 2016) para. 1143.

[142] *Urbaser SA and Consorcio de Aguas Bilbao Bizkaia, Bilbao Biskaia Ur Partzuergoa v The Argentine Republic*, ICSID Case No ARB/07/26, Award (08 December 2016) para. 1144.

[143] *Tethyan Copper Company Pty Limited v Islamic Republic of Pakistan*, ICSID Case No ARB/12/1, Decision on Jurisdiction and Liability (10 November 2017) paras. 1418–1419.

[144] *Limited Liability Company Amto v Ukraine*, SCC Case No 080/2005, Award (26 March 2008) para. 35.

[145] *Limited Liability Company Amto v Ukraine*, SCC Case No 080/2005, Award (26 March 2008) para. 118.

[146] Germany-Ukraine BIT (1993), Art 11: ('(1) Meinungsverschiedenheiten in bezug auf Kapitalanlagen zwischen einer der Vertragsparteien und einem Staatsangehörigen oder einer Gesellschaft der anderen Vertragspartei sollen, soweit möglich, zwischen den Streitparteien gütlich beigelegt werden. (2) Kann die Meinungsverschiedenheit innerhalb einer Frist von sechs Monaten ab dem Zeitpunkt ihrer Geltendmachung durch eine der beiden Streitparteien nicht beigelegt

considered that the counterclaim '*is a dispute between* [Respondent] *and Claimants "with regard to* [Claimants'] *investments"; further, it is a component of the larger dispute that Claimants have consented to submit to this arbitration*'.[147] Therefore, the tribunal acknowledged jurisdiction over the counterclaim.

In the *Metal-Tech v Uzbekistan* case, one of the claimant's arguments was that Uzbekistan lacked standing to bring a claim.[148] Indeed, pursuant to Article 8 Israel-Uzbekistan BIT (1994), the institution of arbitral proceedings was granted at the investor's behest.[149] However, given the wording of the provision, the tribunal considered that its jurisdiction was not '*restricted to disputes initiated by an investor against a Contracting Party. It covers any dispute about an investment*'.[150] In the case of *Oxus v Uzbekistan,* pursuant to Article 8 UK-Uzbekistan BIT (1993), the submission of a claim to international arbitration was subject to the investor's discretion. Based on this provision, the tribunal held that '*the Parties' consent to arbitration under the BIT only cover claims from investors against the host State, but not claims from the host State against the investors*' but it also contemplated an outside-treaty caveat to such rule namely '*to the possible exception of counter-claims having a close connection with the investor's claims*'.[151]

Finally, the tribunal deciding in a similar direction was constituted for the *David Aven v Costa Rica* case. The tribunal recognised that other arbitral tribunals have traditionally declined jurisdiction over counterclaims, yet there were recent decisions in the opposite direction.[152] In spite of the underlying treaty granting standing to submit claims only to the investor,[153] the *David Aven v Costa* tribunal relied on the

werden, so *wird sie auf Verlangen des Staatsangehörigen oder der Gesellschaft der anderen Vertragspartei einem Schiedsverfahren unterworfen. . .*') (emphasis added).

[147] *Inmaris Perestroika Sailing Maritime Services GmbH and Others v Ukraine*, ICSID Case No ARB/08/8, Award (01 March 2012) para. 432.

[148] *Metal-Tech Ltd v Republic of Uzbekistan*, ICSID Case No ARB/10/3, Award (04 October 2013) para. 400.

[149] Israel-Uzbekistan BIT (1994), Art 8: ('1. Each Contracting Party hereby consents to submit to the ICSID for settlement by conciliation or arbitration under the Convention, any legal dispute arising between that Contracting Party and a national or company of the other Contracting Party concerning an investment of the latter in the territory of the former (. . .) 3. If any such dispute should arise and cannot be resolved, amicably or otherwise, within three (3) months from written notification of the existence of the dispute, *then the investor affected may institute conciliation or arbitration proceedings by addressing a request* to that effect to the Secretary-General of the Centre, as provided in Article 28 or 36 respectively of the Convention. The Contracting Party which is a party to the dispute shall not raise as an objection at any stage of the proceedings or enforcement of an award the fact that the investor which is the other party to the dispute has received, in pursuance of an insurance contract, an indemnity in respect of some or all of his or its losses') (emphasis added).

[150] *Metal-Tech Ltd v Republic of Uzbekistan*, ICSID Case No ARB/10/3, Award (04 October 2013) para. 410.

[151] *Oxus Gold v Republic of Uzbekistan*, UNCITRAL Case, Award (17 December 2015) para. 948.

[152] *David R Aven and Others v Republic of Costa Rica*, ICSID Case No UNCT/15/3, Award (18 September 2018) para. 736.

[153] DR-CAFTA, Art 10.16 in conjunction with Art 10.18.

Urbaser v Argentina decision and on the declaration of Michael Reisman in the *Roussalis v Romania* case, sustaining that there was no '*reason of principle to declare inadmissible a counterclaim in which the Respondent State claims that the foreign investor has breached obligations falling within the scope of* [the tribunal's jurisdiction]'.[154]

All in all, utilising the state's lack of standing for submitting a claim as an obstacle for counterclaims might rather be an oversimplification. Conferring the right to initiate arbitration exclusively on the investor may simply underscore the states' consent to resort to arbitration.[155] Particularly, considering the unique functioning of treaty-based investment arbitration whereby consent is achieved in two stages: *first*, the state provides its prospective and generalised consent; *second*, the investor consents normally by filing its notice of arbitration. The state cannot initiate arbitral proceedings against the investor based on the treaty simply because the investor's consent would be lacking. This is reaffirmed by the wording of the IIAs discussed above, whereby the initiation of arbitral proceedings was open to the state only because those treaties required investors to have previously consented to arbitration. In other words, treaty-based investment arbitration necessitates the investor to be the moving party (or as in certain treaties, to provide its consent in advance) since its consent is the missing piece to form an arbitration agreement.

As such, for state counterclaims, the investor would have already consented to arbitration and initiated proceedings. Thus, one cannot equate both situations: state claims and state counterclaims. Accordingly, subjecting the possibility of raising counterclaims to the legal standing to initiate proceedings is not only unreasonable but also inconsistent with the system's functioning.

In this context, some authors suggest that the nub of the matter is whether the dispute resolution clause in the treaty contains a broad wording as to include, for instance 'all disputes', within the tribunal's jurisdiction, rather than the legal standing to initiate proceedings.[156] This issue of the tribunal's jurisdiction over certain

---

[154] *David R Aven and Others v Republic of Costa Rica*, ICSID Case No UNCT/15/3, Award (18 September 2018) paras. 737–742.

[155] Kjos (2013), pp. 140–141. For a different opinion, considering that in such cases the state parties purposefully decided to grant exclusive access to arbitration to investors *see*, Hoffmann (2013), p. 450; Vöneky (2020), p. 351.

[156] Ishikawa (2017), p. 726: ('It is submitted here that the scope of arbitrable disputes as expressed in the dispute resolution clause is of crucial importance. If it is limited to disputes arising from the host State's alleged breach of IIA obligations, then it is an indication of the contracting parties' intention to exclude jurisdiction over counterclaims, arguably showing their preference to resolve their claims against investors in national courts. Conversely, if it is broadly defined. . .it strongly suggests that the contracting parties consent to jurisdiction over disputes giving rise to counterclaims'); Atanasova et al. (2014), p. 377: ('In view of the uncertain tenure of reserving the right to initiate proceedings only to investors, and due to the specific structure of investment treaty arbitration, it would be too strict a reading to discard the possibility of counterclaims by a host state on this basis alone'); Clodfelter and Tsutieva (2018), para. 17.61: ('it has been submitted that, in the absence of additional limiting language (i.e. a narrowly worded dispute settlement clause), a one-sided locus standi cannot be construed as necessarily excluding counterclaims').

kind of disputes and its impact on the possibility to raise counterclaims is addressed in the next section.

3.3.1.1.2 What Kind of Disputes Are within the Tribunal's Jurisdiction: (Solely) Treaty Breaches?

The second kind of formulations in dispute settlement treaty provisions, which might be construed (or have been construed) as restricting a tribunal's jurisdiction over counterclaims, relates to the types of disputes that may be submitted to investment arbitration. Some IIAs establish that 'any kind of dispute' or 'all disputes' arising out of a protected investment may be submitted to investment arbitration.[157] Other IIAs restrict investment arbitration to the violation of the substantive standards of protection embedded in the respective treaty.[158] For the purpose of clarity, the former

---

[157] *See* for instance: Japan-Egypt BIT (1977), Art 11 ('any legal dispute'); Sweden-Egypt BIT (1978) Art 6 ('a dispute...in connection with an investment'); Sweden-Serbia BIT (1978) Art 6 ('a dispute...in connection with an investment'); Singapore-BLEU BIT (1978), Art 9(1) ('any legal dispute'); UK-Sri Lanka BIT (1980), Art 8(1) ('any legal disputes'); Romania-Sri Lanka BIT (1981), Art 7(1) ('any legal dispute'); France-Pakistan BIT (1983), Art 8(1) ('tout différend'); St Lucia-Germany BIT (1985), Art 10(1) ('investment disputes'); Sri Lanka-China BIT (1986), Art 13(1) ('any dispute'); Germany-Belarus BIT (1993), Art 11 ('Meinungsverschiedenheiten in bezug auf Kapitalanlagen'); China-Saudi Arabia BIT (1996), Art 8(1) ('Disputes concerning investments'); Indonesia-Bangladesh BIT (1998), Art VIII(1) ('Any dispute'); Israel-Armenia BIT (2000), Art 8(1) ('any legal dispute'); Austria-Iran BIT (2001), Art 11 ('any dispute'); Finland-Uruguay BIT (2002), Art 9(1) ('cualquier controversia de naturaleza legal'); Guatemala-Italy BIT (2003), Art 9(1) ('cualquier controversia sobre inversiones'); Thailand-Jordan BIT (2005), Art 11(1) ('dispute with respect to investments'); Italy-Bahrain BIT (2006), Art 10(1) ('Any legal dispute'); Netherlands-Algeria BIT (2007), Art 9 ('tout différend'); Panama-Sweden BIT (2008), Art 8(1) ('toda diferencia'); Moldova-Estonia BIT (2010), Art 11(1) ('any dispute'); Armenia-Iraq BIT (2012), Art 8(1) ('Disputes arising between');Russia-Cambodia BIT (2015), Art 8-(1) ('disputes...in connection with an investment'); Turkey-Cambodia BIT (2018), Art 9-(1) ('disputes...in connection with his investment'); Nicaragua-Iran BIT (2019), Art 12(1) ('cualquier controversia').

[158] *See* for instance: Hungary-Denmark BIT (1988), Art 9(2) ('any dispute arising under Article 5 [Expropriation]'); Poland-Kuwait BIT (1990), Art 10(2)(b) ('a dispute concerning expropriation'); UK-Czech and Slovak Republic BIT (1990), Art 8(1) ('Disputes...concerning the obligation of [a Contracting Party] under Articles 2(3), 4, 5 and 6 of this Agreement'); ECT (1994), Art 26(1) ('Disputes...which concern an alleged breach of an obligation...under Part III [of the Treaty]'); Germany-Ghana BIT (1995), Art 12(1) ('Streitigkeiten...hinsichtlich einer Verpflichtung der [Vertragspartei] aufgrund dieses Vertrags'); Ghana-Malaysia BIT (1996), Art 7(1) ('Disputes...concerning an obligation of [a Contracting Party] under this agreement'); Croatia-Canada BIT (1997), Art XII(1) ('in breach of this Agreement'); France-Mexico BIT (1998), Art 9(1) ('disputes concerning an alleged breach of an obligation of [a Contracting Party] under this Agreement'); Turkey-Greece BIT (2000), Art VII(1) ('disputes...concerning an obligation...under this agreement'); India-Bahrain BIT (2004), Art 9(1) ('any dispute...under this Agreement'); Mexico-Trinidad and Tobago BIT (2006), Art 11 ('controversias...derivadas de un presunto incumplimiento de una obligación...en el Capitulo II'); China-Malta BIT (2009), Art 9(1) ('investment dispute regulated by this Agreement'); Japan-Colombia BIT (2011), Art

group of clauses will be referred to as '*broad/broadly drafted*' whereas the latter group will be indicated as '*narrow/narrowly drafted*'.

On that account, it has been propounded that dispute settlement provisions in IIAs restricting the tribunal's jurisdiction to the violation of the treaty (which usually do not foresee investors' obligations but rather only states' obligations) hinder the possibility of state counterclaims.[159] In contrast, dispute settlement provisions in IIAs couched in broad terms are 'more conducive' to state counterclaims.[160] The latter kind of provisions are deemed to be wide enough to cover a more comprehensively range of issues not necessarily governed by the treaty itself like for example tort claims.[161]

The reason behind the differentiation of broad and narrow provisions is placed on the consensual character of arbitration. Besides, in treaty-based investment arbitration not only consent is framed by the terms of treaty, but it also tends to be focused on the investor's one-sided rights.[162] Hence, narrowly worded dispute settlement provisions in IIAs display states' consent to exclude state counterclaims, placing any investor's violation outside the scope of tribunal's jurisdiction.[163] Certainly, efficiency considerations may tilt the tribunal towards allowing state counterclaims in

27 ('that the disputing Party has breached an obligation under Chapter II'); Switzerland-Tunisia BIT (2012), Art 11 ('concerning an alleged breach of this Agreement'); Canada-Benin BIT (2013), Art 23 ('the respondent Contracting Party has breached an obligation under Chapter II'); Colombia-France BIT (2014), Art 15 ('una supuesta violación de una obligación del presente Acuerdo'); Austria-Kyrgyzstan BIT (2016), Art 13 ('an alleged breach of an obligation of the [Contracting Party] under this Agreement'); Israel-Japan BIT (2017), Art 24(2) ('the [Contracting Party] has breached an obligation under [this Treaty]'); Singapore-Myanmar BIT (2019), Art 11-(1) ('concerning an alleged breach of an obligation of [a Party] under this Agreement').

159 Kjos (2007), p. 611: ('The fact that the arbitration agreement only encompasses host State obligations does create an obstacle for host State counter-claims. Since the parties have not agreed to settle through arbitration disputes concerning investor obligations, any grievance against the investor would not have a basis in the parties' arbitration agreement, and would consequently seem to fall outside the jurisdiction of the tribunal'); Lalive and Halonen (2011), p. 147: ('By contrast, a clause that limits jurisdiction to claims brought under the BIT itself would in all likelihood not suffice for counterclaims to be introduced, as BITs generally impose no obligations on investors, only on states'). Similarly, Bjorklund (2014), pp. 265–266.

160 Douglas (2009), para. 488: ('when the consent of the contracting state parties to investor/state arbitration in an investment treaty is couched in broad terms, there is nothing in principle to exclude a tribunal's *ratione materiae* jurisdiction over counterclaims'); Bjorklund (2013), p. 468: ('Some ISDS provisions are quite broad and confer on tribunals the authority to hear any "dispute between an investor of one Contracting Party and the other Contracting Party in connection with an investment," or some similar formulation. Such a clause appears to be more conducive to counterclaims compared to narrow ISDS clauses that limit arbitrable claims to those alleging the breach of a treaty provision'); Jain (2013), p. 146: ('If the scope of the dispute settlement procedure extends to all obligations, consent for counterclaims may be presumed').

161 Douglas (2009), para. 253. Similarly, Schreuer (2014), pp. 7–10. For a different opinion, *see* Steingruber (2020), p. 630.

162 Kjos (2007), pp. 599–600.

163 Sharpe and Jacob (2018), pp. 352–353.

investment arbitration, nevertheless, such considerations pale in comparison to the narrowly worded provisions in a treaty.[164]

Consequently, although one may argue that the state's legal standing is not conclusive of the exclusion of state counterclaims in treaty-based investment arbitration, a narrowly worded dispute settlement provision in the treaty may fit the bill. It could even be suggested that a combination of both a limited legal standing and a narrow treaty provision is more likely to result in the exclusion of state counterclaims from the tribunal's jurisdiction.[165]

Various arbitral tribunals have dealt with narrowly worded dispute resolution clauses and rejected counterclaims because of it. In the *Roussalis v Romania* case, one of the arguments to decline jurisdiction over counterclaims was that the treaty limited the range of disputes to only those arising out of obligations of the host state under the treaty.[166] This decision however seems to encompass the combination of lack of the state's legal standing, applicable law and the scope of disputes to dismiss the counterclaims at the jurisdictional stage.[167] In the *Rusoro Mining v Venezuela* case, one of the reasons for denying jurisdiction over the counterclaim was that pursuant to the dispute resolution provision of the underlying treaty, the '[t]*ribunal's power is limited to adjudicating disputes which arise from the BIT, and the obligations allegedly breached by Rusoro do not derive from and have no connection with the Treaty*'.[168]

Similarly to the approach of the *Roussalis v Romania* tribunal, the decision seems to be grounded on a combination of factors such as, the applicable law, the lack of cause of action against investors and the restricted scope of 'arbitrable' disputes.[169] Here, it must be noticed that by 'arbitrable' disputes the tribunal simply referred to the scope of disputes that according to the treaty may be subject to arbitration.

In the case of *Karkey v Pakistan*, siding with the tribunal's decision on *Roussalis v Romania*, the tribunal declined jurisdiction over the counterclaims, among other reasons, given the restricted scope of the dispute resolution provision.[170] However, Article VII Pakistan-Turkey BIT (1995) does not define what kind of disputes may

[164] Popova and Poon (2015), p. 230.

[165] Kjos (2007), p. 614: ('This leads us to conclude that whereas the sole reference to the investor's locus standi would not necessarily be conclusive with regard to the admissibility of counterclaims; the combined features of a limited jurisdiction ratione personae and a limited jurisdiction ratione materiae are more likely to have such effect'). Similarly, Hoffmann (2013), pp. 450–451.

[166] *Spyridon Roussalis v Romania*, ICSID Case No ARB/06/1, Award (07 December 2011) para. 869.

[167] *Spyridon Roussalis v Romania*, ICSID Case No ARB/06/1, Award (07 December 2011) paras. 869–875.

[168] *Rusoro Mining Ltd v Bolivarian Republic of Venezuela*, ICSID Case No ARB(AF)/12/5, Award (22 August 2016) para. 628.

[169] *Rusoro Mining Ltd v Bolivarian Republic of Venezuela*, ICSID Case No ARB(AF)/12/5, Award (22 August 2016) para. 623–629.

[170] *Karkey Karadeniz Elektrik Uretim AS* v Islamic Republic of Pakistan, ICSID Case No ARB/13/1, Award (22 August 2017) para. 1013.

be subject to arbitration. To the contrary, Article VII(1) of the BIT simply refers to '[d]*isputes between one of the Parties and an investor of the other Party, in connection with the investment*' without limiting jurisdiction to the substantive standards of protection of the treaty in question. Thus, considering the broad consent to arbitration, the tribunal might have seen an obstacle to its jurisdiction where there was none.

The *Anglo American v Venezuela* tribunal was faced with a specific limitation in its jurisdiction. Pursuant to Article 8(3) UK-Venezuela BIT (1995), '[t]*he jurisdiction of the arbitral tribunal shall be limited to determining whether there has been a breach by the Contracting Party concerned of any of its obligations under this Agreement*'. Accordingly, the tribunal considered that such provision reflected a clear intention to restrict the scope of disputes, thus, excluding host state counterclaims.[171]

When the dispute resolution provision is broadly drafted as to the disputes subject to arbitration, tribunals have reached opposite conclusions. For instance, the *Tethyan v Pakistan* tribunal interpreted a broadly couched dispute resolution provision in Article 13 Australia-Pakistan BIT (1998), as indicative of the parties' consent to extend the tribunal's jurisdiction not only to treaty violations, but also to counterclaims based on investment contracts or on the regulatory framework for the investment.[172] Similarly, the *Gardabani v Georgia* tribunal construed the underlying Article 9 Netherlands-Georgia BIT (1998) as "sufficiently broad" to encompass counterclaims based on contractual instruments.[173]

Interestingly, the *Paushok v Mongolia* tribunal paid lip service to the broad wording of Article 6 Russia-Mongolia BIT (1995), and considered that the counterclaims related to taxes were neither within the purview of arbitral tribunals nor connected to the main claim.[174] Here, the tribunal mistakenly confused the requisite jurisdiction with connection (as many other tribunals), but most importantly, the *Paushok v Mongolia* tribunal misconstrued its mandate in treaty-based investment arbitration.[175]

---

[171] *Anglo American PLC v Bolivarian Republic of Venezuela*, ICSID Case No ARB(AF)/14/1, Award (18 January 2021) paras. 526–528.

[172] *Tethyan Copper Company Pty Limited v Islamic Republic of Pakistan*, ICSID Case No ARB/12/1, Decision on Jurisdiction and Liability (10 November 2017) para. 1420.

[173] It must be noted that in this case, the application of the umbrella clause as invoked by the claimant also played in favour of jurisdiction over the counterclaim, see *Gardabani Holdings BV and Silk Road Holdings BV v Georgia*, ICSID Case No. ARB/17/29, Award (27 October 2022) para. 374.

[174] *Sergei Paushok, CJSC Golden East Company and CJSC Vostokneftegaz Company v The Government of Mongolia*, UNCITRAL Case, Jurisdiction and Liability (28 April 2011) paras. 694 et seqq.

[175] Further on this *see* Sect. 4.3.3.1.2.

On a slightly different direction, the *Hamester v Ghana* tribunal took notice that consent was limited to disputes relating to the state's obligations under the treaty.[176] However, the Tribunal highlighted that Article 12 Germany-Ghana BIT (1995) contemplated the possibility of a state party to be aggrieved and thus entitled to refer the dispute to arbitration.[177] It thus seems that the tribunal was open to adjudge host state counterclaims despite the restrictive wording on the types of disputes subject to arbitration.

This overview of case law displays three different approaches. First, when the treaty restricts the kind of disputes subject to arbitration, tribunals in cases such as *Roussalis v Romania*, *Rusoro Mining v Venezuela* and *Anglo American v Venezuela* have declined jurisdiction over counterclaims, whereas broadly drafted dispute resolution provisions, such as in the *Tethyan v Pakistan* case may lead to an opposite conclusion. Second, even if having open dispute resolution provisions *vis-à-vis* the kind of disputes subject to arbitration, tribunals, such in the *Karkey v Pakistan* case, may be reluctant to adjudge counterclaims. Third, the *Hamester v Ghana* tribunal did not see as an obstacle the allegedly restricted definition of disputes in the treaty given the other indications pointing to the state's possibility to raise complaints.

3.3.1.2 Applicable Law to the Substance of a Counterclaim as a Jurisdictional Barrier?

While Chap. 5 will elaborate on the applicable law to the substance of an environmental counterclaim, this section puts forward that an applicable law provision does not constitute a jurisdictional barrier for state counterclaims in treaty-based investment arbitration. The concept of 'applicable law' in treaty-based investment arbitration is usually used for three situations namely the substance of the dispute, the agreement to arbitrate, and the arbitration procedure.[178] With regards to counterclaims, the applicable law to the substance of the counterclaim has appeared as an obstacle, particularly when it does not match the treaty's applicable law provisions.

In this sense, some tribunals have taken into account applicable law provisions as one of the reasons for declining jurisdiction over counterclaims. In the *Amto v Ukraine* case, the respondent host state requested compensation for alleged non-material injury to its reputation.[179] The tribunal opened its reasoning with the '*jurisdiction of an Arbitral Tribunal over a State party counterclaim under an investment treaty depends upon the terms of the dispute resolution provisions of*

---

[176] *Gustav F W Hamester GmbH & Co KG v Republic of Ghana*, ICSID Case No ARB/07/24, Award (18 June 2010) para. 353.

[177] *Gustav F W Hamester GmbH & Co KG v Republic of Ghana*, ICSID Case No ARB/07/24, Award (18 June 2010) para. 354.

[178] McLachlan et al. (2017), para. 398. Other authors may differentiate between applicable law in procedure, jurisdiction, privilege among others, *see* Thomas and Dhillon (2014), p. 975.

[179] *Limited Liability Company Amto v Ukraine*, SCC Case No 080/2005, Award (26 March 2008) para. 35.

the treaty...'.[180] The tribunal dismissed the counterclaim on non-material injury to reputation because there was no basis on the applicable law provision in the treaty for it, since it only referred to the treaty itself (the ECT (1994)) and public international law.[181] It may thus be assumed that the applicable law provision in the ECT (1994) was indeed a jurisdictional barrier for this tribunal.

In the *Roussalis v Romania* case, one of the arguments to decline jurisdiction over counterclaims was that the applicable law provision referred exclusively to the treaty itself and public international law, both of which did not foresee obligations of the investors.[182] Similarly in the *Rusoro Mining v Venezuela* case, one of the reasons for denying jurisdiction over the counterclaim was that '*the Tribunal must decide the dispute in accordance with the Treaty and the principles of international law, and the dispute underlying the counterclaim – that Rusoro breached the mine plan – and cannot be adjudicated by applying the Treaty or principles of international law*'.[183]

Finally, another example is the *Naturgy v Colombia* case. Here, the counterclaim was based on the claimants' alleged mismanagement of the domestic company Electricaribe SA ESP.[184] However, the tribunal considered that '*the Treaty simply does not appear to govern the investor's management of its investment in a regulated sector in accordance with the requirements of national law. Nor does Respondent indicate where in the Treaty such an issue is addressed*'.[185] This was not the only ground given by the tribunal to deny jurisdiction, but the line of reasoning certainly shows the characterisation of applicable law to the counterclaim as a jurisdictional issue.

The term 'jurisdiction' denotes the tribunal's power to entertain a claim,[186] which is rooted in the parties' consent. Likewise, provisions on applicable law may be the result of the exercise of the autonomy that the parties enjoy.[187] Accordingly, it has been stated that a tribunal exceeds the boundaries of its powers (jurisdiction) if it does not respect the parties' agreement on the applicable law to the substance, which

[180] *Limited Liability Company Amto v Ukraine*, SCC Case No 080/2005, Award (26 March 2008) para. 118.

[181] *Limited Liability Company Amto v Ukraine*, SCC Case No 080/2005, Award (26 March 2008) para. 118.

[182] *Spyridon Roussalis v Romania*, ICSID Case No ARB/06/1, Award (07 December 2011) para. 871.

[183] *Rusoro Mining Ltd v Bolivarian Republic of Venezuela*, ICSID Case No ARB(AF)/12/5, Award (22 August 2016) para. 628.

[184] *Naturgy Energy Group SA and Naturgy Electricidad Colombia SL (formerly Gas Natural SDG SA and Gas Natural Fenosa Electricidad Colombia SL) v Republic of Colombia*, ICSID Case No UNCT/18/1, Award (12 March 2021) para. 582.

[185] *Naturgy Energy Group SA and Naturgy Electricidad Colombia SL (formerly Gas Natural SDG SA and Gas Natural Fenosa Electricidad Colombia SL) v Republic of Colombia*, ICSID Case No UNCT/18/1, Award (12 March 2021) para. 582 (footnotes omitted).

[186] Waibel (2015), p. 1213. Similarly, Douglas (2009), paras. 291 et seqq.

[187] Kjos (2013), p. 70.

'*constitute*[s] *part of the definition of the tribunal's mandate*'.[188] Should the tribunal disregard the specific substantive law agreed upon by the parties, the resulting award may be annulled under the ICSID Convention[189] or refused to be enforced under the New York Convention.[190] Similarly, if tribunals mischaracterise the law applicable to the issues before it, this would open the door for possible annulments or setting aside.[191] Therefore, a tribunal should not blatantly disregard the applicable law provisions since they embody one piece of the parties' agreement. Nevertheless, those provisions' role as a jurisdictional barrier to state counterclaims may be overstated due to three reasons:

First, the permissible legal bases for a claim (or a counterclaim for that matter) are defined in the jurisdictional title, which reflects the kind of disputes a tribunal can entertain, rather than by applicable law provisions.[192] In light of this, the latter cannot alter the former. Illustratively, the relation between applicable law provisions and the jurisdictional title was addressed by the tribunal in the *OSPAR Arbitration* case. Article 32(1) OSPAR Convention subjects to arbitration *only* disputes relating to the interpretation and application of the convention, whereas Article 32(6) (a) OSPAR Convention foresees that the tribunal '*shall decide according to the rules of international law and, in particular, those of the OSPAR Convention*'. As held by the tribunal, the latter provision did not intend to extend a tribunal's jurisdiction to other obligations they parties may have assumed under other instruments of international law beside the OSPAR Convention.[193] Otherwise, it '*would transform* [the consent in the OSPAR Convention] *into an unqualified and comprehensive jurisdictional regime in which there would be no limit* ratione materiae *to the jurisdiction of a tribunal*'.[194] This reasoning suggests that an applicable law provision in a treaty cannot expand the explicit powers the parties have bestowed on arbitral tribunals. By the same token, a narrow applicable law provision could not in turn restrict an otherwise broad jurisdictional title.

---

188 *Hussein Nuaman Soufraki v The United Arab Emirates*, ICSID Case No ARB/02/7, Decision on Annulment (05 June 2007) paras. 37–45; *Amco Asia Corporation and others v Republic of Indonesia*, ICSID Case No ARB/81/1, Decision on Annulment in Resubmitted Proceeding (17 December 1992) para. 7.19; *Empresas Lucchetti SA and Lucchetti Peru SA v The Republic of Peru*, ICSID Case No ARB/03/4, Decision on Annulment (05 September 2007) para. 98.

189 Schreuer et al. (2009), Art 52, mn. 195.

190 Borris and Hennecke (2019), mn. 235.

191 Hepburn (2017), pp. 105–108.

192 Atanasova (2019), pp. 399–400. Dafina Atanasova further argues that applicable law provisions play a subsidiary role in the determination of the permissible legal bases, however, this situation is not completely clear.

193 *Dispute Concerning Access to Information under Article 9 of the OSPAR Convention (Ireland v United Kingdom of Great Britain and Northern Ireland)*, PCA Case No 2001-03, Final Award (02 July 2003) para. 85.

194 *Dispute Concerning Access to Information under Article 9 of the OSPAR Convention (Ireland v United Kingdom of Great Britain and Northern Ireland)*, PCA Case No 2001-03, Final Award (02 July 2003) para. 85.

Second, an arbitral tribunal may be perfectly constituted and it may render its decision on merits even if the underlying IIA does not contain an applicable law provision. In fact, applicable law provisions are not ubiquitous to all IIAs. Although newer treaties are more detailed and usually contain such provisions,[195] older treaties still in force lack a reference to the applicable law.[196] In the absence of an agreement on applicable law, other instruments may confer considerable leeway on the tribunal to determine the proper applicable law to the substance of the dispute,[197] for instance Article 42 ICSID Convention,[198] Article 35 UNCITRAL Arbitration Rules (2013),[199] Article 27 SCC Arbitration Rules (2017),[200] and Article 21 ICC Arbitration Rules (2021),[201] among others. Certainly, the tribunal ought to explain the reasons for selecting a particular applicable law.[202] But this shows that the absence of parties' agreement on applicable law does not affect the tribunal's power to decide

[195] From an empirical study, Dafina Atanasova concludes that applicable law provisions are more common in recent treaties, *see* Atanasova (2019), p. 407.

[196] As to 2012 slightly over 32% of IIAs with ISDS contain clauses on applicable law *see* Pohl et al. (2012). Even more recent treaties with ISDS may not contain applicable law provisions, *see* for instance: Korea-Cameroon BIT (2013); Israel-Myanmar BIT (2014); Colombia-France BIT (2014); Kyrgyzstan-Kuwait BIT (2015); Ethiopia-UAE BIT (2016); Morocco-Nigeria BIT (2016); Nicaragua-Iran BIT (2019); Uzbekistan-Korea BIT (2019); Kazakhstan-Singapore BIT (2018).

[197] De Brabandere (2014), pp. 123–124.

[198] ICSID Convention, Art 42: ('(1) The Tribunal shall decide a dispute in accordance with such rules of law as may be agreed by the parties. In the absence of such agreement, the Tribunal shall apply the law of the Contracting State party to the dispute (including its rules on the conflict of laws) and such rules of international law as may be applicable. (2) The Tribunal may not bring in a finding of non liquet on the ground of silence or obscurity of the law. (3) The provisions of paragraphs (1) and (2) shall not prejudice the power of the Tribunal to decide a dispute *ex aequo et bono* if the parties so agree').

[199] UNCITRAL Arbitration Rules (2013), Art 35: ('1. The arbitral tribunal shall apply the rules of law designated by the parties as applicable to the substance of the dispute. Failing such designation by the parties, the arbitral tribunal shall apply the law which it determines to be appropriate. 2. The arbitral tribunal shall decide as amiable compositeur or ex aequo et bono only if the parties have expressly authorized the arbitral tribunal to do so. 3. In all cases, the arbitral tribunal shall decide in accordance with the terms of the contract, if any, and shall take into account any usage of trade applicable to the transaction').

[200] SCC Arbitration Rules (2017), Art 27: ('(1) The Arbitral Tribunal shall decide the merits of the dispute on the basis of the law(s) or rules of law agreed upon by the parties. In the absence of such agreement, the Arbitral Tribunal shall apply the law or rules of law that it considers most appropriate. (2) Any designation by the parties of the law of a given state shall be deemed to refer to the substantive law of that state, not to its conflict of laws rules. (3) The Arbitral Tribunal shall decide the dispute *ex aequo et bono* or as *amiable compositeur* only if the parties have expressly authorised it to do so').

[201] ICC Arbitration Rules (2021), Art 21: ('1) The parties shall be free to agree upon the rules of law to be applied by the arbitral tribunal to the merits of the dispute. In the absence of any such agreement, the arbitral tribunal shall apply the rules of law which it determines to be appropriate. 2) The arbitral tribunal shall take account of the provisions of the contract, if any, between the parties and of any relevant trade usages. 3) The arbitral tribunal shall assume the powers of an amiable compositeur or decide ex aequo et bono only if the parties have agreed to give it such powers').

[202] Such explanation turns the resulting award less vulnerable for annulment, *see* Kjos (2013), p. 82.

the dispute in treaty-based investment arbitration. In other words, an agreement on applicable law to the substance does not constitute a *conditio sine qua non* for the tribunal's jurisdiction.

Third, given the variety of issues dealt with in treaty-based investment arbitration, many arbitral tribunals have been compelled to apply domestic law to certain issues of the disputes, even in cases of narrowly worded applicable law provisions.[203] Indeed, treaty-based investment arbitration is not a self-contained regime,[204] and irrespective of the applicable law provision, a tribunal might be directed to both international and domestic law to settle a single dispute.[205] For instance, issues of property rights over the investment must be referred to domestic law of the state where the assets are located because public international law does not comprise property law.[206] Necessarily, the role of applicable law provisions in treaty-based investment arbitration appears relevant when discussing the cause of action for an environmental counterclaim, which will be addressed in detail in Chap. 5.

Be that as it may, the scope of the tribunal's jurisdiction remains to be framed by the jurisdictional title, whereas the applicable law plays only a secondary role. Therefore, it does not seem tenable to consider that applicable law provisions pose jurisdictional barriers to counterclaims by themselves, but rather that any barrier will be found in the jurisdictional title as such. An argument to the contrary would exacerbate the already blurred function of applicable law clauses in treaty-based investment arbitration.

3.3.1.3 The ICSID Convention and a Tribunal's Jurisdiction Over Counterclaims

The ICSID Convention warrants a separate analysis given that it specifically addresses counterclaims. In particular, Article 46 ICSID Convention provides:

---

[203] *Fraport AG Frankfurt Airport Services Worldwide v Republic of The Philippines*, ICSID Case No ARB/11/12, Award (10 December 2014) para. 298; *Bayview Irrigation District et al v United Mexican States,* ICSID Case No ARB(AF)/05/1, Award (19 June 2007) paras. 109–118; *Mobil Investments Canada Inc and Murphy Oil Corporation Inc v Canada,* ICSID Case No ARB(AF)/07/4, Decision on Liability and on Principles of Quantum (22 May 2012) paras. 354–355.

[204] Simma and Pulkowski (2015), p. 361. Similarly, Douglas (2003), pp. 195 et seqq.

[205] *Asian Agricultural Products Ltd v Republic of Sri Lanka*, ICSID Case No ARB/87/3, Award (27 June 1990) para. 21; *BG Group Plc v Republic of Argentina*, UNCITRAL Case, Award (24 December 2007) para. 100; *CMS Gas Transmission Company v The Republic of Argentina*, ICSID Case No ARB/01/8, Award (12 May 2005) para 116. In a more nuanced approach and considering the treaty nature of the claims, the *Azurix v Argentina* tribunal approached Argentinian domestic law only as an 'element of inquiry', however, without specifying what that means, see *Azurix Corp v The Argentine Republic*, ICSID Case No ARB/01/12, Award (14 July 2006) para. 67.

[206] Douglas (2009), paras. 101 et seqq.; Bjorklund (2014), pp. 273–274; Asteriti (2015), p. 265. This was equally recognised by investment tribunals, for instance, *EnCana Corporation v Republic of Ecuador*, LCIA Case No UN3481, Award (3 February 2006) para. 184.

> Except as the parties otherwise agree, the Tribunal shall, if requested by a party, determine any incidental or additional claims or counterclaims arising directly out of the subject-matter of the dispute provided that they are within the scope of the consent of the parties and are otherwise within the jurisdiction of the Centre.

The ICSID Arbitration Rules (2006) duplicate the provision of the Convention in its Rule 40[207] (Rule 48 in the newly adopted rules of 2022[208]), adding on time limits for the presentation of 'ancillary claims'. Whilst Article 46 ICSID Convention seems to address the arbitral tribunal,[209] Rule 40 ICSID Arbitration Rules (2006) (or Rule 48 ICSID Arbitration Rules (2022)) seems to address the disputing parties. In any case, and despite its apparent simple wording, Article 46 ICSID Convention has been a serious bone of contention. Accordingly, this section addresses the drafting history of Article 46 ICSID Convention and the issue of consent [Sect. 3.3.1.3.1]. Subsequently, this section delves into the doctrine of 'ipso facto' importation of consent [Sect. 3.3.1.3.2] and its interaction with Article 26 ICSID Convention [Sect. 3.3.1.3.3]. Finally, it analyses the apparently extra requirement of '*otherwise within the jurisdiction of the Centre*' [Sect. 3.3.1.3.4].

3.3.1.3.1 Drafting History of Article 46 ICSID Convention and the Issue of Consent

Originally, in the ICSID *travaux préparatoires*, the provision on counterclaims read '[e]*xcept as the parties otherwise agree, the Tribunal shall have the power to hear and determine incidental or additional claims or counter-claims arising directly out of the subject-matter of the dispute*'.[210] Some delegates to the drafting committee expressed that such a provision could eventually expand a tribunal's jurisdiction

---

[207] ICSID Arbitration Rules (2006), Rule 40 Ancillary Claims: ('(1) Except as the parties otherwise agree, a party may present an incidental or additional claim or counter-claim arising directly out of the subject-matter of the dispute, provided that such ancillary claim is within the scope of the consent of the parties and is otherwise within the jurisdiction of the Centre. (2) An incidental or additional claim shall be presented not later than in the reply and a counter-claim no later than in the countermemorial, unless the Tribunal, upon justification by the party presenting the ancillary claim and upon considering any objection of the other party, authorizes the presentation of the claim at a later stage in the proceeding. (3) The Tribunal shall fix a time limit within which the party against which an ancillary claim is presented may file its observations thereon').

[208] ICSID Arbitration Rules (2022), Rule 48 Ancillary Claims: ('Unless the parties agree otherwise, a party may file an incidental or additional claim or a counterclaim ("ancillary claim") arising directly out of the subject-matter of the dispute, provided that such ancillary claim is within the scope of the consent of the parties and the jurisdiction of the Centre. (2) An incidental or additional claim shall be presented no later than in the reply, and a counterclaim shall be presented no later than in the counter-memorial, unless the Tribunal decides otherwise. (3) The Tribunal shall fix time limits for submissions on the ancillary claim').

[209] Not only due to its obvious wording, but also given the Convention's structure, whereby Article 46 ICSID Convention is located in Chapter IV Arbitration, Section 3 Powers and Functions of the Tribunal.

[210] History of the ICSID Convention, Vol I (ICSID Publication 1968) 204.

beyond the parties' agreement. The chairman of the drafting committee, Aaron Broches, reassured that the idea was not to '*extend the competence of the tribunal beyond what the parties had agreed. That section only made it unnecessary for parties making additional claims or counterclaims to start new procedures*'.[211] However, he acknowledged that it was appropriate to clarify that any incidental claim is subject to the 'overriding principle of consent', thus, no extension of the tribunal's competence would be possible.[212]

This prompted the redrafting of the article in two occasions: first, it was proposed to add '*provided that they are within the jurisdiction of the Centre and within the scope of the consent of the parties*'. However, it was considered that such phrase might cause misunderstanding suggesting that consent and jurisdiction are 'separate and distinct factors'.[213] Second, Aaron Broches suggested the phrase—which was finally adopted—'*provided that they are within the scope of the consent of the parties and are otherwise within the jurisdiction of the Centre'*. This change was meant to highlight that consent was at the core of jurisdiction, but that there might be other jurisdictional elements preventing the tribunal to decide the incidental or additional claim.[214]

As such, the rationale behind the inclusion of Article 46 ICSID Convention, which specifically mentions counterclaims, was to avoid unnecessary separate proceedings.[215] Moreover, one may argue that this provision creates a rebuttable presumption in favour of the tribunal's power to decide counterclaims, which can be disproven by the absence of one of the elements of Article 46 ICSID Convention.[216] However, the *travaux préparatoires* show the careful consideration given to the requisite consent, upon which the tribunal's jurisdiction is based. This might be the cause for having consent mentioned in two different limbs of the article: first, by opening with 'except as the parties otherwise agree'; and second, by stating 'provided that they are within the scope of the consent'. This duality was not addressed during the drafting process, but the principle of *effet utile* suggests that each expression must have a meaning.

The first limb of the article regarding consent—'except as the parties otherwise agree'—suggests that the tribunal's power to decide on counterclaims might be modified by the parties' agreement.[217] Accordingly, the underlying instrument could exclude counterclaims outright or restrict its use for certain issues/cases. To

---

[211] History of the ICSID Convention, Vol II-1 (ICSID Publication 1968) 270.

[212] History of the ICSID Convention, Vol II-1 (ICSID Publication 1968) 337, 422 and 573.

[213] History of the ICSID Convention, Vol II-2 (ICSID Publication 1968) 948.

[214] History of the ICSID Convention, Vol II-2 (ICSID Publication 1968) 987.

[215] Kryvoi (2012), p. 223. Similarly, Kalnina and Godbole (2019), mn. 4.430.

[216] Jain (2013), p. 138: ('the framers of the Convention intended to create a rebuttable presumption in favour of the permissibility of counterclaims. This presumption could be rebutted by the consent of the parties'). Similarly, Asteriti (2015), p. 258; Ishikawa (2017), p. 725; Clodfelter and Tsutieva (2018), paras. 17.24 and 17.61.

[217] Schreuer et al. (2009), Art 46, mn. 6 et seqq.

the author's knowledge, there are no treaties explicitly excluding the instrument of counterclaims in its entirety. There are certain IIAs, whereby certain issues have been banned from being raised as counterclaims,[218] but these are the minority nonetheless.

The second limb of the article regarding consent—'provided that they are within the scope of the consent'—covers the arbitration agreement as a whole and its compatibility with the specific counterclaim. Accordingly, this requirement does not demand an additional or specific agreement on counterclaims, but rather it demands that the existing consent covers the specific counterclaim.[219] As mentioned above, this expression was added given the concerns on the expansion of the tribunal's jurisdiction beyond the parties' agreement. Thus, the requirement of consent is highlighted as the core of the tribunal's jurisdiction.[220]

The foregoing demonstrates that consent under Article 25 ICSID Convention differs from consent under Article 46 ICSID Convention. Thus, even though a tribunal may have jurisdiction under Article 25 ICSID Convention, whereby one of the requirements is consent of the parties, this does not necessarily entail that there is consent over a counterclaim under Article 46 ICSID Convention.[221] Otherwise, the requirement of consent under Article 46 ICSID Convention would lose its meaning.[222] Accordingly, the most reasonable interpretation of Article 46 ICSID Convention suggests that counterclaims under the ICSID Convention constitute a procedural mechanism, which would be permitted only if it is covered by the instrument of consent.[223]

In the context of treaty-based investment arbitration, this means that an arbitral tribunal has the power to adjudge counterclaims as a general rule, which is relevant given the absence of provisions on that regard in most of the IIAs, but the wording of the specific dispute resolution provision (or jurisdictional title) would be determinative for admitting counterclaims in each case.[224] Certainly, consent to arbitration under the ICSID Convention was conceived either through a direct agreement

[218] *See* for instance: NAFTA (1994), Art 1137(3); ECT (1994), Art 15(3); US-Uruguay BIT (2005), Art 28(7); Colombia-US TPA (2006), Art 10.20(7); Peru-US TPA (2006), Art 10.20(7); Korea-US FTA (2007), Art 11.20(9); US-Rwanda BIT (2008), Art 28(7); Israel-Japan BIT (2017), Art 24(12); Canada-Moldova BIT (2018), Art 36; Uzbekistan-Korea BIT (2019), Art 11(9); Australia-Uruguay BIT (2019), Art 14(13); Morocco-Japan BIT (2020), Art 16(13).

[219] Pathak (2019), p. 109.

[220] Schreuer et al. (2009), Art 46, mn. 87; Kalnina and Godbole (2019), mn. 4.443.

[221] Bubrowski (2013), p. 218. For a different opinion suggesting that Article 46 ICSID Convention does not impose an additional requirement on consent, but rather, as long as there is consent under Article 25 ICSID Convention, the requirement is fulfilled, *see* Vohryzek-Griest (2009), pp. 90–91.

[222] Kjos (2007), p. 617: ('If the bringing of a claim could in and of itself be construed as consent to counter-claims, this clause would lose its meaning. Accordingly, and in line with the maxim *interpretatio fienda est ut res magis valeat quam pereat*, the fact that the investor presents a claim ought not to be construed to create, in and of itself, the consent necessary for the host State to present counter-claims against the investor').

[223] Bjorklund (2013), p. 472.

[224] Clodfelter and Tsutieva (2018), para. 17.45.

between the host state and the investor (*eg* by means of a concession agreement referring to ICSID), or by a unilateral consent given by the state, which would be subsequently accepted by the investor (*eg* law-based or treaty-based investment arbitration).[225]

While no discussion was held about the state's ability to submit claims for that matter during the drafting process, the Convention as such was conceived to strike a balance between the foreign investor and the host state, whereby either one of them was able to bring claims under the Convention against the other.[226] Yet, the requisite consent under Article 46 ICSID Convention points back to the instrument of consent to the tribunal's jurisdiction and its scope *vis-à-vis* the specific counterclaim.[227] Consequently, the ICSID Convention appears neutral to the admission of counterclaims since the decisive analysis on consent will always focus on the dispute settlement provision.

3.3.1.3.2 The Doctrine of 'Ipso Facto' Importation of Consent in the ICSID Convention

Another point regarding counterclaims under the ICSID Convention pertains to the 'ipso facto' importation of consent developed by the arbitrator Michael Reisman in his declaration dated 28 November 2011. Given his disagreement with the other members of the *Roussalis v Romania* tribunal, his declaration reads as follows:

> I regret that I cannot join my colleagues in that part of our decision which rejects jurisdiction over counterclaims "arising directly out of the subject-matter of the dispute," the first time it has been so rejected on the ground of absence of consent. I understand the line of their analysis but, in my view, *when the States Parties to a BIT contingently consent, inter alia, to ICSID jurisdiction, the consent component of Article 46 of the Washington Convention is ipso facto imported into any ICSID arbitration which an investor then elects to pursue*. It is important to bear in mind that such counterclaim jurisdiction is not only a concession to the State Party: Article 46 works to the benefit of both respondent state and investor. In rejecting ICSID jurisdiction over counterclaims, a neutral tribunal - which was, in fact, selected by the

[225]History of the ICSID Convention, Vol II-1 (ICSID Publication 1968) 274 and 275. The Executive Directors of the ICSID Convention further confirmed this point, see Report of the Executive Directors on the ICSID Convention dated 18 March 1965, para. 24. To this point see additionally, Newcombe and Paradell (2009), p. 44; Parra (2012), p. 25; Schreuer et al. (2009), Art 25, mn. 382 et seqq.

[226]Based on the World Bank Executive Directors Report on the ICSID Convention, Gustavo Laborde posits that the equal access to arbitration was always in the mind of the drafters, *see* Laborde (2010), p. 100.

[227]Lalive and Halonen (2011), pp. 146–149. There is one author defending the possibility of a treaty conflict between the ICSID Convention and the underlying investment treaty concerning counterclaims, *see* Jain (2013), pp. 141 et seqq. This position is inaccurate. Whilst the ICSID Convention defines the outer limits of jurisdiction, the specific IIA defines the scope and limits of the tribunal's jurisdiction in the particular case. Moreover, the ICSID Convention itself allows to contract out the tribunal's power to decide counterclaims, which may be done through an IIA. Thus, no conflict with regards to counterclaims is possible between the two instruments.

> claimant - perforce *directs the respondent State to pursue its claims in its own courts where the very investor who had sought a forum outside the state apparatus is now constrained to become the defendant.* (And if an adverse judgment ensues, that erstwhile defendant might well transform to claimant again, bringing another BIT claim.) *Aside from duplication and inefficiency, the sorts of transaction costs which counter-claim and set-off procedures work to avoid, it is an ironic, if not absurd, outcome*, at odds, in my view, with the objectives of international investment law.[228]

This very succinct, but sharp statement suggests that by consenting to proceedings under the ICSID Convention, thereby consenting to Article 46 thereof, there is an 'ipso facto' importation of consent to counterclaims. Before delving into the implications of this theory, some background might be enlightening.

The *Roussalis v Romania* case arose from the claimant's alleged failure to comply with its obligation of a post-purchase investment of USD 1.4 million in the Romanian company Continent Marine Enterprise SA embedded in a privatisation agreement.[229] The claimant argued that its investment was subsequently subjected to a series of acts amounting to indirect expropriation.[230] In turn, Romania counterclaimed against the claimant and its locally incorporated company for the failure to invest the said amount and for the misappropriation of assets, as well as against the investment for the increase of capital which was allegedly null and void.[231]

The claimant challenged the admissibility of the counterclaim on several grounds: (i) the tribunal's jurisdiction concerns only breaches of the BIT and not issues of Romanian law; (ii) an umbrella clause does not cover respondent's rights; (iii) the dispute resolution clause in the BIT refers exclusively to obligations owed by the state to the investors; (iv) the counterclaim is addressed to the local incorporated company and the investment, which are not part of the proceedings; (v) the respondent did not exhaust local remedies.[232] The tribunal concluded it lacked jurisdiction over the counterclaims given the absence of consent. This decision was mainly based on two points: on the one hand, the jurisdiction of the tribunal was limited to claims brought by the investor according to Article 9(1) Greece-Romania BIT (1997).[233] On the other hand, pursuant to Article 9(4) Greece-Romania BIT (1997) the applicable law referred exclusively to the BIT and public international law, which do not

---

[228] *Spyridon Roussalis v Romania*, ICSID Case No ARB/06/1, Declaration Michael Reisman (28 November 2011) (emphasis added).

[229] *Spyridon Roussalis v Romania*, ICSID Case No ARB/06/1, Award (07 December 2011) paras. 8–9.

[230] *Spyridon Roussalis v Romania*, ICSID Case No ARB/06/1, Award (07 December 2011) para. 10.

[231] *Spyridon Roussalis v Romania*, ICSID Case No ARB/06/1, Award (07 December 2011) paras. 747–755.

[232] *Spyridon Roussalis v Romania*, ICSID Case No ARB/06/1, Award (07 December 2011) paras. 817–841.

[233] *Spyridon Roussalis v Romania*, ICSID Case No ARB/06/1, Award (07 December 2011) para. 869.

contain obligations for investors.[234] Evidently, one of the arbitrators, Michael Reisman, did not share the same opinion and posited an 'ipso facto' importation of consent in his abovementioned declaration.

Interestingly, the entire tribunal in *Antoine Goetz v Burundi* supported Michael Reisman's declaration in the *Roussalis v Romania* case and followed the 'ipso facto' importation of consent under the ICSID Convention. The tribunal started by developing on the inspiration of Article 46 ICSID Convention but highlighting that the term 'consent' did not add anything given that such requirement was required for the jurisdiction of the tribunal under Article 25 ICSID Convention.[235] The tribunal thus seemed to have ignored the ordinary meaning of Article 46 ICSID Convention, which expressly refers to consent to counterclaims. Furthermore, by downgrading the requisite consent in such manner, the *Antoine Goetz v Burundi* tribunal stepped afoul of the drafters' profuse discussion on consent as a core element for counterclaims under the Convention.

Additionally, the tribunal asserted that, in accordance with the spirit and purpose of the ICSID Convention, by accepting the offer to arbitrate in the treaty, there was an 'ipso facto' importation of consent to counterclaims.[236] Thus, the *Antoine Goetz v Burundi* tribunal concluded to have jurisdiction over Burundi's counterclaim.[237] This line of argument used by Michael Reisman and the *Antoine Goetz v Burundi* tribunal may be called as the '*doctrine of ipso facto importation of consent*'.[238] Such doctrine has provoked intense discussions and the opinion is divided between those in favour and those against.

On the side of the doctrine's supporters, some suggest that at its core, the issue of counterclaims under the ICSID Convention reveals three questions: how to interpret parties' consent, what other sources of consent there might be, and what policy concerns entail the majority's decision in *Roussalis v Romania.*[239] In this sense, it is suggested that consent under the Article 46 ICSID Convention should not be limited to the underlying treaty provision on dispute settlement since consent to counterclaims does not need to feature in the same instrument of consent to the main

---

[234] *Spyridon Roussalis v Romania*, ICSID Case No ARB/06/1, Award (07 December 2011) para. 871.

[235] *Antoine Goetz and others v Republic of Burundi*, ICSID Case No ARB/01/2, Award (21 June 2012) paras. 273–274: ('Modifiant légèrement cette rédaction, les auteurs de la Convention ont précisé que le consentement des parties était en outre requis pour que le Tribunal arbitral ait compétence. Mais cette condition n'ajoute rien puisque ce consentement est l'une des conditions de la compétence du Tribunal').

[236] *Antoine Goetz and others v Republic of Burundi*, ICSID Case No ARB/01/2, Award (21 June 2012) paras. 278–280.

[237] It must be highlighted that in spite of relying explicitly on Michael Reisman's Declaration, the jurisdiction of the *Antoine Goetz v Burundi* tribunal was based on different and broadly-worded dispute resolution clause namely Article 8 BLEU Burundi BIT (1989), thus, it does not seem to be a complete departure from the majority in the *Roussalis v Romania* case, *see* Jain (2013), p. 145.

[238] Rivas (2015), p. 802.

[239] Kalicki and Silberman (2012), p. 9.

claim.[240] Others submit that a sort of 'implied' consent to counterclaims under the ICSID Convention exists as long as the underlying treaty does not explicitly exclude counterclaims, following Michael Reisman's declaration and the tribunal's decision in *Antoine Goetz v Burundi*.[241] Arguments on judicial economy and efficiency have also been put forward to condemn the majority's decision in *Roussalis v Romania* and to endorse Michael Reisman's declaration.[242] Finally, it has been suggested as well that there are compelling reasons within the ICSID framework, such as the exclusivity of ICSID jurisdiction, to reject the decision of the *Roussalis v Romania* tribunal and to prefer Michael Reisman's declaration.[243]

On the side of the doctrine's detractors, some suggest that the doctrine amounts to an illegitimate amendment of the underlying IIAs,[244] or a disregard of parties' consent to arbitration.[245] It has also been posited that Michael Reisman's declaration embodies policy considerations on how the system should be, when he could have used arguments on efficiency or judicial economy, thereby availing himself of contextual or teleological interpretations at least.[246] Other opponents, with a more cautious approach, acknowledge the policy concerns raised by Michael Reisman, but highlight that from the perspective of treaty interpretation, the 'ipso facto' importation of consent does not find place in Article 46 ICSID Convention,[247] particularly when the investment treaty envisages a narrowly drafted dispute resolution clause.[248]

---

[240] Kalicki and Silberman (2012), pp. 13–14.

[241] Bravin and Kaplan (2013), pp. 190 et seqq.

[242] Asteriti (2015), pp. 259–260.

[243] Douglas (2013), p. 433: ('The majority of the tribunal considered that in view of the tribunal's limited jurisdiction over claims, it followed that "the BIT does not provide for counterclaims to be introduced by the host state in relation to obligations of the investor" because the "meaning of "dispute" is the issuance of compliance by the State with the BIT". This reasoning should not be endorsed. A limitation upon the scope of the host state's consent to arbitration in respect of the investor's claims does not necessarily apply to the host state's counterclaims; indeed, there are compelling reasons militating against such a conclusion in the ICSID context, especially given that once a notice of arbitration is filed it must be the exclusive forum for resolving the dispute as noted earlier. The host state's consent to ICSID arbitration requires the full application of Article 47 insofar as it vests the tribunal with the power to adjudicate counterclaims with the required factual nexus to the dispute. Professor Reisman's dissent on this point is to be preferred') (footnotes omitted).

[244] Atanasova et al. (2014), p. 358: ('The assertion that consent of the parties to a dispute under arbitral rules enshrining the possibility of counterclaims suffices for the counterclaims to be within the tribunal's jurisdiction, amounts to illegitimate amendment of the applicable treaties and legal instruments').

[245] de Nanteuil (2018), p. 379.

[246] Jain (2013), p. 142–143.

[247] Dudas (2016), pp. 392–393; Clodfelter and Tsutieva (2018), paras. 17.40 et seqq.; Atanasova et al. (2014), pp. 367 et seqq.; Kalnina and Godbole (2019), mn. 4.456.

[248] Pathak (2019), p. 114.

Furthermore, the doctrine of 'ipso facto' importation of consent has been even disparaged, uttering that the *Antoine Goetz v Burundi* tribunal '*chose to exercise jurisdiction for reasons of policy*'.[249] This latter assertion seems imprecise. The underlying IIA in *Antoine Goetz v Burundi* was BLEU-Burundi (1989), whose Article 8 foresees a broadly worded dispute resolution provision.[250] Consequently, the decisions in *Roussalis v Romania* and in *Antoine Goetz v Burundi* seem reconcilable.[251] The tribunal in the latter, despite endorsing Michael Reisman's declaration, was in fact based on a broad dispute resolution provision allowing it to entertain counterclaims.

As the foregoing analysis shows, the doctrine of 'ipso facto' importation of consent is questionable at best. Certainly, there are some valuable aspects to remark from Michael Reisman's declaration, which are in line with the purpose of counterclaims. However, Article 46 ICSID Convention cannot substitute the dispute resolution provisions in IIAs simply for policy purposes. A careful exercise of treaty interpretation must always be undertaken to determine the scope of consent given by the parties *vis-à-vis* counterclaims.

3.3.1.3.3 Does Article 26 ICSID Convention Tilt the Balance?

Zachary Douglas commends Michael Reisman's declaration in *Roussalis v Romania*, although without alluding to the doctrine of 'ipso facto' importation of consent. Instead, he infers the parties' consent from the interpretation of Article 26 ICSID Convention, which states '[c]*onsent of the parties to arbitration under this Convention shall, unless otherwise stated, be deemed consent to such arbitration to the exclusion of any other remedy*'. Zachary Douglas considers that such Article would be deprived of meaning if a tribunal's jurisdiction was restricted to the claimant's claim exclusively.[252] He thus concludes that the scope of consent cannot be limited to the investor's claims with the exclusion of counterclaims since '*once a notice of arbitration is filed it must be exclusive forum for resolving the disputes*'.[253]

[249] Kalnina and Godbole (2019), mn. 4.454.

[250] BLEU-Burundi (1989), Art 8 ('(1) Pour l'application du présent article, un différend relatif à un investissement est défini comme un différend concernant: a) l'interprétation ou l'application d'un accord particulier d'investissement entre une Partie contractante et un investisseur de l'autre Partie contractante; b) l'interprétation ou l'application de toute autorisation d'investissement accordée par les autorités de l'Etat hôte régissant les investissements étrangers; c) l'allégation de la violation de tout droit conféré ou établi par la présente Convention en matière d'investissement. (2) Tout différend relatif aux investissements fait l'objet d'une notification écrite, accompagnée d'un aide-mémoire suffisamment détaillé établi à l'initiative de l'investisseur de l'une des Parties, à l'autre Partie contractante 3. Si le différend ne peut être réglé dans les trois mois à compter de la notification écrite visée au paragraphe 1, il est soumis, à la demande de l'investisseur concerné, pour conciliation ou arbitrage au CIRDI...').

[251] Steingruber (2013), p. 296; Ishikawa (2017), pp. 723–24; Scherer et al. (2021), pp. 421–422.

[252] Douglas (2013), p. 429.

[253] Douglas (2013), p. 433.

The rationale of Article 26 ICSID Convention indicates that parties would not have recourse to other national or international fora as soon as both parties have consented to ICSID arbitration.[254] However, the caveat is that parties may agree otherwise.[255] Such agreement need not be explicit, for instance, there might be tacit consent when the parties do not argue the exclusivity of ICSID jurisdiction before the non-ICSID forum.[256] In practice, parties usually raise Article 26 ICSID Convention requesting provisional measures, particularly to stop parallel proceedings. Nevertheless, there is no discernible trend in this regard. In the *Tokios Tokelés v Ukraine* case, the tribunal ordered both parties to refrain from, suspend or discontinue domestic or other proceedings relating to the investor or its investment in Ukraine.[257] In *Ceskoslovenska Obchodni Banka AS v The Slovak Republic*, the claimant requested the suspension of domestic bankruptcy proceedings against a claimant's subsidiary, which was granted by the tribunal.[258]

A similar request to stop domestic bankruptcy proceedings was submitted by the investor in the *Plama v Bulgaria* case, however, with a different result. The tribunal denied the requested provisional measure on several grounds: first, the proceedings before the court differed in nature to the proceedings before the arbitral tribunal; second, the parties on both proceedings did not coincide; third, there was no risk of aggravating the dispute if the provisional measure was not granted; fourth, the requested provisional measure was neither urgent nor necessary.[259] An interesting approach was adopted by the *SGS v Pakistan* tribunal, which acknowledged that:

> It would be inequitable if, by reason of the invocation of ICSID jurisdiction, the Claimant could on the one hand elevate its side of the dispute to international adjudication and, on the other, preclude the Respondent from pursuing its own claim for damages by obtaining a stay of those proceedings for the pendency of the international proceedings, if such international proceedings could not encompass the Respondent's claim.[260]

However, the *SGS v Pakistan* tribunal finally ordered to stop the domestic arbitration between the parties until it had decided on jurisdiction because it would be '*wasteful of resources for two proceedings relating to the same or substantially the same*

[254] Haridi (2019), mn. 2.256.

[255] *SGS Société Générale de Surveillance SA v Republic of The Philippines*, ICSID Case No ARB/02/6, Decision of the Tribunal on Objections to Jurisdiction (29 January 2004) para. 147.

[256] Schreuer et al. (2009), Art 26, mn. 54 and 140.

[257] *Tokios Tokelés v Ukraine*, ICSID Case No ARB/02/18, Order No 1 (01 July 2003) paras. 1–7.

[258] *Ceskoslovenska Obchodni Banka AS v The Slovak Republic*, ICSID Case No ARB/97/4, Procedural Order No 4 (11 January 1999).

[259] *Plama Consortium Limited v Republic of Bulgaria*, ICSID Case No ARB/03/24, Order (06 September 2005) paras. 42–46.

[260] *SGS Société Générale de Surveillance SA v Islamic Republic of Pakistan*, ICSID Case No ARB/01/13, Procedural Order No 2 (16 October 2002) [reproduced in (2003) 18(1) ICSID Review 293–306] 302.

matter to unfold separately while the jurisdiction of one tribunal awaits determination'.[261]

The request for stopping parallel proceedings is one of the most common provisional measures sought after in investment arbitration,[262] which might prove Zachary Douglas' point on the interpretation of Article 26 ICSID Convention. At the same time, one may construe narrowly drafted provisions on dispute settlement as the consent under Article 26 ICSID Convention against the exclusivity of ICSID jurisdiction, directing counterclaims to a different forum. This brings about two conclusions: on the one hand, the interpretation of consent (as encompassing counterclaims or not) remains the decisive factor for a tribunal's power to entertain counterclaims. On the other hand, claimant investors might wish to be mindful of their arguments regarding counterclaims as it may be inequitable (if not an abuse of process) objecting to counterclaims for being outside the scope of the tribunal's jurisdiction, and subsequently wielding Article 26 ICSID Convention for the stay of other proceedings where the respondent host state seeks to have its counterclaim heard.

3.3.1.3.4 ICSID and 'Otherwise Within the Jurisdiction of the Centre': Old Wine in a New Bottle?

As mentioned above, the starting point for counterclaims under the ICSID Convention is Article 46 thereof. Particularly, this provision sets that the tribunal shall determine counterclaims '*provided that they are within the scope of the consent of the parties and are otherwise within the jurisdiction of the Centre*'. An almost identical formulation is used in Rule 40 ICSID Arbitration Rules (2006) (and in Rule 48 ICSID Arbitration Rules (2022)). This brings about Article 25 ICSID Convention, which refers to the four requirements for the jurisdiction of the Centre namely (i) a legal dispute; (ii) arising directly out of an investment; (iii) between a Contracting State and a national of another Contracting State; (iv) which the parties to the dispute consent in writing to submit to the Centre.

The term 'consent' is explicitly mentioned under both Article 46 and Article 25 ICSID Convention. However, this corresponds to the drafters' intention to highlight the importance of consent with respect to counterclaims.[263] The other elements of jurisdiction under Article 25 ICSID Convention, albeit relevant for counterclaims, play only a secondary role. This is supported by the ICSID *travaux préparatoires*. When concerns were raised with regards to the language of Article 46, which suggested that consent and jurisdiction were not the same, Aaron Broches

[261] *SGS Société Générale de Surveillance SA v Islamic Republic of Pakistan*, ICSID Case No ARB/01/13, Procedural Order No 2 (16 October 2002) [reproduced in (2003) 18(1) ICSID Review 293–306] 304.

[262] Commission and Moloo (2018) para. 3.27.

[263] *See* Sect. 3.3.1.3.1.

opined that '*consent of the parties is a most essential element of the jurisdiction of the Centre... the language he had suggested emphasized that consent in the hardcore of jurisdiction while the other elements were secondary*'.[264] In the same vein, another delegate observed that '*although consent of the party would be an essential condition for the jurisdiction of the Centre, there might be other reasons why the parties might not have the right to have recourse to the jurisdiction of the Centre*', for instance, when the dispute does not pertain to an investment.[265]

Thus, Article 46 ICSID Convention presupposes jurisdiction, which cannot be extended via counterclaims. In other words, the existence of jurisdiction covering the counterclaims is a precondition for the operation of Article 46.[266] Although the main purpose seems simple, the interaction between Article 25 and Article 46 ICSID Convention is far from straightforward. Particularly, there are two problems to consider: the possible overlap of requirements and the double assessment of jurisdiction.

The first problem is the possible overlap between the requirements of Article 25 and the requirements of Article 46 ICSID Convention, specifically the requisite '*arising directly out of an investment*' and the requisite '*arising directly out of the subject matter of the dispute*'.[267] Christopher Schreuer draws an example for the differentiation between both articles: a counterclaim may be within the Centre's jurisdiction without arising of the subject-matter of dispute when it is based on a different investment operation.[268] However, in practice, the line might become blurry.

In the *Amco v Indonesia* case, the respondent raised a counterclaim based on tax fraud allegedly committed by the investor. The tribunal dismissed the counterclaim because '[t]*he obligation not to engage in tax fraud is clearly a general obligation of law in Indonesia. It was not specially contracted for in the investment agreement and does not arise directly out of the investment*'.[269] Thus, it concluded that a counterclaim on tax fraud exceeded its jurisdiction *ratione materiae* as per Article 25(1) ICSID Convention.[270] While the prohibition of committing tax fraud was '*property-independent*', which may undermine its connection with the investment,[271] one may only speculate to what extent the tribunal's reasoning was leaning to the lack of connection between the main claim and the counterclaim rather than the jurisdictional requirements of Article 25 ICSID Convention.

---

[264] History of the ICSID Convention, Vol II-2 (ICSID Publication 1968) 987.

[265] History of the ICSID Convention, Vol II-2 (ICSID Publication 1968) 987.

[266] Schreuer et al. (2009), Art 46, mn. 86.

[267] Clodfelter and Tsutieva (2018), para. 17.65.

[268] Schreuer et al. (2009), Art 46, mn. 73.

[269] *Amco Asia Corporation and others v Republic of Indonesia*, ICSID Case No ARB/81/1, Decision on Jurisdiction in Resubmitted Proceeding (10 May 1988) para. 126.

[270] *Amco Asia Corporation and others v Republic of Indonesia*, ICSID Case No ARB/81/1, Decision on Jurisdiction in Resubmitted Proceeding (10 May 1988) paras. 122–127.

[271] Douglas (2009), para. 475.

In the *Metal-Tech v Uzbekistan* case, the tribunal started is analysis by referring to Article 25 ICSID Convention but considered that only consent was relevant for the case at hand.[272] Specifically, the tribunal recalled that in accordance with the underlying treaty, the offer to arbitrate was limited to investments meeting the legality requirement.[273] However, the tribunal found that the claimant's investment did not meet the legality requirement and that counterclaims could not extend a tribunal's jurisdiction.[274] Thus, the tribunal rejected jurisdiction over both claims and counterclaims. The tribunal seemed particularly preoccupied with the scope of consent and framed the entire discussion around it, thus, the reference to Article 25 ICSID Convention could have been spared especially because Article 46 ICSID Convention already foresees consent as an independent requirement for counterclaims.

In the *Fraport v The Philippines* case, the tribunal, after finding that the investment was made in violation of domestic law, held that the '*illegality of the investment at the time it is made goes to the root of the host State's offer of arbitration under the treaty*'.[275] The tribunal therefore declined jurisdiction over the claim in accordance with Article 25(1) ICSID Convention and the underlying treaty, whereas for the counterclaims, it declined jurisdiction given the lack of connection with the subject-matter of the dispute pursuant to Article 46 ICSID Convention.[276] Despite emphatically referring to the scope of consent *vis-à-vis* the illegality of an investment, the *Fraport v The Philippines* tribunal decided to reject the counterclaims based on the connection requirement set out in Article 46 ICSID Convention. Certainly, the tribunal did not elaborate further on the counterclaims and their requirements, however, it could have pointed to '*otherwise within the jurisdiction of the Centre*' or simply consent as the *Metal-Tech v Uzbekistan* tribunal and reaching the same conclusion.

The second problem pertains to the question of whether a tribunal, which has found jurisdiction over the main claim, must examine its jurisdiction *de novo* and independently for counterclaims using Article 25 ICSID Convention as a benchmark. Some authors consider that the tribunal's jurisdiction over counterclaims must be separately evaluated pursuant to Article 25 ICSID Convention.[277] This means that the tribunal would need to establish whether the particular counterclaim complies

---

[272] *Metal-Tech Ltd v Republic of Uzbekistan*, ICSID Case No ARB/10/3, Award (04 October 2013) para. 408.

[273] *Metal-Tech Ltd v Republic of Uzbekistan*, ICSID Case No ARB/10/3, Award (04 October 2013) para. 411.

[274] *Metal-Tech Ltd v Republic of Uzbekistan*, ICSID Case No ARB/10/3, Award (04 October 2013) paras. 412–413.

[275] *Fraport AG Frankfurt Airport Services Worldwide v Republic of The Philippines*, ICSID Case No ARB/11/12, Award (10 December 2014) para. 467.

[276] *Fraport AG Frankfurt Airport Services Worldwide v Republic of The Philippines*, ICSID Case No ARB/11/12, Award (10 December 2014) para. 468.

[277] Clodfelter and Tsutieva (2018), para. 17.65; Pathak (2019), p. 112; Kalnina and Godbole (2019), mn. 4.434; Shao (2021), p. 165.

with the requirements of Article 25 ICSID Convention regardless of the jurisdiction over the main claim. In this sense, and considering the requisite of consent 'in writing', a counterclaim would be subject to an explicit consent of the parties.[278] Conversely, some posit that as long as the main claim satisfies the jurisdictional requirements of Article 25 ICSID Convention, the respective counterclaim should also fall within the ICSID jurisdiction.[279]

In this regard, the decisions in *Burlington v Ecuador* and *Tethyan v Pakistan* may glimpse an appropriate answer. In the *Burlington v Ecuador* case, the disputing parties had expressly agreed to the submission of counterclaim.[280] Thus, it was for the tribunal to decide on the remaining elements under Article 46 ICSID Convention. Succinctly, by referring to the conditions of the mentioned provision, the tribunal found that:

> These conditions are met here: (i) the counterclaims arise directly out of the subject-matter of the dispute, namely Burlington's investment in Blocks 7 and 21; (ii) they are within the scope of the Parties' consent to ICSID arbitration which is manifested in the agreement just referred to; and (iii) they also fall within the jurisdiction of the Centre as circumscribed by Article 25 of the ICSID Convention (legal dispute arising out of an investment, and nationality requirement).[281]

The *Burlington v Ecuador* tribunal did not undertake a detailed analysis of the requirements under Article 25 ICSID Convention *vis-à-vis* the counterclaims. Instead, it simply stated that the counterclaims fell within the jurisdiction of the Centre. A plausible explanation may indicate that the tribunal considered unnecessary to repeat its analysis on Article 25 ICSID Convention which had been completed *vis-à-vis* the main claims.

In the *Tethyan v Pakistan* case, despite recognising the requisite 'within the jurisdiction of the Centre' in Article 46 ICSID Convention as an independent jurisdictional requirement referring to Article 25 ICSID Convention, the tribunal expressly conceded that an analysis under the latter partially overlaps with an analysis under the former.[282] Nevertheless, the tribunal succinctly addressed all requirements under Article 25 ICSID Convention with respect to the counterclaim, and it found all of them were met.[283]

It seems unlikely that an independent analysis of Article 25 ICSID Convention with respect to counterclaims would render different results once the tribunal has addressed the requirements of Article 46 ICSID Convention and has acknowledge

[278] Pathak (2019), p. 111.

[279] Lalive and Halonen (2011), p. 144.

[280] *Burlington Resources Inc v Republic of Ecuador*, ICSID Case No ARB/08/5, Decision on Ecuador's Counterclaims (07 February 2017) paras. 6 and 60.

[281] *Burlington Resources Inc v Republic of Ecuador*, ICSID Case No ARB/08/5, Decision on Ecuador's Counterclaims (07 February 2017) para. 62.

[282] *Tethyan Copper Company Pty Limited v Islamic Republic of Pakistan*, ICSID Case No ARB/12/1, Decision on Jurisdiction and Liability (10 November 2017) para. 1427.

[283] *Tethyan Copper Company Pty Limited v Islamic Republic of Pakistan*, ICSID Case No ARB/12/1, Decision on Jurisdiction and Liability (10 November 2017) paras. 1429–1433.

jurisdiction over the main claim. Furthermore, a literal interpretation of Article 46 ICSID Convention requiring a *de novo* and independent assessment of the Centre's jurisdiction pursuant to Article 25 ICSID Convention may further lead to absurd situations. For instance, treaty provisions on cooling-off periods or notices of intent prior to the submission to arbitration might be considered conditions attached to consent to the Centre's jurisdiction that ought to be equally fulfilled in case of counterclaims. Accordingly, a respondent would have to exhaust the waiting period for being able to file a counterclaim, whilst the proceeding on the main claim would continue its course. Such a situation would be absolutely inimical to the procedural efficiency counterclaims represent.

The foregoing analysis does not intend to render the phrase '*otherwise within the jurisdiction of the Centre*' of Article 46 ICSID Convention otiose, but rather to prove that such phrase might be overestimated. This provision does not require *de novo* and independent assessment of the Centre's jurisdiction pursuant to Article 25 ICSID Convention over counterclaims, otherwise there might be an overlap with the other elements of Article 46 ICSID Convention or simply encumber the proceedings. Instead, as evinced from the ICSID *travaux préparatoires*[284] the phrase '*otherwise within the jurisdiction of the Centre*' stems from the drafters' extreme caution as to avoid any expansion of the tribunal's scope of jurisdiction, which is supported by the overriding principle of consent. In the same vein, it is thus unfortunate that pursuant to Article 6(4) of the Resolution of 31 August 2019 on Equality of Parties before International Investment Tribunals,[285] the 18th Commission of the *Institut de Droit International* has explicitly tied back Article 46 ICSID Convention with Article 25 ICSID Convention, which according to the foregoing analysis adds nothing to the assessment of a tribunal's power to adjudge counterclaims.

3.3.2 The Case of Contractual Counterclaims in Treaty-Based Investment Arbitration

When discussing treaty-based and contract-based investment arbitration in 2007, James Crawford asserted that the state's counterclaims arising from an investment contract should be permitted in the context of a treaty-based arbitration as long as the said contract falls within the scope of the dispute and there is a connection with the main claim.[286] He further stated that such conclusion '*seems desirable as a matter of policy as well as law. Despite the inherently asymmetrical character of a BIT, BIT*

[284] *See* Sect. 3.3.1.3.1.

[285] *See* this book "Annex 4: *Article 6 of the Resolution on the 'Equality of Parties before International Investment Tribunals of the 18th Commission of the Institut de Droit International*".

[286] Crawford (2007), p. 17. Similarly, Kryvoi (2012), p. 240.

tribunals should be able to hear closely connected investment counterclaims arising under the investment contract'.[287]

Considering the purposes of counterclaims, James Crawford's proposition appears reasonable. Unfortunately, contractual counterclaims by the state in treaty-based investment arbitration face some hurdles, which might impinge on the tribunal's jurisdiction to decide such counterclaims. This section consequently revises the possible obstacles for this type of counterclaims in the context of treaty-based investment arbitration, starting by the dispute resolution clause in the underlying treaty [Sect. 3.3.2.1], followed by the analysis on forum selection clauses in investment contracts [Sect. 3.3.2.2], and concluding with non-consenting third parties [Sect. 3.3.2.3].

3.3.2.1 The Limited Scope of the Dispute Resolution Provision in the Treaty

The differentiation between treaty claims and contract claims represents a bone of contention,[288] and contractual counterclaims in treaty-based investment arbitration contain both: a claimant bringing a treaty claim, whereas the respondent submitting a contractual counterclaim. Thus, the question here is whether a treaty-based tribunal would have jurisdiction over such contractual counterclaim.

The starting point for assessing a tribunal's jurisdiction is certainly the dispute resolution provision in the specific treaty. Accordingly, if the provision in question explicitly contemplates the possibility to submit contract claims, then the tribunal constituted upon such provision would have jurisdiction to decide contract claims. However, IIAs are not usually so specific and the dispute resolution provision thereof must be interpreted. Some tribunals and annulment committees have suggested that broadly drafted dispute resolution provisions in a treaty could encompass contract claims. For instance, the annulment committee in *Vivendi v Argentina* pointed into that direction as long as the contract is related to the protected investment.[289] Similar views have been expressed by the tribunals in *SGS v Paraguay*[290]

[287] Crawford (2007), p. 17.

[288] Cremades (2012), p. 95.

[289] *Compañía de Aguas del Aconguija SA and Vivendi Universal SA v Argentine Republic*, ICSID Case No ARB/97/3, Decision on Annulment (03 July 2002) para. 55: ('Article 8 deals generally with disputes "relating to investments made under this Agreement between one Contracting Party and an investor of the other Contracting Party." It is those disputes which may be submitted, at the investor's option, either to national or international adjudication. Article 8 does not use a narrower formulation, requiring that the investor's claim allege a breach of the BIT itself. Read literally, the requirements for arbitral jurisdiction in Article 8 do not necessitate that the Claimant allege a breach of the BIT itself: it is sufficient that the dispute relate to an investment made under the BIT').

[290] *SGS Société Générale de Surveillance SA v The Republic of Paraguay*, ICSID Case No ARB/07/29, Decision on Jurisdiction (12 February 2010) para. 129.

and *SGS v The Philippines*.[291] These decisions suggest that the definition of investment under the treaty ought to be broad enough as well.

Therefore, it has been submitted that, as a general rule, 'pure' contract claims are excluded from a tribunal's jurisdiction based on a treaty unless both the definition of investment and the dispute resolution provision in the treaty are wide enough.[292] In a more nuanced approach, Eric De Brabandere proposes that the analysis of whether contract claims can be decided by a treaty-based tribunal cannot be limited to the wording of the dispute resolution clause but rather it should focus on the treaty as a whole and its objective.[293]

The same reasoning should apply for contractual counterclaims submitted by the state. Should the treaty provision on dispute settlement be broadly worded, the tribunal constituted upon it ought to have jurisdiction to adjudge contractual counterclaims. Ironically, this brings back the above discussion on the interpretation of the dispute settlement provisions in IIAs and their capability to encompass state counterclaims. As a result, one may conclude that the answer to whether a treaty-based tribunal has jurisdiction over a contractual counterclaim will depend on the interpretation of the respective treaty provision.

The 18th Commission of the *Institut de Droit International* seems to hold a slightly different opinion in this regard. Pursuant to Article 6(3) of the Resolution of 31 August 2019 on Equality of Parties before International Investment Tribunals, the tribunal's jurisdiction over a counterclaim is not dependent on invoking the same jurisdictional title.[294] Thus, in treaty-based arbitration, a host state could raise a counterclaim based on an arbitration clause contained in an investment contract.[295] This approach would certainly streamline the tribunal's analysis on jurisdiction over counterclaims. However, in practice, the situation remains the same: the tribunal ought to interpret the dispute resolution provision in the treaty and assess whether its jurisdiction could expand to a counterclaim based on a different instrument.

3.3.2.2 Forum Selection Clauses in Investment Contracts and the Doctrine of Forum Non Conveniens

Besides the scope of the treaty provision, the most prominent obstacle that a respondent state may face when submitting a contractual counterclaim before a treaty-based tribunal arises when the said investment contract contemplates a forum selection clause directing the parties to an adjudicating body other than an

[291] *SGS Société Générale de Surveillance SA v Republic of The Philippines*, ICSID Case No ARB/02/6, Decision of the Tribunal on Objections to Jurisdiction (29 January 2004) para. 131.

[292] Dumberry (2012), p. 234. Similarly, Schreuer (2005), p. 296.

[293] De Brabandere (2014), pp. 46–47.

[294] *See* this book "Annex 4: *Article 6 of the Resolution on the 'Equality of Parties before International Investment Tribunals of the 18th Commission of the Institut de Droit International*".

[295] Steingruber (2020), p. 618.

international arbitral tribunal. Here, unlike in the *Vivendi v Argentina* case, there is no problem on the characterisation of contract breach or treaty breach. The claimant investor submits an alleged treaty breach, whereas the respondent state submits an alleged contract breach. The problem however lies in the fact that the tribunal in such disputes is based on an IIA, whilst the contract, upon which the respondent state bases its counterclaim, contains a forum selection clause for a different adjudicative body.

Certainly, the contractual forum selection clause should not affect the jurisdiction of a treaty-based arbitral tribunal insofar the claimant investor is claiming the violation of the treaty rather than the contract.[296] The subject-matter in a treaty breach differs from the subject-matter in a contract breach, thus, a forum selection clause may apply for the latter but not for the former.[297] This means that the mere existence of a forum selection clause cannot operate as a waiver of the treaty-based dispute settlement mechanism.[298]

However, given the contractual nature of the respondent state's counterclaim, it would be covered by a forum selection clause in the respective contract. Following the reasoning of the *SGS v The Philippines* tribunal with respect to contractual disputes, a dispute settlement provision in a treaty '*should not, unless clearly expressed to do so, override specific and exclusive dispute settlement arrangements made in the investment contract itself*'.[299] Indeed, the differentiation between contract claim and treaty claim for the purposes of a tribunal's jurisdiction may restrict the possibility of the respondent state to submit a contractual counterclaim in treaty-based investment arbitration.[300] On this note, the tribunals in *Saluka v Czech Republic, Al-Warraq v Indonesia* and *Oxus v Uzbekistan* have dismissed some counterclaims, which arose from a contractual relationship with an independent dispute resolution clause.

---

[296] Schreuer (2005), p. 293: ('forum selection clause contained in a contract between the investor and the host state does not affect the competence of a tribunal based on a BIT, since the two proceedings are based on different causes of action even though they may arise from the same set of facts').

[297] *Azurix Corp v The Argentine Republic*, ICSID Case No ARB/01/12, Decision on Jurisdiction (08 December 2003) para. 79. Similarly, *Compañía de Aguas del Aconguija SA and Vivendi Universal SA v Argentine Republic*, ICSID Case No ARB/97/3, Decision on Annulment (03 July 2002) para. 105.

[298] Magnarelli (2020), p. 78. Interestingly, the *Lanco v Argentina* tribunal considered that a forum selection clause directing the contract parties to local courts, which by law are not subject to agreement or waiver, does not constitute a previously agreed dispute settlement procedure barring the jurisdiction of a treaty-based tribunal, see *Lanco International Inc v The Argentine Republic*, ICSID Case No ARB/97/6, Decision on Jurisdiction (08 December 1998) paras. 25–27.

[299] *SGS Société Générale de Surveillance SA v Republic of The Philippines*, ICSID Case No ARB/02/6, Decision of the Tribunal on Objections to Jurisdiction (29 January 2004) para. 134.

[300] Ben Hamida (2005), pp. 268–269: ('L'on note également que la distinction contract claim/BIT claim selon laquelle un tribunal arbitral statuant sur le fondement d'un traité international ne peut statuer que sur les violations du traité commises par l'État peut limiter la possibilité pour l'État d'introduire des demandes reconventionnelles sur le fondement du contrat').

In the *Saluka v Czech Republic* case, the respondent host state based some of its counterclaims on a share purchase agreement allegedly breached by the claimant's parent company.[301] One of the obstacles to the tribunal's jurisdiction over those counterclaims was found in Article 21 of the said shares purchase agreement, which contained an arbitration clause. Relying on the *ad hoc* annulment committee in *Vivendi v Argentina*, the tribunal concluded that it '*cannot in this arbitration entertain a counterclaim based on a dispute arising out of or in connection with, or the alleged breach of, an agreement which ... contains its own mandatory arbitration provision*'.[302] Interestingly, both the treaty and the investment contract provided for the UNCITRAL Arbitration Rules and the seat of arbitration was in Switzerland (Geneva and Zürich respectively). Thus, the appropriateness of rejecting the counterclaims on that ground is at least questionable given the similarities of the arbitration agreements.

In the *Al-Warraq v Indonesia* case, the respondent host state requested damages for the losses incurred given the claimant's allegedly fraudulent transactions.[303] However, the tribunal considered that those losses arose from the claimant's failure to comply with the Asset Management Agreement, which in turn was subject to the jurisdiction of the courts of England or arbitration at the Singapore International Arbitration Centre.[304] Similarly, in the *Oxus v Uzbekistan* case, the tribunal dismissed the respondent's counterclaims based on a Special Dividend Agreement because of the forum selection clause therein, which referred all disputes out of such agreement to the courts of Uzbekistan.[305] This tribunal thus considered that the '*special dispute resolution clause constitutes a sort of carve-out from a potential jurisdiction under the BIT and deprives the Arbitral Tribunal of any jurisdiction over such counter-claims*'.[306]

These decisions elucidate the principle of *pacta sunt servanda* and the doctrine of *forum non conveniens*. In light of the principle of *pacta sunt servanda*, the contractual forum selection clause should be respected and enforced, by which a contractual counterclaim ought to be dismissed by the treaty-based arbitral tribunal.[307] One may thus argue that the parties' interests in concluding a forum selection clause should not yield to judicial economy's considerations.[308]

---

301 *Saluka Investments BV v The Czech Republic*, UNCITRAL Case, Decision on Counterclaims (07 May 2004) para. 47.

302 *Saluka Investments BV v The Czech Republic*, UNCITRAL Case, Decision on Counterclaims (07 May 2004) paras. 52–57.

303 *Hesham Talaat M Al-Warraq v The Republic of Indonesia*, UNCITRAL Case, Award (15 December 2014) paras. 465ff.

304 *Hesham Talaat M Al-Warraq v The Republic of Indonesia*, UNCITRAL Case, Award (15 December 2014) para. 671.

305 *Oxus Gold v Republic of Uzbekistan*, UNCITRAL Case, Award (17 December 2015) paras. 957–958.

306 *Oxus Gold v Republic of Uzbekistan*, UNCITRAL Case, Award (17 December 2015) para. 958.

307 Kjos (2007), p. 619.

308 Berger (1999), p. 77.

Consequently, the treaty claims would be heard by the treaty-based arbitral tribunal, whereas the contractual counterclaims would be decided in accordance with the specific contractual dispute resolution clause.[309] Considering the consensual nature of the tribunal's jurisdiction, the easiest (and perhaps simplest) solution would be to rescind the contractual forum selection clause and to agree that a single tribunal decides claims and counterclaims altogether.[310]

The doctrine of *forum non conveniens* represents the inherent power of a court to decline the exercise of jurisdiction in cases where the claim may be more appropriately decided by a different court or tribunal.[311] This doctrine seems to originate in the United Kingdom and later be adopted by the US courts,[312] and has permeated arbitration.[313] In fact, the *Salini v Argentina* tribunal recognised the applicability of the doctrine of *forum non conveniens* in treaty-based investment arbitration.[314]

Accordingly, a treaty-based tribunal could not arrogate jurisdiction over such contractual counterclaim disregarding the forum selection clause governing the underlying contract. Absent compelling reasons against its applicability (for instance, given fraud or undue influence at the conclusion of the arbitration agreement), the forum selection clause should govern the specific contract/dispute.[315] A silver lining for contractual counterclaims in treaty-based investment arbitration could nevertheless exist. For instance, in cases where the line between treaty/contractual claim is blurred, taking into account the interest of procedural economy, the tribunal could decide to adjudicate the respondent state's counterclaim based on a contract with a forum selection clause.[316]

3.3.2.3 Non-Consenting Third Parties

A final point appertains to the identity of parties to the dispute and the parties to the investment contract. In the framework of contractual counterclaims in treaty-based

---

[309] Lalive and Halonen (2011), pp. 151–152; Kryvoi (2012), pp. 240–241; Bubrowski (2013), pp. 224–225.

[310] Kjos (2007), p. 620. Similarly, Bubrowski (2013), p. 225. On an analogous point with respect to set-offs and diverging forum selection clauses *see*, Berger (1999), p. 78.

[311] Blair (1929), p. 1.

[312] Barret (1947), pp. 386 et seqq. A similar suggestion on the origins of the doctrine *see*, Blair (1929), pp. 20 et seqq.

[313] Rogers (1988), p. 249.

[314] It must be noted that in that case the tribunal concluded that there were no compelling reasons to decline the exercise of jurisdiction *see*, *Salini Impregilo SpA v Argentine Republic*, ICSID Case No ARB/15/39, Decision on Jurisdiction and Admissibility (23 February 2018) paras. 165–173.

[315] Rogers (1988), p. 242.

[316] Kjos (2013), p. 146. One example where the line between contractual and treaty claims is blurred could be the case of umbrella clauses. In that case, a sense of 'fairness' would suggest that the same treaty-based tribunal should decide the contractual counterclaim *see* Lalive and Halonen (2011), p. 152.

investment arbitration, the issue of non-consenting third parties may be twofold: on the one hand, the claimant investor may have concluded the investment contract through a local subsidiary with independent legal personality. On the other hand, the respondent state may have concluded the investment contract through a subdivision, territorial entity, or agency with independent legal personality. The question thus arises whether such an investment contract may be the basis for a counterclaim in treaty-based investment arbitration despite the different parties involved.

This evokes the 'privity of contract' notion, which dictates that contractual obligations and rights only operate between the contracting parties.[317] Although the notion of privity of contract has its origins in common law, civil law jurisdictions developed a similar concept inherited from Roman law.[318] Transposed to investment arbitration, privity of contract suggests that the disputing parties and the contracting parties ought to be the same.[319] This rarely occurs in investment arbitration because most of the times investors deal with territorial entities or administrative agencies in their investment contracts which normally have a different legal personality under domestic law.[320]

Accordingly, in the framework of treaty-based investment arbitration, the availability of contractual counterclaims may be hindered by the presence of separate legal entities, territorial subdivisions, state-owned enterprises or national funds as the contracting parties.[321] Some treaty-based tribunals have even taken into consideration the different contracting parties to either reject requests for staying proceedings or for denying objections to the tribunal's jurisdiction.[322]

In the context of counterclaims arising of contractual relationships entered into by different parties, tribunals have reached different conclusions. In the *Klöckner v Cameroon* case, the respondent host state invoked, as one jurisdictional basis for the counterclaims, Article 21 of the Establishment Agreement.[323] This Agreement had been concluded between *Société Camerounaise des Engrais* or 'Socame' (a Cameroonian company initially established by the claimant) and the State of Cameroon. The claimant argued that there was no consent to arbitration between the disputing parties under the mentioned Establishment Agreement, given that it had

[317] Newman (1983), p. 339.

[318] However, the notion of privity of contract has been reconsidered and many options for a third-party beneficiary exist in both Common Law and Civil Law traditions. In this regard and for a comprehensive study on privity of contract *see* Merkin (2000); Hallebeck and Dondorp (2008).

[319] Magnarelli (2020), p. 3.

[320] Voss (2011), p. 139.

[321] Bubrowski (2013), p. 217. Similarly, Kryvoi (2012), p. 240.

[322] See for instance, *Impregilo SpA v Islamic Republic of Pakistan*, ICSID Case No ARB/03/3, Decision on Jurisdiction (22 April 2005) para. 289; *Aguas del Tunari, SA v Republic of Bolivia*, ICSID Case No ARB/02/3, Decision on Jurisdiction (21 October 2005) para. 114.

[323] *Klöckner Industrie-Anlagen GmbH and others v United Republic of Cameroon and Société Camerounaise des Engrais*, ICSID Case No ARB/81/2, Award (21 October 1983) 14 [reproduced in R Rayfuse (ed), *ICSID Reports vol 2* (CUP 1994) 3–163].

been concluded by a different company.[324] The tribunal acknowledged jurisdiction by referring to the notion of foreign control under Article 25 ICSID Convention and stated:

> This Agreement, although formally signed between the Government and Socame, was in fact negotiated between the Government and Klöckner. . .Moreover, it is undeniable that it was manifestly concluded in the interest of Klöckner, at a time when Klöckner was Socame's majority shareholder. The Establishment Agreement reflected the contractual relationship between a foreign investor, acting through a local company, and the host country of this foreign investment.[325]

In the *Saluka v Czech Republic* case, one of the main objections raised by the claimant was that some counterclaims were against Nomura Europe, who was a parent company of the claimant not involved in the arbitral proceedings.[326] The tribunal highlighted as a cardinal principle that the parties to the counterclaim must be the same as the parties to the main claim.[327] However, as a preliminary matter, the tribunal had already stated it would '*initially proceed on the assumption, but without deciding, that the relationship between Saluka and Nomura Europe is sufficiently close to enable the Tribunal's jurisdiction in proceedings instituted by Saluka to extend to claims against Nomura*'.[328] The tribunal dismissed the counterclaims before analysing this point in depth.

In the *Paushok v Mongolia* case, the respondent submitted a set of counterclaims against KOO Golden East-Mongolia (a gold mining company owned by the claimants) for alleged violation of tax laws and license agreements.[329] However, the tribunal determined that KOO Golden East-Mongolia was not a party to the dispute and its obligations could not be transposed into treaty obligations.[330] A last example is found in the *Al-Warraq v Indonesia* case. Relying on the *Saluka v Czech Republic* case, the tribunal considered as a 'cardinal' principle that the parties to the counterclaim must be the same as the parties to the main claim.[331] Given that the

[324] *Klöckner Industrie-Anlagen GmbH and others v United Republic of Cameroon and Société Camerounaise des Engrais*, ICSID Case No ARB/81/2, Award (21 October 1983) 15 [reproduced in R Rayfuse (ed), *ICSID Reports vol 2* (CUP 1994) 3–163].

[325] *Klöckner Industrie-Anlagen GmbH and others v United Republic of Cameroon and Société Camerounaise des Engrais*, ICSID Case No ARB/81/2, Award (21 October 1983) 17 [reproduced in R Rayfuse (ed), *ICSID Reports vol 2* (CUP 1994) 3–163].

[326] *Saluka Investments BV v The Czech Republic*, UNCITRAL Case, Decision on Counterclaims (07 May 2004) para. 42.

[327] *Saluka Investments BV v The Czech Republic*, UNCITRAL Case, Decision on Counterclaims (07 May 2004) para. 49.

[328] *Saluka Investments BV v The Czech Republic*, UNCITRAL Case, Decision on Counterclaims (07 May 2004) para. 44.

[329] *Sergei Paushok, CJSC Golden East Company and CJSC Vostokneftegaz Company v The Government of Mongolia*, UNCITRAL Case, Jurisdiction and Liability (28 April 2011) para. 678.

[330] *Sergei Paushok, CJSC Golden East Company and CJSC Vostokneftegaz Company v The Government of Mongolia*, UNCITRAL Case, Jurisdiction and Liability (28 April 2011) para. 686.

[331] *Hesham Talaat M Al-Warraq v The Republic of Indonesia*, UNCITRAL Case, Award (15 December 2014) para. 669.

counterclaim involved other parties' actions (First Gulf Asia Holdings Limited and Mr. Rafat Ali Rizvi), who were not present in the arbitration, the tribunal rejected the counterclaims.[332] Interestingly, for this tribunal the identity of parties was part of the merits rather than the jurisdiction over counterclaims,[333] but most importantly, this tribunal did not consider the caveat made by the *Saluka v Czech Republic* tribunal on sufficiently close relation between legal entities.

It is moreover striking that separate corporate legal personality is easily side-lined to the benefit of the investor, but strictly upheld when the accountability of the investor is at stake.[334] Thus, the notion of privity of contract should not be construed strictly where the circumstances of the case entail a high degree of complexity.[335] Therefore, some flexibility on privity should be encouraged in order to preserve the legitimacy of investor-state arbitration.[336] This implies a moderate approach for contractual counterclaims in treaty-based investment arbitration. In that sense, for cases where the claimant investor bears a different legal personality that the company concluding the investment contract, the contractual counterclaim could be allowed if there is a sufficient connection between the contracting company and the claimant investor, for instance, as forming a single economic reality.[337]

Based on principles of equity and good faith, a treaty-based tribunal could interpret its jurisdiction over a contractual counterclaim as involving a non-consenting third party, which is nonetheless connected to the claimant investor as a single economic reality.[338] In fact, given that foreign investment normally involves complex corporate structures, such 'economic approach' seems to be appropriate not only for counterclaims but also for various situations.[339]

For cases where the respondent state bears a different legal personality from the state entity concluding the investment contract, the contractual counterclaim could be allowed by recourse to the criteria of attribution. Accordingly, if the act of concluding the investment contract by the territorial subdivision, agency, state-

---

[332] *Hesham Talaat M Al-Warraq v The Republic of Indonesia*, UNCITRAL Case, Award (15 December 2014) para. 669.

[333] *Hesham Talaat M Al-Warraq v The Republic of Indonesia*, UNCITRAL Case, Award (15 December 2014) para. 683.

[334] Miles (2013), p. 152. Particularly, Kate Miles points to the SD Myers decision, whereby the tribunal stated that it 'does not accept that an otherwise meritorious claim should fail solely by reason of the corporate structure adopted by a claimant in order to organise the way in which it conducts its business affairs' *see*, *SD Myers Inc v Government of Canada*, UNCITRAL Case, Partial Award (13 November 2000) para. 229.

[335] Magnarelli (2020), p. 126.

[336] Magnarelli (2020), p. 130.

[337] Pathak (2019), pp. 117 et seqq. For a different opinion considering that the corporate veil cannot be lifted without a modification of domestic law *see*, Shao (2021), pp. 174–175.

[338] Pathak (2019), p. 119.

[339] For instance, as advanced by August Reinisch with respect to *res judicata* and *lis pendens*, the triple identity test, particularly the identity of parties, should reflect the economic realities of foreign investment, *see* Reinisch (2004), pp. 56 et seqq.

owned enterprise, or a national fund is attributable to the respondent state by the principles of customary international law on attribution, there should be no limitation on the respondent state to file a contractual counterclaim. In this light, the functional test on attribution may be used to determine whether the specific state entity was acting as an agent of the state or discharging an essential governmental function when concluding the investment contract.[340] Should the answer be positive, the treaty-based tribunal could assume jurisdiction over a contractual counterclaim involving a different state entity, which was nonetheless exercising governmental authority when concluding the investment contract. This approach could be even extended beyond investment contract relations, in cases where the tribunal might be hesitant to adjudge a counterclaim involving third parties such as in the *Alex Genin v Estonia* case.[341]

Interestingly, the *Hamester v Ghana* tribunal used the test of attribution between a state company and the state to reject a counterclaim. Here, the respondent's counterclaim arose out of a joint venture agreement concluded by the claimant and the Ghana Cocoa Board.[342] The tribunal rejected the counterclaim because the respondent state was not a party to the agreement, and the actions of the Ghana Cocoa Board were not attributable to the state.[343] Should the attribution analysis have led to a different answer, the tribunal may have admitted the counterclaim. Similarly, in the *Al-Warraq v Indonesia* case, the tribunal held that respondent's alleged loss was seemingly suffered by a state bank, and the respondent did not prove subrogation or other right to recover those losses.[344] *A contrario*, should the respondent have proven a right to recover on behalf of the bank, for instance through attribution criteria, the result may have been different.

---

[340] With regards to exercise of governmental authority as an attribution test in public international law, *see* Crawford (2019), p. 528. With regards to the functional test on attribution in the context of investment arbitration *see*, *Emilio Agustín Maffezini v The Kingdom of Spain*, ICSID Case No ARB/97/7, Decision on Jurisdiction (25 January 2000) paras. 75 et seqq.; *Bayindir Insaat Turizm Ticaret Ve Sanayi AS v Islamic Republic of Pakistan*, ICSID Case No ARB/03/29, Award (27 August 2009) paras. 111–130; *Deutsche Bank AG v Democratic Socialist Republic of Sri Lanka*, ICSID Case No ARB/09/2, Award (31 October 2012) paras. 401–407.

[341] The *Alex Genin v Estonia* tribunal expressed its concerns, albeit *obiter dictum,* that the respondent might not have been the appropriate party to raise the counterclaim on illegally diverted money but rather the liquidation committee of the locally incorporated company *see*, *Alex Genin, Eastern Credit Limited, Inc and AS Baltoil v The Republic of Estonia*, ICSID Case No ARB/99/2, Award (25 June 2001) fn. 101. Thus, the tribunal could have availed itself of attribution criteria with regards to Estonia and the liquidation committee to eventually determine whether Estonia was actually entitled to raise the counterclaim on the illegally diverted money.

[342] *Gustav F W Hamester GmbH & Co KG v Republic of Ghana*, ICSID Case No ARB/07/24, Award (18 June 2010) paras. 351–352.

[343] *Gustav F W Hamester GmbH & Co KG v Republic of Ghana*, ICSID Case No ARB/07/24, Award (18 June 2010) para. 356.

[344] *Hesham Talaat M Al-Warraq v The Republic of Indonesia*, UNCITRAL Case, Award (15 December 2014) para. 670.

Certainly, one may be reluctant to avail of an economic analysis to circumvent the corporate veil or to use attribution criteria in public international law to quash the differentiation between the state and state entities. In fact, the *Tethyan v Pakistan* decision stressed this issue. Pakistan raised three counterclaims: one based on the IIA; other based on a joint venture agreement concluded with the autonomous province of Balochistan; the last one based on local regulations enacted by Balochistan.[345] However, the tribunal refused to use attribution criteria to equate the Pakistani State with the province of Balochistan. Thus, it concluded that Pakistan was not entitled to bring those counterclaims but rather Balochistan.[346] The tribunal failed to provide any reason supporting such conclusion.

Even though the analysis of the single economic unity (or the attribution criteria in case of the respondent) might theoretically overcome the disparity of legal personalities, one must pay heed to new norms on this regard, for instance, the VIAC Investment Arbitration Rules (2021). Particularly, Article 9(3) thereof states that a tribunal '*may return the counterclaim to the Secretariat to be addressed in separate proceedings if*. . .*the parties are not identical*'. While it is in the tribunal's discretion to return the counterclaim, such provisions may be construed as curtailing the analysis of the single economic unity or the use of attribution criteria.

3.3.3 Revising the Interpretation of Consent to Environmental Counterclaims in Treaty-Based Investment Arbitration

The traditional appraisal of counterclaims evinces that neither the state's legal standing to submit claims nor the narrow applicable law provisions represent a major hurdle for a tribunal's jurisdiction over the respondent's counterclaims. Conversely, the narrowly worded dispute settlement treaty provisions might do so. While *jurisprudence constante* in this regard is not clearly discernible, one cannot ignore that limitations on the kind of disputes a tribunal may decide upon have been interpreted on several occasions as the determinative factor to dismiss counterclaims on jurisdictional grounds [Sect. 3.3.3.1]. There are two options to overcome such barrier, making treaty-based investment arbitration amenable to environmental counterclaims: either by means of treaty interpretation [Sect. 3.3.3.2] or by the implementation of prospective solutions [Sect. 3.3.3.3].

[345] *Tethyan Copper Company Pty Limited v Islamic Republic of Pakistan*, ICSID Case No ARB/12/1, Decision on Jurisdiction and Liability (10 November 2017) para. 1375.

[346] *Tethyan Copper Company Pty Limited v Islamic Republic of Pakistan*, ICSID Case No ARB/12/1, Decision on Jurisdiction and Liability (10 November 2017) para. 1421.

3.3.3.1 Jurisprudence Constante on the Interpretation of Tribunals' Jurisdiction over Counterclaims?

It is undisputed that no binding precedent or *stare decisis* doctrine exists in investment arbitration, yet, arbitral tribunals often rely on previous decisions of other tribunals to support their findings.[347] This conveys an ideal of consistency and harmonious development within international investment law.[348] This phenomenon has been denominated as *jurisprudence constante*, which is a practice from civil law traditions according to which, a line of cases deciding an issue in a certain manner may influence the interpretation of the same issue in the future.[349]

Although one may criticise the appropriateness of using the concept of *jurisprudence constante* in investment arbitration,[350] it is argued that the development of a persuasive and consistent system of decisions builds up the expectations on how treaty provisions should be construed, turning investment arbitration into an instrument of global governance.[351] Considering that the rule of law demands consistency and predictability within a legal system,[352] *jurisprudence constante* may contribute to it. Accordingly, investment arbitral tribunals are encouraged to consider existing

[347] Bungenberg and Titi (2015), pp. 1507–1508.

[348] *Saipem SpA v The People's Republic of Bangladesh*, ICSID Case No ARB/05/07, Decision on Jurisdiction and Recommendation on Provisional Measures (21 March 2007) para. 67: ('it has a duty to seek to contribute to the harmonious development of investment law and thereby to meet the legitimate expectations of the community of States and investors towards certainty of the rule of law'). Similarly, see *Mathias Kruck and others v Kingdom of Spain*, ICSID Case No ARB/15/23, Decision on Jurisdiction (16 April 2021) para. 114: ('While there can be no doctrine of binding precedent among the *ad hoc* tribunals adjudicating upon investment disputes, the consistency and predictability of legal decisions is a goal of the most fundamental importance. No tribunal is an island entire of itself. It is one element of a much more extensive, evolving system for the protection of parties' rights; and individual tribunals are, rightly, slow to depart from principles and analyses that are generally accepted and established within the system'); *Astrida Benita Carrizosa v Republic of Colombia,* ICSID Case No ARB/18/5, Award (19 April 2021) para. 22: ('. . . subject to the text of the treaty or to compelling grounds to the contrary, it should adopt legal solutions firmly established in a series of consistent cases, thereby contributing to the harmonious development of international').

[349] Kaufmann-Kohler (2007), pp. 359–60; Bjorklund (2008), p. 272.

[350] De Brabandere (2014), pp. 97–98: ('The fact that states have chosen international arbitration as a dispute settlement method needs to be respected, and this implies that each case will be examined *de novo* based on the specific factual and legal circumstances of the case ... *Stare decisis* and *jurisprudence constante* very often presuppose a hierarchical system of courts and tribunals... The very fact that states have chosen to establish a horizontal system of ad hoc arbitration with no appellate mechanism by necessary implication results in a system whereby each arbitral tribunal assesses the case without any obligation to consider or apply previous case law').

[351] Schill (2010), pp. 18–19.

[352] Reinisch (2016), pp. 291–307. It is important to note the approach of Thomas Schultz, who posits that consistency entails a relative value since it depends on what is kept 'consistent' *see* Schultz (2014), p. 298.

lines of consistent awards on similar issues, but their decision-making cannot depart from the particularities of the underlying treaty and applicable law.[353]

In the case of counterclaims and the tribunals' jurisdiction to adjudge them, no *jurisprudence constante* can be discerned. On the one hand, decisions declining jurisdiction given state's legal standing to submit a claim or applicable law clauses prove unconvincing. On the other hand, jurisdictional barriers based on the kind of disputes subject to the tribunal's jurisdiction seem reasonable but no consistent case law has arisen on this regard. Despite the divergences, one may assume *arguendo* that tribunals constrain themselves from adjudging counterclaims when the underlying treaty contains a narrowly drafted dispute resolution provision on the types of disputes subject to arbitration. Such rationale may indicate a sort of *jurisprudence constante* and future tribunals might as well follow suit.

However, even in such scenario, previous decisions on jurisdiction over counterclaims ought not to be followed blindly. Consistency does not mandate the same outcome, and the tribunals should critically examine the particularities and legal soundness of the previous decisions *vis-à-vis* the case at hand.[354] This implies that consistency cannot be upheld at the expense of any other legitimate interests,[355] but rather consistency should be pursued '*only when doing so furthers a benign, desirable regime.*'[356] Therefore, awards are to be critically evaluated in order to promote the development and legitimacy of the system.[357] Certainly, this might bring about a body of inconsistent decisions, however, that is exactly the purpose: promoting discourse and operating as a system of 'checks and balances' as long as the diverging decision presents a careful analysis for its deviation.[358]

Given the theoretical framework of investment arbitration, it must be stressed that the investment protection in the broader sense represents a means to achieve a public goal, thus, it '*should not be championed at the expense of other governmental priorities*',[359] which might include environmental protection. This demands a revision of tribunals' approach to counterclaims, specifically, environmental counterclaims and their jurisdiction to adjudge them. In other words, even though *jurisprudence constante* on a tribunal's jurisdiction over counterclaims with respect to narrowly drafted dispute resolution provisions could be tenable, the underlying

[353] Diel-Gligor (2017), p. 109.

[354] Paulsson (2018), para. 4.16.

[355] Schultz (2014), p. 298: ('it is not more important for a rule to be settled than to be right'). Similarly, Diel-Gligor (2017), p. 107.

[356] Schultz (2014), p. 316.

[357] Paulsson (2018), para. 4.64.

[358] Diel-Gligor (2017), pp. 153–155. Jan Paulsson might disagree since this issue pertains a matter of jurisdiction and treaty interpretation, whereby the tribunal's analysis is less fact-specific, thus inconsistent decisions might be more problematic, see on this regard, Paulsson (2018), para. 4.16, fn. 6. However, as long as tribunals analyse their jurisdiction cautiously, a deviation from previous cases should not be worrisome.

[359] Van Harten (2007), p. 145.

public interest on protecting the environment prompts a critical analysis of the particular treaty.

3.3.3.2 Interpreting Environmental Counterclaims within the Jurisdiction of Arbitral Tribunals

Each IIA and its dispute resolution provisions must be examined on their own, which might impede transferring the reasoning from one case to another.[360] The main purpose of treaty interpretation is to give effect to the parties' intention, which in principle is reflected in the plain text of the treaty as a whole, considering the circumstances surrounding its conclusion.[361] In this vein, there are three treaty aspects that should guide the tribunal's interpretation of jurisdictional provisions in investment arbitration amenable to environmental counterclaims: *first*, the underlying treaty provision on dispute resolution is only a starting point for finding jurisdiction over environmental counterclaims [Sect. 3.3.3.2.1]. *Second*, the treaty's context, object and purpose provisions in the underlying IIA may supplement the tribunal's analysis [Sect. 3.3.3.2.2]. *Third*, environmental interests might permeate a tribunal's analysis on its jurisdiction [Sect. 3.3.3.2.3].

3.3.3.2.1 The Jurisdictional Title as a Single Piece of the Puzzle

The analysis of a tribunal's jurisdiction *vis-à-vis* environmental counterclaims must necessarily start with the treaty text, particularly its dispute resolution provision. As discussed above, those provisions do not generally refer to counterclaims at all but tribunals have construed the scope of the jurisdictional title as an indication of the permissibility or not of counterclaims. It is thus indispensable to engage in treaty interpretation, whereby a court or tribunal must not be restricted to a literal interpretation nor can it rewrite the treaty under the disguise of treaty interpretation.[362] In this regard, Gerald Fitzmaurice suggested a balance between the letter and spirit of the treaty, eloquently describing them as '*opposite poles of an electro-magnetic field*'.[363]

Article 31 of the Vienna Convention on the Law of Treaties (VCLT) provides the general rule of interpretation, reflecting customary international law, whereby paragraph 1 thereof states: '[a] *treaty shall be interpreted in good faith in accordance*

[360] Paulsson (1995), p. 236. As recognised by Gerald Fitzmaurice, there are no absolute principles of interpretation and each issue must be decided on its merits, *see* Fitzmaurice (1986), p. 791.

[361] Fitzmaurice (1986), p. 793.

[362] *Case Concerning the Aerial Incident of July 27th, 1955 (Israel v Bulgaria)* (Preliminary Objections) [1959] ICJ Rep 127, Joint Dissenting Opinion by Judges Sir Hersch Lauterpacht, Wellington Koo and Sir Percy Spender, 183.

[363] Fitzmaurice (1986), p. 797.

with the ordinary meaning to be given to the terms of the treaty in their context and in the light of its object and purpose'. Accordingly, Article 31(1) VCLT presents a set of elements that must be used in combination rather separately, without any ranking among them, when interpreting a treaty provision,[364] considering as well authentic means of interpretation and relevant rules of international law as indicated pursuant to Article 31(2) to (4) VLCT. In spite of this, the logical order suggests to start with the ordinary meaning, followed by context, object and purpose, etc.[365] However, this might not be a straightforward exercise, particularly when the treaty fails to mention the issue at stake. Silence or absent terms entail one of the most difficult interpretation processes.[366] Contrasting conclusions may be reached from treaty silence but in all cases the recourse to the entire treaty might be necessary.[367]

Possibly, treaty negotiations might not have considered procedural aspects in detail such as the possibility to bring counterclaims during investment arbitration.[368] Dispute resolution provisions in IIAs alone might not be conclusive to determine whether the parties' consent covers environmental counterclaims, thus, recourse to other indications in the respective treaty becomes indispensable. Similar conclusions should be reached with respect to narrowly drafted dispute resolution provisions, whereby the kind of disputes subject to arbitration appears restricted to a state's obligations or simply treaty breaches. Even if such narrowly worded provisions could be deemed as to limiting the possibility of counterclaims, such 'ordinary meaning' would have to be confirmed by the treaty's context, object and purpose in accordance with the rules of treaty interpretation.[369] Whilst the main claim ought to revolve around the disputes envisaged under the dispute settlement provision, the question whether such restriction extends to environmental counterclaims can only be answered by interpretation recourse to the context of the particular IIA, and its object and purpose. All in all, the treaty dispute resolution provision is only the starting point.

---

[364] Gardiner (2015), p. 162; Dörr (2018), mn. 38. Similarly, *Aguas del Tunari, SA v Republic of Bolivia*, ICSID Case No ARB/02/3, Decision on Jurisdiction (21 October 2005) para. 91.

[365] Villiger (2009), Art 31, mn. 30–31.

[366] Gardiner (2015), p. 165.

[367] Gardiner (2015), pp. 165–166.

[368] Dudas (2016), p. 402. Some may even suggest that states had not realised the implications of the structure and language used in their investment treaties *see*, Methymaki and Tzanakopoulos (2017), p. 156.

[369] Gardiner (2015), p. 185: ('the ordinary meaning is the starting point of an interpretation, but only if it is confirmed by investigating the context and object and purpose, and if on examining all other relevant matters (such as whether an absurd result follows from applying a literal interpretation) no contra-indication is found, is the ordinary meaning determinative').

3.3.3.2.2 Treaty Indications for Environmental Counterclaims: Analysing the Treaty's Context, Object and Purpose

Examining the treaty context, its object and purpose is a necessary step in treaty interpretation. In regard to a tribunal's jurisdiction over counterclaims, some authors have already suggested that many factors have a role to play on the interpretation of the dispute resolution provision, such as other provisions in the treaty, or even the applicable arbitration rules.[370] This section thus analyses how an IIA's context, object and purpose may indicate that an arbitral tribunal based thereupon may adjudge environmental counterclaims.

Context, and the treaty's object and purpose serve as qualifiers of the ordinary meaning of a term, avoiding strictly literal interpretations.[371] Considering that the terms of a treaty are not placed in isolation,[372] they must be interpreted in the light of their context,[373] which are provided by the entire treaty, including its structure, headings, contrasting provisions, preamble, annexes among others.[374]

The identification of a treaty's object and purpose might be more cumbersome since a single treaty might as well comprise several objects and purposes.[375] One may argue that the VCLT formulates 'object and purpose' in the singular, thus, it refers to a single overarching notion referring to the treaty as a whole.[376] However, such approach might not be appropriate and instead all objects and purposes expressed in the treaty must be considered and balanced out for the purpose of interpretation.[377] In any case, the use of a treaty's object and purpose infuses flexibility and common sense in the law of treaties.[378] Yet, it must neither override the text of the treaty,[379] nor establish a reading incompatible with the text.[380] This entails that such exercise of interpretation requires a careful analysis of the treaty text

[370] Atanasova et al. (2014), pp. 377–378.

[371] Gardiner (2015), pp. 197 and 211.

[372] Villiger (2009), Art 31, mn. 10.

[373] Dörr (2018), mn. 43.

[374] Villiger (2009), Art 31, mn. 10; Gardiner (2015), p. 210.

[375] Gardiner (2015), p. 216.

[376] Klabbers (2006), mn. 6–7.

[377] Dörr (2018), mn. 54: ('Since, however, in practice, the object of interpretation is always a specific provision, or a part of such, rather than the treaty as a whole, this global view is bound to diminish the value of teleological interpretation. Therefore, in the case of multi-purpose treaties all goals that are expressed in the terms of the treaty are to be taken into account, and in the end that which conforms best with the grammatical and systematic considerations on the term in question will prevail in the process of interpretation').

[378] Klabbers (2006), mn. 21–22.

[379] Gardiner (2015), p. 211.

[380] Dörr (2018), mn. 57.

since a treaty's object and purpose cannot operate as independent source of meaning contradicting the plain treaty language.[381]

Accordingly, the context of dispute resolution provisions in IIAs, as well as the treaty's object and purpose may provide some indications permitting tribunals to positively find jurisdiction over environmental counterclaims in investment arbitration. These indications are categorised in two groups: treaty provisions excluding certain types of counterclaims and treaty provisions providing for the protection of the environment or promoting sustainable development as a goal.

3.3.3.2.2.1 Provisions Excluding Certain Types of Counterclaims

A considerable number of IIAs prevent respondent host states from raising as counterclaims that the claimant has received or will receive indemnification from an insurance or guarantee.[382] Certainly, those treaty provisions do not constitute a general authorisation of counterclaims, but they may constitute an indication in favour of their permissibility.[383] Accordingly, an interpretation *a contrario* may suggest that those IIAs permit host states to submit counterclaims except for the reasons of indemnification pursuant to an insurance.[384] Thus, those provisions constitute a factor to consider when interpreting the scope of consent to arbitrate and the ensuing jurisdiction of the tribunal.[385] Interestingly, in the *David Aven v Costa Rica* case, the respondent asserted that only counterclaims on indemnification already received by the claimant pursuant to an insurance were explicitly excluded by the underlying treaty (*eg* Article 10.20.7 of the DR-CAFTA), thus, its

[381] *The United States of America and the Federal Reserve Bank of New York v The Islamic Republic and Bank Markazi*, Case A28, Decision No DEC 130-A28-FT (19 December 2000) 36 Iran-US CTR 5, para. 58: ('Even when one is dealing with the object and purpose of a treaty, which is the most important part of the treaty's context, the object and purpose does not constitute an element independent of that context. The object and purpose is not to be considered in isolation from the terms of the treaty; it is intrinsic to its text. It follows that, under Article 31 of the Vienna Convention, a treaty's object and purpose is to be used only to clarify the text, not to provide independent sources of meaning that contradict the clear text').

[382] *See* for instance: NAFTA (1994), Art 1137(3); ECT (1994), Art 15(3); Kazakhstan-Netherlands BIT (2002), Art 8(3); US-Uruguay BIT (2005), Art 28(7); Colombia-US TPA (2006), Art 10.20(7); Peru-US TPA (2006), Art 10.20(7); Korea-US FTA (2007), Art 11.20(9); US-Rwanda BIT (2008), Art 28(7); Israel-Ukraine BIT (2010), Art 10; Mexico-Kuwait BIT (2013), Art 16; Australia-China FTA (2015), Art 9.16(8); Canada-Mongolia BIT (2016), Art 36; Israel-Japan BIT (2017), Art 24(12); Canada-Moldova BIT (2018), Art 36; Uzbekistan-Korea BIT (2019), Art 11(9); Australia-Uruguay BIT (2019), Art 14(13); Morocco-Japan BIT (2020), Art 16(13); Israel-UAE BIT (2020), Art 23(1); Japan-Georgia BIT (2021), Art 23(15).

[383] Alvarez (2000), p. 410; Huber (2020), p. 329. Similarly, Lahlou et al. (2019), p. 54.

[384] Rivas (2015), pp. 814–816. Ben Hamida (2003), para. 280; Ben Hamida (2005), p. 270. For a different opinion considering that an *a contrario* interpretation of treaty provisions excluding certain types of counterclaims may lead to inequality *vis-à-vis* the claimant investors, *see* Mitra and Donde (2016), p. 122.

[385] Kjos (2013), p. 146.

environmental counterclaim would fall within the tribunal's jurisdiction.[386] This aided the tribunal, which acknowledged *prima facie* jurisdiction before dismissing the counterclaim on procedural grounds.[387]

Some authors however doubt that such provisions can override a narrowly worded arbitration provision, and only in cases of doubt those provisions may speak in favour of counterclaims.[388] Although it is an understandable position, it must be highlighted that a narrowly worded arbitration provision (for instance, limiting the kind of disputes subject to arbitration) is only one indication with regards to counterclaims. Unless explicit wording in that direction, narrowly worded arbitration provisions do not constitute a definitive exclusion of counterclaims.

In any case, an *a contrario* interpretation must be reconcilable with its context, and the treaty's object and purpose.[389] In this regard, as remarked by arbitrator Mauro Rubino-Sammartano in his dissenting opinion in the *Gavazzi v Romania* case, it '*would be hard to accept that the BIT's Contracting Parties intended to give rise to parallel proceedings before different courts and tribunals, by preventing the Host State from asserting its rights against the investor in a counterclaim*'.[390] It thus stands to reason that if the underlying treaty aims at providing the foreign investor with a neutral forum for the resolution of investment related disputes, the same investor should not be drawn to national courts for related issues that could constitute a counterclaim of the respondent host state.[391]

Furthermore, the treaty provisions excluding certain types of counterclaims would be meaningless if a host state could never submit a counterclaim against the investor.[392] In support of this, the general rule of interpretation in Article 31 VCLT implies that preference should be given to an interpretation which gives meaning to the text rather than an interpretation which deprives it of all meaning,[393] also known as the principle of *effet utile* or effectiveness. This principle arises from two elements of the article: interpretation in good faith, on the one hand, and in light of the treaty's

---

[386] *David R Aven and Others v Republic of Costa Rica*, ICSID Case No UNCT/15/3, Award (18 September 2018) paras. 693–694.

[387] *David R Aven and Others v Republic of Costa Rica*, ICSID Case No UNCT/15/3, Award (18 September 2018) paras. 728 et seqq.

[388] Atanasova et al. (2014), p. 378. Similarly, suggesting that those treaty provisions must be assessed against the rest of the entire treaty *see*, Steingruber (2020), p. 616.

[389] *Question of the Delimitation of the Continental Shelf between Nicaragua and Colombia beyond 200 Nautical Miles from the Nicaraguan Coast (Nicaragua v Colombia)* (Preliminary Objections) [2016] ICJ Rep 100, para. 35. Similarly, Dörr (2018), mn. 50.

[390] *Marco Gavazzi and Stefano Gavazzi v Romania*, ICSID Case No ARB/12/25, Dissenting Opinion (14 April 2015), para. 42(i).

[391] Magnarelli (2020), p. 126.

[392] Bubrowski (2013), p. 222: ('In fact, the express exclusion of claims of a certain nature would be superfluous if the host state could never file a counterclaim. It seems rather that the contracting parties only wanted to exclude the host state's right to initiated proceedings while preserving its right to respond to the investor's claim by filing a counterclaim').

[393] Gardiner (2015), pp. 168–169; Dörr (2018), mn. 52; Villiger (2009), Art 31, mn. 7.

object and purpose, on the other hand.[394] In conclusion, in order to provide meaning to those treaty provisions excluding certain kind of counterclaims, it should be interpreted that other types, such as environmental counterclaims, are within the jurisdiction of the arbitral tribunals.

3.3.3.2.2.2 Provisions for the Protection of the Environment or the Promotion of Sustainable Development

From the perspective of treaty interpretation, preambles may represent the context and the treaty's object and purpose.[395] Certainly, treaty preambles might be less clear and precise than substantive treaty provisions but '*where there is doubt over the meaning of a substantive provision, the preamble may justify a wider interpretation or at least rejection of a restrictive one*'.[396] Yet, the interpretation of jurisdictional provision in a treaty under the light of the preamble must be carefully undertaken. In this vein, the *Land, Island, and Maritime Frontier Dispute*[397] is apposite. In this case, Honduras argued that the ICJ's jurisdiction was not limited to determining the legal situation of maritime spaces, but rather it included the delimitation of such spaces, since the treaty's object and purpose was to dispose *completely* of the disputes.[398] The Court rejected the argument since it could go beyond the common intention as expressed in the treaty.[399] As such, an interpretation in light of the preamble cannot disregard the express wording of the jurisdictional title.

As mentioned above, IIAs have started to incorporate the protection of the environment and/or the promotion of sustainable development.[400] Given the flexibility of its content, sustainable development may function as a valuable hermeneutical tool conferring on the adjudicative body a wider margin of appreciation for construing the content of the provision to be interpreted.[401]

In this context, the interpretation of IIAs provisions might be informed by the mentioning of sustainable development or environmental protection as an objective protected under the treaty including dispute settlement provisions. Thus, when the underlying treaty does not contain an express exclusion of counterclaims but it does provide for environmental protection or sustainable development as one of the

---

[394] ILC YB [1966] vol II, part II, A/CN.4/SER.A/1966/Add.1, 'Draft Articles on the Law of Treaties, with Commentaries' (177–274) 219, para. 6.

[395] Gardiner (2015), p. 205; Dörr (2018), mn. 49.

[396] Gardiner (2015), p. 206.

[397] *Land, Island, and Maritime Frontier Dispute (El Salvador v Honduras: Nicaragua intervening)* (Judgment) [1992] ICJ Rep 351.

[398] *Land, Island, and Maritime Frontier Dispute (El Salvador v Honduras: Nicaragua intervening)* (Judgment) [1992] ICJ Rep 351, para. 375.

[399] *Land, Island, and Maritime Frontier Dispute (El Salvador v Honduras: Nicaragua intervening)* (Judgment) [1992] ICJ Rep 351, para. 376.

[400] *See* Chap. 1.

[401] Barral (2012), p. 393.

objectives pursued by the contracting parties, the arbitral tribunal should consider this as an indication for the permissibility of environmental counterclaims.

3.3.3.2.3 Looking at the Big Picture: Can Environmental Interests Permeate the Interpretation of Jurisdictional Provisions?

Environmental protection has undoubtedly permeated international investment law during the last years.[402] Accordingly, some authors have proposed interpretative tools to reconcile substantive standards of investment protection with competing public interests (*eg* the protection of the environment) such as systematic integration of international law, proportionality, or deferential standard of review.[403] Particularly, in case of environmental considerations, the principle of systematic integration in accordance with Article 31(3)(c) VCLT may steer tribunal's interpretation task towards an investment regime amenable to environmental protection.[404] This interpretative approach seems limited for the substantive treaty provisions, whereas its application to jurisdictional titles is not yet clear. The question thus arises whether environmental considerations could permeate the interpretation of jurisdictional provisions in IIAs favouring the introduction of environmental counterclaims.

Article 31(3)(c) VCLT provides that in treaty interpretation '*there shall be taken into account, together with the context*...*any relevant rules of international law applicable in the relations between the parties*'. This article embodies the principle of interpretation known as systematic integration, which conceives treaties within the broader realm of international law.[405] Accordingly, despite their actual subject-matter, treaties must be interpreted and applied against the background of public international law.[406] One may argue that the principle of systematic integration '*furnishes the interpreter with a master key*',[407] which allows to cross specialised fields of international law with the objective of finding a common place.[408] This might be helpful in hard cases where the four corners of the treaty do not provide a definitive answer.[409] In any case, Article 31(3)(c) VCLT remains an interpretative tool for the treaty in question, thus, it cannot be used as a back door for incorporating

[402] *See* Chap. 1.

[403] Schill and Djanic (2018), pp. 44–48.

[404] Bjorklund (2014), p. 282; Asteriti (2016), p. 181.

[405] ILC YB [2006] vol II, pt. II, A/CN.4/SER.A/2006/Add.l (Part 2), 'Fragmentation of International Law: Difficulties Arising from the Diversification and Expansion of International Law' (175–184) 180, para. 17.

[406] McLachlan (2005), p. 280; Dörr (2018), mn. 92.

[407] McLachlan (2005), p. 319.

[408] Dörr (2018), mn. 94.

[409] McLachlan (2005), p. 281.

other obligations of international law,[410] or for the modification of the treaty in question either.[411]

The application of Article 31(3)(c) VCLT involves three relevant aspects: *first*, the relevant time—whether the reference to international law is at the moment of the treaty conclusion or at the moment of interpretation depends on the wording of the treaty provision under interpretation.[412] *Second*, the meaning 'applicable' to the relation between the parties—this term appears flexible including rules of a binding character (another treaty, customary international law, general principles of law), but also other rules that are at least implicitly tolerated by the parties may become relevant under Article 31(3)(c) VCLT.[413] *Third*, the relevant parties—whether the provision refers to all treaty parties or only to the disputing parties. While one may suggest a strict reading concluding that the relevant rules must be applicable to *all* treaty parties,[414] the ILC suggests a broader reading, otherwise, the use of Article 31(3)(c) VCLT as an aid to interpretation becomes practically impossible in a multilateral context.[415] There is an extra layer of complexity in treaty-based investment arbitration since one of the parties to the dispute (the investor) is not even a treaty party. One may suggest that for the purpose of Article 31(3)(c) VLCT, the relevant parties ought to be the disputing parties (host state and investor).[416] Given the difficulties of finding international rules applicable to both the host state and investors, the application of Article 31(3)(c) VLCT would probably not add anything for the purpose of interpretation. However, Article 31(3)(c) VLCT could still be relevant in the inter-state context.

In practice, Article 31(3)(c) VCLT may have a bearing on the interpretation of an adjudicator's jurisdiction, as well as on the introduction of environmental considerations in the decision-making process. With respect to the interpretation of an

[410] Gardiner (2015), p. 330: ('The extent of the international law inquiry is confined to the context of the treaty provision, aiding its interpretation and, ultimately, its application. Such application continues to represent application of the treaty to the situation, not direct application of international law to it').

[411] Yotova (2017), p. 185.

[412] ILC YB [2006] vol II, pt. II, A/CN.4/SER.A/2006/Add.l (Part 2), 'Fragmentation of International Law: Difficulties Arising from the Diversification and Expansion of International Law' (175–184) 180, para. 22: ('International law is a dynamic legal system. A treaty may convey whether in applying article 31 (3) (c) the interpreter should refer only to rules of international law in force at the time of the conclusion of the treaty or may also take into account subsequent changes in the law.'). Similarly, McLachlan (2005), pp. 316–317; Gardiner (2015), pp. 295–298; Dörr (2018), mn. 108; *Legal Consequences for States of the Continued Presence of South Africa in Namibia (South West Africa) notwithstanding Security Council Resolution 276 (1979)* (Advisory Opinion) [1971] ICJ Rep 16, para. 53.

[413] Luke (2019), p. 169. Linderfalk (2008), p. 345; Dörr (2018), mn. 96 et seqq.

[414] Linderfalk (2008), p. 362.

[415] ILC, Report of the Study Group of the ILC on 'Fragmentation of International Law: Difficulties Arising from the Diversification and Expansion of International Law' (13 April 2006) UN Doc A/CN.4/L.682, para. 450.

[416] Baetens (2019), fn. 96.

adjudicator's jurisdiction, the *Oil Platforms* case[417] is enlightening. In this case, the ICJ's jurisdiction under the 1955 Treaty[418] was limited to disputes as to the *interpretation or application* of the treaty. However, considering other provisions of the same treaty and having recourse to Article 31(3)(c) VCLT, the Court determined that its jurisdiction was not limited to treaty breaches but it also could consider whether the US action constituted an unlawful use of force under customary international law.[419] The Court finally found that the US action did not constitute a lawful use of force without entering into the discussion of US state responsibility under international law for such finding.

One may suggest that if the Court would have analysed US responsibility for the unlawful use of force, it would have transgressed its jurisdiction.[420] Yet, this view might misconceive Article 31(3)(c) VCLT and its use for the interpretation of dispute settlement provisions, especially, given that the Court had arrogated jurisdiction to decide whether the US action constituted an unlawful use of force via systematic integration. Therefore, the *Oil Platforms* judgment shows that the interpretative role of Article 31(3)(c) VCLT is not limited to substantive treaty provisions, but rather it can be expanded to other provisions, such as those defining the scope of jurisdiction of a court or tribunal. At the end, the VCLT does not differentiate between substantive and jurisdictional treaty provisions. Consequently, Article 31(3)(c) VCLT may play a role in the interpretation of the scope of a tribunal's jurisdiction with regards to environmental counterclaims.

As such, the *Iron Rhine Railway* case can be hailed as a milestone for the introduction of environmental considerations through Article 31(3)(c) VCLT. The tribunal considered that the emerging principles of environmental protection were relevant to the relations between the parties (*ie* Belgium and the Netherlands) and thus they might be referred to for the interpretation of the underlying treaties in the dispute.[421]

Considering that a myriad of IIAs do not foresee environmental protection, one may wonder whether arbitral tribunals constituted upon those treaties would

[417] *Oil Platforms (Iran v United States of America)* (Merits) [2003] ICJ Rep 161.

[418] Treaty of Amity, Economic Relations, and Consular Rights between the United States of America and Iran of 1955, Art XXI(2): ('Any dispute between the High Contracting Parties as to the interpretation or application of the present Treaty, not satisfactorily adjusted by diplomacy, shall be submitted to the International Court of Justice, unless the High Contracting Parties agree to settlement by some other pacific means').

[419] *Oil Platforms (Iran v United States of America)* (Merits) [2003] ICJ Rep 161, paras. 41–42. This reasoning arose some compelling dissents from Judge Buergenthal and Judge Higgins, and perhaps unnecessarily as pointed out by Campbell McLachlan *see* McLachlan (2005), p. 309: ('The Court may well have found itself placing undue weight on a principle of interpretation to make this point, in view of the jurisdictional constraints under which it was working. But, as Judge Simma reminds us, the rules of custom and Charter with which the Court was concerned were in any event of a peremptory character, and so their impact could not properly be ignored').

[420] Yotova (2017), p. 191.

[421] *Iron Rhine Railway Arbitration (Belgium v The Netherlands)*, Award (24 May 2005) XXVII RIAA 35, paras. 58–60.

consider environmental concerns as the *Iron Rhine Railway* tribunal did in its decision.[422] As elaborated above, sustainable development (as an objective to aspire to) reflects customary law,[423] which can be utilised as an interpretative tool via Article 31(3)(c) VCLT. Given that the content of sustainable development nevertheless remains quite flexible, it appears as a valuable hermeneutical tool, providing the interpreter with a wide margin of appreciation in determining the sense of the rule subject to interpretation.[424]

Article 31(3)(c) VCLT may therefore incorporate not only environmental considerations but also the concept of sustainable development in the treaty interpretation process which constitutes the core of environmental counterclaims in investment arbitration. Yet, this might require support by other references in the IIA to environmental law,[425] or even in multilateral frameworks such as the ICSID Convention, where the concept of sustainable development might be read into the goal of economic development.[426] In any case, it must be reminded that treaty interpretation is not intended to 're-write' the treaty,[427] and by using Article 31(3)(c) VCLT the interpreter must carefully consider the weight given to external sources relied upon for the purpose of interpretation.[428]

In sum, when an arbitral tribunal is faced with the question whether it has jurisdiction to adjudge an environmental counterclaim in investment arbitration, this requires an exercise of interpretation of the scope of its jurisdictional mandate as reflected in the underlying treaty provision on dispute settlement. Additionally, the tribunal may consider environmental considerations and the concept of sustainable development as hermeneutical tools pursuant to Article 31(3)(c) VCLT, which altogether should tilt the balance in favour of construing the dispute settlement provision as covering the possibility of environmental counterclaims.

3.3.3.3 Prospective Solutions: Paving the Path Towards Environmental Counterclaims

As evinced from the exercise of treaty interpretation, tribunals might find certain indications in favour of finding environmental counterclaims within their

---

[422] Miles and Lawry-White (2019), p. 12.

[423] *See* Chap. 1.

[424] Barral (2012), p. 393.

[425] Yotova (2017), pp. 195–197.

[426] Miles and Lawry-White (2019), p. 12: ('Moreover, in relation to the ICSID Convention, the concept of sustainable development might be read into its economic development objectives. The practice of inter alia tribunals and the ICJ has considered that economic development must be interpreted in an evolutionary manner, i.e. taking into account current standards').

[427] *Case Concerning the Aerial Incident of July 27th, 1955 (Israel v Bulgaria)* (Preliminary Objections) [1959] ICJ Rep 127, Joint Dissenting Opinion by Judges Sir Hersch Lauterpacht, Wellington Koo and Sir Percy Spender, 183.

[428] McLachlan (2005), p. 310.

jurisdiction. However, these indications do not constitute conclusive proof and must be balanced out with contrary indications suggesting the opposite conclusion. For instance, and as elaborated by the *Naturgy v Colombia* tribunal, detailed treaty provisions on dispute resolution might suggest that the contracting states have deliberately omitted counterclaims within the purview of arbitral tribunals. [429]

The problem stems from the wording of investment treaties, for which only states are to blame for constraining themselves in the dispute settlement provisions when negotiating the respective treaties.[430] Thus, it may be necessary that states explicitly clarify or redraft the jurisdictional scope of arbitral tribunals as to cover environmental counterclaims. This approach will be prospective in nature and will be limited in application for disputes arising after the clarification or redraft has been completed. There are three options in this regard: *first*, by means of authentic or authoritative interpretation of dispute settlement provisions [Sect. 3.3.3.3.1]. *Second*, through treaty drafting or amendment amenable to environmental counterclaims [Sect. 3.3.3.3.2]. *Third*, by imposing acceptance to possible environmental counterclaims as a domestic requirement for admission of the investment [Sect. 3.3.3.3.3].

3.3.3.3.1 Authentic or Authoritative Interpretation of Dispute Settlement Provisions

The interpretation of investment treaties follows the rules of public international law, whereby the contracting parties themselves can subsequently interpret the content or scope of treaty provisions (also known as authentic interpretation), or they can delegate the interpretative authority to a third party (also known as authoritative interpretation). Consequently, states could pursue either authentic or authoritative interpretation of dispute settlement provisions to define whether environmental counterclaims are within the purview of arbitral tribunals.

3.3.3.3.1.1 Authentic Interpretation and Environmental Counterclaims

Contracting states are the masters of their treaty.[431] Thus, they hold the power to construe it, vesting their interpretations with the same legal value as the treaty itself.[432] Accordingly, when treaty parties reach an agreement on the interpretation of a treaty provision after the conclusion of the said treaty, this constitutes an

---

[429] *Naturgy Energy Group SA and Naturgy Electricidad Colombia SL (formerly Gas Natural SDG SA and Gas Natural Fenosa Electricidad Colombia SL) v Republic of Colombia*, ICSID Case No UNCT/18/1, Award (12 March 2021) para. 616.

[430] Magnarelli (2020), p. 116.

[431] Villiger (2009), Art 31, mn. 16.

[432] Berner (2016), p. 875: ('Authentic interpretation is law-making in all but name. This distinct type of law-making rests on a simple premise. The entity that makes the law a fortiori has the power to construe it. Furthermore, it can vest its constructions with the same legal value as the original norm').

authentic interpretation and must be read into the treaty.[433] This rule found its way into the VCLT and is contemplated under Article 31(3)(a) thereof.

In the framework of international investment law, it is submitted that a constructive dialogue through subsequent agreements creates an interpretative balance and promotes more legitimate investment treaty interpretations.[434] In this sense, the contracting states could issue joint interpretations of their treaty, or they could seek clarification of treaty provisions through exchange of diplomatic notes.[435] In practice, some IIAs have formed joint commissions for the interpretation of the underlying treaty terms. For instance, NAFTA (1994) constituted the Free Trade Commission, whose interpretations of NAFTA (1994) provisions were considered binding upon tribunals in investor-state arbitration.[436]

Although joint interpretations may entail a legitimising factor in investment arbitration,[437] arbitral tribunals might be wary of the implications thereof.[438] Furthermore, given the dual role states have in international investment law (treaty parties and possible disputing parties), one may suggest some constraints, especially in ongoing cases, and the persuasiveness of the subsequent agreement on interpretation must be assessed against the background of its timing and reasonableness.[439]

Furthermore, subsequent agreements need not follow the formal requirements of a treaty, but they must demonstrate the common intention of the parties as to the understanding of the provision in question.[440] As held by the *Methanex v US* tribunal '[i]*t follows from the wording of Article 31(3)(a)* [VCLT] *that it is not envisaged that the subsequent agreement need be concluded with the same formal requirements as a treaty; and indeed, were this to be the case, the provision would be otiose*'.[441] Under this light, minutes, memoranda of understanding or letters could constitute subsequent agreements but it would be necessary to assess whether the state officials had the authority to make an agreement binding their states or whether the common understanding has been put into effect reflecting 'subsequent practice' in conformity with Article 31(3)(b) VLCT.[442]

Certainly, Article 31(3)(a) VCLT presupposes that all parties to the treaty are on agreement on the intended interpretation. Nevertheless, before reaching an

---

433 ILC YB [1966] vol II, part II, A/CN.4/SER.A/1966/Add.1, 'Draft Articles on the Law of Treaties, with Commentaries' (177–274) 221, para. 14.

434 Roberts (2010), p. 225.

435 Titi (2017), pp. 39–43.

436 NAFTA (1994), Art 1131(2) and Art 2001(2)(c).

437 See in this regard, van Aaken (2015), pp. 19–47.

438 For instance, whether the interpretation may in fact be an amendment without observing the treaty amendment process, whether the interpretation affects ongoing cases among others *see*, Methymaki and Tzanakopoulos (2017), pp. 173 et seqq.

439 Roberts (2010), pp. 211–212.

440 Dörr (2018), mn. 75.

441 *Methanex Corporation v United States of America*, UNCITRAL Case, Award (03 August 2005) Part II, Ch B, para. 20.

442 Gardiner (2015), p. 245.

agreement, the question is whether the treaty parties are bound by a duty to cooperate and to strive finding a clearer meaning of their treaty and their provisions.[443] One may argue that they are bound by such a duty, which stems from various principles of international law such as performing a treaty in good faith.[444]

Considering that the main barrier on counterclaims in investment arbitration has been found in the dispute settlement provisions in IIAs, it is understandable that some authors might call for affirmative action by the states, for instance, rendering interpretative notes on existing investment treaties.[445] Therefore, states could engage in the interpretation of their IIAs, particularly the dispute resolution provisions thereof, and provide explicitly that an arbitral tribunal based upon them has jurisdiction to adjudge environmental counterclaims of the respondent state.

Although in practice '*few treaty parties have reached explicit interpretive agreements and few tribunals have relied on such agreements*',[446] the potential for subsequent interpretative agreements when it comes to interpreting dispute resolution provisions as encompassing environmental counterclaims cannot be overstated. Future arbitral tribunals would have a clear indication of the parties' consent towards environmental counterclaims and most likely they would find no qualms about deciding on them.

3.3.3.3.1.2 Authoritative Interpretation and Environmental Counterclaims

In contrast to authentic interpretation, when the parties delegate the interpretative function to a third party (for instance a court or a tribunal), the treaty interpretation produced by the third party is known as *authoritative interpretation*.[447] States may seek to retain certain control over treaty interpretation claims. Accordingly, they may have decided to include state-to-state arbitration in investment treaties,[448] which has gained more relevance in the last years.[449]

There are two types of treaty interpretation concerning IIAs a state-to-state arbitral tribunal may render: claims for interpretation of the treaty on abstract questions (purely interpretative questions or abstract interpretation claim) or claims for interpretation of the treaty based on existing disputes (concrete interpretation claim).[450] Abstract interpretation claims seek to clarify the meaning of a treaty provision, isolated from any specific dispute based on that provision.[451] Concrete interpretation claims refer to specific disputes between the state parties on the

[443] Clodfelter (2014), p. 189.

[444] Clodfelter (2014), pp. 189–190.

[445] See in this regard, Kalicki and Silberman (2012), p. 15.

[446] Roberts (2010), pp. 215–216.

[447] Hernández (2015), 174 et seqq.

[448] Hazarika (2021), p. 63. Similarly, Kulick (2017), p. 144.

[449] Posner and Walter (2015), pp. 381 et seqq.

[450] Hazarika (2021), pp. 63 et seqq.

[451] Lourie (2015), p. 513.

interpretation of a treaty provision, thus, they may refer to a forthcoming, existing or decided investor-state dispute and the treaty provisions relied upon.[452]

For both abstract and concrete interpretation claims, the relevant question here is whether the resulting state-to-state arbitral award would be binding upon future investor-state arbitral tribunals. One may argue that even in the absence of a treaty provision granting such binding effect, interpretative awards of state-to-state tribunals should be regarded as binding upon investor-state arbitral tribunals, otherwise those awards would be deprived of any practical value.[453] However, even if investor-state arbitral tribunals do not consider themselves bound by interpretative awards of state-to-state tribunals based on the same IIA, those awards can at least be regarded as 'highly persuasive' in the interpretation process.[454] This might be different for pluri- or multilateral investment treaties since the state-to-state arbitration may not comprise all contracting states, thus, the resulting interpretative award would not reflect the will of all contracting states.[455]

Certainly, state-to-state arbitration based on IIAs may present an opportunity for rebalancing investment commitments and other policy goals.[456] It also provides a level playing field for developing states, who otherwise might be trumped in negotiations with dominant and more powerful states.[457] Yet, there is no guarantee that the state-to-state tribunal will decide in certain direction.[458]

Therefore, for the purpose of environmental counterclaims, contracting states to an IIA should first strive to reach a common interpretation of the underlying dispute resolution provision for investor-state disputes as encompassing the possibility of environmental counterclaims. If they cannot reach an agreement, they could resort to state-to-state arbitration with an interpretation claim (either abstract or concrete) in this regard. There is however uncertainty about the interpretation the state-to-state tribunal may take: either accepting or rejecting that the treaty dispute resolution provision for investor-state disputes covers possible environmental counterclaims. At this point, one may consider that it would be simpler to roll the dice with the investor-state tribunal instead of with the state-to-state tribunal. Yet, the latter option might have lasting effects given the ensuing 'authoritative interpretation' character of its awards, which might bring some consistency and guidance for future tribunals.

---

452 Hazarika (2021), p. 68.

453 Potestà (2015), p. 267. Similarly, Kulick (2015), p. 456.

454 Hazarika (2021), pp. 118–119.

455 Kulick (2017), p. 150. In this regard, Angshuman Hazarika suggests that in cases of multilateral treaties, the state-to-state arbitral award could be used as supplementary means of interpretation affecting all contracting parties *see* Hazarika (2021), pp. 82–83.

456 Lubambo (2016), p. 241: ('However, [state-state investment arbitration] constitutes an additional opportunity for both home and host states to provide balance to investment treaty commitments and fine-tune their investment policies').

457 Hazarika (2021), pp. 82–83.

458 Alschner (2015), p. 330.

3.3.3.3.2 Drafting or Amending Treaties Amenable to Environmental Counterclaims

The second option consists of engaging in treaty drafting or amendment which would turn dispute settlement provisions in IIAs amenable to environmental counterclaims. In general, arbitral tribunals have declined jurisdiction over counterclaims in investment arbitration given the language of the dispute settlement provisions in the underlying IIAs. Accordingly, some authors have proposed the amendment of existing treaties or new drafting for future ones, which expressly incorporates the possibility of counterclaims by the host state.[459] This would not only bring about legal certainty[460] and reduce the risk of tribunals disallowing counterclaims based on treaty language,[461] but would also rebalance investment commitments with other policies such as environmental protection.[462] Under this option, a general reference to counterclaims would suffice to encompass environmental counterclaims. UNCTAD has suggested in its World Investment Report 2012 that the negotiation of '*sustainable-development-friendly IIAs*' may imply the inclusion of the host state's right to submit a counterclaim against the claimant investor.[463]

The question is however how those treaty provisions expressly establishing the possibility of counterclaims would look like. The earliest suggestion for explicitly including counterclaims within the purview of arbitral tribunals in treaty-based investment arbitration consists of the IISD Model Investment Agreement (2006). Succinctly, Article 18(e) thereof provides that a '*host state may initiate a counterclaim before any tribunal established pursuant to this Agreement for damages resulting from an alleged breach of the Agreement*'. Whilst the drafters of this provision belaboured the possibility for host states to initiate arbitration against investors as well, this option was considered to encroach on building domestic judicial procedures.[464] Irrespective of whether such concern is justified, host state claims would have faced the hurdle of investors' lack of consent to arbitration defeating their purpose.

The formulation of Article 18(e) IISD Model Investment Agreement (2006) seems to have served as inspiration for African model investment treaties. Article 19(2) SADC Model BIT (2012) provides in similar wording the possibility for the

[459] See for instance, Kalicki and Silberman (2012), p. 15; Asteriti (2015), p. 264; Schill and Djanic (2018), p. 53; Clodfelter and Tsutieva (2018), para. 17.96; Zin (2020), p. 241; Choudhury (2020), p. 56.

[460] Bubrowski (2013), p. 228.

[461] Scherer et al. (2021), p. 420.

[462] Asteriti (2016), p. 181; Gleason (2021), p. 440.

[463] Such inclusion is coupled with incorporating specific environmental commitments for investors within the treaty when making and operating the investment, but also at a post-operation stage *see*, UNCTAD (2012), p. 135.

[464] Mann et al. (2006), p. 30.

host state to submit counterclaims against the investor.[465] Article 43(2) PAIC (2016) introduces a similar permission for host state counterclaims,[466] but in a slightly broader language since investor-state arbitration is not the only method of dispute settlement foreseen under PAIC (2016). This latter option is deemed to clear any doubt about tribunals' jurisdiction over counterclaims and to serve as an enforcing mechanism of investors' obligations such as on the protection of the environment or human rights.[467] A different example is provided by the COMESA Investment Agreement (2007). Within the framework of investor-state disputes, Article 28-(9) thereof contemplates:

> A member against whom a claim is brought by a COMESA investor under this Article may assert as a defence, counterclaim, right of set off or other similar claim, that the COMESA investor bringing the claim has not fulfilled its obligations under this Agreement, including the obligations to comply with all applicable domestic measures or that it has not taken all reasonable steps to mitigate possible damages.

COMESA departs from the model treaties discussed above in the sense that it does not foresee investors' obligations as part of the treaty. Only a reference in Article 13 thereof is made to '*all applicable domestic measures*' which is later reproduced in Article 28(9) concerning counterclaims. Notwithstanding this deviation, COMESA explicitly refers to counterclaims, which should suffice for the purpose of an arbitral tribunal's jurisdiction.

Similar to these African IIAs, other IIAs give contracting states *carte blanche* to submit counterclaims. These are the Slovak Republic-UAE BIT (2016), the Slovak Republic-Iran BIT (2016), and the Colombia-UAE BIT (2017). The Slovak Republic-UAE BIT (2016) provides that the '*respondent may present an incidental or additional claim or counter-claim arising out of the investment*'.[468] Although in the context of damages, the possibility of host state counterclaims is further reiterated in Article 22(6) Slovak Republic-UAE BIT (2016), which states '[w]*here a tribunal makes a final award against respondent or against claimant in the light of a*

---

[465] SADC Model BIT (2012), Art 19(2): ('A Host State may initiate a counterclaim against the Investor before any tribunal established pursuant to this Agreement for damages or other relief resulting from an alleged breach of the Agreement').

[466] PAIC (2016), Art 43: ('(1)Where an investor or its investment is alleged by a Member State party in a dispute settlement proceeding under this Code to have failed to comply with its obligations under this Code or other relevant rules and principles of domestic and international law, the competent body hearing such a dispute shall consider whether this breach, if proven, is materially relevant to the issues before it, and if so, *what mitigating or off-setting effects this may have* on the merits of a claim or on any damages awarded in the event of such award. (2) *A Member State may initiate a counterclaim* against the investor before any competent body dealing with a dispute under this Code for damages or other relief resulting from an alleged breach of the Code') (emphasis added).

[467] Mbengue and Schacherer (2017), pp. 444–445.

[468] Slovak Republic-UAE BIT (2016), Art 17(3).

defence, counterclaim, right of set off or other similar claim pursuant to Section C of this Agreement, the tribunal may award, separately or in combination'.[469]

The Slovak Republic-Iran BIT (2016) has included two express references to counterclaims: Article 14(3) thereof provides that the respondent may assert counterclaims for the claimant's non-compliance with domestic law (similar to the COMESA provision), whereas Article 17 seeks to pre-empt issues with claimant's consent to arbitration. This provision requires that, in order to pursue arbitration, the investor must provide its express and written consent to counterclaims by the host state.[470] It thus opens the possibility of counterclaims since any jurisdictional constraints a tribunal may encounter in regard to counterclaims are unravelled by the investor's explicit consent. Considering that consent to claims and to counterclaims need not be contained in a single instrument,[471] such approach might be further utilised by other states in the future.

Finally, the Colombia-UAE BIT (2017) took a similar approach. Article 13-(3) thereof requires, as a condition to submit to arbitration, that the investor accepts the possibility of facing claims from the prospective respondent state:

> In order to submit a claim to arbitration under this Section, the Investor must present Forms 1 (a) or 1(b) of Annex II, as applicable, with the Investor's acceptance of the possibility of facing claims by the Respondent against them.

Most likely, Colombian negotiators were the driving force behind this treaty provision considering that the Colombia Model BIT (2017) presents not only a similar provision, but also further references to the possibility of lodging respondent's claims against the investor.[472] Although all provisions therein mention '*claims raised by the Respondent State*' instead of counterclaims, it has been posited that such provisions amount to an express intention of including counterclaims within a tribunal's purview.[473] The drawback of these IIAs is that no investors' obligations were included.

Other examples of treaty provisions incorporating the possibility of counterclaims are the Argentina-UAE BIT (2018) and BLEU Model BIT (2019). Whilst Article 28(4) Argentina-UAE BIT (2018) simply states that the respondent may submit a counterclaim directly related to the dispute, Article 19(D)(2)(a) BLEU Model BIT (2019) has incorporated the requirement for the submission to arbitration of giving express and written consent to the possibility of counterclaims by the host state. A

---

[469] Slovak Republic-UAE BIT (2016), Art 22(6).

[470] Slovak Republic-Iran BIT (2016), Art 17(1): ('The claimant may submit the claim to arbitration if, cumulatively: (a) the claimant gives express and written consent: . . . (ii) that the Host State may pursue any defense, counterclaim, right of set off or other similar claim pursuant to Article 14 of this Agreement in arbitration under this Section. . .').

[471] Kalicki and Silberman (2012), p. 14.

[472] See the provisions of the Colombia Model BIT (2017) concerning: 'Scope of Application of Investor-State Dispute Settlement' paragraph 2; 'Submission of a claim before a Court of Law or Arbitral Tribunal' paragraph 6(a); and 'Disputes and Claims raised by the Respondent State'.

[473] Duggal et al. (2019), p. 235.

last group of IIAs have explicitly included the possibility for the respondent host state to raise counterclaims but limited to the cases where the investor's claims are based on the breach of investment authorisations or contracts. This is the case of, for instance, the CPTPP (2018)[474] and the China-Mauritius FTA (2019).[475]

All the above-mentioned examples might serve as templates for amending existing treaties or for drafting future treaties, which may allow arbitral tribunals to adjudge counterclaims by the host state. Nevertheless, treaty drafting or amendment faces certain drawbacks. *First*, treaty negotiations are rather slow, so counterclaims would continue to struggle with jurisdictional barriers in the immediate future.[476] *Second*, treaty reform is particularly more cumbersome for existing treaties, given the considerable number of treaties already in circulation,[477] and their corresponding sunset or survival clauses.[478] *Third*, a major deterrent may constitute the transaction costs associated with amending old treaties or negotiating new ones.[479]

Be that as it may, ISDS reform has been in the crosshairs of UNCITRAL for the last couple of years,[480] which facilitates the discussion on treaty reform more amenable to environmental counterclaims. Working Group III could thus work on a new model dispute settlement provision for IIAs that states could use as a template when concluding their own treaties. This could provide, for instance, that all disputes concerning a protected investment are subject to arbitration, adding a final clarification that the '*arbitral tribunal constituted thereunder shall have jurisdiction to decide counterclaims arising directly out of the subject-matter of the dispute*'.[481] It might even be further suggested that, similarly to the Slovak Republic-Iran BIT (2016) and the Colombia-UAE BIT (2017), an investor must provide its explicit consent to possible counterclaims in order to submit to arbitration.

With regard to existing IIAs, similar language might be conceived but the crux of the matter would be how to engage in the process of treaty modification. In this scenario, there are two possible courses of action: either modifying each particular IIA one-by-one or modifying several IIAs by means of a multilateral/plurilateral treaty. Whilst a one-by-one modification seems untenable given the number of IIAs, the latter option could be realised by means of an opt-in convention expanding the

---

[474] CPTPP (2018), Art 9.19(2): ('When the claimant submits a claim pursuant to [an investment authorisation or an investment agreement], the respondent may make a counterclaim in connection with the factual and legal basis of the claim or rely on a claim for the purpose of a set off against the claimant').

[475] China-Mauritius FTA (2019), Art 8.24(4): ('When the claimant submits a claim pursuant to [an investment agreement], the respondent may make a counterclaim in connection with the factual and legal basis of the claim or rely on a claim for the purpose of a set off against the claimant').

[476] Rivas (2015), p. 781.

[477] Kendra (2013), p. 587.

[478] Schill and Djanic (2018), p. 44.

[479] Roberts (2010), pp. 192–193.

[480] *See* Sect. 2.2.1.2.3.

[481] On this, see the proposal of EI—IILCC Study Group on ISDS Reform (2022), p. 54.

dispute resolution provisions for the purpose of arbitrating the investor's conduct.[482] The mechanism of an opt-in convention has been already suggested to the Working Group III for addressing a manifold of aspects in ISDS reform, drawing inspiration from the UN Convention on Transparency in Treaty-based Investor-State Arbitration (Mauritius Convention) or the Multilateral Convention to Implement Tax Treaty Related Measures to Prevent Base Erosion and Profit Shifting (BEPS Convention).[483] Certainly, an opt-in convention is a more ambitious project, but it could cover other aspects of ISDS reform as well.

Explicit references to counterclaims might equally be used if the UNCITRAL Working Group opts for a standing court for the settlement of investment disputes. The instrument creating the standing court should expressly include the possibility of submitting counterclaims, and the corresponding power of the court to decide those counterclaims. Thus, it is suggested that the provision establishing the scope of jurisdiction of the court could include a paragraph as follows: '[t]*he Court constituted thereunder shall have jurisdiction to decide counterclaims arising directly out of the subject-matter of the dispute*'.[484] In the same vein, the conditions for submitting to the jurisdiction of the court could explicitly state that the investor must provide its consent to possible counterclaims of the host state. These reform options would allow counterclaims from the outset, which necessarily would encompass environmental counterclaims. Thus, the prospective claimant investor would be aware that, by initiating proceedings, it would be consenting to the possibility of counterclaims.

3.3.3.3.3 Adding Admission Requirements at the Domestic Level?

A last option for environmental counterclaims might find place in licensing procedures under domestic law. When exploring the possibility of direct claims of host state and host state nationals against the foreign investor, Jose Daniel Amado, Jackson Shaw Kern and Martin Doe Rodriguez have considered to demand the investor's consent to arbitration in cases of licencing procedures.[485] In industries

[482] Amado et al. (2018), pp. 93 et seqq. They propose an opt-in convention to subject the standing offer to arbitrate in IIAs to the condition that investors must consent to possible claims from the host state or nationals of the host state. However, an opt-in convention could simply modify the dispute resolution provisions as to include explicit language on the tribunal's jurisdiction over counterclaims.

[483] *See* UNCITRAL, Possible reform of investor-State dispute settlement (ISDS) Submission from the European Union and its Member States (24 January 2019a) UN Doc A/CN.9/WG.III/WP.159/Add.1, paras. 35–37; UNCITRAL, Possible reform of investor-State dispute settlement (ISDS) Submission from the Government of Colombia (14 June 2019b) UN Doc A/CN.9/WG.III/WP.173, paras. 4ff; UNCITRAL, Possible reform of investor-State dispute settlement (ISDS) Submission from the Government of Ecuador (17 July 2019c) UN Doc A/CN.9/WG.III/WP.175, paras. 28–33.

[484] On this, see the proposal of EI—IILCC Study Group on ISDS Reform (2022), p. 56.

[485] Amado et al. (2018), pp. 82–84.

prone to cause some injury in the host state, enterprises are usually subject to licensure requirements pursuant to domestic law.[486] Thus, the inclusion of the investor's consent to arbitration as a requirement for the issuance of licenses could be easily achieved via domestic law modifications.

Following a similar logic, licencing procedures for foreign investors operating in an industry with foreseeable environmental impact might require an *ex ante* consent to counterclaims by the host state in treaty-based investment arbitration for possible environmental damages. Since an investor's consent to claims and counterclaims need not appear in the same instrument, such option seems tenable. As the requirement of the investor's consent would be included in domestic law of the host state, this would avoid the lengthy and costly renegotiation of investment treaties. Nevertheless, there are two points that must be taken into consideration namely whether the state has committed to pre-establishment obligations via IIAs and whether the inclusion of the investor's consent through domestic law may constitute an abuse.

On the one hand, treaties with pre-establishment obligations are admittedly few but this seems to be changing through the conclusion of comprehensive regional trade agreements with investment chapters.[487] In this sense, an obligation on foreign investors to provide consent to possible environmental counterclaims in investment arbitration may be considered at odds with the national treatment standard covering the pre-establishment phase since domestic investors might not be required to provide a similar consent.

On the other hand, the modification of domestic law as to require investor's consent to possible counterclaims may be misused by host states foreseeing a possible claim in investment arbitration. Certainly, states enjoy a wide discretion on the foreign investment's pre-establishment phase and they might include restrictions on admission of certain investments.[488] Furthermore, a requirement of the investor's consent in a licencing procedure would most certainly precede any foreseeable dispute between the investor and the state. Finally, the amendment of licencing procedures might require a legislative process which would not be readily available for the state facing an investment claim. However, a tribunal should be cautious if such requirement is introduced during the operation of the investment project and as a condition for renewing existing licences. In this case, arbitrators should consider if there were foreseeable disputes at the moment of the legislative change.

---

[486] Amado et al. (2018), p. 83.

[487] de Mestral (2015), p. 687.

[488] de Mestral (2015), pp. 685–686.

3.4 Interim Conclusions

The scope of consent constitutes the centrepiece of a tribunal's analysis over its jurisdiction to adjudge environmental counterclaims in investment arbitration. Irrespective of the tribunal's inherent powers or the applicable arbitration rules, every tribunal ought to assess its jurisdiction over environmental counterclaims as reflected in the respective dispute resolution provision. Whilst the framework of contract-based investment arbitration might be more supportive of finding jurisdiction over environmental counterclaims, the framework of treaty-based investment arbitration may have created obstacles on two fronts: the restrictive appraisal of IIAs *vis-à-vis* counterclaims and the possible exclusion of contractual counterclaims from treaty-based investment arbitration.

With respect to the restrictive appraisal of IIAs *vis-à-vis* counterclaims, tribunals have misconceived jurisdictional requirements over counterclaims particularly with respect to the lack of the state's legal standing to submit claims and the applicable law provisions in IIAs. In contrast, the kind of disputes subject to arbitration as defined by the respective treaty may indeed prevent a tribunal from adjudging environmental counterclaims in treaty-based investment arbitration. This is so even in the framework of the ICSID Convention where the Convention's wording and drafting history emphasise the pivotal role of consent for counterclaims.

With respect to the possible exclusion of contractual counterclaims from treaty-based investment arbitration, this is explained by the existence of dispute resolution provisions in IIAs with a limited scope or the presence of a forum selection clause in the respective investment contract. Another potential obstacle for contractual counterclaims in treaty-based investment arbitration is the difference between parties to the dispute and parties to the investment contract. Yet, one could rely on an analysis of a single economic unity (for investors) or on the attribution criteria in public international law (for the respondent) to overcome such difference.

While there is no *jurisprudence constante* with respect to a tribunal's jurisdiction to decide environmental counterclaims, the limitations on the kind of disputes a tribunal may decide upon has been interpreted on several occasions as the determinative factor to dismiss counterclaims. This demands a critical revision on how tribunals should interpret dispute resolution provisions in IIAs. Like any other treaty provision, they ought to be interpreted in accordance with the VCLT. Accordingly, a tribunal can find some indications in favour of the adjudication of environmental counterclaims for instance by assessing their context and the respective treaty's object and purpose, or by relying on systematic integration. This exercise could thus consider provisions excluding certain types of counterclaims, provisions setting out environmental protection or sustainable development as part of the treaty's objectives, and emerging principles on environmental law or any environmental instruments applicable between the treaty parties.

Certainly, prospective solutions such as authentic or authoritative interpretations, treaty drafting or modification, or perhaps imposing the requisite consent over counterclaims in domestic law could clearly clarify the tribunal's jurisdiction to rule upon environmental counterclaims. However, one must be mindful that these options might not feasible in the near future.

References

Alschner W (2015) The return of the home state and the rise of "embedded" investor-state arbitration. In: Lalani S, Polanco Lazo R (eds) The role of the state in investor-state arbitration. Brill Nijhoff, Leiden, pp 293–333

Alvarez HC (2000) Arbitration under the north American free trade agreement. Arbitr Int 16(4): 393–430

Amado JD, Kern JS, Rodriguez MD (2018) Arbitrating the conduct of international investors. Cambridge University Press, Cambridge

Asteriti A (2015) Environmental law in investment arbitration: procedural means of incorporation. J World Invest Trade 16(2):248–273

Asteriti A (2016) Climate change policies and foreign investment: some salient legal issues. In: Levashova Y, Lambooy T, Dekker I (eds) Bridging the gap between international investment law and the environment. Eleven, The Hague, pp 145–186

Atanasova D (2019) Applicable law provisions in investment treaties: forever midnight clauses? J Int Disp Settlement 10:396–422

Atanasova D, Martínez Benoit A, Ostřanský J (2014) The legal framework for counterclaims in investment treaty arbitration. J Int Arbitr 31(3):357–391

Baetens F (2019) Combating climate change through the promotion of green investment: from Kyoto to Paris without regime-specific dispute settlement. In: Miles K (ed) Research handbook on environment and investment law. Edward Elgar Publishing, Cheltenham, pp 107–130

Bain E (2018) When some are more equal than others: the need for a more substantive conception of "equality of the parties" in investment arbitration. In: Sachs LE, Johnson LJ (eds) Yearbook on international investment law & policy 2015–2016. Oxford University Press, Oxford, pp 292–326

Barral V (2012) Sustainable development in international law: nature and operation of an Evolutive legal norm. Eur J Int Law 23(2):377–400

Barret EL (1947) The doctrine of forum non conveniens. Calif Law Rev 35(3):380–422

Ben Hamida W (2003) L'arbitrage Transnational Unilatéral: Réflexions sur une Procédure réservée à l'initiative d'une Personne Privée contre une Personne Publique. Dissertation, Université Pantheon-Assas Paris II

Ben Hamida W (2005) L'arbitrage Etat-investisseur cherche son equilibre perdu: Das quelle mesure l'Etat peut introduire des demandes reconventionnelles contre l'investisseur privé. International Law FORUM du Droit International 7(4):261–272

Berger KP (1999) Set-off in international economic arbitration. Arbitr Int 15(1):53–84

Berner K (2016) Authentic interpretation in public international law. Zeitschrift für ausländisches öffentliches Recht und Völkerrecht (ZaöRV) 76(4):845–878

Bilanová A (2020) Environmental counterclaims in investment arbitration. Eur Investment Law Arbitr Rev 5:400–411

Binder P (2013) Analytical commentary to the UNCITRAL arbitration rules. Sweet & Maxwell, London

Bjorklund AK (2008) Investment treaty arbitral decisions as jurisprudence Constante. In: Picker C, Bunn I, Arner D (eds) International economic law: the state and future of the discipline. Hart Publishing, Portland, pp 265–280

Bjorklund AK (2013) The role of counterclaims in rebalancing investment law. Lewis Clark Law Rev 17(2):461–480

Bjorklund AK (2014) Applicable law in international investment disputes. In: Giorgetti C (ed) Litigating international investment disputes: a Practitioner's guide. Brill Nijhoff, Leiden, pp 261–286
Bjorklund AK, Brosseau J (2019) Sources of inherent powers. In: Ferrari F, Rosenfeld F (eds) Inherent powers of arbitrators. Juris, New York, pp 1–58
Blackaby N, Partasides C, Redfern A, Hunter M (2022) Redfern and Hunter on international arbitration, 7th edn. Oxford University Press, Oxford
Blair P (1929) The doctrine of forum non Conveniens in Anglo-American law. Columbia Law Rev 29(1):1–34
Borris C, Hennecke R (2019) Article V. In: Wolff R (ed) New York convention: article-by-article commentary, 2nd edn. Hart/Beck/Nomos, München, pp 250–279
Bravin MN, Kaplan AB (2013) Arbitrating closely related counterclaims at ICSID in the wake of Spyridon Roussalis v. Romania. Yearb Int Arbitr 3:185–198
Brilmayer L, Giorgetti C, Charlton L (2017) International claims commissions: righting wrongs after conflict. Elgar International Law, Cheltenham
Brown C (2010) Procedure in investment treaty arbitration and the relevance of comparative public law. In: Schill SW (ed) International investment law and comparative public law. Oxford University Press, Oxford, pp 659–688
Bubrowski H (2013) Balancing IIA arbitration through the use of counterclaims. In: de Mestral A, Lévesque C (eds) Improving international investment agreements. Routledge, New York, pp 212–229
Bungenberg M, Titi C (2015) Precedents in international investment law. In: Bungenberg M, Griebel J, Hobe S, Reinisch A (eds) International investment law: a handbook. CH Beck/Hart/Nomos, Baden-Baden, pp 1505–1516
Carlston KS (1972) The process of international arbitration. Greenwood Press, Westport
Caron DD, Caplan LM (2013) The UNCITRAL arbitration rules: a commentary, 2nd edn. Oxford University Press, Oxford
Cheng B (1953) General principles of law: as applied by international courts and tribunals. Stevens and Sons Limited, London
Choudhury B (2020) International investment law and non-economic issues. Vanderbilt J Transnatl Law 53(1):1–78
Clodfelter MA (2014) Do states have a duty to cooperate in the interpretation of investment treaties? Am Soc Int Law Proc 108:188–190
Clodfelter MA, Tsutieva D (2018) Counterclaims in investment treaty arbitration. In: Yannaca-Small K (ed) Arbitration under international investment agreements: a guide to the key issues, 2nd edn. Oxford University Press, Oxford, pp 417–445
Commission J, Moloo R (2018) Procedural issues in international investment arbitration. Oxford University Press, Oxford
Crawford J (2007) Treaty and contract in investment arbitration. In: The 22nd Freshfields lecture on international arbitration, London 29 November 2007
Crawford J (2019) Brownlie's principles of public international law, 9th edn. Oxford University Press, Oxford
Cremades B (2012) Litigating annulment proceedings the vivendi matter: contract and treaty claims. In: Gaillard E, Banifatemi Y(eds) Annulment of ICSID awards. Juris, New York, pp 87–96
Croft C, Kee C, Waincymer J (2013) A guide to the UNCITRAL arbitration rules. Cambridge University Press, Cambridge
De Brabandere E (2014) Investment treaty arbitration as public international law: procedural aspects and implications. Cambridge University Press, Cambridge
de Mestral A (2015) Pre-entry obligations under international law. In: Bungenberg M, Griebel J, Hobe S, Reinisch A (eds) International investment law: a handbook. CH Beck/Hart/Nomos, Baden-Baden, pp 685–699

de Nanteuil A (2018) Counterclaims in investment arbitration: old questions, new answers? Law Pract Int Courts Tribunals 17(2):374–392
Diel-Gligor K (2017) Towards consistency in international investment jurisprudence: a preliminary ruling system for ICSID arbitration. Brill Nijhoff, Leiden
Dolzer R, Kriebaum U, Schreuer C (2022) Principles of international investment law, 3rd edn. Oxford University Press, Oxford
Dörr O (2018) Article 31. In: Dörr O, Schmalenbach K (eds) Vienna convention on the law of treaties: a commentary, 2nd edn. Springer, Heidelberg, pp 559–616
Douglas Z (2003) The hybrid foundations of investment treaty arbitration. Br Yearb Int Law 74(1): 151–289
Douglas Z (2009) The international law of investment claims. Cambridge University Press, Cambridge
Douglas Z (2013) The enforcement of environmental norms in investment treaty arbitration. In: Dupuy PM, Viñuales JE (eds) Harnessing foreign investment to promote environmental protection: incentives and safeguards. Cambridge University Press, Cambridge, pp 415–444
Dudas S (2016) Chapter 14: treaty counterclaims under the ICSID convention. In: Baltag C (ed) ICSID convention after 50 years: unsettled issues. Kluwer Law International, Alphen aan den Rijn, pp 385–406
Duggal KAN, García Clavijo DF, Trujillo S, Rincon MC (2019) Colombia's 2017 Model IIA: something old, something new, something borrowed. ICSID Rev 34(1):224–240
Dumberry P (2012) International investment contracts. In: Gazzini T, De Brabandere E (eds) International investment law: sources of rights and obligations. Brill/Nijhoff, Leiden, pp 215–244
EI—IILCC Study Group on ISDS Reform (2022) Reform of investor-state dispute settlement: current state of play at UNCITRAL. Zeitschrift für Europarechtliche Studien 25(1):15–74
Fitzmaurice G (1986) The law and procedure of the international court of justice, vol II. Grotius Publications Ltd, Cambridge
Fontanelli F (2018) Jurisdiction and admissibility in investment arbitration: the practice and the theory. Brill, Leiden
Gardiner RK (2015) Treaty interpretation, 2nd edn. Oxford University Press, Oxford
Gleason T (2021) Examining host-state counterclaims for environmental damage in investor-state dispute settlement from human rights and transnational public policy perspectives. Int Environ Agreements Polit Law Econ 21:427–444
Hallebeck JJ, Dondorp H (2008) Contracts for a third-party beneficiary: a historical and comparative account. Brill/Nijhoff, Leiden
Hanefeld I, de Jong A (2019) Inherent powers to streamline the proceedings. In: Ferrari F, Rosenfeld F (eds) Inherent powers of arbitrators. Juris, New York, pp 247–268
Haridi SA (2019) Article 26. In: Fouret J, Gerbay R, Alvarez GM (eds) The ICSID convention, regulations and rules: a practical commentary. Edward Elgar Publishing, Cheltenham, pp 227–243
Harrison J (2016) Environmental Counterclaims in Investor-State Arbitration: Perenco Ecuador Ltd v Republic of Ecuador, ICSID Case No ARB/08/6, Interim Decision on the Environmental Counterclaim, 11 August 2015. J World Investment Trade 17:479–488
Hazarika A (2021) State-to-state arbitration based on international investment agreements: scope, utility and potential. Springer, Cham
Hepburn J (2017) Domestic law in international investment arbitration. Oxford University Press, Oxford
Hernández G (2015) Interpretative authority and the international judiciary. In: Bianchi A, Peat D, Windsor M (eds) Interpretation in international law. Oxford University Press, Oxford, pp 166–188
Hoffmann AK (2013) Counterclaims in Investment Arbitration ICSID Rev 28(2):438–453

Holzer AM (2022) Inhärente Befugnisse internationaler Schiedsgerichte: Eine Untersuchung anhand der investitionsschiedsgerichtlichen Kompetenz zur Wiederbefassung (reconsideration) mit Teilentscheidungen. Nomos, Baden-Baden

Huber S (2020) Die Stellung von Unternehmen in der Investitionsschiedsgerichtsbarkeit (unter besonderer Berücksichtigung von Korruptionsproblemen): Unternehmen als gleichberechtigte Verfahrensparteien? In: Reinisch A, Hobe S, Kieninger EM, Peters A (eds) Unternehmensverantwortung und Internationales Recht. CF Müller, Heidelberg, pp 303–338

Hussin A (2019) Environmental counterclaims under the CPTPP: lessons for Asia from recent investor-state jurisprudence. Transnational Dispute Management 5 <https://www.transnational-dispute-management.com/article.asp?key=2673> Accessed 10 Jan 2023

Ishikawa T (2017) Marco Gavazzi and Stefano Gavazzi v Romania: a new approach to determining jurisdiction over counterclaims in ICSID arbitration? ICSID Rev 32(3):721–728

Jain AG (2013) Consent to counterclaims in investor-state arbitration: a post-Roussalis analysis. Int Arbitr Law Rev 16(5):135–147

Kalicki J, Silberman MB (2012) Case comment: Spyridon Roussalis v Romania. ICSID Rev 27(1): 9–15

Kalnina E, Godbole A (2019) Article 46. In: Fouret J, Gerbay R, Alvarez GM (eds) The ICSID convention, regulations and rules: a practical commentary. Edward Elgar Publishing, Cheltenham, pp 413–432

Kaufmann-Kohler G (2007) Arbitral precedent: dream, necessity or excuse? Arbitr Int 23(3): 357–378

Kendra T (2013) State counterclaims in investment arbitration – a new lease of life? Arbitr Int 29(4): 575–606

Kjos HE (2007) Counterclaims by host state in investment dispute arbitration "without privity". In: Kahn P, Wälde T (eds) Les aspects nouveaux du droit des investissements internationaux/New Aspects of International Investments Law. Brill Nijhoff, Leiden, pp 597–628

Kjos HE (2013) Applicable law in investor-state arbitration: the interplay between national and international law. Oxford University Press, Oxford

Klabbers J (2006) Treaties, object and purpose. In: Wolfrum R (ed) Max Planck encyclopedia of public international law. Oxford University Press, Oxford

Kryvoi Y (2012) Counterclaims in investor-state arbitration. Minnesota J Int Law 21(2):216–252

Kulick A (2015) Investment arbitration, investment treaty interpretation, and democracy. Cambridge Int Law J 4(2):441–460

Kulick A (2017) State-state investment arbitration as a means of reassertion of control: from antagonism to dialogue. In: Kulick A (ed) Reassertion of control over the investment treaty regime. Cambridge University Press, Cambridge, pp 128–152

Laborde G (2010) The case for host state claims in investment arbitration. J Int Disp Settlement 1(1):97–122

Lahlou Y, Willard R, Craven M (2019) The rise of environmental counterclaims in mining arbitration. In: Fry J, Bret LA (eds) The guide to mining arbitrations. Law Business Research, London, pp 51–67

Lalive P, Halonen L (2011) On the availability of counterclaims in investment treaty arbitration. Czech Yearb Int Law 2:141–156

Larschan B, Mirfendereski G (1986) The status of counterclaims in international law, with particular reference to international arbitration involving a private party and a foreign state. Denver J Int Law Policy 15:11–48

Linderfalk U (2008) Who are "the parties"? Article 31, paragraph 3(c) of the 1969 Vienna convention and the "principle of systematic integration" revisited. Neth Int Law Rev 55(3): 343–364

Lourie G (2015) Diplomatic protection under the state-to-state arbitration clauses of investment treaties. In: Klausegger C, Klein P, Kremslehner F, Petsche A, Pitkowitz N, Power J, Welser I, Zeiler G (eds) Austrian yearbook on international arbitration 2015. Manz'sche Verlags- und Universitätsbuchhandlung, Alphen aan den Rijn, pp 511–542

Lubambo M (2016) Is state-state investment arbitration an old option for Latin America? Confl Resol Q 34(2):225–247

Luke E (2019) Environment and human rights in an investment law frame. In: Miles K (ed) Research handbook on environment and investment law. Edward Elgar Publishing, Cheltenham, pp 150–174

Magnarelli M (2020) Privity of contract in international investment arbitration: original sin or useful tool? Kluwer Law International, The Hague

Mann H, von Moltke K, Peterson LE, Cosbey A (2006) IISD model international agreement on Investment for Sustainable Development: negotiators' handbook, 2nd edn. International Institute for Sustainable Development, Winnipeg

Mbengue MM, Schacherer S (2017) The "Africanization" of international investment law: the pan-Africa investment code and the reform of the international investment regime. J World Investment Trade 18:414–448

McLachlan C (2005) The principle of systematic integration and Article 31(3)(c) of the Vienna Convention. Int Comp Law Q 54(2):279–320

McLachlan C, Shore L, Weiniger M (2017) International investment arbitration: substantive principles, 2nd edn. Oxford University Press, Oxford

Merkin R (2000) Privity of contract. Routledge, New York

Methymaki E, Tzanakopoulos A (2017) Masters of puppets? Reassertion of control through joint investment treaty interpretation. In: Kulick A (ed) Reassertion of control over the investment treaty regime. Cambridge University Press, Cambridge, pp 155–181

Miles K (2013) The origins of international investment law: empire, environment and the safeguarding of capital. Cambridge University Press, Cambridge

Miles W, Lawry-White M (2019) Arbitral institutions and the enforcement of climate change obligations for the benefit of all stakeholders: the role of ICSID. ICSID Rev 34(1):1–31

Mitra T, Donde R (2016) Claims and counterclaims under Asian multilateral investment treaties. In: Choukroune L (ed) Judging the state in international trade and investment law. Springer, Singapore

Nacimiento P, Scharaw B, Covi A, Tussupov A (2021) Counterclaims in investment arbitration. In: Bungenberg M, Giegerich T (eds) 'Europa lässt nicht mit einem Schlag herstellen' 70 Jahre Europa-Institut der Universität des Saarlandes. ZEuS Special Issue, Nomos, Baden-Baden, pp 165–186

Newcombe A, Paradell L (2009) Law and practice of investment treaties: standards of treatment. Kluwer Law International, Alphen aan den Rijn

Newman RH (1983) The doctrine of Privity of contract: the common law and the contracts (Privity) act 1982. Auckland Univ Law Rev 4(4):339–360

Parra AR (2012) The history of ICSID. Oxford University Press, Oxford

Pathak H (2019) Consenting to counterclaims under the ICSID convention. Pepperdine Disp Resol Law J 19(1):101–126

Paulsson J (1995) Arbitration without privity. ICSID Rev 10(2):232–257

Paulsson J (2018) The role of precedent in investment treaty arbitration. In: Yannaca-Small K (ed) Arbitration under international investment agreements: a guide to the key issues, 2nd edn. Oxford University Press, Oxford, pp 81–100

Paulsson J, Petrochilos G (2017) UNCITRAL arbitration. Kluwer Law International, Alphen aan den Rijn

Pohl J, Mashigo K, Nohen A (2012) Dispute Settlement Provisions in International Investment Agreements: A Large Sample Survey. OECD Working Papers on International Investment 2012/02 <https://doi.org/10.1787/5k8xb71nf628-en> Accessed 10 Jan 2023

Popova IC, Poon F (2015) From perpetual respondent to aspiring counterclaimant? State counterclaims in the new wave of investment treaties. BCDR Int Arbitr Rev 2(2):223–260

Posner TR, Walter MC (2015) The abiding role of state-state engagement in the resolution of investor-state disputes. In: Kalicki JE, Joubin-Bret A (eds) Reshaping the investor-state dispute settlement system: journeys for the 21st century. Brill Nijhoff, Leiden p, pp 381–393

Potestà M (2015) Towards a greater role for state-to-state arbitration in the architecture of investment treaties? In: Lalani S, Polanco Lazo R (eds) The role of the state in investor-state arbitration. Brill Nijhoff, Leiden, pp 249–273
Rau AS (2008) Arbitral jurisdiction and the dimensions of "consent". Arbitr Int 24(2):199–264
Reed LF, Davis JE (2015) Who is a protected investor? In: Bungenberg M, Griebel J, Hobe S, Reinisch A (eds) International investment law: a handbook. CH Beck/Hart/Nomos, Baden-Baden, pp 614–637
Reinisch A (2004) The use and limits of res judicata and Lis Pendens as procedural tools to avoid conflicting dispute settlement outcomes. Law Pract Int Courts Trib 3(1):37–78
Reinisch A (2016) The rule of law in international investment arbitration. In: Pazartzis P, Gavouneli M (eds) Reconceptualising the rule of law: in global governance, resources, investment and trade. Bloomsbury, Portland, pp 291–308
Renteln AD (1987) Encountering counterclaims. Denver J Int Law Policy 15:379–394
Rivas JA (2015) ICSID treaty counterclaims: case law and treaty evolution. In: Kalicki JE, Joubin-Bret A (eds) Reshaping the investor-state dispute settlement system: journeys for the 21st century. Brill Nijhoff, Leiden p, pp 779–827
Roberts A (2010) Power and persuasion in investment treaty interpretation: the dual role of states. Am J Int Law 104(2):179–225
Rogers A (1988) Forum non Conveniens in arbitration. Arbitr Int 4(3):240–254
Romano CPR (2007) The shift from the consensual to the compulsory paradigm in international adjudication: elements for a theory of consent. New York Univ J Int Law Polit 39(4):791–872
Scherer M, Bruce S, Reschke J (2021) Environmental counterclaims in investment treaty arbitration. ICSID Rev 36(2):413–440
Schill SW (2010) International investment law and comparative public law – an introduction. In: Schill SW (ed) International investment law and comparative public law. Oxford University Press, Oxford, pp 3–38
Schill SW, Djanic V (2018) Wherefore art thou? Towards a public interest-based justification of international investment law. ICSID Rev 33(1):29–55
Schreuer C (2005) Investment treaty arbitration and jurisdiction over contract claims: the vivendi I case considered. In: Weiler T (ed) International investment law and arbitration: leading cases from the ICSID, NAFTA, bilateral treaties and customary international law. Cameron May, London, pp 281–324
Schreuer C (2014) Jurisdiction and applicable law in investment treaty arbitration. McGill J Disp Resol 1:1–25
Schreuer C, Malintoppi L, Reinisch A, Sinclair A (2009) The ICSID convention: a commentary, 2nd edn. Cambridge University Press, Cambridge
Schultz T (2014) Against consistency in investment arbitration. In: Douglas Z, Pauwelyn J, Viñuales JE (eds) The foundations of international investment law: bringing theory into practice. Oxford University Press, Oxford, pp 297–316
Shao X (2021) Environmental and human rights counterclaims in international investment arbitration: at the crossroads of domestic and international law. J Int Econ Law 24(1):157–179
Sharpe JK, Jacob M (2018) Counterclaims and state claims. In: Beharry CL (ed) Contemporary and emerging issues on the law of damages and valuation in international investment arbitration. Brill/Nijhoff, Leiden, pp 347–369
Simma B, Pulkowski D (2015) Two worlds, but not apart: international investment law and general international law. In: Bungenberg M, Griebel J, Hobe S, Reinisch A (eds) International investment law: a handbook. CH Beck/Hart/Nomos, Baden-Baden, pp 361–371
Sourgens FG (2017) Supernational law. Vanderbilt J Transnatl Law 55:155–216
Steingruber AM (2012) Consent in international arbitration. Oxford University Press, Oxford
Steingruber AM (2013) Antoine Goetz and others v Republic of Burundi: consent and arbitral tribunal competence to hear counterclaims in treaty-based ICSID arbitrations. ICSID Rev 28(2): 291–300

Steingruber AM (2020) Counterclaims: a critical analysis of Article 6 of the 2019 The Hague resolution of the Institut de Droit International on the "equality of parties before international investment tribunals". ICSID Rev 35(3):595–645
Sullivan J, Kirsey V (2017) Environmental policies: a shield or a sword in investment arbitration? J World Invest Trade 18(1):100–130
Thirlway H (2013) The law and procedure of the international court of justice: fifty years of jurisprudence. Oxford University Press, Oxford
Thomas C, Dhillon HK (2014) Applicable law under international investment treaties. Singapore Acad Law J 26:975–998
Titi C (2017) Non-adjudicatory state-state mechanisms in investment dispute prevention and dispute settlement: joint interpretations, filters and focal points. Braz J Int Law 14(2):37–49
Tomuschat C (2012) Article 36. In: Zimmermann A, Tams CJ, Oellers-Frahm K, Tomuschat C (eds) The statute of the international court of justice: a commentary, 2nd edn. Oxford University Press, Oxford
van Aaken A (2015) Delegating interpretative authority in investment treaties: the case of joint administrative commissions. In: Kalicki JE, Joubin-Bret A (eds) Reshaping the investor-state dispute settlement system: journeys for the 21st century. Brill Nijhoff, Leiden p, pp 21–47
Van Harten G (2007) Investment treaty arbitration and public law. Oxford University Press, Oxford
Villiger ME (2009) Commentary on the 1969 Vienna convention on the law of treaties. Martinus Nijhoff Publishers, Leiden
Vohryzek-Griest A (2009) State counterclaims in investor-state disputes: a history of 30 years of failure. Revista Colombiana de Derecho Internacional 15:83–123
Vöneky S (2020) Die Stellung von Unternehmen in der Investitionsschiedsgerichtsbarkeit unter besonderer Berücksichtigung von Korruptionsproblemen: Unternehmen als völkerrechtlich gleichberechtigte Verfahrensparteien? In: Reinisch A, Hobe S, Kieninger EM, Peters A (eds) Unternehmensverantwortung und Internationales Recht. CF Müller, Heidelberg, pp 339–398
Voss JO (2011) The impact of investment treaties on contracts between host states and foreign investors. Martinus Nijhoff, Leiden
Waibel M (2015) Investment arbitration: jurisdiction and admissibility. In: Bungenberg M, Griebel J, Hobe S, Reinisch A (eds) International investment law: a handbook. CH Beck/Hart/Nomos, Baden-Baden, pp 1212–1287
Wälde TW (2010) Equality of arms in investment arbitration: procedural challenges. In: Yannaca-Small K (ed) Arbitration under international investment agreements: a guide to the key issues, 1st edn. Oxford University Press, Oxford, pp 161–188
Webster TH (2019) Handbook of UNCITRAL arbitration, 3rd edn. Sweet & Maxell, London
Yotova R (2017) Systematic integration: an instrument for reasserting the State's control in investment arbitration. In: Kulick A (ed) Reassertion of control over the investment treaty regime. Cambridge University Press, Cambridge, pp 182–208
Zin SM (2020) Reappraising access to justice in ISDS: a critical review on state recourse to counterclaim. In: Anderson AM, Beaumont B (eds) The investor-state dispute settlement system: reform, replace or status quo? Kluwer Law International, Alphen aan den Rijn, pp 225–246

Other Documents

History of the ICSID Convention, Vol I (ICSID Publication 1968)
History of the ICSID Convention, Vol II-1 (ICSID Publication 1968)
History of the ICSID Convention, Vol II-2 (ICSID Publication 1968)
ILA Committee on International Commercial Arbitration., 'Inherent and Implied Powers of International Arbitral Tribunals: Recommendations' (Resolution No 4/2016) <https://www.ila-hq.

org/images/ILA/docs/No.4_Resolution_2016_InternationalCommercialArbitration.pdf> Accessed 10 January 2023
ILC (13 April 2006) Report of the Study Group of the ILC on 'Fragmentation of International Law: Difficulties Arising from the Diversification and Expansion of International Law'. UN Doc A/CN.4/L.682.
ILC YB [1966] vol II, part II, A/CN.4/SER.A/1966/Add.1, 'Draft Articles on the Law of Treaties, with Commentaries' (177–274)
ILC YB [2006] vol II, pt II, A/CN.4/SER.A/2006/Add.l (Part 2), 'Fragmentation of International Law: Difficulties Arising from the Diversification and Expansion of International Law' (175–184)
Report of the Eighteenth Commission of the *Institut de Droit International* (Rapporteur Professor Campbell McLachlan) on the 'Equality of Parties before International Investment Tribunals' <https://www.idi-iil.org/app/uploads/2019/06/Commission-18-Equality-of-parties-before-international-investment-tribunals-McLachlan-Travaux-La-Haye-2019.pdf> Accessed 10 January 2023
Report of the Executive Directors on the ICSID Convention dated 18 March 1965
UNCITRAL (05 October 2006) Report of the Working Group on Arbitration and Conciliation on the work of its forty-fifth session. UN Doc A/CN.9/614
UNCITRAL (20 March 2007) Report of the Working Group on Arbitration and Conciliation on the work of its forty-sixth session. UN Doc A/CN.9/619
UNCITRAL (09 March 2009) Report of Working Group II (Arbitration and Conciliation) on the work of its fiftieth session. UN Doc A/CN.9/669
UNCITRAL (24 January 2019) Possible reform of investor-State dispute settlement (ISDS) Submission from the European Union and its Member States. UN Doc A/CN.9/WG.III/WP.159/Add.1
UNCITRAL (14 June 2019) Possible reform of investor-State dispute settlement (ISDS) Submission from the Government of Colombia. UN Doc A/CN.9/WG.III/WP.173
UNCITRAL (17 July 2019) Possible reform of investor-State dispute settlement (ISDS) Submission from the Government of Ecuador. UN Doc A/CN.9/WG.III/WP.175
UNCTAD (2012) World Investment Report 2012: Towards a New Generation of Investment Policies. UN Publication

Chapter 4
The Assessment of the Connection Requirement for Environmental Counterclaims

After finding jurisdiction to adjudge environmental counterclaims in investment arbitration, an arbitral tribunal must further assess the connection of the particular counterclaim with the main claim. Should the environmental counterclaim not be (closely) linked to the claimant's claim, the tribunal might refrain from adjudicating the said counterclaim's merits. Virtually all arbitral tribunals concur with counterclaims having to fulfil the connection requirement, but only a handful of them have dismissed counterclaims based exclusively on the lack of such connection.[1]

Accordingly, this Chapter analyses the requisite connection for counterclaims and its implications for the particular case of environmental counterclaims. With this purpose, the first section explores the justifications for the requirement of connection between the counterclaim and the main claim [Sect. 4.1]. The second section appertains to the proper characterisation of the requisite connection [Sect. 4.2]. The third section deals with the dilution of the connection requirement into various balancing factors and the implications for environmental counterclaims [Sect. 4.3]. Finally, the fourth section presents conclusions on the nature and application of the connection requirement, as well as its relevance for environmental counterclaims [Sect. 4.4].

[1] See *Saluka Investments BV v The Czech Republic*, UNCITRAL Case, Decision on Counterclaims (07 May 2004) para. 81; *Sergei Paushok, CJSC Golden East Company and CJSC Vostokneftegaz Company v The Government of Mongolia*, UNCITRAL Case, Jurisdiction and Liability (28 April 2011) paras. 694 et seqq.; *Fraport AG Frankfurt Airport Services Worldwide v Republic of The Philippines*, ICSID Case No ARB/11/12, Award (10 December 2014) para. 468; *Oxus Gold v Republic of Uzbekistan*, UNCITRAL Case, Award (17 December 2015) para. 956. Although in *obiter dictum*, the *Naturgy v Colombia* tribunal considered that given the lack of close connection, the counterclaims would nevertheless fail, see *Naturgy Energy Group SA and Naturgy Electricidad Colombia SL (formerly Gas Natural SDG SA and Gas Natural Fenosa Electricidad Colombia SL) v Republic of Colombia*, ICSID Case No UNCT/18/1, Award (12 March 2021) para. 623.

A. E. Alvarado-Garzón, *Environmental Counterclaims in Investment Arbitration*,
EYIEL Monographs - Studies in European and International Economic Law 34,
https://doi.org/10.1007/978-3-031-46391-4_4

4.1 Justifications for the Requisite Connection in Counterclaims: Beyond the Explicit Rules

An environmental counterclaim must indisputably fulfil the requirement of close connection with the main claim.[2] However, the rationale behind such requirement is often overlooked. From a comparative perspective, the connection requirement for counterclaims appears ubiquitous in different mechanisms of international dispute resolution. This is the case for the ICJ, since, according to the latest version of the Rules of Court and the Court's jurisprudence, a counterclaim must be directly connected with the subject-matter of the main claim.[3] Similarly, the ITLOS Rules of Procedure require the counterclaim to be directly connected with the subject-matter of the main claim.[4]

In the framework of the IUSCT, both the Claims Settlement Declaration and the tribunals constituted thereunder recognise the requisite connection as fundamental for the submission of counterclaims.[5] Although in the context of international commercial arbitration the connection requirement may not be explicitly foreseen, arbitral tribunals may nevertheless demand a close link between the counterclaim and the main claim.[6] Therefore, this section explores whether there is an explicit rule on connection for counterclaims under different instruments used for investment arbitration [Sect. 4.1.1]. Second, this section posits that even in the absence of such an explicit rule, arbitral tribunals must always assess the requisite connection as an inherent element of counterclaims [Sect. 4.1.2].

4.1.1 Finding Commonalities in Different Instruments

Neither investment contracts nor IIAs delve into procedural details such as the requirements for submitting counterclaims. There might be explicit restrictions on which kind of counterclaims are permitted.[7] However, from the IIAs surveyed in this book, only a few explicitly mention the connection requirement of counterclaims.[8] The requisite connection nevertheless appears in three instruments related to investment arbitration namely: in the ICSID Framework [Sect. 4.1.1.1]; in the UNCITRAL Arbitration Rules [Sect. 4.1.1.2]; and in the Resolution on the 'Equality of Parties

[2] Shao (2021), p. 168.

[3] *See* Sect. 2.1.1.

[4] *See* Sect. 2.1.4.2.

[5] *See* Sect. 2.1.2.4.

[6] *See* Sect. 2.1.3.2.

[7] *See* Sect. 3.3.3.2.2.1.

[8] *See* for instance: Slovak-UAE BIT (2016), Art 17(3); Argentina-UAE BIT (2018), Art 28(4).

before International Investment Tribunals' of the 18th Commission of the *Institut de Droit International* [Sect. 4.1.1.3].

4.1.1.1 ICSID Framework

Article 46 ICSID Convention and Rule 40 ICSID Arbitration Rules (2006) (or Rule 48 ICSID Arbitration Rules (2022)) set forth that the counterclaim must arise '*directly out of the subject-matter of the dispute*'. This formulation resembles the requirements of the Centre's jurisdiction in Article 25 ICSID Convention, whereby the legal dispute must arise '*directly out of an investment*'. In order to differentiate between both requirements, Christoph Schreuer points out that a counterclaim may arise out of an investment (pursuant to Article 25 ICSID Convention) without arising out of the subject-matter of the dispute (pursuant to Article 46 ICSID Convention), for instance, when the counterclaim pertains to a different investment operation between the same parties.[9] Thus, the tribunal ought to first ascertain whether it has jurisdiction over the counterclaim, and only afterwards, it would determine whether the counterclaim is connected to the main claim.[10]

However, the line between '*arising out of an investment*' and '*arising out of the subject-matter of the dispute*' might get blurred in practice.[11] This might explain the possible overlap between Article 25 and 46 ICSID Convention in this regard.[12] Be that as it may, the requisite connection has been modestly developed by several arbitral tribunals in investment arbitration and its content will be elaborated upon below.

4.1.1.2 UNCITRAL Arbitration Rules

The UNCITRAL Arbitration Rules present an evolution in their requirements shifting the focus from the requisite connection to the requisite consent. As mentioned above, Article 19(3) UNCITRAL Arbitration Rules (1976) foresaw that counterclaims ought to arise '*out of the same contract*'.[13] This requirement might be at odds with treaty-based investment arbitration, since a dispute need not arise from a contractual relation, or it may even involve a myriad of contracts concluded by different (but related) legal entities.

In this context, the *Saluka v Czech Republic* tribunal sought to interpret the requirement of '*out of the same contract*' in Article 19(3) UNCITRAL Arbitration Rules (1976) for the purposes of treaty-based investment arbitration. The tribunal

[9] Schreuer et al. (2009), Art 46, mn. 73.

[10] Schreuer et al. (2009), Art 46, mn. 74.

[11] Clodfelter and Tsutieva (2018), para. 17.27.

[12] *See* Sect. 3.3.1.3.4.

[13] *See* Sect. 3.1.3.2.

undertook the assessment of other awards rendered under the ICSID Convention and the IUSCT Claims Settlement Declaration[14] and concluded that such requirement expressed the 'general legal principle' that a counterclaim ought to be closely connected with the main claim.[15] The *Paushok v Mongolia* tribunal followed this reasoning.[16] Although these decisions might have finally exaggerated the content of the 'close connection' requirement thereby dismissing the respective counterclaims in both cases,[17] they certainly revealed a point of discussion for the later UNCITRAL Working Group II entrusted with the revision of the said rules.

Whereas the *Saluka* and *Paushok* interpretation of Article 19(3) UNCITRAL Arbitration Rules (1976) seems to align with the provisions in the ICSID framework *ie* denoting a connection with the main claim, there are some authors suggesting a broader interpretation. Particularly, instead of referring to the main claim, they recommend that the requisite '*out of the same contract*' in Article 19(3) UNCITRAL Arbitration Rules (1976) should be read as '*out of the same investment*' for the purposes of treaty-based investment arbitration.[18] Nevertheless, as with the ICSID framework, the differentiation between 'out of the same investment' and 'out of the main claim' may not be evident in practice. Thus, the crux of the matter lies in the actual assessment of connection, the factors involved, and the impact on the viability of counterclaims in investment arbitration.

Mindful of the challenges Article 19(3) UNCITRAL Arbitration Rules (1976) posed on counterclaims in treaty-based investment arbitration,[19] the UNCITRAL Working Group II opted to introduce the single requirement of '*provided that the arbitral tribunal has jurisdiction over it*' in the newly adopted Article 21-(3) UNCITRAL Arbitration Rules (2013). One could argue that these rules no longer

[14] *Saluka Investments BV v The Czech Republic*, UNCITRAL Case, Decision on Counterclaims (07 May 2004) paras. 65 et seqq.

[15] *Saluka Investments BV v The Czech Republic*, UNCITRAL Case, Decision on Counterclaims (07 May 2004) para. 76.

[16] *Sergei Paushok, CJSC Golden East Company and CJSC Vostokneftegaz Company v The Government of Mongolia*, UNCITRAL Case, Jurisdiction and Liability (28 April 2011) paras. 688–693.

[17] *See* Sect. 4.3.3.

[18] Douglas (2009), para. 494: ('It is therefore preferable to interpret the reference to "contract" in Article 19(3) of the UNCITRAL Rules as a reference to the source of the rights forming the object of the claim. In the investment treaty context, that is the investment, and hence a symmetry between the tribunal's jurisdiction over primary claims and counterclaims is achieved by interpreting the reference to "contract" in Article 19(3) as equivalent to "investment" in this context'); Clodfelter and Tsutieva (2018), paras. 17.82: ('. . .While investment per se is not the source of the rights (the treaty is), replacing the "contract" with "investment" would most effectively modify the rules for investment arbitration, consistent with the object of most dispute settlement provisions, that is, to resolve investment disputes').

[19] UNCITRAL, Report of the Working Group on Arbitration and Conciliation on the work of its forty-fifth session (05 October 2006) UN Doc A/CN.9/614, paras. 93–96.

require connection between the counterclaim and the main claim.[20] However, ignoring the requirement of connection might be irreconcilable with counterclaims' purpose.[21]

As a result, while the UNCITRAL Arbitration Rules (2013) have omitted the requirement of connection for counterclaims, tribunals might be arguably inclined to consider whether the particular counterclaim fulfils such requirement as a general rule nonetheless.[22] Such analysis would vary greatly among different tribunals as it would be strictly case-by-case based.[23]

4.1.1.3 Resolution on the 'Equality of Parties Before International Investment Tribunals' of the 18th Commission of the Institut de Droit International

The 18th Commission of the *Institut de Droit International* acknowledged that the principle of equality of parties demanded a close connection between the counterclaim and the main claim.[24] Accordingly, Article 6 Resolution on the 'Equality of Parties before International Investment Tribunals' of the 18th Commission of the *Institut de Droit International* proposes as one requirement of admissibility that a counterclaim must '*arise directly out of the subject-matter of the investment*'.[25] Perhaps with the aim of defining this requirement, the same provision further streamlines two important clarifications: *first*, the requisite connection is fulfilled when the counterclaim concerns the same investment giving rise to the main claim [Sect. 4.1.1.3.1]. *Second*, this requirement does not necessitate 'legal' connection [Sect. 4.1.1.3.2].

[20] Anning (2021), p. 1308. In the same sense, arguing that in the absence of an explicit mention in the arbitration rules, the tribunal should not burden the respondent with the connection requirement *see* Kendra (2013), p. 582.

[21] On this *see* Sect. 4.1.2.

[22] Clodfelter and Tsutieva (2018), para. 17.92; Marisi (2020), p. 246.

[23] Atanasova et al. (2014), p. 364. Similarly, Report of the Eighteenth Commission of the *Institut de Droit International* (Rapporteur Professor Campbell McLachlan) on the 'Equality of Parties before International Investment Tribunals' para. 192 <https://www.idi-iil.org/app/uploads/2019/06/Commission-18-Equality-of-parties-before-international-investment-tribunals-McLachlan-Travaux-La-Haye-2019.pdf> accessed 10 January 2023.

[24] Report of the Eighteenth Commission of the *Institut de Droit International* (Rapporteur Professor Campbell McLachlan) on the 'Equality of Parties before International Investment Tribunals' paras. 187 and 202 <https://www.idi-iil.org/app/uploads/2019/06/Commission-18-Equality-of-parties-before-international-investment-tribunals-McLachlan-Travaux-La-Haye-2019.pdf> accessed 10 January 2023.

[25] *See* this book "Annex 4: *Article 6 of the Resolution on the 'Equality of Parties before International Investment Tribunals of the 18th Commission of the Institut de Droit International*".

4.1.1.3.1 Connection When the Counterclaim Concerns the Same Investment

Neither an investment treaty, an arbitration rule, nor an arbitral tribunal has referred to '*arise directly out of the subject-matter of the investment*' as a requirement for counterclaims. One may thus argue that the 18th Commission borrowed from the ICSID Convention the concepts of '*arising out of an investment*' (Article 25) and '*arising out of the subject-matter of the dispute*' (Article 46) but blurred their distinction.[26] Although such argument seems tenable, it appears that the 18th Commission's intention was, from the outset, to link the connection requirement to the underlying investment. Indeed, Article 6(5) Resolution on the 'Equality of Parties before International Investment Tribunals' of the 18th Commission of the *Institut de Droit International* explicitly states that the requirement of connection is fulfilled when the counterclaim concerns the same investment giving rise to the main claim.

In contrast with the ICSID framework, the Resolution on the 'Equality of Parties before International Investment Tribunals' of the 18th Commission of the *Institut de Droit International* detaches itself from a seemingly narrower construction of '*subject-matter of the dispute*' and establishes an apparently more objective point of reference *ie* the same investment. Such effort is commendable for proposing a clearer threshold with respect to the connection requirement.

4.1.1.3.2 'Legal' Connection Is Not Indispensable

The Resolution on the 'Equality of Parties before International Investment Tribunals' of the 18th Commission of the *Institut de Droit International* brings about a second clarification with respect to the connection requirement, specifically, pertaining to the so called 'legal' connection. Pursuant to Article 6(5) thereof, it is not necessary that '*the counterclaim be founded upon the same legal instrument or cause of action asserted by the claimant*'. Although the dichotomy between legal and factual connection has certainly evolved,[27] the clarification represents a milestone in the understanding of counterclaims in investment arbitration, whereby the legal basis of counterclaims should not be a sole obstacle for their viability.

---

[26] Steingruber (2020), pp. 626–627.

[27] *See* Sect. 4.3.3.1.

4.1.2 *Connection as an Inherent Requirement for Counterclaims*

Unlike the instruments discussed in the section above, all other arbitration rules used for the settlement of investment disputes do not contain a connection requirement. For instance, neither Article 5(5) ICC Arbitration Rules[28] nor Article 9(1) SCC Arbitration Rules[29] mentions that a counterclaim must be connected to the main claim. In this context, one may question whether a counterclaim formulated under these arbitration rules must comply with the requisite connection.[30]

Considering that arbitration is based on the parties' consent, choosing a set of rules that ignores the requirement of connection for counterclaims could be seen as a manifestation of the will of the parties. Thus, it could be argued that if the arbitration rules do not impose a connection requirement for counterclaims, the tribunal should not impose such requirement by its own motion, unless the said requirement is deemed an inherent element of counterclaims.[31] The latter seems to be the position of the *Saluka v Czech Republic* tribunal, which after assessing the instrument of counterclaims in other frameworks[32] concluded that the condition, according to which a counterclaim ought to be closely connected with the main claim, reflected

[28] ICC Arbitration Rules (2021), Art 5(5): ('. . . Any counterclaims made by the respondent shall be submitted with the Answer and shall provide: a) a description of the nature and circumstances of the dispute giving rise to the counterclaims and of the basis upon which the counterclaims are made; b) a statement of the relief sought together with the amounts of any quantified counterclaims and, to the extent possible, an estimate of the monetary value of any other counterclaims; c) any relevant agreements and, in particular, the arbitration agreement(s); and d) where counterclaims are made under more than one arbitration agreement, an indication of the arbitration agreement under which each counterclaim is made. The respondent may submit such other documents or information with the counterclaims as it considers appropriate or as may contribute to the efficient resolution of the dispute').

[29] SCC Arbitration Rules (2017), Art 9(1): ('The Secretariat shall send a copy of the Request for Arbitration and any attached documents to the Respondent. The Secretariat shall set a time period within which the Respondent shall submit an Answer to the SCC. The Answer shall include: . . . (iii) a preliminary statement of any counterclaims or setoffs, including an estimate of the monetary value thereof; (iv) where counterclaims or set-offs are made under more than one arbitration agreement, an indication of the arbitration agreement under which each counterclaim or set-off is made').

[30] For instance, given the absence of a connection requirement for ancillary claims in the ICSID Additional Facility Rules, Henri Alvarez speculates whether such rules provide a broader scope for counterclaims *see* Alvarez (2000), p. 412. Similarly, Laura Rees-Evans posits that if neither the treaty provisions nor arbitration rules foresee the connection requirement, an investor could theoretically circumvent such requirement *see* Rees-Evans (2020), pp. 378 et seqq.

[31] de Nanteuil (2018), p. 386: ('if the parties refer to arbitration rules that do not introduce the connection requirement for counterclaims, it is not certain that such a requirement could be imposed by the tribunal. The only possibility to re-introduce it would be to consider that it is inherent to counterclaims and that there is no need to formally state it to make it applicable').

[32] *Saluka Investments BV v The Czech Republic*, UNCITRAL Case, Decision on Counterclaims (07 May 2004) paras. 65 et seqq.

a '*general legal principle*'.[33] In the same vein, the *Amto v Ukraine* tribunal considered in *obiter dictum* that the admission of a counterclaim hinges upon, among other requirements, the relationship with the main claim,[34] despite the fact that the underlying SCC Arbitration Rules did not provide for the requisite connection.

The requirement of connection for counterclaims is deeply rooted in the purpose of such a procedural mechanism. Counterclaims strive to provide procedural or judicial economy in a particular dispute settlement mechanism,[35] and the connection requirement epitomises such objective.[36] The idea of a close link between the claim and the counterclaim is to create a procedural synergy for a more efficient resolution of both claims in a single proceeding. Although not explicitly, the same considerations permeate all procedural rules which contemplate the procedural mechanism of counterclaims.[37] Arbitral tribunals must therefore assess the connection requirement irrespective of the existence of a treaty provision or an arbitration rule in that regard,[38] particularly because such requisite is inherent to the underlying purpose of counterclaims.

4.2 The Characterisation of the Connection Requirement: An Unsettled Debate

The proper characterisation of the connection requirement begets an inexorable debate: while the majority of tribunals seem to hold this requirement as a jurisdictional matter, most authors seem prompt to categorise it as an admissibility issue. In this vein, this section seeks to puzzle out the relevance of the jurisdiction/admissibility distinction in investment arbitration [Sect. 4.2.1], and explores the appropriate classification for the requisite connection in counterclaims as a non-jurisdictional requirement [Sect. 4.2.2].

[33] *Saluka Investments BV v The Czech Republic*, UNCITRAL Case, Decision on Counterclaims (07 May 2004) para. 76.

[34] *Limited Liability Company Amto v Ukraine*, SCC Case No 080/2005, Award (26 March 2008) para. 118.

[35] For the full discussion on the rationale behind counterclaims, *see* Sect. 2.2.2.

[36] Kjos (2007), p. 621; Marisi (2020), p. 245.

[37] Renteln (1987), p. 390.

[38] For a different opinion, considering that tribunals, vested with jurisdiction to adjudicate counterclaims, should be reluctant to dismiss a counterclaim that failed the connection requirement *see* Anning (2021), p. 1313. Such proposition might nevertheless have a deleterious effect since there might be situations in which a tribunal should decline the exercise of properly vested jurisdiction, which is precisely what the connection requirement seeks to preserve.

4.2.1 *Jurisdiction and Admissibility in Investment Arbitration: A Square Peg in a Round Hole?*

The concepts of 'jurisdiction' and 'admissibility' are certainly well entrenched in domestic procedural laws and in the practice of the ICJ, however, their applicability in investment arbitration is at least subject to contentions.[39] The differentiation between these two concepts is not only absent in IIAs and procedural arbitration rules used for investment arbitration,[40] but also their malleable content creates a 'twilight zone' between them.[41] Accordingly, this section streamlines the reasons motivating the importation of the jurisdiction/admissibility distinction [Sect. 4.2.1.1], and the challenges of using such distinction in investment arbitration [Sect. 4.2.1.2].

4.2.1.1 Reasons for Introducing the Distinction Between Jurisdiction and Admissibility

The discourse at the ICJ may elucidate the juxtaposition of jurisdiction and admissibility. Here, a plea of lack of jurisdiction prevents the Court from rendering any decision at all, whereas a plea of inadmissibility aims at the dismissal of the claim on a ground different than its merits.[42] In other words, jurisdiction rests on the requirement of consent and admissibility lies in other requirements for the submission of a claim that stem either from general rules of public international law or specific agreements between the parties.[43] The Court has reaffirmed this distinction in decisions such as *Oil Platforms*[44] and *Certain Questions of Mutual Assistance*.[45]

The ICJ has certainly a statutory basis for this distinction since, for instance, Article 79 of the Rules of Court[46] expressly mentions the concepts of jurisdiction and admissibility in the context of preliminary objections. Yet, neither the Rules of

---

[39] Pauker and Winston (2021), p. 189; Scherer et al. (2021), p. 424.

[40] Gouiffès and Ordonez (2015), p. 111.

[41] The first description of jurisdiction and admissibility in investment arbitration as constituting a twilight zone was coined by Jan Paulsson *see* Paulsson (2005), pp. 608 et seqq.

[42] Fitzmaurice (1986), pp. 438–439.

[43] Tomuschat (2012), para. 119.

[44] *Oil Platforms (Iran v United States of America)* (Merits) [2003] ICJ Rep 161, para. 29.

[45] *Certain Questions of Mutual Assistance in Criminal Matters (Djibouti v France)* (Judgment) [2008] ICJ Rep 177, para. 48.

[46] ICJ Rules of Court, Art 79: ('1. Following the submission of the application and after the President has met and consulted with the parties, the Court may decide, if the circumstances so warrant, that questions concerning its jurisdiction or the admissibility of the application shall be determined separately. 2. Where the Court so decides, the parties shall submit pleadings concerning jurisdiction or admissibility within the time-limits fixed, and in the order determined, by the Court. Each pleading shall contain the party's observations and submissions, including any evidence on which it relies, and shall attach copies of supporting documents').

Court, the Statute of the ICJ nor any other instrument offers a definition for those concepts, which might guide their interpretation. The Court holds admissibility as a safeguard to its judicial function,[47] or for avoiding an undue prejudice on a disputing party.[48] This in theory could help to differentiate between jurisdictional and admissibility concerns, though in practice, the borderline becomes blurred.[49]

Unlike the ICJ, investment treaties, arbitration rules, and other pertinent instruments for investment arbitration fail to mention the jurisdiction/admissibility divide. Nevertheless, this has not prevented the two concepts from pervading the jargon and deliberations of investment tribunals and scholars. Some suggest that while jurisdiction concerns the authority of a tribunal to adjudicate, admissibility pertains to the tribunal's power to decline the adjudication of the case despite having the authority to rule upon it.[50] Accordingly, an objection to jurisdiction questions the adjudicator's power to decide.[51] Whereas an objection to admissibility confronts the suitability of a particular case for adjudication on the merits,[52] either for temporary or permanent defects of the claim.[53]

In this context, Jan Paulsson has proposed as a 'lodestar' for the differentiation between jurisdiction and admissibility the following question: '*is the objecting party taking aim at the tribunal or at the claim?*'[54] If the objection aims at challenging the tribunal's power to adjudicate, it is a jurisdictional objection, whereas if the objection aims at the suitability of the claim to be adjudged, it is an objection on admissibility.[55] Some authors prefer to frame the distinction in the following terms: all conditions agreed upon by the parties are jurisdictional, once fulfilled, they vest the tribunal with the power to adjudicate; conversely, questions of admissibility entail an exercise of discretion for refusing to adjudicate.[56] Yet, the question remains: is there a legal basis upon which a tribunal might refuse to exercise properly vested jurisdiction? Three scenarios could be conceived: when there is an explicit/implicit rule granting discretion in this regard; when there is an inherent power; or when a rule of public international law demands it.[57]

In arbitral practice, Keith Highet in his dissenting opinion to the *Waste Management v Mexico* case is hallmarked as the first arbitrator expounding the

[47] *Case concerning the Northern Cameroons (Cameroon v United Kingdom)* (Preliminary Objections) [1963] ICJ Rep 15, 38.

[48] Certain Phosphate Lands in Nauru (Nauru v Australia) (Preliminary Objections) Judgment of 26 June 1992, ICJ Reports 1992, p 240, para. 35.

[49] Tomuschat (2012), para. 120.

[50] Shany (2014), p. 796.

[51] Williams (2008), p. 919.

[52] Douglas (2009), para. 310.

[53] Waibel (2015), p. 1213.

[54] Paulsson (2005), p. 616.

[55] Paulsson (2005), p. 617.

[56] Shany (2014), p. 787; Fontanelli (2018), p. 124.

[57] Shany (2014), p. 796.

differentiation in the following terms: '[j]*urisdiction is the power of the tribunal to hear the case; admissibility is whether the case itself is defective—whether it is appropriate for the tribunal to hear it.*'[58] The distinction between jurisdiction and admissibility seems to have gained traction in other tribunals, such as in *Hochtief v Argentina* and the seminal *Abaclat v Argentina*. Whilst in the former, the tribunal drew the distinction in terms of attributes (jurisdiction is an attribute of the tribunal and admissibility is an attribute of the claim),[59] the latter tribunal considered that lack of jurisdiction and inadmissibility bring about different consequences with regards to the defect, the reviewability of the decision, and the possibility of resubmission.[60]

Consequently, the jurisdiction/admissibility divide in investment arbitration has led some authors to propose far reaching consequences for the disputing parties when classifying certain objections as to the tribunal's jurisdiction or the claim's admissibility.[61] Nevertheless, there are two points worth expanding upon in this regard: the reviewability of decisions, and the tribunal's discretion on admissibility decisions. With respect to reviewability, it is argued that a decision on jurisdiction can be challenged before a reviewing authority (*ad hoc* annulment committee in ICSID Arbitration; court at the seat of arbitration; court at the place of enforcement), whereas a decision on admissibility is final and not subject to review.[62] Yet, the tribunal's classification on jurisdictional/admissibility objections does not curtail the

[58] *Waste Management Inc v United Mexican States*, ICSID Case No ARB(AF)/98/2, Dissenting Opinion of Keith Highet (08 May 2000) para. 58.

[59] *Hochtief AG v The Argentine Republic*, ICSID Case No ARB/07/31, Decision on Jurisdiction (24 October 2011) para. 90: ('Jurisdiction is an attribute of a tribunal and not of a claim, whereas admissibility is an attribute of a claim but not of a tribunal. A distinction may also be drawn between questions of admissibility and questions of receivability. A tribunal might decide that a claim of which it is seised and which is within its jurisdiction is inadmissible (for example, on the ground of lis alibi pendens or forum non conveniens); or it might refuse even to receive and become seised of a claim that is within its jurisdiction because of some fundamental defect in the manner in which the claim is put forward').

[60] *Abaclat and Others v Argentine Republic*, ICSID Case No ARB/07/5, Decision on Jurisdiction and Admissibility (04 August 2011) para. 247: ('Although a lack of jurisdiction or admissibility may both lead to the same result of a tribunal having to refuse to hear the case, such refusal is of a fundamentally different nature and therefore carries different consequences: (i) While a lack of jurisdiction *stricto sensu* means that the claim cannot at all be brought in front of the body called upon, a lack of admissibility means that the claim was neither fit nor mature for judicial treatment; (ii) Whereby a decision refusing a case based on a lack of arbitral jurisdiction is usually subject to review by another body, a decision refusing a case based on a lack of admissibility can usually not be subject to review by another body; (iii) Whereby a final refusal based on a lack of jurisdiction will prevent the parties from successfully re-submitting the same claim to the same body, a refusal based on admissibility will, in principle, not prevent the claimant from resubmitting its claim, provided it cures the previous flaw causing the inadmissibility').

[61] For instance, Michael Waibel identifies seven consequences of the distinction between jurisdiction and admissibility, including, whether new developments after the date of the request for arbitration may be taken into account, whether objections may be waived, whether the tribunal can analyse objections *proprio motu*, among others *see* Waibel (2015), pp. 1274 et seqq.

[62] Paulsson (2005), p. 601; Douglas (2009), para. 307; Gouiffès and Ordonez (2015), p. 108.

reviewing authority's power to reclassify the objections as it deems appropriate and correspondingly to revise otherwise mislabelled jurisdictional decisions.[63]

Some authors considered that in the ICSID framework the reviewability of decisions in terms of jurisdiction does not mark any difference since annulment lies in the gravity of the mistake rather than on the classification of such mistake.[64] In this sense, admissibility decisions would still be reviewable if the tribunal has mistakenly exercised its jurisdiction with respect to the admissibility issue, for instance, by failing to state reasons or departing from a fundamental rule of procedure. Conversely, in non-ICSID proceedings, admissibility decisions may not fall within the scope of review in domestic laws or under the grounds for refusal of enforcement pursuant to Article V New York Convention.[65] Here, a distinction between jurisdiction and admissibility requirements might in fact affect reviewability of the decision.

With respect to the tribunal's discretion on admissibility decisions, it is posited that an international adjudicator enjoys certain flexibility when rendering a ruling on admissibility since the tribunal would refrain from exercising its properly vested jurisdictional powers.[66] Besides serving as case filter, admissibility matters may operate as a policy tool, which balances the adjudicator's legal powers, the institutional interests of the dispute settlement mechanism and other prevailing concerns.[67] This explains that admissibility decisions, as with procedural decisions, are rooted in principles such as procedural fairness and efficiency,[68] in contrast to jurisdictional decisions centred at the scope of parties' consent.

4.2.1.2 Challenges to the Jurisdiction/Admissibility Divide: Beyond the 'Admissibility' Label

The utilisation of the distinction between jurisdiction and admissibility in investment arbitration has nevertheless found some resistance. Some investment tribunals have even questioned the usefulness of such distinction.[69] Some authors argue that admissibility is a 'chameleonic' concept, which may have a different meaning

[63] Waibel (2015), p. 1277; Fontanelli (2018), p. 126.

[64] Reinisch (2017), p. 25; Fontanelli (2018), p. 164.

[65] Fontanelli (2018), pp. 164 et seqq.

[66] Shany (2014), p. 800; Waibel (2015), p. 1219.

[67] Shany (2014), p. 780.

[68] Hwang and Lim (2018), p. 267.

[69] See for instance: *CMS Gas Transmission Company v The Republic of Argentina*, ICSID Case No ARB/01/8, Decision on Jurisdiction (17 July 2003) para. 41; *Enron Corporation and Ponderosa Assets LP v Argentine Republic*, ICSID Case No ARB/01/3, Decision on Jurisdiction (14 January 2004) para. 33; *Urbaser SA and Consorcio de Aguas Bilbao Bizkaia, Bilbao Biskaia Ur Partzuergoa v The Argentine Republic*, ICSID Case No ARB/07/26, Decision on Jurisdiction (19 December 2012) paras. 112 et seqq.

under similar situations,[70] and which confers a degree of discretion upon arbitral tribunals affecting the consistency of the investor-state dispute settlement system.[71] Even if there might be some reasons according to which a tribunal vested with jurisdiction should refuse to hear a claim (inadmissibility), there is no clarity on how to identify those conditions or requirements that might render a claim inadmissible, which in turn affects the predictability of investment arbitration.[72] Some others argue that the distinction is normatively useless or inessential since not only there are requirements passing (rebranded) equally as jurisdiction or admissibility issues,[73] but also given the difficulties drawing a line between the two concepts.[74]

Those concerns evince some of the underlying problems with dividing objections into jurisdiction and admissibility. Hence, it is necessary to explore the major flaws of the jurisdiction/admissibility divide. *First*, one of the reasons of the 'twilight zone' between jurisdiction and admissibility lies in the disagreement among tribunals about the proper categorisation of some matters.[75] For instance, tribunals in *Lauder v Czech Republic*, *SGS v Pakistan*, and *Bayindir v Pakistan* have deemed the requirement of engaging in consultations with the host state before submitting to arbitration as a procedural (admissibility) rule,[76] whereas tribunals in *Impregilo v Argentina* and *Daimler v Argentina* regarded the same requirement as pertaining to a tribunal's jurisdiction.[77] This brings about a common occurrence for the disputing parties, who find plenty support in case law and literature: the claimant would argue that any missing requirement for submitting a claim pertains to admissibility and can be consequently obviated, and the respondent would contend that such missing requirement has a jurisdictional character and must consequently bar the claim.[78]

Accordingly, some detractors of the jurisdiction/admissibility divide argue that most of the issues typically framed as admissibility objections may be reshuffled into either jurisdictional aspects or merits. In the majority of cases, a tribunal should assess objections pertaining to, for instance, cooling off periods, denial of benefits, or exhaustion of local remedies as jurisdictional issues, and only in limited cases, such as objections concerning reflective losses or absence of damages, the tribunal

---

[70] Hwang and Lim (2018), p. 265.

[71] Söderlund and Burova (2018), p. 559.

[72] Reinisch (2017), pp. 41–43.

[73] Fontanelli (2018), p. 123.

[74] Gouiffès and Ordonez (2015), p. 117.

[75] Waibel (2015), p. 1274.

[76] *Ronald S Lauder v The Czech Republic*, UNCITRAL Case, Final Award (03 September 2001) paras. 187 et seqq; *SGS Société Générale de Surveillance SA v Islamic Republic of Pakistan*, ICSID Case No ARB/01/13, Decision on Jurisdiction (06 August 2003) para. 184; *Bayindir Insaat Turizm Ticaret Ve Sanayi AS v Islamic Republic of Pakistan*, ICSID Case No ARB/03/29, Decision on Jurisdiction (14 November 2005) para. 100.

[77] *Impregilo SpA v Argentine Republic*, ICSID Case No ARB/07/17, Award (21 June 2011) paras. 79 et seqq; *Daimler Financial Services AG v Argentine Republic*, ICSID Case No ARB/05/1, Award (22 August 2012) paras. 192 et seqq.

[78] Fontanelli (2018), p. 171.

would decide on the merits stage.[79] Even if the tribunal decides those latter objections at an earlier stage, the decision would be '*properly speaking a decision on the merits of the case, which the tribunal exercised its case management discretion to hear at a preliminary stage*'.[80]

Second, resorting to the concepts of jurisdiction and admissibility, their discourse and application by the ICJ might not be appropriate in investment arbitration. If considered from the perspective of reviewability of decisions, certainly the ICJ does not provide a fitting example since there is no reviewing authority to the Court's decisions in contrast to the possibility of challenging arbitral awards before *ad hoc* annulment committees or domestic courts.[81] Furthermore, and perhaps more importantly, the permanency of the ICJ compared with the *ad hoc* nature of arbitral tribunals is a differentiating factor that cannot be ignored. Once the arbitral tribunal has declined to decide a case, it becomes *functus officio* and will cease to exist, regardless whether its decision is grounded on lack of jurisdiction or inadmissibility of the claim.[82] Thus, in arbitration, the resubmission of a claim, which previously was not ripe for adjudication (admissibility), would have to undergo once again the process of constitution of the tribunal, and likely different arbitrators as the ones previously dismissing the case.

Such concern is nevertheless surmountable in some cases. Arbitral tribunals may avail themselves of their powers on case management to avoid an outright dismissal of a claim, whose only missing requirement could be subsequently complied with. For example, in case of uncompleted waiting periods, it is suggested a staying of proceedings or suspension until such requirement is met, unless the underlying IIA provides otherwise.[83] By this means, the tribunal does not bypass or 'downgrade' jurisdictional requirements by labelling them as admissibility issues, nor does it become *functus officio* preventing it from entertaining the case after the requirement is fulfilled.[84] Certainly, a staying of proceedings would be unsuitable for other requirements such as the nationality of the investor, but it is arguably an efficient solution for 'curable' unmet requirements to avoid an unnecessary resubmission and reconstitution of the tribunal.[85]

Third, Jan Paulsson's lodestar of dividing objections aimed at the tribunal (jurisdiction) and at the claim (admissibility) might be insufficient in practice. Arguably, there is no clear guidance on how to identify each objection, which

[79] Söderlund and Burova (2018), p. 556.

[80] Hwang and Lim (2018), p. 268.

[81] Paulsson (2005), pp. 603–604.

[82] Söderlund and Burova (2018), p. 528; Fontanelli (2018), p. 11.

[83] Pauker and Winston (2021), pp. 198–199.

[84] Pauker and Winston (2021), pp. 199–201.

[85] Pauker and Winston (2021), pp. 201–205. For a different opinion, considering that the discretion to halt proceedings is not given for objections to the tribunal's jurisdiction *see* Hwang and Lim (2018), p. 267. In this author's view, the possibility of staying proceedings responds to the inherent powers of an adjudicator on case management in order to preserve the integrity of the proceedings, which has nothing to do with a jurisdiction/admissibility divide.

renders the division ambiguous at best.[86] Some authors propose instead to assess whether the objection targets the consent of the parties as expressed in the jurisdictional title.[87] Otherwise, it is feasible that Jan Paulsson's test could potentially produce conflicting results, for instance, by interpreting whether a waiting period pertains to the tribunal's jurisdiction or admissibility.[88]

Fourth, and perhaps more critically, the distinction on jurisdiction and admissibility in investment arbitration may impinge on the parties' consent. According to Christer Söderlund and Elena Burova, this distinction entails a pernicious effect by giving '*leeway for tribunals to apply a measure of discretion to issues which are in fact jurisdictional or to stop at something which is less than dispositive of the particular issue*'.[89] Consequently, a tribunal would enjoy discretion to ignore parties' consent as expressed in the dispute settlement clauses in total disregard of the ordinary meaning of the treaty provisions.[90]

Understandably, either through a successful objection to jurisdiction or to admissibility, the practical result is the same, '*which is that the tribunal withholds itself from examining the merits of the claim*'.[91] One may thus argue that, although there is no restriction on labelling some procedural issues as admissibility, the ultimate finding should be framed as a jurisdictional decision, whereby the tribunal decides to exercise its adjudicative power or not.[92] Yet, the rationale behind a category of 'admissibility decisions' might be worth preserving. Essentially, as the *ad hoc* annulment committee in *Orascom v Algeria* recently stated: '[e]*ven when the consent has been granted, there may be situations in which it would be inappropriate for an international court or tribunal to exercise its jurisdiction*'.[93]

Admissibility decisions reflect an ideal of judicial propriety. In other words, aiming at preserving the legitimacy of the proceedings, the rule of law, or even the effectiveness of the decisions rendered.[94] For instance, tribunals should decline to adjudicate a case submitted through abusive tactics such as multiplication of claims or nationality shopping. This has a sanctioning effect to some dubious claims and it might deter future claimants from engaging in similar practices.[95] These are '*genuine admissibility issues*' because they '*touch upon the integrity of investment treaty arbitration as a dispute resolution system, being a considerable factor to be taken*

---

[86] Hwang and Lim (2018), p. 277.

[87] Hwang and Lim (2018), p. 278.

[88] Velarde Saffer and Lim (2014), pp. 90–91.

[89] Söderlund and Burova (2018), p. 527.

[90] Söderlund and Burova (2018), p. 538.

[91] Hwang and Lim (2018), p. 266.

[92] Söderlund and Burova (2018), pp. 556–557.

[93] *Orascom TMT Investments Sàrl v People's Democratic Republic of Algeria*, ICSID Case No ARB/12/35, Decision on Annulment (17 September 2020) para. 256.

[94] Shany (2014), p. 801.

[95] Fontanelli (2018), p. 98.

into account when a tribunal considers whether to exercise its existing jurisdiction'.[96]

Therefore, admissibility decisions encompass considerations of procedural fairness and efficiency, which pervade a variety of procedural decisions.[97] In this vein, one may wonder if it is necessary to carve out some procedural decisions and to label them as admissibility issues. Some authors doubt there is anything to gain from the classification of certain procedural decisions as admissibility.[98] However, irrespective of the classification as admissibility or simply as procedural decisions, preserving the legitimacy of the proceedings and the rule of law, or promoting procedural fairness are sufficient reasons to decline properly vested jurisdiction.

4.2.2 *The Connection Requirement for Counterclaims as a Non-Jurisdictional Requirement: Entering Into the Tribunal's Discretion*

The distinction between admissibility and jurisdiction remains a tug of war, which has permeated the discourse on the requirement of connection between the main claim and the counterclaim. Accordingly, this section firstly explores the evolution of the connection requirement as regards to its classification [Sect. 4.2.2.1], and secondly revises the appropriateness of such classification [Sect. 4.2.2.2].

4.2.2.1 The Evolution of the Connection Requirement

Arbitral tribunals in early cases of counterclaims in investment arbitration did not take a stance as to the characterisation of the connection requirement in terms of jurisdiction or admissibility. A first indication in this regard appeared only in 2004 with the *Saluka v Czech Republic* case. After a profuse examination of the connection requirement, the tribunal considered that some of the counterclaims failed to meet this requirement, and consequently, it declined jurisdiction over them.[99] Similarly, in an effort to assess its jurisdiction over counterclaims, the *Paushok v Mongolia* tribunal found indispensable to determine whether there was a close connection between the claim and the counterclaim.[100] Understandably, some

96 Pauker and Winston (2021), p. 205.

97 Hwang and Lim (2018), p. 267.

98 Hwang and Lim (2018), p. 268.

99 *Saluka Investments BV v The Czech Republic*, UNCITRAL Case, Decision on Counterclaims (07 May 2004) paras. 79–80.

100 *Sergei Paushok, CJSC Golden East Company and CJSC Vostokneftegaz Company v The Government of Mongolia*, UNCITRAL Case, Jurisdiction and Liability (28 April 2011) para. 693: ('In considering whether the Tribunal has jurisdiction to consider the counterclaims, it must therefore decide whether there is a close connection between them and the primary claim from which they arose or whether the counterclaims are matters that are otherwise covered by the general law of Respondent').

authors deemed these decisions to be an initial classification of the connection requirement as a jurisdictional issue instead of admissibility.[101]

Tribunals in the *Fraport v The Philippines* case and in the *Oxus v Uzbekistan* case have endorsed such conception of the connection requirement and declined jurisdiction over counterclaims that failed to prove a sufficient link with the main claim or subject-matter of the dispute.[102] More recently, the *Iberdrola v Guatemala* tribunal held a similar view. Although this tribunal never went into the intricacies of the requisite connection, it laid down its jurisdiction over counterclaims in two prongs:

> it does not appear seriously disputed – and rightly so – that an investment tribunal has jurisdiction over a counterclaim if two requirements are satisfied, i.e. the disputing parties have given their consent to arbitrate counterclaims and there is a close connection between the claims and the counterclaim[103]

There is a minority of cases considering that the connection requirement constitutes an admissibility rather than a jurisdictional issue. The *Antoine Goetz v Burundi* tribunal distinguished between the jurisdictional requirements pursuant to Article 25 ICSID Convention (*la competénce du Centre*) and the connection requirement for counterclaims according to Article 46 ICSID Convention (*la recevabilité des demandes reconventionnelles*).[104] Similarly, the *Metal-Tech v Uzbekistan* tribunal held that one of the requirements for entertaining counterclaims under the ICSID Convention was the connection between the claim and the counterclaim, which '*is generally deemed an admissibility and not a jurisdictional requirement*'.[105] Eventually, the tribunal refrained from assessing the connection requirement in depth because it found no jurisdiction over the counterclaims.[106]

In contrast to the prevailing practice of considering the connection requirement as a jurisdictional issue, authors have framed this requirement as a matter of admissibility. In this sense, the enquiry on whether a tribunal may entertain a counterclaim branches into two parts: firstly, on the scope of consent as the jurisdictional threshold and secondly on the connection between claim and counterclaim as the admissibility threshold.[107] Particularly in the ICSID framework, whereby Article 25 ICSID

---

[101] Kalnina and Godbole (2019), mn. 4.458.

[102] *Fraport AG Frankfurt Airport Services Worldwide v Republic of The Philippines*, ICSID Case No ARB/11/12, Award (10 December 2014) para. 468; *Oxus Gold v Republic of Uzbekistan*, UNCITRAL Case, Award (17 December 2015) paras. 954 et seqq.

[103] *Iberdrola Energía SA v The Republic of Guatemala (II)*, PCA Case No 2017-41, Award (24 August 2020) para. 384.

[104] *Antoine Goetz and others v Republic of Burundi*, ICSID Case No ARB/01/2, Award (21 June 2012) para. 283.

[105] *Metal-Tech Ltd v Republic of Uzbekistan*, ICSID Case No ARB/10/3, Award (04 October 2013) para. 407.

[106] *Metal-Tech Ltd v Republic of Uzbekistan*, ICSID Case No ARB/10/3, Award (04 October 2013) para. 413: ('. . . this Tribunal has no jurisdiction over the counterclaims. It will thus abstain from reviewing whether the counterclaims meet the second requirement of Article 46 dealing with admissibility and demanding a connection with the claims').

[107] Kendra (2013), p. 593. Similarly, Anning (2021), p. 1292.

Convention conveys the requirements for the '*jurisdiction of the Centre*', one may argue that the requisite connection for counterclaims under Article 46 ICSID Convention must reflect a different kind of requirements namely one of admissibility.[108]

Even Article 46 ICSID Convention itself distinguishes between the requirements of connection, the scope of consent and '*otherwise within the jurisdiction of the Centre*'. As mentioned above, the latter two arise from the drafters' extreme caution as preventing ancillary claims from overstepping the tribunal's jurisdictional limits,[109] whereas the connection requirement on the other hand seems to have a different nature. Otherwise, a terminological absurd would occur if a counterclaim fails in jurisdiction given the lack of connection, notwithstanding having been found within the scope of consent and '*the jurisdiction of the Centre*'.[110] The lack of connection might preclude the particular tribunal to adjudge the ancillary claim but it would not necessarily prevent other tribunals from entertaining it as a separate claim in other proceedings.[111]

To illustrate the difference between the jurisdictional requirements and the requisite connection, Christoph Schreuer envisages a counterclaim that fulfils the requirements of Article 25 ICSID Convention but does not arise from the subject-matter of the dispute, for instance, because it pertains to a different investment operation between the same parties.[112] Accordingly, given that the connection requirement might hardly be deemed as a jurisdictional issue, authors fall back into the admissibility characterisation.[113]

The characterisation of the connection requirement for counterclaims under the Resolution on the 'Equality of Parties before International Investment Tribunals' of the 18th Commission of the *Institut de Droit International* is perhaps more complex. On a first note, Article 6(2) sets forth that '[i]*n order to be admissible, such a counterclaim must*' be within the tribunal's jurisdiction and arise out of the subject-matter of the investment. Here, the term 'admissible' is not loaded with legal constructions on reviewability or discretion discussed above, but it rather reflects the general idea of permissibility. In other words, when a counterclaim is allowed.

---

[108] Lalive and Halonen (2011), p. 144; Sharpe and Jacob (2018), pp. 356 et seqq.

[109] *See* Sect. 3.3.1.3.4.

[110] Kalnina and Godbole (2019), mn. 4.458.

[111] Atanasova et al. (2014), pp. 379–380: ('The authors consider that the criterion of close connection is conceptually better viewed as an admissibility requirement (...) In international dispute settlement, it is generally understood that once a counterclaim is not sufficiently connected to the main claim, the respondent is not precluded from lodging a separate claim in other proceedings (assuming other conditions are met). This suggests that jurisdiction would normally exist for the issues raised by the counterclaim, if they were brought in separate proceedings. This conclusion is not affected by the fact that in the investment treaty context, this scenario is not likely to occur due to the usual lack of consent on the part of the investor before the claim is lodged') (footnotes omitted).

[112] Schreuer et al. (2009), Art 46, mn. 73.

[113] de Nanteuil (2018), p. 385. Similarly, Bubrowski (2013), pp. 226–227.

The 18th Commission might have mistakenly introduced two connection requirements: one arising directly out of the subject matter of the investment (Article 6(2)(b)); another arising out of the subject matter of the dispute (Article 6(5)). As stated above, the 18th Commission might have strived to redefine the connection requirement and to steer the discussion towards the same investment.[114] Considering that the existence of a protected investment has a jurisdictional character, one may argue that under the Resolution on the 'Equality of Parties before International Investment Tribunals' of the 18th Commission of the *Institut de Droit International*, the connection requirement for counterclaims also has a jurisdictional character.[115] Yet, considering the connection requirement as a jurisdictional issue is not entirely satisfactory. In fact, the Resolution's preparatory work evinces that the members of the 18th Commission were of the opinion that the connection between claim and counterclaim '*is properly to be regarded as a requirement of admissibility*'.[116]

4.2.2.2 Revising the Classification of the Connection Requirement

The lack of connection between claim and counterclaim will necessarily lead to the counterclaim's dismissal. One may thus wonder whether classifying this requirement as jurisdictional or not has any consequence at all.[117] Yet, the (proper) classification of this requirement influences the tribunal's analysis, which in turn might lead to a more lenient approach with respect to counterclaims in general and to environmental counterclaims in particular. Thus, this monograph posits that the connection requirement does not have a jurisdictional character.

On the one hand, jurisdiction pertains to the parties' consent to arbitration, whereas admissibility (or procedural decisions for critics of the terminology) entails the overall preservation of the proceedings' legitimacy.[118] Whilst parties' consent is either complied with or not, a tribunal needs certain degree of discretion to assess whether a particular aspect might affect judicial propriety. On the other hand, the requisite connection epitomises the principles of procedural or judicial economy and even a better administration of justice.[119] Therefore, a tribunal would not determine whether there is connection, but rather whether the existing connection (or lack thereof) has an effect on procedural efficiency and due process. Such analysis requires a balancing exercise that jurisdictional questions do not permit. A tribunal

[114] *See* Sect. 4.1.1.3.1.

[115] Steingruber (2020), p. 603.

[116] Report of the Eighteenth Commission of the *Institut de Droit International* (Rapporteur Professor Campbell McLachlan) on the 'Equality of Parties before International Investment Tribunals' para. 191 <https://www.idi-iil.org/app/uploads/2019/06/Commission-18-Equality-of-parties-before-international-investment-tribunals-McLachlan-Travaux-La-Haye-2019.pdf> accessed 10 January 2023.

[117] For instance *see* Sinha and Fusea (2021), p. 63.

[118] *See* Sect. 4.2.1.2.

[119] *See* Sect. 4.1.2.

should thus enjoy certain flexibility for assessing the connection requirement, and ultimately for allowing the counterclaim[120] (insofar it has found jurisdiction over it).

As a result, the connection requirement plays the role of filtering out those counterclaims, which do not serve procedural economy or the administration of justice.[121] The reasoning of the *Urbaser v Argentina* tribunal is apposite in this regard. Argentina submitted a counterclaim for alleged failure to sufficiently invest in the water concession (investment).[122] After finding jurisdiction over the counterclaim and while assessing the sufficient nexus between the claim and the counterclaim, the tribunal held:

> It would be wholly inconsistent to rule on Claimants' claim in relation to their investment in one sense and to have a separate proceeding where compliance with the commitment for funding may be ruled upon in a different way. Reasonable administration of justice cannot tolerate such a potential inconsistent outcome.[123]

This reasoning evinces that when assessing the connection requirement, an arbitral tribunal considers the overall impact of admitting the counterclaim on the administration of justice. Such an analysis demands certain discretion, not offered when assessing jurisdictional issues. One may thus conclude that the connection requirement escapes a characterisation as a jurisdictional matter and rather falls into the territory of admissibility or procedural decisions.

This classification of the connection requirement suggests three consequences for counterclaims: *first*, as reasoned by the *Alemanni v Argentina* tribunal, logic dictates that jurisdictional objections are analysed before any admissibility objections (or procedural issues for that matter).[124] This does not vary for the case of counterclaims. Whilst the jurisdictional enquiry will determine whether a tribunal is entitled to adjudicate the particular counterclaim at all, the connection analysis hinges on the tribunal's discretion to admit a counterclaim, which is certainly delimited by its jurisdictional powers. Thus, a tribunal ought to assess whether it has jurisdiction over a counterclaim and only if it does, it may analyse the connection requirement as

[120] Kjos (2013), p. 153; Anning (2021), p. 1307. Similarly, Philippe Fouchard, Emmanuel Gaillard and Berthold Goldman endorse a flexible assessment of the connection requirement pursuant to Article 46 ICSID Convention given the risks of an unnecessary multiplication of proceedings *see* Fouchard et al. (1999), para. 1222.

[121] Kjos (2013), p. 147.

[122] *Urbaser SA and Consorcio de Aguas Bilbao Bizkaia, Bilbao Biskaia Ur Partzuergoa v The Argentine Republic*, ICSID Case No ARB/07/26, Award (08 December 2016) para. 36.

[123] *Urbaser SA and Consorcio de Aguas Bilbao Bizkaia, Bilbao Biskaia Ur Partzuergoa v The Argentine Republic*, ICSID Case No ARB/07/26, Award (08 December 2016) para. 1151.

[124] *Giovanni Alemanni and Others v The Argentine Republic*, ICSID Case No ARB/07/8, Decision on Jurisdiction and Admissibility (17 November 2014) para. 260.

a second step.[125] Interestingly, the *Tethyan v Pakistan* tribunal ignored this order and proceeded with its analysis on the connection requirement in the first place.[126]

Certainly, the order of the factors does not alter the result, but such change is procedurally inefficient and methodologically erroneous. Procedurally inefficient because the assessment of the connection requirement is heavily fact-based,[127] warranting a critical analysis of the evidence, which is normally left to the merits stage of the proceedings. Switching jurisdiction with connection might then entail double work for the arbitrators. Methodologically erroneous because when assessing the connection requirement, the tribunal would exercise a judicial discretion, which may not exist according to the jurisdictional title.

Second, given the order of analysis over counterclaims, should a tribunal find lack of jurisdiction over a counterclaim, it would usually dismiss it without delving into the connection requirement. Nevertheless, some authors and even tribunals have hypothesised whether a closely connected counterclaim could overcome any jurisdictional restriction. For instance, some commentators on the ICSID Convention and the proceedings thereunder observe that closely connected counterclaims may always fall within the parties' consent, even in cases of narrow or limited dispute settlement provisions.[128] Similarly, Zachary Douglas concedes that limitations upon the scope of consent in IIAs, *eg* referring to treaty breaches exclusively, should not apply to a host state's counterclaims, as long as the latter's factual matrix directly relates to the main claim.[129]

In the same vein, the tribunals in *Oxus v Uzbekistan* and *Naturgy v Colombia* have considered the possibility that a closely connected counterclaim could overcome jurisdictional restraints. Such hypothesis is not only untenable but is also caused by a misinterpretation of the *Saluka v Czech Republic* case. Initially, the *Oxus v Uzbekistan* tribunal discussed an alleged principle, according to which a closely connected counterclaim may be adjudged by a tribunal, even if the underlying IIA does not cover claims of the state against the investor.[130] The *Oxus v Uzbekistan* tribunal attributed the conception of such a principle to the *Saluka v Czech Republic* case.[131] Similarly, after finding no jurisdiction over respondent's counterclaim, the *Naturgy v Colombia* tribunal explored the possible exception that '*an international tribunal can accept jurisdiction over state counterclaims that are closely connected to the investor's main claim, even if the applicable treaty does not expressly extend*

---

[125] Kendra (2013), p. 590.

[126] *Tethyan Copper Company Pty Limited v Islamic Republic of Pakistan*, ICSID Case No ARB/12/1, Decision on Jurisdiction and Liability (10 November 2017) paras. 1412 et seqq.

[127] *See* Sect. 4.3.3.1.3.

[128] Shihata and Parra (1999), p. 320; Schreuer et al. (2009), Art 46, mn. 94.

[129] Douglas (2013), p. 433.

[130] *Oxus Gold v Republic of Uzbekistan*, UNCITRAL Case, Award (17 December 2015) para. 948.

[131] *Oxus Gold v Republic of Uzbekistan*, UNCITRAL Case, Award (17 December 2015) para. 952.

jurisdiction over such counterclaims'. [132] The *Naturgy v Colombia* tribunal relied both on the *Oxus v Uzbekistan* and *Saluka v Czech Republic* cases for justifying such possible exception. However, the *Saluka v Czech Republic* tribunal never conceived this exception for the tribunal's jurisdiction over counterclaims. Instead, the *Saluka v Czech Republic* tribunal held:

> The Tribunal is satisfied that those provisions [*referring to the connection requirement under different instruments*], as interpreted and applied by the decisions which have been referred to, reflect a general legal principle as to the nature of the close connexion which a counterclaim must have with the primary claim if a tribunal with jurisdiction over the primary claim is to have jurisdiction also over the counterclaim.[133]

Such passage does not suggest that the connection requirement may replace a narrowly drafted dispute resolution provision. It rather ascertains the existence of the requisite connection as a matter of principle, while explicitly underscoring that the tribunal ought to have jurisdiction over both claim and also counterclaim. Certainly, both tribunals in *Oxus v Uzbekistan* and *Naturgy v Colombia* did not go as far as admitting the existence of a closely connected counterclaim upon which they did not have jurisdiction. However, it cannot be overstated that, given the different nature of the requirements of consent and connection for counterclaims, the latter cannot remedy the lack of the former.

Third, and closely related to the previous point, parties' consent over a particular counterclaim might obviate the requirement of connection. This is equally true for cases of explicit or tacit consent after the dispute arose. Accordingly, in the cases of *Benvenuti v Congo, RSM v Grenada* and *Balkan Energy v Ghana* (for contract-based arbitration), and in *Alex Genin v Estonia*, *Desert Line v Yemen*, *Occidental v Ecuador*, and *Perenco v Ecuador* (for treaty-based arbitration), where tacit consent to counterclaims was granted,[134] the respective tribunals omitted any enquiry about the connection requirement and analysed directly the merits of each counterclaim.

Arguably, in the *Burlington v Ecuador* case, where the parties had explicitly agreed on counterclaims, the tribunal took the same path. The tribunal, by enumerating the other conditions for counterclaims under Article 46 ICSID Convention, simply stated that those conditions, including the connection requirement, were met.[135] One may critique that the tribunal oversimplified its task, and regarded the parties' consent as equally satisfying the connection requirement.[136] Yet, this is nothing to frown upon. The tribunal's considerations for the connection requirement hinge on procedural or judicial efficiency, which explains the tribunal's discretion in

[132] *Naturgy Energy Group SA and Naturgy Electricidad Colombia SL (formerly Gas Natural SDG SA and Gas Natural Fenosa Electricidad Colombia SL) v Republic of Colombia*, ICSID Case No UNCT/18/1, Award (12 March 2021) para. 622.

[133] *Saluka Investments BV v The Czech Republic*, UNCITRAL Case, Decision on Counterclaims (07 May 2004) para. 76.

[134] *See* Sect. 3.1.2.

[135] *Burlington Resources Inc v Republic of Ecuador*, ICSID Case No ARB/08/5, Decision on Ecuador's Counterclaims (07 February 2017) para. 62.

[136] Anning (2021), p. 1299.

its analysis. Whereas consent is the overriding principle in international arbitration which might dispense of the tribunal's discretion. Even if a counterclaim is not sufficiently connected to the main claim, the disputing parties may nevertheless agree to submit both counterclaim and main claim to the same tribunal. Thus, in cases of explicit or tacit consent to counterclaims, a tribunal might obviate any analysis on the connection requirement.

4.3 The Dilution of the Connection Requirement in Investment Arbitration and its Impact on Environmental Counterclaims

Probably the most controversial requirement for counterclaims across the different mechanisms of international dispute resolution is the connection between a counterclaim and the main claim. This section thus seeks to decipher the content of such requirement in investment arbitration and its impact on environmental counterclaims raised by the respondent host state. In this context, this section firstly focuses on the differentiation between 'legal' and 'factual' connection, whose origins hearkens back to the jurisprudence of the ICJ and the IUSCT [Sect. 4.3.1]. Subsequently, it analyses the (possible) effects of the connection requirement in contract-based investment arbitration and the respective viability of environmental counterclaims [Sect. 4.3.2]. Finally, it delves into the shifting trend towards balancing factors for the requisite connection in treaty-based investment arbitration and the respective viability of environmental counterclaims [Sect. 4.3.3].

4.3.1 A Dichotomy of Legal and Factual Connection: Looking at Its Origins

Only few investment arbitration tribunals have delved into the content of the connection requirement for counterclaims. However, the distinction between legal and factual connection seems to be borrowed from the ICJ framework and buttressed by the jurisprudence of the IUSCT. For instance, the *Antoine Goetz v Burundi* tribunal asserted that Article 46 ICSID Convention was inspired by Article 80 of the ICJ Rules of Court,[137] and by analogy, relied on the development of the requisite

[137] *Antoine Goetz and others v Republic of Burundi*, ICSID Case No ARB/01/2, Award (21 June 2012) para. 273: ('Le Tribunal observe que l'article 46 de la Convention et l'article 40 du Règlement d'arbitrage sont directement inspirés de l'article 80 du Règlement de procédure de la Cour internationale de Justice qui, à l'époque de l'élaboration du Règlement d'arbitrage, disposait qu'«*[u]ne demande reconventionnelle peut être présentée pourvu qu'elle soit en connexité directe avec l'objet de la demande de la partie adverse et qu'elle relève de la compétence de la Cour*»'). This opinion is shared by Kendra (2013), p. 577. However, there is no record in the ICSID *travaux préparatoires* or elsewhere supporting this position.

connection at the ICJ.[138] Similarly, in the *Saluka v Czech Republic* case, given the absence of previous awards based on the UNCITRAL Arbitration Rules and similar treaty provisions, the tribunal sought guidance from the jurisprudence of the IUSCT with respect to the requirement of connection between a counterclaim and the main claim.[139] The *Paushok v Mongolia* tribunal followed suit.[140] This suggests that the distinction between legal and factual connection might have permeated investment arbitration from other frameworks of international dispute settlement.

Interestingly, the requirement of connection between a counterclaim and the main claim can be traced back to the PCIJ.[141] However, only during the drafting of the PCIJ Rules of Court of 1936 the content of such requirement was discussed, but the judges could not agree on whether it implied a connection in fact, in law or both.[142] Thus, until date, the ICJ Rules of Court simply provide that the counterclaim must be '*directly connected with the subject-matter of the claim*'. The Court usually construes this requirement as demanding a connection in fact and in law.[143] Yet, the debate is not completely settled as for instance Judge Caron considered that the Rules of Court demand connection either in fact or in law.[144] Factual connection with the main claim may be proven if the facts occurred during the same time, in the same geographical area, or when the claim and the counterclaim refer to the same type of conduct.[145] Legal connection, on the other hand, requires that the claim and

[138] *Antoine Goetz and others v Republic of Burundi*, ICSID Case No ARB/01/2, Award (21 June 2012) paras. 284–285.

[139] *Saluka Investments BV v The Czech Republic*, UNCITRAL Case, Decision on Counterclaims (07 May 2004) paras. 68 et seqq.

[140] *Sergei Paushok, CJSC Golden East Company and CJSC Vostokneftegaz Company v The Government of Mongolia*, UNCITRAL Case, Jurisdiction and Liability (28 April 2011) paras. 690 et seqq.

[141] *See* Sect. 2.1.1.1.

[142] Series D, Acts and Documents concerning the Organization of the Court, Third Addendum to No 2, Elaboration of the Rules of Court of March 11th, 1936, Fourteenth Meeting (29 May 1934), 111.

[143] *Application of the Convention on the Prevention and Punishment of the Crime of Genocide (Bosnia and Herzegovina v Yugoslavia)* (Order on Counterclaims) [1997] ICJ Rep 243, para. 33; *Oil Platforms (Iran v United States of America)* (Order on Counterclaim) [1998] ICJ Rep 190, para. 37; *Armed Activities on the Territory of the Congo (Democratic Republic of the Congo v Uganda)* (Order on Counterclaims) [2001] ICJ Rep 660, para. 36; *Certain Activities Carried Out by Nicaragua in the Border Area (Costa Rica v Nicaragua), Construction of a Road in Costa Rica along the San Juan River (Nicaragua v Costa Rica)* (Order on Counterclaims) [2013] ICJ Rep 200, para. 32.

[144] *Alleged Violations of Sovereign Rights and Maritime Spaces in the Caribbean Sea (Nicaragua v Colombia)* (Order on Counterclaims) [2017] ICJ Rep 289, Dissenting Opinion of Judge ad hoc Caron, para. 18.

[145] *Certain Activities Carried Out by Nicaragua in the Border Area (Costa Rica v Nicaragua), Construction of a Road in Costa Rica along the San Juan River (Nicaragua v Costa Rica)* (Order on Counterclaims) [2013] ICJ Rep 200, para. 32; *Alleged Violations of Sovereign Rights and Maritime Spaces in the Caribbean Sea (Nicaragua v Colombia)* (Order on Counterclaims) [2017] ICJ Rep 289, para. 25. Similarly, *Oil Platforms (Iran v United States of America)* (Order on Counterclaim) [1998] ICJ Rep 190, paras. 38–39.

counterclaim seek the same legal remedy or rely on the same legal principles or instruments.[146]

The connection requirement in the context of the IUSCT has been addressed as well.[147] However, the provision referring to this requirement reads differently since pursuant to Article II(I) of the Claims Settlement Declaration a counterclaim must arise '*out of the same contract, transaction or occurrence that constitutes the subject matter of that national's claim*'. Accordingly, in the *TCSB Inc v Iran* case, the IUSCT drew a differentiation between a legal relationship arising out of the application of the law, and a contractual relation arising out of the contract, and concluded that only the latter falls within the scope of the Claims Settlement Declaration as an admissible counterclaim.[148] Such distinction has been followed in subsequent cases,[149] which may be portrayed as a characterisation of legal connection.

4.3.2 Environmental Counterclaims in Contract-Based Investment Arbitration: The Content of the Connection Requirement

Environmental counterclaims in contract-based investment arbitration necessitate to fulfil the requirement of connection. However, the aforementioned distinction between legal and factual connection might undermine the compliance with such requirement in cases where the environmental obligation does not arise from the same investment contract underlying the main claim. Accordingly, this section critically explores the content and effects of the connection requirement in contract-based investment arbitration [Sect. 4.3.2.1] and subsequently provides an assessment on the viability of environmental counterclaims [Sect. 4.3.2.2].

---

[146] *Certain Activities Carried Out by Nicaragua in the Border Area (Costa Rica v Nicaragua), Construction of a Road in Costa Rica along the San Juan River (Nicaragua v Costa Rica)* (Order on Counterclaims) [2013] ICJ Rep 200, para. 32; *Alleged Violations of Sovereign Rights and Maritime Spaces in the Caribbean Sea (Nicaragua v Colombia)* (Order on Counterclaims) [2017] ICJ Rep 289, para. 25. Similarly, *Oil Platforms (Iran v United States of America)* (Order on Counterclaim) [1998] ICJ Rep 190, paras. 38–39.

[147] *See* Sect. 2.1.2.4.

[148] *TCSB Inc v The Islamic Republic of Iran*, Case 140, Chamber 2, Award No 114-140-2 (16 March 1984) 5 Iran-US CTR 160.

[149] *Sylvania Technical Systems Inc v The Islamic Republic of Iran*, Case 64, Award No 180-64-1 (27 June 1985) 8 Iran-US CTR 298; *Questech Inc v The Ministry of National Defence of the Islamic Republic of Iran*, Case 59, Award No 191-59-1 (20 September 1985) 9 Iran-US CTR 170; *International Technical Products Corporation and ITP Export Corporation v The Islamic Republic of Iran and others*, Case 302, Chamber 3, Award No 196-302-3 (24 October 1985) 9 Iran-US CTR 206; *Houston Contracting Company v National Iranian Oil Company, National Iranian Gas Company, and the Islamic Republic of Iran*, Case 173, Chamber 3, Award No 378-173-3 (22 July 1988) 20 Iran-US CTR 3, paras. 117 et seqq.

4.3.2.1 The Effects of the Connection Requirement in Contract-Based Investment Arbitration

Given that contract-based investment arbitration is akin to international commercial arbitration, it is feasible that the same considerations on the permissibility of counterclaims apply.[150] Thereby, considerations on procedural efficiency, reduction of transaction costs and avoidance of contradictory decisions demand an assessment on the connection between the counterclaim and the main claim.[151] This certainly reflects the premise of this Chapter as characterising the connection requirement as inherent to the procedural mechanism of counterclaims. This seemingly undisputed premise however does not address the distinction between 'legal' and 'factual' connection and how it affects counterclaims in contract-based investment arbitration.

In principle, the connection requirement presents no complexity in the context of contract-based investment arbitration when the investor and the host state claim on the basis of the same investment contract.[152] This common source of claims and counterclaims would necessarily satisfy both legal and factual connection. Even if the counterclaim is based on a different but related investment contract as the main claim, it is possible that the connection requirement is nonetheless fulfilled without much hurdles. For instance, in the *Klöckner v Cameroon* case, despite the fact that the claim and the counterclaim were based on different contracts appertaining to a fertiliser factory in Cameroon, the tribunal deemed such contracts to be constituting '*one and the same bilateral relationship*', thus, all obligations arising of those contracts '*had a common origin, identical sources, and an operational unity*'.[153] Accordingly, the tribunal found no qualms about allowing the counterclaims given the interdependency of the investment contracts. This approach is similar to the practice of the IUSCT, according to which claims and counterclaims may arise from different contracts as long as they represent a single transaction.[154]

Only recently, by directly citing the *Klöckner v Cameroon* award on this point, the tribunal in *Grenada Private Power v Grenada* considered that when it is

[150] *See* Sect. 2.2.1.1.

[151] Koller (2008), p. 83.

[152] See for instance: Rivas (2015), p. 784; Asteriti (2015), p. 261; Clodfelter and Tsutieva (2018), para. 17.35. Similarly with respect to the ICSID Convention *see* Fouchard et al. (1999), para. 1222.

[153] *Klöckner Industrie-Anlagen GmbH and others v United Republic of Cameroon and Société Camerounaise des Engrais*, ICSID Case No ARB/81/2, Award (21 October 1983) 65 [reproduced in R Rayfuse (ed), *ICSID Reports vol 2* (CUP 1994) 3-163].

[154] *American Bell International Inc v The Islamic Republic of Iran, The Ministry of Defense, The Ministry of Post, Telegraph and Telephone, and the Telecommunications Company of Iran*, Case 48, Chamber 3, Interlocutory Award No ITL 41-48-3 (11 June 1984) 6 Iran-US CTR 74; *Westinghouse Electric Corporation v The Islamic Republic of Iran, The Islamic Republic of Iran Air Force, Iran Air, The National Iranian Oil Company*, Case 389, Chamber 2, Interlocutory Award No ITL 67-389-2 (12 February 1987) 14 Iran-US CTR 104, paras. 7 et seqq.

impractical to "unbundle" claim and counterclaim arising from the same contractual relationship, counterclaims were to be allowed.[155] Certainly, the *Klöckner v Cameroon* tribunal did not address the distinction between legal and factual connection and rightly so since such categorisation does not find place in the ICSID Convention. The tribunal simply referred to '*a common origin, identical sources, and an operational unity*', which suggests a balancing exercise of connecting factors rather than a check list for assessing the requirement of connection.

However, the situation may differ when the counterclaim is based either on a source other than the contract, for instance, on domestic law. In the *Amco v Indonesia* case, the respondent based its counterclaim on its domestic law regarding tax fraud rather than on the same contract. Admittedly, the *Amco v Indonesia* tribunal framed the discussion into the requirement of '*within the jurisdiction of the Centre*' rather than into the connection requirement, but its reasoning has influenced subsequent tribunals with respect to legal connection between the claim and the counterclaim by stating that:

> it is correct to distinguish between rights and obligations that are applicable to legal or natural persons who are within the reach of a host State's jurisdiction, as a matter of general law; and rights and obligations that are applicable to an investor as a consequence of an investment agreement entered into with that host state.[156]

Since the prohibition of committing tax fraud was considered to arise out of general law, the tribunal rejected the counterclaim. Interestingly, such classification of obligations arising out of general law and obligations arising out of an investment agreement evokes the prior jurisprudence of the IUSCT,[157] which nevertheless might not be an appropriate comparator given the specific wording of Article II (1) of the Claims Settlement Declaration. Even if the classification was appropriate, the *Amco v Indonesia* tribunal acknowledged that general law could generate an investment dispute and be within the jurisdiction of ICSID.[158] This caveat has been often overlooked by subsequent tribunals as elaborated below.[159] In the same vein, the *Elsamex v Honduras* tribunal refrained from adjudging counterclaims based on

---

[155] *Grenada Private Power Limited and WRB Enterprises, Inc v Grenada*, ICSID Case No ARB/17/13, Award (12 March 2020) para. 359.

[156] *Amco Asia Corporation and others v Republic of Indonesia*, ICSID Case No ARB/81/1, Decision on Jurisdiction in Resubmitted Proceeding (10 May 1988) para. 125.

[157] *See* Sect. 2.1.2.4.

[158] *Amco Asia Corporation and others v Republic of Indonesia*, ICSID Case No ARB/81/1, Decision on Jurisdiction in Resubmitted Proceeding (10 May 1988) para. 125.

[159] *See* Sect. 4.3.3.

tort or otherwise outside the contract relationship, while admitting the counterclaims based on the same investment contract as the main claim.[160]

Despite the fact that both the *Amco v Indonesia* and *Elsamex v Honduras* tribunals framed their analyses as jurisdictional issues, rejecting a counterclaim simply on the basis of its legal source does not seem tenable since such strict limitation finds no place in the ICSID Convention. Instead, an approach closer to the reasoning of the *Klöckner v Cameroon* tribunal is recommended, whereby the tribunal may balance different connecting factors before reaching a conclusion. Thus, a 'legal' connection by itself cannot be the only determinative factor for the admissibility of counterclaims, especially if a 'factual' connection inclines the balance in favour of adjudging both claim and counterclaim in the same proceedings for the purpose of procedural or judicial economy. This suggests a dilution of this requirement's content ousting a strict binary classification. In practice, tribunals would enjoy considerable leeway to explore what factors may indicate connection and what factors do not do so, and balance them against each other to determine whether a close connection of the counterclaim with the main claim exists (or is warranted).

4.3.2.2 Assessing the Viability of Environmental Counterclaims with Respect to the Connection Requirement

While Chap. 5 will elaborate on the legal source to an environmental counterclaim, this section advances that the dilution of the connection requirement facilitates the admissibility of environmental counterclaims in contract-based investment arbitration. In principle and despite the scarcity of contract-based investment tribunals analysing the connection requirement for counterclaims, it seems unassailable that environmental counterclaims based on contractual obligations would not face much (if any) hurdles on the requisite connection in contract-based investment arbitration. The situation is however less clear in cases where the respondent host state does not base its environmental counterclaim on the investment contract, but rather, for instance, on domestic law.

In this context, by assuming that the connection requirement entails the assessment of a series of factors linking the main claim with the counterclaim, such as the origin of the obligations, the geographic impact, the timing of the alleged breaches, the centrality (or importance) of the obligations, among others, environmental counterclaims have better prospects. Should the environmental obligation arise from a different instrument than the contract, this will be a factor to consider, but it would not necessarily defeat the counterclaim by itself since many other factors may play in its favour.

[160] *Elsamex SA v Republic of Honduras*, ICSID Case No ARB/09/4, Award (16 November 2012) para. 304.

4.3.3 Environmental Counterclaims in Treaty-Based Investment Arbitration: The Content of the Connection Requirement

The connection requirement might be one of the major obstructions to counterclaims in treaty-based investment arbitration. Nevertheless, the reformulation of this requirement's content may influence a tribunal's decision on environmental counterclaims. For this reason, this section investigates a dilution of the connection requirement starting from a strict legal connection as an indispensable requirement to a more nuanced approach whereby various factors are balanced to determine connection [Sect. 4.3.3.1]. Afterwards, the effects of this new conception of the requisite connection are scrutinised *vis-à-vis* the viability of environmental counterclaims [Sect. 4.3.3.2].

4.3.3.1 The Requisite Connection: A Shifting Trend Towards Balancing Factors

The connection requirement of counterclaims in treaty-based investment arbitration has been a serious bone of contention. The discussion started with the *Saluka v Czech Republic* tribunal, whose decision has been both followed and heavily criticised. Therefore, this section explores the initial line of case law, which required that a counterclaim and the main claim ought to be based on the same legal instrument [Sect. 4.3.3.1.1]. Then, it presents the criticisms of such a strict conception of the connection requirement [Sect. 4.3.3.1.2]. This section concludes by elaborating a more flexible perspective, whereby a series of balancing factors determine whether a sufficient connection between claim and counterclaim exists [Sect. 4.3.3.1.3].

4.3.3.1.1 A Strict Legal Connection: An Initial Line of Case Law

The *Saluka v Czech Republic* decision constitutes a milestone for counterclaims in treaty-based investment arbitration, especially for its analysis on the connection requirement. After seeking guidance from other frameworks with respect to counterclaims, *ie* ICSID and IUSCT cases,[161] the tribunal relied on the *Klöckner v Cameroon* decision and rejected a set of counterclaims given the absence of a '*common origin, identical sources, and an operational unity*'.[162] In addition, the tribunal held that those counterclaims were based on obligations applicable as a

[161] *Saluka Investments BV v The Czech Republic*, UNCITRAL Case, Decision on Counterclaims (07 May 2004) paras. 64 et seqq.

[162] *Saluka Investments BV v The Czech Republic*, UNCITRAL Case, Decision on Counterclaims (07 May 2004) para. 79.

matter of general law, thus, they were inadmissible,[163] which evokes the *Amco v Indonesia* reasoning mentioned above. The *Saluka v Czech Republic* decision on counterclaims suggests that the connection requirement demands a legal connection between the counterclaim and the main claim.[164] This forces respondent host states to identify a legal basis within the respective IIA,[165] which brings to mind the ICJ distinction between connection in fact and in law.

This approach has been adopted by other tribunals. For instance, in the *Paushok v Mongolia* case, the respondent raised seven counterclaims based on its domestic law—*eg* windfall profit taxes, fees, levies, environmental violations among others.[166] Since the main claim was based on the violation of the underlying BIT, whereas the counterclaims were based on the violation of Mongolia's domestic legislation, the tribunal considered that no 'reasonable nexus' existed that could justify the admission of the counterclaims.[167] The tribunal added that the counterclaims covered issues of public law, which were of the exclusive jurisdiction of domestic courts.[168]

Interestingly, from this initial line of case law, there was a seemingly divergent opinion on the connection requirement by the *Antoine Goetz v Burundi* tribunal. The main claim sought redress for damages suffered by the investors, inter alia, given the indirect expropriation of the African Bank of Commerce (ABC). The respondent counterclaimed that ABC had failed to comply with the conditions of operation in the free economic zone, hence causing economic damages to the state.[169] Given that the counterclaim arose out of the same investment and the failure to comply with the conditions of the free economic zone, which led to the suspension of the bank licence and subsequent closure, the tribunal considered that the connection requirement was fulfilled.[170] As such, the counterclaim's legal source was the licence, whereas the claim's legal source was the underlying treaty, but this did not prevent the tribunal from admitting the counterclaim. However, the *Antoine Goetz v Burundi* decision

[163] *Saluka Investments BV v The Czech Republic*, UNCITRAL Case, Decision on Counterclaims (07 May 2004) para. 79.

[164] See for instance: Lalive and Halonen (2011), p. 154; Ng (2018), p. 4; *Urbaser SA and Consorcio de Aguas Bilbao Bizkaia, Bilbao Biskaia Ur Partzuergoa v The Argentine Republic*, ICSID Case No ARB/07/26, Award (08 December 2016) fn. 425.

[165] Gleason (2021), p. 430.

[166] *Sergei Paushok, CJSC Golden East Company and CJSC Vostokneftegaz Company v The Government of Mongolia*, UNCITRAL Case, Jurisdiction and Liability (28 April 2011) para. 678.

[167] *Sergei Paushok, CJSC Golden East Company and CJSC Vostokneftegaz Company v The Government of Mongolia*, UNCITRAL Case, Jurisdiction and Liability (28 April 2011) para. 694.

[168] *Sergei Paushok, CJSC Golden East Company and CJSC Vostokneftegaz Company v The Government of Mongolia*, UNCITRAL Case, Jurisdiction and Liability (28 April 2011) para. 694.

[169] *Antoine Goetz and others v Republic of Burundi*, ICSID Case No ARB/01/2, Award (21 June 2012) para. 267.

[170] *Antoine Goetz and others v Republic of Burundi*, ICSID Case No ARB/01/2, Award (21 June 2012) paras. 282–285.

did not echo in other tribunals, and the appraisal that identity of source between the claim and the counterclaim is necessary has largely prevailed.

Subsequently, the *Gavazzi v Romania* tribunal confirmed the prevailing view on legal connection by rejecting a counterclaim because, among other reasons, it was based upon Romanian law, whereas the claimant's claims were based on breaches of the underlying BIT.[171] The *Anglo American v Venezuela* tribunal also considered the identity of legal basis between the main claim and the counterclaim as an added factor for the adjudication of the counterclaim. Here, since the main claim was based on alleged treaty violations, whereas the counterclaim was based on the violation of Venezuelan domestic law, the tribunal dismissed the counterclaim.[172] In sum, these cases conceived a legal connection between the claim and the counterclaim as a *sine qua non* requirement for counterclaims, which is fulfilled only when claim and counterclaim are based on the same legal instrument/legal source (a 'strict legal connection').

Such conception would virtually exclude all counterclaims in treaty-based investment arbitration cases, whereby the claimant investor submits its claim based on a treaty obligation.[173] Having in mind that there exists usually a '*vacuum of justiciable obligations of the investor*' in investment treaties,[174] counterclaims based on contractual obligations or the respondent's domestic legislation would automatically become inadmissible before a treaty-based arbitral tribunal.[175] However, the identity of legal source as the only decisive element is a misconception of the requisite connection.

4.3.3.1.2 Criticisms to the Strict Legal Connection

There are three criticisms to the abovementioned strict conception of legal connection for counterclaims, which undermine its validity. *First*, the initial reliance on the IUSCT jurisprudence and on early ICSID cases does not do justice to the specific context of treaty-based investment arbitration. *Second*, there is a complete lack of textual support in IIAs, the ICSID Convention or any set of arbitration rules indicating that counterclaims require a 'strict' legal connection. *Third*, requiring identity of legal source for the claim and the counterclaim might undermine broadly worded dispute resolution provisions.

---

[171] *Marco Gavazzi and Stefano Gavazzi v Romania*, ICSID Case No ARB/12/25, Decision on Jurisdiction, Admissibility and Liability (21 April 2015) para. 161: ('... the subject-matter of the counterclaim, *i.e.*, violations of Romanian domestic law, do not directly arise from the breaches of the BIT, being the subject-matter of the present proceedings').

[172] *Anglo American PLC v Bolivarian Republic of Venezuela*, ICSID Case No ARB(AF)/14/1, Award (18 January 2021) paras. 529–530.

[173] Lalive and Halonen (2011), p. 154; Douglas (2013), p. 431; Atanasova et al. (2014), p. 382; Kalnina and Godbole (2019), mn. 4.470.

[174] Amado et al. (2018), pp. 15–16.

[175] Anning (2021), p. 1306.

First, the uncritical reliance on the IUSCT jurisprudence, and on the ICSID cases of *Klöckner v Cameroon* and *Amco v Indonesia* might be incorrect.[176] Certainly, one may argue that the cited decisions were contract-based, whereas the *Saluka v Czech Republic* and *Paushok v Mongolia* cases were treaty-based,[177] or that the applicable instruments both in the IUSCT and ICSID explicitly demanded the connection requirement in contrast to the UNCITRAL Arbitration Rules.[178] However, the major flaw consists of the tribunals' lack of context when referring to other frameworks of international dispute resolution. For instance, despite the explicit wording of Article II(I) of the Claims Settlement Declaration requiring counterclaims to arise out of the same contract, the IUSCT has interpreted that related contracts could also serve as the legal basis for an admissible counterclaim.[179] That was the case in *American Bell v Iran*[180] or *Westinghouse Electric v Iran*,[181] where the IUSCT suggested certain flexibility when assessing the connection requirement. Moreover, the *Saluka v Czech Republic* tribunal obviated an important caveat of the *Amco v Indonesia* decision, whereby it is acknowledged that general law could create an investment dispute.[182] Thus, simply dismissing a counterclaim for its legal source does not precisely reflect the *Amco v Indonesia* reasoning.

The *Paushok v Mongolia* tribunal added fuel to the fire by excluding counterclaims arising out of domestic public law from ever being connected to treaty-based investment claims.[183] To support its decision, the tribunal relied on the IUSCT case

[176] Atanasova et al. (2014), p. 380.

[177] Lalive and Halonen (2011), p. 153: ('In the authors' opinion Saluka's reliance on Klöckner was incorrect, as a the latter was a contractual arbitration, and different considerations thus applied. The language in the Klöckner decision referring to claims and counterclaims that are aimed at the 'accomplishment of a single goal' is simply misplaced and inappropriate in an investment treaty context where the parties to the arbitration have rarely been engaged in a joint enterprise in the way that contractual parties often have'). In the same sense *see* Kendra (2013), p. 582: ('This test appears strict when viewed alongside the UNCITRAL rules, which on their face do not include any such requirement of a closeness of relationship with the principal claims').

[178] Clodfelter and Tsutieva (2018), para. 17.93: ('However, in the absence of an express requirement in Article 21(3) UNCITRAL, there is no reason to insist on the narrow approach of requiring the identity of legal basis of the counterclaim. At the same time, there is a problem with applying the expansive approach to the connection test').

[179] In the same sense, arguing a flexible interpretation of Article II of the Claims Settlement Declaration IUSCT *see* Ben Hamida (2003), para. 281.

[180] *American Bell International Inc v The Islamic Republic of Iran, The Ministry of Defense, The Ministry of Post, Telegraph and Telephone, and the Telecommunications Company of Iran*, Case 48, Chamber 3, Interlocutory Award No ITL 41-48-3 (11 June 1984) 6 Iran-US CTR 74.

[181] *Westinghouse Electric Corporation v The Islamic Republic of Iran, The Islamic Republic of Iran Air Force, Iran Air, The National Iranian Oil Company*, Case 389, Chamber 2, Interlocutory Award No ITL 67-389-2 (12 February 1987) 14 Iran-US CTR 104, paras. 7 et seqq.

[182] Douglas (2009), para. 499.

[183] Atanasova et al. (2014), p. 382: ('The tribunal in *Paushok v. Mongolia* created further confusion on the matter . . . [t]he decision seems to deny that matters covered by general domestic law can ever be closely connected, thus views the issue in a mutually exclusive, binary perspective. The tribunal in effect reformulated the test on admissibility of counterclaims by adding yet another formal criterion: the counterclaims cannot arise out of general domestic law').

of *Computer Sciences v Iran*, where a counterclaim on a tax clearance certificate was dismissed holding that tax laws are limited to domestic court's jurisdiction since they '*are manifestations of* jus imperii *which may be exercised only within the borders of a state*' and are '*typically enormously complex, so much so that their enforcement is frequently assigned to specialized courts or administrative agencies*'.[184] This might reflect the position of domestic courts in states such as Canada and Switzerland, where courts will most likely find judgments based on foreign criminal and tax laws unenforceable.[185]

Such uncritical 'importation' from the IUSCT's decisions to treaty-based investment arbitration is nevertheless inappropriate because: (i) the IUSCT jurisprudence is not as strict as depicted, since in cases such as *Houston Contracting Company v Iran* and *TCSB Inc v Iran*, contractual stipulations creating tax-related obligations (or public law-related obligations for that matter) gave rise to valid counterclaims[186]; (ii) the very concept of 'foreign' domestic law is alien to international arbitration since, unlike national courts, arbitral tribunals do not have *lex fori*[187]; (iii) by its nature, treaty-based investment arbitration deals with the exercise of sovereign authority[188] (or acts *jus imperii*), where even taxation measures have been adjudged.[189] In fact, it is questionable that a '*generally accepted principle*' exists prohibiting international tribunals from adjudicating domestic public law issues, such as those related to environmental damages.[190] Even in states where the rule of refusing enforcement of judgments based on foreign criminal or tax laws constitutes precedent, the justification for such a rule is unconvincing and should not be expanded to other public law areas such as environmental matters.[191] In addition,

[184] *Computer Sciences Corporation v The Government of the Islamic Republic of Iran and others*, Case 65, Chamber 1, Award No 221-65-1 (16 April 1986) 10 Iran-US CTR 269, 56; *Houston Contracting Company v National Iranian Oil Company, National Iranian Gas Company, and the Islamic Republic of Iran*, Case 173, Chamber 3, Award No 378-173-3 (22 July 1988) 20 Iran-US CTR 3, para. 120.

[185] Strebel (1999), pp. 69 et seqq., and 90 et seqq.

[186] *TCSB Inc v The Islamic Republic of Iran*, Case 140, Chamber 2, Award No 114-140-2 (16 March 1984) 5 Iran-US CTR 160. Similarly, *Houston Contracting Company v National Iranian Oil Company, National Iranian Gas Company, and the Islamic Republic of Iran*, Case 173, Chamber 3, Award No 378-173-3 (22 July 1988) 20 Iran-US CTR 3, para. 120.

[187] Kaufmann-Kohler (2005), p. 633.

[188] *See* Sect. 2.2.1.2.2.

[189] See for instance: *Marvin Roy Feldman Karpa v United Mexican States*, ICSID Case No ARB (AF)/99/1, Award (16 December 2002) paras. 7 et seqq.; *RosInvestCo UK Ltd v The Russian Federation*, SCC Case No V079/2005, Final Award (12 September 2010) paras. 456 et seqq.; *Tza Yap Shum v The Republic of Peru*, ICSID Case No ARB/07/6, Award (07 July 2011) paras. 173 et seqq.

[190] Shao (2021), p. 170.

[191] Neither public policy of the host state (since it would always be assessed) nor territorial sovereignty (since there is not exercise of sovereignty on a different state's territory but rather a submission to the court) seem to justify the reliance on the rule of non-enforcement of foreign judgements based on foreign public law *see* Strebel (1999), pp. 112 et seqq.

this should not present a problem at the enforcement stage either. Should the counterclaim succeed, the tribunal would impose pecuniary obligations on the claimant investor for its breach. The enforcing court would neither apply nor enforce the underlying obligation the investor has breached but rather enforce the obligation imposed in the award to pay damages to the respondent host state.[192] Thus, the *Paushok v Mongolia* tribunal has misconstrued the role of domestic public law in treaty-based investment arbitration and thereby overly restricting the possibility of counterclaims.

Second, there is no reference in IIAs, the ICSID Convention, or any set of arbitration rules suggesting that the connection requirement implies exclusively or determinatively the identity of sources grounding the claim and the counterclaim. For instance, Article 19(3) UNCITRAL Arbitration Rules (1976) required counterclaims to arise '*out of the same contract*', which some authors suggested that must be read as '*out of the same investment*' in treaty-based arbitration.[193] This certainly implies a connection requirement, but without suggesting an identity of legal source between the claim and the counterclaim. In turn, Article 21(3) UNCITRAL Arbitration Rules (2013) rephrased the abovementioned article on counterclaims and introduced '*that the arbitral tribunal has jurisdiction over* [the counterclaim]'.[194] Whilst the requirement of connection need not be explicitly mentioned to be applicable,[195] but once again, nothing suggests that connection is only achieved via claim and counterclaim having the same legal source. Thus, the connection requirement under the UNCITRAL Arbitration Rules (2013) must be considered neither narrowly nor expansively.[196]

Article 46 ICSID Convention contemplates the connection requirement by stating that a counterclaim must arise '*directly out of the subject-matter of the dispute*'. However, no reference to the identity of legal source between the claim and the counterclaim is found. Accordingly, some authors have propounded that a requirement of legal connection cannot be read into Article 46 ICSID Convention, otherwise the drafters would have explicitly included it.[197] Instead, in the ICSID framework the connection requirement would be fulfilled if the counterclaim arises out of the same investment,[198] or pertains to the same rights and obligations involved in the main claim.[199] Additionally, one may argue that the Explanatory Notes to the ICSID Arbitration Rules of 1968 suggest that only a factual connection is required. Particularly, Note B to Rule 40 ICSID Arbitration Rules of 1968 states:

[192] Bubrowski (2013), pp. 225–226. Similarly, Asteriti (2015), pp. 262–263.

[193] Douglas (2009), para. 494; Clodfelter and Tsutieva (2018), paras. 17.82–17.87.

[194] *See* Sect. 4.1.1.2.

[195] *See* Sect. 4.1.2.

[196] Clodfelter and Tsutieva (2018), para. 17.93.

[197] Lalive and Halonen (2011), p. 144.

[198] Clodfelter and Tsutieva (2018), para. 17.36. Similarly, Douglas (2009), para. 501.

[199] Kalnina and Godbole (2019), mn. 4.470.

> B. Consequently, ancillary claims are subject to three preliminary conditions (the first two of which appear in Article 46 of the Convention)
>
> (a) To be admissible such claims must arise "directly" out of the "subject-matter of the dispute" (French version: "l'objet du différend"; Spanish version: "la diferencia"). The test to satisfy this condition is *whether the factual connection* between the original and the ancillary claim is so close as to require the adjudication of the latter in order to achieve the final settlement of the dispute, the object being to dispose of all the grounds of dispute arising out of the same subject matter.[200]

This Note B to Rule 40 ICSID Arbitration Rules of 1968 was invoked by Pakistan in the *Tethyan v Pakistan* case to argue that its counterclaim need not arise out of the same legal instrument as the main claim.[201] Although the tribunal did not address the non-binding nature of the Explanatory Notes, it considered that the ICSID Convention simply referred to a 'sufficient nexus' requirement,[202] without further qualification. Accordingly, the requisite connection in Article 46 ICSID Convention does not reveal a narrow conception of legal connection demanding an identity of legal source between the claim and the counterclaim.

Additionally, the Resolution on the 'Equality of Parties before International Investment Tribunals' of the 18th Commission of the *Institut de Droit International* also rejects the strict conception of legal connection since, pursuant to Article 6(5) thereof, it is not necessary that '*the counterclaim be founded upon the same legal instrument or cause of action asserted by the claimant*'. The Commission considered the view of barring counterclaims that were based in an instrument other than the treaty,[203] but it opted for an explicit rule on connection, which could be met by a counterclaim arising out of the same investment.

Third, equating the requirement of connection between the counterclaim and the main claim with the identity of legal source/instrument undermines the scope of broad treaty provisions on dispute settlement, whereby '*any kind of dispute*' arising out of an investment may be submitted to arbitration.[204] In such cases the treaty-based arbitral tribunal has been conferred a wide range of powers to adjudge issues even if arising out of domestic legislation. The requisite nexus would thus be simply

[200] Rules of Procedure for Arbitration Proceedings in effect on 1 January 1968, Arbitration Rule 40, Note B(a) (adopted by Administrative Council on 25 September 1967) <https://icsid.worldbank.org/sites/default/files/ICSID%20Regulations%20and%20Rules%201968%20-%20ENG.pdf> accessed 10 January 2023 (emphasis added).

[201] *Tethyan Copper Company Pty Limited v Islamic Republic of Pakistan*, ICSID Case No ARB/12/1, Decision on Jurisdiction and Liability (10 November 2017) para. 1413.

[202] *Tethyan Copper Company Pty Limited v Islamic Republic of Pakistan*, ICSID Case No ARB/12/1, Decision on Jurisdiction and Liability (10 November 2017) paras. 1413–1414.

[203] Report of the Eighteenth Commission of the *Institut de Droit International* (Rapporteur Professor Campbell McLachlan) on the 'Equality of Parties before International Investment Tribunals' paras. 207–211 <https://www.idi-iil.org/app/uploads/2019/06/Commission-18-Equality-of-parties-before-international-investment-tribunals-McLachlan-Travaux-La-Haye-2019.pdf> accessed 10 January 2023.

[204] Douglas (2009), paras. 496; Waibel (2015), p. 1240.

fulfilled if the counterclaim refers to the investment rights at dispute,[205] regardless of the disparity of legal source. Otherwise, imposing a strict legal connection requirement between the counterclaim and the main claim for the admissibility of the former, would be inimical to such broad consent given by the parties. In sum, the foregoing analysis reveals that a strict conception of legal connection requiring identity of legal source between the claim and the counterclaim must be revaluated.

4.3.3.1.3 Balancing of Factors

Although a strict conception of legal connection might not be appropriate, this does not mean that the entire connection requirement is composed of a 'factual' connection. Accordingly, one may suggest that the tribunal must indeed consider both legal and factual elements of connection in order to determine whether the requisite connection between claim and counterclaim exists.[206] Those factual and legal elements however constitute only *factors* for the tribunal's analysis rather than an exhaustive list of elements that the counterclaim must fulfil.[207] In other words, a legal connection alone represents only an element to look at, rather than a determinative prerequisite for counterclaims.[208]

Accordingly, the requirement of connection begets a mixed analysis of both facts and law, whose weight would be balanced by the tribunal and whose only limitation is set by the same investment at the core of the dispute.[209] Thus, it is conceivable that even in the complete absence of a legal connection, a strong factual connection could tip the scales in favour of admitting a counterclaim, as long as it preserves the purpose of judicial/procedural economy among others.[210] The *Urbaser v Argentina* tribunal rendered the first award in this direction. This tribunal certainly addressed both aspects namely connection in fact and in law. However, it also recognised that the sole analysis of the factual link between claim and counterclaim might have been enough. In this regard, it stated:

> The Tribunal observes that the factual link between the two claims is manifest. Both the principal claim and the claim opposed to it are based on the same investment, or the alleged

[205] Douglas (2009), para. 501.

[206] Kalnina and Godbole (2019), mn. 4.470.

[207] Shao (2021), p. 169.

[208] Clodfelter and Tsutieva (2018), para. 17.35.

[209] Atanasova et al. (2014), pp. 386–387.

[210] Kjos (2007), p. 626; Hoffmann (2013), p. 452. Similarly, Douglas (2013), p. 433: ('It follows from this discussion that the legal basis of the claim is not dispositive for determining the scope of the tribunal's jurisdiction over counterclaims. So long as the factual matrix for the counterclaim directly relates to the dispute between the parties concerning the investment in question, the legal basis for the host state's counterclaim could be a contractual obligation, a domestic regulatory obligation and so on').

> lack of sufficient investment, in relation to the same Concession. This would be sufficient to adopt jurisdiction over the Counterclaim as well.[211]

The *Urbaser v Argentina* tribunal also highlighted that legal connection is fulfilled by the counterclaim insofar is not grounded on domestic law exclusively.[212] This brings to mind the traditional conception of legal connection as entailing an identity of legal sources between the claim and the counterclaim. Yet, the tribunal's decision of admitting the counterclaim went beyond the simple dichotomy of legal/factual connection. Rather, the tribunal profusely elaborated on the nature of the right to water, which was at the core of the concession (investment), and its alleged violation by the investor, which gave rise to the counterclaim.

The *Tethyan v Pakistan* tribunal took a step further. In this case, whilst the main claim arose out of the underlying Australia-Pakistan BIT (1998), one of the counterclaims was based on the terms of a joint venture agreement. With respect to the requisite connection, the tribunal stated that '*there is no general rule pursuant to which there cannot be a sufficient nexus within the meaning of Article 46(1) of the ICSID Convention and Rule 40(1) of the ICSID Arbitration Rules between an investor's treaty claims and a host State's non-treaty counterclaims*'.[213] The tribunal further asserted that such connection exists if the treaty claim required the examination of other instruments, upon which the counterclaims were grounded.[214] This shows a clear detachment from the strict legal connection view, granting some leeway to the admission of counterclaims.

Finally, the *Naturgy v Colombia* tribunal, albeit rejecting the counterclaims, seems to have comprehensively analysed different factors for the determination of connection. The tribunal first stated that the counterclaims are not related to the main claims since they only referred to the general operation of the investment and it summarised its findings as follows:

> None of Respondent's claims are based on the Treaty, much less on the Treaty obligations asserted by Claimants. Moreover, the compensation sought by the Respondent in its counterclaims is different in nature and based on different factual and legal grounds than the compensation sought by Claimants in the main claims. In the circumstances, the Tribunal does not find that Respondent's counterclaims bear a sufficiently close connection. [215]

This decision on counterclaims in treaty-based investment arbitration provides different factors, which in the tribunal's view, rebut a close connection between

[211] *Urbaser SA and Consorcio de Aguas Bilbao Bizkaia, Bilbao Biskaia Ur Partzuergoa v The Argentine Republic*, ICSID Case No ARB/07/26, Award (08 December 2016) para. 1151.

[212] *Urbaser SA and Consorcio de Aguas Bilbao Bizkaia, Bilbao Biskaia Ur Partzuergoa v The Argentine Republic*, ICSID Case No ARB/07/26, Award (08 December 2016) para. 1151.

[213] *Tethyan Copper Company Pty Limited v Islamic Republic of Pakistan*, ICSID Case No ARB/12/1, Decision on Jurisdiction and Liability (10 November 2017) para. 1414.

[214] *Tethyan Copper Company Pty Limited v Islamic Republic of Pakistan*, ICSID Case No ARB/12/1, Decision on Jurisdiction and Liability (10 November 2017) para. 1414.

[215] *Naturgy Energy Group SA and Naturgy Electricidad Colombia SL (formerly Gas Natural SDG SA and Gas Natural Fenosa Electricidad Colombia SL) v Republic of Colombia*, ICSID Case No UNCT/18/1, Award (12 March 2021) para. 623.

the main claim and the counterclaim. This may be deemed as a more comprehensive analysis in contrast to the initial line of case law, where the tribunals simply relied on the distinction between legal and factual connection. Yet, identity of legal source between the claim and the counterclaim still plays an important role.

Without falling into the truism of affirming that the connection requirement must thus be ascertained on a case-by-case basis, this section posits that a binary differentiation between legal and factual connection adds nothing to the debate. Indeed, one may argue that a clear-cut distinction between those two concepts is only theoretical, considering that such issues would most probably be intertwined in most of the cases.[216] However, this view would leave the requirement of connection deprived of any apparent content, which should not be simply up to each tribunal to define.

In this regard, there are certain standards or guidelines, which may steer the analysis of connection including: a temporal and geographic link between claim and counterclaim; a counterclaim need not be based on the same legal instrument as the main claim; the centrality of the investor's obligation in the investment project is to be considered; among others.[217] In any case, an exhaustive list of connecting factors is neither conceivable nor desirable. Tribunals should be mindful that the fulfilment of the connection requirement would hinge on the weight of each of the possible factors found in the particular case. This should provide the tribunal with some flexibility. Accordingly, counterclaims' underlying purpose of promoting judicial/procedural economy would finally prompt the admission of counterclaims provided there is an overwhelming amount of connecting factors between the main claim and the counterclaim.

4.3.3.2 Assessing the Viability of Environmental Counterclaims with Respect to the Connection Requirement

While Chap. 5 will elaborate on the applicable law to the substance of an environmental counterclaim, this part posits that the dilution of the connection requirement facilitates environmental counterclaims in treaty-based investment arbitration. On the one hand, it has been argued that the inclusion of environmental obligations upon investors in IIAs may smooth the way for the admissibility of environmental counterclaims based on those obligations since the claim and the counterclaim would share the same legal source.[218] However, and as mentioned above, there are various reasons to suggest that environmental counterclaims may be viable even if they are based on instruments other than the underlying IIA.

In this regard, the *Burlington v Ecuador* and *Perenco v Ecuador* cases are apposite. In the *Burlington v Ecuador* case, the respondent raised, among others,

[216] de Nanteuil (2018), p. 388.

[217] Anning (2021), pp. 1313 et seqq.

[218] Anning (2021), p. 1316.

an environmental counterclaim based on tort liability for environmental harm in accordance with Ecuadorian legislation,[219] whereas claimant's claims were based on the US-Ecuador BIT (1993). In spite of this disparity of legal source, the tribunal found no qualms with the connection requirement and simply asserted that '*the counterclaims arise directly out of the subject-matter of the dispute, namely Burlington's investment in Blocks 7 and 21*'.[220] The tribunal does not seem to have balanced a series of connecting factors for reaching this conclusion, but this certainly evinces that a 'strict' legal connection is not the utterly decisive factor for the adjudication of environmental counterclaims.

In the *Perenco v Ecuador* case, the respondent also filed an environmental counterclaim based on tort liability for environmental harm in accordance with Ecuadorian legislation, whereas the claimant's claims were based on Participation Contracts and the France-Ecuador BIT (1994). Here, the tribunal did not expound its jurisdiction over such counterclaim or any other requirement for the admissibility of the same. However, it placed a great importance on the redress of environmental damages in investment arbitration.[221] Although the tribunal did not directly address the requirement of connection, it is feasible that the value of environmental protection could have played a major role in this regard despite the disparity of legal source between claims and counterclaims.

These two cases bring about three conclusions relevant for the viability of environmental counterclaims with respect to the connection requirement. *First*, the disparity of the legal source between claim and counterclaim should not be fatal for the connection requirement. This suggests that a tribunal, instead of being restricted to the binary distinction of legal/factual connection, enjoys a broader scope of analysis to assess and balance the connecting factors tilting towards the admission of environmental counterclaims.

Second, as suggested by Xuan Shao, the policy behind the protection of the environment may militate in favour of the admissibility of environmental counterclaims.[222] This is drawn from the ICJ case *Application of the Convention on Genocide*, particularly from Judge Lauterpacht's Separate Opinion, where he opined that the policy underlying the prohibition of genocide (which was the basis of the counterclaim) supported a broader view on the connection requirement, thus, on the

[219] *Burlington Resources Inc v Republic of Ecuador*, ICSID Case No ARB/08/5, Decision on Ecuador's Counterclaims (07 February 2017) para. 224.

[220] *Burlington Resources Inc v Republic of Ecuador*, ICSID Case No ARB/08/5, Decision on Ecuador's Counterclaims (07 February 2017) para. 62.

[221] *Perenco Ecuador Ltd v Republic of Ecuador and Empresa Estatal Petróleos del Ecuador (Petroecuador)*, ICSID Case No ARB/08/6, Interim Decision on the Environmental Counterclaim (11 August 2015) para. 34: ('Proper environmental stewardship has assumed great importance in today's world. The Tribunal agrees that if a legal relationship between an investor and the State permits the filing of a claim by the State for environmental damage caused by the investor's activities and such a claim is substantiated, the State is entitled to full reparation in accordance with the requirements of the applicable law').

[222] Shao (2021), p. 170.

ultimate admissibility of the counterclaim.[223] Certainly, Judge Lauterpacht was not referring to the identity of the legal source for the claim and the counterclaim since both were based on the Convention on Genocide, but rather to the fact that there were different victims, motivations, locations among others.[224] Arguably, no procedural efficiency could be served by admitting a counterclaim whose factual matrix greatly differs to the main claim. Be that as it may, the protection of the environment and the overall utility of environmental counterclaims[225] should constitute connecting factors to consider and to be balanced out when assessing whether an environmental counterclaim is closely connected to the main claim in treaty-based investment arbitration.

Third, the fact that both tribunals in *Burlington v Ecuador* and *Perenco v Ecuador* have ruled upon environmental counterclaims based on domestic principles of constitutional law and environmental protection (albeit the main claims having a different legal source) elucidates that treaty-based tribunals are equipped to admit and adjudge environmental counterclaims.[226] Conversely, one may argue that environmental issues should be of domestic courts' exclusive domain, impinging on the connection requirement. Yet, such considerations rather appertain to the justifications for having investment tribunals adjudging environmental issues as a matter of policy, which Chap. 5 will address below.

---

[223] *Application of the Convention on the Prevention and Punishment of the Crime of Genocide (Bosnia and Herzegovina v Yugoslavia)* (Order on Counterclaims) [1997] ICJ Rep 243, Separate Opinion Judge Lauterpacht, para. 14: ('it is not possible to require that the facts underlying a counter-claim in respect of genocide must have their direct connection with the individual and specific acts forming the basis of the principal claim of genocide. It is sufficient that the acts invoked as constituting the basis of the counter-claim should be directly connected with the principal claim by reason of their occurrence in the course of the same conflict. Indeed, it may be suggested that the policy underlying the prohibition of genocide favours this broader view since the particular obligations of respect for human rights embodied in the Genocide Convention are ones which rest with equal weight upon all persons involved. It is upon this basis that I agree with the conclusion of the Court that the Yugoslav counter-claim is admissible').

[224] *Application of the Convention on the Prevention and Punishment of the Crime of Genocide (Bosnia and Herzegovina v Yugoslavia)* (Order on Counterclaims) [1997] ICJ Rep 243, Separate Opinion Judge Lauterpacht, paras. 8 et seqq.

[225] *See* Sect. 2.2.3.

[226] Report of the Eighteenth Commission of the *Institut de Droit International* (Rapporteur Professor Campbell McLachlan) on the 'Equality of Parties before International Investment Tribunals' para. 211 <https://www.idi-iil.org/app/uploads/2019/06/Commission-18-Equality-of-parties-before-international-investment-tribunals-McLachlan-Travaux-La-Haye-2019.pdf> accessed 10 January 2023.

4.4 Interim Conclusions

While the scope of consent constitutes the centrepiece of a tribunal's analysis on environmental counterclaims, the requisite connection represents the tribunal's compass. Only few instruments in investment arbitration refer to the close connection between the counterclaim and the main claim. Yet, tribunals should always scrutinise the connection requirement as an inherent feature of the procedural mechanism of counterclaims. As such, it is of the utmost importance to consider the proper characterisation of the connection requirement, its content and ultimate relevance for environmental counterclaims.

With respect to the characterisation of the connection requirement, tribunals and authors have unfortunately been engaged in a protracted tug of war framing the requisite connection either as a jurisdictional or as an admissibility issue. One may argue that a distinction between jurisdiction and admissibility in investment arbitration is theoretically flawed. However, it is clear that in certain cases a tribunal should decline to exercise properly vested jurisdiction for reasons of procedural fairness or judicial propriety, irrespective of such decision's label as a non-jurisdictional, admissibility, or procedural decision. This is precisely the scope of analysis on the requisite connection because a tribunal would not determine whether there is connection, but rather whether the existing connection is sufficient to promote procedural efficiency. Such analysis requires a degree of judicial discretion and flexibility that jurisdictional questions do not permit.

Thus, the proper characterisation of the connection requirement for counterclaims is as a non-jurisdictional, admissibility, or procedural issue. This entails three consequences: *first*, a tribunal must assess its jurisdiction over counterclaims prior to an analysis on connection. *Second*, the requisite connection cannot remedy the lack of jurisdiction. *Third*, parties' consent may override any consideration on the connection requirement.

With respect to the content of the connection requirement, there is a traditional division between legal and factual connection. This division seems to be borrowed from the ICJ and IUSCT jurisprudence, and its use in investment arbitration should be taken with a pinch of salt. More critically, many tribunals have narrowed down the content of the connection requirement to a strict legal connection, whereby a counterclaim is connected to the main claim only if both are based on the same legal instrument/legal source. Such position is incorrect for three reasons: *first*, the initial reliance on the IUSCT jurisprudence and on early ICSID cases does not do justice to the specific context of treaty-based investment arbitration. *Second*, there is a complete lack of textual support in IIAs, the ICSID Convention or any set of arbitration rules indicating that counterclaims require a 'strict' legal connection. *Third*, requiring identity of legal source for the claim and the counterclaim might undermine broadly worded dispute resolution provisions.

All in all, the identity of legal source by itself cannot be the only determinative factor for the admissibility of counterclaims, especially if other connecting factors incline the balance in favour of adjudging both claim and counterclaim in the same proceedings. This suggests a dilution of the connection requirement into various balancing factors. In this sense, tribunals enjoy considerable leeway to assess those factors, and to balance them against each other to determine whether a close connection of the counterclaim with the main claim exists. As such, this balancing exercise should render environmental counterclaims more viable as environmental protection with respect to the particular investment and the overall utility of environmental counterclaims can play in favour of admitting the counterclaim.

References

Alvarez HC (2000) Arbitration under the north American Free Trade Agreement. Arbitr Int 16(4): 393–430

Amado JD, Kern JS, Rodriguez MD (2018) Arbitrating the conduct of international investors. Cambridge University Press, Cambridge

Anning M (2021) Counterclaims admissibility in investment arbitration: the case of environmental disputes. In: Chaisse J, Choukroune L, Jusoh S (eds) Handbook of international investment law and policy. Springer, Singapore, pp 1277–1326

Asteriti A (2015) Environmental law in investment arbitration: procedural means of incorporation. J World Investment Trade 16(2):248–273

Atanasova D, Martínez Benoit A, Ostřanský J (2014) The legal framework for counterclaims in investment treaty arbitration. J Int Arbitr 31(3):357–391

Ben Hamida W (2003) L'arbitrage Transnational Unilatéral: Réflexions sur une Procédure résérvée à l'initiative d'une Personne Privée contre une Personne Publique. Dissertation, Université Pantheon-Assas Paris II

Bubrowski H (2013) Balancing IIA arbitration through the use of counterclaims. In: de Mestral A, Lévesque C (eds) Improving international investment agreements. Routledge, New York, pp 212–229

Clodfelter MA, Tsutieva D (2018) Counterclaims in investment treaty arbitration. In: Yannaca-Small K (ed) Arbitration under international investment agreements: a guide to the key issues, 2nd edn. Oxford University Press, Oxford, pp 417–445

de Nanteuil A (2018) Counterclaims in investment arbitration: old questions, new answers? Law Pract Int Courts Trib 17(2):374–392

Douglas Z (2009) The international law of investment claims. Cambridge University Press, Cambridge

Douglas Z (2013) The enforcement of environmental norms in investment treaty arbitration. In: Dupuy PM, Viñuales JE (eds) Harnessing foreign investment to promote environmental protection: incentives and safeguards. Cambridge University Press, Cambridge, pp 415–444

Fitzmaurice G (1986) The law and procedure of the international court of justice, vol II. Grotius Publications Ltd, Cambridge

Fontanelli F (2018) Jurisdiction and admissibility in investment arbitration: the practice and the theory. Brill, Leiden

Fouchard P, Gaillard E, Goldman B (1999) Fouchard, Gaillard, Goldman on international commercial arbitration. Kluwer Law International, The Hague

Gleason T (2021) Examining host-state counterclaims for environmental damage in investor-state dispute settlement from human rights and transnational public policy perspectives. Int Environ Agreements Polit Law Econ 21:427–444

Gouiffès L, Ordonez M (2015) Jurisdiction and admissibility: are we any closer to a line in the sand? Arbitr Int 31(1):107–122

Hoffmann AK (2013) Counterclaims in Investment Arbitration. ICSID Rev 28(2):438–453

Hwang M, Lim SC (2018) The chimera of admissibility in international arbitration. In: Kaplan N, Moser MJ (eds) Jurisdiction, admissibility and choice of law in international arbitration: Liber Amicorum Michael Pryles. Kluwer Law International, Alphen aan den Rijn, pp 265–288

Kalnina E, Godbole A (2019) Article 46. In: Fouret J, Gerbay R, Alvarez GM (eds) The ICSID convention, regulations and rules: a practical commentary. Edward Elgar Publishing, Cheltenham, pp 413–432

Kaufmann-Kohler G (2005) The arbitrator and the law: does he/she know it? Apply it? How? And a few more questions. Arbitr Int 21(4):631–638

Kendra T (2013) State counterclaims in investment arbitration – a new lease of life? Arbitr Int 29(4): 575–606

Kjos HE (2007) Counterclaims by host state in investment dispute arbitration "without privity". In: Kahn P, Wälde T (eds) Les aspects nouveaux du droit des investissements internationaux/new aspects of international investments law. Brill Nijhoff, Leiden, pp 597–628

Kjos HE (2013) Applicable law in investor-state arbitration: the interplay between national and international law. Oxford University Press, Oxford

Koller C (2008) The arbitration agreement and Arbitrability – contemplations on set-off and counterclaim in international commercial arbitration. In: Klausegger C, Klein P, Kremslehner F, Petsche A, Pitkowitz N, Power J, Welser I, Zeiler G (eds) Austrian yearbook on international arbitration 2008. Man'zsche Verlags und Universitätsbuchhandlung, Alphen aan den Rijn, pp 59–85

Lalive P, Halonen L (2011) On the availability of counterclaims in investment treaty arbitration. Czech Yearb Int Law 2:141–156

Marisi F (2020) Environmental interests in investment arbitration: challenges and directions. Kluwer Law International, Alphen aan den Rijn

Ng M (2018) Can human rights counterclaims succeed in investment treaty arbitration? Transnational Dispute Management 5 <https://www.transnational-dispute-management.com/article.asp?key=2600> Accessed 10 Jan 2023

Pauker SA, Winston B (2021) The concept of (in)admissibility in investment treaty arbitration: limited yet indispensable. ICSID Rev 36(1):189–218

Paulsson J (2005) Jurisdiction and admissibility. In: Aksen G, Briner RG (eds) Global reflections on international law, commerce and dispute resolution: Liber Amicorum in honour of Robert Briner. ICC Publishing, Paris, pp 601–617

Rees-Evans L (2020) The protection of the environment in international investment agreements – recent developments and prospects for reform. Eur Invest Law Arbitr Rev 5:357–391

Reinisch A (2017) Jurisdiction and admissibility in international investment law. Law Pract Int Courts Trib 16(1):21–43

Renteln AD (1987) Encountering counterclaims. Denver J Int Law Policy 15:379–394

Rivas JA (2015) ICSID treaty counterclaims: case law and treaty evolution. In: Kalicki JE, Joubin-Bret A (eds) Reshaping the investor-state dispute settlement system: journeys for the 21st century. Brill Nijhoff, Leiden, pp 779–827

Scherer M, Bruce S, Reschke J (2021) Environmental counterclaims in investment treaty arbitration. ICSID Rev 36(2):413–440

Schreuer C, Malintoppi L, Reinisch A, Sinclair A (2009) The ICSID convention: a commentary, 2nd edn. Cambridge University Press, Cambridge

Shany Y (2014) Jurisdiction and admissibility. In: Romano CPR, Alter KJ, Shany Y (eds) The Oxford handbook of international adjudication. Oxford University Press, Oxford, pp 779–805

Shao X (2021) Environmental and human rights counterclaims in international investment arbitration: at the crossroads of domestic and international law. J Int Econ Law 24(1):157–179

Sharpe JK, Jacob M (2018) Counterclaims and state claims. In: Beharry CL (ed) Contemporary and emerging issues on the law of damages and valuation in international investment arbitration. Brill/Nijhoff, Leiden, pp 347–369

Shihata IFI, Parra AR (1999) The experience of the International Centre for Settlement of investment disputes. ICSID Rev 14(2):299–361

Sinha V, Fusea G (2021) Counterclaims in investment arbitration: key threshold issues for claimants, respondents and tribunals. Roman Arbitr J 15:54–79

Söderlund C, Burova E (2018) Is there such a thing as admissibility in investment arbitration? ICSID Rev 33(2):525–559

Steingruber AM (2020) Counterclaims: a critical analysis of article 6 of the 2019 the Hague resolution of the Institut de droit international on the "equality of parties before international investment tribunals". ICSID Rev 35(3):595–645

Strebel FD (1999) The enforcement of foreign judgements and foreign public law. Loyola Los Angeles Int Comp Law J 21:55–130

Tomuschat C (2012) Article 36. In: Zimmermann A, Tams CJ, Oellers-Frahm K, Tomuschat C (eds) The statute of the international court of justice: a commentary, 2nd edn. Oxford University Press, Oxford

Velarde Saffer LM, Lim J (2014) Judicial review of investor arbitration awards: proposals to navigate the twilight zone between jurisdiction and admissibility. Disp Resol Int 8(1):85–93

Waibel M (2015) Investment arbitration: jurisdiction and admissibility. In: Bungenberg M, Griebel J, Hobe S, Reinisch A (eds) International investment law: a handbook. CH Beck/Hart/Nomos, Baden-Baden, pp 1212–1287

Williams DAR (2008) Jurisdiction and admissibility. In: Muchlinski P, Ortino F, Schreuer C (eds) The Oxford handbook of international investment law. Oxford University Press, Oxford, pp 868–931

Other Documents

PCIJ (29 May 1934) Series D—Acts and Documents concerning the Organization of the Court, Third Addendum to No 2, 'Elaboration of the Rules of Court of March 11th, 1936' (Fourteenth Meeting)

Report of the Eighteenth Commission of the *Institut de Droit International* (Rapporteur Professor Campbell McLachlan) on the 'Equality of Parties before International Investment Tribunals' <https://www.idi-iil.org/app/uploads/2019/06/Commission-18-Equality-of-parties-before-international-investment-tribunals-McLachlan-Travaux-La-Haye-2019.pdf> Accessed 10 January 2023

UNCITRAL (05 October 2006) Report of the Working Group on Arbitration and Conciliation on the work of its forty-fifth session. UN Doc A/CN.9/614

Chapter 5
Searching a Cause of Action for Environmental Counterclaims

Once the arbitral tribunal has acknowledged jurisdiction over the environmental counterclaim and established the sufficient connection with the main claim, finding an appropriate cause of action (or legal basis) becomes crucial. Not only would the cause of action define the scope of the respective environmental obligation, but it might also set out the consequences for its breach. Arguably, an investor might be subject to regulations, guidelines or standards of conduct embedded in international or domestic law with respect to the protection of the environment. Yet, this does not ensure the finding of an appropriate legal basis for an environmental counterclaim.

This Chapter assesses possible causes of action for an environmental counterclaim in investment arbitration and the appropriateness of bestowing an arbitral tribunal with the power to entertain such counterclaims. Accordingly, the first and second sections analyse what environmental obligations could give rise to counterclaims in contract-based investment arbitration [Sect. 5.1] and in treaty-based investment arbitration [Sect. 5.2]. The third section delves into the appropriateness of tribunals in investment arbitration deciding environmental counterclaims with respect to technical/procedural issues and from a policy perspective [Sect. 5.3]. Finally, the last section presents some conclusions on an appropriate cause of action for environmental counterclaims in investment arbitration [Sect. 5.4].

A. E. Alvarado-Garzón, *Environmental Counterclaims in Investment Arbitration*, EYIEL Monographs - Studies in European and International Economic Law 34,
https://doi.org/10.1007/978-3-031-46391-4_5

5.1 Investors' Environmental Obligations in Contract-Based Investment Arbitration

This section explores a viable cause of action for environmental counterclaims in contract-based investment arbitration. As mentioned above, investment contracts embody a synallagmatic relation between the foreign investor and the host state.[1] Accordingly, the first and foremost obvious source of environmental obligations on the investor consists of the investment contract itself [Sect. 5.1.1]. Nevertheless, tribunals may also search possible environmental obligations out of the contractual choice of law clause or (if different) the host state's domestic law [Sect. 5.1.2]. Consequently, domestic environmental law would delineate the scope of the respective environmental obligation, which could be nevertheless affected by the application of stabilisation clauses [Sect. 5.1.3].

5.1.1 Environmental Obligations within the Investment Contract

An investment contract foresees reciprocal obligations between the investor and the host state. Thus, a counterclaim by the host state may find its cause of action on one (or more) of those obligations incumbent upon the investor in contract-based investment arbitration.[2] If such obligations impose certain duties on the investor towards the environment (contractual environmental obligations), these may constitute the legal basis for an environmental counterclaim.[3]

Those contractual environmental obligations may operate in three different ways: *first*, they may create *sui generis* obligations to protect and preserve the environment in accordance with the content of the investment contract. This sort of environmental obligations would be subject to the same rules of contract interpretation as the entirety of the contract. Thus, their content, scope and consequences for their breach would be strictly guided by contractual principles. *Second*, they may reflect the respective duties towards the environment already incorporated in domestic law. In this case, the content of the environmental obligation would most likely be delineated by the development of the similar provision in domestic law. *Third*, they may incorporate international environmental standards. Although it is theoretically possible for an investment contract to explicitly include international environmental

[1] *See* Sect. 2.2.1.1.

[2] de Nanteuil (2018), p. 391.

[3] Viñuales (2015), p. 1724.

obligations,[4] the viability of an environmental counterclaim based upon such clauses is less clear.

As will be discussed below,[5] international environmental law does not seem to impose obligations directly on investors. Thus, either by reference or direct transcription in the investment contract, international environmental provisions might not function as the basis for a counterclaim by the host state against the claimant investor. Certainly, international environmental law could be reformulated/operationalised within the contract, though in this case, it is not the international environmental provision, but rather the newly reformulated (or *sui generis*) contractual environmental obligation serving as legal basis or cause of action.

5.1.2 The Interaction of Contractual Choice of Law Clauses and the Host State's Domestic Law on Environmental Matters

Should the investment contract lack any environmental obligations upon the investor, there is still the possibility of finding such obligations in the law of the host state. Based on the premise set out by the PCIJ in the *Serbian Loans* case, which stated that '[a]*ny contract which is not a contract between States in their capacity as subjects of international law is based on the municipal law of some country*',[6] the law governing the investment contract must be the domestic law of a state.[7] The crucial question is which domestic law applies to the investment contract. Certainly, an explicit choice of law clause in the respective contract renders the quest on applicable law quite straightforward. In the absence of such clause, the procedural rules agreed by the parties may enable the tribunal to determine the applicable law,[8] or the tribunal could also apply the pertinent rules on conflict of laws.[9]

By means of choice of law clauses, investment contracts usually refer to the law of the host state as the applicable law[10] but they may also refer to the law of a third

[4]This seems to be the view from authors such as Zachary Douglas and Arnaud de Nanteuil *see* Douglas (2013), pp. 434–435; de Nanteuil (2018), p. 391.

[5]*See* Sect. 5.2.2.2.

[6]*Case concerning the Payment of various Serbian Loans issued in France (France v the Kingdom of Serbs, Croats and Slovenes)* (Judgment) (12 July 1929) PCIJ Rep Series A No 20, 41.

[7]Arguably, certain aspects of the investment contract could be subjected to a law other than national law *eg* transnational law, UNIDROIT Principles, *lex mercatoria, see* Spiermann (2008), pp. 106–107.

[8]Viñuales (2015), p. 1722. Similarly, De Brabandere (2014), pp. 123–124.

[9]Walter (2015), pp. 83–84.

[10]Bjorklund (2014), p. 272.

state.[11] Similarly, the procedural rules or the pertinent rules of conflict of laws may lead the tribunal to determine that the governing law of the investment contract is either the host state's law or, at least theoretically, a third state's law. Yet, a choice of law (or the determination by the tribunal on the governing law of the contract) does not extend beyond the contractual relationship, thus, it would not cover matters such as liability in tort.[12]

As such, tort for environmental damage would be governed by the appropriate rules on conflict of laws. Instructively, various conflict rules in different states designate the law of the state where the tort occurred (or *lex loci* rule) as the appropriate applicable law for torts, although with certain modifications or exceptions.[13] At the EU level and directly applicable to the EU member states, Article 7 Regulation (EC) No 864/2007 (Rome II) envisages an explicit rule for environmental damage.[14] However, this provision simply refers to the general rule: the law of the state where the damage occurred. Since a respondent host state would raise an environmental counterclaim due to environmental damage caused in its territory, the applicable law ought to be the host state's domestic law. Needless to say, the arbitration clause must be broad enough to encompass counterclaims based on tort, otherwise, such as in the *Elsamex v Honduras* case,[15] the tribunal might reject an environmental counterclaim based on tort.

5.1.3 *Environmental Law Obligations and the Impact of Stabilisation Clauses*

A last point on contract-based investment arbitration pertains to the content of the investor's environmental obligations under domestic law and the impact of stabilisation clauses. Some scholars suggest that domestic environmental law usually implements international environmental law.[16] One may thus argue that there is certain harmonisation in this regard. However, there are two factors that hinder such harmonisation of domestic environmental law: the diverse acceptance/ratification of

[11] Dolzer et al. (2022), p. 416; Viñuales (2015), p. 1722. This option is however rare as many elements of the investment would be connected to the host state's law, but it may happen for instance in cases of loan agreements, construction or in licensing arrangements *see* Begic (2005), p. 17.

[12] Douglas (2009), para. 260; Alvik (2019), p. 283. In the context of commercial contracts (arguably comparable to investment contracts), Gary Born and Cem Kalelioglu hold a different opinion suggesting that choice of law clauses should be interpreted expansively as presumptively including non-contractual matters *see* Born and Kalelioglu (2021), pp. 108 et seqq.

[13] For a comparative study on this issue *see* Symeonides (2021), pp. 35–62.

[14] Regulation (EC) No 864/2007 of the European Parliament and of the Council of 11 July 2007 on the law applicable to non-contractual obligations (Rome II), Art 4 and Art 7.

[15] *See* Sect. 3.2.

[16] Viñuales (2012), p. 392; Douglas (2013), p. 434.

international environmental instruments and their wording. As will be elaborated below, those instruments of international law on environmental protection not only have a diverse degree of ratification and accession, which results in a multitude of standards, but also their wording can be extremely vague on terms of scope, which results in different degrees of application.[17]

As such, the environmental obligations under domestic law vary from state to state, rendering the content of such obligations highly fact-specific. For instance, establishing permissible thresholds of pollution is a highly relative undertaking depending on the time, ecosystem affected, technology available among others, which requires a tailor-made legislative choice by the respective states.[18] Even within the same state, there might be different interpretations of the applicable environmental law.[19]

This divergence is further exacerbated by the existence and application of stabilisation clauses in investment contracts. In a nutshell, stabilisation clauses are contractual commitments not to interfere with the regulatory framework an investment project was based upon.[20] Thus, protecting the investment contract, and the investor's rights thereunder, from subsequent regulations or legislative acts.[21] This does not mean the state is prohibited from enacting such acts, but rather that their effect on the particular contract is limited.[22] There are two main categories of stabilisation clauses: *freezing clauses*, which make new laws and regulations inapplicable to the contract or the investment, and *equilibrium clauses*, which oblige to renegotiate the contract to restore the economic balance in light of the new laws or regulations.[23] Some of these clauses have appeared in contract-based investment arbitrations were counterclaims have been filed, for instance, in the *Klöckner v Cameroon* case,[24] and in the *Atlantic Triton v Guinea* case.[25] As the effects of

---

[17] *See* Sect. 5.2.2.2.

[18] de Sadeleer (2020), pp. 49–50.

[19] For the examples of *Perenco v Ecuador* and *Burlington v Ecuador, see* Sect. 5.2.1.1.

[20] Begic (2005), p. 84; Cotula (2006), p. 119.

[21] Comeaux and Kinsella (1994), p. 23; Bernardini (1998), pp. 414–415.

[22] It must be noted that in some states like Germany, stabilisation clauses might be unconstitutional if they freeze the laws in a certain sector for the benefit of some investors, *see* Bungenberg (2023), pp. 195–196.

[23] Accordingly, these clauses reveal a procedural character rather than the substantive result of the renegotiation *see* Luttrell and Murphy (2019), p. 16. Similarly, Alvik (2019), p. 293.

[24] The tribunal considered that the Establishment Agreement assured stability in the terms of '*no legislative or regulatory disposition entering into force at a date subsequent to that of the signature of the present Agreement shall have the effect of restricting its provisions*' *see*, *Klöckner Industrie-Anlagen GmbH and others v United Republic of Cameroon and Société Camerounaise des Engrais*, ICSID Case No ARB/81/2, Award (21 October 1983) 25 [reproduced in R Rayfuse (ed), *ICSID Reports vol 2* (CUP 1994) 3-163].

[25] The tribunal reproduced Article 14 of the Management Agreement as '[t]*he term "law" in the present Agreement refers to Guinean law. However, Guinean law would be applicable only insofar as it is not incompatible with the terms of the present Agreement, and where it is not more restrictive than the law in force at the date of entry into force of the present Agreement*' *see*, *Atlantic Triton*

those stabilisation clauses on the counterclaims had not been at stake, both tribunals in *Klöckner v Cameroon* and *Atlantic Triton v Guinea* did not address the issue.

In any case, the relevance of stabilisation clauses appears more clearly with respect to environmental legislation. New environmental obligations in domestic law may be prompted by the availability of new technologies, new techniques in the assessment of environmental damages, the emergence of new international environmental standards, new perspectives on the environmental impact of certain industries, thus, an investor might wish to secure its position at the moment of conclusion of the contract with a stabilisation clause.[26] For instance, investors might strive to shift the costs of implementing new environmental legislations to the host state.[27] While this affects the development of environmental protection, it also impacts the possible cause of action of an environmental counterclaim in contract-based investment arbitration.

Particularly, freezing clauses insulate the specific investment contract from more stringent environmental laws. From a policy perspective, this excludes large segments of the economic activity (such as extractive industries) in detriment of the aimed goal of environmental protection.[28] In this context, counterclaims would need to search for a cause of action on derogated environmental legislation, which most likely will prove itself less rigorous than the newly implemented laws.

In case of equilibrium clauses, the higher costs on an investment project caused by new environmental regulations might lead to the renegotiation of the investment contract or the compensation of the investor.[29] These considerations distort environmental policies as the state may be persuaded to either refrain from enacting new environmental legislation or to opt for lax regulations, which by the same token are less effective at protecting the environment.[30] Yet, a possibility to curb those effects would be to include a caveat in the stabilisation clause for environmental laws.[31] In this context, counterclaims could be based on the stringent environmental laws. However, the offsetting costs mandated by an equilibrium clause might frustrate the expected gain from a successful environmental counterclaim.

Company Limited v People's Revolutionary Republic of Guinea, ICSID Case No ARB/84/1, Award (21 April 1986) 23 [reproduced in R Rayfuse (ed), *ICSID Reports vol 3* (CUP 1995) 13–44].

[26] Wälde and Ndi (1996), pp. 230–231.

[27] Report for IFC and UN Special Representative of the Secretary-General for Business and Human Rights (SRSG) on 'Stabilization Clauses and Human Rights' (27 May 2009) <https://www.ifc.org/wps/wcm/connect/0883d81a-e00a-4551-b2b9-46641e5a9bba/Stabilization%2BPaper.pdf?MOD=AJPERES&CACHEID=ROOTWORKSPACE-0883d81a-e00a-4551-b2b9-46641e5a9bba-jqeww2e> accessed 10 January 2023.

[28] Miles (2013), pp. 205 et seqq.

[29] Cotula (2006), p. 128.

[30] Cotula (2006), p. 129.

[31] This proposal seeks to strike a balance between the evolution of environmental law and the stability of an investment regime. However, as Lorenzo Cotula concedes, how would arbitrators interpret such commitments remains to be seen, Cotula (2006), pp. 134 et seqq.

Consequently, a stabilisation clause, in contrast to a choice of law clause, might affect the legal source for environmental counterclaims in contract-based investment arbitration. While the effect of such clause is not prohibitive of counterclaims, it would impact the environmental legislation applicable to the counterclaim or the resulting relief/compensation a host state may receive from an investor's environmental damage.

5.2 Investors' Environmental Obligations in Treaty-Based Investment Arbitration

Unlike investment contracts, treaty-based investment arbitration is based on the premise of the asymmetrical relationship between foreign investors and host states.[32] Accordingly, the search for a suitable cause of action for environmental counterclaims in treaty-based investment arbitration does not appear straightforward. Despite the entangled operation of international law and domestic law, this section assesses the viability of incorporating environmental obligations an investor may have as the legal basis for an environmental counterclaim in treaty-based investment arbitration. In this context, the first section addresses the possibility of incorporating environmental obligations of the investor arising from domestic law [Sect. 5.2.1]. The second section focuses on the possibility of finding environmental obligations upon the investor in the broader spectrum of international law [Sect. 5.2.2].

5.2.1 Environmental Obligations from Domestic Law: Outstripping the Role of Domestic Law?

Searching a cause of action in domestic law, particularly an investor's environmental obligations, might be the only way for counterclaims, considering the perceived absence of such obligations either in public international law or in IIAs.[33] Domestic laws are well-placed to regulate the conduct of corporations and to develop criteria of liability, exceptions or limitations, remedies among others.[34] Understandably, environmental counterclaims in treaty-based investment arbitration are often based on compliance with the host state's domestic law.[35]

---

[32] *See* Sect. 2.2.1.2.

[33] Krajweski (2021), p. 107. Similarly arguing in favour of domestic law as the basis for investors' obligations *see* Shao (2021), p. 159.

[34] Shao (2021), p. 164.

[35] Tan and Chong (2020), p. 187; Gleason (2021), p. 430.

Certainly, the principle of territorial sovereignty imposes upon every investor the obligation to comply with the host state's domestic law.[36] However, whether the investor's failure to comply with such obligation is actionable in treaty-based investment arbitration is a different question.[37] This section thus explores first the traditional understanding of an investor's breach of domestic law in treaty-based investment arbitration with emphasis on domestic environmental laws [Sect. 5.2.1.1]. Subsequently, it analyses options for the operationalisation of domestic law as a legal basis for an environmental counterclaim [Sect. 5.2.1.2].

5.2.1.1 Investors' Breach of Domestic Law: Traditional Understanding and the Potential for Domestic Environmental Laws

An investor may breach the host state's domestic law either when making the investment or afterwards during its operation.[38] Whilst the former usually affects the admissibility of the investor's claim, the latter may influence the decision on merits or the quantification of the damage.[39] It is not uncommon that a respondent host state argues some sort of investor's misconduct as a defence, but it is usually restricted to objections as to the tribunal's jurisdiction.[40]

With respect to violations when making the investment, many IIAs require the investment to be made in accordance with the domestic law of the host state (legality requirement).[41] Even though such provisions might not explicitly be framed as obligations, they have been understood as obliging investors to comply with domestic law.[42] This is the case of, for example, Article 1 Germany-Philippines BIT (1997), which includes in the definition of investment, the acceptance of such investment '*in accordance with the respective laws and regulations of either Contracting State*'. Based on this provision, the *Fraport v The Philippines* tribunal considered that investments made in breach of domestic law were not protected under the BIT as they fall short of the *ratione materiae* requirement for

[36] Generally, on the principle of territorial sovereignty *see* Crawford (2019), pp. 191 et seqq. On the foreign investor's obligation to abide by domestic law stemming from territorial sovereignty *see* Kryvoi (2012), p. 245.

[37] Bjorklund (2013), fn. 24.

[38] Kriebaum (2010), p. 329.

[39] Diel-Glior and Hennecke (2015), p. 575. However, Anna Kozyakova criticises that the investor's misconduct in course of its investment activities as a matter for the merits is rather a merely *obiter dictum* without any real elaboration by tribunals *see* Kozyakova (2021), p. 149.

[40] Hussin (2019), p. 2.

[41] *See* for instance: Turkey-Afghanistan BIT (2004), Art 1(2); Albania-Bosnia and Herzegovina BIT (2008), Art 1(1); China-Argentina BIT (1992), Art 1(1); Barbados-Canada BIT (1996), Art I(f); Croatia-Canada BIT (1997), Art I(d); Cyprus-Egypt BIT (1998), Art 1(1).

[42] Bernasconi-Osterwalder (2021), p. 473.

jurisdiction.[43] This however does not mean that any breach of domestic law affects a tribunal's jurisdiction because, as highlighted by the *Kim v Uzbekistan* tribunal, the investor's illegal conduct must be assessed in light of its seriousness and the significance of the breached obligation.[44] As such, a balance emerges whereby illegal investments should not be protected, but at the same time, host states cannot use any kind of illegality to avoid their treaty obligations.[45]

Even in the absence of a treaty provision, some tribunals have opined that an investment made contrary to the law is not protected.[46] For instance, after finding that the investor misrepresented its financial and managerial capacities, the *Plama v Bulgaria* tribunal determined that the investor could not avail itself of investment treaty protection.[47] This has been labelled as the 'clean hands' doctrine.[48]

Conversely, violations of domestic law during the operation of the investment may impact the decision on merits. For instance, in the *Jan Oostergetel v Slovakia* case, the respondent argued that the investor breached its duty to pay taxes and misled tax authorities, which the tribunal considered as allegations relating to the management of the investment to be assessed at the merits stage.[49] Consequently, the tribunal referred to the investor's misconduct as a factor to deny the existence of any legitimate expectations, thus dismissing the claim on the merits.[50]

With respect to domestic environmental law in particular, it is apposite to question what the consequences of a violation might be: would the breach of an environmental obligation be assessed in light of its seriousness, would such a breach affect the tribunal's jurisdiction or have an impact on the merits of the claim, or could

---

[43] *Fraport AG Frankfurt Airport Services Worldwide v The Republic of The Philippines*, ICSID Case No ARB/03/25, Award (16 August 2007) paras. 396 et seqq.

[44] *Vladislav Kim and others v Republic of Uzbekistan*, ICSID Case No ARB/13/6, Decision on Jurisdiction (08 March 2017) para. 404. Similarly, *Cortec Mining Kenya Limited, Cortec (Pty) Limited and Stirling Capital Limited v Republic of Kenya*, ICSID Case No ARB/15/29, Award (22 October 2018), para. 320: ('The Tribunal endorses the application of the Kim principle of proportionality to an assessment of the impact of alleged illegalities. Omission of a minor regulatory requirement, such as the act of Mr. Langwen on 8 July 2013 to issue an ordinary letter rather than use Form 3 of Schedule 1 of the Environmental (Impact Assessment and Audit) Regulations, or inadvertent misstatements, will not have the same impact as an investment "created" in defiance of an important statutory prohibition imposed in the public interest').

[45] Kozyakova (2021), p. 134.

[46] *Phoenix Action Ltd v The Czech Republic*, ICSID Case No ARB/06/5, Award (15 April 2009) para. 101; *SAUR International SA v Republic of Argentina*, ICSID Case No ARB/04/4, Decision on Jurisdiction and Liability (06 June 2012) para. 308; *Yukos Universal Limited (Isle of Man) v The Russian Federation*, UNCITRAL, PCA Case No 2005-04/AA227, Award (18 July 2014) para. 1352.

[47] *Plama Consortium Limited v Republic of Bulgaria*, ICSID Case No ARB/03/24, Award (27 August 2008) paras. 143 et seqq.

[48] Dumberry (2020), para. 4.103; Llamzon (2015), p. 316.

[49] *Jan Oostergetel and Theodora Laurentius v The Slovak Republic*, UNCITRAL Case, Decision on Jurisdiction (30 April 2010) paras. 174–176.

[50] *Jan Oostergetel and Theodora Laurentius v The Slovak Republic*, UNCITRAL Case, Final Award (23 April 2012) paras. 237 et seqq.

a breach of domestic environmental law serve as the cause of action for a counterclaim in treaty-based investment arbitration?[51] Practice shows that environmental breaches can be raised ubiquitously.

For instance, in the *Cortec v Kenya* case, the tribunal found that the investor's mining license was void *ab initio* as it violated domestic environmental laws that declared the mining site as protected.[52] Taking into consideration the requirement that protected investments must be made in accordance with Kenyan law, the tribunal declined jurisdiction.[53] Indicatively, the *Quiborax v Bolivia* tribunal found that the environmental irregularities were '*minor breaches of law*', which did not merit the revocation of the concessions (expropriation).[54] This suggests that serious violations of environmental law may have justified the revocation.[55]

Finally, in the *Burlington v Ecuador* and *Perenco v Ecuador* cases, the tribunals had recourse to Ecuadorian environmental law to assess the merits of the respective environmental counterclaims.[56] These tribunals received expert reports on the functioning of Ecuadorian environmental law, deliberated on its content and decided on issues such as the applicable legal framework,[57] the definition of environmental harm,[58] the existence of time limits for environmental claims,[59] or the switch from

---

[51] Sullivan and Kirsey (2017), p. 124.

[52] *Cortec Mining Kenya Limited, Cortec (Pty) Limited and Stirling Capital Limited v Republic of Kenya*, ICSID Case No ARB/15/29, Award (22 October 2018) paras. 343 et seqq.

[53] *Cortec Mining Kenya Limited, Cortec (Pty) Limited and Stirling Capital Limited v Republic of Kenya*, ICSID Case No ARB/15/29, Award (22 October 2018) paras. 332 et seqq.

[54] *Quiborax SA, Non Metallic Minerals SA and Allan Fosk Kaplún v Plurinational State of Bolivia*, ICSID Case No ARB/06/2, Award (16 September 2015) paras. 219–220.

[55] Sullivan and Kirsey (2017), p. 127.

[56] *Burlington Resources Inc v Republic of Ecuador*, ICSID Case No ARB/08/5, Decision on Ecuador's Counterclaims (07 February 2017) paras. 72–74; *Perenco Ecuador Ltd v Republic of Ecuador and Empresa Estatal Petróleos del Ecuador (Petroecuador)*, ICSID Case No ARB/08/6, Interim Decision on the Environmental Counterclaim (11 August 2015) paras. 65 et seqq.

[57] Both tribunals delved into the transition to the Constitution of 2008, the applicability of RAOHE or Environmental Regulation for Hydrocarbon Operations [*Reglamento Ambiental para las Operaciones Hidrocarburíficas en el Ecuador de 2001*], TULAS or Unified Text of Secondary Environmental Legislation [*Texto Unificado de Legislación Ambiental Secundaria*] and the Environmental Management Law [*Ley de Gestión Ambiental de 1999*] see, *Perenco Ecuador Ltd v Republic of Ecuador and Empresa Estatal Petróleos del Ecuador (Petroecuador)*, ICSID Case No ARB/08/6, Interim Decision on the Environmental Counterclaim (11 August 2015) paras. 317 et seqq; *Burlington Resources Inc v Republic of Ecuador*, ICSID Case No ARB/08/5, Decision on Ecuador's Counterclaims (07 February 2017) paras. 159 et seqq.

[58] Both tribunals concluded that environmental harm required a *significant* loss, diminution, detriment or impairment to the environment see, *Perenco Ecuador Ltd v Republic of Ecuador and Empresa Estatal Petróleos del Ecuador (Petroecuador)*, ICSID Case No ARB/08/6, Interim Decision on the Environmental Counterclaim (11 August 2015) paras. 327 et seqq; *Burlington Resources Inc v Republic of Ecuador*, ICSID Case No ARB/08/5, Decision on Ecuador's Counterclaims (07 February 2017) paras. 276 et seqq.

[59] *Perenco Ecuador Ltd v Republic of Ecuador and Empresa Estatal Petróleos del Ecuador (Petroecuador)*, ICSID Case No ARB/08/6, Interim Decision on the Environmental Counterclaim

fault-based liability to strict liability.[60] Accordingly, these cases evince that domestic environmental law can serve as a legal basis for an environmental counterclaim in treaty-based investment arbitration.

5.2.1.2 Domestic Environmental Law for Counterclaims in Treaty-Based Investment Arbitration: Finding the Appropriate Anchor

Before an investor's breach of domestic environmental law may provide the cause of action for a counterclaim, one may wonder whether the particular IIA needs to refer to the use of domestic law in such a manner. To this point, the *Oxus v Uzbekistan* tribunal held as a premise that '*a mere breach of domestic law is not sufficient to trigger an international liability*' of the claimant under the underlying treaty.[61] Accordingly, some authors suggest that the IIA must incorporate an obligation upon investors to respect domestic law stating that its violation constitutes a breach of the treaty.[62] Others further propose that if the investor does not dispute the applicability of domestic law or if the treaty provision on applicable law refers to domestic law, domestic environmental law might find its way to support a counterclaim.[63]

If the investor does not dispute the applicability of domestic environmental law for a counterclaim, tribunals should not have many qualms applying such law. Indeed, this could be construed as implicit consent to the applicable law to the environmental counterclaim. However, if the applicability of domestic environmental law is in dispute, the tribunal ought to investigate whether the investment treaty provides any anchor for the incorporation of domestic environmental law as a cause of action for a counterclaim. This section explores two possible options (or anchors) for the application of domestic law serving as the legal basis for counterclaims in treaty-based investment arbitration: treaty provisions on applicable law referring to domestic law [Sect. 5.2.1.2.1], and the creation of treaty provisions with a direct *renvoi* to domestic law obligations [Sect. 5.2.1.2.2].

(11 August 2015) paras. 360–364; *Burlington Resources Inc v Republic of Ecuador*, ICSID Case No ARB/08/5, Decision on Ecuador's Counterclaims (07 February 2017) para. 255.

[60] *Perenco Ecuador Ltd v Republic of Ecuador and Empresa Estatal Petróleos del Ecuador (Petroecuador)*, ICSID Case No ARB/08/6, Interim Decision on the Environmental Counterclaim (11 August 2015) paras. 353–359; *Burlington Resources Inc v Republic of Ecuador*, ICSID Case No ARB/08/5, Decision on Ecuador's Counterclaims (07 February 2017) paras. 247–248.

[61] *Oxus Gold v Republic of Uzbekistan*, UNCITRAL Case, Award (17 December 2015) para. 939.

[62] Vohryzek-Griest (2009), p. 118; Scherer et al. (2021), pp. 428 et seqq.

[63] Gleason (2021), p. 432.

5.2.1.2.1 Applicable Law Provisions: A False Anchor for Counterclaims Based on Domestic Environmental Law

The *Rusoro Mining v Venezuela* award shows the potential effect of applicable law provisions on counterclaims. Considering Article XII(7) Canada-Venezuela BIT (1996), which restricted the applicable law to the treaty and principles of international law,[64] the *Rusoro Mining v Venezuela* tribunal dismissed a counterclaim on alleged damage to natural resources and improper mining practices because, among other things, such counterclaim '*cannot be adjudicated by applying the Treaty or principles of international law*'.[65]

Therefore, authors quite often suggest that in treaty-based investment arbitration, the availability of counterclaims, whose legal basis is domestic law, depends on the treaty applicable law provision stipulating domestic law.[66] Considering that a claimant investor's consent covers the dispute resolution method (arbitration) and extends to the applicable law provisions,[67] one may argue that treaty provisions encompassing domestic law as part of the applicable law to the dispute are 'counterclaim-friendly'.[68] On the other side of the debate, a perhaps more radical position downplays applicable law provisions arguing that irrespective of the applicable law embedded in the treaty, investors are always subject to the domestic law of the state, thus, the latter could always base a counterclaim on its domestic law.[69] Neither of these positions seems to be correct.

As mentioned above, applicable law provisions are not ubiquitous to all IIAs.[70] Investment treaties with applicable law provisions to the substance of the disputes evince broadly two categories: some treaties foresee a comprehensive applicable law rule indicating the domestic law of the disputing state, the treaty itself, and public international law (broadly worded).[71] Other treaties restrict the applicable law to the

---

[64] Canada-Venezuela BIT (1996), Art XII(7): ('A tribunal established under this Article shall decide the issues in dispute in accordance with this Agreement and applicable rules of international law. An interpretation of this Agreement to which both Contracting Parties have agreed shall be binding upon the tribunal').

[65] *Rusoro Mining Ltd v Bolivarian Republic of Venezuela*, ICSID Case No ARB(AF)/12/5, Award (22 August 2016) para. 628.

[66] Lalive and Halonen (2011), p. 150; Bjorklund (2014), pp. 262–263; Gleason (2021), p. 432; Thomé (2021), p. 682.

[67] De Brabandere (2014), p. 125.

[68] Atanasova et al. (2014), p. 374.

[69] Mitra and Donde (2016), p. 116.

[70] *See* Sect. 3.3.1.2.

[71] *See* for instance: BLEU-Burundi (1989), Art 8(5); Netherlands-Czech Republic BIT (1991), Art 8(6); Spain-Argentina BIT (1991), Art X(5); Italy-Bahrain BIT (2006), Art 10(4)(c); India-UAE BIT (2013), Art 10(7)(d); Colombia-Turkey BIT (2014), Art 12(9); San Marino-Azerbaijan BIT (2015), Art 12(5); Argentina-Chile FTA (2017), Art 8.36(1); Ethiopia-Qatar BIT (2017), Art 16(3); Turkey-Cambodia BIT (2018), Art 9(5); UAE-Uruguay BIT (2018), Art 11(13); Kyrgyzstan-India BIT (2019), Art 23.3.

treaty itself and public international law (narrowly worded).[72] Indicatively, domestic law features in around 50% of applicable law provisions in IIAs.[73]

One could assume applicable law provisions (either narrow or broad) would match the respective dispute settlement provisions (classified as well as narrow and broad) in the same treaty, but in practice this is not always the case.[74] Accordingly, there are four categories that reflect either a match or mismatch: some treaties contain both a narrow dispute resolution provision and a narrow applicable law provision.[75] Some others contemplate a broad dispute resolution provision and a broad applicable law provision.[76] Yet, there are treaties where there is a mismatch either because they foresee a narrow dispute resolution provision with a broad applicable law provision[77] or they contain a broad dispute resolution provision with a narrow applicable law provision.[78]

Applicable law provisions in investment treaties thus reveal a chaotic spectrum, which may lead to consider these provisions as 'midnight clauses' meaning that they '*are agreed upon hastily at the end of long negotiations over the substantive provisions*', whose significance and interpretation challenges only surface when a dispute arises.[79] Be that as it may, one may question whether different wordings of IIAs with respect to applicable law actually have an effect on the function both public international law and domestic law play in treaty-based investment arbitration. As mentioned above, domestic law always plays a role notwithstanding the

---

[72] *See* for instance: ECT (1994), Art 26(6); NAFTA (1994), Art 1131(1); China-Malta BIT (2009), Art 9(5); Japan-Colombia BIT (2011), Art 31; Canada-Benin BIT (2013), Art 35; Canada-Côte d'Ivoire BIT (2014), Art 32(1); Austria-Kyrgyzstan BIT (2016), Art 18(1); Israel-Japan BIT (2017), Art 24(11); Singapore-Myanmar BIT (2019), Art 15(1); Japan-Georgia BIT (2021), Art 23(12).

[73] This estimate follows a survey of over 1000 treaties (both of old and new) *see* Atanasova (2019), p. 408.

[74] Schreuer (2014), p. 13.

[75] *See* for instance: NAFTA (1994), Arts 1116 and 1131; ECT (1994), Arts 26(1) and 26(6); China-Malta BIT (2009), Arts 9(1) and 9(5); Japan-Colombia BIT (2011), Arts 27(2) and 31; Canada-Benin BIT (2013), Arts 23 and 35; Austria-Kyrgyzstan BIT (2016), Arts 13 and 18(1); Israel-Japan BIT (2017), Arts 24(2) and 24(11); Canada-Moldova BIT (2018), Arts 20 and 32.

[76] *See* for instance: France-Argentina BIT (1991), Arts 8(1) and 8(4); Spain-Argentina BIT (1991), Arts X(1) and X(5); Italy-Bahrain BIT (2006), Arts 10(1) and 10(4)(c); BLEU-Guatemala BIT (2005), Arts 10(1) and 10(4); BLEU-Nicaragua BIT (2005), Arts 12(1) and 12(5); Moldova-Estonia BIT (2010), Arts 11(1) and 11(3); Turkey-Cambodia BIT (2018), Arts 9(1) and 9(5).

[77] *See* for instance: BLEU-Burundi (1989), Arts 8(1)(c) and 8(5); Argentina-Italy BIT (1990), Arts 8(1) and 8(7); Spain-El Salvador BIT (1995), Arts 11(1) and 11(3); Spain-Guatemala BIT (2002), Arts 11(1) and 11(3); Colombia-Turkey BIT (2017), Arts 12(2) and 12(9); Ethiopia-Qatar BIT (2017), Arts 16(1) and 16(3); Argentina-Chile FTA (2017), Arts 8.24(2) and 8.36(1); Turkey-Burundi BIT (2017), Arts 10(1) and 10(6).

[78] This rare combination is found in the Italy Model BIT (2003) and a handful of treaties based thereupon *see*: Italy Model BIT (2003), Art X(1) and X(4); Guatemala-Italy BIT (2003), Arts 9(1) and 9(4); Nicaragua-Italy BIT (2004), Arts X(1) and X(4); Italy-Dominican Republic BIT (2006), Arts XI(1) and XI(4); Italy-DRC BIT (2006), Arts X(1) and X(4)(a).

[79] Atanasova (2019), p. 396.

applicable law provisions.[80] Yet, by default, the role of domestic law is completely different and limited in comparison to public international law.[81] It is thus argued that domestic law and public international law must apply to their own ambit and, for instance, the former cannot justify the breach of the latter.[82] Neither can public international law solve questions *eg* of property law. Certainly, after establishing the content of the host state's domestic law, the tribunal can find whether such domestic law needs to be supplemented or corrected by international law.[83]

Given the differentiated roles of public international law and domestic law, and considering that tribunals might be forced to assess certain issues via a law that is not part of the applicable law provisions, one may wonder what the actual role of applicable law provisions in treaty-based investment arbitration is. One might argue that applicable law provisions may exceptionally provide the permissible legal bases for a claim *only if* the jurisdictional title has failed to do so.[84] In this sense, the applicable law provisions would have a sort of 'feedback effect' on the scope of the jurisdictional title.[85] However, it is difficult to imagine such situation as the kind of disputes a tribunal may entertain is always described in the dispute resolution provisions of the IIAs.

Then, one could consider that applicable law provisions in IIAs embody the law for incidental determinations.[86] The difference between incidental and principal determinations is clarified by the following example: the principal determination is to find whether there is a violation of the fair and equitable treatment standard, whereas an incidental determination might be whether the investor legally acquired the licence to operate (*eg* mining licence).[87] The former would be governed by the respective IIA and public international law, the latter would be governed by domestic law.

As such, either by considering applicable law provisions as providing the permissible legal bases for a claim when the jurisdictional title has failed to do so, or as

---

[80] *See* Sect. 3.3.1.2.

[81] De Brabandere (2014), pp. 122 et seqq.

[82] Bjorklund (2014), pp. 280–281.

[83] Begic (2005), p. 163. Similarly in case law, see *Southern Pacific Properties (Middle East) Ltd v Arab Republic of Egypt*, ICSID Case No ARB/84/3, Award (20 May 1992) para. 84; *Compañia del Desarrollo de Santa Elena SA v Republic of Costa Rica*, ICSID Case No ARB/96/1, Final Award (17 February 2000) para. 64.

[84] Bartels (2011), pp. 120 et seqq. Similarly, Atanasova (2019), pp. 399–400.

[85] Waibel (2015), p. 1222.

[86] On this point, Lorand Bartels makes a distinction between 'incidental norms' and 'principal norms' *see* Bartels (2011), p. 117: ('Principal norms are those norms used by a tribunal to make principal determinations. These determinations that a tribunal is authorized to make by its relevant jurisdictional instruments. By contrast, incidental norms are norms used by a tribunal to make the additional determinations necessary for it to be able to make principal determinations. To identify whether a norm is principal or incidental, it is necessary to identify the precise question being asked of a tribunal in any given case'). Similarly and based on Lorand Bartels' distinction *see* Atanasova (2019), pp. 403 et seqq.

[87] Bjorklund (2014), pp. 275 et seqq.

determining the law for incidental determinations, there seems to be a misunderstanding among treaty drafters on the role of those provisions.[88] On the one hand, applicable law provisions usually replicate the law for principal determinations embedded in the jurisdictional title.[89] New treaties in particular elaborate in detail the scope of tribunals' jurisdiction, thus, applicable law provisions covering the same issue become redundant.[90] On the other hand, even if the applicable law provision fails to mention the domestic law of the host state or excludes it completely, this would not prevent tribunals from using such law for incidental determinations as it might be necessary to solve the dispute. Therefore, overly restrictive applicable law provisions become unworkable.[91]

Equally unworkable appears the emerging trend in treaty drafting that consists of the characterisation of domestic law of the contracting party involved in the dispute 'as a fact' for the purposes of the settlement of investment disputes. Given the CETA Opinion rendered by the Court of Justice of the European Union,[92] this is one of the fundamental aspects advanced by the EU in its new investment treaties with investment court systems, particularly for the compatibility with EU law.[93] There are as well some recent IIAs foreseeing traditional investment arbitration, which instruct tribunals to consider domestic law exclusively as a matter of fact.[94] This is hardly an innovation. The classification of domestic law 'as a fact' has its origins in public international law,[95] and investment tribunals have sometimes adopted the same position even in the absence of explicit treaty language in that direction.[96] However,

---

[88] Atanasova (2019), p. 415.

[89] The only exception to this would be the Italy Model BIT (2003) and the handful of cases based thereupon, *see* fn. 78 above.

[90] Atanasova (2019), pp. 418–419.

[91] Schreuer (2014), p. 25. Similarly, Atanasova (2019), pp. 417–418.

[92] Opinion 1/17 (*CETA Opinion*) [2019] ECLI:EU:C:2019:341, paras. 130–131.

[93] CETA (2016), Art 8.31(2); EU-Singapore IPA, Art 3.13(2); EU-Vietnam IPA, Art 3.42(2); EU-Mexico Global Agreement, Resolution of Investment Disputes, Art 15(2).

[94] *See* for instance: Lithuania-Turkey BIT (2018), Art 12(13); China-Mauritius FTA (2019), Art 8.29(1); Hungary-Cabo Verde BIT (2019), Art 9(7–8); Belarus-Hungary BIT (2019), Art 9(8); Hungary-Kyrgyzstan BIT (2020), Art 9(8); Morocco-Japan BIT (2020), Art 16(7); Colombia-Spain BIT (2021), Art 26(2).

[95] *Case concerning Certain German Interests in Polish Upper Silesia (Germany v Poland)* (Merits) (25 May 1926) PCIJ Rep Series A No 07, 19; *Frontier Disputer (Benin v Niger)* (Judgment) [2005] ICJ Rep 90, para. 28.

[96] *See* for instance: *International Thunderbird Gaming Corporation v The United Mexican States*, UNCITRAL Case, Award (26 January 2006) para. 127; *Bayindir Insaat Turizm Ticaret Ve Sanayi AS v Islamic Republic of Pakistan*, ICSID Case No ARB/03/29, Award (27 August 2009) para. 135; *AES Summit Generation Limited and AES-Tisza Erömü Kft v The Republic of Hungary*, ICSID Case No ARB/07/22, Award (23 September 2010) para. 7.6.6; *Electrabel SA v Republic of Hungary*, ICSID Case No ARB/07/19, Decision on Jurisdiction, Applicable Law and Liability (30 November 2012) para. 4.129.

such classification is at least questionable[97] and particularly inapt for investment law as it trivialises the role of domestic law.[98]

All in all, applicable law provisions in IIAs seem trapped in a futile function and their future inclusion in investment treaties should be reconsidered. This systematic concern turns applicable law provisions into a false anchor for counterclaims seeking to find a cause of action in domestic environmental law. Instead of a controversial and broad applicable law provision, environmental counterclaims need a direct *renvoi* to domestic law obligations upon the investor to find a suitable cause of action as elaborated in the next section.

5.2.1.2.2 Treaty Provisions with a Direct Renvoi to Domestic Law Obligations

The situation might be different when the treaty expressly refers to the investor's obligations in accordance with the host state's domestic law. Whilst the tribunal in the *OSPAR Arbitration* case was very protective of the scope of jurisdiction in its interaction with the applicable law provision,[99] it also considered that a direct *renvoi* to different instruments other than the underlying treaty could potentially expand the tribunal's jurisdiction as to cover disputes over such other instruments.[100] Yet, neither the investment's legality requirement nor provisions confirming the state's power to enact domestic law may fill the bill.

Particularly, in the *Urbaser v Argentina* case, the legality requirement embedded in Article I(2) of the Spain-Argentina BIT (1992),[101] which simply states that an investment must be acquired or made in accordance with the host state's laws, was touched upon for the purpose of counterclaims. The tribunal concluded that such provision only determines the treaty's scope of application without containing '*an investor's obligation to comply with the host State's legislation when pursuing its investment with the effect that the host State would have a right to trigger the*

---

[97] Crawford (2019), pp. 49–50; *Trail smelter case (United States of America v Canada)*, Award (16 April 1938 and 11 March 1941) III RIAA 1905, 1949.

[98] Douglas (2009), paras. 115–120; Hepburn (2017), pp. 105 et seqq. For a different opinion considering that domestic law as a 'matter of fact' might indeed be applied by an international tribunal, for instance, by allocating burden of proof on the disputing parties *see* Scheu (2022), mn. 63.

[99] *See* Sect. 3.3.1.2.

[100] *Dispute Concerning Access to Information under Article 9 of the OSPAR Convention (Ireland v United Kingdom of Great Britain and Northern Ireland)*, PCA Case No 2001-03, Final Award (02 July 2003) para. 85.

[101] Spain-Argentina BIT (1991), Art I(2) ('El término "Inversiones" designa todo tipo de haberes, tales como bienes y derechos de toda naturaleza, adquiridos o efectuados de acuerdo con la legislación del país receptor de la inversion y en particular…').

application of the BIT and its arbitration clause in case of a violation of its domestic law'.[102]

Similarly, in the *Tethyan v Pakistan* case, the legality requirement figured once again in the analysis of counterclaims, this time in the form of Article 1(1)(a) Australia-Pakistan BIT (1998).[103] Here, the tribunal construed such provision in the following terms:

> [It] cannot give rise to an obligation and a corresponding liability of the investor *vis-à-vis* the host State. . .[it] does not give rise to an obligation of either the Contracting Parties or the investor. An investment that violates the host State's laws and investment policies and thus does not fulfill the admission requirement is not an "*investment*" for the purposes of the Treaty and is thus not subject to the standards of protection under the Treaty. Therefore, the non-fulfillment can be invoked by the host State as a defense against claims of the investor based on a violation of any standard of protection; however, it cannot give rise to a liability of the investor for a loss of opportunity as Respondent claims.[104]

The *David Aven v Costa Rica* case evinces a similar situation with respect to provisions confirming the state's power to enact domestic law. Article 10.9(3)(c)[105] and 10.11[106] CAFTA-DR (2004) were the relevant provisions, which in a nutshell reaffirm the states' power to adopt, maintain or enforce environmental measures. The tribunal thus concluded that such provisions do not '*provide that any violation of state-enacted environmental regulations will amount to a breach of the Treaty which could be the basis of a counterclaim*'.[107]

The foregoing suggests that not any provision referring to domestic law may serve as an anchor for environmental counterclaims. The provision must explicitly address the investor as the bearer of obligations under domestic law and whose compliance must go beyond acquiring and making the investment to also cover the

---

[102] *Urbaser SA and Consorcio de Aguas Bilbao Bizkaia, Bilbao Biskaia Ur Partzuergoa v The Argentine Republic*, ICSID Case No ARB/07/26, Award (08 December 2016) para. 1185.

[103] Australia-Pakistan BIT (1998), Art 1(1)(a): ('"investment" means every kind of asset, owned or controlled by investors of one Party and admitted by the other Party subject to its law and investment policies applicable from time to time and includes').

[104] *Tethyan Copper Company Pty Limited v Islamic Republic of Pakistan*, ICSID Case No ARB/12/1, Decision on Jurisdiction and Liability (10 November 2017) paras. 1444–1445.

[105] CAFTA-DR (2004), Art 10.9(3)(c): ('Provided that such measures are not applied in an arbitrary or unjustifiable manner, and provided that such measures do not constitute a disguised restriction on international trade or investment, paragraphs 1(b), (c), and (f), and 2(a) and (b), shall not be construed to prevent a Party from adopting or maintaining measures, including environmental measures: (i) necessary to secure compliance with laws and regulations that are not inconsistent with this Agreement; (ii) necessary to protect human, animal, or plant life or health; or (iii) related to the conservation of living or non-living exhaustible natural resources.').

[106] CAFTA-DR (2004), Art 10.11: ('Nothing in this Chapter shall be construed to prevent a Party from adopting, maintaining, or enforcing any measure otherwise consistent with this Chapter that it considers appropriate to ensure that investment activity in its territory is undertaken in a manner sensitive to environmental concerns').

[107] *David R Aven and Others v Republic of Costa Rica*, ICSID Case No UNCT/15/3, Award (18 September 2018) para. 743.

ensuing investment operation.[108] In these terms, one may thus posit that such treaty provision could elevate domestic law obligations to the international level, providing an anchor for counterclaims.[109] Such treaty provision would operate similarly to umbrella clauses but with respect to investor's obligations.[110] Considering that the investor giving its consent to treaty-based investment arbitration would be equally bound by such treaty provision referring to domestic law obligations, this could open the door for counterclaims based on those domestic law obligations.[111]

This possibility has been explored by the *Al-Warraq v Indonesia* tribunal. Here, the underlying treaty *ie* Article 9 OIC Investment Agreement (1981) stated: '[t]*he investor shall be bound by the laws and regulations in force in the host state and shall refrain from all acts that may disturb public order or morals or that may be prejudicial to the public interest. He is also to refrain from exercising restrictive practices and from trying to achieve gains through unlawful means*'. Based on this provision, the *Al-Warraq v Indonesia* tribunal concluded that the treaty obliged the investor to respect the law of the host state, which raised '*this obligation from the plane of domestic law (and jurisdiction of domestic tribunals) to a treaty obligation binding on the investor in an investor state arbitration*'.[112]

This remains one of a kind decision as no other tribunal has followed the same reasoning when deciding on counterclaims based on domestic law.[113] One may actually argue that the distinctiveness of the *Al-Warraq v Indonesia* case is ascribed to the underlying Article 9 OIC Investment Agreement (1981), which was particularly supportive for the tribunal's conclusion.[114] Certainly, no other counterclaim has been based on an IIA with a similar provision compelling investors to comply with domestic law. Thus, the question is whether, as a general rule, such type of provisions could actually support the finding of a counterclaim's legal basis in the host state's domestic law.

Even if not expressly set out in the IIA, investors are always obliged to comply with the domestic law of the host state.[115] Yet, treaty provisions imposing observance of domestic law, rather than being redundant, could strengthen investor's domestic law obligations and transform their violation into an issue for treaty-based

[108] One may consider a provision on compliance with domestic law as insufficient and rather suggest that treaties explicitly establish an obligation on investors to undertake their activities consistent with international and domestic environmental law *see* Sattorova (2019), p. 25.

[109] Asteriti (2015), p. 271: ('if umbrella clauses can internationalise contractual undertakings and place them under the umbrella of the treaty, by analogy the duty of the investor to comply with the domestic legal obligations might equally be placed under the treaty and provide the jurisdictional hook to allow a direct claim, or a counterclaim, by the state'). Similarly, Shao (2021), p. 164.

[110] Krajweski (2021), p. 119.

[111] Newcombe and Marcoux (2015), pp. 531–32. Similarly, Zin (2020), p. 244.

[112] *Hesham Talaat M Al-Warraq v The Republic of Indonesia*, UNCITRAL Case, Award (15 December 2014) para. 663.

[113] Popova and Poon (2015), p. 235.

[114] Magnarelli (2020), p. 117.

[115] Bjorklund (2013), fn. 24; Mitra and Donde (2016), p. 116.

investment arbitration.[116] In this sense, IIAs could be modernised by explicitly linking environmental obligations in domestic law to counterclaims,[117] and the scope of the investors obligations would certainly depend on the respective domestic law.[118] In practice, this sort of provisions have been increasingly included in IIAs,[119] but disputes thereunder have not arisen yet.

Another anchor could be strictly procedural. Both Article 14(3) Slovak Republic-Iran BIT (2016),[120] and Article 43 PAIC (2016)[121] regulate the possibility for the respondent host state of filing counterclaims, and in both cases there is an explicit reference to the investor's obligations under domestic law as the legal basis of a counterclaim. Arguably, in the case of PAIC (2016), the availability of legal bases is larger by the reference to international law as well.[122] Be that as it may, both provisions foresee a direct *renvoi* to the investor's obligations under the respective domestic law, with the added advantage of already linking such obligations to the host state's counterclaims.

Finally, there are two concerns that would unfold with respect to the application of domestic law as a legal basis for counterclaims in treaty-based investment arbitration: *first*, with respect to the definition of 'law' as it may indicate a formal approach (law is adopted by the parliament) or substantive approach (law may also include decrees and regulations of the government or precedent set out by courts).[123]

---

[116] Krajweski (2021), p. 119.

[117] Gleason (2021), p. 440.

[118] Krajweski (2021), p. 120.

[119] *See* for instance: Kyrgyzstan-India BIT (2019), Art 11(i); Belarus-India BIT (2018), Art 11(i); Argentina-UAE BIT (2018), Art 14(a); Ethiopia-Qatar BIT (2017), Art 14; Ethiopia-UAE BIT (2016), Art 11(1); Argentina-Qatar BIT (2016), Art 11. This is also reflected in the newest version of Model BITs, *see* for instance: The Netherlands Model BIT (2019), Art 7(1); Morocco Model BIT (2019), Art 18(1); BLEU Model BIT (2019), Art 18(1); Canada Model BIT (2021), Art 16; India Model BIT (2015), Art 11(i).

[120] Slovak Republic-Iran BIT (2016), Art 14(3): ('The *respondent may assert as a defense, counterclaim, right of set off or other similar claim that the claimant has not fulfilled its obligations under this Agreement to comply with the Host State law* or that it has not taken all reasonable steps to mitigate possible damages. For avoidance of any doubt, if the tribunal does not dismiss the claim under paragraph 2 above, it shall take such violations into account when assessing the claim if raised as a defense, counterclaim, right of set off or other similar claim by the respondent') (emphasis added).

[121] PAIC (2016), Art 43: ('(1)Where an investor or its investment is alleged by a Member State party in a dispute settlement proceeding under this Code *to have failed to comply with its obligations under this Code or other relevant rules and principles of domestic and international law*, the competent body hearing such a dispute shall consider whether this breach, if proven, is materially relevant to the issues before it, and if so, what mitigating or off-setting effects this may have on the merits of a claim or on any damages awarded in the event of such award. (2) *A Member State may initiate a counterclaim against the investor* before any competent body dealing with a dispute under this Code for damages or other relief resulting from an alleged breach of the Code') (emphasis added).

[122] In this sense *see* Mbengue and Negm (2019), p. 266.

[123] Steingruber (2020), p. 634.

Second, with respect to the timing of enactment as the state could pre-emptively enact a new regulation with the sole purpose of filing a counterclaim.[124] The former would pertain to the functioning of the specific legal system and become a technical issue of how to determine domestic law. Whereas the latter might be a too sweeping suspicion, based on a presumption of misuse by the host state. In any case, should that situation occur, the tribunal itself could resort to general principles of law such as abuse of rights or more generally good faith to address the timing of enactment. There is thus no need to curtail the applicability of domestic law from the outset.

All in all, treaty provisions imposing the obligation upon investors to comply with the host state's domestic law, or treaty provisions foreseeing counterclaims with domestic law as a possible legal basis may theoretically provide a viable anchor for counterclaims, whose legal basis is domestic environmental law. Possibly, a combination of both treaty provisions might be necessary. Yet, since those provisions have not been tested by an arbitral tribunal, their utilisation as an anchor for counterclaims and the assessment of domestic law can only be speculated at this point.

5.2.2 Environmental Obligations from International Law: An Unexploited Opportunity

The second option for environmental counterclaims in treaty-based investment arbitration is to find a cause of action in the broader spectrum of international law. To this point, the *Oxus v Uzbekistan* tribunal held as a premise that the respondent must establish '*what are exactly the international obligations that Claimant is said to have breached*' as well as '*the specific actions of Claimants which are in breach of such international obligations*'.[125] This option faces a first challenge consisting on the general assumption that international law does not (or cannot) impose obligations upon investors.[126] Should such assumption prove correct, substantiating an environmental counterclaim on international law would turn implausible.

Against this backdrop, this section firstly scrutinises whether public international law may impose obligations upon non-state actors such as foreign investors [Sect. 5.2.2.1]. Secondly, it delves into international environmental law as a possible cause of action for environmental counterclaims in treaty-based investment arbitration [Sect. 5.2.2.2]. Thirdly, it explores the role of IIAs with respect to international environmental obligations [Sect. 5.2.2.3].

[124] Steingruber (2020), p. 634.

[125] *Oxus Gold v Republic of Uzbekistan*, UNCITRAL Case, Award (17 December 2015) para. 939.

[126] Kryvoi (2012), pp. 244–245; Sinha and Fusea (2021), p. 65.

5.2.2.1 International Obligations on Non-State Actors: Legal Foundations

The role of non-state or private actors in the international sphere has gained increasing attention. Undoubtedly, non-state actors enjoy some substantive and procedural rights granted directly by instruments of international law.[127] Conversely, much ink has been spilled about the imposition of international obligations upon such non-state actors without a satisfactory common understanding on this issue. Although states might voice their commitment to strengthen control over private actors, particularly multinationals, their domestic regulations and international treaties often pay lip service to such commitment.

However, the legal foundations for international obligations exist and they constitute the groundwork for fostering international environmental obligations upon global actors such as foreign investors. Accordingly, this section first unravels the traditional debate on international legal personality and international obligations, which does nothing but obscure the possibility of imposing obligations upon non-state actors from international law [Sect. 5.2.2.1.1]. Subsequently, the possible sources of obligations on private actors are addressed [Sect. 5.2.2.1.2]. This brings about the clarification of the concepts of 'responsibility', 'accountability' and 'liability' with respect to non-state actors, which unfortunately are often used interchangeably [Sect. 5.2.2.1.3].

5.2.2.1.1 Unravelling the Mixture of International Legal Personality and International Obligations

Originally, states were considered the only 'subjects' of international law, whereas individuals and other entities recognised by domestic law (such as corporations) were deemed merely as 'objects' of international law.[128] Even in the realm of international investment law, where claimant investors may directly claim against the respondent state, some authors argue that this does not transform investors into full or partial subjects of international law.[129] Accordingly, the lack of international obligations on corporate actors was linked to the perceived lack of international legal personality of those actors.[130] However, relegating private actors as mere 'objects' is untenable[131] and rather misconceives their status under international law.

---

[127] For instance, the rights granted by investment treaties or the right to property and privacy under human rights conventions, *see* Ben Hamida (2003), para. 298; Zerk (2006), pp. 75–76; Dörr (2020), p. 137.

[128] Zerk (2006), p. 73; Kryvoi (2012), p. 234.

[129] Vöneky (2020), p. 372.

[130] Muchlinski (2008), p. 655.

[131] Douglas (2009), para. 7.

In the *Reparations Case*, the ICJ considered the international legal personality of the United Nations to stem from the purpose assigned to the organisation by the UN Charter, the possibility to conclude international agreements, the possibility to enjoy rights and be subject to obligations in international law, as well as the right of action to enforce its rights.[132] In this sense, all these characteristics seem to comprise the elements for considering an entity to enjoy international legal personality.[133] The ICJ further recognised that international legal personality does not equate an organisation to a state, nor does it mean that its legal personality and rights are the same as a state.[134] This already evinces that the division between subjects and objects might be more nuanced than originally devised. Moreover, the role of non-state actors in fields such as international economic law urges the reconsideration of subjectivity in international law, perhaps towards an assessment of the degree to which international law recognises the existence of other participants at the international level.[135]

As such, one may argue that foreign investors' right of action and protected rights under IIAs would support the finding of the investors' international legal personality but only for the purpose of the respective IIA.[136] Their international legal personality is thus *limited* to the precise terms of the underlying IIA, *derivative* from the contracting states' will as expressed in said treaty, and *passive*, as investors are not direct negotiators of IIAs.[137]

However, the international legal personality of investors does not reveal whether they can be burdened with international obligations or whether they can be liable before an international tribunal for the breach of those obligations.[138] Given that states create international law, there is no barrier for them to directly allocate certain responsibilities to corporations and other non-state actors,[139] including environmental obligations.[140] In fact, already in the *Danzig* Case, the PCIJ had laid down that states could create rights and obligations upon privates via an international agreement.[141] This understanding has already permeated treaty-based investment arbitration. The *Urbaser v Argentina* tribunal has famously stated:

---

[132] *Reparation for Injuries suffered in the Service of the United Nations* (Advisory Opinion) [1949] ICJ Rep 174, 178–179.

[133] Zerk (2006), p. 73.

[134] *Reparation for Injuries suffered in the Service of the United Nations* (Advisory Opinion) [1949] ICJ Rep 174, 179.

[135] Zerk (2006), p. 74.

[136] Alvarez (2011), p. 12; Dumberry (2013), pp. 183–184.

[137] Dumberry (2013), p. 186.

[138] Karavias (2019), p. 64. Similarly, Alvarez (2011), p. 31.

[139] Vazquez (2005), p. 930; Zerk (2006), p. 262; Dörr (2020), p. 138.

[140] Nollkaemper (2006), p. 194.

[141] *Jurisdiction of the Courts of Danzig* (Advisory Opinion) (03 March 1928) PCIJ Rep Series B No 15, 17–18: ('But it cannot be disputed that the very object of an international agreement, according to the intention of the contracting Parties, may be the adoption by the Parties of some definite rules creating individual rights and obligations and enforceable by the national courts. That there is such

> A principle may be invoked in this regard according to which corporations are by nature not able to be subjects of international law and therefore not capable of holding obligations as if they would be participants in the State-to-State relations governed by international law. While such principle had its importance in the past, it has lost its impact and relevance in similar terms and conditions as this applies to individuals.[142]

Subsequently, the *David Aven v Costa Rica* tribunal explicitly shared the same view.[143] This reasoning does not suggest that private actors such as investors and states are subject to the same obligations, save for some exceptions, for instance, the obligation to abstain from violating human rights equally applies to investors and states.[144] Consequently, for the purposes of counterclaims it is irrelevant to discuss the international legal personality of investors, since the crux of the matter is rather which international obligations investors are subject to.

5.2.2.1.2 Where to Find International Obligations on Non-State Actors?

Obligations on non-state actors under customary international law do not seem to exist given the lack of uniform state practice in this regard.[145] Some authors thus argue that if states aim at subjecting foreign investors to international obligations, they must establish so expressly.[146] However, like with any other treaty provision, there is an exercise of treaty interpretation, which will determine whether the treaty does impose obligations on private actors[147] or whether the treaty simply obliges the contracting states to implement and enforce private obligations within their legal systems.[148] Accordingly, Markos Karavias proposes three conditions for finding obligations of private corporations under international law[149]: *first*, the obligation must stem directly from international law, this means no recourse to domestic legislation is required. *Second*, the violation of such obligation by the corporation

---

an intention in the present case can be established by reference to the terms of the *Beamtenabkomen*').

[142] *Urbaser SA and Consorcio de Aguas Bilbao Bizkaia, Bilbao Biskaia Ur Partzuergoa v The Argentine Republic*, ICSID Case No ARB/07/26, Award (08 December 2016) para. 1194.

[143] *David R Aven and Others v Republic of Costa Rica*, ICSID Case No UNCT/15/3, Award (18 September 2018) para. 738.

[144] Gleason (2021), p. 434. For a different opinion criticising the *Urbaser v Argentina* tribunal on this regard *see* Crow and Escobar (2018), p. 99.

[145] HRC, Report of the Special Representative of the Secretary-General (SRSG) on the issue of human rights and transnational corporations and other business enterprises, 'Business and Human Rights: Mapping International Standards of Responsibility and Accountability for Corporate Acts' (09 February 2007) UN Doc A/HRC/4/035, paras. 33–34.

[146] Sinha and Fusea (2021), p. 73.

[147] Dörr (2020), p. 138.

[148] Vazquez (2005), pp. 940–941.

[149] Karavias (2013), pp. 10 et seqq.

must bring about its responsibility under international law. *Third*, liability ought to be found via the application of international law.

Treaties imposing obligations on non-state actors have lagged behind in contrast to instruments granting rights on those private actors, for instance, in human rights or investment law.[150] There are nevertheless, two examples worth mentioning[151]: (i) Articles 101 and 102 of the Treaty on the Functioning of the European Union (TFEU) which directly impose competition law obligations upon corporations operating in the EU; (ii) the Rome Statute of the International Criminal Court, which sets out the individual responsibility for crimes included thereunder.[152]

Even though international law may impose obligations upon corporations, it often addresses the conduct of non-state actors either *indirectly* or through *non-binding instruments*. An indirect regulation exists where international law compels states to regulate the conduct of non-state actors within their national legal systems.[153] Non-binding instruments are categorised as soft law and enjoy a political rather than legal authority.[154]

With respect to indirect regulation, some examples are the Basel Convention on the Control of Transboundary Movements of Hazardous Wastes and their Disposal (1989) obliging states to prevent and punish the contravention of the convention,[155] the Convention Criminalizing Bribery of Foreign Public Officials in International Business Transactions (1997), which requires states to criminalise bribery when occurring in their territory,[156] or the United Nations Convention against Transnational Organized Crime (2000) commanding states to implement legislative acts and to sanction participation in criminal organisations or money laundering.[157] As such, international law heavily relies on domestic law for regulating the conduct of corporations, and the failure to control non-state actors as commanded by those

[150] Dörr (2020), p. 137. In the particular case of investment law, one may argue that the discussion on possible investor's misconduct was off the agenda during the creation of IIAs and the development of treaty-based investment arbitration *see* Kozyakova (2021), pp. 60–64.

[151] A third category of obligations on non-state actors is proposed by Oliver Dörr with respect to the protection of human rights embedded in the Universal Declaration of Human Rights and some regional instruments, however, by his own admission, those duties are too vague to be regarded as actual obligations *see* Dörr (2020), p. 137.

[152] During the negotiations of the Rome Statute, the possibility of including private entities in the scope of application was discussed but rapidly dropped as it proved divisive *see* Karavias (2019), p. 50.

[153] Vazquez (2005), p. 930; Dörr (2020), p. 144.

[154] Nollkaemper (2006), p. 191.

[155] Basel Convention on the Control of Transboundary Movements of Hazardous Wastes and their Disposal (1989), Art 4(4).

[156] Convention Criminalizing Bribery of Foreign Public Officials in International Business Transactions (1997), Art 1.

[157] United Nations Convention against Transnational Organized Crime (2000), Arts 5–11.

conventions entails the responsibility of the state rather than the responsibility of the respective non-state actor under international law.[158]

With respect to non-binding instruments, some examples include the ILO Tripartite Declaration of Principles concerning Multinational Enterprises and Social Policy of 1977 as amended in 2017, the Principles of the UN Global Compact 2000, the Guidance on Social Responsibility (ISO 26000:2010), the OECD Guidelines for Multinational Enterprises of 2011, or the UN Guiding Principles on Business and Human Rights of 2011. Particularly in the field of human rights, the refusal to incorporate direct obligations from international law to corporations has instead resulted in the support of standard setting.[159] These instruments do not bind corporations and on many occasions their adherence is voluntary, yet their significance cannot be underestimated. Those guidelines or standards not only highlight that international law may directly address the conduct of corporations but may also inform the states' new legislative efforts and judicial practice.[160]

Certainly, the breach or simple non-observance of those instruments does not carry any legal consequence. However, there might be responsibility through reception, in other words, when those instruments are incorporated or referred to via domestic or international law placing legal consequences for their violation.[161] Indeed, one may argue that the implementation of soft law instruments applicable to corporations may '*blur the lines between the strictly voluntary and mandatory spheres for participants*' creating a sort of '*shared responsibility*' between states and non-state actors.[162]

5.2.2.1.3 Distinguishing Responsibility, Liability and Accountability of Non-State Actors

A final clarification on the legal foundations of international obligations on non-state actors (particularly corporations) pertains to the distinction between the concepts of 'responsibility', 'liability' and 'accountability', which are often used interchangeably. Particularly, the concept of responsibility of corporations in international law may refer either to the obligations applicable to corporations or to the legal consequences for the failure to fulfil those obligations.[163] By analogy of the terminology

---

[158] Nollkaemper (2006), p. 186.

[159] UNCHR, Interim Report of the Special Representative of the Secretary-General on the Issue of Human Rights and Transnational Corporations and other Business Enterprises, 'Promotion and Protection of Human Rights' (22 February 2006) UN Doc E/CN.4/2006/97, paras. 55 et seqq.

[160] Morgera (2020), p. 288.

[161] Dörr (2020), p. 154.

[162] HRC, Report of the Special Representative of the Secretary-General (SRSG) on the issue of human rights and transnational corporations and other business enterprises, 'Business and Human Rights: Mapping International Standards of Responsibility and Accountability for Corporate Acts' (09 February 2007) UN Doc A/HRC/4/035, paras. 61–62.

[163] Nollkaemper (2006), pp. 181–182.

adopted by the special rapporteur to the ILC, Roberto Ago, with respect to state responsibility,[164] the first understanding of corporate responsibility describes primary rules, whereas the second understanding of corporate responsibility relates to secondary rules.

Accordingly, the first understanding of corporate responsibility refers to the expectation that private companies should be more responsive to the society's needs in the broader sense rather than solely to their shareholders' wishes.[165] As such, corporate behaviour should align to internationally recognised values.[166] In this sense, the concept of corporate social responsibility (CSR) is indicative. CSR encompasses the idea of certain social obligations that should (or already do) attach to corporations.[167] Thus, 'responsibility' in this context defines obligations applicable to corporations irrespective of their binding or non-binding status.

The second understanding of corporate responsibility concerns the legal consequences for the failure to fulfil international obligations. However and until date, international law does not conceive any rules in this regard.[168] By comparison, the Articles on the Responsibility of States for Internationally Wrongful Acts (ARSIWA) reflect the customary rules on the legal consequences arising out of states' failure to fulfil their international obligations (state responsibility). However, these rules on state responsibility as a whole are not well suited for corporate responsibility.[169] Given that the nature and purpose of state authority differs to the nature and purpose of corporations, ARSIWA cannot be transplanted to the responsibility of corporations[170] or to the responsibility of any other non-state actor for that matter.

Yet, there are two options to fill the gap of rules on the responsibility of corporations: *first*, relying on the general principle delineated by the PCIJ in the *Chorzów Factory* case, according to which '[i]*t is a principle of international law, and even a general conception of law, that any breach of an engagement involves an*

[164] ILC, Second Report on State Responsibility by Mr. Roberto Ago, Special Rapporteur, on 'The Origin of International Responsibility' (20 April 1970) UN Doc A/CN.4/233, para. 11: ('[i]n its previous drafts, the Commission has generally concentrated on defining the rules of international law which, in one sector of inter-State relations or another, impose particular obligations on States, and which may, in a certain sense, be termed 'primary', as opposed to other rules – precisely those covering the field of responsibility – which may be termed 'secondary', inasmuch as they are concerned with determining the consequences of failure to fulfil obligations established by the primary rules').

[165] Morgera (2020), p. 16.

[166] Morgera (2020), p. 17.

[167] Miles (2013), p. 217.

[168] Karavias (2019), p. 60; Dörr (2020), p. 143. Similarly, referring to the absence of international rules on civil or criminal responsibility of corporations *see* Nollkaemper (2006), pp. 191 et seqq.

[169] Gattini (2016), p. 123.

[170] Nollkaemper (2006), pp. 191 et seqq.

obligation to make reparation'.[171] Certainly, this principle provides a rudimentary regime for corporate responsibility, but it could be further furnished with selected and relevant rules of ARSIWA that fit the analysis on corporate behaviour.[172] *Second*, examining what domestic laws provide on corporate responsibility in similar circumstances.[173]

The concept of liability is of paramount importance with respect to environmental damage caused by corporations. For instance, the Convention on Civil Liability for Damage resulting from Activities Dangerous to the Environment of 1993, the Convention on Third Party Liability in the Field of Nuclear Energy of 1960 (Paris Convention), or Protocol to amend the International Convention on Civil Liability for Oil Pollution Damage of 1984 (London Protocol)[174] refer to 'liability' instead of 'responsibility' for environmental damage. But this does not mean that both concepts are synonymous. In fact, the ILC clarified the use of both concepts with respect to state responsibility and considered that '*the term "responsibility" should be used only in connexion with internationally wrongful acts and that, with reference to the possible injurious consequences arising out of the performance of certain lawful activities, the more suitable term "liability" should be used*'.[175] In the same light, corporate liability should be confined to the obligation to repair damages arising out of lawful acts, whereas corporate responsibility should be limited to the obligation to repair damages arising of an unlawful conduct.

The concept of accountability of corporations alludes to transparency *vis-à-vis* the society at large. This entails that the corporate decisions and operations are examined and judged by the public, which creates a sort of 'social direction' of the corporation, incentivised by this openness.[176] With this purpose, there exist some monitoring mechanisms or platforms for voicing complaints against corporations at the international level, though without an adjudicatory nature. For instance, the UN Global Compact Office may receive allegations that a participating corporation is abusing or misrepresenting the principles and aims of the UN Global Compact, including the involvement in severe environmental damage.[177] If the Office considers the allegations not to be frivolous, it establishes a dialogue platform with the concerned

---

[171] *Case concerning the Factory at Chorzów (Germany v Poland)* (Merits) (13 September 1928) PCIJ Rep Series A No 17, 29.

[172] Dörr (2020), p. 144.

[173] Alvarez (2011), p. 26.

[174] The regimes of international civil liability for environmental damage will be discussed in more detail below *see* Sect. 5.2.2.2.2.1.

[175] ILC YB [1973] vol I, A/CN.4/Ser.A/1973, 'Draft Report on State Responsibility' (210–220) 211, para. 37.

[176] Morgera (2020), pp. 19–20.

[177] UN Global Compact Integrity Measures Policy & FAQ, 'Frequently Asked Questions' (2015) <https://www.unglobalcompact.org/library/1831> accessed 10 January 2023.

participating company, but should the latter refuse to engage, it might be removed from the list of participants.[178]

Another example is found in the International Finance Corporation (IFC), which counts with the Compliance Advisor/Ombudsman (CAO) as an oversight authority allowing individuals and communities affected by IFC-supported business activities to raise their concerns.[179] For this purpose, the CAO may engage in collaborative dispute resolution, compliance and advisory functions related to the environmental and social impacts of projects financed by the IFC.[180] This type of accountability mechanisms for private companies contributes to the credibility of international standard setting as they strike a balance between the interests of the society at large that may be affected by corporate environmental damages and the interests of corporations to be protected from unfounded allegations.[181]

5.2.2.2 International Environmental Law: An Unfinished Cause of Action?

Some authors consider the possibility of finding a cause of action for counterclaims in treaty-based investment arbitration in international environmental law, as long as the obligations thereunder apply directly to investors.[182] Against this backdrop, this section sheds some light on the underpinnings of international environmental law [Sect. 5.2.2.2.1] and on whether international environmental law actively regulates the conduct of private actors [Sect. 5.2.2.2.2]. Subsequently, this section casts some doubts on the re-conceptualisation of environmental protection as a matter of human rights or as transnational public policy for the purposes of counterclaims in treaty-based investment arbitration [Sect. 5.2.2.2.3]. Finally, the evocative example of the Alien Tort Claims Act in the US (ATCA) and its relation with international environmental obligations will be touched upon [Sect. 5.2.2.2.4].

---

[178] UN Global Compact, 'Integrity Measures Policy' (2022), pp. 2–4 <https://ungc-communications-assets.s3.amazonaws.com/docs/publications/PDF_Integrity%20Measures_English_01.12.2022.pdf> accessed 10 January 2023.

[179] IFC, 'International Finance Corporation's Policy on Environmental and Social Sustainability' (01 January 2012) para. 55 <https://www.ifc.org/wps/wcm/connect/7141585d-c6fa-490b-a812-2ba87245115b/SP_English_2012.pdf?MOD=AJPERES&CVID=kiIrw0g> accessed 10 January 2023.

[180] IFC, 'IFC/MIGA Independent Accountability Mechanism (CAO) Policy' (28 June 2021) para. 8 <https://www.ifc.org/wps/wcm/connect/d3e7f1c4-fd6b-40fd-ae76-fb028916611d/IFC-MIGA-Independent-Accountability-Mechanism-CAO-Policy.pdf?MOD=AJPERES&CVID=nFDGwP2> accessed 10 January 2023.

[181] Morgera (2013), p. 353.

[182] Scherer et al. (2021), p. 431.

5.2.2.2.1 Underpinnings of International Environmental Law

International environmental law is a relatively recent development in the broader spectrum of public international law and subject to a state of steady dynamic evolution.[183] It reflects the developments in scientific knowledge, the use of new technologies and their impacts on the environment as well as changes at the political and institutional level.[184] In general, environmental law does not seek to prohibit all kinds of pollution generated by humankind, but rather to allow activities that might be injurious to the environment within certain thresholds and adhering to certain standards, given the environment's capacity to regenerate.[185]

The milestones on international environmental law are the Declaration on the Human Environment of 1972 (Stockholm Declaration)[186] and the Rio Declaration. Both declarations comprise a series of principles for the preservation of the environment without legally binding force. Nevertheless, their role in the development of international environmental law cannot be underestimated as they influence consistent state practice, promoting the conclusion of binding treaty commitments.[187] In this line, there are a myriad of international instruments addressing issues of environmental protection, which vary greatly in scope, normative character, acceptance or ratification, among others.

Some examples with widespread coverage are the Convention on International Trade in Endangered Species of Wild Fauna and Flora[188]; the Convention on Long-Range Transboundary Air Pollution[189]; the Convention on the Conservation of Antarctic Marine Living Resources[190]; the Vienna Convention for the Protection of the Ozone Layer[191] and its associated Montreal Protocol on Substances that deplete the Ozone Layer[192]; the Basel Convention on the Control of Transboundary

[183] Boyle (1999), p. 62.

[184] Sands et al. (2018), p. 21.

[185] de Sadeleer (2020), p. 126.

[186] Report of the United Nations Conference on the Human Environment (1973) UN Doc A/CONF.48/14/Rev.1 (Declaration on the Human Environment).

[187] Boyle (1999), p. 64.

[188] Convention on International Trade in Endangered Species of Wild Fauna and Flora (adopted 03 March 1973, entry into force 01 July 1975) 993 UNTS 243, with 184 contracting parties.

[189] Convention on Long-Range Transboundary Air Pollution (adopted 13 November 1979, entry into force 16 March 1983) 1302 UNTS 217, with 51 contracting parties.

[190] Convention on the Conservation of Antarctic Marine Living Resources (adopted 20 May 1980, entry into force 07 April 1982) 1329 UNTS 47, with 32 contracting parties.

[191] Vienna Convention for the Protection of the Ozone Layer (adopted 22 March 1985, entry into force 22 September 1988) 1513 UNTS 293, with 198 contracting parties [Ozone Layer Convention].

[192] Montreal Protocol on Substances that deplete the Ozone Layer (adopted 16 September 1987, entry into force 01 January 1989) 1522 UNTS 3, with 198 contracting parties [Montreal Protocol on Ozone Layer].

Movements of Hazardous Wastes and their Disposal[193]; the Convention on Biological Diversity[194]; the United Nations Convention to Combat Desertification in those Countries Experiencing Serious Drought and/or Desertification, Particularly in Africa[195]; the Stockholm Convention on Persistent Organic Pollutants[196]; the United Nations Framework Convention on Climate Change (UNFCCC)[197] and its associated instruments such as the Kyoto Protocol[198] and the Paris Agreement.[199]

Despite this multitude of instruments, the underpinnings of international environmental law seemingly lie in three main principles: the polluter-pays principle, the principle of prevention and the precautionary principle. *First*, The polluter-pays principle has been aptly condensed in the Rio Declaration in the following terms:

> National authorities should endeavour to promote the internalization of environmental costs and the use of economic instruments, taking into account the approach that the polluter should, in principle, bear the cost of pollution, with due regard to the public interest and without distorting international trade and investment.[200]

The polluter-pays principle thus seeks to protect the environment through the internalisation of environmental costs by the polluter,[201] thus preventing the society at large to be burdened with those costs.[202] It is argued that its application has a multifaceted ripple effect: promoting the use of less-polluting technology, establishing a fairer distribution of environmental costs, and having a pedagogical effect both on producers and consumers.[203] The polluter-pays principle certainly

---

[193] Basel Convention on the Control of Transboundary Movements of Hazardous Wastes and their Disposal (adopted 22 March 1989, entry into force 05 May 1992) 1673 UNTS 57, with 189 contracting parties.

[194] Convention on Biological Diversity (adopted 05 June 1992, entry into force 29 December 1993) 1760 UNTS 79, with 196 contracting parties [Convention on Biological Diversity].

[195] United Nations Convention to Combat Desertification in those Countries Experiencing Serious Drought and/or Desertification, Particularly in Africa (adopted 14 October 1994, entry into force 26 December 1996) 1954 UNTS 3, with 197 contracting parties.

[196] Stockholm Convention on Persistent Organic Pollutants (adopted 22 May 2001, entry into force 17 May 2004) 2256 UNTS 119, with 185 contracting parties [Convention on Persistent Organic Pollutants].

[197] United Nations Framework Convention on Climate Change (adopted 09 May 1992, entry into force 21 March 1994) 1771 UNTS 107, with 197 contracting parties [UNFCCC].

[198] Kyoto Protocol to United Nations Framework Convention on Climate Change (adopted 11 December 1997, entry into force 16 February 2005) 2303 UNTS 162, with 192 contracting parties.

[199] Paris Agreement to United Nations Framework Convention on Climate Change (adopted 12 December 2015, entry into force 04 November 2016) 3156 UNTS, with 193 contracting parties.

[200] Rio Declaration, Principle 16.

[201] Kulick (2012), p. 226.

[202] Khan (2015), p. 640. Although this is the original understanding, one may consider that the compensation for environmental damage is an extension of the polluter-pays principle *see* Atapattu (2006), pp. 439–440 and 472.

[203] Khan (2015), pp. 640–641.

finds reflection in several environmental conventions, whereby the contracting parties call for its application.[204]

However, the polluter-pays principle itself has an elusive meaning and it requires legislative choices for its effective implementation. States must therefore define 'pollution' (whether linked to authorised thresholds of discharges or to the existence of environmental damage), and the 'polluter' (whether operator, licence-holder, representatives).[205] Even if states furnish those concepts with a defined scope either through an international convention or domestic law, the polluter-pays principle leaves certain issues open: how much must be paid as compensation, which is intrinsically difficult to calculate as environmental damage can only be approximately translated into monetary terms[206]; whether it is a strict or fault-based liability; or how to address causation in cases of diffuse pollution, whereby the adequate causality and the equivalence of conditions (joint and several liability) are the dominant theories.[207] For instance, the EU Directive 2004/35/CE conceives a regime of strict liability for operators in the activities listed thereunder.[208] However, with respect to the causal link in diffuse environmental damage, there is '*broad discretion*' for the EU member states to determine how to establish such link, including presumptions.[209]

Second, the principle of prevention compels states to take action at an early stage and ensures that activities within their jurisdiction or control do not cause environmental damage.[210] Its origins can be traced back to the customary law principle of no harm,[211] formulated by the *Trail Smelter* tribunal in the following terms:

---

[204] *See* for instance in the preamble of: International Convention on oil pollution preparedness, response and cooperation (adopted 30 November 1990, entry into force 13 May 1995) 1891 UNTS 77; Convention on the Transboundary Effects of Industrial Accidents (adopted 17 March 1992, entry into force 19 April 2000) 2105 UNTS 457; Convention on Civil Liability for Damage Resulting from Activities Dangerous to the Environment (adopted 21 June 1993) ETS No 150. Others conventions incorporate directly the principle as part of the treaty provisions, *see* for instance: Convention on the Protection and Use of Transboundary Watercourses and International Lakes (adopted 17 March 1992, entry into force 06 October 1996) 1936 UNTS 269, [Convention on Transboundary Watercourses] Art 2(5)(b); Convention for the Protection of the Marine Environment of the North-East Atlantic (adopted 22 September 1992, entry into force 25 March 1998), 2354 UNTS 67, [OSPAR Convention] Art 2(2)(b).

[205] de Sadeleer (2020), pp. 46 et seqq.

[206] Various environmental resources do not have a market value, which turns their valuation into a rough estimate at best *see* Hanley (2002), pp. 29 et seqq.

[207] de Sadeleer (2020), pp. 53 et seqq.

[208] Directive 2004/35/CE of the European Parliament and of the Council of 21 April 2004 on environmental liability with regard to the prevention and remedying of environmental damage [2004] OJ L143/56.

[209] Case C-378/08 *Raffinerie Mediterranee* [2010] ERG Judgment (09 March 2010) ECLI:EU:C:2010:126, paras. 54–58.

[210] Kulick (2012), p. 228.

[211] de Sadeleer (2020), p. 86.

> Under the principles of international law, no state has the right to use or permit the use of its territory in such a manner as to cause injury by fumes in or to the territory of another or the properties or persons therein, when the case is of serious consequence and the injury is established by clear and convincing evidence.[212]

The no harm principle was used as a primary norm to establish responsibility for damage caused to another state,[213] thus falling short of a preventive nature.[214] However, the no harm principle was adopted in Principle 21 Stockholm Declaration and Principle 2 Rio Declaration,[215] whose formulations opened the door for the principle of prevention. The difference between the principle of prevention and the principle of no harm is that the latter focuses more on determination of liability for damage already caused, whereas the former on the avoidance of environmental damage.[216] Thus, the principle of prevention is usually connected with a duty of due diligence.[217]

As such, the principle of prevention finds reflection in various instruments of international law.[218] Similarly to the polluter-pays principle, the normative content of the principle of prevention remains open-textured. This principle thus may beget a plethora of instruments, from monitoring mechanisms to outright bans, including the setting of nuisance thresholds of pollution, the mandate to use the best available technology, the performance of an environmental impact assessment, among others.[219]

---

[212] The principle of no harm is usually formulated as in the wording of the *Trail Smelter* tribunal *see*, *Trail smelter case (United States of America v Canada)*, Award (16 April 1938 and 11 March 1941) III RIAA 1905, 1965.

[213] Dupuy and Viñuales (2018), p. 64.

[214] de Sadeleer (2020), p. 87.

[215] Stockholm Declaration, Principle 21 and Rio Declaration, Principle 2 state with an identical wording: ('States have, in accordance with the Charter of the United Nations and the principles of international law, the sovereign right to exploit their own resources pursuant to their own environmental and developmental policies, and the responsibility to ensure that activities within their jurisdiction or control do not cause damage to the environment of other States or of areas beyond the limits of national jurisdiction').

[216] Dupuy and Viñuales (2018), p. 66. One could even argue that the principle of prevention is not limited to transboundary harm but also to damage within the state's own jurisdiction *see* Sands et al. (2018), p. 212.

[217] *Pulp Mills on the River Uruguay (Argentina v Uruguay)* (Judgment) [2010] ICJ Rep 14, para. 101.

[218] *See* for instance: UNCLOS, Arts 192 et seqq.; Ozone Layer Convention, Arts 2(2)(b); UNFCCC, Art 3; Convention on the Conservation of Migratory Species of Wild Animals (adopted 23 June 1979, entry into force 01 November 1983) 1651 UNTS 333, Art III(4); Protocol on Environmental Protection to the Antarctic Treaty (adopted 04 October 1991, entry into force 14 January 1998) 2941 UNTS 9, Art 3(2).

[219] de Sadeleer (2020), pp. 125 et seqq.

Third, the precautionary principle seeks to guide states on the application of environmental law when there is scientific uncertainty.[220] Its most famous formulation is found in Principle 15 Rio Declaration, which states:

> In order to protect the environment, the precautionary approach shall be widely applied by States according to their capabilities. Where there are threats of serious or irreversible damage, lack of full scientific certainty shall not be used as a reason for postponing cost-effective measures to prevent environmental degradation.[221]

In an nutshell, the lack of scientific certainty on the environmental effects of an activity does not excuse states from taking preventive measures.[222] This implies that there is a potential hazard, but the damage has not yet materialised and no incontestable proof attests that it will eventually materialise.[223] However, the principle does not cover situations where the risk of damage is insignificant or purely hypothetical.[224] The precautionary principle also finds reflection in various instruments of international law.[225] The difference between the principle of prevention and the precautionary principle is that the former seeks to prevent foreseeable and known harm, whereas the latter aims at preventing harm that cannot be fully assessed given the scientific uncertainty.[226]

The precautionary principle endures a normative ambiguity. Particularly, its application is defined by sectoral policies, for instance, fishing, food safety, climate change among others, which renders the principle malleable depending on the technological capabilities and the political needs in each specific field.[227] In addition, the precautionary principle is subject to a debate about its nature and normative basis.[228] Thus, its precise legal implications are difficult to delineate.[229]

---

[220] Sands et al. (2018), p. 230.

[221] Rio Declaration, Principle 15.

[222] Atapattu (2006), p. 284; Kulick (2012), p. 229; Dupuy and Viñuales (2018), p. 70.

[223] Atapattu (2006), p. 206; de Sadeleer (2020), p. 135.

[224] Marisi (2020), p. 78.

[225] *See* for instance: Montreal Protocol on Ozone Layer, Preamble; UNFCCC, Art 3(3); Convention on Biological Diversity, Preamble; Convention on Persistent Organic Pollutants, Preamble; OSPAR Convention, Art 2(a) and Annex I, Art 3(3)(c); Convention on Transboundary Watercourses, Art 2(5)(a).

[226] Atapattu (2006), p. 207; Kulick (2012), p. 229.

[227] de Sadeleer (2020), p. 359.

[228] For instance, the WTO doubts that the precautionary principle is a general principle of law or customary law *see, European Communities — Measures Concerning Meat and Meat Products (Hormones)—Appellate Body Report* (16 January 1998) WT/DS26/AB/R and WT/DS48/AB/R, para. 123; *European Communities — Measures Affecting the Approval and Marketing of Biotech Products—Panel Report* (29 September 2006) WT/DS291/R, WT/DS292/R, WT/DS293/R, paras. 7.88–7.89. However, given its express inclusion in Article 191(2) TFEU, the precautionary principle is considered a principle of EU law *see*, Case T-13/99 *Pfizer Animal Health v Council* [2002] CFI Judgment (11 September 2002) ECLI:EU:T:2002:209, paras. 114–115.

[229] Dupuy and Viñuales (2018), p. 70.

All in all, the polluter-pays principle, the principle of prevention and the precautionary principle appear abstract and indeterminate, requiring further specification for their effective application. In this sense, Nicolas de Saladeer categorises them as '*rules of indeterminate nature*', whose direct applicability necessitates operationalisation (in international agreements or domestic law) in sufficiently prescriptive terms.[230]

5.2.2.2.2 Does International Environmental Law Actively Regulate the Conduct of Private Actors?

Undeniably, several international environmental law instruments have acknowledged the crucial role of non-state actors when it comes to the protection of the environment. The Stockholm Declaration opens with the recognition that citizens, communities and enterprises bear responsibilities towards the environment.[231] Similarly, at the UN Conference on Environment and Development, it was stressed that enterprises have responsibilities towards the environment to the extent their operation has an impact on it.[232] Such mentions however remain highly aspirational.

It is therefore posited that the grip of international environmental law on enterprises is usually indirect: it addresses states, which subsequently need to implement it into their respective domestic laws.[233] This is the case of, for instance, the obligation to undertake an environmental impact assessment under international law: states are the addressees of such obligation, but its application has an impact on the activities of corporations. Consequently, one may divide the shortcomings of international environmental law *vis-à-vis* non-state actors into two groups: upstream factors, which pertain to the nature of the obligations as non-specific, ambiguous or non-self-executing; and downstream factors, such as the lack of proper implementation or reduced local capacity to enforce such obligations.[234] Nevertheless, there are two categories of instruments that directly address the conduct of non-state actors and their impact on the environment. These are

[230] de Sadeleer (2020), pp. 453 et seqq.

[231] Stockholm Declaration, Preamble, para. 7: ('To achieve this environmental goal will demand the acceptance of responsibility by citizens and communities, and by enterprises and institutions at every level, all sharing equitably in common efforts').

[232] UN Conference on Environment and Development, Resolution A/RES/44/228 adopted at the 85th plenary meeting (22 December 1989), I, para. 10: ('Stresses that large industrial enterprises, including transnational corporations, are frequently the repositories of scarce technical skills for the preservation and enhancement of the environment, that they conduct activities in sectors that have an impact on the environment and, to that extent, have specific responsibilities and that, in this context, efforts need to be encouraged and mobilized to protect and enhance the environment in all countries').

[233] Maljean-Dubois and Richard (2013), p. 71.

[234] Maljean-Dubois and Richard (2013), pp. 77–78.

international regimes on civil liability for environmental damage [Sect. 5.2.2.2.2.1], and CSR instruments in the broader sense [Sect. 5.2.2.2.2.2].

5.2.2.2.2.1 International Regimes on Civil Liability for Environmental Damage

The international regimes on civil liability for environmental damage constitute a segment of international environmental law, addressing the damages caused by non-state actors. These regimes define in detail the responsibilities of natural and legal persons, and the consequences for their breach, in specific fields or activities, where there is a likelihood of environmental damage.[235] This includes hazardous activities, particularly if they may entail potential transboundary effects.[236] The rationale behind these regimes is to harmonise obligations and to establish minimum standards.[237]

Some examples are the Vienna Convention on Civil Liability for Nuclear Damage,[238] whose original definition of 'nuclear damage' did not expressly cover environmental damage, until its protocol changed the definition.[239] The International Convention on Civil Liability for Oil Pollution Damage[240] and its amending protocol,[241] the latter redefining the notion of 'pollution damage' to explicitly include impairment to the environment. The Convention on the Protection of the Black Sea against Pollution,[242] which foresees pollution to the marine environment, but it requires contracting parties to further elaborate rules on liability of natural and juridical persons operating in the Black Sea.[243] The Basel Protocol on Liability and Compensation for Damage Resulting from Transboundary Movements of Hazardous Wastes and their Disposal,[244] whose Article 2 limits the concept of 'damage' with respect to the environment to loss of income deriving from the impairment of the environment. The Protocol on Environmental Protection to the Antarctic

[235] Nollkaemper (2006), p. 188; Morgera (2020), p. 44.

[236] Mistura (2019), para. 23.29.

[237] Dupuy and Viñuales (2018), p. 317; Sands et al. (2018), p. 736.

[238] Vienna Convention on Civil Liability for Nuclear Damage (adopted 21 May 1963, entry into force 12 November 1977) 1063 UNTS 265, with 42 contracting parties.

[239] Protocol to amend the Vienna Convention on Civil Liability for Nuclear Damage (adopted 12 September 1997, entry into force 04 October 2003) 2241 UNTS 270, with 15 contracting parties.

[240] International Convention on Civil Liability for Oil Pollution Damage (adopted 29 November 1969, entry into force 19 June 1975) 973 UNTS 3, with 66 contracting parties.

[241] Protocol of 1992 to amend the International Convention on Civil Liability for Oil Pollution Damage (adopted 27 November 1992, entry into force 30 May 1996) 1956 UNTS 255, with 42 contracting parties.

[242] Convention on the Protection of the Black Sea against Pollution (adopted 21 April 1992, entry into force 15 January 1994) 1764 UNTS 3, with 6 contracting parties [Black Sea Convention].

[243] Black Sea Convention, Arts II(1) and XVI(2).

[244] Basel Protocol on Liability and Compensation for Damage Resulting from Transboundary Movements of Hazardous Wastes and their Disposal (adopted 10 December 1999, not entry into force), with 12 contracting parties.

Treaty,[245] whose Annex VI delineates the regime on liability for 'environmental emergencies'.

All these regimes evince a sectoral/regional application.[246] Yet, they have many features in common: the definition of damage is linked to the activity and limited to certain items; liability is channelled to owners of the installation/ship or operators in control of the activity; strict liability is usually the norm; liability is capped (in amount and time); adequate insurance is required; complementing compensation funds might be envisaged.[247] As such, these instruments appear as a promising tool to address the gap between international environmental law and the conduct of investors, however, there are two major drawbacks. *First*, these regimes face a low rate of ratification, and in most cases they have not even entered into force, which affects their effectiveness.[248] Some authors suggest that there is an inverse relation between the scope of the instrument (activity/financial consequences) and the likelihood to enter into force.[249] *Second*, despite being international instruments, all of them require transposition into domestic law.[250]

This shows states' reluctancy to agree on civil liability regimes for environmental damage at the international level. Even when there are some concluded instruments, they might have not entered into force or their implementation through domestic law would bring the discussion back to environmental obligations of investors under domestic law. Therefore, international regimes on civil liability for environmental damage cannot provide a cause of action for environmental counterclaims in treaty-based investment arbitration.

5.2.2.2.2.2 CSR and the Dawn of Voluntary Standards

The concept of CSR has been subject to multiple definitions, but it essentially embodies the idea that '*each business enterprise, as a member of society, has a responsibility to operate ethically and in accordance with its legal obligations and to strive to minimise any adverse effects of its operations and activities on the environment, society and human health*'.[251] Thus, the role of enterprises breaks the traditional paradigm of solely maximation of profits to an extended social and environmental involvement.[252] Considering that there is no agreement on the scope

---

[245] Protocol on Environmental Protection to the Antarctic Treaty (adopted 04 October 1991, entry into force 14 January 1998) 2941 UNTS, with 32 contracting parties.

[246] The only exception to this is the Convention on Civil Liability for Damage resulting from Activities Dangerous to the Environment adopted in 21 June 1993. However, no state has ratified it, which is very telling of the political will to create a comprehensive regime for different kinds of environmental damage.

[247] Dupuy and Viñuales (2018), pp. 319–322; Mistura (2019), paras. 23.32 et seqq.

[248] Mistura (2019), para. 23.83; Morgera (2020), p. 45.

[249] Sands et al. (2018), p. 771.

[250] Nollkaemper (2006), p. 188; Morgera (2020), p. 44.

[251] Zerk (2006), p. 32. Similarly, Chi (2018), p. 101.

[252] Maljean-Dubois and Richard (2013), p. 82.

and nature of obligations attached to the concept of CSR,[253] it usually captures soft-law commitments.[254]

Various actors such as states, international organisations, NGOs or industry associations have developed CSR instruments, which, despite their soft law nature, have exerted a great influence on enterprises by their internalisation, and on the emergence of domestic regulations.[255] One may argue that CSR instruments arose from the pressure of civil society on the control of enterprises, but CSR seems to hinge strongly on the idea of self-regulation.[256] The most prominent examples have already been mentioned above, including the Principles of the UN Global Compact 2000 and the OECD Guidelines for Multinational Enterprises of 2011. It must be highlighted that the focus on the voluntary/mandatory nature of CSR is misplaced. The focus on the voluntary/mandatory divide ignores that corporate behaviour is motivated by many factors, the mandatory nature of law being only one of them, and it also omits that CSR issues such as occupational health and safety, and environmental protection are already regulated in detail in most jurisdictions.[257]

Moreover, even if CSR instruments are not directly binding on enterprises, this does not mean that their non-compliance is entirely deprived of legal consequences. In the *Kasky v Nike* case, the plaintiff claimed that Nike had falsely advertised that the company's subcontractors in Asia complied with regulations concerning minimum wage, occupational health and safety, and environmental protection.[258] The Supreme Court of California determined that such voluntary statements constituted commercial speech and an enterprise could be sanctioned for not upholding them.[259] By the same token, if an enterprise commits to a CSR instrument, it should not be allowed to walk away from such commitment under the pretext of voluntariness.[260]

As such, it is posited that the development of CSR instruments and their reference in investment law foreshadow the balancing of investor protection with investor responsibilities.[261] However, from the viewpoint of public international law, as long as the obligations on non-state actors are not defined in a more concrete, differentiated and prescriptive manner, the protection of the environment with respect to corporate activity will remain a task for the states.[262] This by no means suggests that

[253] Miles (2013), p. 217.

[254] Morgera (2020), p. 15. Similarly, Thomé (2021), p. 658.

[255] Miles (2013), p. 226.

[256] Maljean-Dubois and Richard (2013), p. 89.

[257] Zerk (2006), pp. 34–35.

[258] *Kasky v Nike Inc,* Case No S087859, Judgment (2 May 2002), [2002] 27 Cal 4th 939.

[259] *Kasky v Nike Inc,* Case No S087859, Judgment (2 May 2002), [2002] 27 Cal 4th 939.

[260] Maljean-Dubois and Richard (2013), p. 92.

[261] Miles (2013), p. 230.

[262] Dörr (2020), p. 158. In this sense, Manjiao Chi suggests that soft-law "may be hardened" through consistent state practice *see* Chi (2018), p. 165. However, this would only bring about consistency instead of concrete and differentiated obligations. It is thus unlikely that this could serve as a legal basis for counterclaims.

CSR instruments need be transformed into sets of precise obligations, as this might stifle the flexibility (and evolution) of standards covered by the overly broad concept of CSR.

Evidently, CSR instruments do not impose environmental obligations on investors by themselves. Yet, one may argue that the underpinnings of international environmental law added to the CSR instruments addressing environmental protection constitute the foundations for investors' obligation under international law to refrain from conduct that undermines or places the environment at risk—a sort of negative obligation.[263] Such negative obligation could serve as a legal basis for an environmental counterclaim in treaty-based investment arbitration, but only in clear evidence of environmental degradation. Otherwise, the obligation remains broad in its content, and its application may face difficulties when assessing the damage as no nuisance thresholds of pollution, guidance on diffuse environmental damage, reparatory measures or else are set.

5.2.2.2.3 A Case for the Re-Conceptualisation of Environmental Protection: Much Ado about Nothing?

Another point on international environmental law pertains to the efforts to reconceptualise environmental protection either as an issue of human rights [Sect. 5.2.2.2.3.1], or as an obligation emanating from transnational public policy [Sect. 5.2.2.2.3.2]. Irrespective of the advantages or disadvantages of fitting environmental protection within either of those categories, this would not provide by itself a cause of action for environmental counterclaims in treaty-based investment arbitration.

5.2.2.2.3.1 A Human Rights' Perspective of Environmental Protection

The protection of the environment and human rights are interwoven. In this sense, one may wonder whether the human being or the environment itself are the ultimate object of protection of environmental laws. There are two theories embodying these conflicting positions[264]: on the one hand, the ecologic anthropocentrism, which suggests that the environment needs protection because it enables the full enjoyment of human rights; on the other hand, ecocentrism, which advances that all forms of life have an intrinsic value and deserve protection by themselves. Yet, since the Brundtland Report in 1987 and the advent of the term '*sustainable development*' it seems that a mixture between both theories is dominant, whereby human kind and the environment cannot be conceived separately reconciling human development and environmental protection as two sides of the same coin.[265]

[263] Scherer et al. (2021), p. 432.

[264] Robles Ustariz (2020), pp. 17–19.

[265] Toca Torres (2011), p. 203.

Environmental protection is thus seen as a vital part of numerous human rights such as the right to life or the right to health.[266] In other words, there is a latent environmental content within existing human rights.[267] Human rights courts have confirmed this on various occasions. In the *López Ostra v Spain* case, the European Court of Human Rights sentenced that pollution affects wellbeing, private and family life.[268] In the *SERAC v Nigeria* case, the African Commission on Human and Peoples' Rights considered the right to health and the right to a satisfactory environment to be intertwined.[269] Thus, it determined that the uncontrolled oil spillage was a violation of human rights of the Ogoni people. In the *Maya Indigenous Community v Belize* case, the Inter-American Commission on Human Rights concluded that the environmental damage caused by development activities affected the community rights to property, which in turn affected their physical, cultural and spiritual well-being.[270] Notably, in such cases, the courts do not tend to apply environmental law, but rather acknowledge that an environmental damage could harm human rights.[271]

This relation between human rights and environmental protection has begotten the debate about the recognition of the human right to a healthy environment. Some authors are critical of the practical utility of recognising a human right to a healthy environment given the difficulties on defining, implementing and enforcing such a right.[272] Some stress the benefits of recognising the human right to a healthy environment, albeit being cautious on the means of implementation.[273] Some others even suggest that there is already such a right under international law.[274]

From the viewpoint of international environmental law, recognising the human right to a healthy environment might bring some positive results. For instance, it would reinforce the idea that human rights necessitate environmental protection for their full enjoyment.[275] The environment would be captured in a separate right, whose protection would not depend on the impairment to other human rights.[276] It

[266] *Case concerning the Gabčíkovo-Nagymaros Project (Hungary v Slovakia)* (Judgment) [1997] ICJ Rep 7, Separate Opinion of Vice-President Weeramantry, 91–92.

[267] Luke (2019), p. 161; Tan and Chong (2020), p. 195.

[268] *López Ostra v Spain*, Application No 16798/90, ECtHR Judgment (09 December 1994) para. 51.

[269] *The Social and Economic Rights Action Center and the Center for Economic and Social Rights (SERAC) v Nigeria*, Case ACHPR/COMM/A044/1, ACHPR Commission Decision (27 May 2002) para. 52.

[270] *Maya indigenous community of the Toledo District v Belize*, Case 12.053, IACHR Report No 40/04, OEA/Ser.L/V/II.122 Doc 5 rev 1 at 727 (2004) paras. 148–150.

[271] Brown (2021), p. 244.

[272] Wirth (1995), p. 617.

[273] In this regard *see* Downs (1993), pp. 351 et seqq.

[274] Robles Ustariz (2020), pp. 37 et seqq.

[275] UNGA, 'Human Rights Obligations Relating to the Enjoyment of a Safe, Clean, Healthy and Sustainable Environment' (19 July 2018) UN Doc A/73/188, para. 39.

[276] Atapattu (2006), p. 34.

could also steer the development of international environmental law and international human rights in a more unified and integrated manner.[277]

Notably, various regional agreements on human rights have already incorporated a human right to a healthy environment to some degree. The African Charter on Human and Peoples' Rights mentions a '*general satisfactory environment*'.[278] The ASEAN Human Rights Declaration refers to '*a safe, clean and sustainable environment*'.[279] Whereas both the Arab Charter on Human Rights and American Convention on Human Rights conceive the right to '*a healthy environment*'.[280] Based on such formulation of a human right to a healthy environment, the Inter-American Court of Human Rights considered it as an autonomous right independent from the environmental content that arise from the protection of other human rights such as the right to life or health.[281]

At the national level, there are over 100 states recognising the right to a healthy environment explicitly or implicitly via constitutions, domestic law or court decisions.[282] However, some of the most powerful and populous countries (China, Japan, US, Australia, Canada) have not followed suit.[283] As such, one may argue that the right to a healthy environment is gaining traction, but there is no sufficient state practice to elevate it as a norm of customary international law,[284] or to otherwise consider it as an universally recognised right.[285] This explains the call of the UN special rapporteur on human rights and the environment in 2018 for the recognition of human right to a healthy environment via three possible avenues: (i) the adoption of a treaty including such right by the UN; (ii) the adoption of a protocol, for instance, to the International Covenant on Economic, Social and Cultural Rights incorporating such right; (iii) a resolution of the UN General

[277] Knox (2019), p. 45.

[278] African Charter on Human and Peoples' Rights (adopted 27 June 1981, entry into force 21 October 1986) 1520 UNTS 217, Art 24: ('All peoples shall have the right to a general satisfactory environment favourable to their development').

[279] Association of Southeast Asian Nations (ASEAN) Human Rights Declaration (adopted 18 November 2012), para. 28: ('Every person has the right to an adequate standard of living for himself or herself and his or her family including: . . .f) The right to a safe, clean and sustainable environment').

[280] Arab Charter on Human Rights (adopted 22 May 2004), Art 38: ('Every person has the right to an adequate standard of living for himself and his family, which ensures their well-being and a decent life, including food, clothing, housing, services and the right to a healthy environment'). Additional Protocol to the American Convention on Human Rights in the Area of Economic, Social, and Cultural Rights (Protocol of San Salvador) (adopted 17 November 1988, entry into force 16 November 1999), Art 11(1): ('Everyone shall have the right to live in a healthy environment and to have access to basic public services').

[281] IACHR Advisory Opinion OC-23/17 (15 November 2017) Series A No 23, paras. 62–63.

[282] Boyd (2018), pp. 19–23.

[283] Knox (2019), p. 42.

[284] Atapattu (2006), p. 21.

[285] Knox (2019), p. 45.

Assembly recognising it, as with the right to water and sanitation in 2010.[286] None of these options has yet materialised.

Be that as it may, the recognition of a human right to a healthy environment may not help in the search of a cause of action for an environmental counterclaim in treaty-based investment arbitration. Human rights obligations are placed on the states. Certainly, the theory of horizontality of human rights or *Drittwirkung* suggests that human rights apply between private parties as well.[287] However, this does not place human rights obligations on non-state actors, but rather focuses state responsibility on its failure to prevent or punish the private actor that violated human rights.[288]

In this sense, in the *López Ostra v Spain* case, the European Court of Human Rights held Spain liable for its failure to protect the applicant's private and family life and health affected by a privately-owned waste treatment plant.[289] Similarly, the Inter-American Court of Human Rights has held that a violation of human rights by a private person may entail the state's responsibility if the state lacked due diligence to prevent or respond to the violation.[290] This does not mean that corporations are not susceptible to human rights. Arguably, they bear the negative obligation to respect human rights of individual right holders, but this does not extend to positive obligations such as to protect or fulfil human rights, otherwise, the non-reciprocal nature of human rights could be altered.[291]

Interestingly, in investment arbitration, the *Urbaser v Argentina* tribunal discussed at length whether corporations could have human rights obligations for the purpose of a counterclaim. Here, the respondent submitted a counterclaim arguing that the investor had failed to make further investments (expansion works) required by the concession contract on water and sewage services, thereby violating among other things, the human right to water and sanitation.[292] By considering the Universal Declaration of Human Rights of 1948,[293] the International Covenant on

[286] UNGA, 'Human Rights Obligations Relating to the Enjoyment of a Safe, Clean, Healthy and Sustainable Environment' (19 July 2018) UN Doc A/73/188, paras. 46–48.

[287] Vazquez (2005), p. 937.

[288] Karavias (2013), p. 44; Morgera (2020), p. 56.

[289] *López Ostra v Spain*, Application No 16798/90, ECtHR Judgment (09 December 1994) paras. 44–58.

[290] *See* for instance: *Case of Velásquez-Rodríguez v Honduras,* IACHR Judgment (29 July 1988) paras. 172 et seqq.; *Case of the 'Street Children' (Villagrán-Morales and others) v Guatemala*, IACHR Judgment (19 November 1999) paras. 139 et seqq.

[291] Karavias (2013), pp. 196–197. Similarly, Crow and Escobar (2018), p. 106.

[292] *Urbaser SA and Consorcio de Aguas Bilbao Bizkaia, Bilbao Biskaia Ur Partzuergoa v The Argentine Republic*, ICSID Case No ARB/07/26, Award (08 December 2016) para. 1156.

[293] Particularly, the tribunal emphasised Article 30 of the Universal Declaration of Human Rights of 1948: ('Nothing in this Declaration may be interpreted as implying for any State, group or person any right to engage in any activity or to perform any act aimed at the destruction of any of the rights and freedoms set forth herein').

Civil and Political Rights of 1966,[294] and the ILO Tripartite Declaration of Principles concerning Multinational Enterprises and Social Policy of 1977, the *Urbaser v Argentina* tribunal held '[a]*t this juncture, it is therefore to be admitted that the human right for everyone's dignity and its right for adequate housing and living conditions are complemented by an obligation on all parts, public and private parties, not to engage in activity aimed at destroying such rights*'.[295]

However, with respect to the human right to water, the *Urbaser v Argentina* tribunal conceded that neither the underlying BIT, nor other treaties or general principles of international law impose an obligation on the investor with regards to the human right to water.[296] Whilst the state is obliged under international law to ensure the right to water to its population, the investor's obligations in this regard stem only from the concession and the regulatory regime in the host state.[297] The *Urbaser v Argentina* tribunal added a final caveat with respect to the prohibition of violating human rights (negative obligation) but dismissed it immediately as it was not the case under analysis.[298]

Following the *Urbaser* reasoning, one may argue that environmental protection could be indirectly subjected to a counterclaim, if the respondent host state submits that an environmental damage constitutes an investor's failure to abstain from affecting human rights *eg* the right to health or life,[299] or the human right to a healthy environment for that matter. This might nevertheless be an overoptimistic reading of the *Urbaser* decision. The tribunal certainly emphasised that the duty-bearer of the human right to water is still the state, irrespective of being able to fulfil such obligation through a concession.[300] Notably, Markus Krawjeski criticises the tribunal's findings as neither Article 30 Universal Declaration of Human Rights nor Article 5 International Covenant on Civil and Political Rights addresses the duty-

---

[294] Particularly, the tribunal emphasised Article 5 of the International Covenant on Civil and Political Rights of 1966: ('Nothing in the present Covenant may be interpreted as implying for any State, group or person any right to engage in any activity or perform any act aimed at the destruction of any of the rights and freedoms recognized herein or at their limitation to a greater extent than is provided for in the present Covenant').

[295] *Urbaser SA and Consorcio de Aguas Bilbao Bizkaia, Bilbao Biskaia Ur Partzuergoa v The Argentine Republic*, ICSID Case No ARB/07/26, Award (08 December 2016) para. 1199.

[296] *Urbaser SA and Consorcio de Aguas Bilbao Bizkaia, Bilbao Biskaia Ur Partzuergoa v The Argentine Republic*, ICSID Case No ARB/07/26, Award (08 December 2016) para. 1207.

[297] *Urbaser SA and Consorcio de Aguas Bilbao Bizkaia, Bilbao Biskaia Ur Partzuergoa v The Argentine Republic*, ICSID Case No ARB/07/26, Award (08 December 2016) paras. 1208 et seqq.

[298] *Urbaser SA and Consorcio de Aguas Bilbao Bizkaia, Bilbao Biskaia Ur Partzuergoa v The Argentine Republic*, ICSID Case No ARB/07/26, Award (08 December 2016) para. 1210.

[299] Gleason (2021), p. 436.

[300] On the one hand, one may posit that the only possibility to find investor's responsibility would have been under the concession contract *see* de Nanteuil (2018), pp. 391–390. On the other one, one may suggest that a simpler approach would have been to rely on domestic law implementing and regulating the right to water *see* Viñuales (2020), para. 102. In either of both scenarios (concession contract or domestic law) the cause of action for the counterclaim would no longer be international law, which steers the discussion into a completely different direction.

bearers of human rights obligations, and the tribunal failed to elaborate on any rule of treaty interpretation to reach that conclusion.[301]

Irrespective of the legal soundness of the *Urbaser* decision, it is difficult to deny that investors have at least a rudimentary negative obligation to respect human rights under international law given the increasing affluence of corporate standards linked to human rights. However, and for the sake of argument, considering that investors have such negative obligation with respect to human rights actually reflects the aforementioned negative obligation to refrain from conduct that undermines or places the environment at risk.[302] Thus, from the perspective of environmental counterclaims, the reformulation of environmental protection as a human rights issue becomes rather inconsequential.

5.2.2.2.3.2 A Transnational Public Policy's Perspective of Environmental Protection

Another point to consider is whether the re-conceptualisation of environmental protection as an issue of transnational public policy would provide a viable cause of action for environmental counterclaims in treaty-based investment arbitration. Supporters of the concept of '*transnational public policy*' hold that it alludes to principles that are recognised by legal systems all around the world (reflecting broad consensus) and need not be confused with the concept of '*international public policy*' as the latter refers to fundamental conceptions of legal order in a particular state.[303] A landmark case in the use of this concept in investment arbitration is the *World Duty Free v Kenya* case, where the tribunal found that bribery was contrary to transnational public policy and consequently declined jurisdiction.[304]

In this light, one may wonder whether the concept of transnational public policy could be used as a source of investors obligation in investment arbitration.[305] Arguably based on such a premise, some authors have theorised the possibility of finding the cause of action for a counterclaim in transnational public policy.[306] This is however not viable for two reasons: *first*, the concept of transnational public policy does not seem to be suitable for treaty-based investment arbitration. *Second*,

---

[301] Accordingly, Markus Krajewski endorses the argument of Philippe Sands' Dissenting Opinion to *Bear Creek v Peru*, and suggests that an investor's behaviour should be assessed in the calculation of damages *see* Krajweski (2021), pp. 124–126.

[302] *See* Sect. 5.2.2.2.2.2.

[303] Hunter and Silva (2013), p. 367.

[304] *World Duty Free Company v Republic of Kenya*, ICSID Case No Arb/00/7, Award (04 October 2006) paras. 138 et seqq.

[305] Proposing that transnational public policy could impose human rights obligations upon investors, which, if violated, would bar the investor from resorting to investment arbitration *see* Marcoux (2020), pp. 809 et seqq.

[306] Huber (2020), p. 329. Going a step further, Ted Gleason suggests that the human right to a healthy environment could constitute transnational public policy, and thereby it could open the possibility of counterclaims for its violation *see* Gleason (2021), pp. 436–439.

assuming *arguendo* that the characterisation of environmental protection as an issue of transnational public policy is feasible, this by itself does not provide a cause of action for environmental counterclaims.

First, the *raison d'être* of transnational public policy is that there are universally recognised norms, which should always apply irrespective of the law applicable to the case, thus, its applicability makes sense for a decentralised regime such as international commercial arbitration.[307] One may say that in public international law the same function is fulfilled by *jus cogens*.[308] As such, *jus cogens* norms might apply to treaty-based investment arbitration as the treaty itself is an instrument of public international law.

This in fact was addressed as *obiter dicta* both in the *Urbaser v Argentina* case and in the *David Aven v Costa Rica* case. The *Urbaser v Argentina* tribunal simply held that *jus cogens* norms should prevail over contrary provisions in the underlying treaty.[309] Whereas the *David Aven v Costa Rica* tribunal stated that investors are not impervious to international law particularly with respect to '*obligations that are the concern of all States*',[310] in other words, *jus cogens*. Consequently, there is then no need to import the category of transnational public policy to serve the same function. Either way, environmental protection has not reached the status of *jus cogens*.[311]

Second, the conceptualisation of an international norm as transnational public policy does not change its application and limits.[312] Thus, nothing would be gained from framing an obligation under public international law as part of the vague concept of transnational public policy. As elaborated above, there are no environmental treaties directly applicable to investors and even the so-called principles of international environmental law require implementation into domestic law. Considering norms of international environmental law as transnational public policy would not change their addressees *ie* states, or their content, which often requires operationalisation in domestic legislation.

Arguably, investors have the negative obligation not to impair the environment under international law, but once again the broadness of such obligation would render the viability of an environmental counterclaim rather limited. This would not change for reconceptualising this negative obligation as an issue of transnational public policy. Consequently, there is no benefit of considering environmental protection as an issue of transnational public policy at least for the purpose of counterclaims.

---

[307] De Brabandere (2020), pp. 850 et seqq.

[308] Gaillard (2010), para. 118.

[309] *Urbaser SA and Consorcio de Aguas Bilbao Bizkaia, Bilbao Biskaia Ur Partzuergoa v The Argentine Republic*, ICSID Case No ARB/07/26, Award (08 December 2016) para. 1203.

[310] Admittedly, the tribunal did not use the term '*jus cogens*', but it referred to the *Barcelona Traction* case, where the ICJ mentioned the prohibition of acts of aggression, genocide and slavery as obligations that concern all states *see*, *David R Aven and Others v Republic of Costa Rica*, ICSID Case No UNCT/15/3, Award (18 September 2018) para. 738.

[311] Fitzmaurice (2001), pp. 132 et seqq.; Viñuales (2012), p. 142.

[312] De Brabandere (2020), p. 864.

5.2.2.2.4 Excursus: The Example of the Alien Tort Claims Act and Environmental Obligations

Finally, the experience of ATCA is illustrative with respect to international environmental obligations upon non-state parties. In principle, states can establish domestic law regimes to hold non-state actors responsible for the breach of international obligations.[313] In the US, this option was originally created by the Judiciary Act of 1789 and allows aliens to claim on tort for the violation of the law of nations or a treaty of the US.[314] As such, one can identify three elements for the submission of a claim under ATCA: (i) the plaintiff is an alien, (ii) suing for tort (iii) on the violation of the law of nations or a US treaty.[315] The last requirement proves fatal for tort claims based on international environmental law as the US has not ratified many environmental treaties, and the notion of '*law of nations*' has been narrowly construed.[316] Case law consistently dismissing tort claims, whose cause of action was international environmental law, supports this point.

In the *Amlon Metals Inc v FMC Corp* case,[317] the plaintiffs argued that the defendant violated the law of nations, particularly the principles of the Stockholm Declaration by delivering goods contaminated with hazardous substances. The District Court for the Southern District of New York dismissed the claim reasoning that the Stockholm Declaration has no specific obligations, but rather it refers to the states' responsibilities towards the environment.[318] In the *Beanal v Freeport-McMoran Inc* case,[319] the plaintiff submitted that the defendant's mining activities in Indonesia had resulted in environmental destruction, violating the polluter-pays principle, the precautionary principle and the proximity principle. The District Court for the Eastern District of Louisiana rejected the environmental tort claims given the lack of consensus on the content and binding status of those principles of

[313] Dörr (2020), p. 145.

[314] Title 28 USC §1350: ('The district courts shall have original jurisdiction of any civil action by an alien for a tort only, committed in violation of the law of nations or a treaty of the United States').

[315] Bridgeman (2003), p. 5.

[316] Morgera (2020), pp. 34 et seqq. An often-quoted case is the *Sosa v Alvarez-Machain* case, whereby the US Supreme Court called for judicial restraint with respect to '*the law of nations*' by requiring that '*any claim based on the present-day law of nations to rest on a norm of international character accepted by the civilized world and defined with a specificity comparable to the features of the 18th-century paradigms we have recognized*' see, *Sosa v Alvarez-Machain and others* [2004] 542 US 692, 725. However, even earlier cases under ATCA seem to have closed the possibility for environmental tort claims.

[317] *Amlon Metals Inc v FMC Corp* [2001] 775 F Supp 668 (SDNY).

[318] *Amlon Metals Inc v FMC Corp* [2001] 775 F Supp 668 (SDNY) 671: ('Plaintiffs' reliance on the Stockholm Principles is misplaced, since those Principles do not set forth any specific proscriptions, but rather refer only in a general sense to the responsibility of nations to insure that activities within their jurisdiction do not cause damage to the environment beyond their borders').

[319] *Beanal v Freeport-McMoRan Inc* [1997] 969 F Supp 362 (ED La).

environmental law, which were deemed to address states rather than corporations.[320] On appeal, the US Court of Appeals of the 5th Circuit confirmed the judgment of first instance, but also called for extreme caution when adjudicating environmental claims under the ATCA as to not displace environmental policies of other states.[321]

In the *Aguinda v Texaco Inc* case,[322] the plaintiffs claimed that the defendant's oil-related activities in Ecuador had contaminated the environment, thus violating environmental norms of 'customary international law'. The District Court for the Southern District of New York focused on the doctrine of *forum non conveniens* and concluded that Ecuadorian courts are capable of adjudicating such claims and that under the ATCA (or otherwise) there was no special public interest to provide plaintiffs with a forum for such claims, thereby rejecting the claim.[323] In the *Sarei v Rio Tinto PLC* case,[324] the plaintiffs submitted that the defendant's copper mining activities in Papua New Guinea had polluted the environment, thus violating the principle of sustainable development and UNCLOS with regards to marine pollution. The District Court for the Central District of California rejected the first argument as the plaintiffs failed to identify '*specific, universal, and obligatory*' norm of international law.[325] With respect to the second argument, the court recognised UNCLOS as representing the law of nations, despite of the US having only signed but not ratified the convention.[326] However, the claim on marine pollution under UNCLOS was dismissed as well by the court given the involvement of the state in the mining operation (act of state doctrine).[327]

---

[320] *Beanal v Freeport-McMoRan Inc* [1997] 969 F Supp 362 (ED La) 384: ('The three principles relied on by Plaintiff, standing alone, do not constitute international torts for which there is universal consensus in the international community as to their binding status and their content. . .More to the point, those principles apply to "members of the international community" rather than non-state corporations. . .A non-state corporation could be bound to such principles by treaty, but not as a matter of international customary law').

[321] *Beanal v Freeport-McMoRan Inc* [1999] 197 F.3d 161 (5th Cir) 167: ('federal courts should exercise extreme caution when adjudicating environmental claims under international law to insure that environmental policies of the United States do not displace environmental policies of other governments. Furthermore, the argument to abstain from interfering in a sovereign's environmental practices carries persuasive force especially when the alleged environmental torts and abuses occur within the sovereign's borders and do not affect neighboring countries').

[322] *Aguinda v Texaco Inc* [2001] 142 F Supp 2d 534 (SDNY).

[323] *Aguinda v Texaco Inc* [2001] 142 F Supp 2d 534 (SDNY) 553: ('the actions in question occurred overwhelmingly in Ecuador, where courts are fully capable of interpreting alleged violations of international law. The United States therefore has no special public interest, under the ATCA or otherwise, in providing a forum for plaintiffs pursuing an international law action against a United States entity that plaintiffs can adequately pursue in the place where the violation actually occurred').

[324] *Sarei v Rio Tinto PLC* [2002] 221 F Supp 2d 1116 (CD Cal).

[325] *Sarei v Rio Tinto PLC* [2002] 221 F Supp 2d 1116 (CD Cal) 1160–1161.

[326] *Sarei v Rio Tinto PLC* [2002] 221 F Supp 2d 1116 (CD Cal) 1161.

[327] *Sarei v Rio Tinto PLC* [2002] 221 F Supp 2d 1116 (CD Cal) 1191.

These cases evince the inherent difficulties of raising an environmental tort claim under the ATCA on two fronts. Procedurally, as there are obstacles such as the doctrine of *forum non conveniens* or the act of the state doctrine which might prevent the court from adjudicating the environmental tort claim.[328] Substantially, as international environmental law is composed of a variety of elements (soft law, rules on inter-state relations, broad and vague language) that might undermine its applicability as a cause of action under the ATCA.[329]

Drawing from this experience, one may conclude that international environmental law might not provide a cause of action against non-state actors given their indeterminacy or their focus on state conduct,[330] although the example of the UNCLOS obligation seems to be a step forward. This confirms the conclusions reached in the previous sections, whereby international environmental law may not be suitable to provide a cause of action for a counterclaim in treaty-based investment arbitration. Arguably, a negative international obligation not to undermine the environment could fit the bill, yet only in cases of clear environmental degradation.

5.2.2.3 Investment Treaties and International Environmental Obligations: An Ill-Fated Relation?

Considering that international environmental law and international investment law have evolved quite independently from each other,[331] the crux of the matter at this point is whether IIAs can operationalise international environmental obligations for the purposes of counterclaims in treaty-based investment arbitration. This section thus analyses: *first*, the direct imposition of investors' environmental obligations via investment treaties [Sect. 5.2.2.3.1]. *Second*, whether the reference to international environmental law in IIAs may provide a valid cause of action for counterclaims [Sect. 5.2.2.3.2].

5.2.2.3.1 Direct Imposition of Investors' Environmental Obligations Via Investment Treaties

Some authors assumed that IIAs do not impose obligations upon foreign investors because the purpose of those treaties is confined to the promotion and protection of

---

[328] Abadie (2004), pp. 768 et seqq.; Jaeger (2010), pp. 525–526; Maljean-Dubois and Richard (2013), p. 79.

[329] Jaeger (2010), pp. 523–524; Maljean-Dubois and Richard (2013), p. 79.

[330] Douglas (2013), pp. 438–440. For a slightly different opinion, considering that the principle of prohibition of significant transboundary environmental harm constitutes customary international law and is thereby enforceable under ATCA *see* Abadie (2004), pp. 775 et seqq.

[331] Viñuales (2012), p. 134. Similarly, Chi (2018), p. 89.

investors and their investments.[332] Moreover, some argue that IIA commitments towards investors are unilateral and that consent to treaty-based investment arbitration neither incorporates substantive standards nor does it make them bilaterally applicable.[333] All this seems to render the search for a cause of action in IIAs for counterclaims well-nigh impossible.[334] From this point of view, it is understandable that an investor's misconduct is often raised as part of a defence on the scope of application of the treaty or simply mentioned by an *amicus curiae*.[335]

As mentioned above, nothing prevents international law from directly imposing obligations on non-state actors. Considering the benefits foreign investors enjoy through IIAs and their active role in the development of international investment law via investor-state dispute settlement, the same IIAs should as well impose certain obligations upon those foreign investors.[336] Furthermore, IIAs are becoming more amenable to environmental protection and sustainable development by express language in their preambles or operative provisions.[337] This treaty language brings sustainable development to the forefront of investment protection as a legitimate goal to pursue through international investment law rather than a simple by-product.[338] This not only steers the conception of international investment law into a different direction, but also paves the way for the inclusion of investors obligations towards the environment directly in IIAs.

However, one must not confuse those references to sustainable development or preambular wordings with obligations upon investors. In this regard, the *David Aven v Costa Rica* case is apposite. As mentioned above, Articles 10.9(3)(c)[339] and 10.11[340] CAFTA-DR (2004) only reaffirm the states' power to adopt, maintain or

---

[332] Bubrowski (2013), p. 216; de Nanteuil (2018), p. 376; Sinha and Fusea (2021), p. 65.

[333] Crawford (2007), p. 14.

[334] Hoffmann (2013), p. 447.

[335] For instance, Patrick Dumberry refers to concerns on human rights violations perpetrated by the investor, which are raised by third parties *see* Dumberry (2013), pp. 189–190.

[336] Miles (2013), p. 359. Similarly, with respect to environmental obligations *see* Bilanová (2020), p. 411.

[337] Boisson de Chazournes (2017), p. 380; Tan and Chong (2020), p. 191.

[338] Schill and Djanic (2018), p. 40.

[339] CAFTA-DR (2004), Art 10.9(3)(c): ('Provided that such measures are not applied in an arbitrary or unjustifiable manner, and provided that such measures do not constitute a disguised restriction on international trade or investment, paragraphs 1(b), (c), and (f), and 2(a) and (b), shall not be construed to prevent a Party from adopting or maintaining measures, including environmental measures: (i) necessary to secure compliance with laws and regulations that are not inconsistent with this Agreement; (ii) necessary to protect human, animal, or plant life or health; or (iii) related to the conservation of living or non-living exhaustible natural resources').

[340] CAFTA-DR (2004), Art 10.11: ('Nothing in this Chapter shall be construed to prevent a Party from adopting, maintaining, or enforcing any measure otherwise consistent with this Chapter that it considers appropriate to ensure that investment activity in its territory is undertaken in a manner sensitive to environmental concerns').

enforce environmental measures. Thus, the tribunal concluded that such provisions '*do not -in and of themselves- impose any affirmative obligation upon investors*'.[341]

Conversely, the International Institute for Sustainable Development (IISD) crafted an early example for IIAs imposing obligations upon foreign investors in the IISD Model Investment Agreement (2005). Part 3 of the Model Agreement is titled '*Obligations and Duties of Investors and Investments*' and contains general obligations on the compliance with the host state's domestic laws[342] such as pre-establishment obligations including the elaboration of environmental and social impact assessments,[343] and the prohibition to engage in corruption.[344]

Most importantly, Article 14 foresees a set of post-establishment obligations and particularly Paragraph (d) thereof states: '[i]*nvestors and investments shall not manage or operate the investments in a manner that circumvents international environmental, labour and human rights obligations to which the host state and/or home state are Parties*'. The rationale of this provision consists of thwarting foreign investors from searching for havens of lax environmental regulation by holding them to international standards.[345] Furthermore, the effectiveness of this provision is limited as the host state and/or home states must have adhered to the referred international environmental obligations.

A similar approach was adopted in the SADC Model BIT (2012). Particularly with respect to environmental obligations, Article 15.3 thereof foresees: '[i]*nvestors and their investments shall not [establish,] manage or operate Investments in a manner inconsistent with international environmental, labour, and human rights obligations binding on the Host State or the Home State, whichever obligations are higher*'. The last sentence of this provision pre-empts a possible conflict between environmental obligations assumed by the host state on the one hand, and those assumed by the home state on the other hand. This is certainly an improvement with respect to the IISD Model Investment Agreement (2005).

The efforts made both in the IISD Model Investment Agreement (2005) and SADC Model BIT (2012) are commendable for the balance they strive to achieve between investment protection and environmental protection. However, one may suggest that a sole negative obligation not to circumvent international environmental obligations might not be sufficient and express references to principles of environmental law and the inclusion of positive investors' obligations towards the environment should be preferred.[346]

Be that as it may, there are three IIAs seemingly inspired by the IISD Model Investment Agreement (2005) with respect to investors' environmental obligations:

---

[341] *David R Aven and Others v Republic of Costa Rica*, ICSID Case No UNCT/15/3, Award (18 September 2018) para. 743.

[342] IISD Model Investment Agreement (2005), Art 11.

[343] IISD Model Investment Agreement (2005), Art 12.

[344] IISD Model Investment Agreement (2005), Art 13.

[345] Mann et al. (2006), p. 26.

[346] Miles (2013), p. 361.

the CARIFORUM-EU EPA (2008), ECOWAS Supplementary Act on Investment (2008), and the Morocco-Nigeria BIT (2016). Only the latter foresees treaty-based investment arbitration.

With respect to the CARIFORUM-EU EPA (2008), Article 72 thereof mandates the contracting states to ensure, under Paragraph (c), that '[i]*nvestors do not manage or operate their investments in a manner that circumvents international environmental or labour obligations arising from agreements to which the EC Party and the Signatory CARIFORUM States are parties*'. This is deemed to create a level playing field on the international plane among environmental obligations.[347] Yet, there is a slight difference in language between the IISD Model Investment Agreement (2005) and CARIFORUM-EU EPA (2008) as the latter primarily addresses the contracting states. This suggests that responsibility would befall the contracting states for failing to ensure compliance rather than the investors.

The ECOWAS Supplementary Act on Investment (2008) follows more closely the IISD Model Investment Agreement (2005) since its Article 14(2) foresees: '... *Investors shall not manage or operate the investments in a manner that circumvents human rights obligations, labour standards as well as regional environmental and social obligations, to which the host State and/or home State are Parties*'. Similarly, with respect to the Morocco-Nigeria BIT (2016), Article 18(4) thereof provides that '[i]*nvestors and investments shall not manage or operate the investments in a manner that circumvents international environmental, labour and human rights obligations to which the host state and/or home state are Parties*'.

These treaties are certainly at the forefront of innovation on the sought balance between investment protection and the countervailing investor's obligations.[348] Nevertheless, it is doubtful whether the imposition of direct treaty obligations is a viable option in the future. In fact, the innovative treaties mentioned above seem to be quite isolated stories. For instance, Markus Krajewski questions the spotlight hogged by the Morocco-Nigeria BIT (2016): he considers the willingness of states to conclude investment treaties with investor's obligations is rather overestimated.[349] The lack of other IIAs adopting similar provisions may speak for itself, but this does not mean future treaties cannot change course even in a piecemeal manner. Yet, given the number of IIAs in force, the usual lengthy treaty negotiations, and the existence of sunset/survival clauses, it is unrealistic to expect that treaty drafting may single-handedly strike such balance between rights and obligations.[350]

Substantially, the IISD Model Investment Agreement (2005), SADC Model BIT (2012), the CARIFORUM-EU EPA (2008), ECOWAS Supplementary Act on

[347] Asteriti (2015), p. 255.

[348] Considering that all these developments are fostered mainly by African states, Jackson Shaw Kern provocatively ponders the question '[w]*ill Africa be the savior of investor-State dispute settlement?*' Jackson Shaw Kern, 'Investors Obligations: Africa Leads the Way' (*Kluwer Arbitration Blog*, 14 June 2020) <http://arbitrationblog.kluwerarbitration.com/2020/06/14/investor-obligations> accessed 10 January 2023.

[349] Krajweski (2021), p. 120.

[350] Schill and Djanic (2018), pp. 43–44.

Investment (2008), and the Morocco-Nigeria BIT (2016) evince a further issue: the investor's obligations are restricted to international environmental law, which does not address private actors but rather states, except for international regimes on civil liability for environmental damage and CSR instruments. As outlined above, the normative value of those instruments is limited either because of their voluntary nature or because of the necessity to be implemented through domestic law. Consequently, the investor's obligations foreseen in those treaties appear vague and imprecise, and at best they can be construed as reflecting the negative obligation not to undermine the environment.

Understandably, it becomes extremely cumbersome to draft a list of investors' obligations in a treaty,[351] addressing not only environmental issues, but also human rights or labour standards, which may explain the limited attempts to include investors' obligations in IIAs. However, should states overcome their reluctance to imposing investors' obligations in IIAs, treaty drafters could further ensure certainty by developing precise obligations with respect to the environment and the consequences for their breach. One option explored by Alessandra Mistura is to incorporate certain features of the international regimes on civil liability for environmental damage in investment treaties.[352] As such, IIAs could define in detail environmental damage, types of liability (for instance, strict liability for hazardous activities or fault-based liability for other activities), preventive measures, the kind of reparation/compensation, liability caps, establishment of causal link, among others.[353] This could be tailored for the purpose of environmental counterclaims, thereby providing guidance to the tribunals on the operability of investors' environmental obligations and reducing (to certain extent) the risks of inconsistency.

Another remark with respect to direct environmental obligations upon investors pertains to the use of the most-favoured nation treatment (MFN) clause. Particularly, whether via an MFN provision in the respective treaty, an investor may seek to sidestep its environmental obligations in an investment treaty.[354] For instance, Godwin Tan and Andrea Chong envisage two scenarios: (i) reliance on MFN to request the exclusion of treaty environmental obligations arguing there is a less favourable treatment in comparison to other IIAs without such provisions; (ii) reliance on MFN to narrow the dispute resolution provision that might permit the tribunal to adjudge environmental counterclaims.[355] The answer to this issue would require an extensive exercise of treaty interpretation of the pertinent MFN provisions. Yet, there are arguments for denying the possibility to either exclude substantive environmental obligations through an MFN standard,[356] or narrow down an otherwise

[351] Dumberry (2013), p. 191.

[352] Mistura (2019), paras. 23.108 et seqq.

[353] Mistura (2019), paras. 23.111 et seqq.

[354] Tan and Chong (2020), p. 196. Similarly, Thomé (2021), p. 667.

[355] Tan and Chong (2020), p. 196.

[356] Considering that the absence of provisions on third treaties cannot not be treated as 'more favourable treatment' for the purpose of an MFN clause see for instance: *CMS Gas Transmission*

broad dispute resolution provision amenable to environmental counterclaims by the same means.[357] Moreover, newer IIAs may render the use of MFN standards for side-stepping environmental obligations even more difficult. They increasingly incorporate environmental considerations into the treaty text, which could be viewed as to a treaty purpose intimately linked to environmental protection, and they tend to devise more detailed MFN clauses with a limited scope of application.

5.2.2.3.2 The Incorporation of International Environmental Law by Referral: A Distant Cause of Action for Counterclaims

Given the overwhelming absence of direct environmental obligations of investors in IIAs, a possibility for finding a cause of action for environmental counterclaims could be the referral from the investment treaty to an international environmental norm. This referral could operate in two manners: either by explicit treaty provisions referring to environmental considerations in CSR and other non-binding standards [Sect. 5.2.2.3.2.1]; or by other means of treaty interpretation [Sect. 5.2.2.3.2.2]. None of these avenues provides a viable cause of action for environmental counterclaims.

5.2.2.3.2.1 Treaty Provisions Mentioning CSR and Other Non-Binding Standards

In lieu of direct obligations on investors, IIAs have experimented with mentioning international standards (including with respect to environmental protection), often in terms of encouragement or best efforts.[358] As early as 1994, concepts such as sustainable development found their way into IIAs, as exemplified by the preamble of the NAFTA (1994). This preambular inclusions are more pronounced in newer treaties,[359] which could be attributed to a demand of society for greater accountability of the private sector.[360] Yet, this trend is rather limited and in any case such mentions cannot be considered as obligations upon the investors to comply with international environmental standards.

More interesting in this regard are those treaty provisions addressing CSR *vis-à-vis* investors, for instance, Article 9.17 CPTPP (2018),[361] Article 16 Chile-

Company v The Republic of Argentina, ICSID Case No ARB/01/8, Award (12 May 2005) para. 377; Suleimenova (2019), p. 114.

[357] Arguing that MFN clauses cannot alter the jurisdictional provisions *see* Douglas (2011), pp. 97 et seqq. For a different opinion *see* Schill (2011), pp. 353 et seqq.

[358] Choudhury (2020), p. 53; Krajweski (2021), p. 116.

[359] *See* for instance the preambles in: Rwanda-UAE BIT (2017); Morocco-Nigeria BIT (2016); Slovak Republic-Iran BIT (2016); Nigeria-Singapore BIT (2016); San Marino-Azerbaijan BIT (2015); Canada-Cameroon BIT (2014).

[360] Bernasconi-Osterwalder (2021), p. 465.

[361] CPTPP (2018), Art 9.17: ('The Parties reaffirm the importance of each Party encouraging enterprises operating within its territory or subject to its jurisdiction to voluntarily incorpórate

Hong Kong BIT (2016),[362] Article 12 Argentina-Qatar BIT (2016),[363] Article 11 Nigeria-Singapore BIT (2016),[364] Article 14 Canada-Mongolia BIT (2016),[365] Article 10(3) Slovak Republic-Iran BIT (2016),[366] or Article 16 Canada-Guinea BIT (2015).[367] One may argue that such provisions appear extremely generic, which might provide a flexible approach to accommodate to emerging concepts in international environmental law, but that might as well undermine certainty in their interpretation.[368] Whether this concern is justified could only be assessed against the background of arbitral awards deciding on this issue. Yet, two recent model BITs and the USMCA (2019) pre-emptively seek to refer to specific instruments of international law to avoid uncertainty.

While Article 17 The Netherlands Model BIT (2019) alludes to the multilateral environmental agreements of the contracting states as well as the UNFCCC, Article

---

into their internal policies those internationally recognised standards, guidelines and principles of corporate social responsibility that have been endorsed or are supported by that Party').

[362] Chile-Hong Kong BIT (2016), Art 16: ('The Parties reaffirm the importance of each Party encouraging enterprises operating within its area to voluntarily incorporate into their internal policies those internationally recognised standards, guidelines and principles of corporate social responsibility that have been endorsed or are supported by that Party').

[363] Argentina-Qatar BIT (2016), Art 12: ('Investors operating in the territory of the host Contracting Party should make efforts to voluntarily incorporate internationally recognized standards of corporate social responsibility into their business policies and practices').

[364] Nigeria-Singapore BIT (2016), Art 11: ('(1) Singapore reaffirms the importance of encouraging enterprises operating within its territory or subject to its jurisdiction to voluntarily incorporate into their internal policies those international recognised standards, guidelines and principles of corporate social responsibility that have been endorsed or are supported by Singapore. (2) Nigeria is to encourage enterprises operating within its territory or subject to its jurisdiction to voluntarily incorporate internationally recognised standards of corporate social responsibility in their practices and internal policies such as statements of principles that have been endorsed or are supported by Nigeria. These principles address issues such as labour, the environment, public health, human rights, community relations and anti-corruption').

[365] Canada-Mongolia BIT (2016), Art 14: ('Each Party should encourage enterprises operating within its territory or subject to its jurisdiction to voluntarily incorporate internationally recognized standards of corporate social responsibility in their practices and internal policies, such as statements of principle that have been endorsed or are supported by the Parties. These principles address issues such as labour, the environment, human rights, community relations and anti-corruption. The Parties should remind those enterprises of the importance of incorporating such corporate social responsibility standards in their internal policies').

[366] Slovak Republic-Iran BIT (2016), Art 10(3): ('Investors and investments should apply national, and internationally accepted, standards of corporate governance for the sector involved, in particular for transparency and accounting practices. Investors and their investments should strive to make the maximum feasible contributions to the sustainable development of the Host State and local community through appropriate levels of socially responsible practices').

[367] Canada-Guinea BIT (2015), Art 16: ('Each Party should encourage enterprises operating within its territory or subject to its jurisdiction to voluntarily incorporate internationally recognized standards of corporate social responsibility in their practices and internal policies, such as statements of principle that have been endorsed or are supported by the Parties. These principles address issues such as labour, the environment, human rights, community relations and anti-corruption').

[368] Tan and Chong (2020), pp. 195–196.

14.17 USMCA (2019) mentions the OECD Guidelines for Multinational Enterprises. The BLEU Model BIT (2019) goes a step further and in its Article 7(2) on CSR refers to the OECD Guidelines for Multinational Enterprises, the United Nations Guiding Principles on Business and Human Rights, and the Recommendation CM/REC(2016) of the Committee of Ministers to Member States on human rights and business. Particularly with respect to these Model BITs, tribunals may consider that those non-binding standards for investors become binding norms via the explicit referral of the IIA.[369] Accordingly, one may argue that these explicit referrals may be used as a model for future treaties seeking to impose obligations on investors.[370] However, similar to preambular references to sustainable development or environmental protection, provisions on CSR are not widespread in the network of existing IIAs. One may argue that states are reluctant to include CSR references as it would require that their domestic laws are equipped to compel investors' compliance with CSR.[371]

Most importantly, while all of these provisions aim at the incorporation of international standards on CSR (some even explicitly outlining environmental protection as part of CSR), they are all formulated in a non-binding manner for investors: either the contracting states ought to 'encourage' investors, or the investors themselves 'should' voluntarily incorporate such standards. One could argue that the analysis of investors' behaviour might be easier under those provisions addressing directly the investor instead of the state, otherwise, the tribunal '*might have to assess first if the state party adopted a policy of encouraging the relevant standards*'.[372] This however does not change the fact that all provisions use an hortatory language and it is hardly conceivable that tribunals would construe them as an obligation to comply with international environmental standards.

Finally, CSR commitments could be reflected in the licence to operate, domestic regulations or even voluntary adherence by the investors in a mandatory manner. Accordingly, one may suggest that this would create a valid cause of action for environmental counterclaims in treaty-based investment arbitration.[373] In this case, however, the cause of action would not be the investment treaty, but rather the particular licence or domestic regulation. Thus, the legal analysis would switch from international obligations to domestic obligations as a cause of action in treaty-based arbitration and the aforementioned intricacies thereof. All in all, the reference to CSR in investment treaties is unsuitable to provide a cause of action for environmental counterclaims.

[369] de Nanteuil (2018), p. 392; Krajweski (2021), p. 116.

[370] Dumberry (2013), p. 191.

[371] Bjorklund (2019), p. 52.

[372] Krajweski (2021), p. 119.

[373] Lahlou et al. (2019), p. 63.

5.2.2.3.2.2 Other Means of Incorporation of Obligations Under International Environmental Law Into Investment Law

Another option to explore for the incorporation of international environmental obligations is treaty interpretation. Particularly, either systematic integration or evolutionary interpretation could arguably fill the gap of environmental obligations in investment treaties. With respect to systematic integration, the *Urbaser v Argentina* case is illustrative: the tribunal referred to Article 31(3)(c) VCLT to take into account other rules of international law, including those on human rights, the latter being relevant for the analysis of the counterclaim.[374] As elaborated above, the interpretation principle of systematic integration embedded in Article 31(3)(c) VLCT conceives that treaties must be interpreted against the broader realm of international law.[375] However, this is an *interpretative tool* and cannot be used as a back door for incorporating other obligations of international law.[376]

Moreover, even if possible to integrate international environmental obligations into the particular investment treaty under consideration, this might not suffice for a cause of action of an environmental counterclaim. Obligations under international environmental law usually address the state or require their operationalisation through domestic law.[377] As such, using systematic integration for incorporating investors' obligations from the broader spectrum of international environmental law into investment law is not only questionable from a methodological point of view,[378] but also futile given the content of international environmental law itself.

With respect to evolutionary interpretation, some authors consider the potential for international environmental norms to re-substantiate treaties with limited environmental elements via an evolutionary interpretation.[379] One may recall the *Pulp Mills* case, whereby the ICJ considered that the treaty obligation to protect and preserve the aquatic environment under Article 41(a) Statute of the River of Uruguay (1975) had to be interpreted as including the obligation to undertake an environmental impact assessment under international law.[380] Similarly, the *Iron Rhine Railway* tribunal made use of an evolutionary interpretation to incorporate into the Treaty Between Belgium and the Netherlands relative to the Separation of their

[374] *Urbaser SA and Consorcio de Aguas Bilbao Bizkaia, Bilbao Biskaia Ur Partzuergoa v The Argentine Republic*, ICSID Case No ARB/07/26, Award (08 December 2016) para. 1200.

[375] *See* Sect. 3.3.3.2.3.

[376] Gardiner (2015), p. 330.

[377] Tan and Chong (2020), p. 189.

[378] Krajweski (2021), p. 107.

[379] Brown (2021), p. 236. Confined to 'sustainable development', Virgine Barral argues that such concept could open up the entire treaty for an evolutionary interpretation even if the term is located in the preamble *see* Barral (2012), p. 395. For a similar point on the possibility to assume an evolutionary interpretation from the context of the treaty provision, including but not limited to the preamble *see* McRae (2019), p. 60.

[380] *Pulp Mills on the River Uruguay (Argentina v Uruguay)* (Judgment) [2010] ICJ Rep 14, para. 204.

Respective Territories (1839) the contemporary costs related to environmental protection for the reactivation of the railway.[381] Albeit being an appealing proposition from the outset of public international law, its usefulness for environmental counterclaims in treaty-based arbitration appears extremely limited.

Evolutionary interpretation has been described as an interpretation that favours the contemporary reading (at the moment of interpretation) rather than a historical reading (at the moment of conclusion) of a norm.[382] Understandably, this only arises in cases where there are '*competing views on whether the meaning of the text of the treaty has changed over time*', also known as the intertemporal question.[383] However, there is nothing special about evolutionary interpretation as it is simply the result of using the ordinary cannons of treaty interpretation in a particular case.[384] To say that the VCLT supports either evolutionary or static interpretation is thus incorrect, as the rules of treaty interpretation are temporally neutral.[385] Accordingly, to determine whether a norm demands an evolutionary or static/historic interpretation, the ICJ in the *Namibia* Advisory Opinion,[386] *Aegean Sea* case,[387] *Gabčíkovo-Nagymaros* case,[388] and the *Navigational and Related Rights* case,[389] has

[381] *Iron Rhine Railway Arbitration (Belgium v The Netherlands)*, Award (24 May 2005) XXVII RIAA 35, paras. 80–84.

[382] Kolb (2019), p. 16.

[383] Djeffal (2019), p. 22.

[384] For further elaboration on this idea *see* Bjorge (2014); Djeffal (2019), pp. 21–33; McRae (2019), pp. 57–58.

[385] Wyatt (2019), pp. 127–146.

[386] *Legal Consequences for States of the Continued Presence of South Africa in Namibia (South West Africa) notwithstanding Security Council Resolution 276 (1979)* (Advisory Opinion) [1971] ICJ Rep 16, para. 53.

[387] *Aegean Sea Continental Shelf (Greece v Turkey)* (Judgment) [1978] ICJ Rep 3, para. 77: ('once it is established that the expression "the territorial status of Greece" was used in Greece's instrument of accession as a generic term denoting any matters comprised within the concept of territorial status under general international law, the presumption necessarily arises that its meaning was intended to follow the evolution of the law and to correspond with the meaning attached to the expression by the law in force at any given time').

[388] *Case concerning the Gabčíkovo-Nagymaros Project (Hungary v Slovakia)* (Judgment) [1997] ICJ Rep 7, para. 112: ('By inserting these evolving provisions in the Treaty, the parties recognized the potential necessity to adapt the Project. Consequently, the Treaty is not static, and is open to adapt to emerging norms of international law').

[389] *Dispute Regarding Navigational and Related Rights (Costa Rica v Nicaragua)* (Judgment) [2009] ICJ Rep 213, para. 64: ('there are situations in which the parties' intent upon conclusion of the treaty was, or may be presumed to have been, to give the terms used — or some of them — a meaning or content capable of evolving, not one fixed once and for all, so as to make allowance for, among other things, developments in international law') and para. 66: ('It is founded on the idea that, where the parties have used generic terms in a treaty, the parties necessarily having been aware that the meaning of the terms was likely to evolve over time, and where the treaty has been entered into for a very long period or is "of continuing duration", the parties must be presumed, as a general rule, to have intended those terms to have an evolving meaning').

emphasised the parties' intention as reflected in the treaty as the crucial element to tip the scales.

In this sense, there are two obstacles for an evolutionary interpretation to invoke international environmental obligations as a cause of action for environmental counterclaims: *first*, evolutionary interpretation could not incorporate environmental norms if the particular treaty excludes by omission such category of norms as this would be deemed to express the contracting parties' intention.[390] As such, although the inclusion of environmental protection or related terms in new IIAs is noticeable, the majority of IIAs remain impervious to environmental considerations by their plain wording. Consequently, there is no room to invoke norms of international environmental law in these treaties.

Second, tribunals and international courts prefer to base an evolutionary interpretation on generic terms of the treaty.[391] For instance, both in the *Aegean Sea* case and the *Navigational and Related Rights* case, the ICJ found that the use of generic terms is an indication of parties' intention that those terms would most likely evolve over time.[392] Certainly, there are such terms in some IIAs, including international standards of CSR, environmental protection, and even sustainable development. However, these generic terms are either framed in the preamble of a treaty or in voluntary provisions addressed to the investors. Thus, as part of the preamble, those generic terms could only serve to incorporate contemporary environmental norms in the relation between the contracting states. As a part of voluntary provisions addressed to the investors, once again the hortatory language used in those provisions might not be construed as an investor's obligation serving as a cause of action for environmental counterclaims irrespective of the contemporary reading of those generic terms.

5.3 How Appropriate Is It for Tribunals in Investment Arbitration to Decide on Environmental Matters?

After exploring the possible avenues for finding a cause of action for environmental counterclaims in investment arbitration, this section delves into the appropriateness of investment arbitral tribunals deciding environmental matters. *First*, it addresses the technical and procedural issues an environmental counterclaim might create [Sect. 5.3.1]. *Second*, it assesses the policy issues involved in the adjudication of environmental matters by a tribunal in investment arbitration [Sect. 5.3.2].

[390] Brown (2021), p. 253.

[391] Brown (2021), p. 255.

[392] *Aegean Sea Continental Shelf (Greece v Turkey)* (Judgment) [1978] ICJ Rep 3, para. 77; *Dispute Regarding Navigational and Related Rights (Costa Rica v Nicaragua)* (Judgment) [2009] ICJ Rep 213, para. 66.

5.3.1 Technical and Procedural Issues

At the level of public international law, international arbitration appears as a suitable option for settling environmental-related disputes given its flexibility and the possibility to tailor the particular procedure.[393] This represents a solid starting point for environmental counterclaims in investment arbitration from the tribunal's perspective. There are nevertheless a variety of technical and procedural issues exclusively related to the environmental components of the dispute that might recurrently arise, including: *first*, the analysis of the respective environmental law. *Second*, the assessment of scientific evidence and expert witnesses. *Third*, the standard and burden of proof for environmental damage.

First, with respect to environmental law, a preliminary concern pertains to the arbitrators' familiarity and expertise on environmental law and the science behind it. However, it is assumed that arbitrators (and counsels) would adapt to any rising demand on environmental expertise in investment disputes.[394] That might be true for environmental counterclaims based on international environmental law or environmental obligations in investment treaties. Yet, for environmental counterclaims based on domestic law the situation differs. Tribunals are usually not expected to be acquainted with the domestic law of the host state.[395] Even if such knowledge could be required, this would only reduce the pool of qualified arbitrators, and in case of nationals of the particular host state, their appointment may only be achieved through agreement of both parties.[396]

In a context where the arbitrators might not be experts on the particular domestic environmental law, there is a need to determine the scope and proper application of such law. Here, the *Brazilian Loans* case[397] becomes apposite. When reasoning on the application of French law to the loans in dispute, the PCIJ held that domestic law must be applied as it would be applied in the particular state.[398] In other words, such

[393] Cases such as the *Indus Waters Kishenganga* between Pakistan and India, or the *South China Sea Arbitration* between The Philippines and China show the inclusion of arbitration in environmental agreements such as the UNFCCC, and the adoption of the PCA Optional Rules for Arbitration of Disputes relating to Natural Resources and/or the Environment *see* Miles and Lawry-White (2019), p. 11.

[394] Tan and Chong (2020), pp. 189–190.

[395] Bilanová (2020), p. 410.

[396] Hepburn (2017), p. 113.

[397] *Case concerning the Payment in Gold of Brazilian Federal Loans contracted in France (France v Brazil)* (Judgment) (12 July 1929) PCIJ Rep Series A No 21.

[398] *Case concerning the Payment in Gold of Brazilian Federal Loans contracted in France (France v Brazil)* (Judgment) (12 July 1929) PCIJ Rep Series A No 21, 124: ('Once the Court has arrived at the conclusion that it is necessary to apply the municipal law of a particular country, there seems no doubt that it must seek to apply it as it would be applied in that country. It would not be applying the municipal law of a country if it were to apply it in a manner different from that in which that law would be applied in the country in which it is in force. It follows that the Court must pay the utmost regard to the decisions of the municipal courts of a country, for it is with the aid of their

law must be placed in its domestic context, for instance, with resort to domestic interpretations and interpretative principles.[399] This approach to domestic law has been followed as well by tribunals in investment arbitration.[400] Accordingly, tribunals may ascertain the scope and proper application of the relevant domestic law relying on primary materials (such as the text of the regulation or law), judicial decisions on their application, drafting history, academic texts, expert witnesses among others.[401] This does not mean, for instance, that the tribunal is bound by domestic case-law on the determination of the content of the law, as in certain circumstances it might be appropriate to depart from it or even to choose between conflicting positions.[402]

Certainly, some newer applicable law provisions in investment treaties foresee some guidance on how to determine domestic law,[403] which could be seen as an innovation in treaty drafting.[404] Yet, the utility of such guidance is doubtful as it is limited to repeat the standard set by the PCIJ in the *Brazilian Loans* case. Conversely, a perhaps more useful suggestion would be the introduction of a preliminary reference from the arbitral tribunal to domestic courts over questions of domestic law (akin to the preliminary ruling procedure in the EU legal order).[405] However, this might excessively stall the arbitral proceedings.

Second, the environmental component of a counterclaim would necessitate the assessment of scientific evidence and expert witnesses. Experts may clarify issues beyond the arbitrators' purview such as the existence and extent of soil and water pollution, the health and environmental risks posed by the investment, the biological significance of the investment site among others.[406] However, the assessment of environmental damage may throw conflicting results as the valuation of environmental resources is usually based on estimates and possibly different valuation methods.[407] Thus, the assessment of such evidence adds to the complexity of the

jurisprudence that it will be enabled to decide what are the rules which, in actual fact, are applied in the country the law of which is recognized as applicable in a given case').

[399] Hepburn (2017), p. 109.

[400] *See* for instance: *Hussein Nuaman Soufraki v The United Arab Emirates*, ICSID Case No ARB/02/7, Decision on Annulment (05 June 2007) para. 96; *Emmis International Holding BV, Emmis Radio Operating BV, MEM Magyar Electronic Media Kereskedelmi és Szolgáltató Kft v The Republic of Hungary*, ICSID Case No ARB/12/2, Award (16 April 2014) para. 175.

[401] Hepburn (2017), pp. 117–119.

[402] Hepburn (2017), pp. 132–133.

[403] *See* for instance: CETA (2016), Art 8.31(2); EU-Singapore IPA, Art 3.13(2); Lithuania-Turkey BIT (2018), Art 12(13); Hungary-Cabo Verde BIT (2019), Art 9(7–8); Belarus-Hungary BIT (2019), Art 9(8); Hungary-Kyrgyzstan BIT (2020), Art 9(8); Colombia-Spain BIT (2021), Art 26(2).

[404] Atanasova (2019), pp. 413–414.

[405] Shao (2021), p. 177. A similar procedure exists in the US known as 'certification', whereby federal courts refer questions of state law to the respective state court, which has also been suggested for investment arbitration *see* Puig and Shaffer (2018), p. 405.

[406] Levine and Peart (2019), pp. 222–223.

[407] Hanley (2002), p. 35.

case.[408] One strategy for the tribunal to streamline and better understand technical issues is flagging questions to the expert in advance of and/or after a hearing.[409] This was the method deployed by the tribunal in the *South China Sea Arbitration*, whereby the tribunal sent prior and post hearing questions to the marine biologists (experts), who were reporting on the alleged damage to coral reefs.[410]

A more challenging issue appears when the party-appointed experts present diverging or contradicting conclusions. This happened in the cases of *Perenco v Ecuador* and *Burlington v Ecuador*. For instance, the *Perenco v Ecuador* tribunal acknowledged a divergence between the respective party-appointed experts with respect to strict or fault-based liability, on joint and several liability, on the imprescriptibility of environmental claims and on remediation criteria.[411] The *Burlington v Ecuador* tribunal faced a similar problem as the respective party-appointed experts disagreed on whether prior the 2008 Constitution there was a rebuttable presumption of fault for environmental claims, whether environmental claims before 2008 were imprescriptible, and whether environmental harm involved permissible limits or background values.[412] Curiously, despite analysing the same legal framework and similar facts, the tribunals in *Perenco v Ecuador* and *Burlington v Ecuador* disagreed with each other on the liability regime for environmental damage applicable prior the 2008 Constitution.[413]

These discrepancies may undermine the credibility of the award, which is troubling considering the public interest involved in environmental protection.[414] Therefore, tribunals must address the conflicting expert evidence for instance, by directly assessing the merits of each expert's opinion, by assessing the form, logic and structure of the report or by considering the credentials of each expert.[415] Tribunals

---

[408] Harrison (2016), p. 480.

[409] Levine and Peart (2019), p. 224.

[410] *The South China Sea Arbitration (The Republic of Philippines v The People's Republic of China)*, PCA Case No 2013-19.

[411] *Perenco Ecuador Ltd v Republic of Ecuador and Empresa Estatal Petróleos del Ecuador (Petroecuador)*, ICSID Case No ARB/08/6, Interim Decision on the Environmental Counterclaim (11 August 2015) paras. 116 et seqq., 160 et seqq., 168 and 183 et seqq.

[412] *Burlington Resources Inc v Republic of Ecuador*, ICSID Case No ARB/08/5, Decision on Ecuador's Counterclaims (07 February 2017) paras. 240, 250 et seqq., and 268 et seqq.

[413] The *Perenco v Ecuador* tribunal considered a fault-based liability for environmental damage with a rebuttable presumption that the regulatory exceedance constitutes a failure on the duty of care, which could be disproven by force majeure, act of a third person or that there was not failure on the duty of care *see*, *Perenco Ecuador Ltd v Republic of Ecuador and Empresa Estatal Petróleos del Ecuador (Petroecuador)*, ICSID Case No ARB/08/6, Interim Decision on the Environmental Counterclaim (11 August 2015) paras. 353–355 and 371 et seqq. For the *Burlington v Ecuador* tribunal, before the 2008 Constitution and at least as from 2002, there was a strict-liability regime on environmental damage, whereby proving the fulfilment of the duty of care would not be enough to exempt the operator from liability *see*, *Burlington Resources Inc v Republic of Ecuador*, ICSID Case No ARB/08/5, Decision on Ecuador's Counterclaims (07 February 2017) paras. 247–248.

[414] Shao (2021), p. 176.

[415] Hepburn (2017), pp. 134 et seqq.

in investment arbitration could also follow the practice encouraged by the ICC and provided for in the IBA Rules on the Taking of Evidence of 'hot-tubbing', which basically entails the meeting of the experts to narrow the issues on which they disagree.[416]

Another option is to fall back on the burden of proof as was the case in the *Allard v Barbados* case.[417] Thus, if the tribunal is not convinced by any of the conflicting reports, it would draw negative inferences for the party that needed to prove the particular issue. An alternative to avoid conflicting reports of party-appointed experts consists of tribunal-appointed experts.[418] Needless to say, the tribunal cannot delegate its authority on the expert, but it must rather consider carefully the report before reaching its own conclusions.[419] Yet, the main risk with this option is the circularity of expert evidence as parties may appoint their own experts to rebut the tribunal-appointed expert, which would necessarily increase costs.[420] Interestingly, the *Perenco v Ecuador* tribunal acknowledged the issue of burden of proof, but decided to appoint its own expert instead.[421]

For the assessment of scientific evidence, one may also suggest having a technical expert siting as one of the arbitrators or site visits of the tribunal.[422] The former option is drawn from the *Indus Waters Kishenganga* case, where one of the arbitrators was a '*highly qualified engineer*' appointed by the Rector of the Imperial College of Science and Technology (London).[423] The latter option has taken place in the *Gabčíkovo-Nagymaros* case[424] and *Burlington v Ecuador* case,[425] where the adjudicators visited the site of the alleged environmental harm and gathered further information for the respective record. Whilst site visits could be implemented in agreement between the tribunal and the parties, having a technical expert as an

416 Hussin (2019), pp. 9–10. Similarly, Miles and Lawry-White (2019), p. 28.

417 *Peter A Allard v The Government of Barbados*, PCA Case No 2012-06, Award (27 June 2016) para. 110: ('given the differences in approach of the experts and the insufficiency of available data, the Claimant has failed to discharge his burden of proof to establish that there was a decline in the parameters of water quality (other than salinity) at the Sanctuary during the Relevant Period').

418 Shao (2021), p. 177.

419 Blackaby and Wilbraham (2016), p. 664.

420 Hepburn (2017), pp. 136 et seq.

421 After acknowledging that the burden of proof might not be completely fulfilled given the disagreements over highly technical issues, the tribunal held '[h]*owever, as the Tribunal is satisfied that there has been some damage for which it seems likely that Perenco is liable, the Tribunal is not disposed to dismiss the counterclaim* in limine' *see*, *Perenco Ecuador Ltd v Republic of Ecuador and Empresa Estatal Petróleos del Ecuador (Petroecuador)*, ICSID Case No ARB/08/6, Decision on Perenco's Application for Dismissal of Ecuador's Counterclaims (18 August 2017) para. 35.

422 Levine and Peart (2019), p. 228.

423 *Indus Waters Kishenganga Arbitration (Pakistan v India)*, PCA Case No 2011-01, Partial Award (18 February 2013) para. 14.

424 *Case concerning the Gabčíkovo-Nagymaros Project (Hungary v Slovakia)* (Judgment) [1997] ICJ Rep 7, para. 10.

425 *Burlington Resources Inc v Republic of Ecuador*, ICSID Case No ARB/08/5, Decision on Ecuador's Counterclaims (07 February 2017) paras. 18 et seqq.

arbitrator might be more complicated. For instance, in the *Indus Waters Kishenganga* case, having a technical expert in the tribunal was a requirement in the underlying treaty.[426] In the absence of such provision is difficult to envisage that the disputing parties would agree on such composition of the tribunal.

Third, the standard and burden of proof for environmental damage should be flexible. In this regard, the ICJ in the *Certain Activities Carried Out by Nicaragua in the Border Area* case recognised that there might be difficulties on proving the existence of environmental damage or causation, however, even in the '*absence of adequate evidence as to the extent of material damage will not, in all situations, preclude an award of compensation for that damage*'.[427] This suggests certain flexibility on evidentiary rules with respect to environmental matters.[428] Finally, one of the major evidentiary problems with environmental damage is the existence of contamination prior to the acts of the concerned party. In this sense, the *Perenco v Ecuador* tribunal held:

> Given the problems of proof when seeking to shift responsibility for tortious claims, it is possible that an operator might end up being found liable for an act of contamination possibly caused by its predecessor. The best way for the contractor to protect its legal interests was for it to comprehensively document the environmental condition of the Blocks at the time that it assumed responsibility for them.[429]

Accordingly, an investor setting out an operation with potential environmental impacts might be advised to document the environmental conditions of the relevant area once it has taken responsibility.[430] As such, it could eventually argue that contamination existed prior to its activity or that its contribution to the environmental damage has been minimal with respect to the conditions preceding the investment.

5.3.2 *Policy Issues*

The policy issues involved in the adjudication of environmental matters by a tribunal in investment arbitration unfold in two categories: on the one hand, an international dimension, which pertains to the direct imposition of international environmental obligations on investors. On the other hand, a domestic dimension, which refers to

[426] The Indus Waters Treaty 1960 between the Government of India, the Government of Pakistan and the International Bank for Reconstruction and Development (adopted 19 September 1960, entry into force 12 January 1961) 419 UNTS 215, Annexure G, para. 4(b)(ii).

[427] *Certain Activities Carried Out by Nicaragua in the Border Area (Costa Rica v Nicaragua)* (Compensation) [2018] ICJ Rep 15, paras. 34–35.

[428] Miles and Lawry-White (2019), p. 28.

[429] *Perenco Ecuador Ltd v Republic of Ecuador and Empresa Estatal Petróleos del Ecuador (Petroecuador)*, ICSID Case No ARB/08/6, Interim Decision on the Environmental Counterclaim (11 August 2015) para. 378.

[430] Hussin (2019), pp. 9–10.

the adjudication of counterclaims based on domestic environmental law by investment tribunals.

With respect to the international dimension, there is a structural imbalance in treaty-based investment arbitration that goes beyond the investor's exclusive right to initiate proceedings: investors enjoy substantive standards of protection under IIAs without corresponding obligations under international law.[431] This has often resulted on a further legitimacy concern, whereby an investor's misconduct is ruled upon exclusively as 'contributory negligence' instead of responsibility.[432] With respect to international environmental law there is an added problem: as seen above, international environmental law is usually formulated in CSR standards for its application to non-state actors. Yet, one may argue that reliance on self-regulation and voluntary standards undermines the rule of law as investors may be uncapable or unwilling to adhere to those international standards.[433] This might cause discontent among the receiving communities of foreign investment risking the viability of investment projects in the future.[434] Therefore, one may be inclined to support the inclusion of direct obligations on non-state actors, particularly investors in international law. However, such obligations ought to be sufficiently clear and precise.[435]

Since nothing impedes international law to do so, states' reluctance to regulate the conduct of non-state actors under international law appears as a political choice rather than an inherent constraint of the legal system.[436] One reason could be that directly imposing international obligations on private actors would disempower states with respect to control and compliance with those obligations.[437] As such, the application of precise international obligations on investors by arbitral tribunals remains a '*noble dream*',[438] but this does not mean that the current state practice cannot switch direction.

With respect to the domestic dimension, there are innumerable concerns over investment tribunals adjudging issues of domestic environmental law, which might not always be justified. For instance, one may suggest that counterclaims in treaty-based investment arbitration should be limited to those grounded in law that the tribunal is acquainted with, particularly with respect to domestic public laws, in order to enhance the legitimacy of the process.[439] This however may represent a skewed perspective of arbitration. In practice, arbitrators decide disputes applying domestic law even if they are not experts on that particular law.[440] Moreover, as

[431] Sattorova (2019), p. 26.
[432] Ho (2019), p. 14.
[433] Ho (2019), p. 15.
[434] Sattorova (2019), p. 26.
[435] Krajweski (2021), p. 128.
[436] Nollkaemper (2006), p. 194; Dörr (2020), p. 142.
[437] Vazquez (2005), p. 950.
[438] Krajweski (2021), p. 128.
[439] Bjorklund (2013), p. 479.
[440] Kaufmann-Kohler (2005), p. 631.

mentioned above, arbitrators have a variety of tools to ascertain the scope and application of domestic law *eg* relying on judicial decisions, drafting history, academic texts or expert witnesses. As such, the arbitrator's knowledge on domestic law by itself does not create legitimacy issues. Thus, restricting counterclaims to only those based on (domestic) law the tribunal has knowledge thereof does not seem to serve any purpose.

One may further caution that by narrowing the function of domestic law in newer applicable law provisions in IIAs, states are becoming more defensive of their courts' jurisdiction to solve domestic law issues.[441] This argument is buttressed if the domestic law confers exclusive jurisdiction to domestic courts to decide environmental matters.[442] Yet, such view may not necessarily be correct. On the one hand, the role and design of the applicable law provisions in IIAs is at least questionable as outlined above. On the other hand, any state concern on the exclusive jurisdiction of its courts over environmental matters seems to fade away with the willing submission of the environmental counterclaim to investment arbitration. In any case, legitimacy concerns about investment tribunals adjudging public interests reflected in public domestic law, *eg* environmental issues, are misplaced, since from the outset, those tribunals are conceived to entertain the state's exercise of sovereign authority.[443]

A more troublesome point pertains to whether the claimant investor is subject to the respective domestic law, which provides the cause of action for the environmental counterclaim. Considering that investors normally operate through subsidiaries, this might be the main challenge for counterclaims based on domestic law, unless there are some reasons for piercing the corporate veil.[444] By analogy of the issue on non-consenting third parties mentioned in Chap. 3, a possibility would be to consider the parent company and its subsidiary as a single economic entity.[445] However, the intricacies of third companies in counterclaims require a deeper analysis that exceeds this book's purview.

Be that as it may, from a policy perspective, there are plenty of reasons for supporting the adjudication of environmental counterclaims based on domestic law by investment tribunals. *First*, environmental considerations are more integrated in the reasoning of investment tribunals, which evinces an understanding of investment law more amenable to environmental protection.[446] This suggests that tribunals are fully receptive to consider the implications on sustainable development of their decisions.[447] *Second*, investment tribunals might be better placed to decide connected environmental counterclaims in lieu of domestic courts because of the

441 Shao (2021), p. 167.

442 Douglas (2013), p. 434.

443 *See* Sect. 2.2.1.2.2.

444 Atanasova et al. (2014), p. 390.

445 *See* Sect. 3.3.2.3.

446 Tan and Chong (2020), p. 197.

447 Bjorklund (2019), p. 64.

disparity of power between the state and the investor in domestic proceedings, the inadequate capacity of some domestic court systems to assess environmental issues and the procedural flexibility embedded in arbitration.[448] Most importantly, by arbitrating environmental counterclaims the risk of circularity (challenge of domestic judgments before investment arbitration) might be lessened, thereby reducing possible costs and avoiding further strain on the domestic judicial systems.[449] *Third*, the examples of *Perenco v Ecuador* and *Burlington v Ecuador* illustrate that investment tribunals are capable of deciding environmental counterclaims based on domestic law,[450] without major inconveniences.

5.4 Interim Conclusions

The assessment of a possible cause of action or legal basis for an environmental counterclaim in investment arbitration constitutes the last step of this monograph. Investors might be subject to a myriad of regulations or guidelines both at the international and domestic level but this does not guarantee the existence of an appropriate cause of action for environmental counterclaims. Certainly, the structure and operation of investment contracts facilitate the possibility of finding (or imposing in the future) environmental obligations upon the investor, whose breach could ground an environmental counterclaim in contract-based investment arbitration. In the absence of such obligations, domestic law of the host state could provide the legal basis necessary for an environmental counterclaim.

In treaty-based investment arbitration, both domestic law and international law enjoy the potential for imposing environmental obligations that serve as a cause of action for environmental counterclaims. In case of environmental obligations stemming from domestic law, they need to be operationalised in the respective IIA via a treaty anchor that brings a domestic law violation to the international level. Applicable law provisions in IIAs referring to domestic law of the host state are not suitable for this purpose. Instead, environmental counterclaims might require treaty provisions imposing the obligation upon investors to comply with the host state's domestic law, treaty provisions foreseeing counterclaims based on domestic law or a combination of both.

In case of environmental obligations stemming from international law, they engender a more complex discussion. Preliminary, one must bear in mind that the debate about international legal personality of non-state actors is irrelevant for

---

[448] Anning (2021), pp. 1318–1322.

[449] Shao (2021), p. 173.

[450] Report of the Eighteenth Commission of the *Institut de Droit International* (Rapporteur Professor Campbell McLachlan) on the 'Equality of Parties before International Investment Tribunals' paras. 207–211 <https://www.idi-iil.org/app/uploads/2019/06/Commission-18-Equality-of-parties-before-international-investment-tribunals-McLachlan-Travaux-La-Haye-2019.pdf> accessed 10 January 2023.

finding international environmental obligations upon investors. Moreover, while the concepts of 'responsibility', 'liability' and 'accountability' are often used interchangeably, those concepts have a defined content in international law with respect to corporations. Against this backdrop, one could theorise about two sources of international law for environmental obligations upon investors: international environmental law and investment treaties.

On the one hand, international environmental law does not actively regulate the conduct of private actors. For instance, the well-established principles of the polluter-pays principle, the principle of prevention and the precautionary principle are abstract and indeterminate, thus falling short of imposing environmental obligations on investors. Certainly, international environmental law instruments might highlight the crucial role of non-state actors for the protection of the environment but they usually address states or require subsequent implementation into domestic legislation such as the international regimes on civil liability for environmental damage. Even CSR instruments do not impose environmental obligations on investors by themselves.

Yet, one could conceive that international environmental law as a whole creates a negative obligation upon the investors, according to which, they are prohibited from severally deteriorating the environment. This negative obligation could support an environmental counterclaim in treaty-based investment arbitration but only in clear evidence of environmental degradation. This evinces the intrinsic difficulties of finding a cause of action in international environmental law for environmental counterclaims in investment arbitration. This does not change by the re-conceptualisation of environmental protection as a matter of human rights or as transnational public policy.

On the other hand, IIAs could directly provide for investors' obligations towards the environment, but only if they are sufficiently clear on their scope and consequences. In contrast, IIA provisions referring to CSR and other non-binding standards cannot provide a viable cause of action for environmental counterclaims. Neither can treaty interpretation supply an IIA with environmental obligations upon investors where the plain wording of the treaty does not establish such obligation. This is so because, *first*, references to CSR and other non-binding standards in IIAs are worded in a hortatory or voluntary manner. *Second*, neither systematic integration nor evolutionary interpretation could incorporate investors' obligations from the broader spectrum of international environmental law into investment law. Systematic integration is an interpretative tool and cannot introduce substantive obligations through the back door. Even if it could, such exercise is futile given that international environmental law does not impose positive obligations on non-state actors. Evolutionary interpretation could not incorporate environmental norms if the particular treaty excludes such category of norms by omission or if the generic terms subject to interpretation are worded in hortatory rather than prescriptive language.

All in all, there might be certain hesitance in all stakeholders on the adjudication of environmental counterclaims in investment arbitration. However, the advantages might outweigh the possible concerns. From a technical perspective, arbitration would provide the necessary tools to properly address the respective environmental issues, and from a policy perspective, investment arbitration might exalt environmental protection at the international level.

References

Abadie P (2004) A new story of David and Goliath: the alien tort claims act gives victims of environmental injustice in the developing world a viable claim against multinational corporations. Golden Gate Univ Law Rev 34:745–796

Alvarez JE (2011) Are corporations "subjects" of international law? Santa Clara J Int Law 9:1–36

Alvik I (2019) Investor-state contracts. In: Krajewski M, Hoffmann RT (eds) Research handbook on foreign direct investment. Edward Elgar, Cheltenham, pp 271–298

Anning M (2021) Counterclaims admissibility in investment arbitration: the case of environmental disputes. In: Chaisse J, Choukroune L, Jusoh S (eds) Handbook of international investment law and policy. Springer, Singapore, pp 1277–1326

Asteriti A (2015) Environmental law in investment arbitration: procedural means of incorporation. J World Invest Trade 16(2):248–273

Atanasova D (2019) Applicable law provisions in investment treaties: forever midnight clauses? J Int Disp Settlement 10:396–422

Atanasova D, Martínez Benoit A, Ostřanský J (2014) The legal framework for counterclaims in investment treaty arbitration. J Int Arbitr 31(3):357–391

Atapattu S (2006) Emerging principles of international environmental law. Transnational Publishers, New York

Barral V (2012) Sustainable development in international law: nature and operation of an Evolutive legal norm. Eur J Int Law 23(2):377–400

Bartels L (2011) Jurisdiction and applicable law clauses: where does a tribunal find the principal norms applicable to the case before it? In: Broude T, Shany Y (eds) Multi-sourced equivalent norms in international law. Hart Publishing, Oxford, pp 115–141

Begic T (2005) Applicable law in international investment disputes. Eleven International Publishing, Utrecht

Ben Hamida W (2003) L'arbitrage Transnational Unilatéral: Réflexions sur une Procédure résérvée à l'initiative d'une Personne Privée contre une Personne Publique. Dissertation, Université Pantheon-Assas Paris II

Bernardini P (1998) The renegotiation of the investment contract. ICSID Rev 13(2):411–425

Bernasconi-Osterwalder N (2021) Inclusion of investor obligations and corporate accountability provisions in investment agreements. In: Chaisse J, Choukroune L, Jusoh S (eds) Handbook of international investment law and policy. Springer, Singapore, pp 463–482

Bilanová A (2020) Environmental counterclaims in investment arbitration. Eur Invest Law Arbitr Rev 5:400–411

Bjorge E (2014) The evolutionary interpretation of treaties. Oxford University Press, Oxford

Bjorklund AK (2013) The role of counterclaims in rebalancing investment law. Lewis Clark Law Rev 17(2):461–480

Bjorklund AK (2014) Applicable law in international investment disputes. In: Giorgetti C (ed) Litigating international investment disputes: a Practitioner's guide. Brill Nijhoff, Leiden, pp 261–286

Bjorklund AK (2019) Sustainable development and international investment law. In: Miles K (ed) Research handbook on environment and investment law. Edward Elgar Publishing, Cheltenham, pp 38–68

Blackaby N, Wilbraham A (2016) Practical issues relating to the use of expert evidence in investment treaty arbitration. ICSID Rev 31(3):655–669

Boisson de Chazournes L (2017) Environmental protection and investment arbitration: yin and Yang? Anuario Colombiano de Derecho Internacional 10:371–400

Born G, Kalelioglu C (2021) Choice-of-law agreements in international contracts. Georgia J Int Comp Law 50(1):44–118

Boyd DR (2018) Catalyst for change: evaluating forty years of experience in implementing the right to a healthy environment. In: Knox JH, Pejan R (eds) The human right to a healthy environment. Cambridge University Press, Cambridge, pp 17–41

Boyle A (1999) Codification of international environmental law and the international law commission: injurious consequences revisited. In: Boyle A, Freestone D (eds) International law and sustainable development: past achievements and future challenges. Oxford University Press, Oxford, pp 61–85

Bridgeman NL (2003) Human rights litigation under the ATCA as a proxy for environmental claims. Yale Human Rights Dev Law J 6:1–44

Brown R (2021) Invoking international environmental norms through treaty interpretation. Law Pract Int Courts Trib 20:235–266

Bubrowski H (2013) Balancing IIA arbitration through the use of counterclaims. In: de Mestral A, Lévesque C (eds) Improving international investment agreements. Routledge, New York, pp 212–229

Bungenberg M (2023) Democracy and international investment law. In: Kröll S, Bjorklund AK, Ferrari F (eds) Cambridge compendium of international commercial and investment arbitration, vol 1. Cambridge University Press, Cambridge, pp 186–210

Chi M (2018) Integrating sustainable development in international investment law: normative incompatibility, system integration and governance implications. Routledge, New York

Choudhury B (2020) International investment law and non-economic issues. Vanderbilt J Transnatl Law 53(1):1–78

Comeaux PE, Kinsella NS (1994) Reducing political risk in developing countries: bilateral investment treaties, stabilization clauses and MIGA & OPIC investment insurance. New York Law School J Int Comp Law 15(1):1–48

Cotula L (2006) Stabilisation clauses and the evolution of environmental standards in foreign investment contracts. Yearb Int Environ Law 17:111–138

Crawford J (2007) Treaty and contract in investment arbitration. In: The 22nd Freshfields Lecture on International Arbitration, London 29 November 2007

Crawford J (2019) Brownlie's principles of public international law, 9th edn. Oxford University Press, Oxford

Crow K, Escobar LL (2018) International corporate obligations, human rights, and the Urbaser standard: breaking new ground. Boston Univ Int Law J 36(1):87–118

De Brabandere E (2014) Investment treaty arbitration as public international law: procedural aspects and implications. Cambridge University Press, Cambridge

De Brabandere E (2020) The (Ir)relevance of transnational public policy in investment treaty arbitration – a reply to Jean-Michel Marcoux. J World Invest Trade 21(6):847–866

de Nanteuil A (2018) Counterclaims in investment arbitration: old questions, new answers? Law Pract Int Courts Trib 17(2):374–392

de Sadeleer N (2020) Environmental principles: from political slogans to legal rules, 2nd edn. Oxford University Press, Oxford

Diel-Glior K, Hennecke R (2015) Investment in accordance with the law. In: Bungenberg M, Griebel J, Hobe S, Reinisch A (eds) International investment law: a handbook. CH Beck/Hart/Nomos, Baden-Baden, pp 566–576

Djeffal C (2019) An Interpreter's guide to static and Evolutive interpretations: solving intertemporal problems according to the VCLT. In: Abi-Saab G, Keith K, Marceau G, Marquet C (eds) Evolutionary interpretation and international law. Hart Publishing, Oxford, pp 21–34

Dolzer R, Kriebaum U, Schreuer C (2022) Principles of international investment law, 3rd edn. Oxford University Press, Oxford

Dörr O (2020) Unternehmensverantwortlichkeit im Völkerrecht. In: Reinisch A, Hobe S, Kieninger EM, Peters A (eds) Unternehmensverantwortung und Internationales Recht. CF Müller, Heidelberg, pp 133–184

Douglas Z (2009) The international law of investment claims. Cambridge University Press, Cambridge

Douglas Z (2011) The MFN clause in investment arbitration: treaty interpretation off the rails. J Int Disp Settlement 2(1):97–113

Douglas Z (2013) The enforcement of environmental norms in investment treaty arbitration. In: Dupuy PM, Viñuales JE (eds) Harnessing foreign investment to promote environmental protection: incentives and safeguards. Cambridge University Press, Cambridge, pp 415–444

Downs JA (1993) A healthy and ecologically balanced environment: an argument for a third generation right. Duke J Comp Int Law 3:351–386

Dumberry P (2013) Corporate investors' international legal personality and their accountability for human rights violations under IIAs. In: de Mestral A, Lévesque C (eds) Improving international investment agreements. Routledge, New York, pp 179–194

Dumberry P (2020) A guide to general principles of law in international investment arbitration. Oxford University Press, Oxford

Dupuy PM, Viñuales JE (2018) International environmental law, 2nd edn. Cambridge University Press, Cambridge

Fitzmaurice MA (2001) International protection of the environment. Recueil des cours l'academie de droit international 293:9–488

Gaillard E (2010) Legal theory of international arbitration. Martinus Nijhoff Publishers, Leiden

Gardiner RK (2015) Treaty interpretation, 2nd edn. Oxford University Press, Oxford

Gattini A (2016) International responsibility of the state and international responsibility of juridical persons for environmental damage: where do we stand? In: Levashova Y, Lambooy T, Dekker I (eds) Bridging the gap between international investment law and the environment. Eleven, The Hague, pp 115–141

Gleason T (2021) Examining host-state counterclaims for environmental damage in investor-state dispute settlement from human rights and transnational public policy perspectives. Int Environ Agreements Polit Law Econ 21:427–444

Hanley N (2002) The economic value of environmental damage. In: Bowman M, Boyle A (eds) Environmental damage in international and comparative law: problems of definition and valuation. Oxford University Press, Oxford, pp 27–40

Harrison J (2016) Environmental counterclaims in investor-state arbitration: Perenco Ecuador Ltd v Republic of Ecuador, ICSID Case No ARB/08/6, Interim Decision on the Environmental Counterclaim, 11 August 2015. J World Invest Trade 17:479–488

Hepburn J (2017) Domestic law in international investment arbitration. Oxford University Press, Oxford

Ho J (2019) The creation of elusive investor responsibility. AJIL Unbound 113:10–15

Hoffmann AK (2013) Counterclaims in investment arbitration. ICSID Rev 28(2):438–453

Huber S (2020) Die Stellung von Unternehmen in der Investitionsschiedsgerichtsbarkeit (unter besonderer Berücksichtigung von Korruptionsproblemen): Unternehmen als gleichberechtigte Verfahrensparteien? In: Reinisch A, Hobe S, Kieninger EM, Peters A (eds) Unternehmensverantwortung und Internationales Recht. CF Müller, Heidelberg, pp 303–338

Hunter MH, Silva GEC (2013) Transnational public policy and its application in investment arbitrations. J World Invest 4(4):367–378

Hussin A (2019) Environmental counterclaims under the CPTPP: lessons for Asia from recent investor-state jurisprudence. Transnatl Disp Manage 5 <https://www.transnational-dispute-management.com/article.asp?key=2673> Accessed 10 Jan 2023

Jaeger K (2010) Environmental claims under the alien tort statute. Berkeley J Int Law 28(2): 519–536

Karavias M (2013) Corporate obligations under international law. Oxford University Press, Oxford

Karavias M (2019) Corporations and responsibility under international law. In: Pazartzis P, Merkouris P (eds) Permutations of responsibility in international law. Brill Nijhoff, Leiden, pp 43–68

Kaufmann-Kohler G (2005) The arbitrator and the law: does he/she know it? Apply it? How? And a few more questions. Arbitr Int 21(4):631–638

Khan MR (2015) Polluter-pays-principle: the cardinal instrument for addressing climate change. Laws 4(3):638–653

Knox JH (2019) The global pact for the environment: at the crossroads of human rights and the environment. Rev Eur Comp Int Environ Law 28(1):40–47

Kolb R (2019) Evolutionary interpretation in international law: some short and less than trail-blazing reflections. In: Abi-Saab G, Keith K, Marceau G, Marquet C (eds) Evolutionary interpretation and international law. Hart Publishing, Oxford, pp 15–20

Kozyakova A (2021) Foreign investor misconduct in international investment law. Springer, Cham

Krajweski M (2021) A nightmare or a Noble dream? Establishing investor obligations through treaty-making and treaty-application. Bus Human Rights J 5:105–129

Kriebaum U (2010) Investment arbitration – illegal investments. In: Klausegger C, Klein P, Kremslehner F, Petsche A, Pitkowitz N, Power J, Welser I, Zeiler G (eds) Austrian yearbook on international arbitration 2010. Manz'sche Verlags- und Universitätsbuchhandlung, Alphen aan den Rijn, pp 307–335

Kryvoi Y (2012) Counterclaims in investor-state arbitration. Minn J Int Law 21(2):216–252

Kulick A (2012) Global public interest in international investment law. Cambridge University Press, Cambridge

Lahlou Y, Willard R, Craven M (2019) The rise of environmental counterclaims in mining arbitration. In: Fry J, Bret LA (eds) The guide to mining arbitrations. Law Bus Res, London, pp 51–67

Lalive P, Halonen L (2011) On the availability of counterclaims in investment treaty arbitration. Czech Yearb Int Law 2:141–156

Levine J, Peart N (2019) Procedural issues and innovations in environment-related investor-state disputes. In: Miles K (ed) Research handbook on environment and investment law. Edward Elgar Publishing, Cheltenham, pp 209–243

Llamzon A (2015) Yukos universal limited (Isle of Man) v The Russian Federation: the state of the "Unclean Hands" Doctrine in international investment law: Yukos as both Omega and Alpha. ICSID Rev 30(2):315–325

Luke E (2019) Environment and human rights in an investment law frame. In: Miles K (ed) Research handbook on environment and investment law. Edward Elgar Publishing, Cheltenham, pp 150–174

Luttrell S, Murphy A (2019) Stabilisation provisions in long-term mining agreements. In: Fry J, Bret LA (eds) The guide to mining arbitrations. Law Business Research, London, pp 13–39

Magnarelli M (2020) Privity of contract in international investment arbitration: original sin or useful tool? Kluwer Law International, The Hague

Maljean-Dubois S, Richard V (2013) The applicability of international environmental law to private enterprises. In: Dupuy PM, Viñuales JE (eds) Harnessing foreign investment to promote environmental protection: incentives and safeguards. Cambridge University Press, Cambridge, pp 69–96

Mann H, von Moltke K, Peterson LE, Cosbey A (2006) IISD model international agreement on investment for sustainable development: negotiators' handbook, 2nd edn. International Institute for Sustainable Development, Winnipeg

Marcoux JM (2020) Transnational public policy as a vehicle to impose human rights obligations in international investment arbitration. J World Invest Trade 21(6):809–846

Marisi F (2020) Environmental interests in investment arbitration: challenges and directions. Kluwer Law International, Alphen aan den Rijn

Mbengue MM, Negm MH (2019) An African View on the CETA Investment Chapter. In Mbengue MM, Schacherer S (eds) ForeignInvestment Under the Comprehensive Economic and Trade Agreement (CETA). Springer, Cham, pp 239–270

McRae D (2019) Evolutionary interpretation: the relevance of context. In: Abi-Saab G, Keith K, Marceau G, Marquet C (eds) Evolutionary interpretation and international law. Hart Publishing, Oxford, pp 57–62

Miles K (2013) The origins of international investment law: empire, environment and the safeguarding of capital. Cambridge University Press, Cambridge

Miles W, Lawry-White M (2019) Arbitral institutions and the enforcement of climate change obligations for the benefit of all stakeholders: the role of ICSID. ICSID Rev 34(1):1–31

Mistura A (2019) Integrating civil liability principles into international investment law: a solution to environmental damage caused by foreign investors? In: Sachs LE, Johnson LJ, Coleman J (eds) Yearbook on international investment law & policy 2017. Oxford University Press, Oxford, pp 446–491

Mitra T, Donde R (2016) Claims and counterclaims under Asian multilateral investment treaties. In: Choukroune L (ed) Judging the state in international trade and investment law. Springer, Singapore

Morgera E (2013) From corporate social responsibility to accountability mechanisms. In: Dupuy PM, Viñuales JE (eds) Harnessing foreign investment to promote environmental protection: incentives and safeguards. Cambridge University Press, Cambridge, pp 321–354

Morgera E (2020) Corporate environmental accountability in international law, 2nd edn. Oxford University Press, Oxford

Muchlinski P (2008) Corporate social responsibility. In: Muchlinski P, Ortino F, Schreuer C (eds) The Oxford handbook of international investment law. Oxford University Press, Oxford, pp 637–690

Newcombe A, Marcoux JM (2015) Hesam Talaat M Al-Warraq v Republic of Indonesia: imposing international obligations on foreign investors. ICSID Rev 30(3):525–532

Nollkaemper A (2006) Responsibility of transnational corporations in international environmental law: three perspectives. In: Winter G (ed) Multilevel governance of global environmental change: perspectives from science, sociology and the law. Cambridge University Press, Cambridge, pp 179–199

Popova IC, Poon F (2015) From perpetual respondent to aspiring counterclaimant? State counterclaims in the new wave of investment treaties. BCDR Int Arbitr Rev 2(2):223–260

Puig S, Shaffer G (2018) Imperfect alternatives: institutional choice and the reform of investment law. Am J Int Law 112(3):361–409

Robles Ustariz MI (2020) El impacto del derecho humano al medio ambiente sano en el derecho internacional de inversions. Universidad Externado de Colombia, Bogotá

Sands P, Peel J, Fabra A, Mackenzie R (2018) Principles of international environmental law, 4th edn. Cambridge University Press, Cambridge

Sattorova M (2019) Investor responsibilities form a host state perspective: qualitative data and proposals for treaty reform. AJIL Unbound 113:22–27

Scherer M, Bruce S, Reschke J (2021) Environmental counterclaims in investment treaty arbitration. ICSID Rev 36(2):413–440

Scheu J (2022) Article 8.31. In: Bungenberg M, Reinisch A (eds) CETA investment law: article-by-article commentary. Hart/Beck/Nomos, Baden-Baden

Schill SW (2011) Allocating adjudicatory authority: most-favoured-nation clauses as a basis of jurisdiction—a reply to Zachary Douglas. J Int Disp Settlement 2(2):353–371

Schill SW, Djanic V (2018) Wherefore art thou? Towards a public interest-based justification of international investment law. ICSID Rev 33(1):29–55

Schreuer C (2014) Jurisdiction and applicable law in investment treaty arbitration. McGill J Disp Resol 1:1–25

Shao X (2021) Environmental and human rights counterclaims in international investment arbitration: at the crossroads of domestic and international law. J Int Econ Law 24(1):157–179

Sinha V, Fusea G (2021) Counterclaims in investment arbitration: key threshold issues for claimants, respondents and tribunals. Roman Arbitr J 15:54–79

Spiermann O (2008) Applicable law. In: Muchlinski P, Ortino F, Schreuer C (eds) The Oxford handbook of international investment law. Oxford University Press, Oxford, pp 89–118

Steingruber AM (2020) Counterclaims: a critical analysis of Article 6 of the 2019 The Hague resolution of the Institut de Droit International on the "Equality of Parties before International Investment Tribunals". ICSID Rev 35(3):595–645

Suleimenova M (2019) MFN standard as substantive treatment. Nomos, Baden-Baden

Sullivan J, Kirsey V (2017) Environmental policies: a shield or a sword in investment arbitration? J World Invest Trade 18(1):100–130

Symeonides SC (2021) Tort law and conflict of laws. In: Bussani M, Sebok AJ (eds) Comparative tort law: global perspectives. Edward Elgar Publishing, Cheltenham, pp 39–69

Tan G, Chong A (2020) The future of environmental counterclaims in ICSID arbitration: challenges, treaties and interpretations. Cambridge Int Law J 9(2):176–200

Thomé H (2021) Holding transnational corporations accountable for environmental harm through counterclaims in investor-state dispute settlement: myth or reality? J World Invest Trade 22: 651–686

Toca Torres CE (2011) Las versiones del desarrollo sostenible. Sociedad e Cultura 14(1):195–204

Vazquez CM (2005) Direct vs. indirect obligations of corporations under international law. Columbia J Transnatl Law 43(3):927–960

Viñuales JE (2012) Foreign investment and the environment in international law. Cambridge University Press

Viñuales JE (2015) Investment law and sustainable development: the environment breaks into investment disputes. In: Bungenberg M, Griebel J, Hobe S, Reinisch A (eds) International investment law: a handbook. CH Beck/Hart/Nomos, Baden-Baden, pp 1714–1738

Viñuales JE (2020) Defence arguments in investment arbitration. In: Viñuales JE, Waibel M (eds) ICSID reports: Volume 18. Cambridge University Press, Cambridge, pp 9–108

Vohryzek-Griest A (2009) State counterclaims in investor-state disputes: a history of 30 years of failure. Revista Colombiana de Derecho Internacional 15:83–123

Vöneky S (2020) Die Stellung von Unternehmen in der Investitionsschiedsgerichtsbarkeit unter besonderer Berücksichtigung von Korruptionsproblemen: Unternehmen als völkerrechtlich gleichberechtigte Verfahrensparteien? In: Reinisch A, Hobe S, Kieninger EM, Peters A (eds) Unternehmensverantwortung und Internationales Recht. CF Müller, Heidelberg, pp 339–398

Waibel M (2015) Investment arbitration: jurisdiction and admissibility. In: Bungenberg M, Griebel J, Hobe S, Reinisch A (eds) International investment law: a handbook. CH Beck/Hart/Nomos, Baden-Baden, pp 1212–1287

Wälde TW, Ndi G (1996) Stabilizing international investment commitments: international law versus contract interpretation. Tex Int Law J 31(2):215–268

Walter A (2015) Investor-state contracts in the context of international investment law. In: Bungenberg M, Griebel J, Hobe S, Reinisch A (eds) International investment law: a handbook. CH Beck/Hart/Nomos, Baden-Baden, pp 80–92

Wirth DA (1995) The Rio declaration on environment and development: two steps forward and one Back, or vice versa. Georgia Law Rev 29(3):599–654

Wyatt J (2019) Intertemporal linguistics in international law: beyond contemporaneous and evolutionary treaty interpretation. Hart Publishing, Oxford

Zerk JA (2006) Multinationals and corporate social responsibility: limitations and opportunities in international law. Cambridge University Press, Cambridge

Zin SM (2020) Reappraising access to justice in ISDS: a critical review on state recourse to counterclaim. In: Anderson AM, Beaumont B (eds) The investor-state dispute settlement system: reform, replace or status quo? Kluwer Law International, Alphen aan den Rijn, pp 225–246

Other Documents

HRC (09 February 2007) Report of the Special Representative of the Secretary-General (SRSG) on the issue of human rights and transnational corporations and other business enterprises, 'Business and Human Rights: Mapping International Standards of Responsibility and Accountability for Corporate Acts'. UN Doc A/HRC/4/035

IFC (01 January 2012) International Finance Corporation's Policy on Environmental and Social Sustainability. <https://www.ifc.org/wps/wcm/connect/7141585d-c6fa-490b-a812-2ba87245115b/SP_English_2012.pdf?MOD=AJPERES&CVID=kiIrw0g> Accessed 10 January 2023

IFC (28 June 2021) IFC/MIGA Independent Accountability Mechanism (CAO) Policy. <https://www.ifc.org/wps/wcm/connect/d3e7f1c4-fd6b-40fd-ae76-fb0289166 11d/IFC-MIGA-Independent-Accountability-Mechanism-CAO-Policy.pdf?MOD=AJPERES&CVID=nFDGwP2> Accessed 10 January 2023

ILC (20 April 1970) Second Report on State Responsibility by Mr Roberto Ago, Special Rapporteur, on 'The Origin of International Responsibility'. UN Doc A/CN.4/233

ILC YB [1973] vol I, A/CN.4/Ser.A/1973, 'Draft Report on State Responsibility' (210-220)

Jackson Shaw Kern (14 June 2020) Investors Obligations: Africa Leads the Way. Kluwer Arbitration Blog, <http://arbitrationblog.kluwerarbitration.com/2020/06/14/investor-obligations> Accessed 10 January 2023

Report for IFC and UN Special Representative of the Secretary-General for Business and Human Rights (SRSG) on 'Stabilization Clauses and Human Rights' (27 May 2009) <https://www.ifc.org/wps/wcm/connect/0883d81a-e00a-4551-b2b9-46641e5a9bba/Stabilization%2BPaper.pdf?MOD=AJPERES&CACHEID=ROOTWORKSPACE-0883d81a-e00a-4551-b2b9-46641e5a9bba-jqeww2e> Accessed 10 January 2023

Report of the Eighteenth Commission of the Institut de Droit International (Rapporteur Professor Campbell McLachlan) on the 'Equality of Parties before International Investment Tribunals'. <https://www.idi-iil.org/app/uploads/2019/06/Commission-18-Equality-of-parties-before-international-investment-tribunals-McLachlan-Travaux-La-Haye-2019.pdf> Accessed 10 January 2023

Report of the United Nations Conference on the Human Environment (1973) UN Doc A/CONF.48/14/Rev.1 (Declaration on the Human Environment)

UNCHR (22 February 2006) Interim Report of the Special Representative of the Secretary-General on the Issue of Human Rights and Transnational Corporations and other Business Enterprises, 'Promotion and Protection of Human Rights' UN Doc E/CN.4/2006/97

UNGA (19 July 2018) Human Rights Obligations Relating to the Enjoyment of a Safe, Clean, Healthy and Sustainable Environment. UN Doc A/73/188

Chapter 6
Conclusions

The conflicting relation between investment law and environmental protection cannot always be avoided. But the instrument of environmental counterclaims in investment arbitration might alleviate such relation. As outlined in Chap. 1, the study of environmental counterclaims poses questions about the societal and practical relevance of seeking redress for environmental damage in investment arbitration, the functioning of such instrument both in contract-based and treaty-based investment arbitration, the suitability of arbitral tribunals to rule upon environmental issues, and the kind of environmental damages that could be redressed. Throughout its Chapters, this monograph sought to address all these questions. Most importantly, given the development of environmental protection in international law, this book seeks to stimulate future discussions, tribunals' analyses, and perhaps the reformulation of jurisdictional, procedural and substantive provisions in investment arbitration.

In this context, the main takeaways from this monograph are summarised as follows: theoretical underpinnings for environmental counterclaims in investment arbitration [Sect. 6.1]. The jurisdiction of arbitral tribunals to adjudge environmental counterclaims [Sect. 6.2]. The connection between an environmental counterclaim and the main claim [Sect. 6.3]. The cause of action for an environmental counterclaim [Sect. 6.4].

6.1 The Theoretical Underpinnings for Environmental Counterclaims

A comparative analysis of counterclaims in various frameworks for international dispute settlement has evinced some common features shared by counterclaims in each of the analysed frameworks. This includes for instance that the underlying instrument of consent must vest the adjudicatory body with jurisdiction to adjudicate

A. E. Alvarado-Garzón, *Environmental Counterclaims in Investment Arbitration*,
EYIEL Monographs - Studies in European and International Economic Law 34,
https://doi.org/10.1007/978-3-031-46391-4_6

the counterclaim. Similarly, a close connection between the counterclaim and the main claim shall exist. Furthermore, it appears that belated counterclaims could exceptionally be admitted by the adjudicatory body. However, a comparative analysis of the requirements for counterclaims must nevertheless be tested through the particular characteristics and functioning of investment arbitration.

In this sense, the most evident differentiation appears between contract-based and treaty-based investment arbitration. On the one hand, the synallagmatic structure of investment contracts places international commercial arbitration and the operation of counterclaims therein as a key point of reference when assessing counterclaims in contract-based investment arbitration. On the other hand, despite the multiple conceptualisations of treaty-based investment arbitration, three overarching characteristics delineate the analysis of counterclaims: the unique process for achieving consent; the adjudication of regulatory disputes; the interaction of multilevel norms.

With respect to the rationale behind the availability of counterclaims, one may consider procedural economy, the proper administration of justice, the equality of parties, or due process, which are similarly displayed by all different frameworks for international dispute settlement as the objectives pursued by counterclaims. However, in investment arbitration, counterclaims are supported by procedural or judicial economy considerations, whereas due process and the rule of law appear immaterial for the availability of such procedural instrument.

Furthermore, although counterclaims constitute a neutral instrument through which the state can advance a variety of interests, the intricate relation between investment law and environmental protection has paved the way for the support of environmental counterclaims in investment arbitration, as a means to address instances of 'pure' environmental damage. This theoretical framework ultimately serves for the deconstruction of the requirements of jurisdiction, connection between main claim and counterclaim, and of cause of action.

6.2 Jurisdiction Over Environmental Counterclaims

The scope of consent constitutes the centrepiece of a tribunal's analysis over its jurisdiction to adjudge environmental counterclaims. Neither a tribunal's inherent powers nor the applicable arbitration rules can confer jurisdiction over environmental counterclaims on an arbitral tribunal. On the one hand, the functioning of contract-based investment arbitration seems particular supportive of finding jurisdiction over environmental counterclaims. On the other hand, treaty-based investment arbitration faces two kinds of obstacles: the restrictive appraisal of IIAs *vis-à-vis* counterclaims and the *prima facie* exclusion of contractual counterclaims.

On the one hand, in several occasions, arbitral tribunals have misconceived jurisdictional requirements over counterclaims, especially with respect to the lack of the state's legal standing to submit claims and the applicable law provisions in IIAs. At the same time, the kind of disputes subject to arbitration might function as an indication of the tribunal's lack of jurisdiction over environmental counterclaims.

This is so even in the framework of the ICSID Convention, where consent for counterclaims is constantly underscored.

On the other hand, the exclusion of contractual counterclaims from treaty-based investment arbitration derives from the existence of limited dispute resolution provisions in IIAs or the existence of a forum selection clause in the respective investment contract. Another potential obstacle for contractual counterclaims in treaty-based investment arbitration is the difference between parties to the dispute and parties to the investment contract. Yet, tribunals could resort to an analysis of a single economic unity (for investors) or the attribution criteria in public international law (for the respondent) to overcome the different legal personalities.

Limitations as to the kind of disputes subject to treaty-based investment arbitration have played a decisive role on the tribunals' jurisdiction over counterclaims. Thus, this book has advanced a critical revision on the interpretation of treaty provisions on dispute settlement. This brings about the assessment of the provision's context and the respective treaty's object and purpose, as well as the possibility for tribunals to avail themselves of systematic integration. Such exercise could provide the tribunal with several indications in favour of the adjudication of environmental counterclaims. For instance, in the form of exclusion of certain types of counterclaims by the treaty, explicit objectives towards environmental protection or sustainable development found in the treaty, and international environmental law applicable between the treaty parties.

Prospective solutions remove the inherent problems of treaty interpretation, particularly by means of authentic or authoritative interpretations, treaty drafting and modification, or perhaps by imposing the requisite consent over counterclaims in domestic law. Whilst based upon these prospective options, tribunals might be more receptive to finding jurisdiction over counterclaims, most of those options would constitute a long-term endeavour and do not appear feasible at this moment.

6.3 Connection Between an Environmental Counterclaim and the Main Claim

While the scope of consent constitutes the centrepiece of a tribunal's analysis on environmental counterclaims, the requisite connection represents the tribunal's compass. In this sense, despite the few instruments in investment arbitration referring to the close connection between the counterclaim and the main claim, tribunals should always scrutinise the connection requirement as an inherent feature of counterclaims. This brings about the proper characterisation of the connection requirement, its content and its relevance for environmental counterclaims.

The characterisation of this requirement is not settled: some frame it as a jurisdictional issue, whereas others frame it as an admissibility issue. Certainly, this monograph does not intend to resolve the disagreements on the appropriateness of the jurisdiction/admissibility divide in investment arbitration. But procedural fairness or judicial propriety may undisputedly prompt tribunals to decline the exercise of properly vested jurisdiction over a claim in certain cases. In such situations, the tribunal must exercise judicial discretion that a strict jurisdictional assessment cannot provide.

Given that the analysis on the requisite connection would be guided by the principle of procedural or judicial economy, a tribunal requires a certain degree of judicial discretion and flexibility only available in non-jurisdictional, admissibility, or procedural decisions. This characterisation of the connection requirements entails that the assessment on jurisdiction over counterclaims precedes the analysis on connection. As such, the requisite connection cannot remedy the lack of a tribunal's jurisdiction over counterclaims. Moreover, parties' explicit consent to counterclaims may obviate an analysis on connection.

The content of the connection requirement usually displays a division between legal and factual connection. Irrespective of the merits of such division, it is concerning that several tribunals have limited themselves to find connection only if the counterclaim and the main claim are based on the same legal instrument/legal source. Such limitation on the connection requirement is incorrect because: *first*, it stems from an uncontextualised initial reliance on the IUSCT jurisprudence, and on early ICSID cases. *Second*, it lacks textual support in IIAs, the ICSID Convention or any set of arbitration rules. *Third*, it might undermine broadly worded dispute resolution provisions in IIAs.

This ultimately suggests a dilution of the connection requirement into various balancing factors. Accordingly, the identity of legal source is only one of various connecting factors, which must be balanced out to determine whether there is a close connection between the counterclaim and the main claim. Thus, this provides tribunals with flexibility in their assessments of the requisite connection, which should render environmental counterclaims more viable, for instance, if the environmental issue stems directly from the investment's operation.

6.4 Cause of Action for an Environmental Counterclaim

The assessment of a possible cause of action or legal basis for an environmental counterclaim in investment arbitration constitutes the last step of this book. Whilst investors might be subject to a myriad of norms both at the international and domestic level, this does not necessarily provide an appropriate cause of action for environmental counterclaims. Once again, the division between contract-based and treaty-based investment arbitration entails different conclusions. In contract-based investment arbitration, investment contracts can provide for obligations upon the investor, whose breach could support an environmental counterclaim. Even in the absence of such obligations in the investment contract, domestic law of the host state could provide the legal basis necessary for an environmental counterclaim.

In treaty-based investment arbitration, domestic law and/or international law could potentially impose environmental obligations on investors that serve as a cause of action for environmental counterclaims. With respect to environmental obligations in domestic law, this monograph argues that such law would necessitate operationalisation via a treaty anchor that brings a breach of domestic law to the international level. In this sense, applicable law provisions in IIAs mentioning domestic law cannot serve this purpose. Rather, one may consider treaty provisions obliging the investor to comply with the host state's domestic law and/or treaty provisions foreseeing counterclaims based on domestic law.

With respect to environmental obligations in international law, the irrelevance of considering the legal personality of non-state actors instead of assessing international obligations actually imposed on those actors should be noted. Furthermore, when searching for international environmental obligations on investors, one ought to be cautious of concepts such as 'responsibility', 'liability' and 'accountability' given their interchangeable use. Be that as it may, international environmental obligations upon investors could stem from international environmental law or investment treaties.

In international environmental law, there is no positive obligation on non-state actors towards the environment. This is so because: *first*, the polluter-pays principle, the principle of prevention and the precautionary principle must be incorporated (*eg* in international agreements or domestic law) in sufficient prescriptive terms in order to create obligations. *Second*, international environmental law instruments usually address states or require subsequent implementation into domestic legislation. This is the case of international regimes on civil liability for environmental damage, which not only face a low ratification rate but must also be implemented into domestic law. *Third*, given that CSR instruments are drafted in an hortatory manner, they fail to create obligations on investors as well.

Arguably, international environmental law comprises a negative obligation not to undermine environmental protection, which could serve as a legal basis for an environmental counterclaim but only in clear evidence of environmental degradation. All these obstacles for international environmental law to provide a cause of action for environmental counterclaims in treaty-based investment arbitration would not be solved by the re-conceptualisation of environmental protection as a matter of human rights or as transnational public policy.

In investment treaties, clear environmental obligations could be devised, which could serve as a cause of action for environmental counterclaims. Conversely, a *renvoi* to an international environmental norm or the incorporation of such norm via treaty interpretation cannot serve as a cause of action for environmental counterclaims. On the one hand, IIA provisions referring to international environmental law are drafted in a non-prescriptive manner. On the other hand, systematic integration and evolutionary interpretation as means of treaty interpretation cannot incorporate investors' environmental obligations from international law. All in all environmental obligations stemming from international law may not readily provide a cause of action for environmental counterclaims in treaty-based investment arbitration.

In any case, it must be stressed that from a technical perspective, investment arbitration can provide the necessary technical and procedural tools to properly address the respective environmental issues arising from an environmental counterclaim. Furthermore, from a policy perspective, investment arbitration might exalt environmental protection at the international level.

Overall, environmental counterclaims in investment arbitration appear as a viable instrument for addressing the tensions between investment law and environmental protection. Undeniably, this instrument has faced (and might continue to face) a multitude of obstacles for its effective use. Yet, by deconstructing the requirements of jurisdiction, connection between main claim and counterclaim, and cause of action, this book provides the tools for the re-conceptualisation of the instrument of counterclaims with the hope of harnessing its utility to achieve appropriate redress for environmental damages caused by foreign investors.

Annexes

Annex 1: Counterclaims with an Environmental Related Issue

A. E. Alvarado-Garzón, *Environmental Counterclaims in Investment Arbitration*,
EYIEL Monographs - Studies in European and International Economic Law 34,
https://doi.org/10.1007/978-3-031-46391-4

No.	Case | Decision	Contract- or Treaty-based	Summary of Dispute	Counterclaim	Jurisdiction over (or Admissibility of) Counterclaims	Decision on the Merits of the Counterclaim
1.	*Sergei Paushok, CJSC Golden East Company and CJSC Vostokneftegaz Company v The Government of Mongolia*, UNCITRAL Case: Jurisdiction and Liability (28/04/2011)	Russia-Mongolia BIT (1995)	The investor owned two gold mining companies, and an oil and gas company in Mongolia. The dispute arose out of respondent's enactment of a law on Windfall Profit Tax that negatively affected the investor. Also from a law limiting the number of foreign nationals employed by a mining company. Subsequently, the investor failed to pay taxes and respondent brought such claim before courts.	The respondent filed seven counterclaims for (i) windfall profits taxes; (ii) foreign worker fees; (iii) taxes, fees and levies by illicitly evading restrictions on intergroup transfers, including non-arm's length transfers; (iv) violation of licence agreements; (v) **violation of environmental obligations towards Mongolia**; (vi) damages for gold smuggling; and (vii) failure to comply with Order from House of Lords.	The tribunal rejected jurisdiction over the counterclaims.	N/A
2.	*Perenco Ecuador Ltd v Republic of Ecuador and Empresa Estatal Petróleos del Ecuador (Petroecuador)*, ICSID Case No ARB/08/6: Interim Decision on the Environmental Counterclaim (11/08/2015) *and* Decision on Perenco's Dismissal of Ecuador's Counterclaims (18/08/2017)	France-Ecuador BIT (1994)	The investor held majority shareholding in two oil blocks under two production sharing contracts concluded with a state-owned enterprise. Additionally, the investor held rights under joint operating agreements concluded with other entities holding interests in such blocks. The dispute arose from legislative measures increasing Ecuador's participation under the participation contracts and raising the tax rate on extraordinary revenues or 'windfall levy' on oil revenues.	The respondent counterclaimed for environmental and infrastructural damages in the operation sites. **With respect to the environmental damages**, the respondent requested damages for soil clean-up, groundwater remediation, and further groundwater studies. Additionally, the respondent argued that the investor abandoned the blocks in violation of environmental universal principles embedded in Ecuadorian Law and Contracts and that the investor had deceived authorities with regard to the environmental damage.	The claimant did not dispute the tribunal's jurisdiction over the counterclaim, and the tribunal expressly acknowledged jurisdiction.	The tribunal upheld the counterclaims.
3.	*Burlington Resources Inc v Republic of Ecuador*, ICSID Case No ARB/08/5: Decision on Ecuador's Counterclaims (07/02/2017)	US-Ecuador BIT (1993)	The investor held rights in production sharing contracts on the exploration and exploitation of oil in two sites located in the Amazon region. The dispute arose from respondent's enactment of legislative measures raising the tax rate on extraordinary revenues or 'windfall levy' on oil revenues. After some years, the investor refused to continue paying the windfall levy, for which the respondent terminated the production sharing contracts and seized the sites.	The respondent counterclaimed for environmental and infrastructural damages in the operation sites. **The environmental counterclaim** focused on soil contamination, mud pits, groundwater and well site abandonment. Whereas the counterclaim on infrastructure consisted of the investor's failure to maintain the infrastructure in good working conditions including tanks, fluid lines and pipelines, generator engines, pumps, electrical system, IT and roads.	The disputing parties agreed on the tribunal's jurisdiction over the counterclaims.	The tribunal upheld the counterclaims.
4.	*Chevron Corporation and Texaco Petroleum Corporation v Ecuador (II)*, PCA Case No 2009-23: Second Partial Award on Track II (30/08/2018)	US-Ecuador BIT (1993)	Texaco Petroleum held rights in an oil concession in Ecuador since 1964. In 2001, Chevron acquired Texaco Petroleum. Once the operation ended, the concessionaire and the state reached the 1995 Settlement Agreement and Remedial Action Plan, which included clean-up operations for environmental harm. The dispute arose out respondent's facilitation of legal proceedings to a local community (Lago Agrio Plaintiffs) claiming damages for the investors' contamination. However, the domestic proceedings were subject to procedural fraud and judicial misconduct, which was neither remedied in appeal or cassation, nor by the Constitutional Court. Therefore, the investors claimed a continuing violation of the underlying treaty (denial of justice), which has left them exposed to enforcement proceedings in multiple jurisdictions.	The respondent submitted that the Lago Agrio Plaintiffs are not parties to the arbitration (nor could they participate), and the decision of the arbitral tribunal could 'gravely' prejudice them. Thus, the respondent counterclaimed ('cross-claimed') for **environmental damage**, unjust enrichment, causation and contributory fault. Additionally, the respondent submitted that if the domestic judgement is found null, Chevron would be immunised as new proceedings would be time-barred under Ecuadorian Law, creating an '*immunity from environmental harm*'.	The tribunal rejected jurisdiction over the counterclaim.	N/A

5.	*David R Aven and Others v Republic of Costa Rica*, ICSID Case No UNCT/15/3: Award (18/09/2018)	CAFTA-DR (2004)	The investor held rights in concession site for a tourist project. The dispute arose out respondent's new inspections, issuance of administrative and judicial decisions which ultimately led to the cancellation of the tourist project. Additionally, one of the investors claimed that he was unjustly prosecuted for breach of environmental laws and subject to Interpol red notice.	The respondent counterclaimed arguing that the investors' works on the project site had **affected the environment, particularly a wetland**. Accordingly, the respondent submitted that the investors caused such damage by (i) the construction of the roads, excavation of ditches, placement of culverts and the removal of the vegetation of the forest; (ii) the increasing soil sedimentation; and (iii) the filling and draining of wetlands. Thus, respondent requested environmental reparation.	The tribunal found *prima facie* jurisdiction but rejected the counterclaim due to lack of formal requirements in its submission.	N/A
6.	*Metro de Lima Linea 2 SA v Republic of Peru (I)*, ICSID Case No ARB/17/3: Decision on Jurisdiction and Liability (06/07/2021)	Contract	Concession contract for the line 2 of the subway in Lima, Peru. However, the project experienced significant delays and cost overruns leading to the dispute.	The respondent counterclaimed that the delays in the concession by the investor caused significant socioeconomic and environmental damages. Particularly, that citizens had incurred additional costs in mobility and suffered limited accessibility to their work places. The Respondent also argued that the delays prompted citizens to continue using their private cars creating **more CO2 emissions causing environmental damage**. Furthermore, the respondent counterclaimed for the contractual penalties.	The claimant did not dispute the tribunal's jurisdiction over the counterclaim, and the tribunal did not address the issue.	The tribunal dismissed counterclaims on the merits as no delays were found to be caused by the claimant. Additionally, the contractual penalties were subject to domestic arbitration.

Annex 2: Other Counterclaims in Chronological Order

No.	Case	Contract- or Treaty-based	Summary of Dispute	Counterclaim	Jurisdiction over (or Admissibility of) Counterclaims	Decision on the Merits of the Counterclaim
1.	*Adriano Gardella SpA v Côte d'Ivoire*, ICSID Case No ARB/74/1: Award (29/08/1977)	Contract	Investment contracts on the construction of a textile factory, and the cultivation of hemp, whose harvesting would be used partly for exports, partly for the textile factory. The dispute arose out of the performance and payment of those contracts.	The respondent counterclaimed for damages arising out of claimant's termination of the contract.	The claimant did not dispute the tribunal's jurisdiction over the counterclaim, and the tribunal did not address the issue.	The tribunal rejected it on merits.
2.	*SARL Benvenuti & Bonfant v People's Republic of the Congo*, ICSID Case No ARB/77/2: Award (08/08/1980)	Contract	Investment contract, whereby the claimant set up a company for manufacturing plastic bottles and producing mineral water. The dispute related to the respondent's breach of the contract and its occupation of the factory.	The respondent counterclaimed for damages for: (i) the non-payment of duties and taxes; (ii) the overpricing of raw materials; (iii) the defaults in the execution of the supply agreement; (iv) the defects relating to the construction of the factory; (v) intangible loss (moral damages).	The claimant did not dispute the tribunal's jurisdiction over the counterclaim, which was acknowledged by the tribunal.	The tribunal rejected it on merits.
3.	*Klöckner Industrie-Anlagen GmbH and others v United Republic of Cameroon and Société Camerounaise des Engrais*, ICSID Case No ARB/81/2: Award (21/10/1983)	Contract	Investment contract, whose object was to supply, erect and manage a fertilizer factory via a joint venture with the host state. The dispute arose because the operation became unprofitable, thus, it was shut down, which the investors claimed to be the respondent's fault.	The respondent counterclaimed for the losses arising out of the investor's abandonment of fertilizer project, including state's initial capital, loans and subsidies, as well as lucrum cessans and non-financial damages (moral damages).	Tribunal upheld jurisdiction over the counterclaim (with one dissenting opinion).	The tribunal rejected it on merits.
4.	*Atlantic Triton Company Limited v People's Revolutionary Republic of Guinea*, ICSID Case No ARB/84/1: Award (21/04/1986)	Contract	Investment contract for the conversion, equipping and operation of three fishing vessels, to establish a fishing industry in Guinea. The dispute arose because the vessels were of the wrong type and size for operating in the country, and the operation suffered from lack of port and repair facilities. Additionally, the investor claimed inadequate storage, insufficient supply of fuel, oil, ice and working capital, leading to the operation's closure after nine months.	The respondent counterclaimed that the investor had engaged in abusive proceedings and had failed its contractual obligations. Thus, the respondent requested damages for the restoration and adaptation of the vessels as a result of claimant's faulty execution of the contract. Additionally, it requested damages for invoices resulting from mechanical breakdowns of the vessels.	Tribunal upheld jurisdiction over counterclaims (except the 'choice of vessels').	The tribunal rejected the rest of the counterclaims on merits.

5.	*Maritime International Nominees Establishment (MINE) v Republic of Guinea*, ICSID Case No ARB/84/4: Award (06/01/1988)	Contract	Operation of a joint venture between the investor and the host state for the shipping of bauxite from Guinea. The dispute arose because, given the respondent's delays, the contract could not be performed.	The respondent counterclaimed for the damages (*ie* fees and legal expenses) incurred during a prior arbitration proceeding and court proceedings in Belgium and Switzerland, despite having agreed to ICSID arbitration.	The claimant did not dispute the tribunal's jurisdiction over the counterclaim, and the tribunal did not address the issue.	The tribunal granted relief for some of the fees and legal expenses incurred in court proceedings.
6.	*Amco Asia Corporation and others v Republic of Indonesia*, ICSID Case No ARB/81/1: Decision on Jurisdiction in Resubmitted Proceeding (10/05/1988)	Contract	Investment contract for the construction and management of a hotel complex. The dispute arose because the state took over the project with its military forces, cancelled the license, and the local courts rescinded the underlying contract.	The respondent counterclaimed for the tax fraud allegedly committed by the investor.	The tribunal rejected jurisdiction over the counterclaim.	N/A
7.	*Southern Pacific Properties (Middle East) Ltd v Arab Republic of Egypt*, ICSID Case No ARB/84/3: Award (20/05/1992)	Egyptian Domestic Law*	Joint project for the development of tourist complexes at the pyramids area near Cairo and at Ras El Hekna. However, there was political opposition to the project, arguably because it would threaten undiscovered antiquities. Consequently, the ministry declared the land surrounding the pyramids as public property, and the approval to the project was withdrawn.	The respondent counterclaimed damages arguing that the investor had the duty to mitigate damages but instead it abandoned the Ras El Hekna project, and refused to consider an alternative option.	The claimant did not dispute the tribunal's jurisdiction over the counterclaim, and the tribunal did not address the issue.	The tribunal rejected it on merits.
8.	*Franz Sedelmayer v The Russian Federation*, SCC Case: Award (07/07/1998)	Germany-Russia (USSR) BIT (1989)	Agreement for the development, installation, production and repair of police equipment. The dispute arose out of the state's first attempt to get control over the locally incorporated company, which was brought to domestic courts, where liquidation was ordered, as well as the transfer of assets to the state. Finally, the buildings and materials therein were seized by the state.	The respondent requested alleged damages caused by the investor to the seized property. However, following a clarification requested by the tribunal, the respondent argued that it was a 'conditional' counterclaim, only to be considered if tribunal finds jurisdiction over the main claim.	The tribunal considered respondent's allegations as a defence rather than a counterclaim.	N/A
9.	*Alex Genin, Eastern Credit Limited, Inc and AS Baltoil v The Republic of Estonia*, ICSID Case No ARB/99/2: Award (25/06/2001)	US-Estonia BIT (1994)	Estonian Innovation Bank (EIB), whose shareholders were Baltoil (Estonia), Eastern Credit (US) and Eurocapital. The investor was the chairman of Estonian Innovation Bank (EIB), as well as its financial institution and sole beneficial owner of all shareholders thereof. The dispute arose because the respondent issued an order to EIB regarding allegedly irregular shareholding, and proceeded with revoking EIB's banking license. This decision was later upheld in domestic courts.	The respondent requested damages for money illegally diverted from EIB by the claimants (including preferential transfer of funds after license, and used of feigned transactions and over-valued stocks), plus the costs of the arbitration.	The claimant did not dispute the tribunal's jurisdiction over the counterclaim. The tribunal only mentioned in *obiter dictum* some concerns on the 'proper parties' to the counterclaim, but did not elaborate.	The tribunal rejected it on merits.
10.	*Patrick Mitchell v Democratic Republic of the Congo*, ICSID Case No ARB/99/7: Award (09/02/2004)	US-Congo (Zaire) BIT (1984)	The dispute arose out of the respondent's seizure with military forces of the premises of the investor's legal consulting firm.	The respondent counterclaimed for the 'nuisances' caused by the investor, for damages arising from the attacks to the reputation of the respondent, and for costs incurred in the state's defence in the litigation proceedings.	The tribunal did not address its jurisdiction over counterclaims.	The tribunal rejected it on merits.
11.	*Saluka Investments BV v The Czech Republic*, UNCITRAL Case: Decision on Counterclaims (07/05/2004)	Netherlands-Czech Republic BIT (1991)	Ownership of a controlling block of shares from a state-owned bank in the host state. The dispute arose out of the imposition of a forced administration upon the investor's banking enterprise by the Czech National Bank.	The respondent counterclaimed for the alleged investor's breach of the shares purchase agreement, by which the investor acquired its investment, for instance, arguing that the investor failed to provide new equity capital, it also failed to procure the underwriting of investment's subordinated bonds that would provide it with new quasi-equity funds. Additionally, the respondent counterclaimed that the investor's parent company provided false information, violated the Czech commercial code, violated 'proper morality' among others.	The tribunal rejected jurisdiction over the counterclaims.	N/A
12.	*Zeevi Holdings v The Republic of Bulgaria and the Privatization Agency of Bulgaria*, UNCITRAL Case No UNC 39/DK: Award (25/10/2006)	Contract	A privatisation agreement to purchase 75% of share capital of Bulgaria's national airline. Subsequently, the respondent took away various exclusive rights from the airline company, arguing that the investor failed to make the promised investments.	The respondent counterclaimed for the failure to invest, misappropriation of proceeds, bad faith, breach of joint venture and investment agreement.	The claimant did not dispute the tribunal's jurisdiction over the counterclaim, and the tribunal did not address the issue.	The tribunal upheld some counterclaims and rejected others on the merits.

13.	*Desert Line Projects LLC v The Republic of Yemen*, ICSID Case No ARB/05/17: Award (06/02/2008)	Oman-Yemen BIT (1998)	Rights under several contracts concluded with the respondent for the construction of asphalt roads in Yemen. The dispute arose out of disagreements as to the sums owed to the investor for the construction, which led to domestic arbitration, the suspension of works and signature of a settlement an agreement.	The respondent counterclaimed for damages resulting from the investor's breach of the settlement agreement, and from the investor's unfulfilled construction obligations and failure to maintain bank guarantees.	The claimant did not dispute the tribunal's jurisdiction over the counterclaim, which was acknowledged by the tribunal.	The tribunal upheld some sums as a set-off and rejected the other counterclaims on the merits
14.	*Limited Liability Company Amto v Ukraine*, SCC Case No 080/2005: Award (26/03/2008)	ECT (1994)	The investor held majority shareholding in Ukrainian company that had concluded several maintenance contracts with the State-owned nuclear energy company 'Energoatom' for the repair of high-voltage electrical equipment. The dispute arose out of the nuclear plant's bankruptcy, falling into default with the investor's contracts. The investor started court proceedings against the state-owned enterprise and won, but the execution was stayed due to the bankruptcy proceedings.	The respondent counterclaimed for the reimbursement of the arbitration costs and related expenses, and additionally requested compensation for non-material injury to its reputation.	The tribunal rejected jurisdiction over the non-material injury and considered that requests for costs do not require a counterclaim.	N/A
15.	*RSM Production Corporation v Grenada*, ICSID Case No ARB/05/14: Award (13/03/2009)	Contract	The investor entered into an agreement, recording its intent to apply for an exploration licence for oil and gas in waters off the islands of Grenada, Petite Martinique and Carriacou and, in the event of commercial discovery, to apply for one or more 'Development Licences'. Subsequently, the respondent refused to grant the exploration licence.	The respondent requested to declare that the investor had fraudulently induced the respondent to enter into the agreement and/or that the investor breached the agreement by not submitting an application for the exploration license in time.	The claimant did not dispute the tribunal's jurisdiction over the counterclaim, but the tribunal expressly acknowledged jurisdiction.	The tribunal rejected it on merits.
16.	*Gustav F W Hamester GmbH & Co KG v Republic of Ghana*, ICSID Case No ARB/07/24: Award (18/06/2010)	Germany-Ghana BIT (1995)	Joint-venture between claimant and a respondent's state-owned company for processing and trading cocoa beans. The purpose of the agreement was to rehabilitate an old cocoa processing factory and to contribute to its modernisation and the purchase of refined products. The dispute arose out of the contractual breaches of the joint-venture obligations by the state-owned company.	The respondent counterclaimed for damages, 'moral or otherwise', and for losses sustained as a result of the investor's conduct.	The tribunal rejected jurisdiction over the counterclaim.	N/A

17.	*M Meerapfel Söhne AG v Central African Republic*, ICSID Case No ARB/07/10: Award (12/05/2011)	Central African Republic-Switzerland BIT (1973)	While most of the case is redacted, the investor had invested in the tobacco industry in the Central African Republic. It appears that the investor claimed for some investigations about tax fraud, interferences with the export of tobacco and subsequent seizure of the company's inventory.	Redacted	The tribunal rejected on jurisdiction tax-related counterclaims as these are subject to the jurisdiction of domestic courts.	The tribunal dismissed on merits the other counterclaims related to failure to contribute to the economy of the state, alleged loss for buying tobacco from local growers and non-material damage.
18.	*Spyridon Roussalis v Romania*, ICSID Case No ARB/06/1: Award (07/12/2011) *and* Michael Reisman's Declaration (28/11/2011)	Greece-Romania BIT (1997)	The investor entered into a privatization agreement with the host state for a state-owned enterprise engaged in the frozen-food warehousing business. Thereby, there was an obligation to make a post-purchase investment of USD 1,4 million, which the investor argued it was complied with, whereas the respondent disputed it.	The respondent counterclaimed for the failure to make the post-purchase investment and for misappropriation of assets.	The tribunal rejected jurisdiction over the counterclaims.	N/A
19.	*Inmaris Perestroika Sailing Maritime Services GmbH and Others v Ukraine*, ICSID Case No ARB/08/8: Award (01/03/2012)	Germany-Ukraine BIT (1993)	The investors entered into a series of contracts with respondent's state-owned institution to operate Khersones (windjammer sail training ships). Under the contracts, the institution used the Khersones to train cadets for Ukraine's national fishery fleet while the investors used it to market sailing tours and other onboard events, as a means to lowering the ship's operational expenses to train cadets. Subsequently, the respondent prohibited the Khersones from leaving the borders of the territorial waters. This prevented the Khersones from making a scheduled departure for the 2006 summer sailing season. The investors never regained control of the Khersones after that date.	The respondent counterclaimed for winter costs it paid during the period when the agreement was in effect.	The tribunal acknowledged jurisdiction over the counterclaim.	The tribunal rejected it on merits.

20.	*Antoine Goetz and others v Republic of Burundi*, ICSID Case No ARB/01/2: Award (21/06/2012)	BLEU-Burundi BIT (1989)	The Goetz Family had several businesses, which were affected by the respondent: the dispute arose out of: (i) African Bank of Commerce in Burundi, to which respondent cancelled the bank's permission to operate in a Free Economic Zone; (ii) airlines, which suffered state cancellation of certain flights, the refusal of access by pilots to the companies' planes, and allegations of customs fraud.	The respondent counterclaimed for damages arising out of the failure of the investor's bank to comply with the conditions to operate in Free Economic Zone. According to the respondent, this caused unfair competition against other local banks and the disruption of the currency financial market.	The tribunal acknowledged jurisdiction over the counterclaim.	The tribunal rejected it on merits.
21.	*Occidental Petroleum Corporation and Occidental Exploration and Production Company v The Republic of Ecuador*, ICSID Case No ARB/06/11: Award (05/10/2012)	US-Ecuador BIT (1993) and Contract	The investors concluded 'participation contracts' with a state agency for the exploration and exploitation of hydrocarbons in the Amazon region. The dispute arose out of the respondent's termination of the contracts ('*caducidad*') and the subsequently seizure of the investors' property.	The respondent counterclaimed for: (i) abuse of rights by initiating arbitral proceedings; (ii) breach of participation contracts pertaining to the waiver to the right to use diplomatic or consular channels; (iii) damages to the data and software and the unavailability of drillings rigs; (iv) failure to pay assignment fee and negotiate new participation contracts; (v) moral damages for investors' malfeasance. The fourth counterclaim was later withdrawn	The claimant did not dispute the tribunal's jurisdiction over the counterclaim, and the tribunal did not address the issue.	The tribunal rejected it on merits.
22.	*Elsamex SA v Republic of Honduras*, ICSID Case No ARB/09/4: Award (16/11/2012) *and* Decision on Jurisdiction (04/06/2010)	Contract	The hurricane 'Mitch' damaged considerably the infrastructure of Honduras in October 1998. Accordingly, the respondent subscribed agreements to secure a credit line from Spain and a credit from Inter-American Development Bank, which among other things had the purpose of reconstructing a highway. The investor won the public tender for the reconstruction of the highway. There were technical variations that required modification of the initial contract. The dispute arose out of disagreements between the investor and the state as to technical specifications, prices, non-foreseen items, quality of the works, warranties etc.	The respondent counterclaimed based on the alleged bad quality of works, which were not duly finished, and the refusal to correct the defects timely. Additionally, respondent counterclaimed for tort arguing that investor revised its inadequate proposal and offered an artificially low price when tendering.	The tribunal upheld jurisdiction over the counterclaims except for the those based on tort.	The tribunal granted relief for claimant's breach of its contractual obligation on the sewer and gutter cleaning. The rest of counterclaims were rejected.
23.	*Metal-Tech Ltd v Republic of Uzbekistan*, ICSID Case No ARB/10/3: Award (04/10/2013)	Israel-Uzbekistan BIT (1994)	The investor entered into a joint-venture with an Uzbek state-owned enterprise to build and operate a plant for the production of molybdenum products. The dispute arose out of disagreement between the parties as to the compliance with the contract. Subsequently, the respondent terminated the raw material supply contract, cancelled the investor's exclusive right to export refined molybdenum oxide, and started criminal proceedings against of the company's management.	The respondent counterclaimed for damages out of the investor's misrepresentations. Particularly loss of revenue for what could have been earned with molybdenum related-activities and for the bankruptcy proceedings of the supplier. Additionally, direct damage from lost tax, custom revenue and foreign exchange, and damages for the increase of unemployment.	The tribunal rejected jurisdiction over the counterclaims.	N/A
24.	*Balkan Energy (Ghana) Limited v Republic of Ghana*, PCA Case No 2010-7: Award (01/04/2014)	Contract	The investor entered into a power purchase agreement with the host state. The dispute arose out of respondent failure to provide adequate site electricity, connection to the national grid through a transmission line, and failure to facilitate the acquisition and installation of equipment.	The respondent counterclaimed for: (i) the investor's breach of the power purchase agreement; and (ii) for the investor's misrepresentations regarding its experience and capability of operating liquid/gas fired power plants. The second counterclaim was later withdrawn.	The claimant did not dispute the tribunal's jurisdiction over the counterclaim, and the tribunal did not address the issue.	The tribunal upheld the counterclaim.
25.	*Fraport AG Frankfurt Airport Services Worldwide v Republic of The Philippines*, ICSID Cas e No ARB/11/12: Award (10/12/2014)	Germany-Philippines BIT (1997)	The investor's direct and indirect shareholding in a company with concession agreement for building and operating an airport terminal. The dispute arose out of the respondent's cancellation of the concession. The domestic courts considered the concession void ab initio.	The respondent counterclaimed for, among others: (i) costs for completing or remediating the airport terminal; (ii) lease payments and real-estate taxes where the terminal was located; (iii) tax benefits that the investor received from terminal's status as special economic zone; (iv) costs for administering the bid and concession; (v) lost revenue for lost opportunity caused by failure of the terminal to become operational; (vii) bribes paid by the investor, fines and ill-gotten gains; (viii) costs and legal expenses.	The tribunal rejected jurisdiction over the counterclaims.	N/A
26.	*Hesham Talaat M Al-Warraq v The Republic of Indonesia*, UNCITRAL Case: Award (15/12/2014)	OIC Investment Agreement (1981)	The investor held shares in several banks located in Indonesia namely CIC, Pikko, Danpac, and Bank Century. The dispute arose out of the decision of respondent's central bank to place Bank Century under administration by a governmental agency, and its bail-out. Riots due to allegedly use of bailout funds for the 2009 presidential campaign ensued. A respondent's inquiry committee declared the bailout illegal and mired in corruption. One member of the board of directors of Bank Century subsequently was arrested and the police issued arrest warrants for the investor for alleged fraudulent activities in the financial sector. The investor was convicted in absence for corruption and money laundry and his assets were confiscated.	The respondent counterclaimed for damages out the investor's unjust enrichment in detriment of the Bank Century and the misuse of the bailout.	Tribunal upheld jurisdiction over the counterclaim.	The tribunal rejected it on merits.

27.	*Marco Gavazzi and Stefano Gavazzi v Romania*, ICSID Case No ARB/12/25: Jurisdiction, Admissibility and Liability (21/04/2015) *and* Dissenting Opinion (14/04/2015)	Italy-Romania BIT (1990)	The investors entered into a privatization agreement of 70% of the shares of a state-owned metallurgical plant in Romania. The dispute arose out of the reschedule of debt of the company, which the investor considered less beneficial than initially informed. Subsequently, the state froze the company's bank accounts for repayment of the debt, which prompted the investors to inject more money to keep the company functioning. Parties went to arbitration, where the investors won, but the award was set aside in the host state. The appeals court terminated the shares purchase agreement but determined that the state should keep money paid by the investors for the shares.	The respondent counterclaimed for damages out of the investors' failure to comply with their investment obligations in the share purchase agreement and their mismanagement of the company.	The tribunal rejected jurisdiction over the counterclaim.	N/A
28.	*Oxus Gold v Republic of Uzbekistan*, UNCITRAL Case: Award (17/12/2015)	UK-Uzbekistan BIT (1993)	The investor held shareholding rights in two mining projects in Uzbekistan. The dispute arose out of the respondent's series of actions which including a reversal of government support and tax privileges, tax audits that interfered with the operation, failure to renew or issue operational licences, a ban on export of silver ores, and the conviction for espionage of a senior employee of the investor.	The respondent counterclaimed for: (i) misrepresentations as to the financing of the mining projects; (ii) waste of natural resources (unprocessed ore); (iii) breach of the special dividend agreement; (iv) engagement in self-dealing and related party transactions; and (v) currency law violations and corresponding failure to provide promised foreign currency and other benefits.	The tribunal rejected jurisdiction over the counterclaims.	N/A
29.	*Rusoro Mining Ltd v Bolivarian Republic of Venezuela*, ICSID Case No ARB(AF)/12/5: Award (22/08/2016)	Canada-Venezuela BIT (1996)	The investor acquired controlling interests in 24 Venezuelan companies, which held 58 gold mining concessions and contracts. The dispute arose out of the respondent's decision to assume control over gold mining activities, by particularly: (i) repealing previous liberal gold export regime, imposing that 60% of quarterly production had to be sold to the respondent's central bank—only up to 30% could be export subject to authorisation; (ii) offering a relaxed regime to state-controlled enterprises; (iii) finally, in 2011 a nationalization decree was promulgated.	The respondent counterclaimed for alleged improper mining practices, which had a detrimental impact on the future viability of the mine. According to the respondent, the investor had deviated from the concession's mining plan, by mining soft rock material located at the surface of the deposits. This implied delaying costs into the future and left mining of deeper and harder ore. Furthermore, the investor incurred in the accumulation of waste material that jeopardized original production targets.	The tribunal rejected jurisdiction over the counterclaim.	N/A
30.	*Urbaser SA and Consorcio de Aguas Bilbao Bizkaia, Bilbao Biskaia Ur Partzuergoa v The Argentine Republic*, ICSID Case No ARB/07/26: Award (08/12/2016)	Spain-Argentina BIT (1991)	The investor entered into a concession for water and sewage services for the Province of Greater Buenos Aires. The dispute arose because the concession was running into a deadlock given the financial crisis. Therefore, the concessionaire requested a new valuation of its tariffs and a review of the concession. However, the respondent allegedly did not seriously committed to negotiations. Finally in 2006, the concession was terminated.	The respondent counterclaimed for alleged failure to provide the necessary investment into the concession, thus violating its commitments and its obligations under international law based on the human right to water.	The tribunal acknowledged jurisdiction over the counterclaim.	The tribunal rejected it on merits.
31.	*Teinver SA, Transportes de Cercanías SA and Autobuses Urbanos del Sur SA v The Argentine Republic*, ICSID Case No ARB/09/1: Award (21/07/2017)	Spain-Argentina BIT (1991)	The investors acquired shares in two national airlines. Given the financial crisis and the devaluation of Argentinian currency, fuel's prices increased and airlines requested airfare increase to cope with it. The respondent promised airfare increase and fuel's subsidies but nothing was enacted. After years of agreements and new regulations, the respondent passed a law for the expropriation of the investors' shares on the airlines.	The respondent counterclaimed for damages out of the investors' mismanagement of the airlines between 2001-2008.	The tribunal rejected the counterclaim because it was unsubstantiated, preventing analysis on jurisdiction.	N/A
32.	*Karkey Karadeniz Elektrik Uretim AS* v Islamic Republic of Pakistan, ICSID Case No ARB/13/1: Award (22/08/2017)	Pakistan-Turkey BIT (1995)	The investor won a bid and concluded a concession for the provision of power generating vessels. The dispute arose out of the respondent's supreme court finding that the concession was in violation of public procurement rules and was thus void. The supreme court also ordered to investigate corruption in the bidding process. Additionally, the investor's bank accounts were frozen and the vessels were detained.	The respondent counterclaimed for the investor's unjust enrichment during the operation of the concession, which was in violation of public procurement rules.	The tribunal rejected jurisdiction over the counterclaim.	N/A
33.	*Tethyan Copper Company Pty Limited v Islamic Republic of Pakistan*, ICSID Case No ARB/12/1: Decision on Jurisdiction and Liability (10/11/2017)	Australia-Pakistan BIT (1998)	The investor held rights in a joint venture agreement concluded with the Province of Balochistan (Pakistan) for the exploration, development and subsequently exploitation of deposits of copper and gold. The dispute arose out of the respondent's refusal to grant a mining licence.	The respondent counterclaimed that the investment was not made in accordance with Pakistani laws and investment policies as set out in the treaty. Additionally, respondent counterclaimed that the investor breached the joint venture because it did not comply with the pre-conditions before filing for the mining licence and failed to complete a feasibility study of the discovered deposits.	The tribunal upheld jurisdiction over the counterclaim based on the treaty. However, it rejected the counterclaims based on contractual obligations (joint venture agreement) and on domestic law.	The tribunal rejected the treaty counterclaim on merits.

34.	*Olin Holdings Ltd v Libya*, ICC Case No 20355/MCP: Award (25/05/2018)	Cyprus-Libya BIT (2004)	The investor invested in a dairy and juice factory in Libya. It obtained all authorizations required and rented the land for the factory. The investor also invested on marketing for launch of the products. The dispute arose when the investor received an eviction order (as a consequence of an expropriation decree) from the municipality of Tripoli, requesting to vacate premises within three days. The investor challenged the order in court and in different proceedings claimed for damages suffered for the expropriation order. The domestic courts decided that no damage was proven.	The respondent counterclaimed for damages out of the investor's abusive claims on expropriation and mistreatment, as well as reputational damage suffered by the respondent.	The tribunal did not address its jurisdiction over counterclaims	The tribunal rejected the counterclaims because lack of evidence.
35.	*Anglo American PLC v Bolivarian Republic of Venezuela*, ICSID Case No ARB(AF)/14/1: Award (18/01/2019)	UK-Venezuela BIT (1995)	The investor held indirect participation of 91.37% of shares in local company (MLDN) engaged in mining nickel and cobalt deposits. MLDN held concessions, which provided that upon termination, certain mining assets would be transferred free of charge to the state. The dispute arose upon the termination of the concessions of MLDN, since the investors claimed that the state took over some mining assets, which were not covered by the transfer provision, thus, expropriating the investment. Additionally, the investor claimed for the discontinuation of VAT refunds.	The state counterclaimed for damages out of the investor's failure to comply with its obligations as a concessionaire in relation to the exploitation taxes and special advantages.	The tribunal rejected jurisdiction over the counterclaim.	N/A
36.	*Grenada Private Power Limited and WRB Enterprises, Inc v Grenada*, ICSID Case No ARB/17/13: Award (12/03/2020)	Contract	The investor was the sole electric utility in Grenada. It acquired shares in local company during privatization process in 1994. Pursuant to the Shares Purchase Agreement (SPA), Grenada was obliged to repurchase the shares under a specified formula. Twenty-two years later, new regulation changed the rate-setting mechanism triggering the right to resell the shares to Grenada but the investor and Grenada could not reach an agreement on the price.	The respondent counterclaimed for alleged unfair prejudice and oppression as a violation of domestic law caused by the claimant's actions.	The tribunal considered that the allegations under the counterclaim "track allegations raised in the defence". The tribunal seems to have implicitly acknowledged jurisdiction as it was impractical to unbundle the claims.	The tribunal dismissed the counterclaims on merits because of lack of evidence.

37.	*Iberdrola Energia SA v The Republic of Guatemala (II)*, PCA Case No 2017-41: Award (24/08/2020)	Spain-Guatemala BIT (2004)	The investor was a majority shareholder in a Guatemalan electricity distribution utility. The dispute arose out of respondent's decision to change the calculation of electricity rates.	The respondent counterclaimed that the investor had abusively initiated multiple proceedings against it, thereby violating the treaty's fork-in-the-road clause. Accordingly, the respondent requested damages arising out of that treaty breach and moral damages.	The tribunal rejected jurisdiction over the counterclaim.	N/A
38.	*Naturgy Energy Group SA and Naturgy Electricidad Colombia SL (formerly Gas Natural SDG SA and Gas Natural Fenosa Electricidad Colombia SL) v Republic of Colombia*, ICSID Case No UNCT/18/1: Award (12/03/2021)	Spain-Colombia BIT (2005)	The investor held ownership of 85.3% over a local company engaged a power distribution and marketing in the Caribbean Coast. The dispute arose out of the respondent's decision to place the company into administrative receivership and its subsequent decision to liquidate it. The investor argued that through regulatory action/inaction the respondent drove the company to a financial precipice, and then instead of safeguarding it, the respondent seized a politically opportune moment to expropriate it. Whereas the respondent argued that the administrative receivership decision was caused by the investor's mismanagement of the company.	The respondent counterclaimed for damages out of the investor's alleged mismanagement of the company, in particular, for: (i) state funds channelled to the company to maintain operation; (ii) negative economic impact in Caribbean Region; (iii) lower than expected tax revenues; (iv) reduction in value of Colombia's shareholding in the company.	The tribunal rejected jurisdiction over the counterclaim.	N/A
39.	*Muhammet Çap & Sehil Inşaat Endustri ve Ticaret Ltd Sti v Turkmenistan*, ICSID Case No ARB/12/6: Award (04/05/2021)	Turkey-Turkmenistan BIT (1992)	The investors operated in the construction business. The locally incorporated company (Sehil) was awarded 64 contracts by different State organs and State-owned companies. Half of those projects were completed but the other half could not be fully performed. The claimants claimed that state entities failed to make payments, forced to take additional works without compensation, imposed delay penalties, engaged in unusual site inspections, and threats and intimidation.	The respondent counterclaimed for delay penalties under some of the contracts, replacement works, uncompleted works, and tax debt.	The tribunal considered that respondent's counterclaims were limited to the case were contractual claims were accepted. However, since the tribunal declined jurisdiction over contractual claims, the counterclaims became moot.	N/A

40.	*BSG Resources Limited, BSG Resources (Guinea) Limited and BSG Resources (Guinea) SÀRL v Republic of Guinea*, ICSID Case No ARB/14/22 (18/05/2022)	Contract and Guinea's Domestic law	The respondent relocated two mining blocks of iron ore to claimants in 2008 and subsequently claimants and respondent signed mining agreements for a different area. In 2010, after a regime change, claimants' permits and concessions were revoked or terminated based on corruption.	Respondent counterclaimed for the economic damages caused by claimants' corrupt dealings to obtain their mining rights. Furthermore, respondent requested moral damages given claimants' false public statements.	Claimants did not dispute the tribunal's jurisdiction over the counterclaim but the tribunal explicitly acknowledged it had jurisdiction.	The tribunal rejected the counterclaim as inadmissible given that government officials benefited from the illicit act. This was aggravated by the respondent's lack of prosecution of the government officials involved in the corruption scheme.
41.	*Gardabani Holdings BV and Silk Road Holdings BV v Georgia*, ICSID Case No. ARB/17/29: Award (27/10/2022)	Netherlands-Georgia BIT (1998)	The investors invested in the electricity sector since the beginning of the 2000s. However, they claimed that the national electricity regulator overrode the tariff-related provisions by adjusting the tariffs applicable to the claimant's investments pursuant to the new tariff-setting methodology. Furthermore, the regulator's interpretation of certain provisions of the agreements caused losses to the claimants' electricity companies in Georgia.	The respondent argued that if contractual claims are allowed under the umbrella clause, the counterclaims based on the same agreements were to be admitted as well.	The tribunal explicitly acknowledged jurisdiction over contractual counterclaims as they formed an integral part of the dispute.	The counterclaim was deemed to succeed on merits, but the tribunal pointed out that they had been already accounted for in the related contractual SCC arbitration.

Annex 3: Counterclaims in Numbers

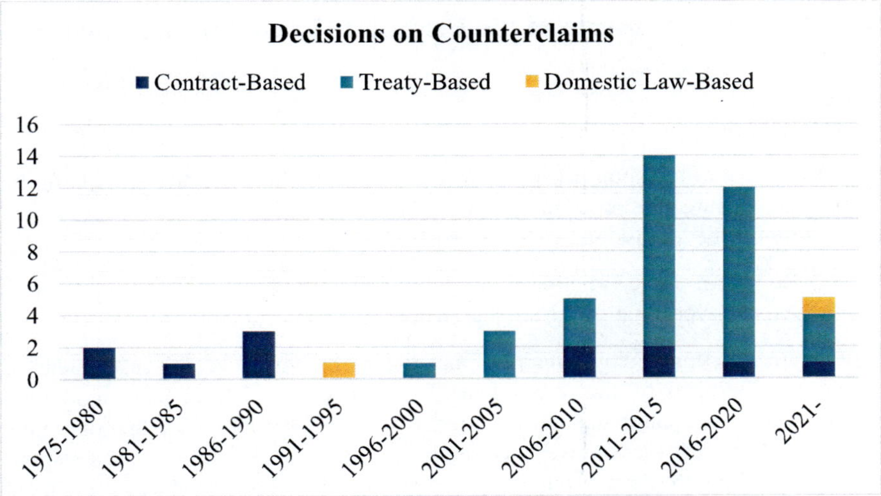

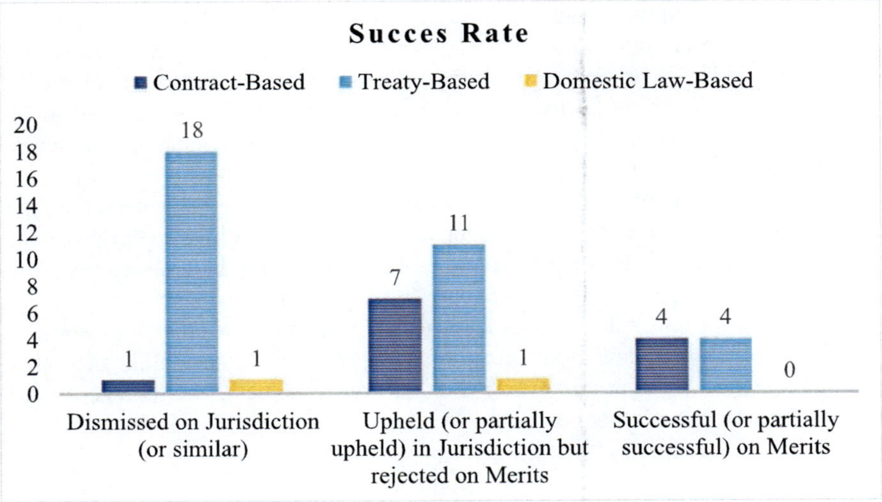

Annex 4: Article 6 of the Resolution on the 'Equality of Parties before International Investment Tribunals' of the 18th Commission of the Institut de Droit International

Article 6
Counterclaims

(1) The ability of a respondent to assert a counterclaim that is admissible before a tribunal ensures the procedural equality of the parties.

(2) In order to be admissible, such a counterclaim must:

(a) Be within the jurisdiction of the tribunal; and,

(b) Arise directly out of the subject matter of the investment.

(3) The jurisdictional requirement is met when, by virtue of the instrument of consent invoked by the respondent, the tribunal would have had jurisdiction over the counterclaim had it been asserted as a primary claim. Whether or not the tribunal has jurisdiction over a counterclaim does not depend upon the respondent invoking the same ground of jurisdiction as that relied upon by the claimant for its claim, nor is the tribunal's jurisdiction limited by the scope of the dispute as framed by the claimant in its Request for Arbitration.

(4) Where the dispute is submitted to arbitration under the ICSID Convention, the requirement in Article 46 that the counterclaim must also be 'otherwise within the jurisdiction of the Centre' means that it must fall within the criteria of Article 25(1) of the Convention by being a 'legal dispute arising directly out of an investment, between a Contracting State. . .and a national of another Contracting State.'

(5) The requirement of sufficiency of connection with the subject matter of the dispute is met where the counterclaim concerns the same investment that gave rise to the claim. It does not require that the counterclaim be founded upon the same legal instrument or cause of action asserted by the claimant.

(6) The tribunal may find a counterclaim to be admissible, whether it is founded upon international law or host State law, provided that it fulfils the other requirements set out in this Article and concerns a subject matter that is capable of submission to arbitration.

List of Cases

Arbitral Decisions in Investment Arbitration (Except Counterclaims)

Abaclat and Others v Argentine Republic, ICSID Case No ARB/07/5, Decision on Jurisdiction and Admissibility (04 August 2011).

Adel A Hamadi Al Tamimi v Sultanate of Oman, ICSID Case No ARB/11/33, Award (03 November 2015).

AES Summit Generation Limited and AES-Tisza Erömü Kft v The Republic of Hungary, ICSID Case No ARB/07/22, Award (23 September 2010).

Aguas del Tunari, SA v Republic of Bolivia, ICSID Case No ARB/02/3, Decision on Jurisdiction (21 October 2005).

Amco Asia Corporation and others v Republic of Indonesia, ICSID Case No ARB/81/1, Decision on Annulment in Resubmitted Proceeding (17 December 1992).

Asian Agricultural Products Ltd v Republic of Sri Lanka, ICSID Case No ARB/87/3, Award (27 June 1990).

Astrida Benita Carrizosa v Republic of Colombia, ICSID Case No ARB/18/5, Award (19 April 2021).

Azurix Corp v The Argentine Republic, ICSID Case No ARB/01/12, Decision on Jurisdiction (08 December 2003).

Azurix Corp v The Argentine Republic, ICSID Case No ARB/01/12, Award (14 July 2006).

Bayindir Insaat Turizm Ticaret Ve Sanayi AS v Islamic Republic of Pakistan, ICSID Case No ARB/03/29, Decision on Jurisdiction (14 November 2005).

Bayindir Insaat Turizm Ticaret Ve Sanayi AS v Islamic Republic of Pakistan, ICSID Case No ARB/03/29, Award (27 August 2009).

Bayview Irrigation District et al v United Mexican States, ICSID Case No ARB (AF)/05/1, Award (19 June 2007).

A. E. Alvarado-Garzón, *Environmental Counterclaims in Investment Arbitration*,
EYIEL Monographs - Studies in European and International Economic Law 34,
https://doi.org/10.1007/978-3-031-46391-4

BG Group Plc v Republic of Argentina, UNCITRAL Case, Award (24 December 2007).

Ceskoslovenska Obchodni Banka AS v The Slovak Republic, ICSID Case No ARB/97/4, Procedural Order No 4 (11 January 1999).

Chemtura Corporation v Government of Canada, UNCITRAL Case, Award (02 August 2010).

CMS Gas Transmission Company v The Republic of Argentina, ICSID Case No ARB/01/8, Decision on Jurisdiction (17 July 2003).

CMS Gas Transmission Company v The Republic of Argentina, ICSID Case No ARB/01/8, Award (12 May 2005).

Compañía de Aguas del Aconguija SA and Vivendi Universal SA v Argentine Republic, ICSID Case No ARB/97/3, Decision on Annulment (03 July 2002).

Compañia del Desarrollo de Santa Elena SA v Republic of Costa Rica, ICSID Case No ARB/96/1, Final Award (17 February 2000).

Cortec Mining Kenya Limited, Cortec (Pty) Limited and Stirling Capital Limited v Republic of Kenya, ICSID Case No ARB/15/29, Award (22 October 2018).

Daimler Financial Services AG v Argentine Republic, ICSID Case No ARB/05/1, Award (22 August 2012).

Deutsche Bank AG v Democratic Socialist Republic of Sri Lanka, ICSID Case No ARB/09/2, Award (31 October 2012).

Electrabel SA v Republic of Hungary, ICSID Case No ARB/07/19, Decision on Jurisdiction, Applicable Law and Liability (30 November 2012).

Emilio Agustín Maffezini v The Kingdom of Spain, ICSID Case No ARB/97/7, Decision on Jurisdiction (25 January 2000).

Emmis International Holding BV, Emmis Radio Operating BV, MEM Magyar Electronic Media Kereskedelmi és Szolgáltató Kft v The Republic of Hungary, ICSID Case No ARB/12/2, Award (16 April 2014).

Empresas Lucchetti SA and Lucchetti Peru SA v The Republic of Peru, ICSID Case No ARB/03/4, Decision on Annulment (05 September 2007).

EnCana Corporation v Republic of Ecuador, LCIA Case No UN3481, Award (3 February 2006).

Enron Corporation and Ponderosa Assets LP v Argentine Republic, ICSID Case No ARB/01/3, Decision on Jurisdiction (14 January 2004).

Fraport AG Frankfurt Airport Services Worldwide v The Republic of The Philippines, ICSID Case No ARB/03/25, Award (16 August 2007).

Giovanni Alemanni and Others v The Argentine Republic, ICSID Case No ARB/07/8, Decision on Jurisdiction and Admissibility (17 November 2014).

Hochtief AG v The Argentine Republic, ICSID Case No ARB/07/31, Decision on Jurisdiction (24 October 2011).

Hussein Nuaman Soufraki v The United Arab Emirates, ICSID Case No ARB/02/7, Decision on Annulment (05 June 2007).

ICS Inspection and Control Services Limited v The Republic of Argentina, PCA Case No 2010-9, Award on Jurisdiction (10 February 2012).

Impregilo SpA v Argentine Republic, ICSID Case No ARB/07/17, Award (21 June 2011).

Impregilo SpA v Argentine Republic, ICSID Case No ARB/07/17, Concurring and Dissenting Opinion of Professor Brigitte Stern (21 June 2011).
Impregilo SpA v Islamic Republic of Pakistan, ICSID Case No ARB/03/3, Decision on Jurisdiction (22 April 2005).
International Thunderbird Gaming Corporation v The United Mexican States, UNCITRAL Case, Award (26 January 2006).
Jan Oostergetel and Theodora Laurentius v The Slovak Republic, UNCITRAL Case, Decision on Jurisdiction (30 April 2010).
Lanco International Inc v The Argentine Republic, ICSID Case No ARB/97/6, Decision on Jurisdiction (08 December 1998).
Loewen Group Inc and Raymond L Loewen v United States of America, ICSID Case No ARB(AF)/98/3, Award (26 June 2003).
Marvin Roy Feldman Karpa v United Mexican States, ICSID Case No ARB(AF)/99/1, Award (16 December 2002).
Mathias Kruck and others v Kingdom of Spain, ICSID Case No ARB/15/23, Decision on Jurisdiction (16 April 2021).
Methanex Corporation v United States of America, UNCITRAL Case, Award (03 August 2005).
Mobil Investments Canada Inc and Murphy Oil Corporation Inc v Canada, ICSID Case No ARB(AF)/07/4, Decision on Liability and on Principles of Quantum (22 May 2012).
Orascom TMT Investments Sàrl v People's Democratic Republic of Algeria, ICSID Case No ARB/12/35, Decision on Annulment (17 September 2020).
Peter A Allard v The Government of Barbados, PCA Case No 2012-06, Award (27 June 2016).
Philip Morris Brands Sàrl, Philip Morris Products SA and Abal Hermanos SA v Oriental Republic of Uruguay, ICSID Case No ARB/10/7 (formerly FTR Holding SA, Philip Morris Products SA and Abal Hermanos SA v Oriental Republic of Uruguay), Request for Arbitration (19 February 2010).
Phoenix Action Ltd v The Czech Republic, ICSID Case No ARB/06/5, Award (15 April 2009).
Plama Consortium Limited v Republic of Bulgaria, ICSID Case No ARB/03/24, Order (06 September 2005).
Plama Consortium Limited v Republic of Bulgaria, ICSID Case No ARB/03/24, Award (27 August 2008).
Quiborax SA, Non Metallic Minerals SA and Allan Fosk Kaplún v Plurinational State of Bolivia, ICSID Case No ARB/06/2, Award (16 September 2015).
Ronald S Lauder v The Czech Republic, UNCITRAL Case, Final Award (03 September 2001).
RosInvestCo UK Ltd v The Russian Federation, SCC Case No V079/2005, Final Award (12 September 2010).
Saipem SpA v The People's Republic of Bangladesh, ICSID Case No ARB/05/07, Decision on Jurisdiction and Recommendation on Provisional Measures (21 March 2007).

Salini Impregilo SpA v Argentine Republic, ICSID Case No ARB/15/39, Decision on Jurisdiction and Admissibility (23 February 2018).

SAUR International SA v Republic of Argentina, ICSID Case No ARB/04/4, Decision on Jurisdiction and Liability (06 June 2012).

SD Myers, Inc v Government of Canada, UNCITRAL Case, Partial Award (13 November 2000).

SGS Société Générale de Surveillance SA v Islamic Republic of Pakistan, ICSID Case No ARB/01/13, Procedural Order No 2 (16 October 2002) [reproduced in (2003) 18(1) ICSID Review 293-306].

SGS Société Générale de Surveillance SA v Islamic Republic of Pakistan, ICSID Case No ARB/01/13, Decision on Jurisdiction (06 August 2003).

SGS Société Générale de Surveillance SA v Republic of The Philippines, ICSID Case No ARB/02/6, Decision of the Tribunal on Objections to Jurisdiction (29 January 2004).

SGS Société Générale de Surveillance SA v The Republic of Paraguay, ICSID Case No ARB/07/29, Decision on Jurisdiction (12 February 2010).

Southern Pacific Properties (Middle East) Ltd v Arab Republic of Egypt, ICSID Case No ARB/84/3, Decision on Jurisdiction (14 April 1988).

Tokios Tokelés v Ukraine, ICSID Case No ARB/02/18, Order No 1 (01 July 2003).

Tza Yap Shum v The Republic of Peru, ICSID Case No ARB/07/6, Award (07 July 2011).

Urbaser SA and Consorcio de Aguas Bilbao Bizkaia, Bilbao Biskaia Ur Partzuergoa v The Argentine Republic, ICSID Case No ARB/07/26, Decision on Jurisdiction (19 December 2012).

Vladislav Kim and others v Republic of Uzbekistan, ICSID Case No ARB/13/6, Decision on Jurisdiction (08 March 2017).

Waste Management Inc v United Mexican States, ICSID Case No ARB(AF)/98/2, Dissenting Opinion of Keith Highet (08 May 2000).

Wena Hotels Limited v Arab Republic of Egypt, ICSID Case No ARB/98/4, Decision on Annulment (05 February 2002).

World Duty Free Company v Republic of Kenya, ICSID Case No Arb/00/7, Award (04 October 2006).

Yukos Universal Limited (Isle of Man) v The Russian Federation, UNCITRAL, PCA Case No 2005-04/AA227, Award (18 July 2014).

Yuri Bogdanov and Yulia Bogdanova v Republic of Moldova, SCC Case No V091/2012, Award (13 April 2013).

PCIJ Decisions

Case concerning Certain German Interests in Polish Upper Silesia (Germany v Poland) (Merits) (25 May 1926) PCIJ Rep Series A No 07.

Case concerning the Factory at Chorzów (Germany v Poland) (Merits) (13 September 1928) PCIJ Rep Series A No 17.

Case concerning the Payment in Gold of Brazilian Federal Loans contracted in France (France v Brazil) (Judgment) (12 July 1929) PCIJ Rep Series A No 21.

Case concerning the Payment of various Serbian Loans issued in France (France v the Kingdom of Serbs, Croats and Slovenes) (Judgment) (12 July 1929) PCIJ Rep Series A No 20.

Jurisdiction of the Courts of Danzig (Advisory Opinion) (03 March 1928) PCIJ Rep Series B No 15.

Rights of Minorities in Upper Silesia (Minority Schools) (Germany v Poland) (Judgment) (26 April 1928) PCIJ Rep Series A No 15.

Status of Eastern Carelia (Advisory Opinion) (23 July 1923) PCIJ Rep Series B No 05.

The Diversion of Water from the Meuse (The Netherlands v Belgium) (Judgment) (28 June 1937) PCIJ Rep Series A/B No 70.

The Mavrommatis Palestine Concessions (Greece v United Kingdom) (Judgment) (30 August 1924) PCIJ Rep Series A No 02.

The Panevezys-Saldutiskis Railway Case (Estonia v Lithuania) (Judgment) (28 February 1939) PCIJ Rep Series A/B No 76.

ICJ Decisions

Aegean Sea Continental Shelf (Greece v Turkey) (Judgment) [1978] ICJ Rep 3.

Alleged Violations of Sovereign Rights and Maritime Spaces in the Caribbean Sea (Nicaragua v Colombia) (Order on Counterclaims) [2017] ICJ Rep 289.

Alleged Violations of Sovereign Rights and Maritime Spaces in the Caribbean Sea (Nicaragua v Colombia) (Order on Counterclaims) [2017] ICJ Rep 289, Declaration of Vice-President Yusuf.

Alleged Violations of Sovereign Rights and Maritime Spaces in the Caribbean Sea (Nicaragua v Colombia) (Order on Counterclaims) [2017] ICJ Rep 289, Dissenting Opinion of Judge ad hoc Caron.

Alleged Violations of Sovereign Rights and Maritime Spaces in the Caribbean Sea (Nicaragua v Colombia) (Order on Counterclaims) [2017] ICJ Rep 289, Joint Opinion of Judges Tomka, Gaja, Sebutinde, Gevorgian and judge ad hoc Daudet.

Alleged Violations of Sovereign Rights and Maritime Spaces in the Caribbean Sea (Nicaragua v Colombia) (Order on Counterclaims) [2017] ICJ Rep 289, Separate Opinion of Judge Greenwood.

Ambatielos Case (Greece v United Kingdom) (Merits: Obligation to Arbitrate) [1953] ICJ Rep 10.

Application of the Convention on the Prevention and Punishment of the Crime of Genocide (Bosnia and Herzegovina v Yugoslavia) (Order on Counterclaims) [1997] ICJ Rep 243.

Application of the Convention on the Prevention and Punishment of the Crime of Genocide (Bosnia and Herzegovina v Yugoslavia) (Order on Counterclaims) [1997] ICJ Rep 243, Declaration of Judge ad hoc Kreca.

Application of the Convention on the Prevention and Punishment of the Crime of Genocide (Bosnia and Herzegovina v Yugoslavia) (Order on Counterclaims) [1997] ICJ Rep 243, Dissenting Opinion Judge Weeramantry.

Application of the Convention on the Prevention and Punishment of the Crime of Genocide (Bosnia and Herzegovina v Yugoslavia) (Order on Counterclaims) [1997] ICJ Rep 243, Separate Opinion Judge Koroma.

Application of the Convention on the Prevention and Punishment of the Crime of Genocide (Bosnia and Herzegovina v Yugoslavia) (Order on Counterclaims) [1997] ICJ Rep 243, Separate Opinion Judge Lauterpacht.

Application of the Convention on the Prevention and Punishment of the Crime of Genocide (Croatia v Serbia) (Merits) [2015] ICJ Rep 3.

Armed Activities on the Territory of the Congo (Democratic Republic of the Congo v Uganda) (Order on Counterclaims) [2001] ICJ Rep 660.

Armed Activities on the Territory of the Congo (Democratic Republic of the Congo v Uganda) (Order on Counterclaims) [2001] ICJ Rep 660, Declaration of Judge Verhoeven.

Armed Activities on the Territory of the Congo (Democratic Republic of the Congo v Uganda) (Merits) [2005] ICJ Rep 168.

Case Concerning Armed Activities on the Territory of the Congo (New Application: 2002) (Democratic Republic of Congo v Rwanda) (Jurisdiction) [2006] ICJ Rep 6.

Case concerning Certain Phosphate Lands in Nauru (Nauru v Australia) (Judgment) [1992] ICJ Rep 240.

Case Concerning the Aerial Incident of July 27 th, 1955 (Israel v Bulgaria) (Preliminary Objections) [1959] ICJ Rep 127, Joint Dissenting Opinion by Judges Sir Hersch Lauterpacht, Wellington Koo and Sir Percy Spender.

Case concerning the Gabčíkovo-Nagymaros Project (Hungary v Slovakia) (Judgment) [1997] ICJ Rep 7.

Case concerning the Gabčíkovo-Nagymaros Project (Hungary v Slovakia) (Judgment) [1997] ICJ Rep 7, Separate Opinion of Vice-President Weeramantry.

Case concerning the Northern Cameroons (Cameroon v United Kingdom) (Preliminary Objections) [1963] ICJ Rep 15.

Certain Activities Carried Out by Nicaragua in the Border Area (Costa Rica v Nicaragua), Construction of a Road in Costa Rica along the San Juan River (Nicaragua v Costa Rica) (Order on Counterclaims) [2013] ICJ Rep 200.

Certain Activities Carried Out by Nicaragua in the Border Area (Costa Rica v Nicaragua), Construction of a Road in Costa Rica along the San Juan River (Nicaragua v Costa Rica) (Order on Counterclaims) [2013] ICJ Rep 200, Declaration of Judge ad hoc Guillaume.

Certain Activities Carried Out by Nicaragua in the Border Area (Costa Rica v Nicaragua) (Compensation) [2018] ICJ Rep 15.

Certain Questions of Mutual Assistance in Criminal Matters (Djibouti v France) (Judgment) [2008] ICJ Rep 177.

Colombian-Peruvian Asylum Case (Colombia v Peru) (Judgment) [1950] ICJ Rep 266.

Corfu Channel Case (United Kingdom v Albania) (Judgment on Preliminary Objection) [1948] ICJ Rep 15.
Dispute Regarding Navigational and Related Rights (Costa Rica v Nicaragua) (Judgment) [2009] ICJ Rep 213.
Frontier Disputer (Benin v Niger) (Judgment) [2005] ICJ Rep 90.
International Status of South-West Africa (Advisory Opinion) [1950] ICJ Rep 128, Separate Opinion by Sir Arnold McNair.
Interpretation of Peace Treaties with Bulgaria, Hungary and Romania (Advisory Opinion) [1950] ICJ Rep 65.
Jurisdictional Immunities of the State (Germany v Italy) (Order on Counterclaim) [2010] ICJ Rep 310.
Jurisdictional Immunities of the State (Germany v Italy) (Order on Counterclaim) [2010] ICJ Rep 310, Dissenting opinion of Judge Cançado Trindade.
Land and Maritime Boundary between Cameroon and Nigeria (Cameroon v Nigeria) (Order) [1999] ICJ Rep 983.
Land and Maritime Boundary between Cameroon and Nigeria (Cameroon v Nigeria, Equatorial Guinea intervening) (Counterclaims) [2002] ICJ Rep 303.
Land, Island, and Maritime Frontier Dispute (El Salvador v Honduras: Nicaragua intervening) (Judgment) [1992] ICJ Rep 351.
Legal Consequences for States of the Continued Presence of South Africa in Namibia (South West Africa) notwithstanding Security Council Resolution 276 (1979) (Advisory Opinion) [1971] ICJ Rep 16.
Oil Platforms (Iran v United States of America) (Order on Counterclaim) [1998] ICJ Rep 190.
Oil Platforms (Iran v United States of America) (Order on Counterclaim) [1998] ICJ Rep 190, Separate Opinion Judge Higgins.
Oil Platforms (Iran v United States of America) (Merits) [2003] ICJ Rep 161.
Pulp Mills on the River Uruguay (Argentina v Uruguay) (Judgment) [2010] ICJ Rep 14.
Question of the Delimitation of the Continental Shelf between Nicaragua and Colombia beyond 200 Nautical Miles from the Nicaraguan Coast (Nicaragua v Colombia) (Preliminary Objections) [2016] ICJ Rep 100.
Reparation for Injuries suffered in the Service of the United Nations (Advisory Opinion) [1949] ICJ Rep 174.

IUSCT Decisions

American Bell International Inc v The Islamic Republic of Iran, The Ministry of Defense, The Ministry of Post, Telegraph and Telephone, and the Telecommunications Company of Iran, Case 48, Chamber 3, Award No 255-48-3 (19 September 1986) 12 Iran-US CTR 170.
American Bell International Inc v The Islamic Republic of Iran, The Ministry of Defense, The Ministry of Post, Telegraph and Telephone, and the

Telecommunications Company of Iran, Case 48, Chamber 3, Interlocutory Award No ITL 41-48-3 (11 June 1984) 6 Iran-US CTR 74.

Computer Sciences Corporation v The Government of the Islamic Republic of Iran and others, Case 65, Chamber 1, Award No 221-65-1 (16 April 1986) 10 Iran-US CTR 269.

Houston Contracting Company v National Iranian Oil Company, National Iranian Gas Company, and the Islamic Republic of Iran, Case 173, Chamber 3, Award No 378-173-3 (22 July 1988) 20 Iran-US CTR 3.

International Technical Products Corporation and ITP Export Corporation v The Islamic Republic of Iran and others, Case 302, Chamber 3, Award No 196-302-3 (24 October 1985) 9 Iran-US CTR 206.

Questech Inc v The Ministry of National Defence of the Islamic Republic of Iran, Case 59, Award No 191-59-1 (20 September 1985) 9 Iran-US CTR 170.

Request for Interpretation: Jurisdiction of the Tribunal with respect to claims by the Islamic Republic of Iran against nationals of the United States of America, Case A/2, Decision No DEC 1-A2-FT (13 January 1982) 1 Iran-US CTR 101.

Request for Interpretation: Jurisdiction of the Tribunal with respect to claims by the Islamic Republic of Iran against nationals of the United States of America, Case A/2, Decision No DEC 1-A2-FT (13 January 1982) 1 Iran-US CTR 101, Dissenting opinion of Mahmoud Kashani, Shafie Shafiel and Seyyed Hossen Enayat.

Sylvania Technical Systems Inc v The Islamic Republic of Iran, Case 64, Award No 180-64-1 (27 June 1985) 8 Iran-US CTR 298.

Sylvania Technical Systems Inc v The Islamic Republic of Iran, Case 64, Award No 180-64-1 (27 June 1985) 8 Iran-US CTR 298, Dissenting Opinion of Seyyed Mohsen Mostafavi.

TCSB Inc v The Islamic Republic of Iran, Case 140, Chamber 2, Award No 114-140-2 (16 March 1984) 5 Iran-US CTR 160.

The Islamic Republic of Iran v The United States of America, Case B1, Interlocutory Award ITL 83-B1-FT (counterclaim) (9 September 2004) 38 Iran-US CTR 77.

The United States of America and the Federal Reserve Bank of New York v The Islamic Republic and Bank Markazi, Case A28, Decision No DEC 130-A28-FT (19 December 2000) 36 Iran-US CTR 5.

Westinghouse Electric Corporation v The Islamic Republic of Iran, The Islamic Republic of Iran Air Force, Iran Air, The National Iranian Oil Company, Case 389, Chamber 2, Interlocutory Award No ITL 67-389-2 (12 February 1987) 14 Iran-US CTR 104.

William L Pereira Associates, Iran v the Islamic Republic of Iran, Case 1, Chamber 3, Award No 116-1-3 (19 March 1984) 5 Iran-US CTR 198, Concurring Opinion of Richard M Mosk.

Decisions of Domestic Courts

Aguinda v Texaco Inc [2001] 142 F Supp 2d 534 (SDNY).
Amlon Metals Inc v FMC Corp [2001] 775 F Supp 668 (SDNY).
Baron v Sunderland Corporation (10 December 1966) [1966] 2 QB 56 (CA).
Beanal v Freeport-McMoRan Inc [1997] 969 F Supp 362 (ED La).
Beanal v Freeport-McMoRan Inc [1999] 197 F.3d 161 (5th Cir).
Bundesgerichthof (*BGH*) [Federal Court of Justice] (Germany) Az: X ZR 23/87, Judgment (26 January 1989).
Kasky v Nike Inc, Case No S087859, Judgment (2 May 2002), [2002] 27 Cal 4th 939.
Occidental Exploration & Production Company v The Republic of Ecuador [2005] EWCA Civ 1116.
Peters Fabrics Inc v Jantzen Inc [1984] 582 F.Supp 1287 (SDNY).
RTK v Sony Ericsson, Case No 1831/12, Supreme Arbitrazh Court (Russia) Decision (19 June 2012).
Sarei v Rio Tinto PLC [2002] 221 F Supp 2d 1116 (CD Cal).
Sosa v Alvarez-Machain and others [2004] 542 US 692.
Stooke v Taylor, Decision (7 August 1880) [1880] 5 QBD 569.
Supreme Court of Cassation (Bulgaria) Case No 1193/2010, Judgment (02 September 2011).
Tote Bookmakers Ltd v Development Property Holding Co Ltd (21 December 1984) [1985] 49 P & CR 232 (Ch).

Other Decisions

Case C-378/08 *Raffinerie Mediterranee* [2010] ERG Judgment (09 March 2010) ECLI:EU:C:2010:126.
Case of the 'Street Children' (Villagrán-Morales and others) v Guatemala, IACHR Judgment (19 November 1999).
Case of Velásquez-Rodríguez v Honduras, IACHR Judgment (29 July 1988).
Case T-13/99 *Pfizer Animal Health v Council* [2002] CFI Judgment (11 September 2002) ECLI:EU:T:2002:209.
Dispute Concerning Access to Information under Article 9 of the OSPAR Convention (Ireland v United Kingdom of Great Britain and Northern Ireland), PCA Case No 2001-03, Final Award (02 July 2003).
Dombo Beheer v The Netherlands, ECtHR Judgment (27 October 1993) Series A No 274.
European Communities — Measures Affecting the Approval and Marketing of Biotech Products—Panel Report (29 September 2006) WT/DS291/R, WT/DS292/R, WT/DS293/R.

European Communities — Measures Concerning Meat and Meat Products (Hormones)—Appellate Body Report (16 January 1998) WT/DS26/AB/R and WT/DS48/AB/R.

IACHR Advisory Opinion OC-23/17 (15 November 2017) Series A No 23.

Indus Waters Kishenganga Arbitration (Pakistan v India), PCA Case No 2011-01, Partial Award (18 February 2013).

Iron Rhine Railway Arbitration (Belgium v The Netherlands), Award (24 May 2005) XXVII RIAA 35.

LFH Neer and Pauline Neer (United States of America v United Mexican States), Award (15 October 1926) IV RIAA 60.

López Ostra v Spain, Application No 16798/90, ECtHR Judgment (09 December 1994).

M/V 'Virginia G' (Panama v Guinea-Bissau), Order (02 November 2012) ITLOS Reports 39, Dissenting Opinion of Judge ad hoc Treves.

M/V 'Virginia G' (Panama v Guinea-Bissau), Order (02 November 2012) ITLOS Reports 39.

Maya indigenous community of the Toledo District v Belize, Case 12.053, IACHR Report No 40/04, OEA/Ser.L/V/II.122 Doc 5 rev 1 at 727 (2004).

Mexico: Tax Measures on Soft Drinks—Report of the Panel (07 October 2005) WT/DS308/R.

Opinion 1/17 (*CETA Opinion*) [2019] ECLI:EU:C:2019:341.

Radio Corporation of America v the National Government of the Republic of China, Award (13 April 1935) III RIAA 1621.

The Pious Fund of the Californias (United States of America v United Mexican States), Award (14 October 1902) IX RIAA 1.

The Prosecutor v Dusko Tadic, ICTY Case No IT-94-1-A, Appellate Judgment (15 July 1999).

The Social and Economic Rights Action Center and the Center for Economic and Social Rights (SERAC) v Nigeria, Case ACHPR/COMM/A044/1, ACHPR Commission Decision (27 May 2002).

The South China Sea Arbitration (The Republic of Philippines v The People's Republic of China), PCA Case No 2013-19.

Trail smelter case (United States of America v Canada), Award (16 April 1938 and 11 March 1941) III RIAA 1905.

BITs, IIAs and Other Investment-Related Agreements

Referred to as	Name of the Agreement	Year of Signature
Italy-Chad BIT (1969)	Agreement between the Italian Republic and the Government of the Republic of Chad for the Protection and Promotion of Investment of Capital	1969
Netherlands-Kenya BIT (1979)	Agreement on Economic Co-operation between the Government of the Kingdom of the Netherlands and the Government of the Republic of Kenya	1970
Netherlands-Malaysia BIT (1971)	Agreement on Economic Co-operation between the Government of the Kingdom of the Netherlands and Malaysia	1971
Central African Republic-Switzerland BIT (1973)	Agreement of Commerce, Promotion and Protection of Investments between the Swiss Confederation and the Central African Republic	1973
UK-Singapore BIT (1975)	Agreement Between the Government of the United Kingdom of Great Britain and Northern Ireland and the Government of the Republic of Singapore for the Promotion and Protection of Investments	1975
Korea-UK BIT (1976)	Agreement between the Government of the Republic of Korea and the Government of the United Kingdom of Great Britain and Northern Ireland for the Promotion and Protection of Investments	1976
Japan-Egypt BIT (1977)	Agreement between Japan and the Arab Republic of Egypt concerning the Encouragement and Reciprocal Protection of Investment	1977
Sweden-Egypt BIT (1978)	Agreement between the Government of Sweden and the Government of the Arab Republic of Egypt on the Mutual Protection of Investments	1978
Sweden-Serbia BIT (1978)	Agreement between the Government of Sweden and the Government of the Socialist Federal Republic of Yugoslavia on the mutual Protection of Investments	1978

(continued)

A. E. Alvarado-Garzón, *Environmental Counterclaims in Investment Arbitration*, EYIEL Monographs - Studies in European and International Economic Law 34,
https://doi.org/10.1007/978-3-031-46391-4

Referred to as	Name of the Agreement	Year of Signature
Singapore-BLEU BIT (1978)	Agreement between the Government of the Republic of Singapore and the Belgo-Luxemburg Economic Union on the Promotion and Protection of Investments	1978
Netherlands-Senegal BIT (1979)	Agreement concerning the Encouragement and the Protection of Investments between the Kingdom of the Netherlands and the Republic of Senegal	1979
UK-Sri Lanka BIT (1980)	Agreement between the Government of the United Kingdom of Great Britain and Northern Ireland and the Government of the Democratic Socialist Republic of Sri Lanka for the Promotion and Protection of Investments	1980
OIC Investment Agreement (1981)	Agreement for the Promotion, Protection and Guarantee of Investment among Member States of the Organisation of the Islamic Conference	1981
Romania-Sri Lanka BIT (1981)	Agreement between the Government of the Socialist Republic of Romania and the Government of the Democratic Socialist Republic of Sri Lanka on the Mutual Promotion and Guarantee of Investments	1981
US-Panama BIT (1982)	Treaty between the United States of America and the Republic of Panama concerning the Treatment and Protection of Investment	1982
France-Pakistan BIT (1983)	Agreement between the Government of the French Republic and the Government of the Islamic Republic of Pakistan on the Encouragement and the Reciprocal Protection of Investments	1983
Senegal-Tunisia BIT (1984)	Agreement between the Government of the Republic of Senegal and the Government of the Tunisian Republic concerning the Promotion and the Reciprocal Protection of Investments	1984
US-Congo (Zaire) BIT (1984)	Treaty between the United States of America and the Republic of Zaire concerning the Reciprocal Encouragement and Protection of Investment	1984
St Lucia-Germany BIT (1985)	Treaty between St Lucia and the Federal Republic of Germany concerning the Encouragement and Reciprocal Protection of Investments	1985
Sri Lanka-China BIT (1986)	Agreement between the Government of the Democratic Socialist Republic of Sri Lanka and the Government of the People's Republic of China on the Reciprocal Promotion and Protection of Investments	1986
UK-Jamaica BIT (1987)	Agreement between the Government of the United Kingdom of Great Britain and Northern Ireland and the Government of Jamaica for the Promotion and Protection of Investments	1987
Malta-BLEU BIT (1987)	Agreement between the Republic of Malta and Belgo-Luxembourg Economic Union concerning the Reciprocal Encouragement and Protection of Investments	1987

(continued)

Referred to as	Name of the Agreement	Year of Signature
Hungary-Denmark BIT (1988)	Agreement between the Government of the Hungarian People's Republic and the Government of the Kingdom of Denmark for the Encouragement and the Reciprocal Protection of Investments	1988
Korea-Italy BIT (1989)	Agreement between the Government of the Republic of Korea and the Government of the Republic of Italy concerning the Encouragement and the Reciprocal Protection of Investments	1989
BLEU-Burundi (1989)	Convention between the Belgian-Luxembourgish Economic Union and the Republic of Burundi concerning the Encouragement and the Reciprocal Protection of Investments	1989
Germany-Russia (USSR) BIT (1989)	Agreement between the Federal Republic of Germany and the Union of Soviet Socialist Republics concerning the Promotion and Reciprocal Protection of Investments	1989
France-Nigeria BIT (1990)	Agreement Between the Government of the French Republic and the Government of the Federal Republic of Nigeria on the Encouragement and the Reciprocal Protection of Investments	1990
Poland-Kuwait BIT (1990)	Agreement between the Republic of Poland and the State of Kuwait for the Promotion and Protection of Investments	1990
UK-Czech and Slovak Republic BIT (1990)	Agreement between the Government of the United Kingdom of Great Britain and Northern Ireland and the Government of the Czech and Slovak Federal Republic for the Promotion and Protection of Investments	1990
Argentina-Italy BIT (1990)	Agreement between the Republic of Argentina and the Republic of Italy on the Promotion and Protection of Investments	1990
Italy-Romania BIT (1990)	Agreement between the Government of the Italian Republic and the Government of Romania for the Promotion and Protection of Investments	1990
Netherlands-Czech Republic BIT (1991)	Agreement on Encouragement and Reciprocal Protection of Investments between the Kingdom of the Netherlands and the Czech and Slovak Federal Republic	1991
Germany-Argentina BIT (1991)	Treaty Between Federal Republic of Germany and the Argentine Republic on the Promotion and Mutual Protection of Investments	1991
France-Argentina BIT (1991)	Agreement between the Government of the French Republic and the Government of the Argentine Republic on the Encouragement and the Reciprocal Protection of Investments	1991
Spain-Argentina BIT (1991)	Agreement for the Promotion and the Reciprocal Protection of Investments between the Kingdom of Spain and the Argentine Republic	1991

(continued)

Referred to as	Name of the Agreement	Year of Signature
Norway-Lithuania BIT (1992)	Agreement between the Government of the Kingdom of Norway and the Government of the Republic of Lithuania on the Promotion and Mutual Protection of Investments	1992
China-Argentina BIT (1992)	Agreement between the Government of the People's Republic of China and the Government of the Argentine Republic on the Promotion and Reciprocal Protection of Investments	1992
Turkey-Turkmenistan BIT (1992)	Agreement between the Republic of Turkey and Turkmenistan concerning the Reciprocal Promotion and Protection of Investments	1992
Germany-Belarus BIT (1993)	Agreement between the Federal Republic of Germany and the Republic of Belarus on the Promotion and Reciprocal Protection of Investments	1993
Germany-Ukraine BIT (1993)	Agreement between the Federal Republic of Germany and the Ukraine on the Promotion and the Reciprocal Protection of Investments	1993
UK-Uzbekistan BIT (1993)	Agreement between the Government of the United Kingdom of Great Britain and Northern Ireland and the Government of the Republic of Uzbekistan for the Promotion and Protection of Investments	1993
US-Ecuador BIT (1993)	Treaty between the United States of America and the Republic of Ecuador concerning the Encouragement and Reciprocal Protection of Investments	1993
US-Estonia BIT (1994)	Treaty Between the Government of the United States of America and the Government of the Republic of Estonia for the Encouragement and Reciprocal Protection of Investment	1994
ECT (1994)	The Energy Charter Treaty	1994
NAFTA (1994)	North American Free Trade Agreement	1994
Israel-Uzbekistan BIT (1994)	Agreement between the Government of the State of Israel and the Government of the Republic of Uzbekistan for the Promotion and Reciprocal Protection of Investments	1994
France-Ecuador BIT (1994)	Agreement between the Government of the French Republic and the Government of the Republic of Ecuador concerning the Encouragement and the Reciprocal Protection of Investments	1994
Russia-Mongolia BIT (1995)	Agreement between the Government of the Russian Federation and the Government of Mongolia on the Promotion and Mutual Protection of Investments	1995
Peru-Germany BIT (1995)	Agreement between the Republic of Peru and the Federal Republic of Germany on the Promotion and Mutual Protection of Investments	1995
Germany-Ghana BIT (1995)	Agreement between the Federal Republic of Germany and the Republic of Ghana on the Promotion and Reciprocal Protection of Capital Investments	1995

(continued)

Referred to as	Name of the Agreement	Year of Signature
Pakistan-Turkey BIT (1995)	Agreement between the Islamic Republic of Pakistan and the Republic of Turkey Concerning the Reciprocal Promotion and Protection of Investments	1995
UK-Venezuela BIT (1995)	Agreement between the Government of the United Kingdom of Great Britain and Northern Ireland and the Government of the Republic of Venezuela for the Promotion and Protection of Investments	1995
Spain-El Salvador BIT (1995)	Agreement for the Promotion and Reciprocal Protection of Investments between the Kingdom of Spain and the Republic of El Salvador	1995
China-Saudi Arabia BIT (1996)	Agreement between the People's Republic of China and the Kingdom of Saudi Arabia on the Reciprocal Promotion and Protection of Investments	1996
Ghana-Malaysia BIT (1996)	Agreement between the Government of the Republic of Ghana and the Government of Malaysia for the Promotion and Protection of Investments	1996
Barbados-Canada BIT (1996)	Agreement between the Government of Canada and the Government of Barbados for the Reciprocal Promotion and Protection of Investments	1996
Canada-Venezuela BIT (1996)	Agreement between the Government of Canada and the Government of the Republic of Venezuela for the Promotion and Protection of Investments	1996
Croatia-Canada BIT (1997)	Agreement between the Government of the Republic of Croatia and the Government of Canada for the Promotion and Protection of Investments	1997
Greece-Romania BIT (1997)	Agreement between the Government of the Hellenic Republic and the Government of Romania for the Promotion and Reciprocal Protection of Investments	1997
Germany-Philippines BIT (1997)	Agreement between the Federal Republic of Germany and the Republic of The Philippines for the Promotion and Reciprocal Protection of Investments	1997
Indonesia-Bangladesh BIT (1998)	Agreement between the Government of the Republic of Indonesia and the Government of the People's Republic of Bangladesh concerning the Promotion and Protection of Investment	1998
France-Mexico BIT (1998)	Agreement between the Government of the Republic of France and the Government of the United Mexican States on the Reciprocal Promotion and Protection of Investments	1998
Egypt-Cyprus BIT (1998)	Agreement between the Arab Republic of Egypt and the Republic of Cyprus for the Promotion and Reciprocal Protection of Investments	1998
Australia-Pakistan BIT (1998)	Agreement between Australia and the Islamic Republic of Pakistan on the Promotion and Protection of Investments	1998
Oman-Yemen BIT (1998)	Agreement for the Reciprocal Promotion and Protection of Investments between the Government of the Sultanate of Oman and the Government of the Republic of Yemen	1998

(continued)

Referred to as	Name of the Agreement	Year of Signature
Netherlands-Georgia BIT (1998)	Agreement on Encouragement and Reciprocal Protection of Investments between Georgia and the Kingdom of the Netherlands	1998
UK-El Salvador BIT (1999)	Agreement between the Government of the United Kingdom of Great Britain and Northern Ireland and the Government of the Republic of El Salvador for the Promotion and Protection of Investments	1999
Israel-Armenia BIT (2000)	Agreement between the Government of the State of Israel and the Government of the Republic of Armenia for the Promotion and Reciprocal Protection of Investments	2000
Turkey-Greece BIT (2000)	Agreement between the Republic of Turkey and the Hellenic Republic concerning the Reciprocal Promotion and Protection of Investments	2000
Austria-Iran BIT (2001)	Agreement on the Reciprocal Promotion and Protection of Investments between the Government of the Republic of Austria and the Government of the Islamic Republic of Iran	2001
Finland-Uruguay BIT (2002)	Agreement concerning the Promotion and Protection of Investments between the Republic of Finland and the Oriental Republic of Uruguay	2002
Kazakhstan-Netherlands BIT (2002)	Agreement on Encouragement and Reciprocal Protection of Investments between the Republic of Kazakhstan and the Kingdom of the Netherlands	2002
Spain-Guatemala BIT (2004)	Agreement between the Kingdom of Spain and the Republic of Guatemala for the Promotion and Reciprocal Protection of Investments	2002
Spain-Albania BIT (2003)	Agreement between the Kingdom of Spain and the Republic of Albania on the Promotion and Reciprocal Protection of Investments	2003
Italy Model BIT (2003)	Italy Model Bilateral Investment Agreement	2003
Guatemala-Italy BIT (2003)	Agreement between the Government of the Republic of Guatemala and the Government of the Italian Republic for the Promotion and Protection of Investments	2003
India-Bahrain BIT (2004)	Agreement between the Government of the Republic of India and the Government of the Kingdom of Bahrain for the Promotion and Protection of Investments	2004
Turkey-Afghanistan BIT (2004)	Agreement between the Republic of Turkey and the Transitional Islamic State of Afghanistan Concerning the Reciprocal Promotion and Protection of Investments	2004
Nicaragua-Italy BIT (2004)	Agreement between the Government of the Republic of Nicaragua and the Government of the Italian Republic on the Promotion and Protection of Investments	2004

(continued)

Referred to as	Name of the Agreement	Year of Signature
CAFTA-DR (2004)	Free Trade Agreement between Central America, the Dominican Republic and the United States of America	2004
Cyprus-Libya BIT (2004)	Agreement on the Promotion and the Reciprocal Protection of Investments between the Government of the Republic of Cyprus and the Great Socialist People's Libyan Arab Jamahiriya	2004
Thailand-Jordan BIT (2005)	Agreement between the Government of the Kingdom of Thailand and the Government of the Hashemite Kingdom of Jordan for the Promotion and Protection of Investments	2005
US-Uruguay BIT (2005)	Treaty Between the United States of America and the Oriental Republic of Uruguay concerning the Encouragement and Reciprocal Protection of Investment	2005
Spain-Colombia BIT (2005)	Agreement between the Kingdom of Spain and the Republic of Colombia for the Promotion and Reciprocal Protection of Investments	2005
BLEU-Guatemala BIT (2005)	Agreement between the Belgo-Luxemburg Economic Union and the Government of the Republic of Guatemala on the Reciprocal Promotion and Protection of Investments	2005
BLEU-Nicaragua BIT (2005)	Agreement between the Belgo-Luxemburg Economic Union and the Republic of Nicaragua on the Reciprocal Promotion and Protection of Investments	2005
IISD Model Investment Agreement (2005)	International Institute for Sustainable Development (IISD) Model International Agreement on Investment for Sustainable Development	2005
Mexico-Trinidad and Tobago BIT (2006)	Agreement between the Government of the United Mexican States and the Government of the Republic of Trinidad and Tobago for the Promotion and Reciprocal Protection of the Investments	2006
Colombia-US TPA (2006)	Trade Promotion Agreement between the Republic of Colombia and the Government of the United States of America	2006
Peru-US TPA (2006)	Trade Promotion Agreement between the Republic of Peru and the Government of the United States of America	2006
Italy-Dominican Republic BIT (2006)	Agreement between the Government of the Italian Republic and the Government of the Dominican Republic on the Promotion and Protection of Investments	2006
Italy-DRC BIT (2006)	Agreement between the Government of the Italian Republic and the Government of the Democratic Republic of Congo on the Promotion and Protection of Investments	2006

(continued)

Referred to as	Name of the Agreement	Year of Signature
Italy-Bahrain BIT (2006)	Agreement between the Government of the Italian Republic and the Government of the Kingdom of Bahrain on the Promotion and Protection of Investments	2006
Netherlands-Algeria BIT (2007)	Agreement on the Encouragement and the Reciprocal Protection of Investments between the Kingdom of the Netherlands and the People's Democratic Republic of Algeria	2007
Korea-US FTA (2007)	Free Trade Agreement Between the Government of the Republic of Korea and the Government of the United States of America	2007
COMESA Investment Agreement (2007)	Investment Agreement for the Common Market for Eastern and Southern Africa (COMESA) Common Investment Area	2007
Panama-Sweden BIT (2008)	Agreement between the Government of the Republic of Panama and the Government of the Kingdom of Sweden on the Promotion and the Reciprocal Protection of Investments	2008
US-Rwanda BIT (2008)	Treaty Between the Government of the United States of America and the Government of the Republic of Rwanda concerning the Encouragement and Reciprocal Protection of Investment	2008
Albania-Bosnia and Herzegovina BIT (2008)	Agreement between Bosnia and Herzegovina and the Council of Ministers of the Republic of Albania on the Reciprocal Promotion and Protection of Investments	2008
CARIFORUM-EU EPA (2008)	Economic Partnership Agreement between the Caribbean Forum (CARIFORUM) States of the one Part and the European Community and its Member States of the other Part	2008
ECOWAS Supplementary Act on Investments (2008)	Supplementary Act A/SA.3/12/08 Adopting Community Rules on Investment and the Modalities for their Implementation with the Economic Community of West African States (ECOWAS)	2008
China-Malta BIT (2009)	Agreement between the Government of the People's Republic of China and the Government of Malta on the Promotion and Protection of Investments	2009
Canada-Czech Republic BIT (2009)	Agreement between Canada and the Czech Republic for the Promotion and Protection of Investments	2009
Japan-Switzerland FTA (2009)	Agreement on Free Trade and Economic Partnership Between Japan and the Swiss Confederation	2009
Moldova-Estonia BIT (2010)	Agreement between the Government of the Republic of Moldova and the Government of the Republic of Estonia on the Promotion and Reciprocal Protection of Investments	2010
Israel-Ukraine BIT (2010)	Agreement Between the Government of the State of Israel and the Government of Ukraine for the Reciprocal Promotion and Protection of Investments	2010

(continued)

Referred to as	Name of the Agreement	Year of Signature
Japan-Colombia BIT (2011)	Agreement between Japan and the Republic of Colombia for the Liberalization, Promotion and Protection of Investment	2011
Switzerland-Tunisia BIT (2012)	Agreement between the Swiss Federal Council and the Government of the Republic of Tunisia on Reciprocal Promotion and Protection of Investments	2012
Armenia-Iraq BIT (2012)	Agreement between the Government of the Republic of Armenia and the Government of the Republic of Iraq for the Encouragement and Reciprocal Protection of Investments	2012
Canada-China BIT (2012)	Agreement between the Government of Canada and the Government of the People's Republic of China for the Promotion and Reciprocal Protection of Investments	2012
SADC Model BIT (2012)	Southern African Development Community (SADC) Model Bilateral Investment Treaty Template	2012
Canada-Benin BIT (2013)	Agreement between the Government of Canada and the Government of the Republic of Benin for the Promotion and Reciprocal Protection of Investments	2013
Korea-Cameroon BIT (2013)	Agreement between the Government of the Republic of Korea and the Government of the Republic of Cameroon for the Promotion and Protection of Investments	2013
India-UAE BIT (2013)	Agreement between the Government of the Republic of India and the Government of the United Arab Emirates on the Promotion and Protection of Investments	2013
Mexico-Kuwait BIT (2013)	Agreement between the Government of the United Mexican States and the Government of the State of Kuwait on the Promotion and Reciprocal Protection of Investments	2013
Guatemala-Trinidad and Tobago BIT (2013)	Agreement between the Republic of Guatemala and the Republic of Trinidad and Tobago on the Reciprocal Promotion and Protection of Investments	2013
Turkey-Gambia BIT (2013)	Agreement between the Government of the Republic of Turkey and the Government of the Republic of the Gambia concerning the Reciprocal Promotion and Protection of Investments	2013
Colombia-France BIT (2014)	Agreement between the Government of the Republic of Colombia and the Government of the French Republic on the Encouragement and the Reciprocal Protection of Investments	2014
Canada-Côte d'Ivoire BIT (2014)	Agreement between the Government of Canada and the Republic of Côte d'Ivoire on Protection of Investments	2014
Canada-Cameroon BIT (2014)	Agreement between Canada and the Republic of Cameroon for the Promotion and Protection of Investments	2014

(continued)

Referred to as	Name of the Agreement	Year of Signature
Israel-Myanmar BIT (2014)	Agreement between the Government of the State of Israel and the Government of the Republic of the Union of Myanmar for the Reciprocal Promotion and Protection of Investments	2014
Colombia-Turkey BIT (2014)	Agreement between the Government of the Republic of Colombia and the Government of the Republic of Turkey concerning the Reciprocal Promotion and Protection of Investments	2014
Switzerland-Georgia BIT (2014)	Agreement between the Swiss Confederation and Georgia on the Promotion and Reciprocal Protection of Investments	2014
Mexico-Panama FTA (2014)	Free Trade Agreement between the United Mexican States and the Republic of Panama	2014
Russia-Cambodia BIT (2015)	Agreement between the Government of the Russian Federation and the Government of the Kingdom of Cambodia on the Promotion and Reciprocal Protection of Investments	2015
Kyrgyzstan-Kuwait BIT (2015)	Agreement between the Government of the Kyrgyz Republic and the Government of the State of Kuwait for the Encouragement and Reciprocal Protection of Investments	2015
San Marino-Azerbaijan BIT (2015)	Agreement between the Government of the Republic of San Marino and the Government of the Republic of Azerbaijan on the Promotion and Reciprocal Protection of Investments	2015
Australia-China FTA (2015)	Free Trade Agreement between the Government of Australia and the Government of the People's Republic of China	2015
Canada-Burkina Faso BIT (2015)	Agreement between the Government of Canada and the Government of Burkina Faso for the Promotion and Protection of Investments	2015
Canada-Guinea BIT (2015)	Agreement for the Promotion and Reciprocal Protection of Investments between Canada and the Republic of Guinea	2015
Japan-Uruguay BIT (2015)	Agreement Between Japan and the Oriental Republic of Uruguay for the Liberalization, Promotion and Protection of Investment	2015
India Model BIT (2015)	India Model Bilateral Investment Agreement	2015
Austria-Kyrgyzstan BIT (2016)	Agreement for the Promotion and Protection of Investment between the Government of the Republic of Austria and the Government of the Kyrgyz Republic	2016
Morocco-Nigeria BIT (2016)	Reciprocal Investment Promotion and Protection Agreement between the Government of the Kingdom of Morocco and the Government of the Federal Republic of Nigeria	2016

(continued)

Referred to as	Name of the Agreement	Year of Signature
Ethiopia-UAE BIT (2016)	Agreement between the Government of the Federal Democratic Republic of Ethiopia and the Government of the United Arab Emirates concerning the Promotion and Reciprocal Protection of Investment	2016
Slovak Republic-UAE BIT (2016)	Agreement between the Slovak Republic and the United Arab Emirates for the Promotion and Reciprocal Protection of Investments	2016
Canada-Mongolia BIT (2016)	Agreement Between Canada and Mongolia for the Promotion and Protection of Investments	2016
Slovak Republic-Iran BIT (2016)	Agreement Between the Slovak Republic and the Islamic Republic of Iran for the Promotion and Reciprocal Protection of Investments	2016
Argentina-Qatar BIT (2016)	The Reciprocal Promotion and Protection of Investments between the Argentine Republic and the State of Qatar	2016
Nigeria-Singapore BIT (2016)	Investment Promotion and Protection Agreement between the Government of the Federal Republic of Nigeria and the Government of the Republic of Singapore	2016
Chile-Hong Kong BIT (2016)	Investment Agreement between the Government of the Hong Kong Special Administrative Region of the People's Republic of China and the Government of the Republic of Chile	2016
PAIC (2016)	Pan African Investment Code	2016
CETA (2016)	Comprehensive Trade and Economic Agreement between Canada and the European Union	2016
Israel-Japan BIT (2017)	Agreement between the State of Israel and Japan for the Liberalization, Promotion and Protection of Investment	2017
Ethiopia-Qatar BIT (2017)	Agreement between the Government of the Federal Democratic Republic of Ethiopia and the Government of the State of Qatar for the Promotion and Reciprocal Protection of Investments	2017
Argentina-Chile FTA (2017)	Free Trade Agreement between Argentina and Chile	2017
Colombia Model BIT (2017)	Colombia Model Bilateral Investment Treaty	2017
Colombia-UAE BIT (2017)	Bilateral Agreement for the Promotion and Protection of Investments between the Government of the Republic of Colombia and the Government of the United Arab Emirates	2017
Rwanda-UAE BIT (2017)	Agreement between the Republic of Rwanda and the United Arab Emirates on the Promotion and Reciprocal Protection of Investments	2017
Turkey-Burundi BIT (2017)	Agreement between the Government of the Republic of Turkey and the Government of the Republic of Burundi concerning the Reciprocal Promotion and Protection of Investments	2017

(continued)

Referred to as	Name of the Agreement	Year of Signature
Turkey-Cambodia BIT (2018)	Agreement between the Government of the Republic of Turkey and the Government of the Kingdom of Cambodia on the Reciprocal Promotion and Protection of Investments	2018
Kazakhstan-Singapore BIT (2018)	Agreement between the Government of the Republic of Kazakhstan and the Government of the Republic of Singapore on the Promotion and Mutual Protection of Investments	2018
UAE-Uruguay BIT (2018)	Agreement between the United Arab Emirates and the Oriental Republic of Uruguay for the Promotion and Reciprocal Protection of Investments	2018
Canada-Moldova BIT (2018)	Agreement between the Government of Canada and the Government of the Republic of Moldova for the Promotion and Protection of Investments	2018
Belarus-India BIT (2018)	Treaty between the Republic of Belarus and the Republic of India on Investments	2018
Argentina-UAE BIT (2018)	Agreement for the Reciprocal Promotion and Protection of Investments between the Argentine Republic and the United Arab Emirates	2018
CPTPP (2018)	Comprehensive and Progressive Agreement for Trans-Pacific Partnership	2018
Lithuania-Turkey BIT (2018)	Agreement between the Government of the Republic of Lithuania and the Government of the Republic of Turkey on the Reciprocal Promotion and Protection of Investments	2018
USMCA (2019)	Agreement between the United States of America, the United Mexican States, and Canada	2019
Uzbekistan-Korea BIT (2019)	Agreement between the Government of the Republic of Uzbekistan and the Government of the Republic of Korea for the Reciprocal Promotion and Protection of Investments	2019
Nicaragua-Iran BIT (2019)	Agreement on Promotion and Reciprocal Protection of Investments between the Government of the Republic of Nicaragua and the Government of the Islamic Republic of Iran	2019
Singapore-Myanmar BIT (2019)	Agreement between the Government of the Republic of Singapore and the Government of the Republic of the Union of Myanmar on the Promotion and Protection of Investments	2019
China-Mauritius FTA (2019)	Free Trade Agreement between the Government of the People's Republic of China and the Government of the Republic of Mauritius	2019

(continued)

Referred to as	Name of the Agreement	Year of Signature
Kyrgyzstan-India BIT (2019)	Bilateral Investment Treaty between the Government of the Kyrgyz Republic and the Government of the Republic of India	2019
Australia-Uruguay BIT (2019)	Agreement between Australia and the Oriental Republic of Uruguay on the Promotion and Protection of Investments	2019
Hungary-Cabo Verde BIT (2019)	Agreement between the Government of Hungary and the Government of the Republic of Cabo Verde for the Promotion and Reciprocal Protection of Investments	2019
Belarus-Hungary BIT (2019)	Agreement between the Government of the Republic of Belarus and the Government of Hungary for the Promotion and Reciprocal Protection of Investments	2019
BLEU Model BIT (2019)	Belgium-Luxembourg Economic Union Model Bilateral Investment Agreement	2019
The Netherlands Model BIT (2019)	The Netherlands Model Bilateral Investment Agreement	2019
Morocco Model BIT (2019)	Morocco Model Bilateral Investment Agreement	2019
Hungary-Kyrgyzstan BIT (2020)	Agreement between the Government of Hungary and the Government of the Kyrgyz Republic for the Promotion and Reciprocal Protection of Investments	2020
Morocco-Japan BIT (2020)	Agreement between the Kingdom of Morocco and Japan for the Promotion and Protection of Investment	2020
Israel-UAE BIT (2020)	Agreement between the Government of the State of Israel and the Government of the United Arab Emirates on Promotion and Protection of Investments	2020
Colombia-Spain BIT (2021)	Agreement between the Republic of Colombia and the Kingdom of Spain for the Promotion and Reciprocal Protection of Investments	2021
Japan-Georgia BIT (2021)	Agreement between Japan and Georgia for the Liberalisation, Promotion and Protection of Investment	2021